Acknowledgements

There are hundreds of people I would like to thank by name, but in the possible hard times ahead, being identified in a book like this may be a little risky.

The "Enemies Within" have proven willing to use the power of the state to harass their opponents. As they get ever more desperate to hold on to power, we can only expect these tactics to intensify.

I just want to say that in my four speaking tours of the United States, I have met so many people who simply blew me away with their kindness, generosity and love of liberty, that I have become a permanently humbled man.

A few however must be named. They deserve it and have all publicly backed me in the past.

Terresa Monroe-Hamilton made this book happen and has been a true friend to me and to her country. I will be eternally grateful to you Terresa.

Oregonians Rodney Stubbs and Tom Hammer made all this possible. They've been with me in the worst of times and the very best of times.

Cliff Kincaid and Max Friedman are both special friends. The kind you make in the trenches. Paul Kengor, Jim Simpson, Matthew Vadum, Curtis Bowers and Glenn Beck are true "warriors of the word." They fight for America every waking moment. George, Wally, Andy, Steve and Rick, have fought and continue to fight for their country.

Regina Thomson and Bill are friends for life.

Bill Jasper, Christian Gomez and Jimmy from Brooklyn, are comrades in the truest sense of the word.

Then there is dear Tracy.

I also want to thank those who are still with us in spirit: Andrew Breitbart, Herb Romerstein, Bob Chandler, Dr. Fred Schwartz and Rep. Larry McDonald of Georgia.

There are many, many more. I know who you are. You know who you are. Let's just keep that information to ourselves shall we?

Trevor Loudon
Christchurch
New Zealand

The Enemies

Communists, socialists
and progressives
in the U.S. Congress

2013-2015 Edition

Trevor Loudon

The views expressed in this book are solely those of the author and do not reflect the views of the publisher, and the publisher hereby disclaims any representation for them.

ISBN-13: 978-1490575179
ISBN-10: 1490575170
Pacific Freedom Foundation, a Nevada Not for Profit Corporation
500 N. Rainbow Blvd., Ste. 300A
Las Vegas, NV 89107
With offices at 3460 Dogwood Dr. S., Salem, OR 97302
www.pacificfreedomfoundation.org

Updates, Errors, Omissions and Redactions of attributed material are welcome. All changes require documentation identifying source, requestors name and address and the page and line number as it appears in this Edition. Changes will be posted when a second edition is published. The redaction policy applies to materials attributed in the book. Redactions will consist of striking through the material and footing the request for redaction by the person or persons responsible for the initial publication. Future publications are subject to the approval of the Author.

United States Library of Congress

Loudon, Trevor

The Enemies Within: Communists, Socialists and Progressives in the United States Congress

Cover and book design by Oleg Atbashian

Table of Contents

Congressional Profiles

Maine

Maryland

Massachusetts

Michigan

Minnesota

Mississippi

Missouri

New York

North Carolina

Ohio

PROLOGUE:
Why I Stand With America

I'm often asked why, as a New Zealander, I should care about the internal politics of the United States.

There are two reasons.

The first is simple gratitude. My country was saved in World War II from probable conquest by the Imperial Japanese Army, by the huge sacrifice of American Servicemen in the Battles of Midway, Guadalcanal and the Coral Sea. Without American blood and steel, my country would have almost certainly have lost its freedom and many of my countrymen would have been slaughtered.

The second reason is related, but a little more selfish. The reality is that if America loses its economic dynamism, its ability to generate huge wealth, it will inevitably also lose its military superiority.

If America loses its position as the world's number one military super power, who will take its place?

The Universe abhors a vacuum. If America is no longer the world's leading military power, someone else will be.

Realistically, that can only be Russia or China, or more likely, an alliance of Russia, China, Iran, North Korea, Cuba, Venezuela, Nicaragua and Vietnam. Such an alliance is already partially built through the little publicized Shanghai Cooperation Organization (SCO). Founded in 2001, the SCO is an economic, political and military alliance binding Russia, China, Kazakhstan, Kyrgyzstan, Tajikistan and Uzbekistan. SCO "Observer" states include Iran, India, Pakistan, Mongolia and Afghanistan. "Dialogue Partners" include Sri Lanka and Belarus.

Add to those the neo-communist ruled countries such as South Africa and Brazil, the Latin American leftist ruled nations such as Ecuador and Argentina, most of the Islamic nations and international Islamic terrorism, and you have a huge potential power bloc. All allied against the United States.

As the U.S. Dollar slowly sinks and America's prestige and power goes with it, Russia, China and Iran grow bolder. America's allies such as Israel, Taiwan, Japan, South Korea, Canada, Australia, Britain, Germany, Poland

and Georgia, can all see the writing on the wall. The message is clear. Every man for himself, or make your peace with the "Evil Axis."

America's allies are looking at the leadership coming out of Washington and they are horrified. If America got into a major war with Russia or China tomorrow, many of them would stay neutral. If Russia, China Iran and all their allies all attacked a weakened and disarmed America in ten years time, it's hard to imagine anyone coming to Uncle Sam's aid. Some current "friends" may even join the anti-U.S. alliance. The Western Alliance would struggle to win World War III today. In another decade, there may be no Western Alliance left to even fight.

If America continues down the current path of impoverishment and disarmament, it is only a matter time before the combined forces of Russia, China, Iran, Cuba, Venezuela, North Korea, Vietnam and their Islamic terrorist protégés come to dominate the planet. Can you imagine consigning your children to living in a world ruled by Russia, China and Iran? Can you envisage what life would be like on a "gangster" run planet?

I live in a tiny country at the bottom of the Pacific. Many of us are very cocky down here. Most of us think that no-one will ever threaten our little paradise. If we think about national security at all, it's mainly about keeping foreign bugs out of our apples or nasty parasites away from our sheep and cattle.

Yet, China is steadily advancing through the Pacific. It now has several footholds in our region, particularly in Fiji, which is our nearest major neighbor in the region except for Australia. Most Kiwis don't care about that because they know the American Navy is always patrolling the region. No one's ever going to challenge America—so they think.

But this view is false. This was made very clear to our Australian neighbors in June of 2012. Song Xiaojun, a "retired" Chinese general, told the Sydney Morning Herald that "Australia has to find a godfather sooner or later."

"Australia always has to depend on somebody else, whether it is to be the 'son' of the U.S. or 'son' of China," Song said, adding that Australia had best choose China because it all "depends on who is more powerful and based on the strategic environment."

That type of choice now faces every major U.S. ally around the globe.

What if the U.S. economy implodes under the weight of its crushing debt? What if America's long-term, but rapidly accelerating slide into socialism, sends the U.S. economy completely out the bottom? Where will the Western Alliance be then? Who will stop the "Evil Axis" from completely dominating the planet?

If Americans are mired in poverty and unemployment, will they have either the stomach or the ability to protect what's left of the free world?

America will certainly continue down that path until it addresses a major problem; an issue almost no one is talking about.

The problem is that for more than 50 years, U.S. radicals, many of them allied to hostile foreign powers, have been systematically infiltrating sympathizers and "useful idiots" into the U.S. House of Representatives and the Senate. There are now large voting blocs in both Houses, who, whether they are conscious of it or not, are effectively an enemy "Fifth Column" in the heart of the U.S. Government.

Until these people are exposed and removed from office, America has no hope of a lasting recovery or maintaining its world leadership role. Until this problem is confronted and dealt with, the very survival of the West is gravely endangered.

Without the U.S. Constitution and the freedoms it protects, America would never have created the bounty it has. Freedom enables prosperity, not "natural resources." Without constitutionally guaranteed liberties, America never would have become the richest, strongest and most benevolent power the world has ever known. And Without America, freedom would surely have perished on this planet decades ago.

That Constitution has never been under more threat than it is today. That threat is primarily internal. The U.S. Constitution is being destroyed before our eyes by the "Enemies Within."

Every Westerner who wants to see freedom flourish on this planet, to see liberty and prosperity spread across the globe, must stand with America now. If America can be turned around, its Constitution restored, its economy re-energized and its military superiority secured, this planet has a very bright future.

However, if America does not confront its internal enemies, very quickly, this planet is heading for a period of unimaginable darkness.

Every Westerner who loves freedom owes a huge debt to America. Many of us wouldn't even be here had it not been for the U.S. military, and the willingness of hardworking American taxpayers to fund it.

I hope this book helps to alert Americans to the greatest threat their nation faces.

Please consider it part of my contribution to the huge debt the world's greatest nation is owed, by the free peoples of Planet Earth.

Trevor Loudon
Christchurch
New Zealand
June 5, 2013

Communism's Big Secret

The international communist movement holds many secrets—one being that it still exists and in many ways, is more powerful than ever before.

However, the biggest secret of communism has to do with its methodology, its means of achieving its goals.

While countless books have been written on "Atom Bomb" spies, charismatic revolutionaries, Kremlinology and the huge death toll of 20th century communism, very few commentators have touched on the greatest impact communism has had on Western society.

The big secret of communism, is the method by which tiny local communist parties, often acting under the direction of foreign powers, are able to get their policies adopted as the "law of the land" in their own country.

How far-fetched is that? How credible is it that a tiny communist party, maybe only a few hundred comrades strong, could influence public policy in a country with tens or maybe even hundreds of millions of voters?

Where is the evidence for such a seemingly implausible claim?

Firstly, I will outline the process and then give examples of the process in action, one from my country New Zealand, then four from the United States.

The Process

The goal of the world communist movement was always to first socialize the entire planet under centralized government control, then to move to a classless, worker controlled society. The second part will never happen, but the centralized control aspect is making steady progress.

After the initial burst of European revolutions all failed in the 1920s, the communist movement began a long-term plan to move individual countries to socialism by force where possible, by infiltration and manipulation when not.

After Eastern Europe and China were communized by force after WWII, communist expansionism was resisted by stiff Western resolve. The Cold War was essentially a stalemate. Communism could only expand peripherally, mainly in the poorer countries of Africa and Asia.

Force was too risky to apply to the main targets of Western Europe and North America. Infiltration and manipulation would have to be amped up. Western Europe, Canada and the United States would have to be socialized from the inside out. The existing order would have to be overturned by a process of subversion. Education, the churches and the media were all targeted. But the key focus, something hardly touched on by scholars, was the systematic infiltration and manipulation of the legislative bodies of each major Western nation.

The communists rightly surmised that if they could influence or manipulate the British Parliament, the German Bundestag and the U.S. Congress, what did it matter how many missiles NATO possessed or how many troops they could mass on the Rhine?

Step One—Policy Formation

During the "Cold War," policy was established in Moscow by the Communist Party of the Soviet Union leadership, in conjunction with the International Department and the KGB. The question was asked by the leadership—what domestic or foreign policy do we want France... or Canada... or Italy... or New Zealand... or the United States to adopt, to move that country more towards socialism or to tilt the balance of power more in our favor?

Since the more apparent than real 'collapse of communism' in the 1990s, communist international policy formation appears to have become more de-centralized.

All the major international communist fronts created by the Soviets in the 1940s and 50s—World Peace Council, World Federation of Trade Unions, Women's International Democratic Federation, World Federation of Democratic Youth and International Association of Democratic Lawyers... are still actively working as a team, promoting the communist "line" wherever they can. Today, they are controlled more by Cuban, Greek and Third World communists, but follow policies almost identical to those of their former Soviet masters.

Currently, most major Western communist parties, including the Communist Party USA, tend to look more to China for leadership, though Russian and former Eastern Bloc communists are still a major part of the international movement.

Step Two—Indoctrination

In Soviet times, thousands of foreign communists were trained every year in many Eastern Bloc academies, particularly Lenin's Institute for Higher Learning, aka Institute of Social Sciences, and the Patrice Lumumba University, in Moscow.

The main purpose of the institutes was to indoctrinate foreign communists into following Moscow's line. A major part of the training was learning how to use their own country's labor movement, peace movement, churches and civil organizations to influence policy formation in their native country's "mainstream" left wing political party—the British Labor Party, the French Socialist Party, the German Social Democrats, the Canadian Liberals or the U.S. Democratic Party.

Interestingly, during the 1980s, no American communists were allowed to train at Lenin's Institute for Higher Learning—it was considered way too dangerous and provocative. Instead, the Soviets would indoctrinate Canadians or even New Zealanders in the appropriate "line," then those cadre would be sent to train the American communists.

Today, this process is more de-centralized with more indoctrination being done "in country, or through the major international front organizations."

Socialists, such as the U.S.'s Democratic Socialists of America, get much of their direction from the Socialist International. That body is now so thoroughly compromised by admitting former communist parties and even bona fide terrorist groups such as Fatah, that its "line" is almost identical to that of the openly communist movement.

Step Three—Implementation

As Lenin said of trade unions—they are the "transmission belts from the Communist Party to the masses." Communist control of the labor movement is the key to the implementation phase of communist policy infiltration into Western countries.

Every major communist party does its level best to take over the local labor movement. There are several reasons for this, but the most important and overlooked one is this… Every mainstream left wing party in the Western democracies is dominated by the labor movement. The unions fund these parties; contribute manpower at election time and bloc vote at their conferences. Labor unions effectively dominate every major left wing political party in every major, and most minor, Western countries.

He who pays the piper calls the tune. Labor unions, by providing the money and the muscle, can dictate party policy and they can usually have a big say in candidate selection.

The process is clear. The international communist movement or the local communist party sets a desired policy, whether it is strengthening labor legislation, state funding of political parties, a more socialist school curriculum, more liberal immigration policies, cancelling a new weapons system, relaxing trade sanctions on Cuba—whatever is paramount on the communist agenda at that time.

The communists and their socialist allies then make these communist policies, UNION POLICIES. The unions then put pressure on the local Labor Party, Socialist Party or Democratic Party, to adopt these union policies as their own. As labor effectively controls these major parties, the process is often not that difficult.

So, communist policies become union policies, which in turn become "mainstream" political party policies.

What the Communist Party wants today, the Labor Party will implement tomorrow. And the vast bulk of the voting public will have no idea that the policies they are voting for originated in Moscow, Havana, Beijing, or in local Communist Party headquarters.

This process has been carried out countless times all over the world. It was much more difficult in the United States for many years because the U.S. labor movement was uniquely led by militant anti-communists like George Meany and Lane Kirkland.

However, the left took over the U.S. labor movement in 1995 and installed Democratic Socialists of America member John Sweeney as President of the AFL-CIO. The next step was to remove the clause from the AFL-CIO constitution banning communists from holding office in AFL-CIO affiliated unions. The communists and socialists came flooding back and now dominate every major union in the U.S.

That is why the move to U.S. socialism has gone into overdrive since the Democrats took power in 2008. They are following a union agenda, foisted upon them by the Communist Party USA and Democratic Socialists of America.

If you want to know what the Democrats will do tomorrow, read the Communist Party's People's World or the Democratic Socialist's Democratic Left today.

Example One:
How the Soviets Destroyed a U.S. Military Alliance

For several decades, my country New Zealand was a staunchly pro-American member of the Australia/New Zealand/United States military alliance (ANZUS).

Older Kiwis in particular were very pro-American. Memories of WWII still lingered. Many remembered the very real fear of a Japanese invasion and the huge sacrifice of American lives that kept us free.

Right up until the early 1980s, it was inconceivable that New Zealand would ever turn its back on our military alliance with the United States.

Stunningly, ANZUS was effectively dead in the water by 1984, when New Zealand's newly elected socialist Labour government banned nuclear warships from the country's harbors. It has not been properly revived to this day.

Nearly three years later, a Nuclear-Free Zone Disarmament and Arms Control Bill passed into law on June 4, 1987. The event has assumed a heroic mythology in New Zealand. Kiwis dared to stand up to the United States and forge its own independent foreign policy. Most New Zealanders still regard that legislation as one of our country's greatest achievements.

So powerful is the myth, that in early 2007, John Key, the new leader of the conservative National Party, made it clear that his party would adhere to the status quo on any potential visit by nuclear-powered warships. He recognized domestic political and cultural realities.

New Zealand "Peace" Movement

The New Zealand anti-nuclear movement didn't arrive from nowhere. It was more than twenty years in the making. The early 1980s though, saw a "mushrooming" of anti-nuke activism.

By late 1986, the NZ peace movement consisted of over 350 disparate groups; this in a population of under four million. One thousand, or one-fifth, of Kiwi physicians belonged to the International Physicians for the

Prevention of Nuclear War. Town councils voted to become nuclear-free, erecting notices at their boundaries that one was entering a nuclear-free zone. By 1987, 70 percent of New Zealand's population was living in such zones.

New Zealand was heralded as a shining example to the world. Its home-grown peace movement had triumphed and is still giving most New Zealanders a sense of pride in their non-aligned status. They had created their own destiny.

"Correlation of forces"

However, even today only a very few New Zealanders realize that the anti-nuclear movement served the strategic interests of the Soviet Union. New Zealand was specifically targeted in a clandestine political operation, designed to remove it from the Western Alliance.

In the late 1970s, policy-makers in the International Department of the Communist Party of the Soviet Union developed doctrine concerning exploiting what they termed the "correlation of forces" within a particular country to achieve a specific outcome. This implied expert direction of the "correlation."

Influencing the unions

A key force to be "correlated" was the New Zealand trade union movement. It would be helpful at this point to outline the changes that were occurring. Tony Neary (now deceased), the conservative leader of the Electrical Workers Union, chronicled the infiltration in a paper he gave at a conference in Washington, D.C. in March of 1987, under the auspices of the Hoover Institute.

Neary claimed that the Soviet Union, through one of its main front organizations, the World Federation of Trade Unions, had successfully infiltrated the New Zealand trade union movement and changed its direction.

He noted that until the mid-1970s, there was a good working relationship between the NZ Federation of Labour (FOL) and the United States labor federation, the AFL-CIO.

The change began in May 1979, when Jim Knox was elected New Zealand FOL President and regular visits by NZ trade unionists to the Soviet Union and other Eastern Bloc countries commenced.

By 1986, known communists from the Moscow-aligned Socialist Unity Party (SUP) and the Maoist-leaning Workers Communist League, along with their sympathizers, had considerable control in seven of the eight largest trade's councils, covering 70 percent of the FOL membership.

Bill Andersen, President of the SUP and the Auckland Trades Council, attended the 27th Congress of the Communist Party of the Soviet Union in March of 1986.

Joint communiqués, signed by Jim Knox on behalf of the FOL and by the heads of visiting Soviet delegations, had been adopted by delegates at the 1984 and 1985 FOL conferences.

Behind Jim Knox was Ken Douglas, the powerful General Secretary of the FOL and Chairman of the SUP. In 1986, he took two months worth of "sick leave" to visit the Soviet Union.

That year, Jim Knox also visited the Soviet Union where, according to the Soviet news agency TASS (on February 22nd), he pledged to "pool efforts in the struggle to prevent a new war with which the imperialist states, above all the United States administration, threatened mankind." He also said: "Soviet peace initiatives are highly appreciated in New Zealand and are supported by broad sections of the population."

TASS (February of 1985) quoted Knox as saying that, "contacts between the trade unions of New Zealand and the USSR grow stronger from year to year. New Zealand trade unionists follow with interest the Soviet people's strides, and come to see for themselves that the socialist system acts in the interests of the working people."

A vignette from that era illustrates the relationship. Each year, the Soviet embassy in Wellington invited delegates from the FOL conference to an embassy function. During the 1986 conference, most delegates attended this reception. To emphasize the importance of the NZ-USSR relationship, at the conference, Jim Knox warmly presented the Soviet delegates with large expensive sheepskin rugs.

The American guest from the AFL-CIO received a small brown paper parcel. From the rostrum, Knox told delegates that the parcel contained a book on New Zealand; but when the American visitor opened the paper, he found a small cheeseboard. The New Zealand Herald reported that "it was a case of hard cheese for the American delegate."[1]

Tony Neary had considerable public respect for the lonely struggle he undertook; but his criticisms of Soviet trade unions as mere appendages of the State were rejected within the FOL. He was regularly accused of seeing "Reds under the bed," to which he responded:[2]

In the New Zealand trade union movement, those who mutter about Reds under the beds must be joking. The Reds are already in the beds and have been there for some years. By now they are sitting up and getting breakfast brought in.

KGB interest

Oleg Gordievsky, a former high-ranking officer of the Soviet security service, the KGB,—who, from 1974, worked as a long-serving undercover agent for the British Secret Intelligence Service (MI6) until his formal defection in 1985—recalled:[3]

> KGB activity in Australasia was ... increased as the result of the election of David Lange's Labour government in New Zealand on an antinuclear programme in 1984.... The [KGB] Centre ... was jubilant at Lange's election....

Gordievsky visited New Zealand on four occasions from 1986 onwards to brief that country's Security Intelligence Service on Soviet clandestine activities in the region. For years, he said, New Zealand:[4]

> ... had been under massive propaganda and ideological attack from the KGB and the [Soviet] Central Committee, and the ruling Labour Party had seemed unaware of the extent to which the fabric of their society was being damaged by subversion....
>
> In its attempts to draw New Zealand into nuclear-free activities, the Soviet authorities had made tremendous efforts to penetrate and strengthen the Labour Party, partly through the local Party of Socialist Unity (in effect the Communist Party of New Zealand) and partly through the Trades Union Congress.

Gordievsky alleged that New Zealand and Australian communists were being run by the International Department of the CPSU. He said:[5]

> "I know the situation in New Zealand very well; only 500 members of the Socialist Unity Party, but they are invaluable because each was ready to do something. It was like the KGB had 500 agents in the country."
>
> He added: "Plus some of them penetrated the trade unions, and then they penetrated the left wing of the NZ Labour Party."

The "peace" push

Their aspirations were spelt out in a Socialist Unity Party Auckland regional newsletter, dated November 12, 1980:

To date in the region the Peace Council has made good progress among trade unions, but more effort must be made to build on this and take the peace question to the factory floor.

Also needed now is to broaden the Peace Council into other areas of the community, join up prominent personalities including MPs, increase church involvement, university involvement, other peace groups, community clubs etc.

Here branches and comrades can act as catalysts. We must be extremely careful that in building the Peace Council, it does not become overburdened with 'SUP' people, or be labeled as just another 'SUP' front.

If our Party is working correctly, only a few comrades, reporting back to the region and branches, and taking forward issues from the same sources, are necessary to ensure effective involvement in the peace movement. The broadest possible base is needed if we are to make the Council effective.

Influencing the Labour Party

In July of 1980, Labour Party council member and unionist, Allan O'Neill, claimed that the Socialist Action League and Socialist Unity Party were infiltrating the Labour Party. "It appears to be a new tactic of these political organizations to get their members into the party, to incite from within and push their own political dogmas."

Other Labour figures made similar accusations, but nothing was done. By the early 1980s, the SUP had gained control of the NZ Federation of Labour and most of the major unions in the engineering, dairy, hotel and transport industries.

These unions were affiliated with the Labour Party and enjoyed bloc voting rights at party conferences. Every financial member of an affiliated union was counted as a member of the Labour Party. This gave affiliated unions thousands of votes each, which, when coordinated, guaranteed the SUP's ability to choose the Labour Party's President, Executive, Policy Council—and to influence policy on that council.

Understandably, the SUP took advantage of this preferential system, so that through the mid to late 1980s, the majority of Labour Party senior officials were SUP sympathizers or secret members. The same infiltration was occurring at branch level, ensuring that the SUP became the leading power bloc in the Labour Party.

SUP members studying at Lenin's Institute in Moscow during the early 1980s, were drilled extensively by their Russian tutors on the advantages to the Soviet Union that could accrue from the election of a Labour Government in New Zealand.

On June 6, 1984, SUP National Secretary George Jackson, addressed a meeting of his party's Hamilton branch. He explained the rationale for supporting Labour in the upcoming national elections. According to a party document, Jackson stated that:

> The Federation of Labour and Combined State Unions, later joined under the Council of Trade Unions banner, have more influence on the Labour Party than for many years. And the trade union structures have the ability to transform economic campaigns to political campaigns.

Infiltrating the infiltrators

It was later revealed by me and Auckland journalist, Bernard Moran, that the SUP was itself infiltrated by a humble truck-driver, who was later selected to attend a specialist course at Lenin's Institute in Moscow.

John Van de Ven, a Dutch immigrant, was stocky, powerfully built and full of restless energy. In the late 1970s, Van de Ven worked as a tanker-driver for Mobil and belonged to the Wellington Drivers' Union run by Ken Douglas. Van de Ven raced through his delivery rounds and received several warnings that his speed was upsetting the union's workplace rules. Undeterred, he raced on until called into the union office and forthrightly informed that if he didn't play by the rules he would lose his union card and would not drive trucks in Wellington again.

"I was mad at being treated like this," Van de Ven told us. "So I decided to get even. I had no firm plans, but I knew the union was run by the SUP and so I thought that if I can get in—then sometime down the track I'll get even. It was as simple as that."

Van de Ven went to the union and apologized for his misdemeanors and offered to assist with menial tasks, even hand out copies of the SUP newspaper, the Tribune. After a year's probationary period as a model unionist, his talents were recognized. Drivers' Union official and senior SUP member, Richie Gillespie, took him aside and said the union had big things planned for him, if he could prove himself.

Fortuitously, in 1977, Van de Ven discovered a legitimate grievance over tire-safety issues on the tankers. When the company refused to make the changes, he led a prolonged strike that paralyzed petrol supplies for weeks around the lower half of the North Island. Finally, Mobil capitulated and conceded that the Drivers' Union, not the company, must have the final say on safety issues.

Ken Douglas, impressed with Van de Ven's leadership, personally invited him to join the SUP. In 1978, he joined the Porirua branch and studied Marxist-Leninist theory under a secret member (who later became a leading member of the Labour Party National Executive). Within two years, he took over the Porirua branch Chairmanship and, in 1981, was the SUP candidate for Porirua at the general election.

Still on course to get even, Van de Ven contacted NZ's Security Intelligence Service (SIS), who asked him to stay in place. He was put on the payroll, assigned a handler and given the code-name "Joe Martin."

Moscow sojourn

Van de Ven's common sense and "street smart" talents were recognized with selection for further training in Moscow from October 29, 1983 to February 12, 1984. He went with three other SUP members and one month later, they were joined by Bill Andersen, George Jackson and Marilyn Tucker (all SUP Central Committee members).

The Moscow course had been shortened because of the developing situation in New Zealand. Van de Ven noted that his and his fellow-delegates' passports had to be surrendered and were not stamped, so as to leave no record of their having been in the Soviet Union. He recalled:

> On arrival in Moscow, we were quarantined for medical checks over four days and given new identities. I became John Van, Jim Thompson became Jimmy Brown, Allan Ware—Allan Wolf, Peter Devlin—Peter Jay.

> This took place in an old mansion near Moscow. The ten acres of woodland was [sic] surrounded by high walls, so that nobody could look in or out. After that, we were transported in a mini-bus with black-curtained windows to the Lenin Institute for Higher Learning in Prospect Leningradski, across the road from Metro Aeroport, an underground station.

> There were 3,500 communists from all over the world, being trained five and half days a week, according to the requirements of their home country. We were assigned three tutors who were specialists on New Zealand. They were a (first name unknown) Venediev, who lectured on the National Question (racial manipulation) and trade unions. He was

also a staff member of the World Marxist Review. Other tutors included Bella Vorontsova (doctorate in history) and Eduard Nukhovich (doctorate in economics), both of whom later visited New Zealand to liaise with SUP branches.

"Peace" was high on the agenda. As one tutor told us: 'We have many clever people in the Soviet Union, but no one has even been able to come up with a weapon potentially as powerful as the peace movement.'

Taking New Zealand out of ANZUS

Van de Ven was told that the reason for the "condensed" 13-week course was that Soviet leader (and former KGB Chief) Yuri Andropov had initiated a strategy for taking a social democratic country out of the Western Alliance, by utilizing the "correlation of forces" provided by the "peace" and labor movement.

This was the time of massive anti-Nuclear marches in Europe, the Greenham Common "peace" protestors in England. Anti-NATO sentiment was sweeping Europe, fuelled by the "peace" movement, local communist parties and professional Soviet propagandists. There was a real fear in some circles that NATO might disintegrate and the Soviets were doing everything they could to make that fear a reality.

New Zealand was given a high priority by the Soviets, for its strategic propaganda potential. The Soviets prioritized countries according to their strategic interest. The United Kingdom, Chile, Argentina and South Africa were Category One. Tiny New Zealand was in Category Two— alongside the then Soviet client-state, India.

The particular circumstances of New Zealand, with a national election in late 1984, were seen as providing a suitable testing ground for this strategy. If it worked as intended, then the concept could be applied to countries such as Denmark. If New Zealand could be broken away from the Western Alliance, the Soviets reasoned that other countries could be persuaded to follow suit.

There were two key aims:

- To get rid of ANZUS.
- For the Labour Government to steer nuclear-free legislation through Parliament.

Van de Ven described the techniques of the strategy as "brilliant," which, when applied within the trade unions, the peace movement and the Labour Party worked as intended. He recalled:

> Our role was to influence and steer the peace movement, not by taking the top jobs, but to be done in such a way that the top people in the various peace groups were seen as reasonably responsible by the average New Zealander.

> So our training consisted of being able to train lesser-known communists, secret members, sympathizers and fellow-travelers, to take over these groups, unite them, but never take the leading roles. My own role was as a 'nuts and bolts' technician.

The overall Project Director was Gennady Yannaev, an engineer by training and later a leading member of the 1991 coup that overthrew Soviet leader Mikhail Gorbachev. Van de Ven got on well with Yannaev and was several times invited to his home for meals and drinks. He found Yannaev a dedicated and honest communist, who frequently vented his disgust at the corruption within the Nomenklatura. He was informally questioned about the other members of the New Zealand delegation, Bill Andersen and Ken Douglas.

Implementation

After training in Moscow, the four SUP members returned to New Zealand and a series of secret meetings with the unions, "peace" movement and the Labour Party began. A secret contract was even signed between the SUP and the Labour Party in the Hotel Workers Union rooms on Marion Street in Wellington.

Terms were struck. In return for SUP/Federation of Labour support in the 1984 General Election, the Labour Party agreed to implement the SUP's Soviet designed anti-nuclear policies. In return for this, the SUP agreed to hold the labor unions in line, while Labour's "right wing" faction would be allowed to sack thousands of Government workers, as part of a much needed program of state spending cuts.

New Zealanders got economic liberalization, tax reform and a more dynamic economy, in return for the destruction of their military alliance with the United States. The SUP betrayed the New Zealand labor movement to serve the strategic interests of their Soviet masters.

John Van de Ven was interviewed by Bernard Moran and Trevor Loudon in February of 1990 and again in 1991.

In 1985, with the Labour Government in power, the NZ SIS cut ties with John Van de Ven. The SIS simply could not trust the new Prime Minister to keep their agent's identity secret.

Hardly one in a thousand New Zealanders would have any inkling that the anti-nuclear policies they are so proud of were designed in Moscow.

The Soviets duped a whole country, just as they have done many times before and since.

Example Two:
The Cesar Chavez Holiday Campaign

The communist movement is big on iconic figures, symbolism and anniversaries. They love to lionize their heroes and glorify their martyrs, almost as much as they love to demonize their enemies.

One of the left's big heroes in the U.S. is the late Cesar Chavez, Founder of the United Farm Workers Union. Chavez, was trained by the Chicago based father of "community organizing," Saul Alinsky, and worked with the Communist Party USA (CPUSA) and Democratic Socialists of America his entire life.

Holiday campaign

The Cesar E. Chavez National Holiday campaign was established by Los Angeles by volunteers who organized and led the effort in California to win the first legal state holiday and day of service and learning in honor Cesar Chavez. The legal holiday bill introduced by then State Senator Richard Polanco (Los Angeles-D) was signed into law by then Governor Gray Davis (D) on August 18, 2000. The holiday is celebrated in California on Cesar E. Chavez's birthday, March 31st.

The California legal holiday set into motion a wave of initiatives resulting in optional and commemorative Cesar Chavez Days in nine additional states (Arizona, Colorado, Illinois, Michigan, New Mexico, Texas, Utah, Wisconsin and Rhode Island).

Cesar Chavez Day brings together "hundreds of thousands who engage in celebrations, service and learning projects, as well as other actions that further the many causes which Cesar Chavez worked for."

The long-term mission of the Cesar E. Chavez National Holiday is to work for national recognition of Cesar E. Chavez on his birthday, March

31st. The organization has formed national, state and local coalitions; organized volunteer committees; and provided education "about the value to our nation of honoring Cesar E. Chavez."

Barack Obama calls for National Holiday for Cesar E. Chavez

April 1, 2008 Washington DC–Evelina Alarcon, Executive Director of Cesar E. Chavez National Holiday welcomed the backing for a Cesar Chavez national holiday from Presidential candidate Senator Barack Obama who issued a statement on Cesar Chavez's birthday Monday, March 31, 2008.

The Cesar E. Chavez National Holiday website even boasts the endorsement of then presidential candidate, Barack Obama, for a national holiday in honor of their hero.[6]

Communist control

The website doesn't advertize the fact, but Evelina Alarcon, the only ever Executive Director of the Cesar E. Chavez National Holiday, was also the long-time Chair of the Southern California District of the Communist Party USA and Secretary of its National Mexican American Equality Commission—the Party body charged with manipulating America's Mexican community.[7]

Alarcon is open with her comrades about the Chavez campaign's potential to build the Party's influence:[8]

> If someone would have asked me one year ago, can my District really lead thousands? I probably would of hesitated. But today, I say yes, because a few comrades in my district are literally leading a movement of thousands in California for the Cesar Chavez holiday. We are a key part of the core of leaders who are coordinating the whole campaign...

> Our participation has opened many formerly closed doors. The California leaders who agreed to my being the public leader and state coordinator of the Cesar Chavez holiday campaign are prominent statewide and even national leaders. Most of them know that I am a Communist. Has this built the Party's influence? Yes. Has it built the Party's credibility? Yes. Is it opening new doors to us in other areas of labor and people's movements? Yes.

The Communist Party origins and intentions of the campaign were confirmed in a 2001 report, "Building the Communist Party USA in the South (PART 2)," by Russell Pelle, Chair Communist Party of Jacksonville, Florida:[9]

> The Party could do much more with agricultural workers, again there is the objective impediment of our small size, which of course cannot be overcome without active mass work. Tactically, we can be more open as communists with these workers and their organizations than might be prudent with other unions, especially at the onset. Thanks to the outstanding, historic work of comrades in California winning the Cesar Chavez Holiday, we have a special edge in working with agricultural workers unions. The Party should organize a southern tour by Comrade Evelina Alarcon to promote the Chavez holiday; comrades should initiate work to build a movement to win a national holiday. Such a project is an avenue for comrades outside the unions to establish working relations with union labor in general and farm labor and the Spanish-speaking community in general.

Using the unions and the Democrats

Alarcon's campaign follows the classic pattern. The Communist Party sets a policy then enlists the help of unions and other sympathizers to promote it. Then they get leftist and communist sympathizing Democrats to promote it inside their party. It then becomes Democrat Party policy, then state or national legislation. Meanwhile, the general public is totally in the dark.

The Holiday campaign's Advisory Council includes several prominent California Democrats, including Alarcon's brother Richard, a former State Senator and at the time, a Los Angeles City Councilor, and Richard Polanco, then Chairman of the California Latino Caucus Institute and author of the California Holiday bill for Cesar Chavez.

Sponsors of the campaign included Pennsylvania Communist Party member and unionist Royce Adams; former U.S. Senator and presidential candidate, John Edwards; Los Angeles Mayor Antonio Villaraigosa; musician Carlos Santana; actors—Edward James Olmos, Martin Sheen, George Lopez, Mike Farrell, Ed Begley, Jr., Lupe Ontiveros and Esai Morales; the Communist Party initiated union groups Coalition of Black Trade Unionists; Coalition of Labor Union Women; Labor Council for Latin American Advancement and the Maoist initiated Asian Pacific American Labor Alliance.

Unions on board include the International Longshore & Warehouse Union, Service Employees International Union Local 1000 (CA), Laborers International Union of North America, the AFL-CIO, American Federation of State, County and Municipal Employees, Communication Workers of America, Farm Labor Organizing Committee and of course, the United Farm Workers of America.

The NAACP and the National Council of La Raza have also signed on.

Obama photo op

In June of 2008, Evelina Alarcon got a great photo-op for her campaign when she presented a poster from the organization to Barack Obama's younger sister, Maya Soetoro-Ng, at a gathering in East Los Angeles:[10]

> Addressing a largely Latino audience in East Los Angeles yesterday, Dr. Maya Soetoro-Ng shared stories about her childhood with her older brother, Barack Obama, and the effect he has had on her life. Held in El Sereno's Hecho en Mexico restaurant, the event drew more than a hundred enthusiastic community activists, local elected officials, and regular citizens...

> Evelina Alarcon, a notable Obama supporter and the sister of long-time Los Angeles politician Richard Alarcon, presented a poster to Obama's sister commemorating the life of Cesar Chavez.

> Alarcon recounted the accomplishments of the late Chicano leader and argued persuasively for honoring his accomplishments with a national holiday. Reminding those in attendance that Barack Obama supports the call to make Cesar Chavez's birthday a national holiday. Alarcon trusts that if Obama is elected president the holiday will become a reality.

> Obama has been quoted recently to say: "As farm workers and laborers across America continue to struggle for fair treatment and fair wages, we find strength in what Cesar Chavez accomplished so many years ago and we should honor him for what he's taught us about making America a stronger, more just, and more prosperous nation. That's why I support the call to make Cesar Chavez's birthday a national holiday. It's time to recognize the contributions of this American icon to the ongoing efforts to perfect our union."

Clearly "designed to draw support to her brother's presidential candidacy" from two key voting blocs—women and Latinos—the event was organized by key California Democrat State Senate Majority Leader

Gloria Romero, State Senator Martha Escutia (ret.), State Board of Equalization Chair Judy Chu, Los Angeles City Controller Laura Chick, Los Angeles City Council member Ed Reyes and Los Angeles Unified School District Vice President Yolie Flores-Aguilar.[11]

That is how a few Communist Party members can build a nationwide campaign and change legislation in several states.

Standing: Evelina Alarcon (left), Maya Soetoro-Ng (right)

Example Three:
Latino Immigrants: Tools to Ensure a "Governing Coalition" for the Left

The U.S. communist movement has long exploited ethnic minorities for revolutionary purposes

According to the Party's own Constitution:[12]

> We are the party of the African American, Mexican American, Puerto Rican, all other Latino American, Native American, Asian American, and all racially and nationally oppressed peoples, as well as women, youth, and all other working people...

> It shall be the duty of all Party members to fight for the full social, political and economic equality of the African-American, Mexican-American, Puerto Rican, Native American Indians, Asian and Pacific Islanders, other oppressed minorities, immigrants and the foreign born, and to promote the unity of all people as essential to the advancement of their common interests.

18

Accordingly, the communists and their socialist allies have long promoted illegal immigration across the Mexican border and have worked tirelessly for "amnesty" for any illegals who manage to settle in the United States.

Bert Corona, Communist Father of the "Immigrants Rights" Movement

Bert Corona (1918-2001), was an icon of the California and Chicano left, and the father of the modern "immigrants rights" movement. Corona was born in 1918 in El Paso, Texas, at the height of the Mexican Revolution. His father was a member of the Partido Liberal Mexicano, an anarcho-syndicalist group and he was murdered when Bert was five.

In the 1930s, Corona was close to International Longshore and Warehouse Union leader and secret communist, Harry Bridges.

According to Communist Party USA member David Bacon:[13]

> Corona came to Los Angeles to study at USC, where he went to work and was caught up in the labor ferment of the late 1930s. He became president of Local 26 of the International Longshore and Warehouse Union, and a political ally of Harry Bridges, one of U.S. labor's most progressive and democratic leaders.

While working for Bridges' union, Corona was identified in Congressional testimony as a Communist Party USA (CPUSA) member. He was identified again in 1975.[14]

Later, Corona helped establish chapters of Saul Alinsky's Community Service Organization and in doing so… he met a young organizer named Cesar Chavez.

In 1964, Corona, Cesar Chavez and future Democratic Socialists of America (DSA) member, Dolores Huerta, forced Congress to end the guest worker "Bracero" Program. The next year, Mexicans and Filipinos went out on strike in Coachella and Delano California and the United Farm Workers was born. That year, in 1965, they went back to Congress. "Give us a law," they said, "that doesn't make workers into braceros or criminals behind barbed wire, into slaves for the growers."[15]

In 1959, Bert Corona and Ed Roybal, a future Democratic Congressmen and the father of current California Congresswoman Lucille Roybal-Allard, met in Fresno to form the Mexican American Political Association (MAPA).

The organization's mission was to support and promote Mexican American candidates within the Democratic Party. The young organization helped set up the Viva Kennedy clubs that, for the first time, brought large numbers of Mexican Americans into a Presidential campaign.

In the 1960s, Corona served as Co-Chair for both Lyndon Johnson's and Bobby Kennedy's presidential campaigns in California. Today, the Communist Party still has strong influence in MAPA, which can still make or break the candidacy of Democratic Party aspirants in the Los Angeles area.[16]

Corona ran MAPA and in 1965, California Governor Edmund "Pat" Brown appointed him to the California Civil Rights Commission. Corona even delivered a nationally televised address at the violence-prone 1968 Democratic Party convention in Chicago.

Soon after, Corona broke with the Democrats and backed the separatist La Raza Unida Party, which was based on the concept of Aztlan, the notion that an occupied Chicano nation in the southwestern U.S. needs to be wrested from the occupying "Anglos."[17]

La Hermandad Mexicana Nacional

Corona was most closely identified with the work of La Hermandad Mexicana Nacional, or the National Mexican Brotherhood. Founded in 1951 in San Diego, the organization originally provided services to immigrants. Over the years, La Hermandad established chapters throughout the country and at one point boasted a membership of 30,000. The focus was organizing trade unions, defending undocumented workers and providing social services to the undocumented.

Corona quickly recognized the urgency of this group's efforts and he helped establish its Los Angeles chapter. For the next four decades, he devoted much of his time to La Hermandad. He was the group's Executive Director when he died.

Corona also used immigrants to protest U.S. involvement in Vietnam. A supporter of Fidel Castro, Corona was one of the few to bemoan the fall of the Berlin Wall.

"Renewed class struggle in these societies will lead to new forms of social arrangements," he said. "The workers of East Germany, for example, aren't about to give up easily many of the supports they had under socialism, such as low rents and free education for their children."

Corona "earned icon status with the left wing of the Democratic Party, becoming a hero to state politicians such as Tom Hayden, Sheila Kuehl, Assemblyman Gil Cedillo and Assembly speaker Antonio Villaraigosa, among others." He maintained a residence in Washington and was even entertained by President Clinton.

Under Corona's leadership, Hermandad was a powerful lobbying force for the City's radical Latinos. During the latter 1980's and 1990's, it secured a staggering $35 million in grants, but eventually collapsed under a mountain of debt.[18]

Defending the "Undocumented"

In the spring of 1974, when La Hermandad was still in its heyday, the organization held a conference at Northridge, where representatives from 10 states met to "discuss problems confronting Mexicans in the United States who had no visas or citizenship documents. The first day, participants discussed how to defend persons detained by immigration authorities and how to help immigrants acquire disability and unemployment insurance and welfare:"

> Over the course of the day, Corona seemed to be everywhere. If not speaking at one of the workshops, he was bustling around making sure everything was running like clockwork.

The next day, participants discussed resolutions from the workshops. Corona "stressed the need to establish a legislative program to campaign against bills that would crack down on the hiring of illegal immigrants and to fight for humane immigration policies and practices."

Corona's patient, disciplined Communist Party training was evident as he sought to calm and neutralize ultra-left elements who might damage the credibility of his organization.

According to participant Carlos Ortega:

> This conference helped us organize at our campus and in the local community. At the same time, La Hermandad was also going through some changes. There had been an influx of student activists, professionals, and community organizers. The ideological nature of these groups brought a strong Marxist appeal, which changed the focus of the organization as Corona knew it. The newer activists wanted to deemphasize the service aspect of the organization and focus on larger ideological issues. At Northridge, there was some support from students who wanted to push a more revolutionary agenda, but many of

us were not convinced how this agenda—which had its merits—would bring immediate results for the undocumented and the poor. I threw my support to Corona and to the idea that organizing could not be accomplished by polishing leftist vocabulary but rather by working hard, speaking to one person at a time, and building an organization.

By 1975, Corona had moved his operation to the San Fernando Valley where Cal State Northridge was located, so he could continue to work with the undocumented. A group of students including Carlos Ortega brought Corona back on campus for a conference to clarify how students should organize and mobilize against deportation raids and repression in general.

"Present-day immigration policies and practices of the government are fundamental characteristics of the capitalist system," he said, "and the only possible way to confront those oppressing us is to organize as one, the alliance of students, workers, and the community." He added: "The student movement only has validity if directly linked with the workers' movement and the movement of people."

Corona, "more than any other person, furthered the ideological struggle against the nativists," according to Rodolfo Acuna, a Marxist professor of Chicano Studies at Cal State Northridge.[19]

> Corona made the issue of immigration and undocumented workers, in particular, a civil and human rights concern.

CASA

Corona also founded another "immigrants' rights" group, Centro de Action Social Autonoma, or CASA for short. Three young activists worked together in CASA—Tony Villar (aka Antonio Villaraigosa), Gil Cedillo and Maria Elena Durazo. All three would go on to become key players in the California "immigrants' rights" movement.

Villaraigosa and Cedillo worked on the CASA newspaper, Sín Fronteras. "At CASA, we wanted to organize the undocumented into unions, instead of seeing them as a threat," Cedillo said.

Villaraigosa worked full time for CASA and did a stint in Cuba with the communist run Venceremos Brigade. He then went into the labor movement and into state politics through the Democratic Party, before assuming his current role as Mayor of Los Angeles—the most pro-illegal immigrant mayor the city has ever seen.[20]

Gil Cedillo, Marxist DREAMER

California State Assembly member Gil Cedillo is close to both the communist and socialist movements.

In May of 1992, the Communist Party USA newspaper, People's Weekly World, published a May Day supplement which included a call to "support our continuing struggle for justice and dignity."

Endorsers of the call included Gilbert Cedillo, Civil Service Advocate and member of SEIU Local 660.[21]

In June of 1996, the Communist Party USA paper, People's Weekly World, held a tribute event in Los Angeles for unionists Jerry Acosta and Gil Cedillo:[22]

> The Southern California Friends of the People's Weekly World tribute to two of Los Angeles' finest labor leaders, Jerry Acosta and Gilbert Cedillo, became a dynamic rally of elected officials, activists, labor and community leaders in solidarity with labor struggles and in the fight to defeat the ultra-right in November...
>
> "The People's Weekly World and all of us in this room feel very strongly about who we honor today," said Evelina Alarcon, chair of the Southern California District and national secretary of the Communist Party USA, one of the emcees of the tribute. "Jerry Acosta and Gilbert Cedillo represent the new fightback vision of the Sweeney, Trumka, Chavez-Thompson leadership in the AFL-CIO. They represent the rank and file that is pushing from the bottom for that new vision!"

In June 2008, the Socialist International (SI) Migrations Committee held a Migrations Reform, Integration, Rights forum in Los Angeles.

Democratic Socialists of America, the SI's main U.S. affiliate, was represented by DSA National Director Frank Llewellyn plus Duane Campbell and Dolores Delgado Campbell of DSA's Anti-Racism and Latino networks. Then California State Senator Gil Cedillo was also in attendance.[23]

Currently, Cedillo employs Conrado Terrazas, son of late Los Angeles Communist Party activist, Mauricio Terrazas, as his Communications Director.[24] [25]

The DREAM Act

On January 11, 2011, Assembly member Gilbert Cedillo (D-Los Angeles), introduced the California DREAM Act in the California State Assembly.

The proposed law would grant qualifying undocumented college students access to institutional financial aid and Cal Grants from the University of California, California State University and Community Colleges.

The California DREAM Act, first introduced by Cedillo in 2006, was introduced in two bills. The first bill would allow students that meet the in-state tuition requirements to apply for and receive specified financial aid administered by California's public colleges and universities. The types of aid these students would be eligible for include: Board of Governors (BOG) Fee Waiver and Institutional Student Aid: a Student aid program administered by the attending college or university (i.e. State University Grant, UC Grant). The second bill would allow students that meet the in-state tuition requirements to apply for and receive Cal Grants by California's public colleges and universities.

Assembly member Gilbert Cedillo announced the introduction of the California DREAM Act with a coalition of business, education and labor leaders including Kelly Candaele, Los Angeles Community College Board of Trustees; Javier Nunez, President, Executive Board, Laborers International Union, Local 300; Kent Wong, Director, UCLA Labor Center, National Council of La Raza; Nancy Ramirez, Western Regional Counsel, MALDEF; Angelica Salas, Executive Director, CHIRLA, LA Dream Team and NAKASEC (National Korean American Service & Education Consortium), Korean Resource Center; Marvin Andrade, Executive Director, CARECEN; Evan Bacalao, Sr. Director of Civic Engagement, NALEO and David Huerta, Regional Vice President, SEIU United Service Workers West.[26]

Here we see the familiar pattern—Marxists and organized labor working through the Democrat Party to promote communist inspired legislation. Of those standing with Cedillo, Kelly Candaele, Kent Wong (a former member of the Communist Workers Party) and Angelica Salas were involved with the Progressive Los Angeles Network, a creation of Democratic Socialists of America.[27]

AB130 was signed by Governor Jerry Brown on June 25, 2011 and AB131 was signed by Brown on October 8, 2011.

California Rep. Linda Sanchez (a board member of the Democratic Socialists of America-controlled Economic Policy Institute) posted an article on the Huffington Post blog on September 17, 2012, co-signed by several leftist California activists and legislators, supporting Barack Obama for president:

We support comprehensive immigration reform and we believe President Obama is on the right track. He favors an immigration policy that rewards hard work and responsibility and lifts the shadow of deportation from young people who were brought here as children, through no fault of their own, and grew up as Americans. And given congressional inaction, the President and the DHS implemented a stop-gap measure that temporarily lifts the shadow of deportation from DREAMers.

The economic recovery is not yet complete, but we recognize President Obama's work to help our communities. From the Latina back in school thanks to expanded Pell Grants to the family that can now afford health care for their child with a preexisting condition, all Latinos need a leader that will stand by his word and respect their pursuit of the American Dream.

Sadly when Mitt Romney speaks to Latinos today he will not answer our Grito de Verdad y Liderazgo because he stands on the wrong side of every Latino voter priority. Latinos know that what we need is a President who will lead our community with respect and value our contributions and that the contrast between Romney's campaign rhetoric and four years of action from this administration is clear: the man we need to lead us is Barack Obama.

Gill Cedillo signed the letter, as did his old CASA comrade Maria Elena Durazo.[28]

Maria Elena Durazo, Labor Leader, Socialist

As Executive Secretary-Treasurer of the Los Angeles County Federation of Labor, CASA veteran Maria Elena Durazo leads the country's largest labor council. She was President of UNITE HERE! Local 11 from 1989-2006, representing more than 440,000 hotel and restaurant workers in Los Angeles. Under Durazo's leadership, Local 11 has "become a vital force in the life of Los Angeles and in the debate over the city's future."

Like Gil Cedillo, Durazo is close to both the communist and socialist movements.

In 1992, she signed the Communist Party May Day pledge alongside Cedillo.[29]

In November 1993, Los Angeles Democratic Socialists of America's Debs-Thomas Dinner, honored Hotel and Restaurant Employees Union leader Maria Elena Durazo.[30]

Maria Elena Durazo receiving award from Jose LaLuz

In 2000, DSA kicked off events at that year's Democratic National Convention by organizing a major panel on the 2000 presidential and Congressional elections. DSA National Director Horace Small played host to DSA leaders Harold Meyerson of LA Weekly, Barbara Ehrenreich, who has been stumping for Ralph Nader, and Cornel West, who was a Co-Chair of the Bill Bradley Presidential primary campaign.

They were joined by panelists Maria Elena Durazo, President of H.E.R.E in LA; John Nichols of the Madison daily Capital Times; and Antonio Villaraigosa, Speaker Emeritus of California's Assembly.

DSAer Lynn Shaw, Vice-Chair of the LA County Democrats, chaired the event.[31]

Maria Elena Durazo was also active in the DSA-inspired Progressive Los Angeles Network.[32]

Changing Demographics and Voting in California

Beginning in 1994, immigrant numbers in California began to grow exponentially. Prior to Proposition 187, the number of new citizens in California each year had been a steady 50,000 to 60,000. In 1994, the number jumped to 118,567. In 1995, it was 171,285. In 1996, it was 378,014.

Also in 1994, the husband and wife team, Miguel Contreras, the leader of the Los Angeles County Federation of Labor and Maria Elena Durazo, then the leader of the Hotel Workers in Los Angeles, began something new: they linked organizing immigrant workers to organizing immigrant voters. And they hired a young immigrant-rights radical named Fabian Nunez to carry their flag.

Nunez served as L.A. Labor's Political Director and eventually became the Speaker of the California Assembly.

The campaigns Durazo, Contreras and consultant Richie Ross developed, organized new union workers and dramatically increased the political impact of Latino voters on California (and national) politics. Their plan tripled the number of registered Latino voters, increased the Democratic share of that vote by 50% and doubled the percentage of the total votes cast in California from Latinos.

> Through the rest of the 1990's our campaigns focused on legislative races in Los Angeles. We succeeded. But it was all small.

In 2000, Maria Elena Durazo pushed for something bigger...

In 2000, the message was controversial. "If you want to make a difference, voting isn't enough. Don't bother voting unless you sign our pledge to get 100% of your family to vote." Latino turnout rose... and accounted for 14% of the votes cast according to the State's voter registration and voting history records.

In 2005, over dinner with some friends, Durazo heard a successful Latina businesswoman bemoaning the low Latino turnout for Antonio Villaraigosa in the March 2005 Democratic Mayoral primary. The woman told Durazo that it was "imperdonable" (unforgivable).

Voting records show that the L.A. Labor Fed's subsequent "Imperdonable" Campaign increased Latino turnout in the Mayoral run-off by 50%, helping Villaraigosa win the election.

In May 2010, Durazo called Richie Ross and others together. Her message was clear. Latinos would end up voting for Democrat gubernatorial candidate Jerry Brown. That would be easy. The "challenge was how to motivate them to vote at all."

According to Ross:[33]

> Fortunately, the Republicans in Arizona wrote a new law.

> When we conducted focus groups, people brought the issue up to us. When we polled it, we found 93% of California Latinos knew about it, 84% said it was more about profiling than immigration, and 73% thought it could happen in California. That view became more believable when Meg Whitman and Steve Poizner in the Republican primary tried to outdo one another as anti-immigrant politicians.

So instead of a campaign where our candidate was a 72-year-old white guy, Maria Elena and the L.A Fed ran a campaign on behalf of "Tuesday"—Martes—and against an opponent—Arizona—that research told us Latinos were motivated to defeat.

Latinos accounted for 22% of the votes cast in California. None of us know how much bigger this trend will be. We do know that Pete Wilson's TV ad got one thing right… they keep coming… to the polls.

Maria Elena Durazo's campaign has changed California voting patterns dramatically, turning the state into a socialist-led Democratic stronghold. The same process is now underway in several other Southwestern states.

Lorrezo Torrez: Arizona's Most Influential Politician?

Lorenzo Torrez (1928-2012), was the long-time organizer of the Arizona Communist Party.

A former copper miner, Torrez joined the CPUSA in 1952 during the protracted Empire Zinc Corporation mine strike in Bayard, New Mexico.[34]

Unemployed, "hounded and harassed" by the FBI, Torrez moved from job to job until he landed a permanent position as a Communist Party organizer in California, organizing in Los Angeles' Latino community. He worked with the Party for over 20 years until he reached 65, chairing the Party's a National Commission for Mexican-American Equality.[35]

Torrez had a big impact on Arizona, and Southwest politics. He paved the way for Communist backed Congressmen Ed Pastor and Raul Grijalva to win Congressional seats in Arizona. He organized opposition to any attempt by Southwestern states to shut down illegal immigration. He also helped to change voting patterns across the entire region.

According to a pre-conference discussion paper, "Special Convention Discussion: Mexican American Equality," written for the Communist Party USA at the May 2010 Convention in New York, by Rosalio Munoz:[36]

> The Communist Party has made historic contributions to the Mexican American people and to their struggles for social justice. It was the first and most persistent and helpful in seeing and working on integrating Mexican Americans into all aspects of U.S. society and in particular class and democratic struggles. It has been foremost in seeing the need for recognizing the plight and need for special steps to be taken in the struggles for equality for Mexican Americans. The more that it has

contributed to, and participated, the more the Party has grown among Mexican Americans.

With the national support of the Party, Comrades Lorenzo and Anita Torres have played historic roles in this work in ideological, economic, and political struggles in the Party and in mass work, in educational and organizational efforts. With their retirement, there is a clear need to carry on their work.

In the early seventies, Lorenzo and Anita were called on to focus their work in the key population, economic and political area for Mexican Americans. They spoke the language of the people both in English and Spanish. They worked along with other Black and white comrades like Bill Taylor and Rose Chernin, especially among the young Chicano workers and community, and got active in the mass work and struggle. They then built their work in another key area, Arizona, and dealt with the work on a national basis. They helped Mexican Americans see their future in building coalitions, and fighting for peace. This type of concentration work, in line with our size and organizational capability, is what is needed for continued work.

In 1974, Torrez moved with his family to Tucson where he served as Chair of the Arizona Communist Party for more than 30 years. He also led the party's Chicano Equality Commission and was a member of the CPUSA National Committee.

He built the Arizona Party into an influential organization in "all the progressive movements of Arizona."

According to Arizona Party member Steve Valencia, "Lorenzo changed the political landscape of Arizona. For him, the liberation of the working class and equality for the Mexican American people were inherently tied together."

In 2004, Lorenzo Torrez and his comrade Rosalio Munoz were entrusted by the CPUSA with swinging the Latino vote in the Southern states behind the Democratic Party:[37]

> TUCSON, Ariz.—Communist Party leaders and activists met here to discuss plans to bring out the broadest possible Mexican American and Latino vote to defeat the ultra right in the November elections and to strengthen the CPUSA's work among this section of the population. The participants at the meeting, held in the Salt of the Earth Labor College on May 15-16, came chiefly from the Southwest and the West Coast.

Lorenzo Torrez, chair of the Party's Mexican American Equality Commission, reviewed the Commission's work in the recent period. He proposed the organizing of a left-center Latino coalition to mobilize the progressive sentiments of U.S. Latinos. Rosalío Muñoz, CPUSA organizer in Southern California, reported on Latinos and the elections. He noted that the presidential race will be decided in key "battleground states." A number of these, such as Arizona, New Mexico, and Colorado, are states where Mexican Americans are concentrated, he said.

Muñoz proposed that the CPUSA put out literature in both Spanish and English explaining what is at stake for Latinos in the upcoming elections.

José A. Cruz, editor of Nuestro Mundo, the Spanish-language section of the People's Weekly World, discussed ways of improving the paper's coverage of critical issues in the Mexican American and Latino communities.

Munoz was one of several communists active in the Latino Congreso 2007, which was designed partly to influence the 2008 election cycle. According to an article written for Communidad by Munoz and Joelle Fishman of the Communist Party USA Political Action Commission:

Some 2000 Latino leaders and activists from throughout the United States came together in Los Angeles October 5-9 to iron out a plan of action and a social justice program of issues for the 2008 elections with the goal of bringing out 10 million Latino voters that can play a decisive role in the presidential and congressional elections.

Latinos can be decisive in determining the presidential electoral in the key battle ground states of "Florida, New Mexico, Arizona, Colorado and Nevada ... and congressional elections in twenty states" that can change the political direction of the country said Antonio Gonzalez President of the Southwest Voter Registration Project in opening up the 2nd National Latino Congreso convened by 10 national Latino organizations and hundreds of state and local groups from 22 states.

"We are going to mobilize massively to reach record levels of Latino vote" on the key issues of immigration reform, the war, greening cities, health care and climate change declared Gonzalez. While recognizing that "today we don't have a critical mass to affect that change", Gonzalez said this can be achieved with "conscious thinking, planning and organizing" leading up to the 2008 elections." "We have big issues not only as Latinos but as citizens of the world", he concluded.[38]

Torrez fought almost to the end of his life to organize undocumented immigrant workers. "Lorenzo urged us to join every action against SB-1070 and struggle to repeal that racist law," said Steve Valencia referring to the recall defeat of Arizona Senate President Russell Pearce, the author of the SB-1070, Arizona's anti-illegal immigration law.[39]

Eliseo Medina, "Building a Progressive Majority"

Eliseo Medina is one of the U.S.'s most influential labor union officials. He was described by the Los Angeles Times as "one of the most successful labor organizers in the country" and was named one of the "Top 50 Most Powerful Latino Leaders" in Poder Magazine. He is currently leading the Service Employees International Union efforts to achieve comprehensive immigration reform that "rebuilds the nation's economy, secures equal labor and civil rights protections for workers to improve their wages and work conditions and provides legal channels and a path to citizenship."

Medina is both the country's most influential "immigration reform" activist and a Marxist. He is an Honorary Chair of Democratic Socialists of America.[40]

Medina's career as a labor activist began in 1965 when, as a 19-year-old grape-picker, he participated in the United Farm Workers' strike in Delano, California. Over the next 13 years, Medina worked alongside labor leader and civil rights activist Cesar Chavez and honed his skills as a union organizer and political strategist; eventually rising through the ranks to serve as the United Farm Workers' National Vice President.[41]

Medina learned voting strategies from Fred Ross; a Saul Alinsky trained activist and the brains behind Cesar Chavez. Ross was to eventually have an impact on the national stage.

Fred Ross conceived the voter outreach strategy that not only elected Communist Party affiliate Ed Roybal as Los Angeles' first Latino Council member in 1949, but also laid the groundwork for the Obama campaign's Latino voter outreach campaign in 2008.

Ross trained United Farm Workers organizers Marshall Ganz, Miguel Contreras (Maria Elena Durazo's husband) and Eliseo Medina in voter outreach strategies to reach "occasional" voting Latinos and these three took what they learned to California politics.

Ganz and Medina then brought this voter outreach model to the Obama campaign.[42]

In 2008, Eliseo Medina even served on Barack Obama's National Latino Advisory Council, while his DSA comrade, Jose LaLuz, served as Chairman of Latinos for Obama and personally campaigned in Colorado and New Mexico registering, educating and mobilizing voters right up until Election Day.

Latino Voters Key to Obama Win in Battleground States

According to the Communist Party's People's Weekly World of September 19, 2008:

> Latino Voters Key to Obama Win in Battleground States

> The historic Nov. 4th presidential election is less than two months away, and a monumental battle is heating up in a few crucial swing states, as some nine million Latino voters prepare to cast their ballot, which could be the deciding factor for an Obama win.

> Latinos are the fastest growing minority group in the U.S. at 15 percent of the population and represent nine percent of eligible voters. But many agree the Latino vote could be the key bloc that could lead to an Obama victory, especially in battleground states where Latinos make up at least 10 percent of the voting population...

> Latino voters represent 35 percent of the electorate in New Mexico, 11 percent in Colorado, 12 percent in Nevada and 14 percent in Florida. According to the poll Obama is expected to win the majority of Latino voters in California, which is the state with the largest Latino population.

> Jose LaLuz is the chairperson for Latinos for Obama and is campaigning in Colorado and New Mexico registering, educating and mobilizing voters until Election Day. He is also the director of the Leadership Academy with the American Federation of State, County and Municipal Employees Union.

> LaLuz spoke with the People's Weekly World during an AFL-CIO labor forum at the Democratic National Convention in Denver.

> "Well over 60 percent of Latino voters are supporting Obama—closer to 66 percent now, ...The right wing is pulling all its dirty tricks even in the Latino community. We all realize that Bush used appeals to 'family values,' religion and the sanctity of marriage, etc. to get white workers

and Reagan Democrats to back him last time...Well they are using the same stuff, the same tactics in the Latino communities. When you combine this with their attention on swing states we find they are waging an especially big push against Obama in the Mexican and Chicano communities in Colorado and New Mexico..."

LaLuz explained his tactics to the People's Weekly World:

The Obama campaign is working in both New Mexico and Colorado, among other states, telling Latino voters about McCain's terrible stands on the economy and about the horrible role Republicans have played and continue to play on immigration... "We are showing how the companies and outfits that exploit Latino workers are the people behind McCain."

Between now and Election Day LaLuz said that the Obama campaign is registering voters in New Mexico and Colorado and developing lists of tens of thousands of Latino supporters for Obama.

"Those lists will constitute the people we bring out on Election Day."

Medina is also friendly with the Communist Party.

As Keynote speaker, Eliseo Medina received a standing ovation at the People's Weekly World banquet in Berkeley on Nov. 18, 2001, when he sharply criticized Republicans for killing an economic stimulus program that would have "benefited working families".

Medina thanked the World and Nuestro Mundo for continued coverage of labor struggles.

"Wherever workers are in struggle," Medina said, "they find the PWW regularly reporting issues and viewpoints that are seldom covered by the regular media. For us, the PWW has been and always will be the people's voice."

While welcoming federalization of airport security screeners, Medina criticized Congress' new requirement that screeners must now be U.S. citizens—though this is not required of airline pilots or members of the military. He said immigration laws should be changed to grant immigrants equal rights.

"[K]eep a sense of purpose," he urged the audience, maintain a "sense of outrage."

"Fight back," he said, "against those who use the post-Sept. 11 crisis to scapegoat immigrants and minorities, to make the rich richer and the poor poorer, and destroy what remains of government capacity to serve the great majority of people in this country."

Changing Labor

Medina's biggest contribution to the "immigrants' rights" movement is his work in changing organized labor's immigration outlook.

Before the AFL-CIO was taken over by Democratic Socialists of America in 1995, most U.S. labor unions vehemently opposed illegal immigration. Unions correctly saw illegal aliens as a threat to American workers' wages and conditions.

It was a tough sell changing this attitude, but Medina and his Marxist comrades were up to the task. Medina used his base in SEIU to get the ball rolling.

Medina joined SEIU in 1986, where he helped revive a local union in San Diego—building its membership from 1,700 to over 10,000 in five years. He was a key strategist in the Los Angeles strike by SEIU Local 1877's building service workers, who in April 2000 "won the largest wage increase in the 15-year history of SEIU's Justice for Janitors campaign."

Medina has served as International Executive Vice President of the SEIU since 1996, helping make SEIU the fastest-growing union on the West Coast and the largest union in California. Since 1996, more than 1.2 million workers across the country have joined SEIU, the union with the largest membership of immigrant workers in the country.[43]

According to the Democratic Socialists of America website, Eliseo Medina is widely credited with playing a key role in the AFL-CIO's decision to adopt a new policy on immigration a few years ago and was one of the organizers of the Immigrant Workers Freedom Bus Rides in 2003.[44]

Medina worked hand in hand with UNITE HERE President John Wilhelm, to change AFL-CIO immigration policy at the 1999 Los Angeles Convention.[45]

Then, claiming U.S. immigration policy is "broken and needs to be fixed," the AFL-CIO on February 16, 2000, called for a new amnesty for millions of undocumented workers and the repeal of the 1986 law that criminalized hiring them.

The position, adopted unanimously by the federation's Executive Council at its winter meeting in New Orleans, represented a dramatic shift for the AFL-CIO, which had backed the so-called employer sanctions law, 15 years previously.

Eliseo Medina, Vice President of SEIU, "was among the early proponents of the new policy."[46]

According to the SEIU website, Medina has played the leading role in uniting Change to Win and AFL-CIO behind the immigration reform movement:

> Working to ensure the opportunity to pass comprehensive immigration reform does not slip away, Medina led the effort to unite the unions of the Change to Win federation and AFL-CIO around a comprehensive framework for reform. Serving as a leading voice in Washington, frequently testifying before Congress, Medina has also helped to build a strong, diverse coalition of community and national partners that have intensified the call for reform and cultivated necessary political capital to hold elected leaders accountable. Medina has also helped strengthen ties between the Roman Catholic Church and the labor movement to work on common concerns such as immigrant worker rights and access to health care.[47]

"Governing Coalition"

At the "progressive" America's Future Now! conference in Washington, D.C. on June 2, 2009, Eliseo Medina addressed attendees on the necessity of "comprehensive immigration reform." Medina let the cat out of the bag. This has nothing to do with humanitarianism, reuniting families or giving foreigners access to greater opportunities.

This was all about raw political power.

Speaking of Latino voters, Medina said, "When they voted in November, they voted overwhelmingly for progressive candidates. Barack Obama got two out of every three voters that showed up:"

> So I think there's two things that matter for the progressive community.
>
> Number one, if we are to expand this electorate to win, the progressive community needs to solidly be on the side of immigrants, that we'll expand and solidify the progressive coalition for the future...
>
> When you are in the middle of a fight for your life you will remember who was there with you. And immigrants count on progressives to be able to do that.
>
> Number two.
>
> We reform the immigration laws, it puts 12 million people on the path to citizenship and eventually voters. Can you imagine if we have, even the same ratio, two out of three?

> If we have eight million new voters who care about ...... and will be voting. We will be creating a governing coalition for the long term, not just for an election cycle...

In other words, Marxists, like Medina, are using Latino immigrants to put the Democrats into power—forever.[48]

Example 4:
The Vietnam Scam

Over several years, the Committees of Correspondence for Democracy and Socialism (CCDS), and their allies have waged a clever propaganda campaign to win U.S. taxpayer support for their friends in communist ruled Vietnam. The campaign is ongoing, but demonstrates well, how a small communist sect can co-opt senior Democratic Party representatives to promote communist inspired legislation in the U.S. Congress. Playing on emotion and guilt, U.S. taxpayers are being scammed into funding a communist Government that killed more than 50,000 U.S. servicemen and conquered the once sovereign nation of South Vietnam.

The main vehicle for this effort has been the Vietnam Agent Orange Relief and Responsibility Campaign (VAORRC), a project of two heavily communist infiltrated organizations: Veterans for Peace and Vietnam Veterans Against the War. There are also close ties to two international communist front organizations:

> In support of justice for Vietnamese Agent Orange victims, a national coalition of veterans, Vietnamese-Americans and other community leaders announces the formation of the Vietnam Agent Orange Relief and Responsibility Campaign on February 28, 2005.

Right from the start, the organization was dominated by the pro-Vietnam CCDS.

In 2010, VAORRC board members included CCDS affiliates Bill Goodman, Felicia Gustin, Betita Martinez, Jack O'Dell, Paul Shannon, Walter Teague, Ngo Thanh Nhan and Frank Velgara.

Other notable board members included Vinie Burrows, U.S. representative of the international communist front Women's International Democratic Federation; Bill Fletcher, Jr. of Democratic Socialists of America and the Freedom Road Socialist Organization (FRSO); Claire Tran of FRSO; Communist Party affiliate Nadya Williams;

Marjorie Cohn, a former President of the National Lawyers Guild who serves on the board of the old Soviet front organization, the International Association of Democratic Lawyers (IADL); and Jeanne Mirer, International President of the IADL.[49]

The organization is led by Merle Ratner, a former member of the CCDS National Coordinating Committee and Susan Schnall, a former Navy Nurse and Socialist Workers Party hang around, court marshaled for anti-war activism during the Vietnam War. Schnall is currently a Professor in Health Policy and Planning at NYU and a member of Vietnam Veterans Against the War, Veterans for Peace and American Public Health Association.[50] [51]

According to VAORRC's website:[52]

> The U.S. government used Agent Orange, from 1962 to 1971, as part of their war in Vietnam. Agent Orange contains dioxin, one of the deadliest substances known, and continues to cause death and sickness to millions of Vietnamese and to many U.S. veterans of the Vietnam war. Now even more than thirty years after the war, Agent Orange remains in the land and water of Vietnam, causing horrific birth defects to several generation of children.
>
> We support the Vietnamese Agent Orange survivors and their representative, the Vietnam Association for Victims of Agent Orange/Dioxin in their lawsuit against the U.S. chemical companies. Their lawsuit is a historic first effort by Vietnamese victims of Agent Orange to achieve compensation from the manufacturers who profited from this chemical warfare.
>
> We call upon our government to meet its responsibility to compensate the more than three million Vietnamese people suffering from the effects of Agent Orange. The U.S. government has a moral and legal obligation to heal the wounds of war.

Propaganda Campaign

An evening of solidarity with Vietnam was held at the 6th CCDS Convention in San Francisco in July of 2009.

It featured highlights of the recent CCDS sponsored tour of Vietnam and the "ongoing crisis of Agent Orange." Earlier in the day, a documentary film by Clay Claiborne, "Vietnam: American Holocaust," "brought all the bitter horrors and memories of those years back to the surface." Claiborne was part of a CCDS Study Tour to Vietnam in 2008 and "after presenting the film to the Vietnamese, they ran it on nationwide television."

Claiborne even got left wing actor Martin Sheen to narrate his film. Claiborne also planned another documentary on the achievements of Vietnamese socialism after the war.[53]

Martin Sheen, Clay Claiborne

Co-Chaired by Vietnam veteran Paul Cox and Judge Claudia Morcom, the evening was designed to launch a campaign for the U.S. to make reparations to Vietnam for the ongoing impact of the mass poisoning of the population with Agent Orange. Morcom was one of seven international judges on the International People's Tribunal of Conscience in Support of the Vietnamese victims of Agent Orange, which had been organized in Paris in June of 2009 by the International Association of Democratic Lawyers:[54]

> The veterans and their families and friends who spoke from the floor were choked with emotion as they offered accounts not only of what they had seen that happened to the Vietnamese, but also to the veterans who were poisoned, and birth defects on their children as well. CCDS joined the campaign by acclamation.

Lobbying Congress

The groundwork for the public campaign had been laid back in 2007 with the visits to the United States by a Vietnamese delegation, with a second in 2010.

From November 1-14, 2007, Dr. Nguyen Thi Ngoc Phuong, a leading clinician/researcher on the effects of Agent Orange on women and children in Vietnam, from Tu Du Hospital, Ho Chi Minh City, visited Washington, D.C. on a Vietnam Agent Orange Public Health Tour

Dr. Phuong, Vice President of the Vietnam Association for Victims of Agent Orange, toured Washington, D.C. where a policy of the American Public Health Association on Agent Orange (Vietnamese version) was passed on November 6, 2007. Dr. Phuong was accompanied by Merle Ratner and Susan Schnall of the Vietnam Agent Orange Relief & Responsibility Campaign.[55]

Dr. Phuong has held many senior positions in Vietnam's communist government including:

- 2006—Present Vice President, Union of Solidarity Societies of Ho Chi Minh City.
- 2004—Present Vice President, Vietnam Association for Victims of Agent Orange/Dioxin (VAVA).
- 2000—Present Member of the Presidium, Vietnam Fatherland Front.
- 1999—Present Vice President, Vietnam Fatherland Front of Ho Chi Minh City.
- 1999—Present President, Vietnam American Friendship Association of Ho Chi Minh City.
- 1992—1997—Deputy Chair, Commission of the International Relations of the Vietnam National Assembly.
- 1987—1992—Vice Speaker of the Vietnam National Assembly.

The delegation met several members of Congress including John Conyers, Sheila Jackson Lee and Bob Filner.

Members of the U.S. Congress and the U.S. Department of State showed their support for Vietnamese "victims of Agent Orange/Dioxin" during a visit to the U.S. by a delegation from the Vietnam Association of Victims of Agent Orange/Dioxin (VAVA) on November 22nd to December 4th, 2010, at the invitation of Veterans for Peace and the Vietnam Agent Orange Relief & Responsibility Campaign.

The Vietnamese delegation met with the leaderships of the VFP and VAORRC to discuss assistance for Agent Orange victims and future cooperation, "especially when commemorating the 50th Anniversary of the start of the dioxin war against Vietnam on August 10, 1961."

November 6, 2007: Filner's Capitol Hill office. (second from left) Susan Schall, Dr. Nguyen Thi Ngoc Phuong, Bob Filner and Merle Ratner

They also met with Senator Al Franken of Minnesota; Congressman John Conyers, Chairman of the Committee on the Judiciary under the U.S. House of Representatives; Congressman Eni Faleomavaega, Chairman of the Subcommittee on Asia, the Pacific and the Global Environment under the Committee on Foreign Affairs at the U.S. House of Representatives; and again with Bob Filner:

> These U.S. congressmen expressed their support for Vietnamese victims of Agent Orange and welcomed VAVA's efforts to assist the victims. They stated that the U.S. administration must attach more importance to settling the aftermaths of dioxin in Vietnam.

Mr. Faleomavaega said that he regretted not having done enough for the victims in Vietnam and called on both the U.S. and Vietnamese government to take responsibility and address the problem.

During the delegation's meeting with representatives from the U.S. Department of State, the U.S. side "confirmed that the U.S. Department of State gives a high priority to solving the dioxin issue in Vietnam."[56]

During the meetings, the Congressmen showed their support for Vietnamese Agent Orange victims, praising the VAVA for its effective activities to help the victims:[57]

> They also affirmed that the U.S. administration must treasure the addressing of the consequences of AO in the relation between the two countries.

During the meeting with the U.S. Department of State, the Department of State affirmed that the addressing of AO issue in Vietnam was a care and priority, according to delegation leader Lieutenant-general Nguyen Van Rinh.

He also said that the VAVA and the VAORRC would actively work with the U.S. Congress and Government to have greater help for Vietnamese and American AO victims as well as for purifying toxic chemicals in hot areas in Vietnam.

The two organizations came to a joint declaration on increasing cooperation for justice for Vietnamese AO victims.

Filner's Vietnam Visit

San Diego based Rep. Bob Filner was an ideal choice to represent VAORRC and Vietnam's interests in the House of Representatives. Now Mayor of San Diego, Filner was the archetypal "red diaper baby."

Bob Filner is the son of Joseph Filner, formerly a senior official of the Pennsylvania Communist Party, who went on to make a fortune trading metals with the Soviet Union and marketing Soviet products in the United States.[58]

All through his 20 years in Congress, Bob Filner enjoyed a very close relationship with San Diego Democratic Socialists of America.[59]

Congressman Filner, the sponsor of H.R. 2634, the "Victims of Agent Orange Relief Act of 2011," visited Vietnam from January 5th through the 11th in 2012 to study the impact of Agent Orange on the Vietnamese people.

Filner's bill would increase medical funding for Vietnam veterans who were exposed to the chemical and their descendants, along with providing money for health services and cleanup in areas of Vietnam still affected by Agent Orange. At the time, Filner's bill was awaiting debate in a House Foreign Affairs subcommittee.

Congressman Filner was hosted by the Vietnam Association for Victims of Agent Orange/Dioxin (VAVA) and the visit was coordinated by the Vietnam Agent Orange Relief & Responsibility Campaign.

Incredibly, the former Soviet front International Association of Democratic Lawyers "provided funding assistance."[60]

Filner was met at Tan Son Nhat Airport by Senior Lieutenant General Nguyen Van Rinh, Chairman of VAVA and Major General Tran Ngoc Tho, Chairman of the HCMC Association for Victims of Agent Orange.

Filner meeting with Vietnamese Premier Nguyen Tan Dung

On January 4, the first day of his trip, Saigon Giai Phong, a news service billed in English as "The Organ of the Party Committee, the Communist Party of Viet Nam," reported that Filner visited a temple honoring Ho Chi Minh, where he "burned incense to the country's dear leader."

Rep. Filner visited Agent Orange victims in Ho Chi Minh City, Vung Tau, Cu Chi, Danang, Quang Ngai, Quang Ninh and Hanoi. He saw daycare, homecare and rehabilitation projects run by the representative of Vietnam's victims, the Vietnam Association for Victims of Agent Orange/Dioxin.

Congressman Filner met with Vietnam's communist Prime Minister Nguyen Tan Dung and Mrs. Nguyen Thi Kim Ngan, Vice President of the National Assembly, as well as with medical and scientific experts on Agent Orange.

The Franken Delegation

U.S. Sen. Al Franken led a Senate delegation to Vietnam in July of 2010.

The group would "look into environmental remediation of dioxin and the joint funding of medical services for people with disabilities, and meet with Vietnamese government officials to discuss education initiatives, labor issues and trade relations."

Franken was accompanied by Senators Tom Harkin of Iowa, Bernie Sanders of Vermont and Jeff Merkley of Oregon.[61]

While in Vietnam, Tom Harkin was interviewed by Tuoi Tre of the Vietnam Association of Victims of Agent Orange/Dioxin, in which he stated his intention to win more U.S. taxpayers' money for the communist government's cause:

> Iowa Senator Tom Harkin, who as a young U.S. Congress staffer discovered the infamous "tiger cages" at the Saigon regime's Con Dao island prison, talked with Tuoi Tre before he and three other American senators made a July 6 field trip to Da Nang, a hot-spot for Agent Orange in Vietnam.
>
> **Tuoi Tre:** We've heard that you struggled for Vietnam-U.S. relation normalization before 1995...
>
> **Senator Tom Harkin:** There were many difficulties over a long period of time. Many Americans didn't want to establish diplomatic relations with Vietnam because of the previous war, but President Bill Clinton made normalization and establishment of diplomatic ties with Vietnam a priority...
>
> **Tuoi Tre:** Are you going to visit Da Nang because it's a dioxin hot-spot?
>
> **Harkin:** That's my concern. We Americans conducted a chemical war which perhaps didn't directly aim to [harm] humans, but it turned out spraying Agent Orange defoliant can cause prolonged effects on people. My colleagues in the Senate have agreed to allocate funds each year to clean up hot-spots in Da Nang, Bien Hoa and Hue. We're trying to increase that amount.
>
> **Tuoi Tre:** But besides dioxin hot-spots, we still have 3-4 million AO victims!
>
> **Harkin:** I know. That will be the next step. I think we will have to do something for victims. We know dioxin persists in the food chain and affects humans. It is a fact that in the U.S., the Department of Veterans has compensated AO victims who suffer from cancers, blood cancer, Parkinsons, etc., around 15 diseases believed related to their exposure to AO, but not for any cases of disability.

The thing I want to do is to help victims in Vietnam who suffer from AO-related diseases (those recognized in the U.S.) obtain compensation as American victims. The fund for Vietnamese AO victims is now around $3 million a year. We are trying to raise it to $20-30 million a year...[62]

Example Five: "Obamacare"

The Affordable Health Care Act, or "Obamacare" is a classic example of a socialist policy foisted on the American public, by a small but committed Marxist sect. In this case Democratic Socialists of America (DSA) is the main culprit, though they had had considerable assistance from the Communist Party USA and the Institute for Policy Studies.

While DSA is active in the "peace" movement, organized labor, Latino and African-American movements, religion, gay rights, environmentalism and a host of other issues, socialized health care has long been their number one priority. The socialists and Communists understand that socialized medicine gives huge scope for state intrusion into every aspect of an individual's life. It makes more people state dependent (and therefore more likely to vote Democrat), quicker than virtually any other measure.

While "Obamacare" is not yet fully socialized or "single payer" health care; it is a quantum leap down that road. If "Obamacare" is fully implemented, it will be only a matter of time until the left achieves fully socialized health care in the home of the cowed and the land of the formerly free.

Socialists "driving force"

DSA has long been the driving force behind the campaign for socialized medicine in the U.S. It works closely with allies such as U.S. Congressman John Conyers and Senator Bernie Sanders to move the debate in the appropriate direction.[63]

In 1991, Rep. Marty Russo (D-IL) introduced a bill into the U.S. House of Representatives calling for a single, universal, publicly-administered health care program. The Russo Bill attracted the support of many progressive organizations—including DSA:[64]

Supporters are currently pushing for the Russo Bill to reach the floor of the House for a vote. Activists should contact their representatives to encourage their support. Contact your local to find out what other DSAers are doing to support the Russo Bill.

Los Angeles physician Steve Tarzynski, then a member of the DSA National Political Committee and Chair of the DSA National Health Care Task force, revealed the Marxist's agenda and tactics in Democratic Left, January/February 1994:[65]

> We've met some of the modest goals that the national leadership set when DSA decided to make support for a single-payer Canadian-style health care system our major issue.

> DSA members have served on the Clinton Health Care Task Force and in the leadership and rank and file of national and state single-payer coalitions. Perhaps most importantly, in 1991 we organized a twenty-two-city national tour of over forty Canadian health experts (from our sibling party, the New Democrats) that helped to galvanize the single-payer movement into action. No other organization was in a position to carry out such a major tour. We have done a good job as the socialist current within the single-payer movement, but still have significant opportunities to improve DSA locals' level of activism and our recruitment of activists into DSA through this issue. In the coming year, as we close in for the final legislative phase of this fight, the national DSA leadership and the DSA health care task force will focus efforts in these two areas.

> The DSA National Convention in November unanimously adopted a resolution that clearly reaffirmed our support of the McDermott-Conyers-Wellstone single-payer bills (HR1200/S491). It also stipulated DSA's advocacy of a "state option" for single payer in the final legislative package. The resolution also stated that DSA will organize and participate in anti-corporate campaigns targeting private health insurance, pharmaceutical lobbies, and any other corporate or political forces that seek to destroy real reform.

> If a vote is delayed beyond fall 1994, DSA will also work in congressional campaigns that target anti-reform incumbents and that support, single-payer advocates. We will also continue our work in state campaigns to establish single-payer systems.

> The most delicate aspect of our work is how we balance our efforts in improving the Clinton proposal and pushing for single-payer. This is

not a new dilemma for the left. The tension between reform and revolution has existed within every socialist movement in Western industrialized democracies. It will always be with us. The solution lies in putting into practice Michael Harrington's notion "visionary gradualism."

Democratic socialists should project a vision of a moral society based on freedom, equality, and solidarity. We must also understand that reaching such a goal involves a gradual approach over a long period of years, with each reform becoming the foundation for the next. There is no other way, and history alone will judge the pace."

Influencing Obama

DSA claims credit for both indoctrinating Barack Obama into the ideas of socialized health care and for designing "Obamacare."

Retired Chicago physician Quentin Young is an ex-communist and a long-time DSA member. He is the father of the socialized health care movement in the United States and has been working for more than 50 years on the issue through organizations such as Health & Medicine Policy Research Group, Medical Committee for Human Rights and especially his nationwide DSA front, Physicians for a National Health Program.[66]

Quentin Young, Barack Obama (2003)

Quentin Young is a long-time friend and supporter of Barack Obama. He was Obama's personal physician for more than 20 years:[67]

Quentin Young, perhaps the most well-known single-payer advocate in America. He was the Rev. Martin Luther King's doctor when he lived in Chicago and a longtime friend and ally of Barack Obama.

In the 1990s, Barack Obama and Quentin Young were both supporters of "single payer" health care.

As a State Senator, Obama and another leftist colleague, State Representative Willie Delgado, presented The Health Care Justice Act to the Illinois House and Senate.

According to the blog, Thomas Paine's Corner:[68]

> Barack Obama is quite familiar with the concepts and the specific merits of single payer. Back in the late 1990s, when he was an Illinois State Senator representing a mostly black district on the south side of Chicago, he took pains to consistently identify himself publicly with his neighbor Dr. Quentin Young.
>
> He signed on as co-sponsor of the Bernardin Amendment, named after Chicago's late Catholic Archbishop, who championed the public policy idea that medical care was a human right, not a commodity. At that time, when it was to his political advantage, Obama didn't mind at all being perceived as an advocate of single payer.

Quentin Young has supported Obama politically since at least 1995.[69]

> "I knew him before he was political; I supported him when he ran for State Senate. When he was a State Senator he did say that he supported single payer. Now, he hedges. Now he says, if we were starting from scratch, he would support single payer."
>
> "Barack's a smart man. He probably calculated the political cost for being for single payer—the shower of opposition from the big boys—the drug companies and the health insurance companies. And so, like the rest of them, he fashioned a hodgepodge of a health insurance plan."

From a March 2009 Democracy Now! interview with DSA aligned Amy Goodman:[70]

> **Amy Goodman:** You've been a longtime friend of Barack Obama.
>
> Dr. Quentin Young: Yeah.
>
> **Amy Goodman:** How has he changed over the years?
>
> **Dr. Quentin Young:** Well, Barack Obama, as we know, was a community organizer, a very lofty calling, in my book, and he made the decision, when the opportunity came, that he could get more done politically, and he accepted the nomination for the seat in the State Senate. It's not that long ago, really. It's about a six, eight years ago.

Barack Obama, in those early days—influenced, I hope, by me and others—categorically said single payer was the best way, and he would inaugurate it if he could get the support, meaning majorities in both houses, which he's got, and the presidency, which he's got. And he said that on more than one occasion, and it represented the very high-grade intelligence we all know Barack has...

Amy Goodman: This brouhaha over the last week with the White House healthcare summit, 120 people, there were going to be no single-payer advocates. Congressman Conyers asked to go. At first, he was told no. He directly asked President Obama at a Congressional Black Caucus hearing. He asked to bring you and Marcia Angell—

Dr. Quentin Young: Yes.

Amy Goodman:—former Editor-in-Chief of the New England Journal of Medicine. You weren't allowed to go. Do you have President Obama's ear anymore? You have been an ally of his for years, for decades.

Dr. Quentin Young: Well, it's mixed. I think we're friends, certainly. At this gala that you mentioned, which was embarrassing, he did send a very complimentary letter. And I appreciate that, but I'd much rather have him enact single payer, to tell the truth. And we did—it's fair to say, after a good deal of protest, I think we were told there was a—phones rang off the hook. They did allow our national president, Dr. Oliver Fein, to attend with Dr. Conyers—Congressman Conyers. That's fine, but we need many more people representative of the American people at large to get this thing through the Congress, and Baucus, notwithstanding, be overruled.

So DSA is not entirely happy with "Obamacare," but that is far from the end of the health care struggle.

Designing "Obamacare"

John E. McDonough is a Professor of Public Health Practice at the Harvard School of Public Health and Director of the new HSPH Center for Public Health Leadership.

An Obama 2012 campaign video, released on the six year anniversary of "Romneycare's" adoption in Massachusetts, identifies McDonough as one of the architects of both the Romney and Obama plans. "I helped craft and pass Massachusetts health reform in 2006 and the Affordable Care Act in 2010."

The video was designed to make Romney look foolish for campaigning to repeal a national program modeled after the state plan he signed when he was Governor of Massachusetts.

McDonough says that although he was "deeply involved" in the health care legislation passed in Massachusetts and on the national level, both Romney and Obama "would say they had zero contact with me, for different reasons." He explained, "As a progressive health leader in Massachusetts, I helped push Massachusetts health reform in a much more progressive direction than Romney wanted. As part of a large army of U.S. Senate staffers, I never got into the same room as the President—many others outranked me."[71]

The Obama video of course fails to mention that McDonough is a former Chair of Massachusetts Democratic Socialists of America. While claiming he left the organization in the 1980s, on November 22, 2005, Sponsors and Co-Sponsors of Boston Democratic Socialists included Mass-Care, Health Care for All and the Health Care Amendment Campaign. They held a forum, "Which Way for Health Care Reform?" Speakers included John McDonough, Director of Health Care for All.[72]

Without Democratic Socialists of America, there would assuredly be no "Obamacare."

---

1 Tim Donoghue, "Hard Cheese," New Zealand Herald (May 23, 1986) p. 8
2 Tony Neary and Jack Kelleher, "The Price of Principle," (Auckland: Harlen Books, 1986) p. 206
3 Christopher Andrew and Oleg Gordievsky, "KGB: The Inside Story of its Foreign Operations from Lenin to Gorbachev," http://encyclopedia.thefreedictionary.com/Oleg+Gordievsky (London: Hodder & Stoughton, 1990) p. 513
4 Oleg Gordievsky, "Next Stop Execution: The Autobiography of Oleg Gordievsky," (London: Macmillan, 1995) pp. 365-66
5 Gordievsky, quoted by Greg Ansley in the New Zealand Herald (October 15, 1990) Ansley was quoting interviews that Gordievsky had given to Australian journalist James O'Brien, which had appeared in the Melbourne Herald Sun and Brisbane Courier-Mail.
6 KeyWiki, "Cesar E. Chavez National Holiday," KeyWiki, http://www.keywiki.org/index.php/Cesar_E._Chavez_National_Holiday (accessed May 14, 2013)
7 KeyWiki, "Evelina Alarcon," KeyWiki, http://www.keywiki.org/index.php/Evelina_Alarcon (accessed May 14, 2013)
8 Evelina Alarcon, "On the Work of Districts and Clubs," CPUSA, http://www.cpusa.org/on-the-work-of-districts-and-clubs/ (September 22, 2001)
9 Russell Pelle, "Building the Communist Party USA in the South (PART 2)," Yahoo!, http://groups.yahoo.com/group/Communist-Party/message/1067 (2001)

10 LA Progressive, "Barack's Sister Brings the Heat to El Sereno," LA Progressive, http://www.laprogressive.com/2008/06/22/barack%E2%80%99s-sister-brings-the-heat-to-el-sereno/ (June 22, 2008)
11 LA Progressive, "Barack's Sister Brings the Heat to El Sereno," LA Progressive, http://www.laprogressive.com/2008/06/22/barack%E2%80%99s-sister-brings-the-heat-to-el-sereno/ (June 22, 2008)
12 CPUSA, "Constitution of the Communist Party of the United States of America," CPUSA, http://www.cpusa.org/cpusa-constitution/ (accessed June 6, 2013)
13 David Bacon, "El Valiente Chicano," David Bacon, http://dbacon.igc.org/Portrait/07Corona.htm (January 19, 2001)
14 Hearings before the Subcommittee to Investigate the Administration of the Internal Security Act, U.S. Senate, 94th Congress, Part 2 (July 1975) p. 182
15 Democratic Left (Fall 2009)
16 Bert Corona Leadership Institute, "Bert Corona Leadership Institute Profile," Bert Corona Leadership Institute, http://www.bcli.info/profile.htm (accessed May 2010)
17 Lloyd Billingsley, "Union Card for Green Card: The Radical Vanguard in the Los Angeles Labor Movement," http://www.americanpatrol.com/404.html (August 2000)
18 Lloyd Billingsley, "Union Card for Green Card: The Radical Vanguard in the Los Angeles Labor Movement," http://www.americanpatrol.com/404.html (August 2000)
19 Carlos F. Ortega, "The Legacy of Bert Corona," The Progressive (August 2001)
20 Harold Meyerson, "Crunch Time The race to succeed Richard Riordan — and to reshape Los Angeles — comes down to the wire," LA Weekly, http://www.laweekly.com/content/printVersion/33315/ (March 29, 2001)
21 People's Weekly World, "May Day Supplement," People's Weekly World (May 2, 1992)
22 People's Weekly World (June 20, 1996)
23 Socialist International, http://www.socialistinternational.org/viewArticle.cfm?ArticleID=1924&ArticlePageID=1252&ModuleID=18 (accessed June 6, 2013)
24 KeyWiki, "Conrado Terrazas," KeyWiki, http://keywiki.org/index.php/Conrado_Terrazas (accessed June 6, 2013)
25 KeyWiki, "Mauricio Terrazas," KeyWiki, http://keywiki.org/index.php/Mauricio_Terrazas (accessed June 6, 2013)
26 Zorro, "Gil Cedillo introduces the California DREAM Act!," Orange Juice Blog, http://www.orangejuiceblog.com/2011/01/gil-cedillo-introduces-the-california-dream-act/ (January 11, 2011)
27 KeyWiki, "Progressive Los Angeles Network," KeyWiki, http://www.keywiki.org/index.php/Progressive_Los_Angeles_Network (accessed June 6, 2013)
28 Huffington Post blog (September 17, 2012)
29 People's Weekly World, "May Day Supplement," People's Weekly World (May 2, 1992)
30 Democratic Left (January/February 1994) p. 17
31 Democratic Left (Fall 2000)
32 KeyWiki, "Progressive Los Angeles Network," KeyWiki, http://www.keywiki.org/index.php/Progressive_Los_Angeles_Network (accessed June 6, 2013)
33 Richie Ross, "Untold Story: How the Latino Vote Hit Critical Mass," Calbuzz, http://www.calbuzz.com/tag/maria-elena-durazo (November 15, 2010)

34 Tim Wheeler, "Lorenzo Torrez, copper miner, Communist leader, dies at 84," People's World, http://peoplesworld.org/lorenzo-torrez-copper-miner-communist-leader-dies-at-8/, (January 9, 2012)

35 Plansponser website, "Portrait of Retiree: Lorenzo Torrez," Plansponser website (accessed July 5, 2010)

36 Communist Party USA, "Special Convention Discussion: Mexican American Equality," Communist Party USA (April 6, 2010)

37 People's Weekly World (March 6, 2004)

38 Rosalio Munoz and Joelle Fishman, "Latino Congreso Sets 2008 Agenda," LatinoLA, http://www.latinola.com/story.php?story=4725 (October 11, 2007)

39 Tim Wheeler, "Lorenzo Torrez, copper miner, Communist leader, dies at 84," People's World, http://peoplesworld.org/lorenzo-torrez-copper-miner-communist-leader-dies-at-8/, (January 9, 2012)

40 Chicago DSA, "New Ground 96," DSA, http://www.chicagodsa.org/ngarchive/ng96.html (October 2004)

41 SEIU, "Elisio Medena," SEIU, http://www.seiu.org/a/ourunion/eliseo-medina.php (accessed June 6, 2013)

42 Randy Shaw, "National Campaign Urges Obama to Award Presidential Medal of Freedom to Legendary Organizer Fred Ross," BeyondChron Blog, http://www.beyondchron.org/news/index.php?itemid=10980, (February 13, 2013)

43 SEIU, "Elisio Medena," SEIU, http://www.seiu.org/a/ourunion/eliseo-medina.php (accessed June 6, 2013)

44 DSA, "Medina," DSA, http://www.dsausa.org/LatestNews/2004/medina.html (2004)

45 Randy Shaw, "Implications of the SEIU/UniteHere Settlement," Talking Union (July 29, 2010)

46 Nancy Cleeland, "AFL-CIO Calls for Amnesty for Illegal U.S. Workers," SCI SDSU, http://www.sci.sdsu.edu/salton/AFL-CIOAmnestyForIllegals.html (February 17, 2000)

47 SEIU, "Elisio Medena," SEIU, http://www.seiu.org/a/ourunion/eliseo-medina.php (accessed June 6, 2013)

48 Eliseo Medina, "Eliseo Medina Speaks on Immigrants for Votes," YouTube, http://www.youtube.com/watch?feature=player_embedded&v=AK7K0itgQt0 (accessed June 6, 2013)

49 KeyWiki, "Vietnam Agent Orange Relief & Responsibility Campaign," KeyWiki, http://www.keywiki.org/index.php/Vietnam_Agent_Orange_Relief_%26_Responsibility_Campaign (accessed June 6, 2013)

50 KeyWiki, "Merle Ratner," KeyWiki, http://www.keywiki.org/index.php/Merle_Ratner (accessed June 6, 2013)

51 KeyWiki, "Susan Schnall," KeyWiki, http://www.keywiki.org/index.php/Susan_Schnall (accessed June 6, 2013)

52 Vietnam Agent Orange Relief & Responsibility Campaign website, http://www.vn-agentorange.org/about.html (accessed December 13, 2010)

53 Martin Sheen, "Vietnam: American Holocaust," Amazon.com, http://www.amazon.com/Vietnam-American-Holocaust-Martin-Sheen/dp/B001O287YO (accessed June 6, 2013)

54 IADL Law, "INTERNATIONAL TRIBUNAL OF CONSCIENCE IN SUPPORT OF THE VIETNAMESE VICTIMS OF AGENT ORANGE," IADL Law, http://www.iadllaw.org/en/node/353 (May 16, 2009)

55 Vietnam Agent Orange Relief & Responsibility Campaign website, "Vietnam Agent Orange. Public Health Tour Featuring: Dr. Nguyen Thi Ngoc Phuong," Vietnam Agent Orange Relief & Responsibility Campaign website, http://www.vn-agentorange.org/Nov2007_public_health_tour.html (accessed December 12, 2010)

56 Voice of Vietnam News, "US congressmen support Vietnam's Agent Orange victims," Voice of Vietnam News (December 6, 2010)

57 BaoMoi.com, "Vietnamese AO victims receive great support in the US," BaoMoi.com, http://en.baomoi.com/Info/Vietnamese-AO-victims-receive-great-support-in-the-US/3/91846.epi (accessed June 6, 2013)

58 KeyWiki, "Joseph Filner," KeyWiki, http://www.keywiki.org/index.php/Joseph_Filner (accessed June 6, 2013)

59 KeyWiki, "Bob Filner," KeyWiki, http://www.keywiki.org/index.php/Bob_Filner (accessed June 6, 2013)

60 Vietnam Agent Orange Relief & Responsibility Campaign website, "Congressman Bob Filner visits Vietnam for Study Tour on Agent Orange," Vietnam Agent Orange Relief & Responsibility Campaign website (January 5-11, 2012)

61 Joe Kimball, "Al Franken to visit Vietnam with Senate group, then head to Laos," Minn Post (July 1, 2010)

62 Vavanew, "Harkin vows to seek more help for Vietnamese Agent Orange victims," Vava.org (May 16, 2013)

63 Democratic Left magazine, http://www.dsausa.org/dl/Summer_2009.pdf (Summer 2009)

64 Democratic Left (July/August 1991) p. 10

65 Democratic Left (January/February 1994) p. 2

66 KeyWiki, "Physicians for a National Health Program," KeyWiki, http://www.keywiki.org/index.php/Physicians_for_a_National_Health_Program (accessed May 5, 2013)

67 Democracy Now!, "Dr. Quentin Young, Longtime Obama Confidante and Physician to MLK, Criticizes Admin's Rejection of Single-Payer Healthcare," Democracy Now!, http://www.democracynow.org/2009/3/11/dr_quentin_young_obama_confidante_and (March 11, 2009)

68 Thomas Paine's Corner, "Barack Obama Hypocrisy on Health Care," Civil Libertarian, http://civillibertarian.blogspot.com/2007/02/barack-obama-hypocrisy-on-health-care.html (February 2007)

69 Corporate Crime Reporter, "Quentin Young, Early Supporter of Obama, Now Disappointed and Saddened," Corporate Crime Reporter, http://www.corporatecrimereporter.com/obama012808.htm (January 28, 2008)

70 Democracy Now!, "Dr. Quentin Young, Longtime Obama Confidante and Physician to MLK, Criticizes Admin's Rejection of Single-Payer Healthcare," Democracy Now!, http://www.democracynow.org/2009/3/11/dr_quentin_young_obama_confidante_and (March 11, 2009)

71 Cliff Kincaid, "The Socialist Behind Romneycare," Accuracy in Media, http://www.aim.org/aim-column/the-socialist-behind-romneycare/# (August 6, 2012)

72 The Yankee Radical, "Which Way for Health Care Reform?," DSA, http://www.dsaboston.org/yradical/yr2005-11.pdf (November 2005)

Communists

Communist Party USA

The Communist Party USA (CPUSA) is America's oldest and most prestigious Marxist-Leninist organization. It was founded in 1919 and today is active in most states of the union.

In 2002, the CPUSA claimed 20,000 registered members and groups in 28 of the 50 U.S. states. While these figures were probably grossly exaggerated, the party still has strong influence in certain labor unions, churches, civic groups and especially inside the Democratic Party, in its strongholds of New York, Connecticut, Ohio, Illinois, Michigan, Washington State, Oregon, California, Arizona, Missouri and to a degree in Texas and Florida.[1][2]

Communist Party USA Infiltration of the Democratic Party

The latest phase of Communist Party plans to infiltrate and manipulate the Democratic Party began in earnest in the 1970s, and has today, reached a peak of influence not seen since the 1940s. These plans can be illustrated by direct quotes from Communist Party literature.

In 1972, Gus Hall, then Chairman of the CPUSA, wrote in his book, "A Lame Duck in Turbulent Waters," describing what had been the long-time party policy:[3]

> Our electoral policy has for 25 years been expressed in the phrase, 'the three legs of a stool'... The stool was constructed at a time when the Party was under sharp attack... a reflection of the Party's response to the difficulties.

> The flexibility was contained in the idea that no one leg of the stool was the main leg. Depending on the political pressures, one could choose a particular leg or legs. In fact the concept was built on the idea that when the other two legs, namely, the Communist Party and the forces of political independence, got strong enough, then and only then would

the stool sit on three legs. But until that day comes the one operating leg would be the liberal wing of the Democratic Party.

Hall, writing this in 1972, at that time claimed that he had decided the policy was wrong. It is apparent, however, from later quotes and actions of top communists including Hall, that the policy has in fact not only been continued, but augmented.

Gus Hall himself said at the time:[4]

> We are going to work towards independence, but I think it is clear we are going to work with people who for some time will be 'riding two horses' (Communist and Democrat) in the field of political action.

Mitchell on Moving the Democrats Left

Charlene Mitchell, then Executive Director of the African-American Commission of the CPUSA, wrote in the People's Daily World on June 9, 1983:[5]

> To date, most of the debate has centered on the personalities of potential Black candidates and the pros and cons of such a challenge. The thrust of such a candidacy must be to develop the popular electoral base to prevent the Democratic Party from continuing its shift to the right and force a more progressive platform and program in the 1984 campaign.

Mitchell went further in the March 1989 issue of Political Affairs, the monthly theoretical journal of the Communist Party:[6]

> We see building political independence based on the alliance of labor with the African-American community as the aim for changing the relationship of forces in elected office. The Party Program maintains the ultimate expression of this would be a mass anti-monopoly people's party...

> From the standpoint of process, even if it is currently developing primarily through the Democratic Party, the fact that labor, the Rainbow Coalition, and the African-American community are the main generators of the new developments substantiates our policy and our historic approach of basing the building of political independence on the alliance of the trade union movement and the African-American people...

> Should the party strive to play a leading role helping those forces gain and consolidate new positions of strength, even inside the Democratic Party or shouldn't it?, I think it should.

How is our party going to develop its all-sided electoral presence? This cannot and should not repose solely on Communist or Left-independent candidates. Not if there is any intention of emerging as an integral component of the overall progressive coalition. Especially in view of the fact that the Jackson-led progressive wing of the Democratic Party is that coalition's major organized component.

"People's Forces"

The September/October 1988 issue, Political Affairs states:[7]

Beyond the rhetoric, politics in the United States invariably reflects the class struggle. Even as parties of capitalism, the dynamics between and within the Democratic and Republican parties express the interests and demands of competing sections of the ruling class, on the one hand; and cross-purposes of contending class forces vying for control of the Democratic Party, on the other.

During the Reagan-Bush years the Republican Party has become the party of the ultra-Right. Organized forces of the working class and people are almost totally absent from it.

For the last fifty years the Democratic Party has housed a broad mix of class and social forces that are often in conflict with each other. This has given rise to a sometimes subtle, sometimes sharp struggle over direction.

The status and intensity of this struggle depend on the level and strength of the political independence of the labor movement and other people's forces operating inside the (Democratic) party.

Political Affairs for March 1989 contained the following statement:[8]

Organized mass movements, especially the African American community, the Rainbow Coalition, labor on all levels, SANE-Freeze, and other mass organizations—became more independent of the Democratic Party establishment on policy and political direction, but more organizationally involved in the Democratic Party.

The same issue also contained the following:[9]

This much is clear—the overall movement will grow. So will the role of the Rainbow Coalition and the labor movement. And it will unfold in the 1989-1992 quadrennial cycle primarily, but not exclusively—through the medium of the Democratic Party.

CPLAN

In the late 1980's, Communist Party publications also specifically described a party apparatus for directly influencing the votes of Congress and even Congressional and Presidential elections. This was called CPLAN or the Communist Party Legislative Action Network.

This network was organized to influence other mass organizations cooperating with the Communists through the "All Peoples Front" to stimulate telephone networks and letter writing campaigns to influence Congress on legislation and even to reach voters regarding election campaigns.

The May 1987 issue of Political Affairs described CPLAN in more detail:[10]

> Every party organization should assign a comrade to be in touch with the legislative and political action department of the Central Committee. This could be a key for rapid mobilization.
>
> The aim is to activate within a day or two all party organizations, as well as our mass movement's connections, to pressure their Senators and Representatives...
>
> Nationally, CPLAN would be able to generate tens of thousands of letters, telephone calls, mailgrams, etc... There are few questions on which CPLAN cannot make the difference in how at least 5 to 10 Senators or Representatives would vote...
>
> CPLAN is an important means of strengthening the unity of the independent forces, and this could have a great bearing not only on the 100th Congress but on the 1988 electoral struggle.

The same issue of Political Affairs went on to say:

> When account is taken of the Party district and club organizations, as well as the thousands of trade unions, coalitions, and mass organizations on the grassroots, citywide, and national levels that Communists belong to, help lead, are active in, have friends, relatives, and contacts in, then the answer as to how to organize a Party legislative apparatus, as well as the Party's potential for influencing the legislative scene, become clear... the basis for an extraordinary legislative action network that could impact on the 100th Congress in a major way.

Working Through the "Quad Caucus"

The Communist Party aims to exert pressure on "progressive" Democratic Congressmen in the so-called "Quad Caucus" to get desired legislation passed. According to an April 2010 CPUSA Political Action Commission report submitted as part of the discussion leading up to the Communist Party USA's 29th National Convention on May 21-23, 2010:[11]

> The formation this year of the Quad Caucus within Congress is a reflection of a growing demographic and progressive shift within the electorate. The collaboration of the Congressional Black, Hispanic, Asian-Pacific and Progressive caucuses creates a strong counter-force to the conservative element within the Democratic Party. Here, the support for single-payer among a section of members, and the push for "public option" from the majority of members of those caucuses, while unsuccessful, kept the pressure on until a final bill was passed.

> Many of our clubs are located in Congressional Districts of Quad Caucus members. A labor-people's electoral force working within the broad alliance and relating with members of Congress can project specific legislation like passage of the Local Jobs for America Act to restore one million jobs in cities and towns, and bigger goals like shifting military funding to human needs with massive public works job creation.

> Such creative applications of our electoral policy build working relations and respect with the labor/people's forces and further political independence in a fundamental way. Similar approaches can be developed in relation to problematic policies of the Obama administration including the direction for public education, energy resources and military funding.

> As Communists, we look for the key demand that will put the maximum number of people into motion and help to move other demands. At this moment that key demand is for good job creation. Working class families are hanging on to survive this economic crisis. Young people are being shut out of the economy. A huge infusion of funds is required to put people back to work and restart the economy.

> Working with the labor movement, civil rights, environmental and other organizations to create a groundswell that can push positive initiatives through Congress is the most important way to meet needs and prevent a right-wing takeover in the 2010 elections.

Running as Democrats

In 2010, in a report prepared for the Communist Party's 29th National Convention, several members of the Young Communist League USA wrote:[12]

> Currently, the conditions rarely if ever allow us to run open Communists for office. When members do run for office, it is within the auspices of the Democratic Party. Otherwise, we find ourselves supporting progressive (and in some instances not-so-progressive) Democratic candidates. Despite how much many of us would love to run comrades for office as Communists, we all agree that this is how we currently have to function in this political climate.

Working Inside the Democratic Party

The Young Communist League is probably being too cautious. The political climate has in fact changed so much, that in most Communist stronghold states, Communist Party members openly work inside the Democratic Party.

In a report to the National Committee meeting of the Communist Party USA on November 20, 2004 (originally delivered at a YCL conference), Jessica Marshall, YCLUSA National Coordinator, outlined examples of YCL electoral activity, including helping Missouri Democrat John L. Bowman, the League of Pissed Off Voters and the Democratic Party itself:[13]

> It's important to note here that this is a generation of young people that have no particular allegiance to the Democratic Party and show hope for the possibility of further developing independent and progressive voter coalitions and voting blocks. But this generation of voters also was mature enough to recognize the importance of uniting in this year's election to elect John Kerry and defend themselves against a President and Congress that has been wreaking havoc on our lives for quite some time. This represents a tremendous opportunity for the YCL as we continue to grow and work to build broader, progressive coalitions of youth and students.

> Of particular importance to the YCL in our efforts to deepen and broaden our relations with other progressive youth and student organizations, were our YCL Midwest Summer and GOTV election projects. In July, we went to St. Louis where 13 YCLers (5 of whom stayed for the whole month) volunteered alongside the party, Planned

Parenthood, CBTU, SEIU and AFSCME, and others on several campaigns including the victorious campaign of John Bowman who is here today. During that same period we sent 12 volunteers to Cleveland where volunteers worked with the Vote Mob and participated in labor walks.

We worked on everything from phone banking to lit drops and led precincts in Akron for the VoteMob operation... Both the Milwaukee and Chicago YCLers worked in Wisconsin, helping to chaperone a group of 400 high school students on election day who participated in a massive knock and drag effort to get people to the polls, in addition to their work with Vozes, an immigrants rights group, the League of Conservation Voters and ACT on door-knocking and GOTV efforts.

In New York YCLers were delegates and founders of the local organizing committees of the National Hip Hop Political Convention. In Providence, Miami and Chicago YCLers helped head up the League of Pissed Off Voters efforts. YCLers staffed Democratic Party operations and headed up precincts in Ohio and Florida. A YCLer from Virginia was a canvas director for a progressive young candidate in a tight race in Ohio. In Miami, the newly formed club helped ACT organizing efforts at Miami Dade Community College.

The YCLUSA is open about using the Democratic Party to destroy the Republican Party as a political force.

According to a 2007 report by then YCLUSA National Coordinator Erica Smiley:[14]

But even though the ultra-right is in retreat, kicking and screaming and even calling Hillary Clinton's half public-half private healthcare proposal "socialist", they still haven't been defeated. As Communists, we have to finish the task of isolating the ultra-right and completely removing them from power—using the Democrats to finish the job.

Examples of Communists Working Through the Democrats

Clallam County Communists

Communist Party members Tim Wheeler, Joyce Wheeler and Honeybee Wheeler, openly work inside the Clallam County Democrat Party in Washington State.

Clair McCaskill's Communists

In the 2006 election, Missouri Senator Claire McCaskill tried to woo rural support against her Republican opponent Jim Talent.

According to the Communist Party USA paper People's Weekly World:[15]

> McCaskill is challenging conventional wisdom though, spending more time in rural areas than ever before. While working the traditional Democratic base, her connection with rural voters is forcing Talent to spend time and money on what was once thought of as solid Republican turf.

Communist Party USA supporter, John L. Bowman, coordinated the McCaskill campaign:

> Is McCaskill's strategy working? According to Missouri State Rep. John Bowman (D-70), who is coordinating the McCaskill campaign for the St. Louis city and county area, the answer is yes. He told the (Communist Party's Peoples Weekly) World, "We are running one helluva ground campaign. So far it has been planned out and executed very well, even in rural areas." He added, "That Talent, the incumbent, isn't ahead in the polls is uniquely strange. Missouri voters are ready for a change."

> Reaching out to rural voters hasn't changed McCaskill's stance on key issues, though. She is a strong supporter of raising the minimum wage (Proposition B), authorizing stem cell research (Amendment 2) and changing the administration's course in Iraq. Prop. B is supported by more than 70 percent of Missourians, while Amendment 2 is supported by over 60 percent. These two ballot initiatives are expected to help McCaskill gain at least 3 percentage points on Talent.

The McCaskill campaign also received support from state-level races. For example, State Rep. Jeanette Mott Oxford, another Communist Party affiliate, told the People's Weekly World, "Higher turnout in the Jane Bageto (D-94) and the Bob Burns (D-85) races, which are strong Republican areas, will help the McCaskill vote in those areas as well."

According to Pro-Vote organizer, Communist Party USA member Glenn Burleigh, who has managed campaigns for several Missouri Democrats, "These are tough races in areas where choice, LGBT rights and guns can make or break a campaign. We are working to turn the tide against the right wing, but a lot more work needs to be done."

According to John L. Bowman:

> Increased voter registration is also a big part of the statewide turnout strategy. ACORN and Pro-Vote have collectively registered nearly 40,000 new voters in St. Louis and expect a higher than usual turnout in November.
>
> We are knocking on almost 5,000 doors a day, passing out 'Claire facts' and talking to voters about the minimum wage and stem cell initiatives. We're pushing for a big turnout.

"We made history," State Rep. John L. Bowman told the People's Weekly World shortly after Claire McCaskill announced she had defeated "right-wing" Republican incumbent Jim Talent in the hotly contested U.S. Senate race. "We've sent a clear message: 'Enough is enough! It is time for a change!'" Bowman said.[16]

Kucinich's Comrades

Former Ohio Congressman Dennis Kucinich enjoyed Communist Party support his entire career.

In 2005, Ohio Communist Party leader Rick Nagin campaigned unsuccessfully as an Independent for City Council and was heavily criticized in the press over his Communist Party ties. Nagin had resigned as Chairman of the Ohio Communist Party (but had remained a member) to take a position as Executive Assistant to Nelson Cintron Jr., the first Latino on the City Council and a protégé of Dennis Kucinich's.

According to the People's Weekly World:[17]

> Nagin was continuously targeted as a member and former chairman of the Ohio Communist Party, yet his strong showing was impressive and stemmed from a number of factors...
>
> Nagin also had seven and a half years of experience as executive assistant to Nelson Cintron Jr. who represented an adjacent ward. Furthermore, he had been a key organizer for Dennis Kucinich's campaigns for Congress and president and for the 2004 John Kerry presidential campaign.

The Party also backed Kucinich in 2004. One member, Bruce Bostick, even made a video endorsing the Congressman.

In a 2004 report to the CPUSA National Board, the Party's Political Action Committee Chair, Joelle Fishman, wrote a report on Party work in the U.S. Presidential elections. She included a comment on Dennis Kucinich and the Democratic Party National Convention:

> Dennis Kucinich's 50 delegates to the national Democratic convention, will be presenting a platform plank for a Department of Peace, voted favorably by four state conventions, including dramatically in Texas just this week. The efforts of Kucinich together with Jesse Jackson and others, to bring forward more advanced demands, will make an important contribution to the convention. A very special contribution will be made by an expectedly large number of labor union delegates who will work together in one bloc to get a strong platform for jobs, health care, and pensions.

The Communist Party would also be at the convention:[18]

> We project our role at the convention as distribution of the People's Weekly World/Nuestro Mundo and literature to delegates and in free speech areas, and participation in the Kucinich-led issue events. We hope to have reporters inside the convention, we hope to speak with any labor delegates we know in their home states before the convention, and to participate in the Boston Social Forum which will be held the weekend prior to the convention.

In a July 2007 report to the CPUSA's National Committee, Party Chairman Sam Webb urged fellow communists to "have a positive attitude toward the candidacy of Congressman Dennis Kucinich," characterizing the latter as "a leading voice of the broad people's coalition." "The more he [Kucinich] speaks to audiences of the core forces," said Webb, "the better positioned the movement will be to win in 2008 and to fight the good fight in 2009."

Rick Nagin was Labor Coordinator for Dennis Kucinich's 2008 primary campaign.

Dennis Kucinich even endorsed Rick Nagin when he stood unsuccessfully (as a Democrat) in his 2009 Cleveland City Council race:[19]

> I've known Rick Nagin for more than 30 years. He's honest, hard-working and conscientious. The people of Ward 14 have a chance to elect a Councilman who will be totally dedicated to them. What more can you ask for?
>
> I'm proud to join with the AFL-CIO in supporting Rick Nagin.
>
> Dennis Kucinich, Congressman, 10th District

Dan Margolis in New York

In 2006, Dan Margolis was a former Chair of the New York State CPUSA. In addition, he wrote for the People's World, covering local New York City and state issues, as well as events at the United Nations. He joined the Communist Party in 2001.[20]

Margolis has been active in New York City elections, including serving as the mid-Staten Island Coordinator for the 2004 Democratic Party Congressional campaign.

Comrade Lozano in Chicago

In early 2010, Rudy Lozano, Jr. ran unsuccessfully for public office in Chicago on a Democratic Party ticket with running mate Jesus Garcia, a long-time Communist Party affiliate. Garcia was elected as Cook County Commissioner.[21]

Lozano was the individual referred to in this Young Communist League USA 2010 Convention discussion paper:[22]

> Thousands of miles away in Chicago, another younger comrade is running for a similar position. The organization pushing his election, the IPO (Independent Political Organization) shares many of our values and has many of our members (and ex-members) among its ranks. It is a leadership development body for future candidates like our comrade, whose affiliations with the Communist Party are well-known throughout the city even though he is running as a Democrat.

Mark Froemke in Minnesota

Leading North Dakota based Communist Party member and labor union official, Mark Froemke, operates inside the Minnesota Democratic Party affiliate, the Democratic-Farmer-Labor Party, at the highest levels. He has ties to almost all the state's leading politicians, including both Senators and Governor Mark Dayton.

Mark Froemke, Mark Dayton (January 14, 2010)

In October 2009, Mark Froemke was the Fargo Moorehead organizer for the 10 Days of Labor Action campaign for then Minnesota gubernatorial candidate Dayton.[23]

> The time is now. We have an opportunity to build a Better Minnesota by electing Mark Dayton as Governor and all our other labor-endorsed candidates. But, we need your help. That's why on Saturday, October 23, we're kicking off 10 Days of Labor Action.

Froemke has also lobbied Senator Amy Klobuchar on health issues and posed for at least one photo op with her on July 1, 2009.[24]

LaVonne Froemke (left), Amy Klobuchar, Mark Froemke (right)

Communist Party Fronts

The Communist Party has created hundreds of front organizations over the decades, but the most important in modern times are the Coalition of Black Trade Unionists, the Coalition of Labor Union Women and the U.S. Peace Council. All three are used to influence Democratic Party politicians.

Coalition of Black Trade Unionists

Formed in 1972, the CBTU was directly inspired by an earlier Party front, the National Negro Labor Council, which existed from 1950 to '56, when it succumbed to well-justified "red-baiting."

Key leaders of the National Negro Labor Council included Coleman Young (National Executive Secretary and future Democratic Mayor of Detroit), Charles Hayes (Chicago leader, future Democratic Congressman), Cleveland Robinson, George Crockett (future Democratic Congressman) and Erma Henderson from Detroit.

Young and Hayes were both identified Communist Party members, while all of the others were at least close sympathizers.[25]

In the early 1970s, Communist Party union members began to "find their voice through new coalitions such as the Coalition of Black Trade Unionists; the Coalition of Labor Union Women; the Labor Council for Latin American Advancement and the Trade Unionists for Action and Democracy.

TUAD leaders Fred Gaboury, Rayfield Mooty, Debbie Albano and Adelaide Bean, along with Labor Today Editors Jim Williams and Scott Marshall, helped bring these coalitions together. These labor coalitions reflected "rising communist influence in the labor movement."[26]

In September of 1972, more than 1,200 black union officials and rank and file members, representing thirty seven different international and national unions, met in Chicago for two days to discuss the role of black trade unionists in the labor movement.

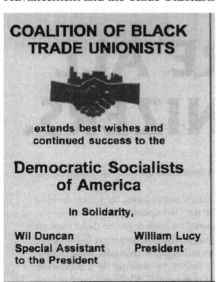

COALITION OF BLACK TRADE UNIONISTS

extends best wishes and continued success to the

Democratic Socialists of America

In Solidarity,

Wil Duncan
Special Assistant
to the President

William Lucy
President

Democratic Left (September/October 1995)

Five black labor leaders, alarmed that the AFL-CIO Executive Council had taken a "neutral" position in the 1972 presidential election between incumbent Richard Nixon and challenger George McGovern, called this founding conference of the Coalition of Black Trade Unionists. They believed AFL-CIO President George Meany had "ignored the voice of black trade unionists." Neutrality, they believed, would contribute to the re-election of Nixon. The call they issued for the conference noted:[27]

> We are concerned that the re-election of Richard Nixon will almost certainly result in four more years of favored treatment for the rich and powerful; continued unemployment; frozen wages; high prices; appointment of additional members of the U.S. Supreme Court who are conservative and insensitive to the rights of workers, minorities, and the poor; more repression and restriction of civil liberties; and the reversal or total neglect of civil rights.

> The delegates made it clear that black workers were ready to share in the power of the labor movement at every level of its policy-making process. CBTU would be a progressive forum for black workers to bring their special issues within unions as well as act as a bridge between organized labor and the black community.

While initiated by communists, socialists were also drawn into the organization. The initial leadership reflected this.

The initial leadership roster included two veterans of the old National Negro Labor Council, communist Charles Hayes and communist sympathizer, later to turn Democratic Socialists of America member, Cleveland Robinson. Chicago unionist Addie Wyatt was there, a long-time Communist Party supporter and a future friend and mentor to a young Barack Obama.[28] [29] [30]

Another Founder, William Lucy, who would lead the organization for decades, was also later to join Democratic Socialists of America.[31]

The CBTU has worked for decades to cultivate black Democratic Party politicians. Speakers at CBTU conferences in recent years have included Senator Barack Obama and "progressive" Congressmen William Lacy Clay (MO), Bennie Thompson (MS) and Keith Ellison (MN).[32]

Coalition of Labor Union Women

The origins of Coalition of Labor Union Women (CLUW) date back to 1973, when seven women activists from seven different unions put out the idea of a union women's coalition. The seven included Addie Wyatt, a

Communist Party supporter and a Founder of the allied Coalition of Black trade unionists; Clara Day, a Teamsters Union leader; and Florence Criley, an electrical workers' leader and wife of communist Richard Criley. Soon they were joined by Barbara Merrill (later a Democratic Socialists of America member), a welfare worker and a Founder of Black Labor Leaders of Chicago. Their work culminated in a national convention to form a "Coalition of Labor Union Women." The convention opened in Chicago on March 22, 1974.

Eight hundred women were expected, but 3,200 came:

> Many were young; some like participant Bea Lumpkin, not so young. Almost all had come at their own expense. Some thought it was a near miracle that so many women participated. It was no miracle. The mass sentiment was there. Union women were fired up and "not taking it anymore." The ground work had been laid in well-attended regional conferences. Lumpkin got into the action earlier in 1973, at the Midwest Regional Conference of Union Women. It was attended by 200 women from 20 different national unions and from 18 states. Men were invited to join too, to help fight for women's rights. Frank Lumpkin was one of the first to join CLUW.

Bea and Frank Lumpkin were both prominent Communist Party leaders.[33]

As with the Coalition of Black Trade Unionists, the communists worked closely with the socialists from the beginning. Feminist Gloria Steinem was a CLUW Founder—and later a member of Democratic Socialists of America.[34]

The socialists, being more acceptable to the public, have often led the organization. DSAer Joyce Miller was a long-time President of the Coalition of Labor Union Women.[35]

Gloria T. Johnson, National President of the Coalition of Labor Union Women, sent Labor Day greetings to Democratic Socialists of America's Democratic Left, Issue 6, 1997:[36]

> The Coalition of Labor Union Women Proudly Salutes the Democratic Socialists of America KEEP UP THE GOOD WORK!

At its founding convention in Chicago, Illinois, CLUW adopted four basic goals of action: to promote affirmative action in the workplace; to strengthen the role of women in unions; to organize the unorganized women; and to increase the involvement of women in the political and legislative process.

The CLUW is considered one of the AFL-CIO's constituency groups, along with the Asian Pacific American Labor Alliance, Coalition of Black Trade Unionists, A. Philip Randolph Institute, Labor Council for Latin American Advancement and Pride At Work.

Several Democratic Party women have been involved with CLUW over the years, one of the most notable being Washington State U.S. Senator Patty Murray.[37]

U.S. Peace Council

The U.S. Peace Council (USPC) was launched as the official U.S. national section of the Soviet front, World Peace Council (WPC) at a November 1979 conference in Philadelphia.

In Democratic Socialists of America member Lawrence S. Wittner's 2003 book, "Toward Nuclear Abolition: A History of the World Nuclear Disarmament," Rob Prince, a 15-year veteran of the Communist Party National Council, describes how he was "part of a nucleus of Communist Party activists" that established the U.S. Peace Council in 1978/79.[38]

By 1983, the USPC Executive Board included several prominent Democrats including Rep. Saundra Graham, Massachusetts State Legislature; Gus Newport, Mayor of Berkeley; Shirley Douglas, Niagara Democratic Club, Oakland, CA; future Congresswoman Barbara Lee of California and future Illinois State Senator and later Obama mentor, Alice Palmer.

These Democrats worked alongside fellow Executive Board members and identified Communist Party activists Sara Staggs, Rob Prince, Michael Myerson, Arnold Braithwaite, Otis Cunningham, James Jackson, Atiba Mbiwan, Pauline Rosen, Jose Soler and Denise Young.[39]

In a brochure distributed at its second convention in November 1981, the U.S. Peace Council explained its support for disarmament and Third World revolutionary organizations:

> The campaign to stop weapons of mass destruction cannot be separated from support for the peoples of Southern Africa, Asia and the Middle East... The movement to defend and consolidate détente is at the same time a movement to halt the forces that seek to crush struggles for liberation. The demand for jobs and rebuilding the cities of our country is simultaneously a demand to reduce the military budget, from which we must get the billions of dollars needed for that task.

The role of the USPC was to influence U.S. elections in favor of the Democrats and build pressure for U.S. disarmament in favor of their beloved Soviet Union. The "line" then, as it is today, was that the U.S. needed to slash military spending in favor of more social spending.

An article in the Communist Party's Daily World, April 27, 1984, p. 10, "N.Y. meet to discuss peace and the elections," gives a flavor of the organization:[40]

> A citywide meeting to discuss the role of the peace and solidarity movements in the 1984 elections has been called by the New York Peace Council for Saturday, May 5.
>
> - Arnold Braithwaite (Communist)—Chairperson of the New York Peace Council. "In this critical year, the N.Y. Peace Council sees as paramount the defeat of Ronald Reagan and elected officials who support his administration and its policies."
> - Miriam Friedlander—New York City Council (and a secret Communist), will speak. "She is the sponsor of Council Resolution 568, which opposed the homeport plan (i.e. for U.S. nuclear missile-armed ships)."
> - A representative from the liberation movement in El Salvador will also speak.
> - Michael Myerson (Communist)—Executive Director of the USPC will speak at the opening session on "The Peace Movement and Elections."
> - Rev. Tony Watkins—Disarmament Coordinator for Clergy and Laity Concerned (CALC) will speak at the closing session on "The Global War Plan and the Need for an Anti-War Movement."

While the Soviet Union has "retreated," the U.S. Peace Council is still in existence, still run by communists and still doing its best to destroy the U.S. military and weaken opposition to the remaining communist countries, Islamic extremism and "Third World" liberation movements.

The USPC works with labor unions and sympathetic Democrats to oppose the wars in Afghanistan, and Iraq, and to cut off military aid to anti-communist allies such as El Salvador, Colombia and South Korea.

In December 2010, Alfred L. Marder was the originator of a U.S. Peace Council "Petition to President Barack Obama and Congress to end the Korean War and Normalize Relations:"[41]

We call on U.S. government to stop its repeated "war games" threatening North Korea, to stop demonizing but rather recognize North Korea as a sovereign nation, to engage the North Korean government in meaningful direct talks to end the Korean War, to sign a peace treaty, to remove all U.S. military bases and troops from South Korea, to negotiate with North Korea to dismantle its nuclear weapons as part of global nuclear abolition, and to normalize diplomatic and trade relations between the two nations.

Marder is a member of the Communist Party's Peace and Solidarity Commission, the Party body charged with running the U.S. "peace movement."[42]

Communist Aligned Senators and Congress Members

Over the last three decades, the Communist Party USA has helped to elect hundreds of sympathetic state legislators, school board members and municipal and county politicians all over the United States. Many are secret Party members posing as Democrats. Most are sympathizers willing to do the Party's bidding in exchange for union money and volunteers at election time.

The Congress and Senate have always been the main targets however, and the party throws all its resources every election cycle into electing as many "progressive" Congress members and Senators as possible.

Disregarding those still in office, Communist Party aligned Congressmen and women in recent years have included:

Patsy Mink (HI); Californians Yvonne Braithwaite Burke, John Burton (now Chair of the California Democratic Party), his brother Phillip Burton, Ron Dellums, Mervyn Dymally, Diane Watson and Lynn Woolsey; Illinois Reps. Charles Hayes, Gus Savage and Harold Washington; Michigander George Crockett; Ohio Rep. Dennis Kucinich; New Yorker's Bella Abzug and Major Owens; and Marylander Parren Mitchell.[43 44 45 46 47 48 49 50 51 52 53 54 55 56 57 58]

Recent Senators with Communist Party connections include Californian Alan Cranston; from Illinois, Carol Moseley Braun and Barack Obama; and from Ohio, Howard Metzenbaum.[59 60 61 62]

Special District Meeting on African American Equality

Search

> Archive / Struggles / African-American Equality

Author: _John Bachtell, National_
Board Member

First published 10/23/2007 15:24 by
{article_topic_desc}

Special District Meeting on African American Equality and
Building the Communist Party and Young Communist League
Chicago, IL September 30, 2007

Opening Remarks By John Bachtell, IL District Organizer

First, I want to acknowledge the collective nature of this report and
preparation for the meeting. Thanks to everyone who contributed.
Secondly, these remarks will not begin to touch on every question,
only a few of the key problems and issues before the district. The rest
is up to you.

--snip--

The African American community, and especially trade unionists have
played a crucial role in the struggle to defeat the ultra right. This
includes massive voter turnout in election after election, but also the
swing state mobilizations in 2004.

This was also reflected in the historic election of Barack Obama. Our
Party actively supported Obama during the primary election. Once
again Obama's campaign reflected the electoral voting unity of the
African American community, but also the alliances built with several
key trade unions, and forces in the Latino and white communities.
It also reflected a breakthrough among white voters. In the primary,
Obama won 35% of the white vote and 7 north side wards, in a
crowded field. During the general election he won every ward in the
city and all the collar counties. This appeal has continued in his
presidential run.

Communists Supported Obama in the 2008 Primaries

Committees of Correspondence

Committees of Correspondence for Democracy and Socialism began in 1991, when approximately one third of the Communist Party USA (CPUSA) membership split from the Party to form a new organization.

In 2000, Committees of Correspondence (CoC or CofC) became Committees of Correspondence for Democracy and Socialism (CCDS).

From the 2004 website of the CCDS came this self-description of the organization:[63]

> We are people of all races and national backgrounds who are committed to the struggle for democracy and socialism. Our name is taken from the history of the U.S. revolutionary war against British colonialism. In the 1770s, Committee of Correspondence were formed in all 13 colonies and became the catalyst for united action against British oppression.

> We, too, seek united action among all who feel the brunt of oppression in the U.S. And we believe that our Committee of Correspondence will, as before, be a catalyst for change.

> Our members are activists in all the social movements of our country—of labor, civil rights, immigrant's rights, women, peace, international solidarity, gay and lesbian rights, environment, youth and students, seniors, and religion. We have come together to help shape a clear cut alternative to the destructive, mean-spirited corporate drive for profit above all else.

> We seek constructive solutions to the problems of poverty and unemployment, racism, sexism, health, education and housing.

Initially, the CoC grew quickly, attracting former Maoists, Trotskyites, anarchists and socialists. The plan was to turn CoC into a communist-led third party to eventually replace the Democrats, but that ambition is on hold right now and working inside the Democrats is common.

The organization discussed its relationship with the Democrats at it 6th Convention, held in San Francisco in July of 2009:[64]

> CCDS's attitude toward organizing a new third party, which was also more prominent in the founding statement, was debated. CCDS has a long-standing "inside/outside" policy on electoral work, which has only been defined in a general way. For a large majority of the organization, this meant working to get Obama elected in various ways.

> Some worked within the Democratic Party organization and others worked for Obama in independent organizations. A number of CCDSers

were opposed to any Democrat and worked for Cynthia McKinney in the Green Party or the Peace and Freedom Party in California.

Still others worked for the Working Families Party in New York where, because of its more progressive election laws, they could vote for Obama on the WFP ticket.

Judging from the positive reports from the delegates' experiences with the election, as well as the documents and resolutions passed, it's clear most of the organization will be engaged in the Obama alliance, although from an independent and critical position.

For those members deeply connected with the labor movement and the movements of oppressed minority communities, most will work on strengthening the left-progressive pole within the Democratic Party at the base. This will heighten the struggle against the "Blue Dog" Democrats and others collaborating with the unreconstructed GOP neoliberals.

Strategically, this position is consistent with preparing the conditions for supplanting the Democrats with a popular and working-class alternative, although not always viewed as such by third party proponents. But it's also clear that the prospects for such a breakaway and wider alliance are not imminent.

"We have our platform and Obama has his," said one delegate, summing up. "They overlap, but they're not the same. We support him where he's right and we oppose and pressure him where he's wrong—and we certainly defend him against the racist assaults from the far right."

Today the Committees of Correspondence are but a few hundred strong and only seriously impacts the electoral process in New York, Northern California and to a degree, in Chicago.

The organization is, however, closely allied to the communist government of Vietnam and does lobby U.S. lawmakers aggressively for U.S. "reparations" to that country for damage done by American forces during the Vietnam War.[65]

Communist Workers Party/Asian Americans for Equality

The Communist Workers Party (CWP) was a Maoist political organization, which grew out of the radical Asian-American youth movement of the Vietnam War era.

Formally founded in 1979, the CWP gained international notoriety in November of that year when 5 of its member were killed in a daylight gun battle with the Ku Klux Klan, in the streets of Greensboro, North Carolina.[66]

Over the next 5 years, the CWP evolved from a militant, "in your face" Maoist grouping, into something far more dangerous.

New Democratic Movement

By the mid-1980s, the CWP was ready to follow China in abandoning open Maoism for a new, much more subtle approach. Working on the theories of Antonio Gramsci, the Italian Communist Party theoretician, business, government and American civil society were no longer to be opposed—they were to be infiltrated.

Any career in government, business, civil society or the church, was to be open to CWP members, as long as they used that position to serve the revolution. The Democratic Party was of course, a major target.

Ben Connors, a lawyer, joined the Communist Workers Party circa 1984.

He wrote an article for the Party's periodical, The Expert Red in February of 1985, on the change in Party tactics from one of traditional Marxist-Leninist agitation, to a conscious program of infiltrating America's institutions:

> Organizing other leftists like ourselves seemed sufficiently important at the time. We came to learn however that it was indeed important, but hardly sufficient. It was time to assume leadership over the whole society... Rather than storm City Hall, we are donning tuxedoes, and preparing to enter through special invitation. We are learning to use our skills in ways that are proving far more dangerous to the ruling class, and far more beneficial to the masses to whom we have dedicated lives of service.

> These days we not only organize but will also begin to deliver. We will not be content to petition the state legislature, we want to be the state legislature. It is truly an exciting time to be an American revolutionary.

> You want me to be a Congressman? Fine, it's what my mother always wanted for me anyway. It's all very legitimate. For other new comrades as well, the road is wide open—we can follow any career path we choose, so long as it helps the Party lead and serve the American people.

At a convention in mid-1985, the CWP formally dissolved itself; in its place a new organization arose, the New Democratic Movement, devoted to establishing "local power bases." Jerry Tung, General Secretary of the former CWP, explained the idea to the assembled faithful. "[O]nce you get people elected or appointed to office, you can award contracts to friends... When you can raise money for political purposes, when you do it in the right place in the right atmosphere, and look right, and the [mainstream] party bosses are there, then that money makes them take you seriously." The meeting closed with a rousing chorus of the "Internationale."

The New Democratic Movement joined the Democratic Party en masse. In New York, comrades working with allies in Democratic Socialists of America, heavily infiltrated the influential Village Independent Democrats and used it as a base to influence Democrat politics across the city.[67]

Asian Americans for Equality

During the 1980s, the CWP set up its power base in New York's Chinatown, in the form of a "community group," Asian Americans for Equality (AAFE).

For years, the two groups shared an office and phone number and CWP veterans still number among Asian-Americans for Equality leaders. One prominent example is AAFE's President from 1982 to 1986: Margaret Chin, now a Democratic New York City Councilor.

For all intents and purposes, Asian Americans for Equality is the continuation of the CWP/NDM.

Built with millions of Federal, state and city dollars, AAFE is now a huge organization, owning property all over Manhattan. AAFE has considerable political clout and close relations with high ranking politicians all over the city.

Its annual banquet in Chinatown received greetings from not only an array of Democratic officeholders, but also such Republicans as Senator Alfonse D'Amato and Representative Bill Green.

New York Senator Chuck Schumer has worked with AAFE, so has Governor Andrew Cuomo and several of the city's Democratic Congressional delegation.[68] [69]

New York City Comptroller and 2013 mayoral hopeful, John Liu, is also a long-time AAFE affiliate.[70]

AAFE also works with networks surrounding pro-China, former CWP members in Los Angeles and the Bay Area, notably around Oakland, California Mayor Jean Quan and with members of the Congressional Asian Pacific American Caucus.[71]

Freedom Road Socialist Organization

The Freedom Road Socialist Organization came out of the Maoist movement of the 1960s. Unlike most other Maoist groups however, FRSO was open to working inside the Democratic Party from early on.

FRSO threw themselves into Jesse Jackson's 1984 bid for the Democratic Party nomination for President. His 1984 and 1988 bids marked the high point of a nearly 20-year period when the Black Liberation Movement's main focus was electoral.

According to Freedom Road, Jackson had the most leftist platform of any major party candidate in the 20th Century. He won support from a "broad array of forces—African Americans, naturally, and other oppressed nationality communities, but also several unions, white family farmers in the Midwest crippled by the Reagan Recession, gays facing the first great wave of AIDS deaths, feminists, students and more. Much of the organized socialist left in the U.S., and an even larger section of unaffiliated reds and revolutionaries, threw themselves into the campaigns:"[72]

> Jackson's newly formed National Rainbow Coalition, billed as an independent form that would fight inside and outside of the Democratic Party for a radical agenda, provided a common project for comrades to work on and around. Now we could test and strengthen the unity we had built. In 1988, Jackson won nearly a third of the delegates, and the "Democratic Party moved hard to co-opt him."

> When Jackson slid into the Democratic Party mainstream he tried to bring his whole campaign with him. But FRSO members joined others fighting to keep their state Rainbows independent until he dissolved them.

While they are still a small organization, FRSO works with the Communist Party and Democratic Socialists of America to influence the Democratic Party when it can.

Writing on the Freedom Road Socialist Organization website in January 2008, Missouri based FRSO National Executive Committee member Jamala Rogers, urged her comrades to work inside the Democratic Party when conditions were suitable—with the eventual goal of breaking away to form a third party:[73]

> Build locally based, independent, progressive mass electoral organizations that can identify, train and run candidates for office within the Democratic Party or as independents, depending on the actual situation at the local level. Such locally based organizations should be seen as a component in laying the basis for an eventual electoral realignment, but should not be created as independent political parties. They must be more than PACs, 527s or think tanks in that they must be a means for real people to interact with the electoral arena in ways other than as objects. Such organizations should seek to give electoral voice to the various progressive social movements that are not, mainly, electoral.

Workers World Party

Founded in 1959, the Workers World Party (WWP) is one of the most hardcore Marxist organizations of any consequence in the U.S. It supports Cuba, Venezuela, North Korea, Iran and even Zimbabwean dictator, Robert Mugabe.

The party is extremely militant and prone to confrontation with the police.

It seldom gets involved in Democratic Party election campaigns, though it did support radical New York City Councilor Charles Barron in his unsuccessful bid for the Democratic nomination in New York's 8th District:[74]

> Barron was attacked for welcoming Zimbabwe President Robert Mugabe to City Hall. Mugabe is a liberator who has distributed land to thousands of Black farmers. That should have been done here following the U.S. Civil War.

> Charles Barron was also attacked for denouncing NATO's colonial war against Libya. Barron defended African leader Moammar Gadhafi, who was tortured to death by U.S.-NATO mercenaries.

> Workers World Party is proud to have supported Charles Barron.

Usually, WWP likes to influence Democrats through the anti-war movement, Iranian solidarity and the like. The Party has run several large front groups, including International Action Center, Act Now to Stop War and End Racism and Youth Against War & Fascism, which often co-opts Democrat officials and Congress members to address their marches and rallies.[75]

1 The Firing Line, Online Forum,
http://thefiringline.com/forums/showthread.php?p=249251 (October 10, 2000)
2 KeyWiki, "Communist Party USA," KeyWiki,
http://www.keywiki.org/index.php/Communist_Party_USA (accessed May 7, 2013)
3 Gus Hall, "A Lame Duck in Turbulent Waters," Communist Party USA (1972)
4 Wilson C. Lucom, "Communists in the Democratic Party," Concerned Voters Inc. (1990) p. 21
5 Charlene Mitchell, People's Daily World (June 9, 1983)
6 Charlene Mitchell, Political Affairs (March 1989)
7 Political Affairs (September/October 1988)
8 Political Affairs (March 1989)
9 Communists in the Democratic Party, p. 26
10 Political Affairs (May 1987)
11 CPUSA Political Action Commission, "Convention Discussion: Building Labor/People's Electoral Power," Communist Party USA,
http://www.cpusa.org/convention-discussion-building-labor-people-s-electoral-power/ (April 13, 2010)
12 YCLers in Transition, "Convention Discussion: A Time to Grow," Communist Party USA, http://www.cpusa.org/convention-discussion-a-time-to-grow/ (February 2, 2010)
13 Jessica Marshall, Communist Party USA,
http://www.cpusa.org/article/articleview/608/1/56/ (November 20, 2004)
14 Scott Marshall, "Workers and oppressed of the world unite, 2.0," People's World,
http://www.peoplesworld.org/workers-and-oppressed-of-the-world-unite-2/ (November 22, 2009)
15 Tony Pecinovsky, "Missourians shifting away from GOP," People's World,
http://transitional.pww.org/missourians-shifting-away-from-gop/ (October 21, 2006)
16 World Combined Sources, "As Ohio goes, so goes the nation," People's World,
http://www.peoplesworld.org/as-ohio-goes-so-goes-the-nation/ (November 10, 2006)
17 People's Weekly World (December 10, 2005)
18 CPUSA, http://www.cpusa.org/article/view/586/ (2004)
19 Dennis Kucinich, "Kucinich Endorsement," Nagin for Council,
http://www.naginforcouncil.com/kucinich_endorsement.html (2009)
20 Dan Margolis, "Dan Margolis," People's World, http://www.peoplesworld.org/dan-margolis (accessed May 7, 2013)
21 KeyWiki, "Jesus Garcia," KeyWiki,
http://www.keywiki.org/index.php/Jesus_Garcia (accessed May 7, 2013)
22 YCLers in Transition, "Convention Discussion: A Time to Grow," Communist Party USA, http://www.cpusa.org/convention-discussion-a-time-to-grow/ (February 2, 2010)

23 CShields, "10 Days of Action!," AFL-CIO,
http://www.mnaflcio.org/blog/2010/10/10-days-action (October 21, 2010)
24 KeyWiki, "Amy Klobuchar," KeyWiki,
http://www.keywiki.org/index.php/Amy_Klobuchar (accessed May 7, 2013)
25 People's Weekly World (February 20, 1993) p. 12
26 Bea Lumpkin, "Joy in the Struggle, My Life and Love," p. 163
27 CBTU, "About CBTU," CBTU, http://www.cbtu.org/history.html (accessed May 7, 2013)
28 Hearings before the Subcommittee to Investigate the Administration of the Internal Security Act, U.S. Senate, 94th Congress, Part 2 (July 1975) p. 182
29 KeyWiki, "Cleveland Robinson," KeyWiki,
http://www.keywiki.org/index.php/Cleveland_Robinson (accessed May 7, 2013)
30 KeyWiki, "Addie Wyatt," KeyWiki,
http://www.keywiki.org/index.php/Addie_Wyatt (accessed May 7, 2013)
31 KeyWiki, "William Lucy," KeyWiki,
http://www.keywiki.org/index.php/William_Lucy (accessed May 7, 2013)
32 KeyWiki, "DSA Supporters," KeyWiki,
http://www.keywiki.org/index.php/Coalition_of_Black_Trade_Unionists#DSA_supporters (accessed May 7, 2013)
33 Bea Lumpkin, "Joy in the Struggle, My Life and Love," p. 163
34 Stowe Vintage, "Famous Women Autographs," Stowe Vinatge,
http://www.stowevintage.com/gpage56.html (accessed May 7, 2013)
35 KeyWiki, "Joyce Miller," KeyWiki,
http://www.keywiki.org/index.php/Joyce_Miller (accessed May 7, 2013)
36 Democratic Left, Issue 6 (1997)
37 KeyWiki, "Patty Murray," KeyWiki,
http://www.keywiki.org/index.php/Patty_Murray (accessed May 7, 2013)
38 Toward Nuclear Abolition: A History of the World Nuclear Disarmament, p. 39
39 KeyWiki, "U.S. Peace Council," KeyWiki,
http://www.keywiki.org/index.php/U.S._Peace_Council (accessed May 8, 2013)
40 Communist Party's Daily World, "N.Y. meet to discuss peace and the elections," Communist Party's Daily World (April 27, 1984) p. 10
41 USPC website, "Sign the USPC Petition on Korea, Petition to President Barack Obama and Congress to end the Korean War and Normalize Relations," USPC website, http://uspeacecouncil.org/?p=526 (December 29, 2010)
42 KeyWiki, "Alfred Marder," KeyWiki,
http://www.keywiki.org/index.php/Alfred_Marder (accessed May 8, 2013)
43 KeyWiki, "Patsy Mink," KeyWiki, http://www.keywiki.org/index.php/Patsy_Mink (accessed May 8, 2013)
44 KeyWiki, "Yvonne Braithwaite Burke," KeyWiki,
http://www.keywiki.org/index.php/Yvonne_Braithwaite_Burke (accessed May 8, 2013)
45 KeyWiki, "John Burton," KeyWiki,
http://www.keywiki.org/index.php/John_Burton (accessed May 8, 2013)
46 KeyWiki, "Phillip Burton," KeyWiki,
http://www.keywiki.org/index.php/Philip_Burton (accessed May 8, 2013)
47 KeyWiki, "Ron Dellums," KeyWiki,
http://www.keywiki.org/index.php/Ron_Dellums (accessed May 8, 2013)
48 KeyWiki, "Mervyn Dymally," KeyWiki,
http://www.keywiki.org/index.php/Mervyn_Dymally (accessed May 8, 2013)

49 KeyWiki, "Diane Watson," KeyWiki,
http://www.keywiki.org/index.php/Diane_Watson (accessed May 8, 2013)
50 KeyWiki, "Lynn Woolsey," KeyWiki,
http://www.keywiki.org/index.php/Lynn_Woolsey (accessed May 8, 2013)
51 KeyWiki, "Charles Hayes," KeyWiki, www.keywiki.org/index.php/Charles_Hayes
(accessed May 8, 2013)
52 KeyWiki, "Gus Savage," KeyWiki, http://www.keywiki.org/index.php/Gus_Savage
(accessed May 8, 2013)
53 KeyWiki, "Harold Washington," KeyWiki,
http://www.keywiki.org/index.php/Harold_Washington (accessed May 8, 2013)
54 KeyWiki, "George Crockett, Jr.," KeyWiki,
http://www.keywiki.org/index.php/George_Crockett (accessed May 8, 2013)
55 KeyWiki, "Dennis Kucinich," KeyWiki,
http://www.keywiki.org/index.php/Dennis_Kucinich (accessed May 8, 2013)
56 KeyWiki, "Bella Abzug," KeyWiki,
http://www.keywiki.org/index.php/Bella_Abzug (accessed May 8, 2013)
57 KeyWiki, "Major Owens," KeyWiki,
http://www.keywiki.org/index.php/Major_Owens (accessed May 8, 2013)
58 KeyWiki, "Parren Mitchell," KeyWiki,
http://www.keywiki.org/index.php/Parren_Mitchell (accessed May 8, 2013)
59 KeyWiki, "Alan Cranston," KeyWiki,
http://www.keywiki.org/index.php/Alan_Cranston (accessed May 8, 2013)
60 KeyWiki, "Carol Moseley Braun," KeyWiki,
http://www.keywiki.org/index.php/Carol_Moseley_Braun (accessed May 8, 2013)
61 KeyWiki, "Barack Obama and the Communist Party," KeyWiki,
http://www.keywiki.org/index.php/Barack_Obama_and_the_Communist_Party
(accessed May 8, 2013)
62 KeyWiki, "Howard Metzenbaum," KeyWiki,
http://www.keywiki.org/index.php/Howard_Metzenbaum (accessed May 8, 2013)
63 KeyWiki, "Committees of Correspondence," KeyWiki,
http://www.keywiki.org/index.php/Committees_of_Correspondence#Portside_publicat
ion (accessed May 8, 2013)
64 CCDS, "Socialism and the Emerging Progressive Majority," CCDS, http://www.cc-
ds.org/convention_2009/Socialism_and_the_Emerging_Progressive_Majority.pdf
(2009)
65 CCDS, "Socialism and the Emerging Progressive Majority," CCDS, http://www.cc-
ds.org/convention_2009/Socialism_and_the_Emerging_Progressive_Majority.pdf
(2009)
66 Greensboro TRC, "Greensboro Truth and Reconciliation Commission Final Report,
Sequence of events on Nov. 3, 1979, Chapter 7," Greensboro TRC,
http://www.greensborotrc.org/1979_sequence.pdf (accessed May 9, 2013)
67 Richard Brookhiser, "The Resistible Rise of Margaret Chin," City Magazine,
http://www.city-journal.org/article02.php?aid=1606, (Spring 1991)
68 KeyWiki, "Charles E. Schumer," KeyWiki,
www.keywiki.org/index.php/Charles_Schumer (accessed May 9, 2013)
69 KeyWiki, "Asian Americans for Equality," KeyWiki,
http://www.keywiki.org/index.php/Asian_Americans_for_Equality (accessed May 9,
2013)
70 KeyWiki, "John Liu," KeyWiki, http://www.keywiki.org/index.php/John_Liu
(accessed May 9, 2013)

71 KeyWiki, "Jean Quan," KeyWiki, http://www.keywiki.org/index.php/Jean_Quan (accessed May 9, 2013)

72 Dennis O'Neil, "A Very Short History of Our Organization," FRSO/OSCL, http://www.freedomroad.org/index.php?option=com_content&view=article&id=725% 3Aa-very-short-history-of-our-organization&catid=171%3Aour-history&Itemid=264&lang=en (August 31, 2010)

73 KeyWiki, "Freedom Road Socialist Organization/Organizacion Socialista del Camino para la Libertad," KeyWiki, http://keywiki.org/index.php/Freedom_Road_Socialist_Organization (accessed May 8, 2013)

74 Stephen Millies, "How they kept Barron out of Congress," Workers World, http://www.workers.org/2012/us/barron_0712/ (July 5, 2012)

75 KeyWiki, "Workers World Party," KeyWiki, http://www.keywiki.org/index.php/Workers_World_Party (accessed May 9, 2013)

Socialists

Democratic Socialists of America

Democratic Socialists of America (DSA) is the largest socialist organization in the U.S. It is the U.S. affiliate of the Socialist International, which despite its name, now incorporates several communist or "former" communist parties.

DSA was formed in 1982 from a merger of the Michael Harrington-led Democratic Socialist Organizing Committee (DSOC) and the smaller New American Movement (NAM), which was in turn formed mainly by former members of Students for a Democratic Society and the Communist Party USA (CPUSA).

Circa 2000, DSA was a national organization of about 7,000 members, of which about 2,000 were academics. Today, after falling away a little, numbers are believed to be back around the 7,000 mark.

There are about 20 larger local chapters, concentrated mainly in New York, Massachusetts, Illinois, Michigan, Georgia and California.

In addition to the national and local groups, there were several Commissions. These groups dealt with specific issues and are not geographically organized. While coming and going, DSA has operated Latino, Anti-Racism, Feminism, Labor, Religion and Socialism, Eco-Socialism and African American Commissions at various times.[1]

"Communist Lite?"

While DSA claims to be socialist rather than communist, the differences are minimal. While the former DSOC did contain some genuinely anti-communist socialists, since the merger with NAM, DSA has moved steadily left.

Today, its program is virtually identical to that of the CPUSA, but the word "Democratic" in DSA's name enables it to penetrate organizations that wouldn't accept more open communists.

DSA follows the ideas of the late Italian Communist Party theoretician Antonio Gramsci. According to Gramsci, "working class revolution" is a dead end. Communism can best be achieved by infiltrating civil society—political parties, churches, labor unions, universities, the media, community groups, etc. to turn them into revolutionary vehicles. It is revolution by stealth.

Orange County California DSA acknowledged its debt to Gramsci in its February 1984, newsletter:

> Antonio Gramsci was a founder of the Italian Communist Party. He developed theories on "open ended Marxism" and independent Euro-Communism. His writings have remained influential among European parties of the left for several decades. They have also formed a vital part of the ideas that brought about the formation of today's DSA.

In DSA's Democratic Left, Spring 2007, DSA National Political Committee member David Green of Detroit, exposed his organization's commitment to Marxism in an article on the Employee Free Choice Act (EFCA)—or "Card Check:"[2]

What distinguishes socialists from other progressives is the theory of surplus value. According to Marx, the secret of surplus value is that workers are a source of more value than they receive in wages. The capitalist is able to capture surplus value through his ownership of the means of production, his right to purchase labor as a commodity, his control over the production process, and his ownership of the final product. Surplus value is the measure of capital's exploitation of labor...

Our goal as socialists is to abolish private ownership of the means of production. Our immediate task is to limit the capitalist class's prerogatives in the workplace...

In the short run we must at least minimize the degree of exploitation of workers by capitalists. We can accomplish this by promoting full employment policies, passing local living wage laws, but most of all by increasing the union movement's power...

The Employee Free Choice Act (EFCA) provides an excellent organizing tool (i.e., tactic) through which we can pursue our socialist strategy while simultaneously engaging the broader electorate on an issue of economic populism.

Today's DSA cooperates with CPUSA, Committees of Correspondence for Democracy and Socialism, Freedom Road Socialist organization and other communist groups. Its deceptive name helps make them the most effective and dangerous Marxist organization now operating in the U.S.

Conquering the Unions

The key to socializing the U.S. is the conquest of organized labor— something that DSA has already pretty much achieved. The U.S. labor movement, once run by strong anti-communists such as Lane Kirkland and George Meany, is now almost entirely in the hands of the socialists and communists.

Circa 1994, AFSCME President Gerald McEntee (a long-time DSA supporter), approached the AFL-CIO with his idea for Project '95, a coalition effort aimed at retaking the House for the Democratic Party, but AFL-CIO President Lane Kirkland wouldn't have a bar of it. In response, McEntee and fellow DSA supporter John Sweeney began canvassing their colleagues about Kirkland's removal.

Soon, they amassed support from a coalition that included not just the core of the old CIO (the Auto Workers, Steelworkers and Mine Workers), but the Machinists, Ron Carey's new-model Teamsters, the Carpenters and the Laborers.[3]

This plot led to the most profound move to the left since the founding of the communist-led Congress of Industrial Organizations in the '30s. By 1995, Sweeney had formally joined DSA and assumed the Presidency of the AFL-CIO.[4]

According to DSA member and Washington Post journalist, Harold Meyerson, the "progressive coalition" of labor unionists which ousted conservative AFL-CIO President Lane Kirkland in 1994-95 and replaced him with John Sweeney, was led by Gerald McEntee, John Sweeney, Richard Trumka and George Kourpias (all identified DSA supporters).[5]

Sweeney immediately removed the anti-communist clause from the AFL-CIO's constitution and the Marxists came flooding back. Today, almost every major labor union in the U.S. is dominated by the left.

The editor of DSA's Democratic Left assured a reader in the Spring/Summer 2000 edition:[6]

> And there's good news: More DSA members and alumni of DSA's Youth Section are moving up through the administrative and organizing reaches of AFL-CIO international unions, and global labor solidarity groups, than ever in recent memory.

In modern America, the unions effectively fund and control the Democratic Party. So, if the socialists can control the unions, they can then dictate the whole direction of the Party, from policy formation to candidate selection.

In an essay in Democratic Left Spring/Summer 2000, then DSA Vice-Chair Harold Meyerson wrote:[7]

> The differences here are magnified because the strategic importance of unions in American politics has increased almost exponentially since John Sweeney took the helm at the AFL-CIO in 1995. It's the unions that have brought the Democrats back to brink of retaking Congressional power.

Dictating to the Democrats

Many, if not most, DSAers are also Democrats and hold high Party offices all over the country—right up to the Congressional level. They operate as a sort of secret society within the Party and by coordinating their efforts, they can have a big say in Democratic Party decisions.

According to an article written in the Boston DSA magazine Yankee Radical, January, 2001, by Mike Pattberg, DSA was intent on taking over the Democrats:[8]

On the other hand, the Communist Party experienced the height of its numbers, power and influence when it abandoned its previous ultra-left course to become the Stalinist wing of the New Deal in the mid-1930s...

In any case, by the early 1960s some within the Socialist Party (including future DSA leaders), adopting a variant of the CP's strategy 25 years earlier, had broken with prevailing labor party orthodoxy... They instead advanced the concept of "Realignment" in the Democratic Party; forging a coalition of labor, blacks and middle-class liberals and radicals to take over the Party by purging (democratically, of course) Southern racists, big-city bosses and other retrograde elements.

Circa 1982, DSA Poster

DSA is quite honest to its members that the Democratic Party is only a means to an end.

From DSA's Democratic Left magazine, Spring/Summer 2000:[9]

DSA is no more loyal to the Democratic Party—which barely exists as a grassroots institution—than are individuals or social movements which upon occasion use its ballot line or vote for its candidates... Veterans of the left will remember that the 1968 Peace and Freedom Party and the 1980 Citizens Party arose at moments of greater left-wing strength and did not significantly alter the national electoral landscape. Nor has, unfortunately, the New Party, which many DSAers work with in states where "fusion" of third party and major party votes is possible (such as the DSA co-sponsored Working Families Party in N.Y. State).

DSA recognizes that some insurgent politicians representing labor, environmentalists, gays and lesbians, and communities of color may choose to run under Democratic auspices, as in the 1988 Jesse Jackson campaign, or operate as Democrats like Senator Paul Wellstone, and the 59 Democratic members of the Congressional Progressive Caucus, one-half of whom are Black and Latino and all of whom possess strong labor backing and operative social democratic politics.

Electoral tactics are only a means for DSA; the building of a powerful anti-corporate and ultimately socialist movement is the end. Where third party or non-partisan candidates represent significant social movements DSA locals have and will continue to build such organizations and support such candidates. DSA honored independent socialist Congressperson Bernie Sanders of Vermont at our last convention banquet, and we have always raised significant funds nationally for his electoral campaigns. At the same time, we were pleased to have Democratic Congressperson and Progressive Caucus member Bob Filner of San Diego introduce Sanders at the convention, and note that Progressive Caucus member Jan Schakowsky (D-IL) will be honored at our annual Debs-Thomas-Harrington dinner this Spring in Chicago...

DSA is not an electoral organization, but rather a democratic socialist political organization which aims to bring socialism into the mainstream of American politics. We endeavor to do so through a two-pronged strategy of education and organizing. Much of our work is cultural and ideological: forums, debates, publications. But our voice can only be heard if we simultaneously play a central, activist role within struggles relevant to working people, communities of color, women, gays and lesbians and other oppressed constituencies. We operate within progressive coalitions as an open socialist presence and bring to these movements an analysis and strategy which recognizes the fundamental need to democratize global corporate power.

DSA strives to be a crucial socialist leaven within a mass movement for social justice. In the 2000 elections, most electorally-active, progressive constituencies will endeavor to elect progressives to Congress and to the state legislatures.

At DSA's November 2009 National Convention in Evanstown, Illinois, the organization resolved to work hard to keep moving the Democrats left:[10]

Finally, DSA will work in 2010 to insure that progressive Democrats who support many of the above items are reelected to Congress or replace right-wing Democratic or Republican incumbents. Only if the Democratic majority in Congress is not just preserved but expanded and moved to the left can any of the above progressive reforms be enacted. DSA PAC will explore hiring an organizer to help our members become more effective in electoral politics, especially in the primary campaigns where we will promote true progressives.

What DSA Wants

In 1997, DSA goals by 2017 included:[11]

A U.S. President from the Progressive Caucus, a 50 member socialist caucus in Congress, successful programs of the likes of universal health care, progressive taxation, social provision and campaign finance reform.

While Obama has never publicly identified with the Progressive Caucus, there is no doubt he is sympathetic with their aims. His moves towards socialized health care, higher taxes on the wealthy, increased welfare, etc., are right out of the DSA playbook.

DSAers in the Democratic Party

Thousands of DSA Marxists have held Democratic Party office over the last 30 years, from local committee to Congressional level. Every year, each DSA local would get a questionnaire from the Head Office asking which positions in the local Democrat Party were held by DSA members and which "progressive" Democrats they had supported for municipal positions, Congress or Senate.

Over time, this long-term infiltration at every level by DSAers has moved the Democratic Party so far left it would be unrecognizable to a Truman or a Kennedy Democrat.

Some Democratic Party operatives who have been involved with Democratic Socialists of America in recent years include:

- Elizabeth Bunn - Michigan Democratic Party Super Delegate, 2008.[12]
- Tim Carpenter - Leader of Progressive Democrats of America.[13]
- David Dinkins - New York City Mayor, in the early 1990s.[14]
- Bob Fitrakis - Former Ohio Congressional candidate. He led the charge against alleged Republican voter fraud in that state after the 2000 elections.[15]
- Matthew Hallinan - Key Bay Area Democrat.[16]
- Millie Jeffrey - Key Michigan and national Democratic Party activist. Responsible for advancing the careers of Michigan Governor Jennifer Grantholm and Senator Debbie Stabenow.

Jeffrey helped Geraldine Ferarro secure the Democratic VP nomination in 1984.[17]

- John Katz - A leader of the Bay Area's Wellstone Democratic Renewal Club.[18]
- David Kusnet - Chief Speechwriter for former President Bill Clinton. Speechwriter for former presidential candidates Walter Mondale and Michael Dukakis.[19]
- John Laird - Former Santa Cruz Mayor and influential California Democratic Party activist.[20]
- Mike Lux - Special Assistant to the President for Public Liaison in the Bill Clinton White House. Led the Obama Transition Team outreach to the "progressive" movement.[21]
- Maryann Mahaffey - Former Detroit City Councilor.[22]
- Hilda Mason - Former Washington, D.C. City Councilor.[23]
- Ruth Messinger - Former New York City Councilor.[24]
- Christine Riddiough - Former Chair of the Gertrude Stein Democratic Club, an influential gay-lesbian Democratic organization in Washington, D.C.[25]
- Lynn Shaw - Former Vice-Chair of the Los Angeles County Democratic Party.[26]
- Jim Scheibel - Former Mayor of St. Paul, Minnesota.[27]
- Paul Schrade - Key California Democratic operative, going back to the Kennedy era.[28]
- Stanley Sheinbaum - Key California Democratic Party funder and influence broker.[29]

DSAers Holding Elected Office:

→United States Representative Ronald Dellums (Berkeley, CA)
→United States Representative Major Owens (Brooklyn, NY)
→New York Mayor David Dinkins
→St Paul (MN) Mayor Jim Schiebel
→Ithaca (NY) Mayor Ben Nichols
→Irvine (CA) Mayor Larry Agran
→Santa Monica (CA) Mayor Jim Conn
→Alaska State Legislator Niilo Koponen (Fairbanks)
→Oregon State Representative Beverly Stein (Portland)
→Michigan State Representative Perry Bullard (Lansing)
→Pennsylvania State Representative Babette Josephs (Philadelphia)
→Manhattan (NY) Borough President Ruth Messinger
→San Francisco President of the Board of Supervisors Harry Britt
→Detroit (MI) City Council President Maryann Mahaffey
→Washington, D.C City Councilperson Hilda Mason
→Cambridge (MA) City Councilperson David Sullivan
→Boston (MA) City Councilperson David Scondras
→Berkeley (CA) City Councilperson Ann Chandler
→Wayne State University (Detroit) Governor Mildred Jeffrey

Democratic Left (Jan. 1990) p. 7

Among the dozens of current and former DSA State Reps. posing as Democrats are:[30]

- Harlan Baker - Former Maine State Rep.[31]
- Babette Josephs - State Rep., Pennsylvania.[32]
- Niilo Koponen - Former Alaska State Rep.[33]
- John McDonough - Former Massachusetts State Rep.[34]
- Michael Paymar - Minnesota State Rep.[35]
- Nancy Skinner - California State Rep.[36]
- Frank I. Smizik - Massachusetts State Rep.[37]
- Bev Stein - Former Oregon State Rep.[38]

DSAers in Congress

Several paid-up DSAers have served as Democrat Reps. in the U.S. Congress in recent years.

Among them were Neil Abercrombie from Hawaii (now Governor of that state), Ron Dellums of California, Carrie Meek from Florida, one term Ohio Rep. Mary Jo Kilroy and Major Owens from New York.[39] [40] [41] [42] [43]

David Bonior of Michigan, once the second highest ranked Democrat in the House and a long-time friend of DSA formally joined the socialists after leaving Congress in 2002.[44]

Several former U.S. Representatives have worked very closely with Democratic Socialists of America, but may not have been formal members. These include Massachusetts Rep. Barney Frank, California Rep. (now San Diego Mayor) Bob Filner, New York Rep. Maurice Hinchey, Massachusetts Rep. Gerry Studds, Pennsylvania Rep. Bob Edgar, New York Rep. Ted Weiss and particularly, Senator Ted Kennedy of Massachusetts.[45] [46] [47] [48] [49] [50] [51]

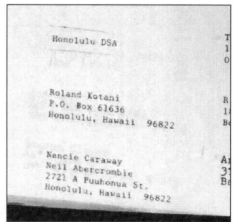

Early 1990s, DSA Hawaii Membership List

Marxism in Michigan

Michigan provides a good illustration of how Democratic Socialists of America has been able to exert influence on the Democratic Party in that state. The same techniques are applied in major cities all over the country.

A revealing article in the Chicago-based socialist journal *In These Times*, lays out DSA strategy and methodology:

> Democratic socialists in southeastern Michigan possess a level of influence within the Michigan Democratic Party of which many American leftists dream. And "they've done it all without compromising their beliefs or values."

> Their success has come from working with, instead of against, local Democrats.

> "It starts out with relationships," says David Green, the chair of the Greater Detroit Democratic Socialists of America (DSA). "Mark Brewer, the chair of the Michigan Democratic Party, has a very good relationship with us. He's spoken to our local several times. The chairs of the county parties, several of them are close friends as well."

DSA openly works with the Democrats to get "progressive" candidates into office:

> Since 1998, Detroit DSA, with about 250 members, has successfully partnered with local county chairs and other Democratic Party officials to promote and elect several progressive candidates to the Michigan state legislature. One of these candidates, State Rep. John Espinoza, was even elected in the heavily conservative "Thumb" region of the state. In 2004, with the backing of Detroit DSA, Espinoza became the first Democrat and the first Latino ever elected to represent Michigan's 83rd District.

> The secret to their success, says Green, is thinking strategically.

> "As a small organization, how can we make a difference? We leverage our forces. We put our efforts towards a progressive Democrat challenging a Republican, or a progressive Democrat challenging a centrist Democrat [in a primary]."

> "We don't pick symbolic victories," Green says, "We pick things we can win."

After deciding whom to support, Detroit DSA carefully chooses tactics that will have the greatest impact, all of which are based on the leftist tradition of on-the-ground, grassroots action.

Green holds initial fundraisers for progressive Democratic candidates in his own home, where he invites friends and allies to come meet the candidates and contribute to their campaigns. These fundraisers bring in several thousand dollars, which, according to Green, is more than enough to get a fledgling statehouse race off the ground, providing crucial support to underfunded progressive candidates entering politics for the first time.

Detroit DSA is not so open with the voting public however and takes pains to hide their socialist affiliations:

To build on the initial fundraising push, a core of Detroit DSA goes door-to-door to distribute literature and answer questions about their candidates. These activists also participate in phone banking and email campaigns. As part of this effort, Green instructs his members not to identify themselves as DSA members, to "avoid the knee-jerk reaction" many still have toward people who self-identify as "socialists."

DSA has had to deal with some "red-baiting," which gives the Democrats a little pause. However, any hesitation enlisting socialist help is really only for public consumption:[52]

Detroit DSA has come under fire from Republicans and Democrats for being a "socialist" organization. Earlier in 2009, the pro-free-market, Michigan-based Mackinac Center for Public Policy asked the question, "Are socialists deciding close state house races?" In addition, in previous elections, Detroit DSA candidates have been "red-baited" by both Republican opponents and mainstream newspapers. Detroit DSA's support became an issue in another statehouse race, in which the Republican candidate commissioned robo calls that accused her opponent, Democrat Vicki Barnett, of being a socialist.

Such red-baiting, has prevented Detroit DSA from getting involved in higher profile races. The group offered to support progressive Democratic candidates in two congressional races in 2008: Gary Peters (9th district) and Mark Schauer (7th district), both of whom went on to victory. Green says that the candidates themselves were happy to have Detroit DSA's involvement, but that "handlers" from the Democratic National Committee (DNC) refused the support, for fear that the candidates would be red-baited or branded as socialists.

Green is confident that the DNC's rejection of his organization's support will change. In the 2008 cycle, support from Detroit DSA helped to push progressive candidates over the top in close races, in traditionally Republican regions, and in races where their candidates were red-baited. They continue to lead living-wage campaigns and other social movements that mainstream Democrats can support without controversy.

Helping the Democrats "Take Control"

Under the heading, "DSAers work for Andy Levin, Lisa Brown," a Greater Detroit Democratic Socialists of America 2006 newsletter reported on a Detroit DSA meeting on November 4, 2006, which stated:[53]

> DSA's goal this election cycle is to help the Democrats take control of both the state house and state senate. We do this work, not because we are sycophants of the Democratic Party, but because only in the context of a Democratic majority do we have the political space necessary to pursue our agenda (e.g., fixing the flawed minimum wage legislation, pursuing universal health care).

Justice Caucus

In 2000, Detroit DSA's energy was directed at electing "progressives" to the State Legislature. The local negotiated directly with these candidates to canvas for them if they agreed to support Living Wage Initiatives and Universal Health Care 2000, as well as to co-sponsor the Single Payer Health Insurance Bill. Also, DSAers got their agreement to help form a Progressive Caucus in the State Legislature. The caucus was named The Justice Caucus, which now serves as a DSA directed power bloc in the Michigan State Legislature. This is very similar to the way the DSA initiated Congressional Progressive Caucus functions in the U.S. House of Representatives.[54]

Democratic Party Conference

In April 2010, Detroit DSA had a room at the Michigan Democratic Party endorsement convention, which was attended by approximately 2000 delegates. DSA was introduced to various candidates who were seeking endorsements and lobbied and voted for their two endorsed candidates—one for Secretary of State (who won) and one for Attorney General (who lost by a narrow margin). They distributed DSA literature (the Economic Justice Agenda and pieces on the financial crisis) to "a large and receptive audience."[55]

PLAN: The Stealth Socialists Who Conquered Los Angeles

PLAN (Progressive Los Angeles Network), was a program conceived and executed by socialists, mostly affiliated with Democratic Socialists of America, to take political control of America's second largest city.

The germ of a plan can be traced back to 1998. On March 11th of that year, Los Angeles Democratic Socialists of America (DSA) leader Steve Tarzynski wrote an email to another Los Angeles DSA leader, journalist Harold Meyerson, discussing a long-term program to "rebuild a progressive movement in our metropolitan area that could challenge for power."

Tarzynski named more than 40 people he thought could be included on an "A-list" of 25 or so leaders/activists/intellectuals and/or "eminent persons" who would gather periodically to theorize/strategize towards the goal in mind.

From:	Tarzynski,Stephen
Sent:	Wednesday, March 11, 1998 11:49 AM
To:	'Meyerson, Harold'
Subject:	RE: HELLO

Great. Let's start then. Here are some of the folks I was thinking should be considered for the "A-list" of the 25 or so leaders/activists/intellectuals and/or "eminent persons" who would gather periodically to theorize/strategize about how to rebuild a progressive movement in our metropolitan area that could challenge for power. I'm sure I've omitted some obvious biggies.

you, me, Karen Bass, Sylvia Castillo, Gary Phillips, Joe Hicks, Richie Rothstein, Steve Cancian, Larry Frank, Torrie Osborn, Rudy Acuna, Arid Anagnos, Abby Arnold, Carl Boggs, Blase Bonpane, Rick Brown, Stanley Sheinbuam, Alice Callahan, Jim Conn, Peter Dreier, Maria Elena Durazo, Miguel Contreras, Mike Davis, Bill Gallegos, Bob Gottlieb, Kent Wong, Russell Jacoby, Bong Hwan Kim, Paula Litt (and Barry?), Peter Olney, Derek Shearer, Clancy Sigal, and Anthony Thigpenn.

Elected officials, as we agreed, are somewhat a breed unto themselves. I would include in this subgroup Mark Ridley-Thomas, Gloria Romero, Jackie Goldberg, Gil Cedillo, Hayden, Villaraigosa, Paul Rosenstein, and even some Congressfolk like Becerra, Waxman, Waters. There are other obvious officials who escape me at the moment, but will not escape you. It may be difficult to get some of these folks to sit in the same room with each other. And their presence in any significant numbers would skew the conversation in certain directions.

I think that we should limit the group to 25 max, otherwise group dynamics begins to break down. I don't know. Maybe we won't even get that many. Let me know what you think and how you think we should proceed. As I said, I would like this to take place in a nice place with good food and drink. And as you said, it should properly be an all day event. Is your fax number 213-465-3220? Steve

To anyone who knows the left, it was clear that Tarzynski had chosen the cream of Los Angeles' socialist "progressive" activists, academics and elected officials. Most were members or supporters of DSA.

Included were prominent activists such as Karen Bass (Community Coalition), Gary Phillips (Southern California Library for Social Studies and Research), journalist/activist Richard Rothstein (a DSA member), Steve Cancian (Coalition for Economic Survival), Larry Frank (National Lawyers Guild), Torie Osborn (Liberty Hill Foundation and a DSA supporter), socialist property magnate Aris Anagnos, Carl Boggs (DSA's Socialist Community School), Central America activist Blase Bonpane (a DSA supporter), Rick Brown (UCLA School of Public Health and a DSA member), Stanley Sheinbaum (philanthropist and a DSA member), Maria Elena Durazo (Hotel and Restaurant Employees Union leader and a DSA supporter), her husband Miguel Contreras (Executive Secretary Los Angeles Federation of Labor), Bill Gallegos (Freedom Road Socialist Organization leader), Kent Wong (Asian labor leader, former member of the Communist Workers Party and a DSA supporter), Russell Jacoby (DSA's Socialist Community School), Bong Hwan Kim (Black Korean Alliance), Paula Litt (philanthropist and a DSA member), Peter Olney (labor unionist, Marxist) and Anthony Thigpenn (Black Radical Congress).

Academics listed included: Rudy Acuna (a political science professor at CalState Northridge), Peter Dreier (Occidental College, and a DSA member), Mike Davis (University of California, Irvine and a former Communist Party member), Robert Gottlieb (media academic) and Derek Sheare (Occidental College and a DSA supporter).

Elected officials included: Jim Conn (a DSA member and past Mayor of Santa Monica); DSA affiliated Los Angeles City Council members Mark Ridley-Thomas and Jackie Goldberg; California State Senators Gloria Romero and Tom Hayden; Communist Party affiliate Gil Cedillo, California Assembly Speaker; Antonio Villaraigosa, Santa Monica Mayor and DSA member Paul Rosenstein and far left Congress members Xavier Becerra, Henry Waxman and Maxine Waters.[56]

Progressive L.A. Conference

Things got really moving with the "Progressive L.A. Conference," held on October 3rd, 1998, at the Keck Theater, Occidental College:

> Progressive LA! A Conference on Social Movements in Los Angeles: Uncovering our History and Envisioning our Future

> The goals of the conference are to illustrate the role of progressives and progressive social movements in Los Angeles from the 1920s to the present and how these movements provide an alternative view of what Los Angeles has been and what it can become. Movements to be

explored in terms of their contribution to this vision include the labor movement · civil rights and civil liberties movements · environmental movement · urban movements (housing, land use, transportation, etc.) · women's and gay/lesbian movements.

Through this exploration, the conference will discuss the conflicts and opportunities for linking movements in order to identify lessons from the past for the future of progressive politics in Los Angeles.

Many of the names from Tarzynski's list addressed the conference, including Miguel Contreras, Torie Osborn, Karen Bass, Anthony Thigpenn, Harold Meyerson, Tom Hayden, Mark Ridley-Thomas and Antonio Villaraigosa. Prominent DSAers on the speaking roster included union leader Paul Schrade, civil libertarian and former communist Frank Wilkinson and housing activist Jan Breidenbach.

Other prominent speakers included Bert Corona, Founder of Hermandad Mexicana and Communist Party veteran turned Democratic Party activist; former communist, turned Democratic Congressman Augustus Hawkins; and leading California civil libertarian Ramona Ripston.[57]

The Progressive LA Conference "was an overwhelming success and gave participants a sense that the growth of a wide variety of progressive social movements had reached an important threshold. As a result, attendees and others within the progressive movement in Los Angeles expressed a desire to participate in further discussion about how to develop a common agenda that is community based, inclusive and brings together the wealth of experience and knowledge of organizers, activists, and researchers."[58]

PLAN

PLAN was founded and built on the success of the 1998 Progressive L.A. Conference which had been co-sponsored by a number of local and national institutions and organizations including Occidental College, The Nation Institute, Liberty Hill Foundation, LA Weekly and the Los Angeles County Federation of Labor.

In 1999, the organizers of the 1998 Conference, consulted dozens of grassroots, community, labor and environmental leaders about how to "capitalize on the conference's momentum. Participants decided to develop a community-driven network that could develop a public policy agenda and action plan for Los Angeles, using the resources and knowledge of public policy experts and the experience and leadership of influential activists and organizers in Los Angeles." This network became the Progressive Los Angeles Network—PLAN.

Members of PLAN's Advisory Board, who had also been on Tarzynski's list, were PLAN Co-Chairs Robert Gottlieb and Peter Dreier, Karen Bass, Rick Brown, Maria Elena Durazo, Harold Meyerson, Torie Osborn, Gary Phillips, Anthony Thigpenn and Kent Wong.

Other notable PLAN advisors were Paul Schrade and Ramona Ripston, DSAer Jan Breidenbach, Antonio Gonzalez (Southwest Voter Registration Education Project), Roger Lowenstein (ACLU Foundation), Sarah Pillsbury (Sanford/Pillsbury Productions), Neal Richman (UCLA Dept. of Urban Planning), Roy Hong (Korean Immigrant Workers Advocates), Amy Schur of ACORN and Robin Toma, a former supporter of the Communist Workers Party.

PLAN's 21 Point Agenda was:

- Ensure public investment yields quality jobs and community benefits.
- Gear job training towards quality jobs.
- Consolidate all economic development functions.
- Increase urban parks and clean up contaminated brown fields.
- Inventory toxic health risks and reduce pesticide use.
- Promote clean fuel vehicles and green energy.
- Institute a Livable City Plan.
- Boost the Housing Trust Fund.
- Require developers to build affordable housing units in all new residential developments.
- Crack down on slum landlords.
- Attract food markets, farmers' markets and community gardens to underserved neighborhoods.
- Launch an annual report, plan of action and policy council on food, hunger and nutrition.
- Improve public transit.
- Promote safe, walkable and bikeable neighborhoods.
- Promote smart growth land use.
- Promote workers' rights to organize.
- Strengthen protections for low-wage workers.
- Strengthen public sector union job opportunities.

- Institute a health care fund or purchasing pool for employers.
- Promote increased electoral participation.
- Ensure full participation on commissions and neighborhood councils.

In a March 2001 article in the LA Weekly, Harold Meyerson signaled that PLAN was ready for political power:

> What has emerged over the past two and a half years is the Progressive Los Angeles Network. With the city approaching this spring's watershed election, in which half the City Council and all three citywide elected officials are termed out of office, PLAN's plan was to hammer out a platform for a progressive Los Angeles. Over the past year, representatives of roughly 50 groups, along with some unaffiliated policy wonks, formed nine task forces to assess and make suggestions for the city's policies in such fields as housing, economic development, transportation and land use, community development, the urban environment, health policy and democracy and participation.

> This Saturday, at Patriotic Hall downtown, PLAN will present its platform—the key recommendations of its task forces for new directions in city policy. Some of these policies have been tried in other cities, like the establishment of an affordable housing trust fund financed in part by a fee imposed on developers of large projects. Some are specific to L.A.'s environment, such as the greening of the L.A. River, and some to our political topography, such as inclusionary criteria for neighborhood councils. And some—conditioning development on living-wage policies, establishing a municipal health-care pool for living-wage workers and employers—would move L.A. further down the road toward a municipal minimum wage and health coverage than any other American city:[59]

> Today, L.A. is poised to become a laboratory for the next century's democracy. No other major city has so polarized an economy and so dynamic a movement for social and economic equity. No other major city will play so large a role in determining the destiny of America's third great wave of immigrants. No other major city is changing so fast. In the struggles of immigrant workers for a living wage, of parents for decent schools and medical care for their kids, of families for homes, of motorists for time, of a city for air it can breathe, the American future is being born.

Working with the Communist Party and their subservient unions, PLAN campaigned hard to elect Antonio Villaraigosa to the Los Angeles mayoralty that year. They fell just short, but did manage to help elect several "progressive" allies to the City Council.

Harold Meyerson argued after the loss that the new "L.A. model" of progressive politics, centered on a powerful labor-Latino alliance, still offered a "blueprint for reviving a sluggish U.S. liberalism." Even the defeat of mayoral candidate Antonio Villaraigosa, "whom he roundly endorsed, hasn't shaken Meyerson's conviction that the Golden State is rapidly shifting leftward, with L.A. at its tectonic midpoint."[60]

Progressive LA: The Next Agenda Conference

PLAN next decided to reach outside of Los Angeles to the wider "progressive" movement. Progressive LA: The Next Agenda Conference was held On October 20, 2001, in Los Angeles at the California Science Center. Organized by PLAN and the Institute for Policy Studies/DSA initiated Institute for America's Future, the Next Agenda Conference was designed to "celebrate recent victories, build upon Los Angeles' progressive momentum and link local issues with a national progressive agenda." The conference would also help "solidify a more strategic and integrated progressive movement in Los Angeles:"

> Timed to expand the work of progressive movements amidst changing political circumstances, "The Next Agenda" conference will focus on five issues [of] significance for the region (and nation): Housing, Living Wage, Parks and Open Space, Immigration issues related to higher education, and Secession. Participants will strategize on advancing campaigns on these issues, and local progressive leaders will present recommendations to key local elected officials in attendance.

Speakers included several people from Tarzynski's 1998 list including California Assemblywoman Jackie Goldberg, Miguel Contreras (head of LA County Federation of Labor), Maria Elena Durazo (HERE Local 11), Torie Osborn (Liberty Hill Foundation), Kent Wong (UCLA Labor Center), Robert Gottlieb and Peter Dreier of Occidental College, and Harold Meyerson, Executive Editor, The American Prospect and contributor to the LA Weekly.

Other notables included Assemblywoman Judy Chu (a former affiliate of the Communist Workers Party); freshmen Los Angeles City Councilors Eric Garcetti, Jan Perry and Ed Reyes; Roxana Tynan of the influential Los

Angeles Alliance for a New Economy; Illinois Congresswoman and one time DSA member Jan Schakowsky and arch "progressives" Robert Borosage and Roger Hickey of the Institute for America's Future.[61]

Villaraigosa Wins!

By 2005, PLAN and its allies had refined their messaging and had deliberately moderated the image of their very radical mayoral candidate, Antonio Villaraigosa.

When the ballots were counted, Villaraigosa was victorious.

According to Harold Meyerson of LA Weekly, it was "L.A.'s liberal operatives who helped put Villaraigosa over the top." His field campaign was captained by Anthony Thigpenn, one of a "cadre of progressive younger African-Americans who are transforming the politics of South-Central." Meyerson also credited Villaraigosa's victory to Parke Skelton, "possibly the most principled political consultant in the business, who has steered to elected office virtually every liberal pol in greater L.A.—among them, Hilda Solis, Eric Garcetti, Jackie Goldberg, Sheila Kuehl, Karen Bass and Martin Ludlow:"[62]

> Having won the city district by district, on Tuesday Parke won it across the board. But the victory is fundamentally Villaraigosa's, and he won it in two stages. The first stage was his campaign of 2001, which set liberal L.A. ablaze with excitement and probably pulled down as many votes as such a liberal campaign could conceivably amass: 46 percent. The second stage, his campaign this year, was deliberately duller, devoted largely to reassuring older African-Americans and San Fernando Valley centrists that he wasn't such a dangerous character after all.

Another PLAN leader, Peter Dreier, wrote in DSA's Democratic Left, Winter 2006, on the "progressive" networks around Mayor Antonio Villaraigosa and Los Angeles Congresswoman (and later Obama Labor Secretary) Hilda Solis:[63]

> Antonio Villaraigosa... He was a union organizer. He was the head of the ACLU. He came out the barrio and grew up very poor. His father was an alcoholic, beat his mother—he overcame incredible obstacles. He dropped out of high school, and went back and then graduated from UCLA. He worked his way up through the labor movement and then was elected to the state legislature, becoming Speaker of the Assembly.
>
> When he was term-limited out of the legislature he ran for the LA City Council and was elected. When he ran for Mayor the first time in 2001

he lost, but he ran again and won in 2005. Now we have a progressive mayor, thanks in large part to this impressive network of grassroots organizations, labor unions and community and environmental organizations. Many of them have lifted up some of their leaders into positions of electoral power. It's a network of activists that work closely with elected officials, like Congresswoman Hilda Solis, and it's just remarkable what L.A. has become.

Once elected, Antonio Villaraigosa still tried to portray a reasonably "moderate" image. The socialists play a long-term game. They take their radical gains when they can, but are always aware of public opinion and wary of potential voter backlash.

Said Peter Dreier, Co-Director of PLAN of Villaraigosa:[64]

> If there are radicals out there who expect him to govern as a radical, then they are going to be very disappointed.

Where are they now?

Antonio Villaraigosa may try to appear moderate (he was even on President Obama's 2008 Transition Team), but in reality he has consolidated power for the Southern California left. A key part of his agenda has been making Los Angeles into an illegal immigrant haven. The left plans to swamp California and other Southern states with Latino immigrants, who they know will vote Democrat, come hell or high water.

In reality, Villaraigosa is no moderate. He is a past supporter of MEChA, a radical Chicano separatist group with a strong Marxist-Leninist underpinning and a veteran of the Venceremos Brigade sojourn in Cuba. He was trained as a young man by Bert Corona, a veteran Communist Party member and a father of the "immigrant's rights" movement.

Looking back at Steve Tarzynski's 1998 list and the key PLAN people, it's interesting to see what they went on to achieve for their cause.

Just after Villaraigosa's 2005 election, Harold Meyerson wrote in the LA Weekly that "newly elected Mayor Antonio Villaraigosa can call on a locally based progressive talent pool that includes such policy activists as Occidental Government Professor Peter Dreier and Nonprofit Housing Advocate Jan Breidenbach (in housing), Roxana Tynan of the Los Angeles Alliance for a New Economy (in development), Larry Frank of UCLA's Labor Center (in work-related issues) and the Liberty Hill Foundation's Torie Osborn (for general administrative genius)".

Larry Frank is, until he leaves the job in July 2013, the Deputy Chief of Staff in the Office of the Mayor of Los Angeles, Antonio Villaraigosa. In that capacity, Frank is responsible for several city departments, including community development, contract administration and the City's workforce development program.

He previously served as Deputy Mayor of Neighborhood and Community Services in Villaraigosa's office, but Torie Osborn took over that job in 2012.[65]

Osborn is responsible for the Department of Neighborhood Empowerment, as well as the Community Development Department, the Mayor's field operations and constituent services, the City's anti-poverty programs and FamilySource Centers, among other areas.[66]

Peter Dreier, a Professor of Politics and Director of the Urban & Environmental Policy Program at Occidental College, played a key role in the Villaraigosa campaigns of 2001 and 2005. He is an influential player in the Democratic Party and an historian of the local "progressive" movement.

Jan Breidenbach, Adjunct Associate Professor at University of Southern California, made city history in 2002, when as the Executive Director of the Southern California Association of Non-Profit Housing and Housing LA, she succeeded in getting the City to set up a $100 million Housing Trust Fund—a key component of the PLAN program. This was achieved over a three year campaign, backed by radical community group ACORN and the Los Angeles labor movement.[67]

Roxana Tynan, who attended Democratic Socialists of America's 2005 National Convention in Los Angeles, now heads up the Los Angeles Alliance for a New Economy; a $4.5 million a year lobby group which has had huge influence on City policy.

Her former boss, another PLAN leader named Madeline Janis, negotiated the nation's first community-benefits agreement, which forces private developers—as a quid pro quo for receiving city subsidies, tax breaks and permits—to provide "living wage jobs" and "affordable housing." She also used her Los Angeles Alliance for a New Economy to stop the world's largest corporation, Wal-Mart, from building a superstore in Inglewood, a working class suburb of Los Angeles:

> In the past several years, she has played a pivotal role in uniting labor, community and environmental leaders, initiating groundbreaking campaigns to create good green jobs and reduce pollution. Under her stewardship, LAANE helped enact an EPA-award-winning program to

remove thousands of polluting diesel trucks that carry cargo from the LA port, the nation's dirtiest, and replace them with clean trucks. Earlier this year, that same coalition pushed the Los Angeles government to adopt a path-breaking recycling program that will improve air quality and upgrade working conditions for sanitation workers and those who work in recycling facilities.

Mayor James Hahn appointed Janis Breidenbach to the powerful nine-member Community Redevelopment Agency (CRA) in 2002. Four years later, Mayor Antonio Villaraigosa re-appointed her, despite efforts by business lobby groups to stop her reappointment.[68]

Another PLAN leader Robin Toma, a former supporter of the ultra militant Communist Workers Party, now heads the influential Los Angeles County Commission on Human Relations, where he polices City Workers and especially the LAPD with "politically correct" restrictions on their ability to do their jobs.

PLAN leader Maria Elena Durazo is now head of the Los Angeles County Federation of Labor, making her one of the most powerful women in California. A long-time associate of Democratic Socialists of America and the Communist Party, Durazo has used her position to change California forever. Through massive union backed voter registration drives and Get Out The Vote efforts amongst Los Angeles' Latino population, she has moved the City Council, Los Angeles and indeed Southern California in general, into an almost impregnable Democratic Party stronghold.[69]

Karen Bass, yet another PLAN leader, is now a Congresswoman, where she joins the three other Los Angeles area representatives on Steve Tarzynski's original list: Xavier Becerra, Henry Waxman and Maxine Waters. Another peripheral PLANner, Judy Chu, now also serves in Congress.

It would be fair to say that Democratic Socialists of America, working through PLAN, has had a substantial impact on Southern California (and by extension, national) politics.[70]

1 KeyWiki, "Democratic Socialists of America," KeyWiki, http://keywiki.org/index.php/DSA (accessed May 4, 2013)
2 Democratic Left magazine, http://www.dsausa.org/dl/Spring_2007.pdf (Spring 2007)
3 Democratic Left (July/August 1995) p. 22
4 Democratic Left (September/October 1995) p. 8
5 KeyWiki, "AFL-CIO," KeyWiki, http://www.keywiki.org/index.php/AFL-CIO (accessed May 4. 2013)

6 Democratic Left, DSA, http://www.dsausa.org/dl/sum2kindex.html (Spring/Summer 2000)

7 Democratic Left, DSA, http://www.dsausa.org/dl/sum2kindex.html (Spring/Summer 2000)

8 Yankee Radical, http://www.dsaboston.org/yradical/yr2001-01.pdf (January 2001)

9 Democratic Left, DSA, http://www.dsausa.org/dl/sum2kindex.html (Spring/Summer 2000)

10 Democratic Left, http://www.dsausa.org/dl/Winter_2010.pdf (Winter 2009)

11 New Ground, 51 (March/April 1997)

12 KeyWiki, "Elizabeth Bunn," KeyWiki, http://www.keywiki.org/index.php/Elizabeth_Bunn (accessed May 12, 2013)

13 KeyWiki, "Tim Carpenter," KeyWiki, http://www.keywiki.org/index.php/Tim_Carpenter (accessed May 12, 2013)

14 KeyWiki, "David Dinkins," KeyWiki, http://www.keywiki.org/index.php/David_Dinkins (accessed May 12, 2013)

15 KeyWiki, "Robert Fitrakis," KeyWiki, http://www.keywiki.org/index.php/Bob_Fitrakis (accessed May 12, 2013)

16 KeyWiki, "Matthew Hallinan," KeyWiki, http://www.keywiki.org/index.php/Matthew_Hallinan (accessed May 12, 2013)

17 KeyWiki, "Mildred Jeffrey," KeyWiki, http://www.keywiki.org/index.php/Mildred_Jeffrey (accessed May 12, 2013)

18 KeyWiki, "John Katz," KeyWiki, http://keywiki.org/index.php/John_Katz (accessed May 12, 2013)

19 KeyWiki, "David Kusnet," KeyWiki, http://www.keywiki.org/index.php/David_Kusnet (accessed May 12, 2013)

20 KeyWiki, "John Laird," KeyWiki, http://www.keywiki.org/index.php/John_Laird (accessed May 12, 2013)

21 KeyWiki, "Mike Lux," KeyWiki, http://www.keywiki.org/index.php/Mike_Lux (accessed May 12, 2013)

22 KeyWiki, "Maryann Mahaffey," KeyWiki, http://www.keywiki.org/index.php/Maryann_Mahaffey (accessed May 12, 2013)

23 KeyWiki, "Hilda Mason," KeyWiki, www.keywiki.org/index.php/Hilda_Mason (accessed May 12, 2013)

24 KeyWiki, "Ruth W. Messinger," KeyWiki, http://keywiki.org/index.php/Ruth_Messinger (accessed May 12, 2013)

25 KeyWiki, "Christine Riddiough," KeyWiki, http://www.keywiki.org/index.php/Christine_Riddiough (accessed May 12, 2013)

26 KeyWiki, "Lynn Shaw," KeyWiki, http://www.keywiki.org/index.php/Lynn_Shaw (accessed May 12, 2013)

27 KeyWiki, "Jim Scheibel," KeyWiki, http://www.keywiki.org/index.php/Jim_Scheibel (accessed May 12, 2013)

28 KeyWiki, "Paul Schrade," KeyWiki, http://www.keywiki.org/index.php/Paul_Schrade (accessed May 12, 2013)

29 KeyWiki, "Stanley Sheinbaum," KeyWiki, www.keywiki.org/index.php/Stanley_Sheinbaum (accessed May 12, 2013)

30 Democratic Left (January 1990) p. 7

31 KeyWiki, "Harlan Baker," KeyWiki, www.keywiki.org/index.php/Harlan_Baker (accessed May 12, 2013)

32 KeyWiki, "Babette Josephs," KeyWiki,
http://www.keywiki.org/index.php/Babette_Josephs (accessed May 12, 2013)
33 KeyWiki, "Niilo Koponen," KeyWiki,
http://www.keywiki.org/index.php/Niilo_Koponen (accessed May 12, 2013)
34 KeyWiki, "John McDonough," KeyWiki,
www.keywiki.org/index.php/John_McDonough (accessed May 12, 2013)
35 KeyWiki, "Michael Paymar," KeyWiki,
http://www.keywiki.org/index.php/Michael_Paymar (accessed May 12, 2013)
36 KeyWiki, "Nancy Skinner," KeyWiki,
http://www.keywiki.org/index.php/Nancy_Skinner (accessed May 12, 2013)
37 KeyWiki, "Frank I. Smizik," KeyWiki,
http://www.keywiki.org/index.php/Frank_I._Smizik (accessed May 12, 2013)
38 KeyWiki, "Beverly Stein," KeyWiki, www.keywiki.org/index.php/Beverly_Stein
(accessed May 12, 2013)
39 KeyWiki, "Neil Abercrombie," KeyWiki,
http://www.keywiki.org/index.php/Neil_Abercrombie (accessed May 12, 2013)
40 KeyWiki, "Ron Dellums," KeyWiki,
http://www.keywiki.org/index.php/Ron_Dellums (accessed May 12, 2013)
41 KeyWiki, "Carrie Meek," KeyWiki, www.keywiki.org/index.php/Carrie_Meek
(accessed May 12, 2013)
42 KeyWiki, "Mary Jo Kilroy," KeyWiki,
www.keywiki.org/index.php/Mary_Jo_Kilroy (accessed May 12, 2013)
43 KeyWiki, "Major Owens," KeyWiki, www.keywiki.org/index.php/Major_Owens
(accessed May 12, 2013)
44 KeyWiki, "David Bonior," KeyWiki,
http://www.keywiki.org/index.php/David_Bonior (accessed May 12, 2013)
45 KeyWiki, "Barney Frank," KeyWiki, www.keywiki.org/index.php/Barney_Frank
(accessed May 12, 2013)
46 KeyWiki, "Bob Filner," KeyWiki, www.keywiki.org/index.php/Bob_Filner
(accessed May 12, 2013)
47 KeyWiki, "Maurice Hinchey," KeyWiki,
www.keywiki.org/index.php/Maurice_Hinchey (accessed May 12, 2013)
48 KeyWiki, "Gerry Studds," KeyWiki, www.keywiki.org/index.php/Gerry_Studds
(accessed May 12, 2013)
49 KeyWiki, "Robert W. Edgar," KeyWiki, www.keywiki.org/index.php/Bob_Edgar
(accessed May 12, 2013)
50 KeyWiki, "Ted Weiss," KeyWiki, www.keywiki.org/index.php/Ted_Weiss
(accessed May 12, 2013)
51 KeyWiki, "Edward Kennedy," KeyWiki,
www.keywiki.org/index.php/Ted_Kennedy (accessed May 12, 2013)
52 Seth A. Maxon, "Mobilized in Motor City How Detroit DSA works in the
Democratic Party to effect change," In These Times,
http://www.inthesetimes.com/article/5317/mobilized_in_motor_city (December 25,
2009)
53 GDDSA Newsletter Archives, http://kincaidsite.com/dsa/nl-archive.html (2006)
54 Democratic Left, http://www.dsausa.org/dl/dlspr2k1.pdf (Summer 2001)
55 Democratic Left, http://www.dsausa.org/dl/Summer_2010.pdf (Summer 2010)
56 KeyWiki, "Progressive Los Angeles Network," KeyWiki,
http://www.keywiki.org/index.php/Progressive_Los_Angeles_Network (accessed June
4, 2013)

57 KeyWiki, "Progressive Los Angeles Network – Schedule," KeyWiki, http://www.keywiki.org/index.php/Progressive_L.A._Conference#Schedule (accessed June 5, 2013)

58 PLAN website, "Progressive Los Angeles Network (PLAN)," PLAN website, http://dornsife.usc.edu/cdd/civic/bmus/The%20Progressive%20Los%20Angeles%20N etwork%20%28PLAN%29.html#TheProgressiveLosAngelesNetwork%28PLAN%29-PLAN%27sAdvisoryBoard, (accessed October 2011)

59 Harold Meyerson, "A Vision for the City: Introduction," LA Weekly, http://www.laweekly.com/2001-03-15/news/a-vision-for-the-city-introduction/2/ (March 7, 2001)

60 Reed Johnson, "Icon of West Coast Liberalism Set to Take On D.C.," Los Angeles Times, http://articles.latimes.com/2001/jun/29/news/cl-16385 (June 29, 2001)

61 KeyWiki, "Progressive LA: The Next Agenda Conference," KeyWiki, http://www.keywiki.org/index.php/Progressive_LA:_The_Next_Agenda_Conference (accessed June 5, 2013)

62 Harold Meyerson, "New Mayor, New City," LA Weekly, http://www.laweekly.com/2005-05-19/news/new-mayor-new-city/ (May 19, 2005)

63 DSA USA, http://www.dsausa.org/dl/Winter_2006.pdf (Winter 2006)

64 Randy Shaw, "Villaraigosa: How He Won and What Progressives Can Expect," BeyondChron, http://www.beyondchron.org/news/index.php?itemid=1165 (May 20, 2005)

65 KeyWiki, "Larry Frank," KeyWiki, http://www.keywiki.org/index.php/Larry_Frank (accessed June 5, 2013)

66 KeyWiki, "Torie Osborn," KeyWiki, http://www.keywiki.org/index.php/Torie_Osborn (accessed June 5, 2013)

67 KeyWiki, "Jan Breidenbach," KeyWiki, http://keywiki.org/index.php/Janis_Breidenbach (accessed June 5, 2013)

68 Peter Dreier, "Madeline Janis: An Extraordinary Activist for the "Long Haul,"' The Huffington Post, http://www.huffingtonpost.com/peter-dreier/madeline-janis-an-extraor_b_3333802.html (May 24, 2013)

69 KeyWiki, "Maria Elena Durazo," KeyWiki, http://keywiki.org/index.php/Maria_Elena_Durazo (accessed June 5, 2013)

70 KeyWiki, "Karen Bass," KeyWiki, http://keywiki.org/index.php/Karen_Bass (accessed June 5, 2013)

"Progressives"

Institute for Policy Studies

The Institute for Policy Studies (IPS) is the oldest and most influential of the far left "think tanks" in Washington D.C. Since its founding in 1963, IPS has consistently followed the Marxist line on foreign policy, defense and the economy and has spawned a large number of spin-offs, alliances and public affairs organizations following the same radical agenda. IPS works closely with several U.S. Marxist groups, but is particularly close to Democratic Socialists of America (DSA).

Soviet Sympathies

During the Cold War, IPS seemed often to be working as an arm of Soviet foreign policy. In 1978, in an article in National Review, Brian Crozier, Director of the London-based Institute for the Study of Conflict, described IPS as the "perfect intellectual front for Soviet activities which would be resisted if they were to originate openly from the KGB."[1]

IPS was always particularly concerned with researching U.S. defense industries and arms sales policies to free world countries under pressure from Soviet-supported terrorist movements. The Director of IPS arms sales research, Michael Klare, was a veteran of the North American Congress on Latin America, a pro-Cuba research group and who also worked with the Center for National Security Studies, an IPS off-shoot affiliated with the Fund for Peace. Klare made frequent trips to Havana to "lecture" on U.S. arms policies to "graduate students" at the University of Havana and has participated in disarmament conferences sponsored by Soviet front World Peace Council (WPC) groups.

From September 29 to October 12, 1975, the World Peace Council sent a delegation on a ten-day tour of the United States of America, where it was "warmly and enthusiastically received."

The delegation was composed of Romesh Chandra, an Indian communist and Secretary General of the World Peace Council; Josef

Cyrankiewicz, former Premier of communist Poland and Chairman of the Polish Peace Committee; Ambassador Harald Edelstam, Swedish Ambassador to Algeria, formerly Ambassador to Chile during the Marxist Allende Presidency; Purabhi Mukherji, General Secretary of the Congress Party of India; James Lamond, Labour member of British Parliament and active member of the Engineering Workers Union; Yacov Lomko, Editor-in-Chief of the Moscow News, leading member of the Soviet Peace Committee and Communist Party USA; and member Karen Talbot, a U.S. member of the WPC Secretariat.

At an informal luncheon given by IPS, the WPC representatives had a probing and lively discussion with those present on "questions of disarmament and detente."[2]

On April 10, 1982, an IPS sponsored group visited Moscow for a week of meetings with high-level Soviet officials "responsible for disseminating disinformation and propaganda for U.S. consumption." The IPS group, led by its principal spokesman, Marcus Raskin, IPS Co-Founder and Senior Fellow, included Robert Borosage, IPS Director, National Lawyers Guild activist and former Director of the Center for National Security Studies; Minneapolis Mayor Donald M. Fraser; Rt. Rev. Paul Moore, Episcopal Bishop of New York; New York lawyer Robert S. Potter; and Roger Wilkins, journalist and Senior Fellow of the Joint Center for Political Studies, which specializes in "black issues."

The IPS group identified only two of the Communist Party of the Soviet Union Central Committee officials they met—Georgi A. Arbatov, head of the Institute of the USA and Canada, a "think tank" that provides research and analysis and also cultivates and develops contacts with Americans at the direction of the KGB and the International Department of the CPSU Central Committee; and Vadim V. Zagladin, First Deputy Chief of the International Department.

In various U.S. interviews, Borosage had floated such standard Soviet themes as the Soviet Union is satisfied by "rough parity" with the United States; that the United States is restarting the arms race; that the Soviets want to go back to SALT II and get U.S. ratification; that if the United States starts another round in the arms race, it will seriously hurt the Soviet economy and ordinary Soviet citizens—but they'll still go ahead, so competition is futile; and the threat that the modern U.S. weapons proposed for deployment are "very dangerous... and would lead to much more dangerous stages that would make both sides insecure, not more secure."

Borosage took pains to say that the Soviets were "skeptical" of the disarmament movement and "they hadn't expected it. It was much more powerful and widespread than they'd ever imagined."[3]

Influencing Government

IPS has had a huge influence on U.S. government policies, particularly since the Carter years. IPS is the ideas factory for the U.S.'s "progressive" movement and for the Democratic Party.

Washington School

The IPS founded the Washington School in 1979, a Marxist-oriented "academy" under the guise of presenting an "alternative" view/voice on both U.S. domestic and foreign policies. They not only gave "fellowships" to hardcore Marxists and known/identified members of the Communist Party USA (CPUSA), but to other loosely affiliated Marxists, socialists and liberals. IPS also recruited members of Congress to teach classes, thus sucking in some liberals who might not have participated if they had knowledge of IPS' Marxist history and funding.

"Information Digest," April 30, 1982, produced a combined "faculty members" list for the years 1979, 1980, the fall of 1981 semester and the spring of 1982 semester. It contains a number of members of Congress, the news media, former U.S. defense officials and key members from labor, pro-communist Latin America guerrilla movement support operations, members of the "Hanoi Lobby," the "PLO Lobby" and the "anti-Defense Lobby."

Some notables on the list included:[4]

- James Abourezk - A former U.S. Senator from South Dakota and an IPS Trustee and leader of the pro-Palestine Liberation Organization lobby.
- Richard Barnet - An IPS Founder and a key member of the Hanoi Lobby who broadcast over Radio Hanoi to American troops during the war. He was a key leader in the "Anti-Defense" and "Anti-Intelligence" lobbies. Barnet also had a long record of supporting communist fronts and causes.
- Robert Borosage - A key IPS Marxist leader who later went on to head the Marxist-oriented Campaign for America's Future, which is partially funded by extreme leftist financier, George Soros.

- Josephine Butler - A local D.C. Marxist who headed CPUSA fronts in the area and had a major role in leading the communist-dominated D.C. Statehood Party, whose Constitution was written by avowed Communist Party D.C.-VA leader, Maurice Jackson.
- Arthur Macy Cox - An arms control "expert" who worked for the Senate and represented the "appeasement" and "détente" wing of the Congressional left.
- Doug Fraser - The former socialist labor leader of the United Auto Workers union.
- Morton Halperin - A former government official, who turned to the left, became a leader of the "Anti-Intelligence Lobby" and later became a leader of George Soros' Open Society Institute.
- Senator Mark Hatfield (R-OR) - A far-left, religious pacifist and advocate of appeasement in foreign affairs. A Republican who was happy to support Communist Party causes.
- Anthony Lake - A leftist member of the State Department, who basically advocated an appeasement policy regarding communism.
- Saul Landau - A veteran Marxist film/documentary maker promoting Marxism in Latin America. A long-time IPS Fellow and supporter of many communist fronts and causes.
- Paul Tsongas (D-MA) - A far left Senator who supported some communist fronts and causes.

IPS Twentieth Anniversary Celebration Committee

In 1983, an IPS Anniversary Celebration Committee was created to celebrate the organization's 20th year. The list was impressive, including many current and former members of Congress.

Then current members were:[5]

- Sen. Gary Hart (D-CO) - later a presidential candidate.
- Sen. Christopher Dodd (D-CT)

Representatives - Present Members

- Les Aspin (D-WI) - later Clinton Secretary of Defense.
- George Brown (D-CA)
- Philip Burton (D-CA)
- George Crockett, Jr. (D-MI)
- Ron Dellums (D-CA)
- Don Edwards (D-CA)

- Walter Fauntroy (D-DC)
- Tom Harkin (D-IA)
- Robert Kastenmeier (D-WI)
- Richard Ottinger (D-NY)
- Leon Panetta (D-CA) - later Obama head of the CIA and Secretary of Defense.
- Patricia Schroeder (D-CO)
- John Seiberling (D-OH)
- Ted Weiss (D-NY)

Influencing Legislation

In 1975, a group of 47 members of Congress, led by John Conyers, asked the IPS to prepare an "alternative budget" to that proposed by President Ford. This request was repeated in 1976 and 1978 by 56 legislators.

The 1978 document called for "a socialist housing program... radical social change in the educational system... a 50% cut in the defense budget" and "disengagement" from America's overseas commitments.

In 1983, 60 Congressmen went back to the IPS with a request for another "alternative" budget.[6]

According to its own website IPS has "always worked closely with and provided analysis and model pieces of legislation to "progressive" members of Congress. Currently, IPS advises the Congressional Progressive Caucus, which, with more than 70 members, is the largest Caucus in Congress".[7]

In the late 1990s, IPS established Progressive Challenge to utilize leftist groups including Democratic Socialists of America, Americans for Democratic Action, United Electrical Workers, NETWORK and National Jobs for All Coalition, etc. to pressure the Progressive Caucus in the "correct" direction.

The IPS sees the Obama administration as a "window of opportunity" to push for "progressive" change.

IPS plans to utilize its "deep ties with the Congressional Progressive Caucus" and the wider social movements to pressure the Obama administration.

In 2008, IPS enlisted 70 writers to produce a document entitled, "Mandate for Change-Policies and Leadership for 2009 and Beyond," which was designed to provide a policy blueprint for President Obama's Administration.[8]

Anti-Militarism

IPS has also opposed the U.S. military, at every opportunity and has consistently worked to undermine the U.S. war effort   action from Vietnam to Afghanistan. This has often earned IPS   the organization the attention of the authorities.

From the IPS website history page:[9]

> As soon as IPS opened its doors in 1963, it plunged into the anti-Vietnam War movement. In 1965, Raskin and Associate Fellow Bernard Fall edited The Vietnam Reader, which became a textbook for teach-ins across the country. In 1967, Raskin and IPS Fellow Arthur Waskow penned "A Call to Resist Illegitimate Authority," a document signed by dozens of well-known scholars and religious leaders that helped launch the draft resistance movement.

> IPS also organized Congressional seminars and published numerous books that challenged the national security state, including Gar Alperovitz's Atomic Diplomacy and Barnet's Intervention and Revolution. The FBI responded by infiltrating IPS with more than 70 informants, wiretapping its phones, and searching through its garbage. The Nixon Administration placed Barnet and Raskin on its "enemies list."

From the IPS website history page:[10]

> In 1991, during the first U.S. military foray in Iraq, IPS produced the pamphlet Crisis in the Gulf, which was widely used by the peace movement. Fellow Gail Christian produced a weekly IPS radio program on the war that was broadcast by three dozen public radio stations across the country.

Another IPS municipal project is Cities for Peace, which is designed to spread nationwide local opposition to the wars in Afghanistan and Iraq:[11]

> IPS also founded Cities for Peace, which coordinated hundreds of city council resolutions against the war and is now organizing resolutions to bring the troops home and against war in Iran.

Campaign for America's Future

Right from the start, Campaign for America's Future (CFAF) was a project of the Institute for Policy Studies (IPS) and Democratic Socialists of America (DSA). The current CFAF Secretary-Treasurer is Robert

Borosage, an IPS Board of Trustees member and former head of the organization. Current CFAF President Roger Hickey hails from another IPS/DSA project, the Economic Policy Institute.[12]

Of the organization's 130 founders, at least 30 were identified DSA members, including former Georgia State Senator Julian Bond, academic activists Richard Cloward and his wife Frances Fox Piven, Progressives for Obama Founder Barbara Ehrenreich, Washington Post journalist Harold Meyerson, Economic Policy Institute President Larry Mishel, former long-time AFL-CIO President John Sweeney and Los Angeles philanthropist and Democratic Party donor, Stanley Sheinbaum.

IPS affiliates on the founding roster included Gar Alperowitz, Ira Arlook, Ann Beaudry, Norman Birnbaum, Heather Booth, David Carley, John Cavanagh, William Domhoff and Chester Hartman.

Other notable founders included:[13]

- Morton Bahr - Communication Workers of America
- Berkley Bedell - Former Member of Congress
- Thomas Buffenbarger - Machinists Union
- Moe Biller - American Postal Workers Union
- Douglas Dority - United Food and Commercial Workers
- Tom Hayden - California Legislature
- Patricia Ireland - National Organization for Women
- Amy Isaacs - Americans for Democratic Action
- David Kusnet - Former White House Speechwriter
- Robert Kuttner - The American Prospect
- Ray Marshall - University of Texas-Austin, Former Secretary of Labor
- Howard Metzenbaum - U.S. Senator
- Nan Orrock - Women Legislator's Lobby, Georgia House of Representatives
- Ron Pollack - Families USA Foundation
- Steve Protulis - National Council of Senior Citizens
- Miles Rapoport - President of Demos, Former Connecticut Secretary of State
- Robert Reich - Brandeis University, Former Secretary of Labor
- Andy Stern - SEIU
- Richard Trumka - AFL-CIO
- Stephen Yokich - United Auto Workers

Conferences

Campaign for America's Future coordinates the U.S. "progressive" movement in a number of ways, but especially through its annual conferences held in Washington D.C. From 2003 through 2008, these were known as the "Take Back America" conferences. Today they are called America's Future Now! Or, as a one off in 2011, Take Back the American Dream.[14]

These annual gatherings attract literally thousands of "progressives," socialists, communists, labor unionists, social movement activists and elected politicians. They are by far the most important "progressive" conferences in America.

Everybody who is anybody on the left attends these events. Notable speakers in recent years include Barack Obama, his Marxist former physician Quentin Young, former Speaker of the House Nancy Pelosi, former Presidential candidate John Edwards, former Obama Labor Secretary Hilda Solis, former Obama "Green Jobs Czar" Van Jones, most of the Congressional Progressive Caucus and dozens of other Democratic Senators and Congress members.[15]

Progressive Democrats of America

Progressive Democrats of America (PDA) was established by affiliates of Democratic Socialists of America (DSA) and the Institute for Policy Studies (IPS), as a means of driving the Democratic Party further to the left.

PDA National Director Tim Carpenter is a former leader of Orange County Democratic Socialists of America. Three current members of PDA's Advisory Board are also DSAers: Bill Fletcher, Jr., Michael Lighty and Quentin Young. Recent IPS affiliated Advisory Board members include Medea Benjamin, Steve Cobble, Jodie Evans, Tom Hayden and Andy Shallal.

Recent or current Congressional Progressive Caucus (CPC) members who have served on PDA's Advisory Board include John Conyers, Donna Edwards, Raul Grijalva, Dennis Kucinich, Barbara Lee, Jim McGovern, Lynn Woolsey and Maxine Waters.

"Inside-Outside" Strategy

PDA operates as an activist network inside the Democratic Party. It has been described as the political arm of the Congressional Progressive Caucus and works closely with that body. PDA uses an "inside-outside" strategy that enables non-Democratic Party members to influence party policy.

According to PDA's website:[16]

> Progressive Democrats of America was founded in 2004 to transform the Democratic Party and our country. We seek to build a party and government controlled by citizens, not corporate elites—with policies that serve the broad public interest, not just private interests. As a grassroots PAC operating inside the Democratic Party, and outside in movements for peace and justice, PDA played a key role in the stunning electoral victory of November 2006. Our inside/outside strategy is guided by the belief that a lasting majority will require a revitalized Democratic Party built on firm progressive principles.

> For over two decades, the party declined as its leadership listened more to the voices of Wall Street than those of Main Street. PDA strives to rebuild the Democratic Party from the bottom up—from every Congressional District to statewide party structures to the corridors of power in Washington, where we work arm in arm with the Congressional Progressive Caucus. In just a couple of years, PDA and its allies have shaken up the political status quo—on issues from the Iraq war to voter rights to economic justice.

An article by PDA Executive Director Tim Carpenter in Democratic Left, Fall 2006 (the official publication of Democratic Socialists of America), profiled the organization:[17]

> Progressive Democrats of America is a rapidly growing, two-year-old, 80,000-strong, 135-chapter organization operating in over 30 states. PDA's board of advisers is a diverse group of committed progressive elected officials and activists.

> Since its founding in Roxbury, Massachusetts, in July 2004, PDA has aggressively worked an "inside/outside" strategy, networking progressive Democratic elected officials inside the Beltway with grassroots Democrats and progressive movement activists across the country.

PDA strategy involves nothing less than a takeover of the Democratic Party from the "grass roots" up:[18]

We will reach our goal by working inside the Democratic Party to return it to its roots as the party that represents the workers and the less fortunate, and by building coalitions outside the Democratic Party on shared issues.

By establishing chapters in all 435 congressional districts, we are creating an information and action conduit that allows us to effectively organize in response to or in support of congressional actions.

We work with the Congressional Progressive Caucus to support and bring forward progressive legislation on the core issues identified by our PDA chapters.

Claimed Successes

Tim Carpenter claimed that PDA had chalked up several achievements in its short life, successfully promoting initiatives by PDA board members John Conyers and James McGovern.

PDA was the driving force in the passage of resolutions opposing the war in Iraq by 8 state Democratic Party meetings. The organization also was instrumental in the passage of resolutions in 10 states calling for the impeachment of President Bush.

PDA is often referred to by Congressional Progressive Caucus Executive Director Bill Goold as the CPC's field operation, because PDA has built relationships with members of Congress by delivering grassroots support for their initiatives—from Rep. John Conyers' investigation of the 2004 Ohio voting fraud to Rep. Jim McGovern's bill to cut off funding for the war in Iraq.

In 2006, PDA worked hard for Marcy Winograd against Jane Harman and for several other "progressive" Democrats:[19]

> While PDA is still only a progressive "pup" compared with big liberal dogs like MoveOn, PDA-backed candidates have taken some big bites out of conventional wisdom and centrist Democratic complacency. In Los Angeles, local PDA leader Marcy Winograd won 37 percent of the primary vote against entrenched pro-war Democrat Rep. Jane Harman with only two months of lead time. In Maryland, the dynamic Donna Edwards appears to have come only a few hundred votes short of toppling the multi-term Rep. Al Wynn in her first bid for public office, and she is seen as well-positioned to prevail in 2008. And in Illinois, with strong PDA support, Christine Cegelis, though outspent 8 to 1, nearly beat the candidate of the inside-the-Beltway Party leadership and

Illinois party machine, Tammy Duckworth, to vie for the seat being vacated by Rep. Henry Hyde.

This fall, in the House, PDA is focusing attention and effort on several strong progressives worthy of note and support in hopes of flipping several seats from red to blue. In California, Jerry McNerny is running a strong race against an incumbent Republican. In Michigan, Tony Trupiano, with one of the nation's strongest grassroots efforts, has his sights on an open seat in a Republican-leaning district. And in New York, anti-nuclear activist John Hall has won the Democratic nomination to challenge a four-term incumbent Republican. In Arizona, while the local PDA primary candidate, Jeff Latas, did not prevail, PDA will now enthusiastically join forces with PDA Board Member Rep. Raul Grijalva and support the nominee, the equally progressive Gabby Giffords, as well as PDA-backed Herb Paine, who won a razor-thin primary victory in a neighboring district.

Altering Congress/Progressive Strategy

Tim Carpenter went on to write that a Democratic victory would give "progressive" Democrats and members of the Congressional Black Caucus and Congressional Progressive Caucus control of many important Congressional positions.

While PDA certainly understands the difference between a "progressive" Democrat and a "centrist" Democrat, the group urged vigorous work on behalf of all Democratic House candidates in November 2006:[20]

> This is because currently elected progressives and members of the Congressional Black Caucus are mostly in safe districts and so have held their seats for several terms, building seniority. Thus, election of a Democratic House majority this year would have absolutely huge ramifications for the progressive community when it comes to controlling committees: At least nine Congressional Progressive Caucus members would become committee chairs and an additional 35 CPC members would become subcommittee chairs!

2012 Election Cycle and Beyond

PDA held its third Progressive Central, a one-day gathering of politicians from the left wing of the Democratic Party and prominent activists from the labor, anti-war and environmental movements, in Washington, D.C., scheduled for January 19, two days in advance of Barack Obama's more prominent inauguration.

The event was intended to kick off PDA's lobbying and organizing efforts for the next four years.

> In a national political context dominated by talk of austerity, PDA is aiming to keep popular progressive demands on the agenda in Congress—issues like universal single-payer healthcare, ending the wars while slashing the defense budget and implementing a financial transactions tax. Emblematic of the group's "inside-outside mission" of translating the demands of existing social movements into action from sympathetic members of Congress, the event featured a mix of Democratic representatives and leaders.

> "When we say inside-outside, if it's the peace issue, we're working inside the Democratic Party to support Barbara Lee (D-Calif.) [who sponsored a bill last session calling for the swift removal of U.S. troops from Afghanistan]. The outside piece would be working with folks like Phyllis Bennis from the Institute for Policy Studies and Medea Benjamin of CODEPINK," Tim Carpenter, PDA's executive director, told In These Times. "We've got to organize demonstrations; we've got to put together candlelight vigils, civil disobedience, the street heat, that's the outside piece. What PDA is trying to do is be that bridge. Every great social movement starts outside the halls of Congress, but if it's successful at the end of the day, it's going to pass legislation."

Carpenter stressed that the event "will launch the group's work for the next four years:"

> That plan, he said, will include monthly letter drops to members of Congress, urging them to support legislation that PDA allies in Congress plan to introduce, such as bills for single-payer universal healthcare or a financial transactions tax. PDA will also organize monthly discussions in Washington with its allies in Congress and the public interest community about the state of progressive legislation, in order to better co-ordinate support for those legislative efforts from PDA's supporters and allies on the local level.

According to Carpenter, PDA has a mailing list of roughly 78,000 people who are concentrated in California, Arizona, Massachusetts, Illinois, Florida and Wisconsin. Meanwhile, "in the halls of Congress, PDA can count on a small handful of allies, most of whom hail from the Congressional Progressive Caucus."

"We're realistic," says Carpenter, who "suggests that recent fiscal policy debates present an opportunity to push for cuts in military spending and a financial transactions tax." "We're going to be playing a lot of defense, but we need to be playing defense with an eye toward moving these questions [forward] and taking the offensive again."

In 2012, all of PDA's incumbent allies—Reps. John Conyers, Donna Edwards, Keith Ellison, Raul Grijalva, James McGovern and Barbara Lee—held their seats.

PDA also benefited from some sympathetic newcomers in the 113th Congress. Out of the 8 non-incumbent Democratic candidates the group endorsed in the 2012 election cycle, 3 picked up seats: Mark Pocan in Wisconsin, Alan Grayson in Florida and PDA's "jewel in the crown," Elizabeth Warren, who would represent Massachusetts in the U.S. Senate.[21]

21st Century Democrats

21st Century Democrats is a Political Action Committee that has supported "progressive" candidates at municipal, county, state and federal levels for more than a quarter of a century. 21st Century Democrats was founded in 1986 by Institute for Policy Studies affiliated Senator Tom Harkin (D-IA) and two Democratic Socialists of America (DSA) supporters, Texas Agriculture Secretary Jim Hightower and Congressman Lane Evans (D-IL).[22]

The socialist current runs deep in the organization.

Long-time Board Chair was one time Democratic Socialists of America member and former Mayor of Saint Paul, Minnesota, Jim Scheibel.[23]

Current 21st Century Democrats Advisory Board members include:[24] [25] [26] [27]

- Carol Moseley Braun - Former U.S. Senator from Illinois, a long-time supporter of the Communist Party USA.
- James Carville - Well known political commentator and Democratic Party strategist.
- Don Fowler - Former Chairman of the Democratic National Committee.
- Robert B. Reich - Former Secretary of the U.S. Department of Labor, Clinton Administration and DSA affiliate.

- Kathleen Kennedy Townsend - Former Maryland Lieutenant Governor and ACORN adviser.
- David Wilhelm - Former Chairman of the Democratic National Committee and former board member of the DSA-influenced Citizen Action of Illinois.

Electing "Progressives"

The mission of 21st Century Democrats is to build a "farm team" of progressive populists who will be the future leaders of the Democratic Party.

According to Advisory Board member Carol Mosely Braun:

> We can turn back the growing power of the extreme right wing in this country by standing with 21st Century Democrats. We need every committed Democrat to get involved—the future of our nation is at stake.

Growing influence

In the 2004 election cycle, it was the 13th largest Political Action Committee in the United States, raising nearly $7 million. Among progressive ideological PACs, it then ranked fourth behind America Coming Together, EMILY's List and MoveOn.org.[28]

Unlike traditional PACs, 21st Century Democrats focuses on recruiting, training and hiring field organizers to organize grassroots campaigns on behalf of candidates for local offices, statewide offices and even targeted presidential swing states. The group also has ties to Democracy for America, which grew out of far leftist Howard Dean's presidential campaign.[29]

21st Century Democrats has helped elect several hundred "progressive" politicians, including U.S. Senators Tim Johnson, Barbara Boxer, Russ Feingold, Jeff Merkley, Martin Heinrich, Elizabeth Warren, Jeanne Shaheen, Tom Udall, Ken Salazar, Jon Tester, John Sarbanes, Kirsten Gillibrand, Walter Mondale, Mary Landrieu and Barack Obama.

Recent Congressional Progressive Caucus members who have benefited from 21st Century Democrats' support include Rick Nolan, Bob Filner, Carol Shea Porter, Alan Grayson, Keith Ellison, Ben Lujan, Chellie Pingree, Andre Carson, Donna Edwards, Raul Grijalva and David Bonior.[30]

Its three main goals are to help elect progressive candidates, train young people about grassroots organizing and lastly, to continue to support our elected officials after Election Day, "through our comprehensive progressive network."

1 The Soviet Peace Offensive, "The War Called Peace," Knology.net, http://www.knology.net/~bilrum/PeaceGrpGloss.htm (1982)
2 World Peace Council Tour USA, WPC Information Centre, Lonnrotinkatu 25 A 5 krs 00180 Helsinki 18 Finland (1975) pp. 6-7
3 The Soviet Peace Offensive, "The War Called Peace," Knology.net, http://www.knology.net/~bilrum/PeaceGrpGloss.htm (1982)
4 "Information Digest" (ID) Publication (April 30, 1982)
5 Human Events (April 2, 1983)
6 Communists in the Democratic Party, p. 71
7 IPS, "IPS History: 1963 to Today," IPS, http://www.ips-dc.org/about/history (accessed May 10, 2013)
8 IPS Ideas for Obama Administration (December 16, 2008)
9 IPS, "IPS History: 1963 to Today," IPS, http://www.ips-dc.org/about/history (accessed May 10, 2013)
10 IPS, "IPS History: 1963 to Today," IPS, http://www.ips-dc.org/about/history (accessed May 10, 2013)
11 IPS, "IPS History: 1963 to Today," IPS, http://www.ips-dc.org/about/history (accessed May 10, 2013)
12 Campaign For America's Future, "About Us," Campaign For America's Future, http://www.ourfuture.org/about (accessed May 12, 2013)
13 KeyWiki, "Campaign for America's Future," KeyWiki, http://www.keywiki.org/index.php/Campaign_for_America%27s_Future (accessed May 12, 2013)
14 KeyWiki, "Take Back the American Dream Conference 2011," KeyWiki, http://www.keywiki.org/index.php/Take_Back_the_American_Dream_Conference_20 11 (accessed May 12, 2013)
15 KeyWiki, "America's Future Now!," KeyWiki, http://www.keywiki.org/index.php/America%27s_Future_Now (accessed May 12, 2013)
16 PDA's website, "About PDA," PDA's website, http://pdamerica.org/about/what-is-pda.php (accessed 2009)
17 Tim Carpenter, "PDA," Democratic Left, http://www.dsausa.org/dl/Fall_2006.pdf (Fall 2006)
18 PDA's website, "About PDA," PDA's website, http://pdamerica.org/about/what-is-pda.php (accessed 2009)
19 PDA's website, "About PDA," PDA's website, http://pdamerica.org/about/what-is-pda.php (accessed 2009)
20 PDA's website, "About PDA," PDA's website, http://pdamerica.org/about/what-is-pda.php (accessed 2009)
21 Cole Stangler, "A People's Inauguration," ITT, http://inthesetimes.com/article/14423/progressive_democrats_hold_a_peoples_inaugur ation, (January 15, 2013)
22 KeyWiki, "21st Century Democrats," KeyWiki, http://keywiki.org/index.php/21st_Century_Democrats (accessed June 5, 2013)
23 KeyWiki, "Jim Scheibel," KeyWiki, http://keywiki.org/index.php/Jim_Scheibel (accessed June 5, 2013)

24 KeyWiki, "Carol Moseley Braun," KeyWiki,
http://keywiki.org/index.php/Carol_Moseley_Braun (accessed June 5, 2013)
25 KeyWiki, "Robert Reich," KeyWiki, http://keywiki.org/index.php/Robert_Reich
(accessed June 5, 2013)
26 KeyWiki, "Kathleen Kennedy Townsend," KeyWiki,
http://keywiki.org/index.php/Kathleen_Kennedy_Townsend
 (accessed June 5, 2013)
27 KeyWiki, "David Wilhelm," KeyWiki,
http://keywiki.org/index.php/David_Wilhelm (accessed June 5, 2013)
28 Sam Attlesey, Lori Stahl, "New Group Seeks to Re-Focus Democratic Message,"
Dallas Morning News (January 23, 1996)
29 Sam Attlesey, Lori Stahl, "New Group Seeks to Re-Focus Democratic Message,"
Dallas Morning News (January 23, 1996)
30 KeyWiki, "21st Century Democrats," KeyWiki,
http://keywiki.org/index.php/21st_Century_Democrats (accessed June 5, 2013)

Foreign Policy/National Security

World Peace Council

The World Peace Council (WPC) was the former Soviet Union's most important international "front." Today it describes itself as "an anti-imperialist, democratic, independent and non-aligned international movement of mass action."[1]

In 1949, the WPC was founded in Prague during a "Peace Congress" sponsored by the Soviets and their Czech and other Eastern European satellites. The organization was planned and controlled by the International Department of the Communist Party of the Soviet Union, in conjunction with the KGB and claimed to represent 600 million "organizers for peace" around the world.

Under Soviet direction, the WPC had two main functions: to influence public opinion and government policies in non-communist countries along lines favorable to Soviet policy goals and to provide logistical support to Soviet-supported terrorist groups.[2]

In 1978, the House Intelligence Committee released a large CIA report on Soviet propaganda and front groups around the world (outside the U.S.) in which the WPC was identified as such a front. It has continued to be so identified in other government reports including State Department documents.

After being expelled from several countries, the WPC set up headquarters in Helsinki. Circa 1990, the WPC was estimated to have an annual budget of more than $40 million, almost all provided by the Soviet Union.[3]

In recent years, the WPC appears to have been mainly run by Greek and Cuban communists.

Influence in the U.S.

Through the Cold War, the WPC toured the U.S. several times, liaising with U.S. communists and cultivating leftist Congressmen and Senators in a concerted propaganda offensive to reduce U.S. defense spending.

In September-October, 1975, the first of several delegation of WPC leaders toured the United States in a major propaganda "effort to coordinate a post-Vietnam drive against American defense preparedness, according to Rep. Larry McDonald (D-GA), in a major report published in the "Congressional Record" of October 8, 1975.[4]

Today, the World Peace Council works less directly. The appropriate propaganda is disseminated to the Communist Party-controlled U.S. Peace Council, which then passes it to Peace Action and United for Peace and Justice, who then work to implement "the line" through public propaganda and influencing sympathetic Congress members.

Socialist International

The Socialist International (SI) is a worldwide organization of around 170 social democratic, socialist and labor parties.

Democratic Socialists of America (DSA) is the only U.S. affiliate of the SI, however the National Democratic Institute for International Affairs, which is led by top Democratic Party figures such as former Clinton Secretary of State Madeleine Albright, former Senator Tom Daschle, former Congressman Sam Gejdenson and former DNC Chairman Howard Dean, is listed on the SI website as an "Associated Organization."[5]

Ever since its inception in 1951, the Socialist International has made cosmetic efforts to distance itself from the communist movement. It continues to do so, sprinkling its calls for socialism and global governance with assurances of support for "democratic" principles.

During the Cold War, the SI aligned itself with communist terrorist Yasser Arafat and the PLO, the Soviet Union's premier terror master. It was also comfortable maintaining close fraternal relations with the communist dictatorships of the Warsaw Pact, Africa, Asia and Latin America. Cuba's Fidel Castro and Nicaragua's Sandinista regimes were SI favorites.

When Gunther Guillaume, companion and closest aide to West German Chancellor Willy Brandt, was exposed as a communist agent of the East German Stasi, Brandt was forced to resign as Chancellor. But Brandt's East Bloc intelligence revelations didn't faze the SI leadership, who allowed him to continue in office as the longest-serving President of the organization.[6]

Willy Brandt was personally close to DSA Founder and long-time leader, Michael Harrington.

When Harrington died in 1989, invited guest speakers at his tribute service included Senator Ted Kennedy and Willy Brandt.

Communists Welcomed

"Reformed" communists and communist parties are welcomed with open arms and hold top posts in the SI. The SI's Commission for a Sustainable World Society is a good example. Its members include Aleksander Kwasniewski, the former President of Poland, who was a leading Communist Party member until it became convenient to switch to the "reform" label. Likewise for CSWS member Sergei Mironov, who was an apparatchik in the Communist Party of the Soviet Union and remains a stalwart supporter of Russia's top KGB man, Prime Minister Vladimir Putin.

Another SI official was Sergei Stanishev, Prime Minister of Bulgaria and Chairman of the Bulgarian Socialist Party (formerly the Bulgarian Communist Party). Still another was Ayaz Mütallibov, the former communist dictator of Soviet Azerbaijan. Also, Nicaraguan President Daniel Ortega, and his communist Sandinista regime have extensive SI connections.[7]

SI currently includes on its membership roster the "former communist" or pro-Soviet parties of Albania, Angola, Armenia, Bulgaria, Hungary, Mongolia, Mozambique, Namibia, Nicaragua, Poland, Romania, Serbia, Slovakia, South Africa and Yemen.

Palestinian terrorist group Fatah is a member, while "former" Marxist insurgent groups such as Western Sahara's Polisario and a whole slew of leftist parties from the old Soviet Bloc enjoy "consultative status."[8]

The Socialist International provides guidance to the many members of Democratic Socialists of America, who regularly attend its conferences and meetings. The U.S. comrades then promote these ideas through their channels in the U.S. labor movement and the Democratic Party.

Council for a Livable World

The Washington D.C. based Council for a Livable World (CLW) has been financing and lobbying pro-disarmament, anti-U.S. military legislators since its foundation in 1962.

Founded by Manhattan Project nuclear scientist, Leo Szilard, and led by leftists such as Jerome Grossman and more lately, former high ranking Democratic Party Congressman David Bonior, CLW has been a key part of America's march to a national defense meltdown.

The CLW has funded hundreds of U.S. Senators and Congressmen in its history, almost all Democrats, with a sprinkling (mainly in the early days) of leftist Republicans.

Leo Szilard founded CLW originally to support pro-disarmament Senators. He reasoned that as even sparsely populated states have two Senators, he could buy the most influence for the least outlay, by funding leftist Senate candidates from small states.

CLW's long-time CEO, Jerome Grossman, claims that by funding Senators at the beginning of their careers, the Council for a Livable World was able to influence them later when needed.

Grossman told a 1996 interviewer:

> Now Council for a Livable World is playing the money game… We try to find obscure people who would make good Senators or Representatives and early on try to give them the initial funding. Now we can't compete with the big money. We only raise a million and a half each election cycle. But that's a million and a half that has no cost to them. Because we get in early, and because it's tied to issues, seems to have some kind of an effect. Then if we elect somebody they're eternally grateful. Then we go and we are able to get a hearing.

Jerome Grossman even claimed he was able to influence Democratic Senator George Mitchell to campaign against President Bush on the B-2 bomber project:

> George Mitchell who's going to be Secretary of State — when he ran for Senator in Maine the first time, he was against a very popular member of the House of Representatives in Maine, a Republican by the name of… Robert Emory. Well, Emory and Mitchell had run for Governor and run for Representative before. He had lost both times. He was considered a terrible politician. He had been a Federal Judge briefly. And he was considered a basket case. He was thirty-six points

behind. We raised fifty, sixty thousand dollars for him. He never stops telling that story. Now it so happens he's a good guy anyway. But in time he was majority leader of the United States Senate. And we could walk in any time and tell him what we wanted. We even got him to oppose the President on the B2 bomber and so forth...

Though by 1996, Grossman was no longer involved in the day to day running at CLW, he still claimed considerable influence in Washington D.C.:

I go to Washington for three days every month. Last time I was there, I saw a few Senators, a few members of the House of Representatives. And I also went in the Pentagon because the Pentagon is now doing another bottom-up review before they put their budget in. Because their budget now is based on fighting two regional wars simultaneously. So they're going through the motions — well, I'm being unfair. They're re-studying it, all right. While I was there I went in to see if I could have some input. I have had input.

Grossman also "conspired" with State Department officials to help with the passing of a controversial Chemical Weapons Treaty:

And then the State Department — wow, there are some [people] there — they want to see the Chemical Weapons Treaty pass. It hasn't been ratified. And [Senator Jesse] Helms won't bring it up. So, I conspire with them. The point is that I get... and people are calling me all day, and I'm calling people all day to find out what goes on...

The CLW's February 1982 fund-raising appeal commenced with a letter entitled, "The Reagan Administration is launching a massive escalation of the nuclear arms race," signed by George Kistiakowsky, Chief Science Adviser to President Eisenhower. The letter stated that the CLW's chief targets were the MX missile and B-1 bomber, and he stated, "We're on Capitol Hill every day, working to reestablish arms control talks, fighting the proliferation of nuclear weapons, lobbying for nuclear arms control agreements." CLW also targeted U.S. chemical weapons funding and campaigning for across-the-board defense cuts with a "media blitz" slated for late May when the Senate would be considering the chemical weapons issue.

According to CLW's own website, "notable achievements to which the Council-supported candidates who were elected have contributed" include:

- Ratifying the Chemical Weapons Convention and Intermediate-Range Nuclear Forces, Conventional Forces in Europe and Strategic Arms Reduction (START) Treaty.
- Establishing a U.S. nuclear testing moratorium in 1992.
- Limiting the deployment of the MX missile and B-2 bomber.
- Blocking deployment of National Missile Defense by the Clinton administration.
- Eliminating funding for the nuclear "Bunker Buster" and "Reliable Replacement Warhead."

Just who has CLW financed and presumably "influenced" over the years?

A few of the several dozen CLW-backed Democratic candidates in 2008 and 2010 were Senators:

- Barbara Boxer
- Chris Coons
- Paul Hodes
- Patty Murray
- Harry Reid
- Al Franken
- Jeff Merkley
- Jeanne Shaheen
- Mark Udall

Earlier Senate victories have included these still prominent Democrats:

- Dianne Feinstein
- Chris Dodd
- Joe Biden
- Dick Durbin
- Tom Harkin
- Barbara Mikulski
- John Kerry
- Hillary Clinton
- Charles Schumer
- Sherrod Brown

Jerome Grossman also knew Barack Obama way before his 2004 Senate race, as this 1994 photo attests.

Barack Obama was closely associated with Chicago Democratic Socialists of America. Jerome Grossman was close to Boston Democratic Socialists of America. Possibly the two met through mutual "comrades" while Obama was studying at Boston's Harvard University in the early 1990s.[9]

Barack Obama, Jerome Grossman; Location Unknown (1994)

CLW Leaders

Several leaders of CLW have connections to other Szilard creations, including the far left sister organizations Bulletin of the Atomic Scientists and Federation of American Scientists, as well as Democratic Socialists of America (DSA) and the far left Washington based "think tank," Institute for Policy Studies (IPS).

Former CLW Board members include:

- Ruth Adams - 1980's Board member (died 2005) - An arms-control activist and a former long-time Editor of the Bulletin of the Atomic Scientists. In 1962, Adams served on the Advisory Board of the Hyde Park Community Peace Center alongside Communist front activists Timuel Black, Robert Havighurst, Sidney Lens and Quentin Young. Comrades Black and Young would both go on to join Democratic Socialists of America and to befriend and mentor a young Chicago lawyer named Barack

Obama. Adams would serve on The Bulletin of the Atomic Scientists in the 1980s with Quentin Young's wife, the late Ruth Young, and also with future Obama "Science Czar," John Holdren. Adams was also a Chair of the Institute for Policy Studies and a supporter of a Communist Party USA (CPUSA) front (with Timuel Black and Quentin Young), the Chicago Committee to Defend the Bill of Rights.

- Bernard Feld - 1980's Board member - A member of Richard Nixon's famed "enemies list," Editor of the Bulletin of the Atomic Scientists and a member of the Soviet friendly, pro-disarmament American Committee on East-West Accord.

- Jerome Frank - 1980's Board member - An affiliate of the Institute for Policy Studies and a member of the Board of Sponsors of the Federation of American Scientists.

- Herbert "Pete" Scoville - 1980's Board member - Former CIA Assistant Director of Scientific Intelligence and Deputy Director for Research and later was Assistant Director of the U.S. Arms Control and Disarmament Agency. Scoville was active with the IPS in anti-NATO and disarmament projects since the 1960s. In January 1978, Scoville participated in the Washington, D.C. meetings of the World Peace Council Bureau, a well documented Soviet front.

- Kosta Tsipis - 1980's Board member - Former Board member of the heavily communist and socialist infiltrated SANE - "A Citizens' Organization for a Sane World." A member of the Board of Directors for the Bulletin of the Atomic Scientists.

- Paul Warnke - 1980's Board member - A leading arms control expert under Democratic administrations in the 1970s and '80s. A Trustee of the Institute for Policy Studies.

Current CLW National Advisory Board members include:

- Julian Bond - Long-time leader of the NAACP and a veteran of the Soviet front World Federation of Democratic Youth Festival in Helsinki, Finland in 1962. Bond is a long-time member of DSA and has been affiliated with several IPS spin-offs and with the communist front Chicago Committee to Defend the Bill of Rights. In November 2006, Bond traveled to Cuba to take a first-hand look at the island's health system and especially to find out about the Latin American Medical School and its nearly 90 U.S. students.

- Tom Downey - A former far left Democratic member of Congress from New York. While in Congress, Downey was affiliated with and supported by the Long Island Progressive Coalition, a front for DSA.
- Patricia Schroeder - A former far left Democratic member of Congress from Colorado. Schroeder was an affiliate of the IPS and a protégé of DSA activist and Democratic Party women's leader, Mildred Jeffrey.

On February 4, 2010, the Council for a Livable World announced that David Bonior would be succeeding Patricia Schroeder as the next Chair of PeacePAC, the organization's arm dedicated to endorsing pro-disarmament candidates for the U.S. House of Representatives. At the time, Bonior commented:[10]

> I am honored to be selected as the next chairman of PeacePAC. I look forward to working with the experts on the committee's Board of Directors to endorse and help elect strong, progressive candidates in the 2010 elections.

David Bonior, the formerly number two Democrat in the U.S. House of Representatives, had most recently been working as a member of the Obama Economic Transition Team to reunify America's two rival labor federations, the AFL-CIO and Change to Win.

Bonior was also a long-time affiliate of both the Institute for Policy Studies and Democratic Socialists of America. Since leaving Congress, Bonior has become an open member of DSA.

Who is Jerome Grossman?

Born in 1917, Jerome Grossman worked in his family business, the Massachusetts Envelope Company, for thirty-five years. After selling his interest in the firm, Grossman accepted a position as the President and National Executive Director of Council for a Livable World, before becoming after 12 years, the Chairman of the organization. He is still officially Chairman Emeritus on the board of the CLW.

While coming from a business background, there is no doubt that Grossman is a socialist at heart.

Grossman told interviewer Nancy Earsy in 1996:

> The dynamics of the modern world under capitalism tend toward the growth of large corporations with semimonopoly positions. That's my basis for supporting a big government, is to control big corporations.

Jerome Grossman grew up in a "liberal" household reading The Nation and watching his father support several Massachusetts leftist politicians:

> By this time he had left the business. When I was twenty-four he gave me the keys, and says, "You run it." So that's what he did. So he was known as a capable, effective, well-respected political person. I'm known as the Massachusetts liberal. Not radical — liberal. Although a lot of people think I'm radical — I'm more radical than they think. But my activities have been along those lines.

Grossman began his own political activism in the 1950s, working through the "peace movement" of the time, but became dissatisfied with lack of progress:

> This in the middle 1950's. And, of course, everybody was still terrified of McCarthyism, unwilling to do anything that appeared to recognize the existence of the Soviet Union and that they had a right to exist. It was interpreted as being against the Cold War. I was against the Cold War and I wanted it resolved. The reason why I wanted it resolved is so that nuclear weapons ought not to be used. So I became involved in National Committee For A Sane Nuclear Policy and various other organizations that were founded virtually every other year in response to various pressures.

> Of course what we were working on then was the nuclear test ban. We're still working on the nuclear test ban to try to complete it. But I was the one who became quite dissatisfied with the fact that we were essentially talking to each other in church basements and academic meetings, middle class, upper class, highly educated people. We weren't reaching the public.

Founded in 1957, the National Committee for a Sane Nuclear Policy became known as SANE and later Peace Action. The organization has been guided by communists and socialists throughout its history.

One of Grossman's most significant projects was the recruitment of Jesuit priest, Fr. Robert Drinan, to run for Congress. Communist fronter Drinan turned out to be one of the most far left Representatives to ever serve in the U.S. Congress. He played a lead role in ending U.S. government investigations into subversive activities. This campaign also led to Grossman's connection to future U.S. Senator and Presidential candidate, the leftist John Kerry:

> We decided that we wanted to elect a member of the House of Representatives who was against the Vietnam War... So we furthered our activities against the Vietnam War by using the most Democratic tactics, by bringing in all of the two thousand anti-Vietnam War activists in the fourth Congressional district; bringing them all into a school for an all-day session and selecting a candidate from people who ran.

> I was a candidate, and I was the likely candidate, until I found a Jesuit priest, Father Robert F. Drinan, the Dean of the Boston College Law School... Okay. So when I heard that Drinan, a well known priest, the Dean of the Boston College Law School, might be interested in running, I called him up immediately and said, "I'm dropping my candidacy; I will work for you." So we nominated him at the caucus, and we elected him. And electing him was part of the process.

> While this was going on I got a telephone call from somebody I had never heard of... This fellow calls me up and he says, "You don't know me, but I have a brother who is a natural politician, and he's over in Vietnam now. He's coming back. And he wants to run in the caucus that you are organizing." And I said, "I already have a candidate." He says, "Yes, but my brother is special." I said, "Who's your brother?" He says, "John Kerry." This was Cameron Kerry who at the time was a junior at Harvard College. He interested me so I said, "Get over here." He hopped a bus and he came over in his sweater and everything. And we talked. John Kerry did run in that caucus and did very, very well in the caucus. I was hard pressed to beat him. But John Kerry, after he lost, he stood up and he said, "I'm going to respect the wishes of the caucus. I'm not going to run in the primary. I will dedicate the rest of the campaign to working for Father Drinan." And that's why I have been a supporter of John Kerry every since.

In 1982, Jerome Grossman was a member of the American Committee on East-West Accord. The ACEWA, based in Washington, D.C., was a tax-exempt "independent educational organization," with the stated aim of "improving East/West relations, with special focus on U.S.-Soviet relations."

One of the key pro-disarmament organizations of the "Cold War," ACEWA, while attempting to maintain an aura of respectability, was riddled with far leftists.

Prominent ACEWA members included:

- Joseph Filner - A former Pennsylvania Communist Party official turned international businessman. Filner focused on metal and technology trading with the Soviet Union and was a major funder of leftist causes. He was the father of recently retired DSA affiliated California Congressman Bob Filner.

- Philip Klutznik - Former U.S. Secretary of Commerce, who later served on far leftist Chicago Mayor Harold Washington's Transition Oversight Committee.

- Bernard Lown - A life-long Communist Party front activist and Co-President of International Physicians for the Prevention of Nuclear War.

- George McGovern - Far left U.S. Senator.

- Erwin Salk - A communist affiliated, F.B.I.-monitored Chicago lawyer and President of the Board of Directors of the Chicago Center for U.S./USSR Relations and Exchanges, where he worked with CPUSA member Larry McGurty and DSA member and future Progressives for Obama supporter, Betty Willhoite.

- Jeremy Stone - President of the far left and pro-disarmament Federation of American Scientists, affiliate of the even further left IPS and son of one time Soviet agent I.F. Stone. In November 1983, the Federation of American Scientists sent a party to the Soviet Union, which included Jeremy Stone and future Obama "Science Czar," John Holdren.

There is some evidence also that Grossman, who was a former member of the Democratic National Committee, may also be a member of Democratic Socialists of America.

In 2010, Steve Grossman, was endorsed by the Boston Democratic Socialists of America in his run for the Massachusetts Treasurer job:

> Son of CPPAX founder Jerome Grossman (one of DSA's first Debs-Thomas honorees), Steve Grossman has strong labor backing and says he will use this office to leverage progressive issues.

Jerome Grossman is also listed on the Advisory Board of the DSA-controlled National Jobs For All Coalition, alongside identified DSA members Elaine Bernard, Noreen Connell, Staughton Lynd, Manning Marable, Lawrence Mishel, Rep. Jerrold Nadler, Juliet Schor, Ruth Sidel, Victor Sidel, Theda Skocpol, Joe Uehlein, Cornel West (Barack Obama's Black Advisory Council, 2008) and William Julius Wilson (a panelist with Obama at a DSA sponsored forum in Chicago in 1996).

Though little known nationally, Jerome Grossman has probably had more influence on U.S. disarmament policy than any living person in the country.[11]

Was Leo Szilard a Soviet Agent?

Leo Szilard was born in Hungary in 1898.

In Budapest, during the 1919 Bela Kun Hungarian Soviet Republic, Szilard founded a socialist student's association to "help clarify political and economic issues." The Hungarian Association of Socialist Students distributed a pamphlet on tax and monetary reform purportedly written by Szilard.

Leo Szilard

Leo Szilard was an enthusiastic supporter of Bela Kun's communist regime. When Kun's government fell, the backlash against communists persuaded Szilard to leave Hungary for Berlin. There he was involved in a study group dedicated to analyzing Soviet affairs.

In London in the 1930s, Szilard helped organize the Academic Assistance Council to aid refugee scholars. He also proposed enlisting Nobel laureates to protest Japan's invasion of Manchuria, the first time the group was politicized in this way. Both causes were legitimate, but both were also heavily infiltrated by communists and sympathizers.

Szilard's best known political efforts involved his mentor, friend and fellow communist sympathizer, Albert Einstein. In New York in 1939, Szilard proposed and drafted a letter from Einstein to President Franklin D. Roosevelt that warned about German nuclear weapons research and urged a U.S. counter-effort.

Their letter prompted Roosevelt to convene a federal Advisory Committee on Uranium (with Hungarian physicists Eugene Wigner, Edward Teller and Szilard as members) that promised money for Enrico Fermi and Szilard to conduct chain-reaction experiments at Columbia University.

But when this funding from Washington hadn't materialized by the spring of 1940, Szilard enlisted Einstein in an effort at political blackmail. He drafted for Einstein a letter warning the White House that if those funds were not forthcoming, Szilard would publish a paper detailing just how a chain reaction in Uranium could work. Soon, Fermi and Szilard received their money.

By 1942, Szilard was working on the Allied effort to develop the Atomic Bomb - the Manhattan Project.

However Szilard was already under suspicion.

General Groves, head of the project, declared Szilard to be detrimental to the project and that he should be arrested and interned for the duration of the war.

Were Groves' suspicions founded?

According to Pavel Sudoplatov, former wartime Director of the Administration for Special Tasks, an elite unit of the Soviet intelligence service, Leo Szilard, Robert Oppenheimer and Enrico Fermi knowingly supplied information to Soviet contacts during their work on the Manhattan Project.

Sudoplatov wrote in his 1994 book, "Special Tasks, Memoirs of an unwanted witness—A soviet Spymaster":

> The most vital information for developing the first Soviet atomic bomb came from scientists engaged in the Manhattan Project to build the American atomic bomb—Robert Oppenheimer, Enrico Fermi, and Leo Szilard.
>
> Oppenheimer, Fermi, Szilard, and Szilard's secretary were often quoted in the NKVD files from 1942 to 1945 as sources for information on the development of the first American atomic bomb. It is in the record that on several occasions they agreed to share information on nuclear weapons with Soviet scientists. At first they were motivated by fear of Hitler; they believed that the Germans might produce the first atomic bomb. Then the Danish physicist Niels Bohr helped strengthen their own inclinations to share nuclear secrets with the world academic community. By sharing their knowledge with the Soviet Union, the chance of beating the Germans to the bomb would be increased.
>
> As early as 1940, a commission of Soviet scientists, upon hearing rumors of a superweapon being built in the West, investigated the possibility of creating an atomic bomb from uranium, but concluded that such a weapon was a theoretical, not a practical, possibility. The same scientific commission recommended that the government instruct intelligence services to monitor Western scientific publications...
>
> We were able to take advantage of the network of colleagues that Gamow had established. Using implied threats against Gamow's relatives in Russia, Elizabeth Zarubina pressured him into cooperating with us. In exchange for safety and material support for his relatives,

Gamow provided the names of left-wing scientists who might be recruited to supply secret information.

Another route was from the mole who worked with Fermi and Pontecorvo. The mole in Tennessee was connected with the illegal station at the Santa Fe drugstore, from which material was sent by courier to Mexico. The unidentified young moles, along with the Los Alamos mole, were junior scientists or administrators who copied vital documents to which they were allowed access by Oppenheimer, Fermi, and Szilard, who were knowingly part of the scheme.

We received reports on the progress of the Manhattan Project from Oppenheimer and his friends in oral form, through comments and asides, and from documents transferred through clandestine methods with their full knowledge that the information they were sharing would be passed on. In all, there were five classified reports made available by Oppenheimer describing the progress of work on the atomic bomb.

Not only were we informed of technical developments in the atomic program, but we heard in detail the human conflicts and rivalries among the members of the team at Los Alamos. A constant theme was tension with General Groves, director of the project. We were told of Grove's conflicts with Szilard. Groves was outraged by Szilard's iconoclastic style and his refusal to accept the strictures of military discipline. The "baiting of brass hats" was Szilard's self-professed hobby. Groves believed that Szilard was a security risk and tried to prevent him from working on the Manhattan Project despite Szilard's seminal contribution to the development of the first atomic chain reaction with Fermi.

Sudoplatov claims that Soviet Spy Chief Lavrenti Beria had post war plans for their Manhattan Project friends:

> After our reactor was put into operation in 1946, Beria issued orders to stop all contacts with our American sources in the Manhattan Project; the FBI was getting close to uncovering some of our agents. Beria said we should think how to use Oppenheimer, Fermi, Szilard, and others around them in the peace campaign against nuclear armament. Disarmament and the inability to impose nuclear blackmail would deprive the United States of its advantage. We began a worldwide political campaign against nuclear superiority, which kept up until we exploded our own nuclear bomb, in 1949. Our goal was to preempt American power politically before the Soviet Union had its own bomb.

Beria warned us not to compromise Western scientists, but to use their political influence.

Comrade Beria's advice turned out to be sound. Szilard's usefulness to the Soviet cause only increased after the war.

One of Szilard's next projects was the strongly pro-disarmament Federation of American Scientists (FAS), started with former communist and alleged spy, Philip Morrison, and communist sympathizer, Harold Urey. FAS was founded in 1945 with a membership of more than 2,000 scientists and an advisory panel that included several more communists or sympathizers, including Robert Oppenheimer, Harlow Shapley and Edward U. Condon , a known associate of several Polish embassy officials.

Leo Szilard was Co-Organizer of the first Pugwash Conference in 1957, a major series of gatherings involving Western and Eastern Bloc scientists, diplomats and politicians.

In 1960, Szilard gained a private audience with Soviet Premier Nikita Khrushchev in New York City. During their two-hour conversation, Szilard gained the Soviet leader's assent for a Moscow-Washington "hotline" to help prevent accidental nuclear war.

Szilard was also an early affiliate of the far left and pro-disarmament Washington D.C. based "think tank," the Institute for Policy Studies.[12]

SANE/Peace Action

SANE, or a Citizens' Organization for a Sane World, was formed in 1957 as the National Committee for a Sane Nuclear Policy. In 1987, it merged with the Nuclear Freeze movement and in 1993 became known as Peace Action. It is the country's largest grassroots "peace" (read anti-U.S. military) organization with a claimed 100,000 members nationwide.

The organization's original goal was to promote U.S. disarmament. SANE launched a series of advertisements in the New York Times. Local groups then "spontaneously" formed around the country to buy space in other newspapers for SANE ads. These small groups served as the basis for local SANE chapters.

In the mid-1980s, SANE and the far left Coalition for a New Foreign and Military Policy, cooperated in compiling a joint computerized mailing list by Congressional Districts and as a media task force against the Reagan defense budget.

The committee's mission was to "develop public support for a boldly conceived and executed policy which will lead mankind away from war and toward peace and justice."[13]

SANE led a number of successful public education projects "including hard-hitting advertising campaigns that brought nuclear disarmament issues to millions of Americans." SANE's first claimed major success was ratification of the Limited Nuclear Test Ban Treaty with the Soviet Union.

SANE was also an early leader in the movement against the war in Vietnam. In 1978, SANE was at the head of a successful campaign which halted the deployment of MX mobile missiles in Utah and Nevada.[14]

Peace Politics

H. Stuart Hughes, Chair of SANE, played a role in a 1960's political campaign that would change Massachusetts and national politics forever.

Opposing Ted Kennedy in the 1962 Massachusetts Democratic Primary was Edward McCormack, nephew of House Speaker John McCormack. Kennedy's Republican opponent was George Cabot Lodge and on the far left was Independent Peace candidate, Harvard Prof. Hughes.

Socialist Jerome Grossman, of the Council for a Livable World, was Hughes' Campaign Manager and Chester Hartman (later with the Institute for Policy Studies) was the organizer of the massive signature drive required to place Hughes on the ballot. According to Grossman:[15]

> Hughes needed 72,000 signatures, a purposely prohibitive number in that era of McCarthyism and nobody in fact had tried to reach it since the law had first been passed.

> In this talented field, Hughes polled 50,013 votes, 2.3% of the votes cast. However, we collected a startling 149,000 signatures in ten weeks for a "peace candidate." The Cuban Missile Crisis arrived in October just before the election. With the integrity that was his hallmark, Hughes went against the popular hysteria: he accused President Kennedy of acting over hastily in imposing the blockade of Cuba, of bypassing the United Nations, and unnecessarily stirring up an atmosphere of national emergency. His position cost Hughes thousands of votes.

> In the process we built a town-by-town organization all over the state, a structure that remains in place today. A clear result has been the

election over recent decades of so many progressive voices to the state's first-rate Congressional delegation, including Michael Harrington, Father Robert Drinan, Gerry Studds, Jim McGovern, Barney Frank, Ed Markey, John Tierney, Michael Capuano and John Kerry.

Marxist Influence

SANE was always a coalition of communists, socialists and liberals, with the leftists firmly in the driver's seat.

SANE's founders included Saturday Review Editor Norman Cousins, American Friends Service Committee member Clarence Pickett and poet and Communist Party USA (CPUSA) sympathizer, Lenore Marshall, among others.

Spokespeople for SANE included liberals such as Dr. Albert Schweitzer and Eleanor Roosevelt, as well as Socialist Party USA leader Norman Thomas and Communist Party sympathizer Dr. Benjamin Spock.[16]

From the beginning, SANE linked issues of peace and "social justice." Supporters such as CPUSA affiliates Harry Belafonte, Ruby Dee and Ossie Davis connected SANE with radical groups across the country.[17] [18]

SANE also cooperated directly with the Soviet front World Peace Council (WPC), co-sponsoring two Capitol Hill appearances by WPC activists in 1981.[19]

SANE's Executive Director was David Cortright, who was a Founder of the WPC affiliated Communist Party-led U.S. Peace Council. Cortright was also a protégé of Institute for Policy Studies (IPS) Founder Marcus Raskin and a staffer of the Center for National Security Studies.[20]

During the 1970s and '80s, known CPUSA members on the SANE Board of Directors, or Advisory Council, included scientist Linus Pauling; California Latino leader Bert Corona; former Martin Luther King adviser Jack O'Dell; Baltimore activist Sam Schmerler and California "peace" activist Irving Sarnoff.

Socialists who would later join Democratic Socialists of America (DSA) included SANE Co-Chair William Winpisinger and Board members California Congressman Ron Dellums, Michigan State Rep. Zolton Ferency and labor leader David Livingston.

Several Institute for Policy Studies affiliates were also involved in the SANE leadership, including IPS Founder Marcus Raskin who served as SANE Co-Chair.

Then Iowa Congressman Tom Harkin and his New York colleague Ted Weiss were also SANE leaders.[21]

The pattern continues today with two DSAers, Larry Wittner of New York and Carol Allen of New Jersey, currently serving on the Peace Action Board of Directors.

Communist Organizer

Judith LeBlanc is the National Field Organizer for Peace Action. From 2005-2008, she was the National Co-Chair of United for Peace and Justice, a peace "umbrella" organization that she helped found with the IPS.

Le Blanc is one of the Vice-Chairs of the CPUSA and chairs its Peace and Solidarity Commission, the body charged with running the U.S. "peace" movement for the Communist Party and its foreign allies.

LeBlanc's other main mission is to pressure U.S. Congress members and Senators to cut U.S. defense spending and massively downsize the military.

When the 2011 Super Committee was charged with identifying potential U.S. government spending cuts, LeBlanc mobilized her resources nationwide to make sure defense spending took the biggest hits. Members of the Super Committee were lobbied relentlessly by LeBlanc's Peace Action comrades to make sure they voted to cut America's ability to defend its citizens.

LeBlanc outlined her strategy on the Peace Action blog:

> The choice is clear. The Super Committee either cuts programs that help the oldest, the youngest and sickest in our society or the Pentagon...

> The creation of a Super Committee to make decisions that will affect generations to come, without a way for the people to be heard, is unprecedented.

> The Super Committee's time line is short for when these decisions will be made and voted on. Between September and November 23, the Super Committee will negotiate a plan that will be sent to the Congress for an up or down vote by December 23.

> Can we leverage the majority opinion, reflected in poll after poll, to make the rich pay their fair share of taxes, close corporate tax loop holes and end the wars to bring the tax dollars home? How do we build a grassroots roar for moving the money from wars and weapons back to our cities and towns?

We must organize, educate and mobilize for real cuts in Pentagon spending to protect community services.

Peace Action says cuts can be made, and it is important that our communities get the facts and bust the myths surrounding cutting Pentagon spending.

Targeting members of the Super Committee, members of subcommittees in both Houses who will weigh in on cuts in Pentagon spending, and the Congress as a whole is a big job, but the economic justice and peace movements have already begun.

Grassroots mobilizing for Congressional town hall meetings and public events in August and continuing into the Fall are creating a stir. People are raising their voices for "Jobs, not more weapon and wars!"

Peace Action is also on the move. We are organizing town hall meetings and bird-dogging the Super Committee members.

Last week we called on our supporters to use social media to send a message to the co-chairs. We Tweeted "Super Com co chairs @PattyMurray @RepHensarling. Start with cuts to Pentagon budget. Protect Social Security, Medicare & Medicaid."

We asked people to go to their Facebook pages: Senator Patty Murray and Representative Jeb Hensarling to raise our concerns. Let's keep that up!

Peace Action Montgomery County, MD, helped to initiate the MD Coalition: Fund Our Communities, Bring the War Dollars Home which is sponsoring a town hall meeting September 20 in Silver Spring to "Take back the Budget Debate." The gathering will map out a plan for action including pressing Representative Chris Van Hollen, a member of the Super Committee.

North Carolina Peace Action is organizing in Durham a Town Hall Meeting to "Bring the War Dollars Home to Fund Our Communities" on Saturday, September 1. Their goal is to line up support from local elected officials who are faced with budget shortfalls, to press the North Carolina Congressional delegation to change Federal spending priorities.

Massachusetts Peace Action has begun to "bird dog" Senator Kerry, one of the members of the Super Committee, with a leaflet and petition making the links between Pentagon spending and meeting the needs of our communities.

The Communist Party USA owes its allegiance not to the United States, but to the international communist movement, currently led by the communist parties of China, Cuba and the Russian Federation.

Judith LeBlanc's and Peace Action's efforts had nothing to do with peace. They are a blatant attempt to exploit U.S. economic problems to shift the balance of military power against the United States and in favor of America's most dangerous enemies.[22]

---

1 WPC, "Information Letter," WPC, http://www.wpc-in.org/informationletter (accessed May 11, 2013)

2 Knology.net, "Peace Group Glossary," Knology.net, http://www.knology.net/%7Ebilrum/PeaceGrpGloss.htm (1982)

3 Communists in the Democratic Party, p. 64

4 Rep. Larry McDonald, "The World Peace Council in Congress: Soviets Lobby for U.S. Disarmament," Congressional Record, http://www.keywiki.org/index.php?title=The_World_Peace_Council_in_Congress:_So viets_Lobby_for_U.S._Disarmament&action=edit&redlink=1 (October 8, 1975) Extension of Remarks, pp. E5329-5331

5 KeyWiki, "Socialist International," KeyWiki, http://www.keywiki.org/index.php/Socialist_International (accessed May 11, 2013)

6 William F. Jasper, "The Grasp of Socialist International," Crossroad, http://www.crossroad.to/articles2/forcing-change/010/11-socialist-international.htm (January 11, 2011)

7 William F. Jasper, "The Grasp of Socialist International," Crossroad, http://www.crossroad.to/articles2/forcing-change/010/11-socialist-international.htm (January 11, 2011)

8 KeyWiki, "Socialist International – Member Parties," KeyWiki, http://www.keywiki.org/index.php/Socialist_International#Member_parties (accessed May 11, 2013)

9 Trevor Loudon, "Nuclear Treason Part 4 Influence of the Council for a Livable World," New Zeal, http://www.trevorloudon.com/2011/02/nuclear-treason-part-4-influence-of-the-council-for-a-livable-world/ (February 11, 2011)

10 Trevor Loudon, "Nuclear Treason Part 3: Who's Who at the Council for a Livable World?" New Zeal, http://www.trevorloudon.com/2011/01/nuclear-treason-part-3-whos-who-at-the-council-for-a-livable-world/ (January 28, 2011)

11 Trevor Loudon, "Nuclear Treason Part 2 Who Is Jerome Grossman?" New Zeal, http://www.trevorloudon.com/2011/01/nuclear-treason-part-2-who-is-jerome-grossman/ (January 25, 2011)

12 Trevor Loudon, "Nuclear Treason Part 1, Who Was Leo Szilard?" Worldview Weekend Interactive Magazine, http://worldviewweekend.com/news/article/nuclear-treason-part-1-who-was-leo-szilard (February 11, 2011)

13 Temple University Libraries, "SANE, Greater Philadelphia Council, Temple University, http://library.temple.edu/collections/urbana/urb50.jsp;jsessionid=2E997D2C81155CD A86B73501F1BD8ACA?bhcp=1 (accessed May 11, 2013)

14 Knology.net, "Peace Group Glossary," Knology.net, http://www.knology.net/~bilrum/PeaceGrpGloss.htm (1982)

15 Jerome Grossman, "Ted Kennedy: His First Election Monday," The Relentless Liberal blog, http://www.articlealley.com/article_811556_13.html (February 16, 2009)
16 KeyWiki, "Benjamin Spock," KeyWiki, http://www.keywiki.org/index.php/Benjamin_Spock (accessed May 11, 2013)
17 KeyWiki, "SANE," KeyWiki, http://www.keywiki.org/index.php/SANE (accessed May 11, 2013)
18 Peace Action, "History," Peace Action, http://www.peace-action.org/history, (accessed May 3, 2013)
19 Knology.net, "Peace Group Glossary," Knology.net, http://www.knology.net/~bilrum/PeaceGrpGloss.htm (1982)
20 Knology.net, "Peace Group Glossary," Knology.net, http://www.knology.net/~bilrum/PeaceGrpGloss.htm (1982)
21 KeyWiki, "SANE," KeyWiki, http://www.keywiki.org/index.php/SANE (accessed May 11, 2013)
22 Trevor Loudon, "Treason? Senior Communist Lobbies "Super Committee" for Defense Cuts," New Zeal, http://www.trevorloudon.com/2011/10/treason-senior-communist-lobbies-super-committee-for-defense-cuts/ (October 23, 2011)

The Caucuses

Congressional Progressive Caucus

The Congressional Progressive Caucus (CPC) was founded in 1991 by Bernie Sanders—the openly socialist then Independent Congressman from Vermont, Democratic Socialists of America (DSA) and the radical Washington D.C. based "think tank," Institute for Policy Studies (IPS).

Sanders' CPC Co-Founders included House members Ron Dellums (a DSA member), Lane Evans, Tom Andrews, Peter DeFazio and Maxine Waters.

Many members were and continue to be linked to DSA and/or the Communist Party USA (CPUSA), IPS or other radical organizations.

From small beginnings, the CPC has grown to embrace more than 70 members of Congress and one in the Senate—Bernie Sanders.

CPC is the largest caucus and the socialist heart of the Democratic Party.[1]

Democratic Socialists of America Influence

Democratic Socialists of America played a role in organizing the CPC. According to Chicago DSA:[2]

> Congressman Bernie Sanders has been charging that these bail-outs to regimes which violate worker and civil rights are illegal under a law passed last year by Sanders and Representative Barney Frank, both leaders of the Progressive Caucus in Congress which DSA has helped to organize.

Several past and current members of CPC have been DSAers, including David Bonior, Ron Dellums, Major Owens, Carrie Meek, Danny Davis, Jan Schakowsky and Jerrold Nadler, while Bob Filner, John Conyers, John Lewis, Eleanor Holmes Norton and Bernie Sanders are among many with strong DSA connections.[3]

According to a DSA flier, the organization works with CPC to promote "progressive change."[4]

DSA is an activist organization, not a political party. From promoting single-payer health care, to combating Congress' war on the poor, to proposing democratic alternatives to the power of the transnational corporations, DSA is in the center of struggles to advance a progressive America. This struggle is carried on not only by prominent leaders, but more importantly, through the work of thousands of DSA members across the country.

As a national organization, DSA joins with its allies in Congress' Progressive Caucus and in many other progressive organizations, fighting for the interests of the average citizen both in legislative struggles and in other campaigns to educate the public on progressive issues and to secure progressive access to the media.

In 1999, the Young Democratic Socialists of James Madison University wrote:[5]

D.S.A. is not a political party, but rather works within the left wing of the Democratic Party and other third parties. D.S.A. is a driving force for the Progressive Caucus in the U.S. House of Representatives (led by Rep. Bernie Sanders, Socialist Congressman of Vermont).

Democratic Socialists of America also works hard to keep the CPC in touch with foreign socialists.

According to DSA's Democratic Left, Winter 1996:[6]

"Says leading DSAer, Christine Riddiough, "DSA supports a 'Better Way,' global dialogue that links parliamentarians of the Left, community activists and Non-Governmental Organizations working against the untrammeled rights of corporations to divide and rule. DSA tries to link the U.S. Congressional Progressive Caucus to parliamentarians of the Left in other countries."[7]

Communist Party on the Progressive Caucus

A 2002 report by Joelle Fishman, Chair, Political Action Committee, Communist Party USA, to the Party's National Board, evaluated the Congressional Progressive Caucus:[8]

Although this Caucus is not large enough to control the Congressional agenda or even to break into the media, the existence of this group of 57 members of Congress, which includes 20 members of the Congressional Black Caucus and six members of the Congressional Hispanic Caucus, provides an important lever that can be used to advance workers' issues and move the debate to the left in every Congressional District in the country.

In a report, "What Can We Learn From the Movement for Health Care Reform?" prepared as part of the discussion leading up to the CPUSA's 29th National Convention on May 21-23, 2010, Communist Party member David Bell wrote on the partial failure of the Party's health care agenda:[9]

> Did we forget the fact that many of the same unions, hundreds of locals, and the rank and file supported single payer? We also turned away from our allies in Congress, the Progressive Caucus, and John Conyers. We did not insist that single payer supporters, including Conyers, be included in the White House summit on health care reform.

Communist regard for the role of the CPC is current and ongoing.

A report praising Barack Obama and the changes wrought by him, as well as the communist connection to the Democratic Party, was delivered at the 14th International Meeting of Communist and Workers Parties, held in Beirut, Lebanon, November 22-25, 2012, by Erwin Marquit, a member of the International Department, CPUSA:[10]

> The Communist Party USA not only welcomes the reelection of President Barack Obama, but actively engaged in the electoral campaign for his reelection and for the election of many Democratic Party congressional candidates. We regarded the 2012 election as the most important in the United States since 1932, an election held in the midst of the Great Depression...

> Faced with a choice between the victory of either the Democratic Party or Republican Party, the Communist Party viewed a victory of the far-right Republican Party as an extreme disaster. In this situation, we saw the necessity of a policy of center-left alliances in order not to separate ourselves from the people's struggles for dealing with the far right onslaught, The basis of such an alliance now includes the labor movement, organizations of African Americans and Latinos, the women's movement, gay and lesbian civil rights groups, and organizations of the elderly and retirees. On some issues, these groups are joined by a few far-sighted elements of capital...

> In our electoral policy, we seek to cooperate and strengthen our relationship with the more progressive elements in [the] Democratic Party, such as the Progressive Caucus in the U.S. Congress, a group of seventy-six members of the Congress co-chaired by Raúl Grijalva, a

Latino from Arizona, and Keith Ellison, an African American Muslim from Minnesota. We also will strengthen our relationship to the Congressional Black Caucus, which has been the point of origin of innovative policies including an end to the U.S. economic blockade of Cuba, and with the Congressional Hispanic Caucus.

In its domestic policy, for example, the Progressive Caucus has put forth a program for using the public sector to deal with unemployment. It has opposed the use of the so called "war on terror" to incarcerate U.S. citizens indefinitely without criminal charges. In its foreign policy, the Progressive Caucus and the Black Caucus are outspoken in their opposition to U.S. imperialist policies abroad. The Progressive Caucus, now that Obama has been reelected, will be playing an important role in contributing to the mobilization of mass activity on critical issues to bring pressure on the Congress and administration to act on them...

While the victory of Obama is a welcome aid for us in our domestic struggles, we still face the challenge of mobilizing mass pressure on his administration to reverse the imperialist character of U.S. foreign policy. The CPUSA will pursue this formidable task vigorously in alliance with domestic progressive forces and with our comrades in the Communist and Workers' Parties and their allies throughout the world.

Institute for Policy Studies/Progressive Challenge

The Congressional Progressive Caucus is heavily influenced by the Institute for Policy Studies.

From the IPS website history page:[11]

Much of IPS's policy work is aimed at the national level, and IPS has always worked closely with, and provided analysis and model pieces of legislation to, progressive members of Congress.

Currently, IPS advises the Congressional Progressive Caucus, which, with more than 70 members, is the largest non-party Caucus.

In the late 1990s, IPS established the Progressive Challenge to utilize leftist groups including Democratic Socialists of America, Americans for Democratic Action, United Electrical Workers, NETWORK, DSA's National Jobs for All Coalition, etc. to pressure the Progressive Caucus in the "correct" direction.[12]

Chicago DSAer Bob Roman writes of a 1998 Chicago Progressive Challenge meeting attended by Illinois Congressmen Jesse Jackson Jr., Luis Gutierrez and Danny Davis:[13]

On the evening of Monday, April 21, the Progressive Challenge came to Chicago. Starting off with a town hall style meeting that brought together about 150 people in the UNITE hall at 333 S. Ashland in Chicago, the meeting was structured to present testimony from representatives of various local organizations to local Congressional members of the Progressive Caucus.

DSA was particularly well represented by the testimony of the Youth Section's International Secretary, Daraka Larimore-Hall. Daraka Larimore-Hall gave an impassioned, coherent presentation that linked the various aspects of DSA's agenda with the project at hand...

The Progressive Challenge is an effort to link the Congressional Progressive Caucus with the larger left grass roots network of single issue, constituent, labor and ideological organizations. The Institute for Policy Studies is very much the keystone organization of this project, which has brought together some 40 organizations including DSA, Americans for Democratic Action, United Electrical Workers, NETWORK, National Jobs for All Coalition to name a few. No one of these groups is a major player inside the Beltway, but together they have captured the attention of the Progressive Caucus and contributed to its growth.

"The Heart and Soul of the Democratic Party"

On Nov. 15, 2010, Earl Ofari Hutchinson of The Huffington Post conducted an interview with Rep. Lynn Woolsey, then House Chair of the Congressional Progressive Caucus. The interview reveals just how influential CPC is inside the Democratic Party:[14]

Earl: Many are not familiar with the Progressive House Caucus. How big is it?

Lynn: We had 83 members before the election. It is bicameral, with House and Senate members. It's by far the largest caucus in Congress. We lost four members this election. But we also gained a couple of new members. We will not have less than 80 members in the next Congress. The Blue Dog Democrats lost almost two-thirds of their members.

Earl: What are the major issues that the Caucus will press Congress and the Obama Administration on?

Lynn: It is clear that we represent the heart and soul of the Democratic Party. So, the first item is jobs. We have to have a robust jobs bill. One that we should have had when President Obama first took office and

149

his popularity was at its height. He had a big majority in the House and Senate. We would have doubled the amount of money allocated for the jobs bill that came out of the House, which the Senate cut to shreds. The other priority is combating the notion that the timetable for ending the Afghanistan War is 2014. The war is killing our budget, killing our people, and killing our relations with our allies.

Earl: The headline article in the Washington Post, Nov. 11, was "Liberals plan to push Obama not to compromise with GOP." Will the Progressive Caucus take the lead in pushing the president not to "compromise" with the GOP?

Lynn: We were the most productive House in recent legislative history in getting key pieces of legislation passed. Unfortunately, it was not enough. We were in such a deep economic hemorrhaging. We stopped that. But to do more we have to be even bolder in our actions. We're going to push the White House to come forth with bold steps. It's not too late now. But it will be in two years. So we're hoping that he recognizes that.

Earl: White House Press Secretary Robert Gibbs blasted liberals and progressives as the "professional Left" for continuing to criticize the president despite what he's tried to accomplish.

Lynn: I totally disagreed with him. I've won office with 70 percent of the vote, and there is a large base of voters that are progressive. This is America, and they do have the right to express themselves. And criticism or not of us, we're not going to stop our criticism on policy issues we disagree with. In fact, in line with the Congressional Black Caucus, the Congressional Hispanic Caucus, and the House Pacific Asian Caucus, we will represent a good majority of the Democrats who remain in the House.

Earl: So no compromise on the core issues?

Lynn: Any idea that we're going to reach across the aisle and surrender our Democratic ideals on jobs, health care, education, and fighting for working people and not the wealthy is not going to happen. We're not going to compromise our votes to support programs just to appear that we're compromising. We're not going to start from the right of center and go further to the right. That's not what the nation needs.

Earl: There were reports that during the health care debate the White House shunned the Progressive Caucus. How accurate is that?

Lynn: No we were not shunned. I still hear the president saying, "Lynn what's our agenda on health care and what's to be done to secure passage." We took groups of representatives to the White House more than once for meetings. We always had an open-door relationship to work with the president and the House leadership. We intend to continue to work with the president. He will have a hard time getting anything done if he doesn't have us with him. And he knows that.

But we're not going to compromise with the right on some lukewarm programs that should have been much bolder. The public option in the health care fight was a good example of that. We still feel it was given away before the health care debate really began. So we're not going to roll over. Most of our members won reelection, and in some ways we'll have an even bigger voice in the next Congress.

Members of the Congressional Progressive Caucus in the 113th Congress

Co-Chairs
- Keith Ellison (D-MN)
- Raúl Grijalva (D-AZ)

Vice Chairs
- Judy Chu (D-CA)
- David Cicilline (D-RI)
- Michael Honda (D-CA)
- Sheila Jackson Lee (D-TX)
- Jan Schakowsky (D-IL)

Whip
- Barbara Lee (D-CA)

Senate Member
- Bernie Sanders (I-VT)

House Members
- Karen Bass (D-CA)
- Xavier Becerra (D-CA)
- Earl Blumenauer (D-OR)
- Suzanne Bonamici (D-OR)
- Corrine Brown (D-FL)
- Michael Capuano (D-MA)
- Andre Carson (D-IN)

- Matt Cartwright (D-CA)
- Donna Christensen (D-VI)
- Yvette Clarke (D-NY)
- William (Lacy) Clay (D-MO)
- Emanuel Cleaver (D-MO)
- Steve Cohen (D-TN)
- John Conyers (D-MI)
- Elijah Cummings (D-MD)
- Danny Davis (D-IL)
- Peter DeFazio (D-OR)
- Rosa DeLauro (D-CT)
- Donna Edwards (D-MD)
- Sam Farr (D-CA)
- Chaka Fattah (D-PA)
- Lois Frankel (D-FL)
- Marcia Fudge (D-OH)
- Alan Grayson (D-FL)
- Luis Gutierrez (D-IL)
- Janice Hahn (D-CA)
- Jared Huffman (D-CA)
- Rush Holt, Jr. (D-NJ)
- Steven Horsford (D-NV)
- Hakeem Jeffries (D-NY)
- Eddie Bernice Johnson (D-TX)
- Hank Johnson (D-GA)
- Marcy Kaptur (D-OH)
- Joe Kennedy III (D-MA)
- Ann McLane Kuster (D-NH)
- John Lewis (D-GA)
- David Loebsack (D-IA)
- Ben Ray Lujan (D-NM)
- Carolyn Maloney (D-NY)
- Ed Markey (D-IL)
- Jim McDermott (D-WA)
- James McGovern (D-IL)

- George Miller (D-CA)
- Gwen Moore (D-WI)
- Jim Moran (D-VA)
- Jerrold Nadler (D-NY)
- Rick Nolan (D-MN)
- Eleanor Holmes Norton (D-DC)
- Frank Pallone (D-NJ)
- Ed Pastor (D-AZ)
- Chellie Pingree (D-ME)
- Mark Pocan (D-WI)
- Jared Polis (D-CO)
- Charles Rangel (D-NY)
- Lucille Roybal-Allard (D-CA)
- Linda Sanchez (D-CA)
- Jose Serrano (D-NY)
- Louise Slaughter (D-NY)
- Mark Takano (D-CA)
- Bennie Thompson (D-MS)
- John Tierney (D-IL)
- Nydia Velazquez (D-NY)
- Maxine Waters (D-CA)
- Mel Watt (D-NC)
- Peter Welch (D-VT)

Congressional Black Caucus

Founded in 1971, the Congressional Black Caucus (CBC) is the oldest of the far left caucuses in the Democratic Party. Until the advent of the Congressional Progressive Caucus in 1991, it was the major transmission belt for socialist and communist influence into the Democratic Party. Of the CBC's 42 current members, 31 are past or current members of the Congressional Progressive Caucus.[15] [16]

Virtually all of the CBC's original founders: Shirley Chisholm, John Conyers, Ron Dellums, Ralph Metcalfe, Parren Mitchell, Charlie Rangel,

Louis Stokes and District of Columbia Delegate Walter Fauntroy, had ties to the communist and socialist movements.[17]

The late Marxist academic, Manning Marable, a leader of both Democratic Socialists of America (DSA) and the Committees of Correspondence for Democracy and Socialism, wrote in 2003:[18]

> That the Congressional Black Caucus is the most progressive organized formation in national politics is not an accident. The CBC's politics are what they are because of the base they reflect.

> To the degree this base socially fragments and deteriorates and becomes splintered from the broad progressive movement is the degree to which the entire progressive movement is weakened.

Soviet Interest

The Soviet Union and its international appendages were always interested in the CBC, seeing it as a means to influence the wider Democratic Party in ways favorable to the socialist cause.[19]

For example, in March 1983, when the Soviets were desperately trying to rein in President Reagan's military buildup, a delegation from the Supreme Soviet of the USSR met for over two hours with John Conyers, Ron Dellums and other members of the CBC in Washington. The Soviet parliamentarians presented an autographed copy to the CBC of the nuclear freeze resolution that had been unanimously passed last December 22nd by the Supreme Soviet and the Central Committee of the Communist Party of the Soviet Union.

Delegation members were Alexander Subbotin, Chairman of the Peace and Disarmament Committee; Yuri Israel, Chairman of the Environmental Control Committee and Alexander Chakovsky, a Foreign Affairs Committee member and also Editor-in-Chief of Literaturnaya Gazeta.

The Soviet nuclear weapons freeze states in part: "We declare that the Soviet Union is prepared, on a basis of reciprocity with the United States of America, to freeze its nuclear arsenal." The Soviets desperately wanted sympathetic Black Congress members to promote their cause on Capitol Hill.

Influence of the Black Press Institute

Alice Palmer and her husband Buzz Palmer established the Black Press Institute (BPI) in Chicago, circa 1982. In a 1986 interview with the Communist Party USA (CPUSA) paper People's Daily World, Alice

Palmer explained BPI's role in influencing decision makers such as the Congressional Black Caucus:[20]

> After the 1960s some of us looked around and observed there was no national Black newspaper... So we started the Black Press Review. We received the Black newspapers from around the country, reprinted articles and editorials that gave a sense of the dynamics and the lives of Black people, and sent them out to the Congressional Black Caucus and other opinion leaders, saying "Look, here is what black America is thinking and doing."
>
> Since then we have moved into organizing forums and dialogues...

BPI's journal, New Deliberations, carried articles such as "Socialism is the Only Way Forward" and "Is Black Bourgeoise Ideology Enough?"

More significantly, most of BPI's nearly 50 board members, including both Palmers, were heavily tied to Soviet communism.[21]

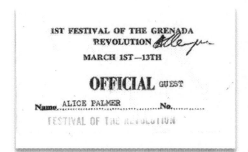

In 1980, Alice Palmer herself was invited by the Maurice Bishop-led government of the Caribbean island of Grenada to attend celebrations marking the first anniversary of the country's Marxist-Leninist "revolution."

In 1983, Alice Palmer traveled to Czechoslovakia to the Soviet front World Peace Council (WPC) Prague Assembly. She also served on the Executive Board of the WPC affiliated U.S. Peace Council, alongside 16 identified members of the CPUSA.[22]

Alice Palmer, as Editor of the Black Press Review, was elected International Organization of Journalists (IOJ) Vice President for North America at the organization's 10th Congress on October 20-23, 1986, in Prague, Czechoslovakia. She also traveled to the Soviet Union and Bulgaria during the same trip. Alice Palmer's IOJ duties were to include coordinating the activities of IOJ chapters in the U.S., Canada, Mexico and the Caribbean.[23]

Other U.S. attendees included Jan Carew of Black Press Institute, CPUSA members Simon Gerson and Jose Soler of the U.S. branch of IOJ, and Gwen McKinney and Leila McDowell of the National Alliance of Third World Journalists.[24]

The IOJ was a Soviet front operation, based in Prague until its expulsion by the Czech government in 1995.[25]

A summary of a paper by Bob Nowell, entitled, "The Role of the International Organization of Journalists in the Debate about the "New International Information Order," 1958-1978," states:[26]

> This paper examines the International Organization of Journalists (IOJ), which it identifies as a Soviet-dominated organization. The paper suggests that the IOJ has capitalized on "Third World" countries' discontent with Western news media by offering itself as the ideological leader and trainer of anti-Western journalists. It then examines the function and methods of the IOJ in the context of post-World War II communist international front organizations; reviews the IOJ's structure, publications, and training centers; and explores its role in shaping "Third World" arguments in the debate about the New Information Order. The paper argues that the IOJ's efforts generally have served Soviet foreign policy on international communications.

During her time as IOJ Vice President, Alice Palmer worked with the highest levels of the Soviet propaganda machine, with the Soviet journal Izvestia, with Romesh Chandra and the WPC and with IOJ leaders such as Kaarle Nordenstreng and Jiri Kubka.

Alice Palmer told the People's Weekly World:[27]

> The IOJ has adopted positions on nuclear weapons, trying to do away with the nuclear threat in the world.

> The IOJ stands not only for peace, but for justice as well. An example of its concern for justice is that [at] the same time I was elected a vice president; a number of African nations were also brought in. This was a real move to bring in people from frontline countries and other nations.

> I will be heading a taskforce on peace and disarmament. And at the conference I was co-moderator, with the editor of Izvestia (a Soviet government publication), of a panel on peace and the news media. We came up with some very good suggestions. A number of the people complimented the Soviet Union for its efforts towards peace in these past few years—the moratorium and other things.

> The IOJ has worked with the World Peace Council, and Kaarle Nordenstreng, Jiri Kubka and other IOJ leaders have worked closely with Romesh Chandra, the president of the World Peace Council.

IOJ delegations visit other countries to report on the peace proposals of the Soviet Union, so that people can hear about it. This by the way is an example of promoting fairness in the media.

The IOJ is the largest journalist organization in the world. Its publications are published in 10 or 15 languages, and it reaches many people all over the world. So you can see that being fair in the media is very important, particularly in the Third World.

Interestingly, Alice Palmer didn't just try to influence the CBC on behalf of the Soviet Union; she also tried to influence a future president of the United States.

By the mid-'90s, Alice Palmer was a Democratic State Senator in Illinois. After deciding to run for Congress, she hired an eager young political aspirant as her Chief of Staff. Palmer promised the young man her State Senate seat when she moved up to Congress.

In 1995, State Senator Palmer introduced her chosen successor at a gathering in the Hyde Park home of former Weather Underground terrorists Bill Ayers and Bernardine Dohrn.

"I can remember being one of a small group of people who came to Bill Ayers' house to learn that Alice Palmer was stepping down from the Senate and running for Congress," said Dr. Quentin Young, a prominent Chicago physician and Democratic Socialists of America member, of the informal gathering at the home of Ayers and his wife, Dohrn. "[Palmer] identified [Obama] as her successor."

"Obama"—Barack Obama that is.[28]

Cuban Connections

Since Soviet communism has taken a Leninist step backwards, Cuba is now the CBC's main foreign friend. Caucus members have been visiting Cuba regularly, since at least Ron Dellums' visit to Havana in 1977, to discuss "health problems" with Fidel Castro. Formal CBC delegations began in 1999.[29]

Castro on the CBC

Writing in Granma on April 7, 2009, Fidel Castro gave a history of the CBC and its relations with Cuba in, "The seven Congress members who are visiting us:"[30]

An important U.S. political delegation is visiting us right now. Its members belong to the Congressional Black Caucus (CBC) which, in practice, has functioned as the most progressive wing of the Democratic Party.

Presently, as a result of the struggles they have waged, the CBC has 42 members. Several of its representatives have maintained very active and constructive positions on Cuba-related topics.

The first Caucus delegation visited us in February 1999 and was headed by Maxine Waters; the second came in January 2000.

Influential members of that Congressional group publicly expressed their positions and carried out other positive actions during the battle for the return of young Elián to his homeland.

In May 2000, another Caucus delegation visited us. It was presided over by the then Caucus President James Clyburn, from North Carolina, and was made up of Bennie Thompson from Mississippi and Gregory Meeks from New York. These congressmen were the first to learn from me of Cuba's disposition to grant a number of scholarships to low-income youths, to be selected by the Congressional Black Caucus, so that they could come to Cuba and study medicine.

Castro went on to comment how the new Obama Administration might relax U.S. restrictions on Cuba, an opinion enthusiastically shared by members of the CBC delegation:

Within the delegation, there are opinions which are shared by all; others are personal points of view. Generally speaking, its members believe that 68% of the U.S. population favors a change of policy toward Cuba.

One of them expressed the need to take advantage of this historical moment, when the presence of an African-American president in the White House coincides with a current of opinion that favors the normalization of relations.

Another representative explained Obama's tremendous significance for the United States and the need for him to be reelected. He said that the president sees himself as a political leader who should govern all social sectors of the country. Nevertheless, he said he was sure that Obama would change Cuba policy, but that Cuba should also help him.

A fourth member of the Caucus said that despite Obama's electoral victory, U.S. society is still racist. He added that Obama represents the only opportunity that nation has to move forward and leave behind all the wrongdoings accumulated by former governments. He said that the president cannot go beyond lifting travel restrictions and allowing remittances by Cuban-Americans, because announcing an end to the blockade or the full normalization of bilateral relations would mean that he would never be reelected. He also confirmed that the anti-Cuban right wing still has enough power to attack him and prevent his reelection.

Finally, speaking frankly during a visit to the Ministry of Foreign Affairs, another legislator stated that the United States should not waste the opportunity of acknowledging that its Cuba policy has been a total failure. He added that his government should apologize to Cuba for all these years of hostility and for the blockade, because only then will we be in a position to move on together towards resolving the bilateral dispute. He affirmed that he would do whatever is possible to eliminate the blockade.

If Castro's version is to be believed, the CBC members were clearly conspiring with the Cuban leader to both help Obama's re-election and change U.S. policy towards Cuba.

Congressional Black Caucus, 113th Congress

- Karen Bass (D-CA) - also a member of the Congressional Progressive Caucus
- Sheila Jackson Lee (D-TX) - also a member of the Congressional Progressive Caucus
- Joyce Beatty (D-OH)
- Sanford D. Bishop, Jr. (D-GA)
- Corrine Brown (D-FL) - also a member of the Congressional Progressive Caucus
- G.K. Butterfield (D-NC)
- Andre Carson (D-IN) - also a member of the Congressional Progressive Caucus
- William "Mo" Cowan (D-MA)
- Donna Christensen (D-VI) - also a member of the Congressional Progressive Caucus
- Yvette Clarke (D-NY) - also a member of the Congressional Progressive Caucus

- William Lacy Clay, Jr. (D-MO) - also a member of the Congressional Progressive Caucus
- Emanuel Cleaver (D-MO) - also a member of the Congressional Progressive Caucus
- James Clyburn (D-SC)
- John Conyers, Jr. (D-MI) - also a member of the Congressional Progressive Caucus
- Elijah E. Cummings (D-MD) - also a member of the Congressional Progressive Caucus
- Danny K. Davis (D-IL) - also a member of the Congressional Progressive Caucus
- Donna Edwards (D-MD) - also a member of the Congressional Progressive Caucus
- Keith Ellison (D-MN) - also a member of the Congressional Progressive Caucus
- Chaka Fattah (D-PA) - also a member of the Congressional Progressive Caucus
- Marcia Fudge (D-OH) - also a member of the Congressional Progressive Caucus
- Al Green (D-TX)
- Alcee Hastings (D-FL) - also a member of the Congressional Progressive Caucus
- Steven Horsford (D-NV) - also a member of the Congressional Progressive Caucus
- Hakeem Jeffries (D-NY) - also a member of the Congressional Progressive Caucus
- Eddie Bernice Johnson (D-TX) - also a member of the Congressional Progressive Caucus
- Hank Johnson (D-GA) - also a member of the Congressional Progressive Caucus
- Robin Kelly (D-IL)
- Barbara Lee (D-CA) - also a member of the Congressional Progressive Caucus
- John Lewis (D-GA) - also a member of the Congressional Progressive Caucus
- Gregory Meeks (D-NY)

- Gwen Moore (D-WI) - also a member of the Congressional Progressive Caucus
- Eleanor Holmes Norton (D-DC) - also a member of the Congressional Progressive Caucus
- Donald M. Payne, Jr. (D-NJ)
- Charles B. Rangel (D-NY) - also a member of the Congressional Progressive Caucus
- Cedric Richmond (D-LA)
- Bobby Rush (D-IL) - a former member of the Congressional Progressive Caucus
- David Scott (D-GA)
- Robert C. Scott (D-VA)
- Terri Sewell (D-AL)
- Bennie Thompson (D-MS) - also a member of the Congressional Progressive Caucus
- Marc Veasey (D-TX)
- Maxine Waters (D-CA) - also a member of the Congressional Progressive Caucus
- Mel Watt (D-NC) - also a member of the Congressional Progressive Caucus
- Frederica Wilson (D-FL) - a former member of the Congressional Progressive Caucus

Congressional Hispanic Caucus

The Congressional Hispanic Caucus (CHP) was founded in December 1976 as a legislative service organization of the House of Representatives. Now it is a bicameral Congressional organization. In the 113th Congress it has 28 members, including one in the U.S. Senate. Nine CHP members are also active in the Congressional Progressive Caucus.[31]

Of the five original founders, Herman Badillo (NY), Baltasar Corrada del Río (PR), Kika de la Garza (TX), Henry B. Gonzalez (TX) and Ed Roybal (CA), Badillo was closely involved with the Democratic Socialist Organizing Committee. As a "recognize Cuba" supporter, Gonzalez was a leftist and sympathetic to the Nicaraguan Sandinistas, and Ed Roybal had a long history with the Communist Party USA.[32] [33] [34]

The pattern has continued over the years as leftists like New York Democrats Jose Serrano and Nydia Velazquez have held leadership positions.

The last two remaining anti-communist Republican members, Cuban-Americans Lincoln Diaz-Balart and Ileana Ros-Lehtinen, quit the Caucus in protest when then Chairman Xavier Becerra traveled to Cuba with CHC comrade and fellow Californian leftist, Esteban Torres, in January of 1997.

Diaz-Balart said the Congressman's trip "to meet with the Cuban tyrant," while Becerra was campaigning for Caucus Chairman, "manifested a gross insensitivity toward the pain of all who have been victims of the Cuban tyranny."

Becerra wrote in his disclosure form of his December 5-10 trip that he had gone there "to study the impact of Helms-Burton and the effects of the embargo on supplies of food and medicine."

The trip was sponsored by a Los Angeles-based leftist group called the Southwest Voter Research Institute, which picked up his $1,800 tab.

Since that time, the Congressional Hispanic Caucus has been completely dominated by the left.[35]

Congressional Hispanic Caucus Members in the 113th Congress

Officers

- Chair, Rubén Hinojosa (D-TX)
- 1st Vice Chair, Ben Ray Luján (D-NM) - also a Congressional Progressive Caucus member
- 2nd Vice Chair, Linda Sanchez (D-CA) - also a Congressional Progressive Caucus member
- Whip, Michelle Lujan Grisham (D-NM)

Current

- Xavier Becerra (D-CA) - also a Congressional Progressive Caucus member
- Tony Cardenas (D-CA)
- Joaquin Castro (D-TX)
- Jim Costa (D-CA)
- Henry Cuellar (D-TX)
- Pete Gallego (D-TX)
- Joe Garcia (D-FL)

- Raúl Grijalva (D-AZ) - also a Congressional Progressive Caucus member
- Luis V. Gutierrez (D-IL) - also a Congressional Progressive Caucus member
- Senator Bob Menendez (D-NJ)
- Grace Napolitano (D-CA)
- Gloria Negrete McLeod (D-CA)
- Ed Pastor (D-AZ) - also a Congressional Progressive Caucus member
- Pedro Pierluisi (D-PR-At Large)
- Silvestre Reyes (D-TX)
- Lucille Roybal-Allard (D-CA) - also a Congressional Progressive Caucus member
- Raul Ruiz (D-CA)
- Gregorio Sablan (D-MP-At Large)
- Loretta Sanchez (D-CA)
- José Serrano (D-NY)
- Albio Sires (D-NJ)
- Nydia Velázquez (D-NY) - also a Congressional Progressive Caucus member
- Juan Vargas (D-CA)
- Filemon Vela (D-TX)

Congressional Asian Pacific American Caucus

The Congressional Asian Pacific American Caucus was established in 1994 by California Congressman Norman Mineta. While it has some moderates in its ranks, most of its leaders from Mineta to Mike Honda, to the incumbent Judy Chu, have been "progressives."[36]

Chu came out of the orbit of the pro-China Communist Workers Party. She has used her position as Caucus leader to increase U.S.-China ties and to build strong links to the Asian Pacific American Labor Alliance, founded by her friend and former Communist Workers Party member, Kent Wong.[37]

According to Kent Wong:[38]

The formation of the Asian Pacific American Labor Alliance (APALA) in 1992 was a milestone in providing a voice for Asian Americans within the labor movement... The establishment of APALA has its roots in the Asian American Movement of the 1960s and 1970s.

Revolutionary movements of the 1960s and 1970s, domestically and internationally nurtured the Asian American Movement... Asian American activists were involved in the civil rights movement and the movement against the Vietnam War... Asian Americans led and joined Marxist study groups around the country. Asian American activists gained inspiration from the Vietnamese struggle for liberation and from the Chinese revolution and the teachings of Mao Zedong.

Asian American activists played prominent roles in a number of emerging Marxist-Leninist organizations in the 1970s... Many Asian American activists left college to work as grass roots organizers in the Asian American community, or to seek jobs in factories, to build a workers movement.

In the 1980s, Asian activists began to set up Asian labor committees in key cities around the country... From 1991 to 1992, there were a series of national meetings of Asian American trade unionists... The founding convention of the Asian Pacific American Labor Alliance in 1992, surpassed everyone's expectations...

It's probably no coincidence that the Congressional Asian Pacific American Caucus was formed just two years after the Marxist-led Asian Pacific American Labor Alliance kicked off.

Currently, CAPAC has 17 members, 7 of which are current or former Congressional Progressive Caucus comrades. Of CAPAC's 24 associate members, 8 come from the Progressive Caucus.[39]

Membership for the 113th Congress

Leadership
- Rep. Judy Chu, Chair (D-CA) - also a member of the Congressional Progressive Caucus
- Rep. Madeleine Bordallo, Vice Chair (D-Guam)
- Rep. Mark Takano, Whip (D-CA) - also a member of the Congressional Progressive Caucus
- Rep. Mike Honda, Chair Emeritus (D-CA) - also a member of the Congressional Progressive Caucus

Executive Board Members

- Sen. Mazie Hirono (D-HI) - former member of the Congressional Progressive Caucus
- Sen. Brian Schatz (D-HI)
- Rep. Xavier Becerra (D-CA) - also a member of the Congressional Progressive Caucus
- Rep. Ami Bera (D-CA)
- Rep. Eni Faleomavaega (D-American Samoa) - former member of the Congressional Progressive Caucus
- Rep. Tulsi Gabbard (D-HI)
- Rep. Al Green (D-TX)
- Rep. Colleen Hanabusa (D-HI)
- Rep. Barbara Lee (D-CA) - also a member of the Congressional Progressive Caucus
- Rep. Doris Matsui (D-CA)
- Rep. Grace Meng (D-CA)
- Rep. Gregorio Sablan (D-Northern Mariana Islands)
- Rep. Bobby Scott (D-VA)

Associate Members

- Rep. Gerry Connolly (D-VA)
- Rep. John Conyers (D-MI) - also a member of the Congressional Progressive Caucus
- Rep. Joseph Crowley (D-NY)
- Rep. Susan Davis (D-CA)
- Rep. Anna Eshoo (D-CA)
- Rep. Marcia Fudge (D-OH) - also a member of the Congressional Progressive Caucus
- Rep. Raul Grijalva (D-AZ) - also a member of the Congressional Progressive Caucus
- Rep. Janice Hahn (D-CA) - also a member of the Congressional Progressive Caucus
- Rep. Zoe Lofgren (D-CA)
- Rep. Carolyn Maloney (D-NY) - also a member of the Congressi-onal Progressive Caucus
- Rep. Alan Lowenthal (D-CA)
- Rep. Jerry McNerney (D-CA)

- Rep. Grace Napolitano (D-CA)
- Rep. Scott Peters (D-CA)
- Rep. Charles Rangel (D-NY) - also a member of the Congressional Progressive Caucus
- Rep. Lucille Roybal-Allard (D-CA) - also a member of the Congressional Progressive Caucus
- Rep. Linda Sanchez (D-CA) - also a member of the Congressional Progressive Caucus
- Rep. Loretta Sanchez (D-CA)
- Rep. Adam Schiff (D-CA)
- Rep. Brad Sherman (D-CA)
- Rep. Adam Smith (D-WA)
- Rep. Jackie Speier (D-CA)
- Rep. Eric Swalwell (D-CA)
- Rep. Chris Van Hollen (D-MD)

Populist Caucus

The Populist Caucus was founded on February 11, 2009, in the U.S. House of Representatives by Democrat Bruce Braley of Iowa. The caucus originally included 26 other Democrats in the House.

According to Braley:

> The middle class is the economic engine of America. Unfortunately, it has seen tough economic times lately, and it's time for a renewed emphasis on those issues that serve to strengthen the middle class and improve the lives of working families. That's why I established the Populist Caucus to focus exclusively on these types of issues.

Braley's Caucus is basically "prairie socialism," drawing from the "populist" movement's widespread influence in the Midwest in the late 19th and early 20th centuries.

Braley wants higher taxes on the rich, socialized health care, more government education, protectionist trade policies and strengthened "consumer protection."

Of the Populist Caucus' 28 members in its last published roster in 2010, 15 were also past or present members of the Congressional Progressive Caucus.

The Populist Caucus is simply Progressive Caucus "lite."[40] [41]

Membership, 2010

Chair

- Rep. Bruce Braley (D-IA) - Founder & Chairman

Vice-Chairs

- Rep. Peter DeFazio (D-OR) - Vice Chair of Communications - also a member of the Congressional Progressive Caucus
- Rep. Rosa DeLauro (D-CT) - Whip Vice Chair - also a member of the Congressional Progressive Caucus
- Rep. Betty Sutton (D-OH) - Vice Chair of Recruitment and Member Outreach
- Rep. Donna Edwards (D-MD) - New Media Vice Chair - also a member of the Congressional Progressive Caucus

Members

- Rep. Leonard Boswell (D-IA)
- Rep. David Loebsack (D-IA) - also a member of the Congressional Progressive Caucus
- Rep. Steve Cohen (D-TN) - also a member of the Congressional Progressive Caucus
- Rep. Peter Welch (D-VT) - also a member of the Congressional Progressive Caucus
- Rep. Keith Ellison (D-MN)
- Rep. Mazie Hirono (D-HI)
- Rep. Linda Sanchez (D-CA) - also a member of the Congressional Progressive Caucus
- Rep. Hank Johnson (D-GA) - also a member of the Congressional Progressive Caucus
- Rep. John Yarmuth (D-KY)
- Rep. Joe Courtney (D-CT)
- Rep. Bob Filner (D-CA) - also a member of the Congressional Progressive Caucus
- Rep. Mike Michaud (D-ME)
- Rep. Jan Schakowsky (D-IL) - also a member of the Congressional Progressive Caucus

- Rep. Louise Slaughter (D-NY) - also a member of the Congressi-onal Progressive Caucus
- Rep. Lloyd Doggett (D-TX)
- Rep. Marcy Kaptur (D-OH) - also a member of the Congressional Progressive Caucus
- Rep. Ben Ray Lujan (D-NM) - also a member of the Congressional Progressive Caucus
- Rep. Henry Waxman (D-CA) - also a member of the Congressional Progressive Caucus
- Rep. Jackie Speier (D-CA)
- Rep. Brad Sherman (D-CA)
- Rep. Dan Lipinski (D-IL)
- Rep. John Garamendi (D-CA)
- Rep. Paul Tonko (D-NY)

---

1 KeyWiki, "Congressional Progressive Caucus," KeyWiki, http://keywiki.org/index.php/Congressional_Progressive_Caucus (accessed May 3, 2013)
2 New Ground, "Reorganized Illinois Citizen Action," Chicago DSA, http://www.chicagodsa.org/ngarchive/ng56.html#anchor1041720 (January/February 1998)
3 KeyWiki, "Congressional Progressive Caucus," KeyWiki, http://keywiki.org/index.php/Congressional_Progressive_Caucus (accessed May 3, 2013)
4 Cliff Kincaid, "Democratic Socialists of America, Greater Detroit local," Cliff Kincaid, http://kincaidsite.com/dsa/ (accessed May 3, 2013)
5 About JMU YDA (accessed May 19, 2010)
6 Democratic Left, DSA (Winter 1996) p. 16
7 Democratic Left, DSA (Winter 1998) p. 26
8 Joelle Fishman, "Report on the 2002 Elections," CPUSA National Committee (February 22, 2002)
9 David Bell, "Convention Discussion: What Can We Learn From the Movement for Health Care Reform?" Communist Party USA, http://www.cpusa.org/convention-discussion-what-can-we-learn-from-the-movement-for-health-care-reform/ (February 2, 2010)
10 Erwin Marquit, "Contribution of the Communist Party, USA, 14th International Meeting of CWP," Solidnet.org, http://www.solidnet.org/usa-communist-party-usa/3139-14-imcwp-contribution-of-cpusa-en, (November 25, 2012)
11 IPS, "IPS History: 1963 to Today," IPS, http://www.ips-dc.org/about/history (accessed May 3, 2013)
12 New Ground, 58, http://www.chicagodsa.org/ngarchive/ng58.html (May/June 1998)
13 New Ground, 58, http://www.chicagodsa.org/ngarchive/ng58.html (May/June 1998)

14 Earl Ofari Hutchinson, "Progressive House Democrat Co-Chair Vows Democrats Won't Roll Over to the GOP," The Huffington Post, http://www.huffingtonpost.com/earl-ofari-hutchinson/progressive-house-democra_b_783414.html (November 15, 2010)

15 Congressional Black Caucus, "Directory," Congressional Black Caucus, http://cbc.fudge.house.gov/members/directory/ (accessed May 3, 2013)

16 KeyWiki, "Congressional Progressive Caucus," KeyWiki, http://www.keywiki.org/index.php/Congressional_Progressive_Caucus (accessed May 3, 2013)

17 KeyWiki, "Congressional Black Caucus," KeyWiki, http://www.keywiki.org/index.php/Congressional_Black_Caucus (accessed May 3, 2013)

18 Committees of Correspondence, "Dialogue," Committees of Correspondence, http://www.cc-ds.org/pub_arch/dialogue_pdf/winter03mitchell.pdf (Winter 2003)

19 Communist Party's Daily World (March 17, 1983) p. 3

20 People's Daily World (December 24, 1986) p. 10

21 KeyWiki, "Black Press Institute," KeyWiki, http://www.keywiki.org/index.php/Black_Press_Institute (accessed May 4, 2013)

22 USPC Conference Brochure, Yale University (November 8-10, 1985)

23 People's Daily World (December 24, 1986) pp. 10-11

24 IOJ's 10th Conference Participant's List

25 Yearbook on International Communist Affairs (1991) p. 437

26 Bob Nowell, "The Role of the International Organization of Journalists in the Debate about the "New International Information Order,"" ERIC, http://www.eric.ed.gov/ERICWebPortal/search/detailmini.jsp?_nfpb=true&_&ERICExtSearch_SearchValue_0=ED189654&ERICExtSearch_SearchType_0=no&accno=ED189654 (accessed May 4, 2013)

27 People's Daily World (December 24, 1986) p. 10

28 Ben Smith, "Obama once visited '60s radicals," Politico, http://www.politico.com/news/stories/0208/8630.html (February 22, 2008)

29 Herb Kaye, "Dialogue Delegation to Cuba," People's Weekly World (December 5, 1998) p. 8

30 Fidel Castro, "Reflections of Fidel, The seven Congress members who are visiting us," Granma, http://www.granma.cu/ingles/2009/april/mar7/Reflections-6april.html (April 7, 2009)

31 Jared Janes, "U.S. Rep. Hinojosa to chair Hispanic caucus," The Brownsville Herald, http://www.brownsvilleherald.com/news/valley/article_ccbc9026-3065-11e2-9685-0019bb30f31a.html (November 16, 2012)

32 KeyWiki, "Herman Badillo," KeyWiki, http://www.keywiki.org/index.php/Herman_Badillo (accessed May 11, 2013)

33 KeyWiki, "Henry Gonzalez," KeyWiki, http://www.keywiki.org/index.php/Henry_Gonzalez (accessed May 11, 2013)

34 KeyWiki, "Ed Roybal," KeyWiki, http://www.keywiki.org/index.php/Ed_Roybal (accessed May 11, 2013)

35 Carol Rosenberg, "Congressional travelers are attracted to Cuba," The Miami Herald, http://www.latinamericanstudies.org/us-cuba/congressional.htm (January 14, 1997)

36 KeyWiki, "Congressional Asian Pacific American Caucus," KeyWiki, http://www.keywiki.org/index.php/Congressional_Asian_Pacific_American_Caucus (accessed May 11, 2013)

37 KeyWiki, "Judy Chu," KeyWiki, http://www.keywiki.org/index.php/Judy_Chu (accessed May 11, 2013)
38 Carol Antonio, "Legacy to Liberation: Politics & Culture of Revolutionary Asian Pacific America," pp. 90-91
39 KeyWiki, "Congressional Asian Pacific American Caucus," KeyWiki, http://www.keywiki.org/index.php/Congressional_Asian_Pacific_American_Caucus (accessed May 11, 2013)
40 Bruce Braley, "Populist Caucus," Bruce Braley website, http://braley.house.gov/issues/populist-caucus, (accessed January 15, 2013)
41 KeyWiki, "Populist Caucus," KeyWiki, http://keywiki.org/index.php/Populist_Caucus (accessed May 11, 2013)

CONGRESSIONAL
BIOGRAPHIES

Eni F.H. Faleomavaega
(Non-Voting Delegate)

Eni F.H. Faleomavaega has been representing the territory of American Samoa as a Non-Voting Delegate in the United States Congress since 1989.

He is a leading member of the Congressional Asian Pacific American Caucus. In 1998, Faleomavaega was a member of the Congressional Progressive Caucus, but is no longer listed as such.[1]

Background

Faleomavaega holds a Master of Law Degree from the University of California at Berkeley and a Juris Doctorate Degree from the University of Houston, Law School. He also holds a B.A. Degree in Political Science and History from Brigham Young University at Provo, Utah and an A.A. Degree from Brigham Young University at Laie, Hawaii.[2]

Faleomavaega served as Staff Counsel to the late Congressman Phillip Burton of California. Burton was one of the most radical Congress members of his era. Burton had ties to the Communist Party USA, to the Soviet controlled World Peace Council and also to the Institute for Policy Studies.[3]

Influence

Faleomavaega was Lieutenant Governor for American Samoa from 1985 to 1988.

Prior to this, he was Deputy Attorney General for American Samoa from 1981 to 1984.

He is a member of the House Committee on Foreign Affairs, where he serves as Ranking Member on the Subcommittee on Asia, the Pacific and the Global Environment, as well as serving on the Subcommittee on the Western Hemisphere.

As a member of the Foreign Affairs Subcommittee on the Western Hemisphere, he has oversight and jurisdiction over countries including Central and South America and Canada.

Faleomavaega is also a member of the House Committee on Natural Resources, where he serves on the Subcommittee on Energy and Mineral Resources and the Subcommittee on Fisheries, Wildlife, Oceans and Insular Affairs.

He is Vice Chair of the Army Reserve Component of the National Guard and Reserve Components Caucus.

He is a member of the Congressional Human Rights Caucus, the Congressional Oceans Caucus and the Congressional Native American Caucus.[4]

Socialist Connection

In July 1996, the Democratic Socialists of America Political Action Committee endorsed Eni Faleomavaega as At Large in that year's Congressional elections.[5]

"Progressive" Connection

Eni Faleomavaega is on the list of Congressional Representatives who have participated in hearings/briefings since 1998 with the very radical Institute for Food and Development Policy/Food First, founded by Frances Moore Lappe (Democratic Socialists of America, Institute for Policy Studies) and Joseph Collins (Institute for Policy Studies), authors of the book: "Food First."[6]

Foreign Policy/National Security

Cuban Trip

Faleomavaega addressed the communist dominated United Nation's Special Committee on Decolonization (C-24) in Havana, Cuba on May 23, 2001:[7]

> I want to thank you, Mr. Chairman... and the members of the United Nations Special Committee on Decolonization for the formal invitation extended to me to participate in this session of the Special Committee. My compliments also go to the leaders and the Government of Cuba for their hospitality in hosting these meetings.

Kazakhstan Visit

In 2006, as Ranking Member of the House International Relations Subcommittee on Asia and the Pacific, Faleomavaega spoke about opposition to nuclear testing in the South Pacific and praised the government of semi-communist Kazakhstan for its "commitment to nuclear disarmament."[8]

China Delegation

U.S. Representative Judy Chu (CA-32), Chairwoman of the Congressional Asian Pacific American Caucus, led the first ever CAPAC Congressional delegation to the People's Republic of China in September of 2011.

Chairwoman Chu was accompanied by CAPAC Executive Board Members Representative Mike Honda and Representative Eni Faleomavaega.[9]

Vietnam "Agent Orange" Support

Faleomavaega was one of several members of the U.S. Congress who showed their support for Vietnamese "Victims of Agent Orange/Dioxin," during a November 2010 visit to the U.S. by a delegation from the Vietnam Association of Victims of Agent Orange/Dioxin.

For several years, the communist Vietnamese government, aided by communist fronts in the U.S., has been trying to fleece the U.S. taxpayers by using the "Agent Orange" issue.

This particular visit was at the invitation of the Communist Party infiltrated Veterans for Peace[10] and the Vietnam Agent Orange Relief & Responsibility Campaign, which is led by Merle Ratner, a leader of the Committees of Correspondence for Democracy and Socialism.[11]

Mr. Faleomavaega said that he regretted not having done enough for the victims in Vietnam and called on both the U.S. and Vietnamese government to "take responsibility and address the problem."[12]

Vietnam Visit

At a meeting with visiting U.S. Congressman Eni Faleomavaega, a member of the U.S. House External Relations Committee in Hanoi on December 19, 2012, Vietnamese Prime Minister Nguyen Tan Dung said he hopes U.S. Congressmen will continue increasing exchanges between the two legislative bodies and the two peoples and support the negotiations of the Trans Pacific Partnership.

Eni Faleomavaega, Vietnamese Prime Minister Nguyen Tan Dung, Dec. 2012

Faleomavaega promised to call on the U.S. Congress to increase the budget for decontamination and supporting Agent Orange/Dioxin victims.[13]

While receiving Eni F.H. Faleomavaega in Hanoi on December 19, 2012, Dung appreciated the Congressman's substantial contributions to Vietnam-U.S. relations over the years:

Faleomavaega has conducted hearings on the impact of Agent Orange/dioxin on Vietnamese people's health and the environment, and demanded that the U.S. government provide more assistance to dioxin victims.

Faleomavaega confirmed that he will continue lobbying the U.S. Congress to increase the budget for Dioxin clean-up efforts and assistance to Dioxin victims living in contaminated areas.[14]

---

[1] WayBackMachine, "Members of the Progressive Caucus," Democratic Socialist of America,
http://web.archive.org/web/19990219104730/www.dsausa.org/pc/pc.members.html
(accessed March 27, 2013)
[2] Eni F.H. Faleomavaega, "Biography," House.gov,
http://www.house.gov/faleomavaega/bio.shtml (accessed March 27, 2013)
[3] KeyWiki, "Phillip Burton," KeyWiki,
http://www.keywiki.org/index.php/Phillip_Burton (accessed March 27, 2013)
[4] Eni F.H. Faleomavaega, "Biography," House.gov,
http://www.house.gov/faleomavaega/bio.shtml (accessed March 27, 2013)
[5] Democratic Left (July/August 1996) p. 21
[6] Food First, "Staff Page," Food First, http://www.foodfirst.org/es/about/staff (accessed March 27, 2013)
[7] Eni F.H. Faleomavaega, "Statement of the Honorable Eni F.H. Faleomavaega, Before the United Nation's Special Committee on Decolonization (C-24)," House.gov,
http://www.house.gov/faleomavaega/speeches/undecolonization.html (May 23, 2001)
[8] Eni F.H. Faleomavaega, "Speeches," House.gov,
http://www.house.gov/faleomavaega/speeches.shtml (accessed March 27, 2013)
[9] CAPAC Press Release, CAPAC Chair Judy Chu Leads Historic First Caucus Congressional Delegation to China, http://capac-chu.house.gov/press-release/capac-chair-judy-chu-leads-historic-first-caucus-congressional-delegation-china, (September 12, 2011)
[10] KeyWiki, "Veterans for Peace," KeyWiki,
http://www.keywiki.org/index.php/Veterans_for_Peace (accessed March 27, 2013)
[11] KeyWiki, "Vietnam Agent Orange Relief & Responsibility Campaign," KeyWiki,
http://www.keywiki.org/index.php/Vietnam_Agent_Orange_Relief_%26_Responsibility_Campaign (accessed March27, 2013)
[12] BaoMoi.com, "Vietnamese AO victims receive great support in the US,"
BaoMoi.com, http://en.baomoi.com/Info/Vietnamese-AO-victims-receive-great-support-in-the-US/3/91846.epi (accessed March 27, 2013)
[13] VOVWORLD, "PM receives US Congressman Eni Faleomavaega," talkvietnam,
http://talkvietnam.com/2012/12/pm-receives-us-congressman-eni-faleomavaega/#.UUaAIjfgKUg, (December 19, 2012)
[14] Vietnamnet, "Government In Brief 20/12," Vietnam Breaking News,
http://vietnambreakingnews.com/2012/12/government-in-brief-2012/#.UUaD6TfgKUg, (December 20, 2012)

Raul Grijalva (D-AZ)

Raul M. Grijalva is a Democratic member of the United States House of Representatives, representing the 3rd District of Arizona. He is a Co-Chair on the Congressional Progressive Caucus, a member of the Congressional Hispanic Caucus and an associate member of the Congressional Asian Pacific American Caucus.[1]

Background

Raul Grijalva's father was a migrant worker from Mexico who entered the United States in 1945 through the Bracero Program and labored on southern Arizona ranches. Grijalva was born in Tucson, Arizona in 1948 and graduated from Sunnyside Magnet High School in 1967. He attended the University of Arizona and earned a Bachelor's Degree in Sociology. At the time, he was inspired into activism by United Farmworkers leader Cesar Chavez—a man trained by the father of "community organizing," Saul Alinsky.

Grijalva himself told the socialist journal, In These Times—"I'm a Saul Alinsky guy, you know, that's where I learned this stuff... There's gotta be some victories regardless of how small they are. Sometimes the victory with this group is going to be keeping the worst from happening."[2]

More than three decades later, in one of his first speeches as a member of the U.S. House of Representatives, Grijalva echoed the Communist Party USA (CPUSA) in calling for a national holiday to honor Cesar Chavez.[3]

Grijalva was a young man at the peak of El Movimiento, the Chicano civil rights movement. He had been primed for activism by his experiences in public school. "I was actually made to feel I wanted to be an Anglo," he told a Tucson newspaper in 1975. "I realized what I was doing and my embarrassment turned to anger."

Grijalva wrote for the Movimiento newspaper Coraje! (the word means both "courage" and "anger"), whose logo was a clenched-fisted Chicano saying, "My race first" and the motto, "Better to die on your feet than live on your knees." In 1969, the paper published a poem Grijalva wrote in outrage at a racist's "clammy hand of hate."

In 1970, Grijalva helped lead a confrontation with the Tucson City Council, demanding that a "people's park" be carved out of a city-owned golf course in a largely Mexican-American neighborhood. After months of protests, some of which turned violent, the group prevailed and the city built a park and community center.

Grijalva became a leader in such radical groups as the Chicano Liberation Committee, which confronted the administration of the University of Arizona with demands for the establishment of a Mexican-American Studies program and the recruitment of Chicano students and faculty.

He was also active in MEChA, Movimiento Estudiantil Chicano de Aztlan, a pro-Cuban student group that called the Southwest "Aztlan," the spiritual home of the Chicano people. The acronym, the Spanish word for "fuse," was evocative of the group's confrontational, nationalist ideology, which took its sharpest formulation in the group's motto: "Por la raza todo, fuera de la raza nada"—"For the race, everything, outside the race, nothing."

Grijalva was so militant that he alienated some members of Tucson's Mexican-American community. After losing in his first bid for elective office, a 1972 run for a seat on the school board, he began to cultivate a less radical image. Grijalva "decided to dissociate himself from RUP" and adopted "a much more middle-of-the-road image and approach" that included outreach to non-Hispanics.[4]

In 1974, Grijalva was elected to the Tucson Unified School District Board and served as a school board member until 1986. From 1975 to 1986, Grijalva was the Director of the El Pueblo Neighborhood Center and in 1987, he was Assistant Dean for Hispanic Student Affairs at the University of Arizona. Grijalva was a member of the Pima County Board of Supervisors from 1989 to 2002 and served as Chairman from 2000 to 2002.[5]

While on the Board of Supervisors, Grijalva managed a $1 billion budget and "ensured that the county was at the forefront of issues such as domestic partner benefits, labor rights and transparent government."[6]

Influence

Grijalva serves on the Committee on Natural Resources, which includes the Subcommittee on Public Lands and Environmental Regulations where he is a Ranking Member, the Subcommittee on Indian and Alaska Native Affairs and the Subcommittee on Energy and Mineral Resources. He also serves on the Committee on Education and The Workforce, which includes the Subcommittee on Early Childhood, Elementary and Secondary Education and the Subcommittee on Health, Education, Labor and Pensions. He is the Vice-Chair on the House LGBT Equality Caucus. He is on several Task Forces/Coalitions including the Sustainable Energy & Environmental Coalition.[7]

According to Raul Grijalva's official Congressional Biography, accessed September 2011:[8]

> As Co-Chair of the Congressional Progressive Caucus (CPC), Raúl has championed affordable health care for every American and has pushed for job creation measures that focus on improving America's infrastructure and economic base. He has announced his support in the 112th Congress for the Fairness in Taxation Act, which would create new tax brackets for millionaires and billionaires who currently enjoy generous loopholes that prevent them from contributing a proportionate amount to our economic recovery.

In August 2008, the Obama Campaign announced the formation of its National Latino Advisory Council, highlighting the continued growth of support Senator Obama was receiving in the Latino community nationwide. Raul Grijalva was an important member of that Council.[9]

In 2011, Raul Grijalva served on the Board of Directors of the Center for Progressive Leadership—a national civic training institute that "seeks to develop diverse leaders who can effectively advance progressive political and policy change." The Center has trained over 6,000 leaders through intensive, leadership programs primarily in state offices in Arizona, Colorado, Michigan, Ohio, Pennsylvania and Wisconsin.[10]

Communist Connections

Raul Grijalva has a long history with the Arizona Communist Party.

Anti-NAFTA Article in Communist Paper

In 1993, Raul Grijalva, identified as a member of the County Board of Supervisors for Pima County, Arizona, wrote an anti-NAFTA article entitled: "North America needs 'fair' trade," for the November 13th edition of the Communist Party USA's People's Weekly World.[11]

People's Weekly World   Saturday, November 13, 1993   7

, everywhere ...

North America needs 'fair' trade

By Raúl Grijalva

In their zeal to defeat NAFTA, some politicians have crossed the line and stoked the flames of resentment and divisiveness. They have tried to capitalize on the fact that hard times have made some Americans fearful and resentful toward immigrants in general, and Mexican people in particular.

Bohlke Connection

Raul Grijalva has worked in the past with Tucson CPUSA supporter Linda Bohlke, including during a campaign against a Tucson property manager.

In 1994, the communist-influenced Southern Arizona People's Law Center listed one of J.C. Harry's federally subsidized apartment complexes, Fry Apartments on S. Fifth Ave., as one of two complexes "in the worst overall state of repair with dangerous structural flaws that seriously threaten the health and safety of households who reside at these properties."

"I think there's a real problem with J.C. Harry in the sense that ultimately they're responsible for the fact that the apartment has run into the ground over the last 20 years," said Linda Bohlke, a community advocate with the Law Center, a "private, nonprofit group focusing on housing and economic rights."

At the request of Pima County Supervisor Raul Grijalva, an item to extend the $25,000 contract of J.C. Harry & Associates, Inc. until next April was pulled from the Council's agenda.

Grijalva wanted the company sanctioned under the county's "Bad Boy Ordinance," which essentially states that the county will not do business with companies accused of practices that harm others.

"I personally don't think we should be doing business with them at all, and if it was solely up to me, we wouldn't," Grijalva said. "I think it's important that we not do business with a company that has rundown apartments in the minority and poor areas while the ones in other areas of town are spotless. They aren't dealing with all properties equally."[12]

In August, residents of the Fry Apartments planned a 'victory' party.

The property manager, J.C. Harry & Associates, resigned August 1st, after weathering two years of pressure.

Resident Joann Madrid, who was coincidentally involved in the CPUSA-dominated Tucson Tenants Union, said she hoped the new manager would invest in much-needed improvements.

Madrid and other residents, aided by the Southern Arizona People's Law Center, had been demanding J.C. Harry clean up what they called slum conditions in the 48-unit complex. Linda Bohlke, who worked for the Law Center, was one of the main campaigners. By the time of the victory party, she had moved to assisting the Tucson Tenants Union.

Supervisor Raul Grijalva was among those who wanted to prevent the landlord from doing further work for the county.

"I felt they had a public responsibility on their part to provide safe living conditions. If they weren't doing it for Fry residents, why should we let them manage property for the county?" Grijalva said.[13]

A letter to the Tucson Citizen, October 15, 2002, on Raul Grijalva accused him of being aided by Tucson activist Linda Bohlke:[14]

> Grijalva is supported by AFSCME, the labor union for City of Tucson and Pima County employees. The principal spokeswoman for AFSCME is Linda Bohlke. Bohlke has supported Grijalva for a long time and

collected nominating signatures for Grijalva in his congressional campaign. Bohlke identifies herself on her voter registration as a Communist.

Communists Paved the Way

Arizona Communist Party Chair Lorenzo Torrez was a "pioneer in the struggle for Mexican American political representation. According to fellow Party member Steve Valencia, "I always say: before Ed Pastor and Raul Grijalva, there was Lorenzo Torrez."

Pastor and Grijalva are Arizona's first two Mexican American members of the U.S. Congress. But Torrez ran for Congress before they ran and also boldly ran against Republican Senator Barry Goldwater.

"Lorenzo told us it is time for these majority Latino districts to be represented by a Mexican American," said Valencia. "He wanted voters to see a Latino name on the ballot."

When Pastor declared his candidacy, Torrez rallied the Tucson Communist Party club to join in the effort. Pastor's victory in 1991 set the state for Grijalva's election in 2002."[15]

"People Gain in Arizona Primaries"

The People's Weekly World, September 21, 2002 issue, carried an article on page 8: "People gain in Arizona primaries." The column by local Party leader, Joe Bernick, dealt mainly with Raul Grijalva's victory in the recent Democratic Party primary:[16]

> The tireless efforts of hundreds of grassroots volunteers dealt a blow to the corporate establishment here and their attempt to dominate Southern Arizona politics in the Sept. 10 primary election.

> Long-time progressive Raul Grijalva routed seven other candidates to win the Democratic nomination for CD-7, one of Arizona's two new Congressional seats.

> Grijalva expects to become only the second Mexican American ever elected to Congress from Arizona, and the first from Southern Arizona. As a Pima County Supervisor and Tucson School Board member Grijalva consistently fought for working peoples' interests.

> The Grijalva campaign was a textbook example of how to conduct a peoples' campaign, beginning with its name: "A whole lot of people for Grijalva." Hundreds of people came out seven days a week, sometimes twice on Saturday, to wear out tons of shoe leather.

Communist Report on Grijalva Victory

At a meeting of the National Board of the CPUSA in South Chicago, on the last weekend of January 2003, an unnamed Arizona AFSCME activist stated: "Using street heat tactics, all of labor worked to back one candidate, Raul Grijalva, in Tucson... And we won!"[17]

Thorpe on Grijalva Campaign

Tucson Communist Party supporter, Susan Thorpe, wrote an article covering the 2002 Grijalva campaign for the People's World, November 8, 2003, page 5, entitled: "Arizona: Grassroots can beat big bucks."[18]

> Nevertheless, here in Tucson, we are gearing up for local elections in 2003 and the presidential election ahead in 2004 by using the same tactics we did in 2002 to get Raul Grijalva elected to Congress.... Congressman Raul Grijalva is proving to be a wonderful voice for the people of Arizona. And our movement and those important connections made during his campaign are still alive in Tucson.

Arizona Together

Arizona made history on November 7, 2006, when its voters became the first in the nation to reject a constitutional ban on same-sex marriage—Proposition 107. Wrote Arizona Communist Party leader and Arizona Together activist, Joe Bernick:[19]

> Why Arizona? How come voters in more liberal states have voted for similar hateful laws while conservative Arizona voted no?

> So how did we do it? The answer is: educating, organizing and mobilizing... Congressman Raul Grijalva appeared on radio ads calling Prop. 107 an attack on working families. The Grijalva campaign worked closely with Arizona Together, using its literature in their extensive door-to-door canvassing.

Grijalva's Daughter Mixes with Communists

On Wednesday, September 15th, 2010, a reception in support of Sunnyside Unified School District School Board member and Communist Party affiliate, Eva Carrillo Dong, was held at Rigo's Mexican Restaurant in Tucson.

Key attendees included Sunnyside board member Magdalena Barajas, the Hon. Dan Eckstrom, County Supervisor Richard Elias, Tucson City

Council Member Richard Fimbres, TUSD board member and daughter of Raul Grijalva, Adelita Grijalva, Tucson City Council member Regina Romero, Joe Bernick, Janet L. Valencia and Steve Valencia. Bernick and both Valencias were all affiliated with the Arizona District Communist Party USA.[20]

"Progressive" Connections

21st Century Democrats Support

Grijalva was endorsed by 21st Century Democrats in the 2002 election cycle—the PAC founded by Institute for Policy Studies and Democratic Socialists of America affiliates and run by DSA member Jim Scheibel for many years.[21]

Take Back America Conferences

Raul Grijalva was on the list of 129 speakers at the 2003, Take Back America conference, which was organized by the Institute for Policy Studies and Democratic Socialists of America-dominated Campaign for America's Future.[22]

Grijalva was back in 2004 and addressed the newly named America's Future Now! conference in 2009.[23]

IPS Awards Ceremony

Every year, the Institute for Policy Studies gives two awards—one domestic and one international—to what are described as "heroes of the progressive movement."

In 2011, the International Award was presented by Raul Grijalva to Bethlehem, The Migrant's Shelter (Mexico). The award ceremony was presented at the National Press Club in Washington, D.C. on October 12th, 2011.[24]

Progressive Democrats of America

In 2009, Raul Grijalva served on the Advisory Board of the Democratic Socialists of America/Institute for Policy Studies-dominated Progressive Democrats of America.[25]

Progressive Democrats of America Endorsement

In 2012, Raul Grijalva (AZ-3) was one of fourteen leftist Congressional and Senate candidates endorsed and supported by Progressive Democrats of America.[26]

The Peoples' Inauguration

Progressive Central: The People's Inauguration was held Saturday, January 19, 2013, at the UDC David A. Clarke School of Law in Washington, D.C. The event was sponsored by Progressive Democrats of America, The Nation, National Nurses United, Democrats.com and Busboys and Poets. The event was advertised and promoted by the IPS.

The 1:00 pm - 2:10 pm session: "Organizing the Progressive Movement Inside and Outside the Democratic Party," was moderated by socialist, John Nichols and featured Rep. Raul Grijalva; Rep. Mark Pocan;

Thom Hartmann, PDA National Board/Radio/TV Host and Author; and Lori Wallach, Public Citizen's Global Trade Watch.[27]

Rep. Raul Grijalva, "Co-Chair of the Congressional Progressive Caucus," told the socialist journal, In These Times, at the event that he was worried his Party leadership might agree to a future budget deal that could include cuts to Social Security.

"I'm concerned. I'm concerned," Grijalva said. "But none of that's going to pass without Democrats, so I think for the Progressive Caucus and our 70-odd members, holding the line can be huge leverage in this discussion. I'm optimistic about the role we can play. This is where the outside-inside [strategy] is so critical, because the pressure from the outside, not just on progressive members of Congress, but on all members of Congress, is going to be critical to holding the line."[28]

Foreign Policy/National Security

Staffers' 2010 Trip to Latin America

Rep. Grijalva sent Daniel Brito to Honduras and El Salvador for three days in May/June 2010. The trip was courtesy of a $4,107.39 grant from the Institute for Policy Studies-connected Center for Democracy in the Americas, to "assess the situation in Honduras and El Salvador and current U.S. policy implications in the countries."[29]

Council for a Livable World

The Council for a Livable World, the anti-military, pro-disarmament PAC, founded by reported Soviet agent, Leo Szilard, supported Grijalva in his 2010 Congressional election campaign.[30]

---

1 KeyWiki, "Raul Grijalva," KeyWiki,
http://keywiki.org/index.php/Ra%C3%BAl_Grijalva (accessed January 12, 2012)
2 Cole Stangler, "Progressive Democrats: Inside and Outside," ITT,
http://www.inthesetimes.com/article/14463/progressive_democrats_inside_and_outsid
e, (January 22, 2013)
3 Center for Immigration Studies, "Raul Grijalva Biography," Center for Immigration
Studies, http://www.cis.org/grijalva, (accessed January 2, 2013)
4 Center for Immigration Studies, "Raul Grijalva Biography," Center for Immigration
Studies, http://www.cis.org/grijalva, (accessed January 2, 2013)
5 Raul M. Grijalva, "Biography," House.gov, http://grijalva.house.gov/biography/
(accessed September 21, 2011)

6 Raul M. Grijalva, "Biography," House.gov, http://grijalva.house.gov/biography/ (accessed September 21, 2011)

7 Raul M. Grijalva, "Committee, Caucus and Task Force Membership," House.gov, http://grijalva.house.gov/committee-caucus-and-task-force-membership/ (accessed September 21, 2011)

8 Raul M. Grijalva, "Biography," House.gov, http://grijalva.house.gov/biography/ (accessed September 21, 2011)

9 Roots Wire, "Patricia Madrid Named Obama's National Latino Advisory Council," Roots Wire, http://rootswire.org/conventionblog/patricia-madrid-named-obamas-national-latino-advisory-council (accessed October 18, 2010)

10 KeyWiki, "Center for Progressive Leadership," KeyWiki, http://www.keywiki.org/index.php/Center_for_Progressive_Leadership (accessed January 31, 2011)

11 People's Weekly World (November 13, 1993) p. 7

12 Rhonda Bodfield, "County criticizes rental manager," Tucson Citizen, http://tucsoncitizen.com/morgue2/1994/04/07/200876-county-criticizes-rental-manager/, (April 7, 1994)

13 Jennifer Katleman, "Tenants celebrate landlord's leaving," Tucson Citizen, http://tucsoncitizen.com/morgue2/1994/08/17/44691-tenants-celebrate-landlord-s-leaving/, (August 17, 1994)

14 Tucson Citizen, "Grijalva not fit to be in Congress," Tucson Citizen, http://tucsoncitizen.com/morgue2/2002/10/15/215143-letters-to-the-editor/, (October 15, 2002)

15 Tim Wheeler, "Lorenzo Torrez, copper miner, Communist leader, dies at 84," People's World, http://peoplesworld.org/lorenzo-torrez-copper-miner-communist-leader-dies-at-8/, (January 9, 2012)

16 People's World (September 21, 2002) p. 8

17 People's Weekly World, "Communist meet heats up in Chicago," People's Weekly World (February 1, 2003)

18 Susan Thorpe, "Arizona: Grassroots can beat big bucks," People's World (November 8, 2003) p. 5

19 Joe Bernick, "How Arizona defeated the hatemongers," People's World, http://peoplesworld.org/how-arizona-defeated-the-hatemongers/ (December 8, 2006)

20 Eva Carrillo Dong, "A Reception for Eva Carrillo Dong for SUSD Governing Board," Facebook, https://www.facebook.com/events/151873911501271/ (September 15, 2010)

21 21st Century Democrats, "Raul Grijalva Biography," 21st Century Democrats, http://21stcenturydems.org/candidates/past-candidates/, (2006)

22 Campaign For America's Future, "Archives – 2003 Speakers," Campaign For America's Future, http://www.ourfuture.org/node/13211 (accessed June 17, 2010)

23 Confabb website, "Take Back America 2003 Speakers," Confabb website, http://now2009.confabb.com/conferences/82401-americas-future-now/speakers (accessed July 13, 2010)

24 IPS website, http://salsa.democracyinaction.org/o/357/p/salsa/event/common/public/?event_KEY=69486, (October 12, 2011)

25 Progressive Democrats of America, "Advisory Board," Progressive Democrats of America, http://pdamerica.org/tools/pda/Adboard.pdf (accessed 2009)

26 KeyWiki, "Raul Grijalva," KeyWiki, http://keywiki.org/index.php/Ra%C3%BAl_Grijalva (accessed January 12, 2012)

27 PDA website, http://hq-
salsa3.salsalabs.com/o/1987/p/salsa/event/common/public/index.sjs?event_KEY=6957
5, (accessed January 15, 2013)
28 Cole Stangler, "Progressive Democrats: Inside and Outside," ITT,
http://www.inthesetimes.com/article/14463/progressive_democrats_inside_and_outsid
e, (January 22, 2013)
29 Legistorm, "Center for Democracy in the Americas – Sponsor of Congressional
Travel," Legistorm,
http://www.legistorm.com/trip/list/by/sponsor/id/10693/name/Center_for_Democracy_
in_the_Americas/page/2.html (accessed August 30, 2010)
30 Council for a Livable World, "Meet the Candidates," Council for a Livable World,
http://livableworld.org/support/meet_candidates/ (accessed January 13, 2012)

Kyrsten Sinema (D-AZ)

Kyrsten Sinema entered Congress with the 2012 elections as an Arizona Democrat for the new 9th District.[1]

Background

Kyrsten Sinema was born in Tucson, Arizona in 1976 and was raised in the Dobson Ranch area, in a conservative Mormon family.

At age 16, Sinema graduated as her high school's valedictorian and went on to earn a Bachelor's Degree in social work from Brigham Young University.[2]

While advocating for "marginalized and oppressed communities in the state," she earned her Master's Degree in Social Work and later went on to graduate Cum Laude with her Juris Doctorate from Arizona State University. In addition, she was hired as an adjunct professor in the School of Social Work at ASU at the age of 26 to teach Master's level courses in fundraising and political and social policy. Kyrsten Sinema was elected to the House of Representatives in 2004, after nearly a decade of professional practice as a social worker and "social justice" advocate.[3]

Sinema was a social worker from 1995 to 2002; she practiced in the Washington Elementary School District before becoming a criminal defense lawyer in 2005. Sinema has also been an adjunct instructor in the Arizona State University School of Social Work since 2003.[4]

She became a Democratic Arizona legislator in 2005 following a stint, in the early 2000s, as the spokesperson for Ralph Nader's Green Party USA.[5]

Influence

Sinema serves on numerous community and national boards, including as Board President of Community Outreach and Advocacy for Refugees, the Center for Progressive Leadership and the Young Elected Officials' Network.

She is the recipient of awards for her political leadership, including the NAACP Civil Rights Award, AZ Hispanic Community Forum Friend of the Year, Planned Parenthood Legislative CHOICE Award, Sierra Club's Most Valuable Player and the AZ Public Health Association Legislator of the Year.[6]

In 2010, Kyrsten Sinema was serving her second term in the State House, teaching at Arizona State University, practicing criminal defense law while consulting with the state on LGBTQ legislation and initiatives.[7]

Sinema was part of a national team of state elected officials who worked to help craft America's new health care law to "meet the needs of states, not the federal government."

Thanks in part to her work in "improving the bill," Sinema was invited by the President to attend the signing in March of 2010.[8]

Circa 2008, Sinema and three colleagues joined together to form a "Progressive Caucus" for the House of Representatives of the Arizona State Legislature.[9]

In the House of Representatives, Sinema serves on the Committee on Financial Services, which includes the Subcommittee on Housing and Insurance and the Subcommittee on Oversight and Investigations.

In 2010, Kyrsten Sinema served on the Board of Directors of the Progressive States Network, a George Soros funded organization which seeks to "transform the political landscape by sparking progressive actions at the state level."[10]

Kyrsten Sinema's first book, "Unite and Conquer: How to Build Coalitions that Win and Last," was released in July of 2009 by Berrett-Koehler Publishers.

Communist Connections

Endorsing Communist Party Causes

Kyrsten Sinema was a signatory to an advertisement: "May Day and Cinco de Mayo greetings," placed in the Communist Party USA (CPUSA) paper People's Weekly World on May 4, 2002. Such ads were traditionally placed in the Communist Party paper every May Day, sponsored by local party clubs, members or supporters:

> Arizona's progressive community extends May Day and Cinco de Mayo greetings to all our friends across the country. We commit ourselves to resist the Bush Administration's drive for ever increasing military spending and a never-ending state of war. We must redouble our efforts to build a people's coalition that will drive the ultra right out of Congress next November.

Co-signing the advertisement with Sinema were CPUSA members Joe Bernick, Jack Blawis, Lem Harris, Lorenzo Torrez, Anita Torrez, Carolyn Trowbridge, Steve Valencia, the Tucson and East Valley Clubs of the Communist Party USA and the party fronts: the Arizona Peace Council and the Salt of the Earth Labor College.

People's Weekly World   Saturday, May 3, 2003   17

nco de Mayo

Day and Cinco de Mayo
. We call for peace with
ncreasing military spend-
st redouble our efforts to
at will struggle to redirect
rather than perpetuating

Daniel Brockert • Anne & Will Brenner
echer • Rolande Baker • Albert Clark
Druan • Andree Diaz • Andrew DeSousa
Sean Fowlkes • Chris Ford • Mike Flower
ne • Tom Hinchion • Martin Hernandez
• Mike Kreta • Sahee Kil • Klara Kelley
lae • Nancy Myers • Bernie Muller
McElwain • Jane Martin & Bob Vint
Pettit • Ellen E. Rojas • Jose Ramos
Smith • Ray Siqueiros • Kyrsten Sinema
lyn Trowbridge • Lorenzo & Anita Torrez
Vietti • Steve Valencia • Julie Valencia

This support for the communist cause was not a "one off" or an aberration. In 2003, Sinema again put her name to the Arizona Communist Party's May Day greetings page.

Arizona Together

Shortly after her election in 2004, Kyrsten Sinema and former State Representative Steve May formed Arizona Together, the statewide coalition to defeat Arizona's same-sex marriage ban, During the course of the two years leading up to the 2006 election, Sinema led the campaign's effort to "raise nearly $3 million, research, craft and deliver a winning message and build a broad-based, statewide coalition of community leaders, organizations and businesses."[11]

Arizona made history on Nov. 7, 2006, when its voters became the first in the nation to reject a constitutional ban on same-sex marriage. Explained Arizona Communist Party USA leader and Arizona Together activist Joe Bernick:[12]

> So how did we do it? The answer is: educating, organizing and mobilizing.

> As soon as proponents started circulating petitions to put 107 on the ballot, opponents brought out their own clipboards, signing up thousands of volunteers. Arizona Together emerged as the campaign committee, chaired by progressive state Rep. Kyrsten Sinema.

"Progressive" Connections

Progressive Democrats for America

Kyrsten Sinema is the only state legislator to serve as a board member of the Institute for Policy Studies (IPS)/Democratic Socialists of America (DSA)-dominated Progressive Democrats of America.[13]

Take Back America Conferences

Kyrsten Sinema was on the list of speakers at the 2008 Take Back America conference, which was organized by the IPS and DSA-initiated Campaign for America's Future.

On March 17, 2008, DSA affiliate Rick Perlstein, State Representative Kyrsten Sinema and Marxist Mike Zielinski spoke in a session entitled: "The Crackup of Conservatism."[14]

Sinema also addressed the succeeding Campaign for America's Future organized America's Future Now conference in 2009.[15]

Foreign Policy/National Security

Anti-Israel Activities

Kyrsten Sinema's anti-Israel activism began in the early 2000s when she organized for the Arizona Alliance for Peace and Justice, a group whose members have denounced Israel's "disproportionate" use of "violence and oppression." The group also criticized U.S. military aid to Israel as well as the expansion of Israeli settlements "into Palestinian lands."

Sinema later urged supporters of the AAPJ to deluge the phone lines of a radio show hosted by "an unapologetic unconditional supporter of Israeli policy."

Sinema formerly served as a spokeswoman for Women in Black, an anti-war group that was founded in part to support Palestinians during the Intifada.[16]

Council for a Livable World Support

Kyrsten Sinema was supported by the far left, anti-U.S. military Council for a Livable World in her successful 2012 Congressional campaign.

According to the Council for a Livable World website:[17]

> Outside of state government, Sinema has been a leader in Arizona's anti-war movement. In the days after the 9/11 attacks, Sinema helped to organize Arizona progressives who were alarmed by widespread calls for invasion. Sinema was at the forefront of Arizona's grassroots opposition to the war in Iraq.

> Sinema's principled opposition to war extends to the movement for a world free of nuclear weapons. As an Arizona state legislator she actively lobbied Senators John McCain (R) and John Kyl (R) for ratification of the New START nuclear reductions treaty. She supports

ratification of the Comprehensive Nuclear Testing Ban and opposes the development of new nuclear weapons.

1 KeyWiki, "Kyrsten Sinema," KeyWiki, http://keywiki.org/index.php/Kyrsten_Sinema (accessed March 31, 2013)
2 Nation Journal, Arizona, 9th District, http://www.nationaljournal.com/congress-legacy/arizona-9th-house-district-20121101, (accessed March 21, 2013)
3 CPL Arizona, "Representative Kyrsten Sinema 2010 Arizona Faculty," Center For Progressive Leadership, http://www.progressiveleaders.org/states/arizona/faculty/sinema.html (accessed February 21, 2010)
4 Nation Journal, Arizona, 9th District, http://www.nationaljournal.com/congress-legacy/arizona-9th-house-district-20121101, (accessed March 21, 2013)
5 Adam Kredo, "Adult Sinema," The Washington Free Beacon, http://freebeacon.com/adult-sinema/, (April 20, 2012)
6 Americans United for Sparation of Church and State – Greater Phoenix Chapter, "Mission Statement," Americans United for Separation of Church and State, http://au-gp.org/?page_id=128 (accessed March 31, 2013)
7 CPL Arizona, "Representative Kyrsten Sinema 2010 Arizona Faculty," Center For Progressive Leadership, http://www.progressiveleaders.org/states/arizona/faculty/sinema.html (accessed February 21, 2010)
8 Kyrsten Sinema, "Making Quality Health Care Affordable," Sinema for Congress, http://kyrstensinema.com/issues/health-care/, (accessed January 30, 2013)
9 Progressive Arizona, "Profiles in Vision Arizona State Reps Form Progressive Legislative Caucus," Progressive Arizona, http://www.progressiveazdems.org/azlege01.html (accessed February 21, 2011)
10 Progressive States Network, "Board of Directors," Progressive States Network, http://www.progressivestates.org/inside_psn/board (accessed September 1, 2010)
11 CPL Arizona, "Representative Kyrsten Sinema 2010 Arizona Faculty," Center For Progressive Leadership, http://www.progressiveleaders.org/states/arizona/faculty/sinema.html (accessed February 21, 2010)
12 Joe Bernick, "How Arizona defeated the hatemongers," People's World, http://peoplesworld.org/how-arizona-defeated-the-hatemongers/ (December 9, 2006)
13 CPL Arizona, "Representative Kyrsten Sinema 2010 Arizona Faculty," Center For Progressive Leadership, http://www.progressiveleaders.org/states/arizona/faculty/sinema.html (accessed February 21, 2010)
14 Campaign For America's Future, "Take Back America 2008 – Agenda," Campaign for America's Future, http://www.ourfuture.org/takebackamerica/2008/agenda/ (accessed May 11, 2010)
15 Confabb website, "America's Future Now 2009 Speakers," Confabb website, http://now2009.confabb.com/conferences/82401-americas-future-now/speakers (accessed on July 13, 2010)
16 Adam Kredo, "Adult Sinema," The Washington Free Beacon, http://freebeacon.com/adult-sinema/, (April 20, 2012)
17 Council for a Livable World, "Kyrsten Sinema," Council for a Livable World, http://livableworld.org/elections/2012/candidates/house/ksinema/ (accessed 2012)

Barbara Boxer (D-CA)

Barbara Boxer is the Junior Democratic member of the United States Senate, representing California.[1]

Background

Barbara Boxer became a United States Senator in January of 1993, after 10 years of service in the House of Representatives and 6 years on the Marin County Board of Supervisors. In November 2010, she was reelected to her fourth term in the Senate.[2]

Boxer grew up in Brooklyn, before moving with her husband, Stewart, to San Francisco in 1965 and then to Marin County in 1968. In 1972, Boxer ran for the Board of Supervisors and lost to an incumbent Republican. She then worked for far left Democratic Congressman John Burton. In 1976, she ran again for the board and won. In 1982, she ran for the House and was easily elected.[3]

She was elected to the U.S. Senate in 1992.

Influence

Senator Boxer was the first woman to Chair the U.S. Senate's Committee on Environment and Public Works.

Boxer also Chairs the Senate Select Committee on Ethics, making her the only sitting Senator to Chair two Senate committees. She is a senior member of the Senate Commerce Committee and the Senate Foreign Relations Committee, where she chairs the first Subcommittee ever to focus on Global Women's Issues.

Senator Boxer is also a member of the Democratic leadership in the Senate, serving as the Chief Deputy Whip since 2005, which gives her the job of lining up votes on key legislation.

Boxer is currently fifteenth in seniority in the United States Senate.[4] [5]

Communist Connections

John Burton Protégé

During the late 1970s, Barbara Boxer worked as an aide to U.S. Representative John Burton—a man often described as Boxer's political mentor. When Burton retired unexpectedly in 1982, Boxer ran for the House and was easily elected.[6]

John and his brother Phillip Burton were two of the most radical representatives to ever serve in the U.S. Congress. Both were tied to the Soviet front World Peace Council (WPC), and to the Communist Party USA (CPUSA).[7] [8]

In 1978, Congressmen John Burton, Ted Weiss, Ron Dellums, John Conyers, Don Edwards, Charles Rangel and others... attended a WPC organized meeting on Capitol Hill.

WPC delegation members included President Romesh Chandra, a leading member of the Communist Party of India; KGB Colonel Radomir Bogdanov and Oleg Kharkhardin of the Communist Party of the Soviet Union International Department.[9] [10]

John Burton, Barbara Boxer

Sponsors of the Communist Party's 1996 Bay Area People's Weekly World Banquet at His Lordship's Berkeley Marina included then California State Assemblyman John L. Burton.[11]

On May 9, 1998, the People's Weekly World held a centennial festive tribute celebrating the life of well known Communist Party scholar and singer, Paul Robeson. Speakers included Communist Party Vice Chair Jarvis Tyner, retired ILWU International Rep. and communist Abba

Ramos, Northern California Communist Party leader Marilyn Bechtel and Northern California Young Communist League Co-Chair Amie Fishman.

Among the event's co-sponsors was then California Senate President Pro Tem John L. Burton—who is incidentally now the Chair of the California Democratic Party.[12]

Burton Inspired "Rage for Justice" Award

Consumer Watchdog hosts the annual Rage for Justice Awards to honor the "heroes and heroines of the public interest movement." The awards are named after Congressman Phillip Burton, one of the "most productive and driven progressive legislators in American history."

The 2008 Award went to U.S. Senator Barbara Boxer. She was introduced by Phillip Buton's equally radical brother, and her old boss and political mentor, John Burton.[13]

Eulogy for Communist Carlton Goodlett

In February of 1997, Barbara Boxer read a tribute to another icon of the Northern California left, Carlton Goodlett, into the Senate Record:

> Mr. President, I rise today to celebrate the life of Dr. Carlton Goodlett. Dr. Goodlett recently passed from this life, leaving it richer and more decent for his presence. The challenge of his voice, conscience, and healing hand is the legacy of a singular man.

> To say that Carlton Goodlett was multitalented is to understate his genuinely remarkable energy and versatility. He was a medical doctor, held a doctorate in psychology and published a newspaper for nearly 50 years. He was local president of the NAACP and worked side by side with many of the giants of the civil rights era…

> At the Sun-Reporter, he nurtured numerous fledgling writers, giving them the opportunity to develop their professional talents while simultaneously providing readers with invaluable insight into a vibrant community at play, at work, in worship, and in struggle. As a physician, he helped guide young men and women into medicine. As a civil rights leader and advocate for peace, he appealed to conscience of leaders and citizens alike.

> Dr. Goodlett considered life and community to be sacred. Though his time has come and gone, his message of hope and fairness endures. For all he did for others, he will forever be treasured and missed.

Boxer failed to mention Goodlett's long-time Communist Party USA membership, his heavy involvement with the Soviet-controlled, anti-US military World Peace Council, his receipt of the Lenin Peace Prize in Moscow, on April 22, 1970, or his ties to Bay Area Marxist cult leader Jim Jones—of Jonestown Massacre infamy.[14]

Succeeded Alan Cranston

When far left Democratic California Senator Alan Cranston retired in 1992, Boxer sought his seat. In the November general election, she defeated Bruce Herschensohn, a Republican whose candidacy unraveled in the final weeks of the race after reports surfaced that he had visited a nude bar.

Interestingly, Cranston, an extreme left legislator, also fell under suspicion of communist ties early in his career.

In World War II, Cranston was Chief of the Foreign Language Division of the Office of War Information, the U.S. information and propaganda organization, which was heavily penetrated by communists.

Cranston recommended that the OWI hire David Karr, as "a senior liaison officer working with other Federal agencies." Karr had been writing for the Communist Party newspaper, The Daily Worker, as well as for Albert Kahn, an author who was later revealed in Congressional testimony to be a Soviet agent.

In spite of this record, Cranston recommended Karr for employment, claiming that he knew he had worked for The Daily Worker, but did not know he was a communist.

After the War, Karr launched a successful career in international finance and became even more active in pro-communist work. In 1975, for example, he arranged a $250 million credit for the Soviet Foreign Trade Bank.

His main contact in Moscow was reported to be Djerman Gvishiani, Deputy Chairman of the Soviet State Committee for Science and Technology and son-in-law of Soviet Premier Kosygin.

Cranston remained a long-time friend of Karr and said later that Karr "had a strong social conscience that made him an intense promoter of Detente."[15]

Throughout his career in the Senate, Cranston was one of the most radical in opposing aid to countries fighting Communist insurgencies such as South Viet Nam and El Salvador, and for refusing to support anti-communist movements in Communist dictatorships such as Nicaragua, Angola, Mozambique, etc.[16]

He was also supported by the anti-U.S. military, Council for a Livable World, founded by reported Soviet agent Leo Szilard.[17]

Socialist Connections

DSA Support in '92

```
DSA  CALIFORNIA                                   1102 N. BRAND BLVD. #20
     DEMOCRATIC SOCIALISTS OF AMERICA                  GLENDALE, CA. 91202

Dear California DSA Member:
     There will be a state meeting of California DSA on Sunday,
August 2, 1992 from 9:00 AM - 5:00 PM at the Student Union of
Stanford University in Palo Alto California.
     The agenda will address:

          DSA's Role in the November Election

          -- the Barbara Boxer Senatorial Campaign

          -- DSA member Rachel Dewey's campaign for
             State Senate in Los Angeles

          -- Opposition to Governor Wilson's vindictive
             initiative slashing payments to welfare
             mothers and their children
```

California Democratic Socialists of America discussed its role in the Barbara Boxer Senate campaign, at an August 2 1992 meeting in the Student Union at Stanford University, Palo Alto.

21ˢᵗ Century Democrats

The mission of 21st Century Democrats, a DSA led Political Action Committee, is to build a "farm team" of progressive populists who will be the future leaders of the Democratic Party.[18]

The organization supported Barbara Boxer in 1998 and in 2010.

"Progressive" Connections

Borosage on Board

Institute for Policy Studies (IPS) leader Robert Borosage has served as an Issues Adviser to several progressive political campaigns, including those of Senators Carol Moseley Braun (a Communist Party supporter and DSA affiliate), Paul Wellstone (a DSA supporter) and Barbara Boxer.[19]

Like some other key people in Boxer's career, Borosage has a lot of time for Moscow.

On April 10, 1982, an IPS-sponsored group visited Moscow for a week of meetings with high-level Soviet officials responsible for disseminating disinformation and propaganda for U.S. consumption. The IPS group was led by its principal spokesman, Marcus Raskin and by Robert Borosage, IPS Director, National Lawyers Guild activist and former Director of the Center for National Security Studies.[20]

Russia Today, the Moscow-funded propaganda channel, aired a special program on February 22, 2012, on how progressives in the U.S. can "Take Back the American Dream" by defeating Republicans. The propaganda effort was broadcast throughout the United States and produced in collaboration with IPS allied groups such as the Campaign for America's Future and Demos.

The "National Teach-In to Take Back the American Dream," featured Democratic Socialists of America affiliate Robert Reich (a former U.S. Secretary of Labor); Heather McGhee of Demos and Robert Borosage of the Campaign for America's Future.[21]

Take Back America Conferences

Barbara Boxer was on the list of 237 speakers at the 2007 Take Back America conference, which was organized by the IPS and DSA initiated Campaign for America's Future.[22]

IPS Inspired Attack Ad

In California's 2010 Senate race, both incumbent Senator Barbara Boxer and Republican challenger, Carly Fiorina, used Executive Excess Reports to attack one another. The Institute for Policy Studies has published these annual reports on CEO pay for 17 years.

Friends of Barbara Boxer cited IPS' Executive Excess 2003 Report in an attack ad on Fiorina.

As the advertisement pointed out, Fiorina laid off 25,700 workers in 2001 and then saw her pay jump 231 percent, from $1.2 million in 2001 to $4.1 million in 2002. Whereas, previous HP heads had strived to avoid layoffs, IPS pay analyst Sarah Anderson described Fiorina as "like the Annie Oakley of the corporate world, coming in with her guns blazing."[23]

CODEPINK

CODEPINK: Women for Peace, a partner organization of the IPS, is a strong supporter of Barbara Boxer, citing her as "our beloved Barbara Boxer" in a 2005 action alert.[24]

Boxer has worked with the group and supported its goals on many occasions. In early 2005, Boxer was the only member of the Senate to oppose certifying the Electoral College result that returned George Bush to office for a second term. CODEPINK hosted rallies and participated in various demonstrations and marches to "defend democracy" against the results of the 2004 elections.

On January 7, 2005, CODEPINK thanked Congresswoman Stephanie Tubbs Jones and Senator Barbara Boxer for their role in objecting to certifying the Electoral College votes. They wrote, "We ended the day at the office of Senator Boxer, singing her songs of thanks for stepping forward."[25]

CODEPINK founder Medea Benjamin is an IPS Trustee and a long-time affiliate of the Communist Party spinoff, Committees of Correspondence for Democracy and Socialism.[26]

Foreign Policy/National Security

Council for a Livable World

The Council for a Livable World supported Barbara Boxer in her 2010 election campaign.[27]

Previous to this, the Council had also supported Boxer in her Senate and House of Representatives campaigns.[28]

The Council certainly got value for their money. In Congress, during the Cold War, Boxer consistently worked to cut military funding for projects such as the Patriot missile and stealth aircraft, and supported a

Congressional Black Caucus recommendation to cut the defense budget in half. In 1991, she sponsored a House resolution demanding prior Congressional approval of all covert U.S. actions overseas—a measure that would have crippled anti-terrorist efforts. This proposal was defeated unanimously.[29]

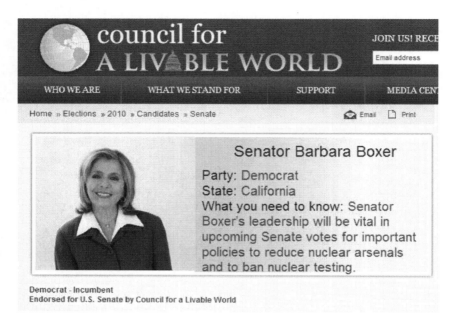

council for A LIVABLE WORLD

JOIN US! RECE

Email address

WHO WE ARE   WHAT WE STAND FOR   SUPPORT   MEDIA CEN

Home » Elections » 2010 » Candidates » Senate   Email   Print

Senator Barbara Boxer

Party: Democrat
State: California
What you need to know: Senator Boxer's leadership will be vital in upcoming Senate votes for important policies to reduce nuclear arsenals and to ban nuclear testing.

Democrat - Incumbent
Endorsed for U.S. Senate by Council for a Livable World

While endorsing her in 2010, the Council said this about Boxer:[30]

> Council for a Livable World has had a long and close relationship with Senator Barbara Boxer... she has been one of the Senate's most steadfast leaders on progressive issues for almost 20 years. Boxer will continue to be a staunch ally of the Council...
>
> She was motivated to enter politics by the assassinations of Martin Luther King, Jr. and Robert Kennedy, as well as her opposition to the Vietnam War... Boxer's intense grassroots activism enabled her to win an open seat in the U.S. House of Representatives in 1982. In that campaign, she emphasized arms control and during her decade in the House, she helped lead the fight for a nuclear freeze and an end to underground nuclear testing.
>
> Senator Boxer, who serves on the Senate Foreign Relations Committee, has significant experience and expertise on other military and foreign policy, always trying to control national security spending. She

discovered the Pentagon's notorious $7,622 coffee maker and was successful in more than a dozen Pentagon procurement reforms. She became a leading member of the Armed Services Committee.

From the outset of the war in Iraq, Senator Boxer has been a vocal opponent and critic of the use of force there. She cast her vote against the war in 2002, repeatedly criticized the Bush Administration's go-it-alone strategy, and supported numerous efforts in Congress to force a redeployment of American troops out of Iraq. She authored amendments in the Senate to end the no-bid contracts given to Halliburton and to require the Pentagon to regularly report on the cost of military operations in Iraq.

She has been an ardent supporter of nuclear arms control treaties, and voted for the Comprehensive Nuclear Test Ban Treaty in 1999. In the most recent Council for a Livable World voting records, she received a 90%, a 91% and a 100%, with two absences producing the only negatives. Senator Boxer has consistently opposed high national missile defence budgets and new nuclear weapons and was one of the few Senators to vote against the U.S.-India nuclear deal, arguing at the time: "The Nuclear Non-Proliferation Treaty is the keystone of our efforts to stop the spread of nuclear weapons throughout the world.

Voted Against Support for "Contras"

The Congressional Record of February 3, 1988, shows that Barbara Boxer was one of the 38 leading Democratic Party Congress members who voted against aid to the Nicaraguan Freedom Fighters—the "Contras"— then fighting against the Marxist-Leninist Sandinista government of Nicaragua.[31]

"Congressional Pink Caucus"

In October 1989, the Nicaraguan Sandinista Government announced that they would no longer comply with the 19 month-old cease-fire agreement with the "Contras." This had been considered a prime step forward for the "peace process" that was progressing slowly as part of the Arias Peace Plan.

A resolution was introduced in Congress deploring the Sandinistas' action. The Senate voted unanimously in favor, but in the House the vote was 379-29. All of the 29 Congress members voting against the resolution were Democrats. Barbara Boxer was one of them.

The Council for Inter-American Security dubbed these 29 people the "Congressional Pink Caucus."[32]

Trip to Cuba

From April 19 to April 22, 2002, Boxer and her husband, Stewart Boxer, visited Cuba to discuss "California trade." The trip was paid for by the Center for International Policy, a project of the Institute for Policy Studies.[33]

At the time, Boxer was serving on the Foreign Relations Committee.[34]

Assisting CODEPINK's "Fallujah Aid"

In December 2004, U.S. Senator Barbara Boxer of California; two Communist Party affiliated Congressmen, Raul Grijalva of Arizona and Dennis Kucinich of Ohio; and "progressive" Rep. Henry Waxman of California, provided diplomatic courtesy letters to a contingent of anti-war groups and individuals desiring to travel to Fallujah, Iraq.

Among those travelling in the contingent were: Rosa Suarez del Solar and her husband Fernando Suarez del Solar; Jeffrey Ritterman, Physicians for Social Responsibility; Jodie Evans, Co-Founder of CODEPINK: Women for Peace; Medea Benjamin, Co-Founder of Global Exchange and CODEPINK; and Hany Khalil, National Organizer of the IPS affiliated United for Peace and Justice.[35]

Fernando Suarez del Solar stated that had it not been for the Congressional help, the tour would have not seen the light of day due to obstacles laid by the Pentagon. The contingent traveled from December 27, 2004, through January 8, 2005.

The contingent delivered $100,000 in cash and $500,000 in humanitarian aid. At the time the diplomatic courtesy letters were issued, Medea Benjamin had stated that the aid was intended for families of the "other side" in Fallujah.[36]

---

1 KeyWiki, "Barbara Boxer," KeyWiki, http://keywiki.org/index.php/Barbara_Boxer (accessed April 23, 2013)
2 Barbara Boxer, "Biography," Senate.gov, http://www.boxer.senate.gov/en/senator/biography.cfm (accessed April 23, 2013)
3 The New York Times, "Barbara Boxer," The New York Times, http://topics.nytimes.com/top/reference/timestopics/people/b/barbara_boxer/index.html , (November 2, 2010)

4 Barbara Boxer, "Biography," Senate.gov,
http://www.boxer.senate.gov/en/senator/biography.cfm (accessed April 23, 2013)
5 Barbara Boxer, "U.S. Senator Barbara Boxer's Senate Committee Assignments,"
Senate.gov, http://www.boxer.senate.gov/en/senator/committees/index.cfm (accessed
April 23, 2013)
6 The New York Times, "Barbara Boxer," The New York Times,
http://topics.nytimes.com/top/reference/timestopics/people/b/barbara_boxer/index.html
, (November 2, 2010)
7 KeyWiki, "John Burton," KeyWiki, http://www.keywiki.org/index.php/John_Burton
(accessed April 24, 2013)
8 KeyWiki, "Phillip Burton," KeyWiki,
http://www.keywiki.org/index.php/Philip_Burton (accessed April 24, 2013)
9 WPC Call from Washington, "World Peace Council Helsinki Finland," p. 4
10 Communists in the Democratic Party, p. 65
11 People's Weekly World (September 21, 1996) p. 2
12 KeyWiki, "John Burton," KeyWiki,
http://www.keywiki.org/index.php/John_Burton (accessed April 24, 2013)
13 Consumer Watchdog, "Phillip Burton Public Service Award," Consumer
Watchdog, http://www.consumerwatchdog.org/rage-justice-awards, (accessed April
12, 2013)
14 KeyWiki, "Carlton Goodlett," KeyWiki,
http://www.keywiki.org/index.php/Carlton_Goodlett (accessed April 24, 2013)
15 Communists in the Democratic Party, p. 37
16 Communists in the Democratic Party, p. 9
17 Council for a Livable World, "Legacy in Congress: Who We've Helped Elect,"
Council for a Livable World,
http://livableworld.org/what/legacy_in_congress_who_weve_helped_elect/ (accessed
April 24, 2013)
18 21st Century Democrats, Facebook Page,
https://www.facebook.com/21stCenturyDemocrats (accessed April 24, 2013)
19 Apollo Alliance Board Bios (accessed November 18, 2010)
20 The War Called Peace, Peace Group Glossary,
http://www.knology.net/~bilrum/PeaceGrpGloss.htm, Published in 1982
21 Full Show 2/21/12: The "National Teach-in to Take Back the American Dream"
Special, Submitted by Thom Hartmann,
http://www.thomhartmann.com/bigpicture/full-show-22112-national-teach-take-back-
american-dream-special,
22 Campaign For America's Future, "Archives – 2003 Speakers," Campaign For
America's Future, http://www.ourfuture.org/node/13211 (accessed June 17, 2010)
23 Kevin Shih, "Both California Senate Candidates Use IPS Reports to Slam Each
Other," IPS website, http://www.ips-
dc.org/blog/both_california_senate_candidates_use_ips_reports_to_slam_each_other,
(September 21, 2010)
24 CODEPINK, "Let us Celebrate 2 MAJOR Victories!" CODEPINK,
http://www.codepinkalert.org/article.php?id=526 (2005)
25 CODEPINK, "Send thanks to Jones and Boxer," CODEPINK,
http://www.codepinkalert.org/article.php/http/article.php?id=250 (January 7, 2005)
26 KeyWiki, "Medea Benjamin," KeyWiki,
http://www.keywiki.org/index.php/Medea_Benjamin (accessed April 24, 2013)

27 Council for a Livable World, "Meet the Candidates," Council for a Livable World, http://livableworld.org/support/meet_candidates/ (accessed April 24, 2013)

28 Council for a Livable World, "Legacy in Congress: Who We've Helped Elect," Council for a Livable World, http://livableworld.org/what/legacy_in_congress_who_weve_helped_elect/ (accessed April 24, 2013)

29 U.S. Senate, "U.S. Senate Roll Call Votes 111th Congress – 2nd Session," U.S. Senate, http://www.senate.gov/legislative/LIS/roll_call_lists/roll_call_vote_cfm.cfm?congress =111&session=2&vote=00081 (March 24, 2010)

30 Council for a Livable World, "Senator Barbara Boxer," Council for a Livable World, http://livableworld.org/elections/2010/candidates/senate/bboxer/, (accessed May 2013)

31 KeyWiki, "Barbara Boxer," KeyWiki, http://keywiki.org/index.php/Barbara_Boxer (accessed April 23, 2013)

32 KeyWiki, "Barbara Boxer," KeyWiki, http://keywiki.org/index.php/Barbara_Boxer (accessed April 23, 2013)

33 LegiStorm, "Barbara Boxer: Trips," LegiStorm, http://www.legistorm.com/trip/list/by/approver/name/Sen_Barbara_Levy_Boxer/id/11/ core_person_id_page/51157/page/3.html (accessed October 13, 2010)

34 CubaNews, "Barbara Boxer, U.S. Senator, Travels to Cuba," CubaNews, http://groups.yahoo.com/group/CubaNews/message/9050 (April 20, 2002)

35 Adam Wild Aba, "Bereaved U.S. Families Share Iraqis Agonies of War," IslamOnline.net (Google cache), http://webcache.googleusercontent.com/search?q=cache:G3gwE9h- 8VYJ:www.islamonline.net/English/News/2005- 01/04/article05.shtml+%22Bereaved+US+Families+Share+Iraqis+Agonies+of+War% 22&cd=1&hl=en&ct=clnk&gl=us (January 4, 2005)

36 Big Peace, "Rep. Waxman Spokeswoman: 'We Do Not Know' If We Aided Fallujah Terrorists with Code Pink Letter," Big Peace, http://bigpeace.com/taylorking/2010/10/16/rep-waxman-spokeswoman-we-do-not- know-if-we-aided-fallujah-terrorists-with-code-pink-letter/ (October 16, 2010)

Karen Bass (D-CA)

Karen Bass is the U.S. Representative for
California's 33rd Congressional District,
winning election in November 2010. She
replaced retiring far left Representative
Diane Watson. Bass is a member of the
Congressional Black Caucus and the
Congressional Progressive Caucus. She is
an associate member of the Congressional
Asian Pacific Caucus.[1]

Background

Karen Bass grew up in the Venice/Fairfax area of Los Angeles. She
graduated from Hamilton High School, Cal State Dominguez Hills and
the University of Southern California, School of Medicine Physician
Assistant Program.

Bass says that from a young age she was "drawn to addressing
injustice in all its forms and standing up for what she believes." As early
as high school, she was volunteering on political campaigns, following the
Civil Rights Movement and protesting the Vietnam War.

She returned to southern California before completing her degree in
Philosophy and instead sought a career that afforded her time to devote
to her political activism, and equally as important, one that also aligned
with her values system. "It's that set of values that led me to a profession
that would help people. That's the same set of values that led me to be an
activist," she said. "So the passion that underlines whether I'm working in
a hospital or whether I'm attending meetings, it's the same drive."

When Bass graduated from CSU Dominguez Hills in 1990, it was also
the year her career and her activism took a new direction. Crack use
among the low income African American communities in Los Angeles

was reaching epidemic proportions and Bass saw too many people affected by it coming through the emergency room.

"A good percentage of what comes in (to the ER), it's either fights or accidents, domestic violence, but all those, if you look at the root of them, there's drugs or alcohol," she said. "So when the crack cocaine epidemic hit, that led me to want to figure out how to address it and so I started Community Coalition, a community-based "social justice organization in South Los Angeles," which she led for 14 years.[2]

Influence

Karen Bass was elected to the California State Legislature in 2005, eventually becoming its 67th Speaker.

Speaker Bass authored legislation that "expands Healthy Families insurance coverage to prevent children from going without health care."[3]

In Congress, Bass was selected by Democratic leader Nancy Pelosi to serve on the prestigious Steering and Policy Committee, which sets the policy direction of the Democratic Caucus. Democratic Whip Steny Hoyer of Maryland appointed Bass to serve as an Assistant Whip.[4]

Bass sits on the Judiciary Committee, which includes the Subcommittee on Crime, Terrorism, Homeland Security and Investigations and the Subcommittee on Courts, the Internet and Intellectual Property. She also sits on the Foreign Affairs Committee, which includes the Subcommittee on Africa, Global Health, Global Human Rights and International Organizations where she is a Ranking Member.[5]

Socialist Connections

Karen Bass has long worked with Democratic Socialists of America (DSA) members and other Los Angeles based leftist groups.

West Coast Socialist Scholars Conference

The West Coast Socialist Scholars Conference of 1993, "New Realities, New Identities; Socialism and Empowerment," was held on April 17, 1993 at the University of California, Los Angeles. Speakers included Karen Bass, plus Bogdan Denitch, Angie Fa and Harold Meyerson (all from DSA), as well as Trotskyite Solidarity activist Mike Davis and Pro-Soviet communist turned Maoist, turned Pro-Soviet communist again, Irwin Silber.

Co-Sponsors were Socialist Community School, Democratic Socialists of America, Committees of Correspondence, Concerned Faculty (UCLA), CrossRoads Magazine, International Socialist Organization, Socialist Organizing Network, Solidarity and the Union of Radical Political Economists.[6]

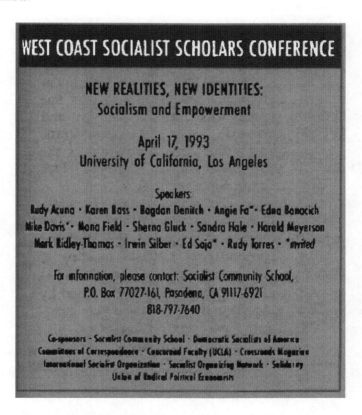

Progressive Los Angeles Network

Circa 2002, Karen Bass, Community Coalition, served on the Advisory Board of the Democratic Socialists of America-dominated Progressive Los Angeles Network. This organization laid the groundwork for the socialist/labor union takeover of Los Angeles politics, since Mayor Antonio Villaraigosa's ascension to power in 2005.[7]

Slumming it with the Sheinbaums

Congresswoman Lynn Woolsey, the first member of Congress to call on the President to bring U.S. troops home from Iraq, was in Los Angeles on February 4th, 2006, for a "very exciting, but critical fundraiser against the most well-known, well-financed challenger she's ever faced."

Facing a serious primary challenge over her anti-Iraq War views, wealthy DSA members Stanley and Betty Sheinbaum hosted a fundraiser for Woolsey in their luxurious Brentwood home.

Karen Bass served on the Host Committee alongside DSA member and actor, Ed Asner.[8]

On September 20, 2009, Southern California ACLU held its 46th annual Garden Party at the home of Stanley and Betty Sheinbaum.

Karen Bass, speaker of the California Assembly, was there to receive the Legislator of the Year Award.[9]

"Progressive" Connections

Liberty Hill Foundation

As of 2009, Karen Bass, Speaker of the House, California State Assembly, was on the Board of Directors of the Liberty Hill Foundation, a Los Angeles based organization seeking to "advance movements" for social change through a combination of grants, leadership training and alliance-building.

Liberty Hill is a partner organization of the Institute for Policy Studies. Its Advisory Board is dominated by Democratic Socialists of America affiliates such as philanthropist Paula Litt, former Santa Monica Mayor Jim Conn, former LA City Councilwoman Jackie Goldberg, academic and Democratic Party activist Peter Dreier, Los Angeles Mayor Villaraigosa, staffer Torie Osborn, labor unionist Paul Schrade and Betty and Stanley Sheinbaum. Two former Communist Workers Party affiliates, LA lawyer Stewart Kwoh and labor academic Kent Wong, also grace the Liberty Hill Advisory Board.[10] [11]

IPS Africa Event

In September 21, 2012, Karen Bass and the Congressional Black Caucus Foundation addressed the Africa Braintrust.

Institute for Policy Studies' Director of Foreign Policy in Focus, Emira Woods, was featured on a panel about "Emerging Threats to Political Stability," in Africa.

Other panelists included: Ambassador Johnnie Carson, Assistant Secretary of State for African Affairs; Amina Salum Ali, Ambassador of African Union to the U.S. and the IPS' Dr. Clarence Lusane, a Professor, American University.[12]

Foreign Policy/National Security

Arab American Institute

The Arab American Institute (AAI) offers internships in Washington for Arab American college students and recent graduates interested in public affairs, advocacy and ethnic politics. The program is part of the Arab American Institute Foundation's "commitment to youth leadership, along with scholarships and awards for public and community service."

The Arab American Institute was founded in 1985 to "nurture and encourage the direct participation of Arab Americans in political and civic life in the United States. AAI provides training and resources for Arab American political effectiveness through participation in party politics, public boards and commissions, city councils and state legislatures, as well as Congressional and presidential elections."

2012 AAI interns were offered positions at the U.S. Department of State, the office of Congresswoman Karen Bass, the Democratic National Committee and the Institute for Policy Studies.[13]

Cuba, Communists and the Venceremos Brigade

In a May 5, 2005 exchange on Yahoo! Group Atzlannet, Los Angeles Communist Party USA organizer Rosalio Munoz revealed his own early connection to Karen Bass and of another communist, Leroy Parra.

He revealed that communists had indeed been part of Bass' movement and that she had been a member of the Venceremos Brigade, whose members traveled to Cuba to do agricultural work in support of the Cuban revolution.[14]

Cuba 1989

On May 19, 1989, Karen Bass discussed her recent trip to Cuba on "Voices of the Left: A Socialist Perspective," a radio show on KPFK 90.7 FM. It was advertised in Los Angeles Democratic Socialists of America's Los Angeles Left, May 1989, page 2. This may refer to the Venceremos Brigade trip discussed above, or it may be talking about an entirely separate visit to the communist run island.[15]

1 KeyWiki, "Karen Bass," KeyWiki, http://keywiki.org/index.php/Karen_Bass (accessed March 31, 2013)
2 Peter Dreier, "From Organizer To Elected Official," The Huffington Post, http://www.huffingtonpost.com/peter-dreier/from-organizer-to-elected_b_124971.html? (September 8, 2008)
3 Karen Bass, "Full Biography," House.gov, http://bass.house.gov/about-me/full-biography (accessed April 15, 2011)
4 Karen Bass, "Full Biography," House.gov, http://bass.house.gov/about-me/full-biography (accessed April 15, 2011)
5 Karen Bass, "Committees and Caucuses," House.gov, http://bass.house.gov/about-me/committees-and-caucuses (accessed April 1, 2013)
6 Democratic Left (March/April 1993)
7 USC, "Black Movements in the US – Fall 2008: The Progressive Los Angeles Network (PLAN)," PLAN website, http://dornsife.usc.edu/cdd/civic/bmus/The%20Progressive%20Los%20Angeles%20Network%20%28PLAN%29.html#TheProgressiveLosAngelesNetwork%28PLAN%29-PLAN%27sAdvisoryBoard, (accessed October 2011)
8 Sharon T., "LA Event Featuring Warren Beatty, Matt Daman for Lynn Woolsey 2/4/06," Care Moo, http://www.care2.com/c2c/groups/disc.html?gpp=6486&pst=347342 (January 31, 2006)
9 ACLU SC website, http://www.aclu-sc.org/events/view/102899/, (accessed September 19, 2011)
10 Liberty Hill, "Board/Advisory Council," Liberty Hill, http://www.libertyhill.org/Page.aspx?pid=242 (accessed April 1, 2013)

11 KeyWiki, "Liberty Hill Foundation," KeyWiki,
http://www.keywiki.org/index.php/Liberty_Hill_Foundation (accessed April 1, 2012)
12 FPIF, "Events, Africa Braintrust 2012," FPIF,
http://www.fpif.org/events/africa_braintrust_2012, (accessed April 1, 2013)
13 Arab American Institute, "2013 Summer Internship Program," Arab American
Institute, http://www.aaiusa.org/page/s/2013-summer-internship-application (accessed
April 1, 2013)
14 Aztlannet News, "Who Killed Neto Falcon," Yahoo! Groups,
http://groups.yahoo.com/group/NetworkAztlan_News/message/11773, (May 5, 2005)
15 KeyWiki, "Karen Bass," KeyWiki, http://keywiki.org/index.php/Karen_Bass
(accessed April 1, 2013)

Xavier Becerra (D-CA)

Xavier Becerra is a Democratic member of the United States House of Representatives, representing the 34th District of California. He is a member of the Congressional Progressive Caucus, the Congressional Hispanic Caucus and serves as an Executive Board member of the Congressional Asian Pacific American Caucus.

Background

Xavier Becerra was born on January 26, 1958. In 1980, Becerra earned his Bachelor of Arts Degree in Economics from Stanford University. He was awarded his Juris Doctorate from Stanford Law School in 1984.[1]

In 1992, after redistricting, incumbent Democratic United States Congressman Matthew Martínez of California's 30th Congressional District decided to run in the newly redrawn 31st District. Becerra, a Freshman Assemblyman, then successfully ran for Congress in the Los Angeles based district.[2]

Becerra announced in July of 2011, that he would run in the newly redrawn California 34th Congressional District which he lives in and contains most of his current district.[3]

Influence

Representative Xavier Becerra serves as Chairman of the House Democratic Caucus, is a member of the powerful Committee on Ways And Means and is a Ranking Member of the Ways and Means Subcommittee on Social Security.

His committee is responsible for formulating our nation's tax, Social Security, Medicare, trade and income security laws. As Chairman of the Democratic Caucus, Becerra wields a strong voice in House Democratic leadership, helping to set priorities and drive the legislative decision making process.[4]

In August of 2008, the Obama Campaign announced the formation of its National Latino Advisory Council, highlighting the continued growth of support Senator Obama is receiving in the Latino community nationwide. Xavier Becerra was a member of the Council, alongside SEIU Vice President, leading Latino immigration activist and Democratic Socialists of America (DSA) leader Eliseo Medina.[5]

Communist Connections

Ed Roybal

Congressman Ed Roybal represented the people of California's 30th Congressional District from 1963 to 1993. Upon his retirement, Roybal supported then Assembly member Xavier Becerra for election to the 30th Congressional District seat. "The two have been close ever since, the elder statesman serving as both friend and mentor to his successor."[6]

Roybal was a long-time ally of the Communist Party USA (CPUSA), particularly close to prominent Los Angeles party member Bert Corona.[7]

Martinez Jobs Bill

In 1994, the Communist Party USA instigated the Martinez Jobs Bill (HR-4708). It was co-sponsored by several Democratic Congressional leftists, including Xavier Becerra.[8]

Evelina Alarcon, Chair of the Southern California Communist Party, was delegated by the CPUSA to co-ordinate the bill's passage through Congress.[9]

Mexican American Political Association Endorsement

Formed in 1959, by Ed Roybal and CPUSA member Bert Corona, the highly influential Mexican American Political Association (MAPA), has remained under Communist Party influence ever since.

Over 130 delegates to the Mexican American Retro Region Primary Endorsing Convention in Los Angeles on April 25, 1992, voted to endorse those Congressional, State Senate, Assembly and County Supervisor candidates who took the strongest pro-labor and pro-immigrant stands.

Guest speakers included two Communist Party affiliates: Maria Elena Durazo, President of Hotel Employees and Restaurant Employees Local 1 and Gilbert Cedillo of Service Employees Local 660.

State Assemblyman Xavier Becerra won MAPA's support to be the Democratic candidate for the 30th District after he pledged support for extending unemployment benefits for the full length of joblessness.[10]

Socialist Connections

DSA Endorsement

In July 1996, the Democratic Socialists of America Political Action Committee endorsed Xavier Becerra in that year's Congressional elections.[11]

Sheinbaum Fundraiser

Congresswoman Lynn Woolsey was in Los Angeles on February 4th, 2006, for a "very exciting, but critical fundraiser. The Host Committee for this fundraiser included Xavier Becerra, radical leaders Tom Hayden and Jodie Evans, and DSA member and actor, Ed Asner.

The fundraiser was at the Stanley and Betty Sheinbaum residence in Brentwood. Both Sheinbaums had been members of Los Angeles DSA's Upton Sinclair Club for rich radicals.[12]

"Progressive" Connection

America's Future Now!

Xavier Becerra was a speaker at the 2010, America's Future Now! Conference which was hosted by the Institute for Policy Studies/Democratic Socialists of America founded Campaign for America's Future.

Foreign Policy/National Security

Controversial Cuba Trip

Becerra's trip to Cuba in January of 1997 caused such a furor that Florida's two Republican Cuban-American Congress members from Dade County: Lincoln Diaz-Balart and Ileana Ros-Lehtinen quit the House Hispanic Caucus in protest.

The trip was sponsored by a Los Angeles-based leftist group called the Southwest Voter Research Institute, which picked up Becerra's $1,800 tab.[13]

Islamic Unity Conference

Speakers from around the globe gathered at the Omni Shoreham Hotel in Washington, D.C. in August of 1998 to discuss Muslim issues at the 2nd International Islamic Unity Conference. Under the auspices of the Islamic Supreme Council of America and its founder, Shaykh Muhammad Hisham Kabbani, religious and political leaders alike gathered to address concerns facing the Islamic community and to "condemn the oppression of Muslims worldwide."

Muslims involved in the process of United States policymaking, gathered for a panel entitled "How to Create Public Policy." Arshi Siddiqui, Legislative Aide to Congressman Xavier Becerra, stressed that Muslim Americans should not only form relationships with Congressmen, but with Congressional staff members as well.[14]

Staffer to Venezuela

Rep. Becerra sent staffer Henry Truong to Marxist led Venezuela for 3 days in February of 2010. The trip was courtesy of a $2,219.70 grant from the Institute for Policy Studies connected Center for Democracy in the Americas, "A fact-finding trip in Venezuela and other Latin American countries with the mission of fostering dialogue and improving U.S. policy and bilateral relations."[15]

---

1 Xavier Becerra, "Biography (English)," Congressman Xavier Becerra, http://becerra.house.gov/index.php?option=com_content&view=article&id=13&Itemid=16 (accessed June 10, 2012)
2 Our Campaigns, "CA District 30," Our Campaigns, http://www.ourcampaigns.com/RaceDetail.html?RaceID=27863 (accessed June 10, 2012)

3 Becerra For Congress, "Rep. Xavier Becerra Announces Intention To Run In The East Los Angeles/Boyle Heights (CA-34) Congressional District," Becerra For Congress, http://xavierbecerra.ngphost.com/node/100 (accessed June 10, 2012)
4 Xavier Becerra, "Biography," House.gov, http://becerra.house.gov/index.php?option=com_content&view=article&id=13:biograp hy-english&catid=8&Itemid=16 (accessed May 15, 2013)
5 KeyWiki, "Xavier Becerra," KeyWiki, http://keywiki.org/index.php/Xavier_Becerra (accessed June 11, 2012)
6 KeyWiki, "Xavier Becerra," KeyWiki, http://keywiki.org/index.php/Xavier_Becerra (accessed June 10, 2012)
7 KeyWiki, "Ed Roybal," KeyWiki, http://www.keywiki.org/index.php/Ed_Roybal (accessed May 30, 2013)
8 KeyWiki, "Xavier Becerra," KeyWiki, http://keywiki.org/index.php/Xavier_Becerra (accessed June 10, 2012)
9 Political Affairs (January 1997) p. 8
10 KeyWiki, "Xavier Becerra," KeyWiki, http://keywiki.org/index.php/Xavier_Becerra (accessed June 10, 2012)
11 KeyWiki, "Xavier Becerra," KeyWiki, http://keywiki.org/index.php/Xavier_Becerra (accessed June 10, 2012)
12 Sharon T., "LA Event Featuring Warren Beatty, Matt Daman for Lynn Woolsey 2/4/06," Care2, http://www.care2.com/c2c/groups/disc.html?gpp=6486&pst=347342 (accessed June 11, 2012)
13 KeyWiki, "Xavier Becerra," KeyWiki, http://keywiki.org/index.php/Xavier_Becerra (accessed June 10, 2012)
14 KeyWiki, "Xavier Becerra," KeyWiki, http://keywiki.org/index.php/Xavier_Becerra (accessed June 10, 2012)
15 LegiStorm, "Center for Democracy in the Americas – Sponsor of Congressional Travel," LegiStorm, http://www.legistorm.com/trip/list/by/sponsor/id/10693/name/Center_for_Democracy_ in_the_Americas/page/2.html (accessed January 21, 2013)

Ami Bera (D-CA)

Ami Bera entered Congress with the 2012 elections as a California Democrat in District 7. The 7th District is located just east of California's capitol city, Sacramento.[1]

Congressman Bera is a member of the "centrist" New Democrat Coalition."[2]

Background

Born and raised in California, Bera earned both his B.S. and M.D. from the University of California, Irvine.

After graduating from medical school in 1991, he did his residency in internal medicine at California Pacific Medical Center, eventually becoming Chief Resident. Bera went on to practice medicine in the Sacramento area, serving in various leadership roles for MedClinic Medical Group. He then served as Medical Director of Care Management for Mercy Healthcare.[3]

Influence

Ami Bera is a member of the House Committee on Science, Space and Technology and the House Committee on Foreign Affairs.[4]

Socialist Connections

Bera has ties to the 5,000 member strong Sacramento Progressive Alliance (SPA), which is run by Democratic Socialists of America (DSA) members Paul Burke and Duane Campbell.[5] [6]

Progressive Forum, Sacramento

During Bera's unsuccessful 2010 run, he was a guest at the Progressive Election Forum, convened by the SPA on October 28, 2010, at Sacramento State University.

The event was sponsored by the Faculty Progressive Alliance, SPA, the Sac State Coalition, CFA-Capitol Chapter and Capitol Area Progressives.[7]

Bera's co-panelist was Jim Shoch, an Associate Professor of Government at Sacramento State and a former Political Director of DSA.[8]

The SPA also endorsed Ami Bera in his successful race in 2012.[9]

Jim Shoch, Ami Bera

"Progressive" Connections

Bera was supported in 2012 by the DSA/Institute for Policy Studies-led Progressive Democrats of America (PDA).[10]

NNU and PDA

Wrote Michael Lighty, Director of Public Policy National Nurses United and PDA Advisory Board Member:[11]

> The RNs of NNU have found a natural alliance with [PDA activists], who never slow in the fight against austerity to win prosperity for all. RNs and PDA activists joined in campaigns across the country for insurgent progressives like Elizabeth Warren, now Senator-elect from Massachusetts, Medicare for All supporter Ami Bera, soon to be Congressman from California...

Michael Lighty is also a former National Organizational Director of Democratic Socialists of America.[12]

PDA Phone Bankers

PDA phone bankers and mail deliverers helped Bera win his very tight race.

From November 1, 2012, through Election Day, Progressive Democrats of America's Phone Bank Director, Mike Fox, organized volunteers across the USA, making thousands of GOTV calls for "progressive candidates," including Dr. Ami Bera—a Medicare for All medical doctor running against 4-term incumbent Dan Lundgren in California's 7th District...[13]

Hosting PDA

According to a New Year 2013 press release from PDA, Bera was a "friend" of the organization and would be hosting a PDA delegation on Capitol Hill:[14]

> Progressive Democrats of America accomplished a lot in 2012—thanks to your help and support. Together, we helped defeat Tea Party extremists and helped elect strong progressives to Congress...

> In just a few days, on January 3rd, our team will be on Capitol Hill as special guests of our newly elected and re-elected progressive candidates including our board members our friends Representatives Alan Grayson, Dr. Ami Bera, and Mark Pocan...

Foreign Policy/National Security

Council for a Livable World, 2012 Victory

The anti-U.S. military Council for a Livable World Political Action Committee claimed 26 House victories in the 2012 election cycle, including Ami Bera.[15]

---

1 Peter Bell, "The New Faces of the 113th Congress," National Journal, http://www.nationaljournal.com/congress-legacy/the-new-faces-of-the-113th-congress-20121105 (November 15, 2012)
2 Ami Bera, "Full Biography," House.gov, http://bera.house.gov/about/full-biography (accessed April 29, 2013)

3 Ami Bera, "Full Biography," House.gov, http://bera.house.gov/about/full-biography (accessed April 29, 2013)

4 Ami Bera, "Full Biography," House.gov, http://bera.house.gov/about/full-biography (accessed April 29, 2013)

5 KeyWiki, "Paul Burke," KeyWiki, http://keywiki.org/index.php/Paul_Burke (accessed May 15, 2013)

6 KeyWiki, "Duane Campbell," KeyWiki, http://keywiki.org/index.php/Duane_Campbell (accessed May 15, 2013)

7 Progressive Forum blog, Progressive Election Forum, http://progressiveforum07.blogspot.co.nz/2010_10_01_archive.html, (October 20, 2010)

8 DSA Letterhead (April 28, 1987)

9 SPA blog, Progressive Alliance Endorsement 2012 (October 28, 2012)

10 KeyWiki, "Ami Bera," KeyWiki, http://keywiki.org/index.php/Ami_Bera (accessed May 15, 2013)

11 PDA Email Blast, "Let's Tax Wall Street, Create Jobs, and Save the Social Security Net," http://salsa3.salsalabs.com/o/1987/t/0/blastContent.jsp?email_blast_KEY=1233025, (accessed May 15, 2013)

12 Democratic Left 3 (July/August 1990) p. 13

13 PRLOG, "Jim Hightower, John Nichols, Michael Lighty and Tim Carpenter in Janesville," PDA, http://www.prlog.org/12014034-jim-hightower-john-nichols-michael-lighty-and-tim-carpenter-in-janesville.html (November 1, 2012)

14 Tim Carpenter, "Happy New Year from PDA!," PDA, http://dir.groups.yahoo.com/group/progressivesforobama/message/6357 (January 1, 2013)

15 Council for a Livable World, "Meet the Candidates," Council for a Livable World, http://livableworld.org/support/meet_candidates/, (accessed April 10, 2013)

Judy Chu (D-CA)

Judy May Chu is a Democratic member of the United States House of Representatives, representing the 27th District of California. In 2011, she was elected as the Chair of the Congressional Asian Pacific American Caucus and she is a Vice Chair of the Congressional Progressive Caucus.[1]

Background

Judy Chu was born July 7, 1953, in Los Angeles, to Judson Chu, a native Californian and his wife, May, whom he brought from China under the War Brides Act. Judy Chu's father worked as an electrical technician for Pacific Bell and her mother was a cannery worker and a member of the Teamsters.[2]

Rep. Chu earned her B.A. in Mathematics from UCLA and her Ph.D. in Psychology from the California School of Professional Psychology.

She taught as a psychology professor at the Los Angeles Community College District for 20 years, including 13 years at East Los Angeles College.[3]

Judy Chu can trace the beginnings of her career as a San Gabriel Valley activist and political leader back to the early 1970s and her freshman year in college.

Intent on a career in computer science, Chu was radicalized in an Asian American studies course.

"It was like a light went off in my head," Chu recalled. She learned "about the history of Asian immigrants and their children, the discrimination and stereotypes they endured and their contributions to American life and culture."

One of the guest speakers was far left radical Pat Sumi, a third-generation Japanese American whose activism included organizing protests against the Vietnam War.

"It was the very first time it occurred to me that an Asian American woman could be a leader," said Chu, who began volunteering with various radical causes, transferred to UCLA and "gave up computers for clinical psychology".[4]

Chu joined the movement to pass the Equal Rights Amendment for women and then taught classes at UCLA on Asian American Women. She was once a Rape Crisis Counselor.[5]

Judy Chu is married to former California State Assembly member, and former student radical Mike Eng.

Influence

When elected to the U.S. House of Representatives for California's 32nd District in July 2009, Chu's first assignment was on the House Education and Labor Committee, where she served on the Subcommittees on Early Childhood, Elementary and Secondary Education and Healthy Families and Communities. Chu's District has since been redrawn as the 27th District.

In the 112th Congress, Rep. Chu served on the House Judiciary Committee, where she is a member of the Crime, Terrorism, and Homeland Security and the Intellectual Property, Competition and the Internet Subcommittees. She is also a member of the House Small Business Committee, where she is leading the Contracting and Workforce Subcommittee as the Ranking Democrat and serves on the Economic Growth, Tax and Capital Access Subcommittee.

Congresswoman Chu is also a strong advocate for "progressive" immigration reform, having been an original co-sponsor of the Comprehensive Immigration Reform (CIR-ASAP) bill introduced by Rep. Luis Gutierrez in 2010.[6]

On February 22, 2012, Obama for America, announced the selection of the campaign's National Co-Chairs, a "diverse group of leaders from around the country committed to re-electing President Obama. The co-chairs will serve as ambassadors for the President, advise the campaign on key issues and help engage and mobilize voters in all 50 states."

Representative Judy Chu was on the list.[7] [8]

Communist Connections

Judy Chu has a 30 year history with the now defunct, pro-China Communist Workers Party (CWP) and its surviving networks.

Federation for Progress

In the early 1980s, Judy Chu was a leader of the Federation for Progress, a front group for the CWP.

The Federation for Progress was an attempt to create a new Marxist united front organization, similar to efforts of the People's Alliance and the National Committee for Independent Political Action.

The FFP put a half-page ad in the "socialist" oriented weekly newspaper, In These Times, in the July 14-27, 1982 issue, p. 8, entitled: "A natural follow-up to June 12: A national conference July 30-August 1 at Columbia Un., in New York City."

It was a follow-up conference to the major "anti-defense lobby" march and protest in New York in June relating to the U.N., Second Special Session on Disarmament.

The FPP Interim Executive Committee included:

Judy Chu—Professor Asian-American Studies, Los Angeles, Michio Kaku—nuclear physicist and CWP affiliate, Manning Marable—Professor of Political Economy and member of Democratic Socialists of America (DSA) and Musheer Robinson—Executive Director, Black and Latin Workers Health & Safety Resource Center, Newark, NJ, also a DSA member.[9]

Letter to Samaranch

The '84 Mobilization for Peace and Justice penned a July 25, 1984 letter to Dr. Juan Antonio Samaranch and Members of the International Olympic Committee:

> We wish to express our outrage at the statements made by members of the International Olympic Committee (IOC) in support of the Racist Apartheid Regime of South Africa, which is seeking to regain membership of the IOC. Moreover we think that appropriate measures should be taken to hasten Mr. Roby's planned retirement and to replace Mr. Roosevelt as members of the IOC.

Judy Chu, UCLA Asian American Studies and Federation for Progress, signed the letter.[10]

Dr. Juan Antonio Samaranch
Members of the International
Olympic Committee
July 25, 1984

We feel these statements are a violation of the Olympic charter and we formally
request that Mr. Roosevelt and Mr. Roby be asked to submit their resignations to
the IOC. It is impossible for them to represent the morals or ideals of fair-
minded sports enthusiasts in the United States.

Sincerely,

Mike Young
'84 Mobilization for
Peace and Justice

Judy Chu, Ph.D.
Federation For Progress

Reverend Eugene Boutilier
Southern California
Ecumenical Council

Dennis Brutus, HLD.
President, South   African
Non-Racial Olympic
Committee (SAN-ROC)

CHAMP and the Calderon Connection

By the early 1980s, Judy Chu and Mike Eng had settled in Monterey Park, which was experiencing an influx of immigrants from China, Taiwan and Hong Kong.

When some long-time residents sought to ban Chinese-language storefront signs, the City Council voted in 1986 to support a resolution endorsing English as the nation's official language. Chu, by then on the school board, and Eng helped to form the Coalition for Harmony in Monterey Park.

"Judy and Mike were always trying to find ways to bring people together," said former Colorado Communist Workers Party leader Jose Calderon, another member of CHAMP, then an academic at Pitzer College in Claremont. The group started "Harmony Days" to celebrate the city's various cultures and they led a petition drive that moved the council to rescind its divisive resolution.

The communist-led group won the campaign, helping to launch Judy Chu into local politics.[11]

Calderon's wife, Marilyn Calderon, later served on Judy Chu's legislative staff in the California Assembly.[12]

When Jose Calderon and several other activists were arrested in a protest over a Pomona College employment dispute in December 2011, Judy Chu stepped in to offer support.

Jose Calderon, Denver (November 1979)

Bryan Urias, a member of Chu's staff, attended the protest on behalf of the Congresswoman.

"She wanted me to be here to let all of you know, to let the workers know, to let Pomona College know, that she is watching what is going on and she is disgusted with the process that happened here," Urias said.

Urias added that Chu had personally called President Oxtoby to ask him to reconsider his decision to terminate employees who could not update their documentation by Dec. 1. He also said that Chu's office intended to help the terminated workers who wanted to fix their documentation and get re-hired by Pomona.[13]

On March 30, 2012, Jose Calderon organized the Annual Latino and Latina Roundtable Cesar Chavez Breakfast at The Avalon, in Pomona:[14]

> In keeping with the tradition of honoring leaders in our region who have exemplified the principles and values of Cesar Chavez, the Roundtable is honoring Congresswoman Judy Chu.

227

Kent Wong and APALA

Chu also works closely with another former CWP member, California labor academic, Kent Wong.

Chu, the Chair of the Congressional Asian Pacific American Caucus— and a long-time activist in her union, American Federation of Teachers, is a strong supporter of Wong's creation, the pro-Marxist Asian Pacific American Labor Alliance.

On May 17, 2002, an Asian Pacific American Labor Alliance public hearing was held at the Monterey Park City Hall. This event was symbolic for the Asian Pacific American Immigrant community because it was the first hearing held over the issues of Asian Pacific American labor. The hearing included two panels of speakers. The first included Kent Wong and Judy Chu.[15]

On Saturday, April 9th, 2011, at the Japanese American National Museum, 369 East 1st St., Los Angeles, the Asian Pacific American Labor Alliance held a hearing on the stories and testimonies of Asian Pacific American workers and their struggles to organize. The hearing featured panels on health care, immigrant rights and the involvement of youth in the labor movement. The event included performances by Progressive Taiko and KIWA's Cultural Resistance Committee drumming group.

Speakers were: Congresswoman Judy Chu, her husband, Assembly member Mike Eng, former student radical Warren Furutani and Kent Wong.[16]

Gathering of Old Communists

An event entitled: "A conversation with Judy Chu and Jean Quan," was held on July 10, 2011 at Empress Pavilion, LA Chinatown. Jean Quan was the serving Mayor of Oakland, California and an identified former member of the Communist Workers Party.[17]

The Host Committee consisted of:

- Rep. Judy Chu, U.S. Congresswoman
- Mike Eng, California Assembly member
- Stewart Kwoh, a Los Angeles lawyer and former CWP associate
- Kent Wong, former CWP member
- Jose Zapata Calderon, former CWP member
- Jai Lee, Kent Wong's wife

Foreign Policy/National Security

Judy Chu, without doubt, is communist China's best friend in the U.S. Congress.

China Trips

Soon after Judy Chu was elected as a Monterey Park City Council member and Mayor, she led a delegation to visit China in 1990 when relations between the two countries were "not normal." She visited China again in 1994 and 1999 as a City Councilwoman.[18]

2011 Delegation to China

In late August 2011, Chu led a delegation, which consisted of fellow Congressional Asian Pacific American Caucus members Mike Honda and Eni Faleomavaega, for a week-long visit to China at the invitation of the Chinese Communist Party's Chinese People's Institute of Foreign Affairs.[19]

Meeting Lu Yongxiang

Senior Chinese Communist Party legislator, Lu Yongxiang, met with U.S. Representative Judy Chu at the Great Hall of the People. Lu, Vice Chairman of the Standing Committee of the National People's Congress, China's top legislative body, reviewed the exchanges that have taken place between the NPC and the U.S. Senate and Congress.

Lu Yongxiang (R), Vice Chairman of the Standing Committee of the National People's Congress, meets with Judy Chu, U.S. Rep for California's 32nd Congressional District, in Beijing (Aug. 20, 2011)

Lu called on China and the United States to "step up dialogues, enhance mutual trust and carry out more extensive cooperation in order to boost the development of China-U.S. ties."

As the "first Chinese-American woman to be elected to the U.S. Congress", Chu said "she pays close attention to her country's relations with China. She said she will play her own part in boosting U.S.-China ties."[20]

School of Transnational Law

During a visit to the School of Transnational Law on Sept. 1, 2011, to discuss the role of caucuses in the U.S. House of Representatives in the legislative process, Chu spoke about her position as the first Chinese American woman in the U.S. House, immigration, reform and improving U.S.-China relations.

"We have more to gain from a relationship than we have to lose—and in fact, we are very much interdependent," Chu said. "We want to make sure that we raise our voices for reason and mutual cooperation between U.S. and China."[21]

Ancestral Home, Jiangmen, Guangdong Province

The last leg of Judy Chu's trip was a visit to her ancestral home of Jiangmen, Guangdong Province:[22]

Going to my home village and the Jiangmen museum of overseas Chinese it exemplified so greatly the hardships of the Chinese experience when they went abroad and had been treated so poorly by the immigration officials and experienced such hardships as they were trying to settle in America.

It just brought home for me what kind of difficulties that my own grandfather and parents must have experienced as they came over.

"Much to Learn from China"

Judy Chu told China Daily, that she wanted to increase understanding between the United States and China, a relationship which Chu said has sometimes been hit by "great anxiety and tension."

"There are some in Congress who are saying negative and angry things about China," Chu said.

"I felt that we needed to have this trip in order to help balance the perspective that is out there. We have more to gain in our relationship between U.S. and China than we have to lose. There is also much that the U.S. can learn from China," she added.

"We need to explain what great progress China has made, with some great advances that we can learn from. For instance, on high-speed rail, we actually rode the high-speed rail from Nanjing to Shanghai and we were incredibly impressed at how China could make these advances when we in the U.S. actually have not been able to get our first high-speed train going," she said.[23]

From the *Life of Guangzhou* Website

"Daughter of China"

Judy Chu told the Life of Guangzhou website:

> I am a daughter of China, now I am coming home. This most incredible eight days visit has made me better understand what China is about. I had a memorable visit to my home village of Jiangmen. I am truly coming home.

Ms. Chu said the most memorable event of the whole trip was visiting her home village Jiangmen. The delegation paid for a visit to Beijing, Nanjing, Shanghai, Guangzhou, Shenzhen and Jiangmen. "China has really made great progress," said Ms. Chu, "21 years ago when I was last in Jiangmen, single lane roads, no bridges cross the river. But this time I see 3-lane highways, magnificent highways, and all kinds of industry."[24]

Supporting China at Home

Committee of 100

The Committee of 100 is a "national, non-profit, non-partisan organization that brings a Chinese American perspective to issues concerning Chinese Americans and U.S.-China relations. Its members—Chinese Americans who have achieved prominence in a variety of fields—work in partnership toward our dual mission:"[25]

> ...to encourage constructive relations between the peoples of the United States and Greater China, and to promote the full participation of Chinese Americans in all fields of American life.

Some Committee of 100 members have past Communist Workers Party ties.

Washington area Committee of 100 members hosted a dinner meeting on November 4, 2009, in honor of Congresswoman Judy Chu. She has spoken at past Committee of 100 conferences and attended the 2008 conference in Los Angeles.[26]

Supporting Chinese Propaganda station

On May 23, 2012, Consul General Qiu Shaofang attended the opening ceremony of the 2012 Global Chinese Broadcasting Cooperation Annual Meeting in Los Angeles. U.S. Congresswomen Judy Chu, China National

Radio President Wang Qiu, Vice Consul General Sun Weide and representatives of more than 30 broadcasting companies arrived at the event.

Global Chinese Broadcasting Cooperation is a "broadcasting network providing real-time radio broadcast, dissemination of information, cultural entertainment and many more features." Consul General Qiu spoke highly of the GCBC. He said that "for the past 9 years since its establishment, it has become one of the windows for the Chinese people and the world to learn about each other. Media is playing an increasingly important role in promoting better understanding and friendship around the world. GCBC is a bridge of communication to let the world know a real and developing China."

Consul General Qiu also talked about current China and U.S. relations; he hoped "GCBC will provide more opportunities for China and American people to communicate, cooperate and to improve bilateral relationships."

Judy Chu positively commented on the important role played by Chinese broadcasting in the Chinese American community in her speech. At the end, China National Radio President Wang Qiu concluded that GCBC will devote its best effort to promote the development of Chinese broadcasting and to raise China's global profile around the world.[27]

"New Age of U.S.-China Relations"

The 2012 Western Region Conference of the pro-communist U.S.- China People's Friendship Association was held Friday, October 26-28, 2012 at the Hilton Hotel in San Gabriel, California:[28]

"New Age of U.S.-China Relations" is the theme of this conference. Invited dignitaries will be from business, politics, NGOs and academia from both countries. Some of the keynote speakers that we are inviting include Madame Xiaolin Li, President of the Chinese Association for Friendship with Foreign Countries, his Excellency Shaofang Qiu, Consul General of China in Los Angeles, and Congresswoman Judy Chu, and her husband Mr. Mike Eng, California State Assembly.

Judy Chu provided "sobering remarks" on the first day of the conference. She offered a history lesson on the Chinese Exclusion Act of 1882, which, according to Chu, prevented Chinese immigrants from becoming naturalized citizens, thus making Chinese "scapegoats for the Americans here." The Congresswoman said, "It was the relationship between the U.S. and China that actually got that act repealed in the first place. So, we must know that we have to value that relationship."[29]

Chinese Diplomat Recognized

Qiu Shaofang, China's Consul General in Los Angeles received a Certificate of Congressional Recognition from U.S. Representative Judy Chu of California for his contribution to U.S.-Chinese relations. The two were attending a reception in September 2012, marking China's National Day holiday.[30]

The Chinese Claim Chu as "Their" Politician

China lays claim to a huge overseas resource—50 million ethnic Chinese, mostly citizens of other countries, who Beijing sees as "sons and daughters of the Chinese nation."

The official Chinese newspaper the People's Daily on Saturday (November 3, 2012) published an article on what it called the participation of "overseas Chinese" in politics.

It cited U.S. Congresswoman Judy Chu of California, emphasizing that she was the only Asian among 35 national campaign Co-Chairpersons for Barack Obama's campaign committee.

Even though the article appeared in English in the paper's online edition, it referred to Chu as Zhao Meixin, using her Chinese name.

The article called Chu an example of a successful overseas Chinese "participating in politics in foreign countries," even though Chu was born in the United States, the granddaughter of an immigrant.

The People's Daily said: "As China's national strength is constantly enhancing, the status of overseas Chinese is also upgraded in the countries they live in."

It said that participation in politics had become an "irresistible trend" for overseas Chinese.

"In order to strengthen exchanges and cooperation with China, more and more overseas Chinese are needed to participate in the local political life," the paper said.

So from China's viewpoint, these ethnic Chinese politicians serve China's national purpose, even though they are elected officials of other countries.[31]

---

1 KeyWiki, "Judy Chu," KeyWiki, http://keywiki.org/index.php/Judy_Chu (accessed April 18, 2013)

2 Wigaable.com, "Former UCSB Activist Judy Chu = 1st Chinese American Woman Elected to Congress," Wigaable.com, http://www.wiqaable.com/2009/07/news-judy-chu-1st-chinese-american.html, (accessed April 18, 2013)

3 Judy Chu, "Biography," House.gov, http://chu.house.gov/about-me/full-biography (accessed April 18, 2013)

4 Wigaable.com, "Former UCSB Activist Judy Chu = 1st Chinese American Woman Elected to Congress," Wigaable.com, http://www.wiqaable.com/2009/07/news-judy-chu-1st-chinese-american.html, (accessed April 18, 2013)

5 Cynematic, "Run, Mama, Run*: Candidate for Congress Judy Chu Answers More Questions, Part 2," MOMocrats, http://momocrats.com/2009/05/06/run-mama-run-candidate-for-congress-judy-chu-answers-more-questions-part-2/, (May 6, 2009)

6 Judy Chu, "Biography," House.gov, http://chu.house.gov/about-me/full-biography (accessed April 18, 2013)

7 Judy Chu, "Obama for America Announces Rep. Judy Chu as National Co-Chair," Judy Chu for Congress, http://www.judychu.org/PDF/120222obamacochairrelease.pdf, (February 22, 2012)

8 KeyWiki, "Obama for America," KeyWiki, http://keywiki.org/index.php/Obama_for_America (accessed April 18, 2013)

9 KeyWiki, "Judy Chu," KeyWiki, http://keywiki.org/index.php/Judy_Chu (accessed April 18, 2013)

10 KeyWiki, "Judy Chu," KeyWiki, http://keywiki.org/index.php/Judy_Chu (accessed April 18, 2013)

11 Wigaable.com, "Former UCSB Activist Judy Chu = 1st Chinese American Woman Elected to Congress," Wigaable.com, http://www.wiqaable.com/2009/07/news-judy-chu-1st-chinese-american.html, (accessed April 18, 2013)

12 Wigaable.com, "Former UCSB Activist Judy Chu = 1st Chinese American Woman Elected to Congress," Wigaable.com, http://www.wiqaable.com/2009/07/news-judy-chu-1st-chinese-american.html, (accessed April 18, 2013)

13 Jeff Zalesin, "15 Arrested in Protests Over Documentation Firings," Student Life, http://tsl.pomona.edu/articles/2011/12/2/news/851-15-arrested-in-protests-over-documentation-firings (December 2, 2011)

14 Wherevent, "Annual Cesar Chavez Breakfast," Wherevent, http://www.wherevent.com/detail/jose-z-calderon-annual-cesar-chavez-breakfast, (accessed April 18, 2013)

15 Esther Cho and Eleanor Choi, "Asian American Studies 197B Spring Quarter 2002, Final Community Internship Reports, Asian Pacific American Labor Alliance—Public Hearing on Labor," Professor Glenn Omatsu's ClassWeb, http://www.sscnet.ucla.edu/aasc/classweb/spring02/aas197b/apala.html (accessed April 18, 2013)

16 Bananafish Blog, "APA Workers' Rights Hearing," Bananafish Blog (April 5, 2011)

17 KeyWiki, "Judy Chu," KeyWiki, http://keywiki.org/index.php/Judy_Chu (accessed April 18, 2013)

18 Chinaview, "Judy Chu becomes first Chinese American congresswoman in U.S.," Chinaview, http://news.xinhuanet.com/english/2009-07/15/content_11713232.htm, (July 15, 2009)

19 People's Daily Online, "Senior Chinese legislator meets U.S. congresswoman," People's Daily Online, http://english.peopledaily.com.cn/90883/7583897.html, (August 30, 2011)

20 People's Daily Online, "Senior Chinese legislator meets U.S. congresswoman," People's Daily Online, http://english.peopledaily.com.cn/90883/7583897.html, (August 30, 2011)
21 Peking University website, "Pro-Vice-Chancellor of Durham University visits Peking University," Peking University website, http://english.pku.edu.cn/News_Events/News/Global/8671.htm, (September 2011)
22 China Daily, "Congresswoman: Nations can learn from each other," China Daily, http://www.chinadaily.com.cn/world/2011-09/05/content_13615075.htm, (accessed April 19, 2013)
23 China Daily, "Congresswoman: Nations can learn from each other," China Daily, http://www.chinadaily.com.cn/world/2011-09/05/content_13615075.htm, (accessed April 19, 2013)
24 Life of Guangzhou, "The 1st American Chinese Congresswoman: I'm Truly Coming Home," Life of Guangzhou, http://www.lifeofguangzhou.com/node_981/node_989/node_994/node_1024/2011/09/20/131648734291072.shtml, (accessed April 19, 2013)
25 KeyWiki, "Committee of 100," KeyWiki, http://www.keywiki.org/index.php/Committee_of_100 (accessed April 19, 2013)
26 Jane Leung Larson, "Committee of 100 Greets Newly-Elected Representative Judy Chu in Washington, D.C.," Committee of 100, http://committee100.typepad.com/committee_of_100_newslett/2009/11/committee-of-100-greets-newly-elected-representative-judy-chu-in-washington-dc.html, (November 2009)
27 Consulate-General Of The People's Republic Of China In Los Angeles, "Engaging Global Audiences and Reaching Potentials – 2012 Global Chinese Broadcasting Cooperation Annual Meeting," Consulate-General Of The People's Republic Of China In Los Angeles, http://losangeles.china-consulate.org/eng/lghd/t938892.htm (June 7, 2012)
28 2012 Western Region Conference of USCPFA, http://uscpfa-wr.org/about.htm,
29 Jim E. Winburn, "U.S.-China Conference Discusses Past, Present Relations," Temple Tribune, http://www.templecitytribune.com/current-news/u-s-china-conference-discusses-past-present-relations/, (October 2012)
30 China Daily Los Angeles, "Diplomat recognized," China Daily Los Angeles, http://usa.chinadaily.com.cn/epaper/2012-09/28/content_15790763.htm, (September 2012)
31 Frank Ching, "The 'sons & daughters of China'," The China Post, http://www.chinapost.com.tw/commentary/the-china-post/frank-ching/2012/11/07/360168/The-sons.htm, (November 7, 2012)

Michael Honda (D-CA)

Michael Honda is a Democratic member of the United States House of Representatives, representing the 17th District of California. He is a member of the Congressional Progressive Caucus and a former chair of the Asian Pacific American Caucus.

Background

Michael Makoto "Mike" Honda was born on June 27, 1941 in California, but spent his early childhood with family in an internment camp in Colorado during World War II. Honda's father served in the Military Intelligence Service, while his mother served as a fulltime homemaker. His family returned to California in 1953, becoming strawberry sharecroppers in San José's Blossom Valley.

In 1965, Honda enrolled in the Peace Corps for two years in El Salvador and returned fluent in Spanish and with a "passion for teaching."

Honda earned Bachelor's Degrees in Biological Sciences and Spanish and a Master's Degree in Education from San José State University. In his career as an educator, he was a science teacher, served as a principal at two public schools and conducted educational research at Stanford University.[1]

In 1971, Honda was appointed by then-Mayor Norman Mineta (later a leftist Congressman) to San Jose's Planning Commission. In 1981, he won his first election, gaining a seat on the San José Unified School Board. In 1990, Honda was elected to the Santa Clara County Board of Supervisors.[2]

Influence

Mike Honda served in the California State Assembly from 1996 to 2000. In 2000, he was elected to the U.S. House of Representatives and serves on the Appropriations Committee, with postings on Commerce, Justice and Science, and Legislative Branch Subcommittees. Honda is also Co-Chair of the Democratic Caucus' New Media Working Group.

In the 112th Congress, Honda was reappointed to House Democratic Senior Whip by then House Minority Whip Steny Hoyer.

Honda is currently the Chairman Emeritus of the Congressional Asian Pacific American Caucus after spending seven years as Chairman. He continues his past work of coordinating with his colleagues in the Congressional Black Caucus and the Congressional Hispanic Caucuses to "champion the causes of under-represented communities by promoting social justice, racial tolerance, civil rights and voting rights. Additionally, as Co-Chair of the House LGBT Caucus, Mike Honda authored immigration legislation to reunite all families, regardless of orientation."[3]

Communist Connections

Lopez Report

In a report given to the National Committee of the Communist Party USA (CPUSA) and dated September 26, 2001, California District Communist Party—Northern Region Chair Juan Lopez, wrote extensively on Honda:[4]

> California was a big bust for Bush and the Republicans.

> Joining with Los Angeles and other Southern California areas, the greater Bay Area counties, where the population is concentrated in Northern California and the labor movement is strongest, helped give Gore a big win in the state.

> Labor organized and mobilized like I've never seen, in some areas working more closely with its allies, especially among African Americans and Mexican Americans. Along with women voters, labor and African Americans and Latinos were the core of the electoral coalition that dealt Bush and the Republicans a devastating defeat in California...

Democrat Mike Honda embodies California's rich multi-cultural, working class experience. He is a union member of the American Federation of Teachers, a former teacher and principal, who comes from a farmworker family of Japanese ancestry and who as a child spent time in an infamous American concentration camp during WW II...

I want to cite one example. On the Saturday before the elections, our paper ran a very good article on the congressional races, highlighting Mike Honda among others, with a big picture of him. I asked if it was OK for me to pass the paper out, outside by the front door as the volunteers came streaming back for lunch. I was told, no!... Better yet: put copies on the tables where the workers would be having lunch and pass them out inside the campaign headquarters to those hanging around.

Fishman Report

A 2002 report by Joelle Fishman, Chair, Political Action Committee, CPUSA to the Party's National Board, called for communist support for two California Congressional candidates—Michael Honda and Barbara Lee:[5]

The priority labor campaigns deserve our support. In addition our work will take us beyond these races to election districts where we have organization and where there are strong pro-labor candidates, African American, Mexican American and Latino candidates such as Rep. Mike Honda and Rep. Barbara Lee.

Every district should consider where we can make a qualitative difference. What are the election campaigns where there is a labor or people's candidate, where we can participate in coalition to build a movement in that election district, and in the process build our Party...

Certainly, we would not be making our special contribution to this crucial election if we were to approach our task in simply a narrow, immediate way. This gigantic election battle must be put into the broader context of the fight for an expansion of democratic rights, voter rights and voter participation. It must be put into the context of building political independence of labor and allies. In addition to union-based get-out-the-vote drives, what does political independence of labor and allies encompass?

Perhaps in the first place, it means adding more Mike Honda's to Congress—electing more union leaders and activists to public office.

Amy Dean Relationship

Mike Honda was very close to Amy Dean, a long-time Communist Party affiliate, when she led the labor movement in his area.[6]

Christopher Gardner

Smacks of Cronyism: Organized labor, personified by South Bay Labor Council leader Amy Dean (center), holds the cards for area Democrats like Assemblyman Mike Honda (left) and others. The labor contingent also hopes to keep relations with the next mayor

Mike Honda, Amy Dean

In the House of Representatives on June 4, 2003, the Santa Clara County Congressional delegation: Anna Eshoo, Zoe Lofgren and Mike Honda, read a tribute into the Congressional Record to Amy Dean, Chief Executive Officer of the South Bay AFL-CIO Labor Council, who was leaving the Bay Area to return to her native Chicago.[7]

> Through Amy Dean's leadership, the South Bay AFL-CIO Labor Council has been extremely successful in working for living wage contracts for city workers, affordable housing requirements in new developments, and health insurance for every child in Santa Clara County.

> Amy Dean has been a tireless and passionate advocate for social justice and has helped to strengthen the labor movement, bringing dignity and hope to countless families, whether they are union or non-union workers.

Amy Dean is also a big fan of Honda's. She told the socialist journal In These Times:[8]

> One of my favorite elected leaders is Mike Honda, a congressman in California. I would do anything for this guy: He takes chances, he takes

risk. He always sticks to his progressive values. Even when he is a minority, he never sways from his values.

APALA Connection

Mike Honda has close ties to the Asian Pacific American Labor Alliance, a radical union grouping founded and supported by members and affiliates of the new re-branded, pro-China, Communist Workers Party.

Honda attended the organization's three day 11th biennial convention on July 22, 2011, in Oakland, California, along with Oakland Mayor Jean Quan, a former member of the Communist Workers Party.[9] [10]

"Progressive" Connections

Writing in Support of IPS Event

Rep. Honda co-wrote an article, for The Huffington Post—"What America Can Learn From El Salvador in Ending Gang Violence about El Salvador," in advance of an Institute for Policy Studies-supported event on January 13, 2013.[11] The article recommended that gang problems might best be solved through negotiation rather than tough law enforcement:

> The Obama administration should take a cue from El Salvador, which has adopted a far less confrontational approach to gangs, and is seeing a drop in gang violence as a result. Both of us have worked and traveled extensively in Central America—El Salvador in particular, which has its own MS-13...
>
> Earlier this year, in an effort to curb the violence, the government in El Salvador negotiated a groundbreaking deal with the Salvadoran MS-13 and a rival gang, Calle-18. In a bold move, mediators in El Salvador essentially extended the framework of humanitarian engagement to gang warfare, brokering a peace treaty between the two gangs and the Salvadoran government. After the deal, homicides decreased by 32 percent and kidnappings by 50 percent, as reported by the New York Times. In May, the gangs extended their truce to school zones and agreed to end forced recruitment of child soldiers...
>
> The U.S.—and gang-plagued Mexico—should heed the progress made in El Salvador and recognize that the standard methods to end violence aren't working. Creative, innovative solutions are needed. This

Salvadoran example is one that should be tried, showing that everyone from the community to local elected officials to law enforcement needs to be brought in to truly end violence on a large scale.

The truce established in El Salvador may be unusual, but it is most certainly benefiting the people of that nation, and may serve as an interim solution to a very real and dangerous epidemic.

The IPS supported function was held on January 16th at an IPS-linked venue: Busboys & Poets, in Washington, D.C.[12]

"Leading with Love"

"Leading with Love" was an event to celebrate five years of the Marxist-led, Institute for Policy Studies "key partner" National Domestic Workers Alliance. It was held in Washington D.C. on November 14, 2012.

Members of the Host Committee included Mike Honda, Ken Grossinger, a one-time Democratic Socialists of America member, Rinku Sen of the communist influenced Applied Research Center, former Maoist and one-time Obama "Green Jobs Czar," Van Jones, Institute for Policy Studies, "partner organization" Demos and Young Communist League convention attendee, Sarita Gupta.[13]

Foreign Policy/National Security

Cuban Visit

In early April 2009, Representative Barbara Lee led a Congressional delegation to Havana for a 4-1/2 hour meeting with Raul Castro, telling reporters, "All of us are convinced that President Castro would like normal relations and would see normalization, ending the embargo, as beneficial to both countries." Reuters reported that Lee's delegation "avoided specifics" with Castro "but were struck by his humor, impressed by his involvement in Third World causes and firm in their belief that he wants to end United States-Cuba enmity.[14]

Michael Honda, from California, also accompanied the delegation.[15]

Staffer's Trip to Venezuela

Rep. Honda sent staffer Michael Shank to Marxist-led Venezuela for three days in February 2010. The trip was courtesy of a $2,219.70 grant from the Institute for Policy Studies-connected Center for Democracy in the Americas, "A fact-finding trip in Venezuela and other Latin American countries with the mission of fostering dialogue and improving U.S. policy and bilateral relations."[16]

2010 Trip to Latin America

Rep. Honda traveled to Honduras and El Salvador for three days in May/June 2010. The trip was courtesy of a $4,107.39 grant from the Institute for Policy Studies-connected Center for Democracy in the Americas, to "Assess the situation in Honduras and El Salvador and current U.S. policy implications in the countries."[17]

China Trip

U.S. Rep. Judy Chu, Chairwoman of the Congressional Asian Pacific American Caucus, led the first ever CAPAC Congressional delegation to the People's Republic of China in September 2011. The primary purpose of the delegation was to promote U.S. exports and improve the U.S.-China relationship.

Chairwoman Chu was accompanied by CAPAC Executive Board Members Rep. Mike Honda (CA-15) and Rep. Eni Faleomavaega (AS).[18]

Council for a Livable World

The anti-U.S. military Council for a Livable World has supported Mike Honda in his successful House of Representatives run as a candidate for the state of California.[19]

---

1 Mike Honda, "About Mike," Congressman Mike Honda, http://honda.house.gov/index.php?option=com_content&view=article&id=12&Itemid=19 (accessed June 15, 2012)
2 Mike Honda, "About Mike," Congressman Mike Honda, http://honda.house.gov/index.php?option=com_content&view=article&id=12&Itemid=19 (accessed June 15, 2012)
3 Mike Honda, "About Mike," Congressman Mike Honda, http://honda.house.gov/index.php?option=com_content&view=article&id=12&Itemid=19 (accessed June 15, 2012)
4 Juan Lopez, "Northern California Elections Report," Communist Party USA, http://www.cpusa.org/northern-california-elections-report/, (September 26, 2001)
5 Joelle Fishman, "CPUSA Report on the 2002 Elections, February 22, 2002, National Committee Meeting," CPUSA (February 2002)
6 KeyWiki, "Amy Dean," KeyWiki, http://www.keywiki.org/index.php/Amy_Dean (accessed May 12, 2013)
7 Congressional Record (June 4, 2003)

8 Amy Dean, "In Person," In These Times,
http://www.inthesetimes.com/community/20questions/5720/amy_dean/ (accessed
January 21, 2012)
9 KeyWiki, "Michael Honda," KeyWiki, http://keywiki.org/index.php/Michael_Honda
(accessed January 21, 2013)
10 KeyWiki, "Asian Pacific American Labor Alliance," KeyWiki,
http://www.keywiki.org/index.php/Asian_Pacific_American_Labor_Alliance
(accessed May 12, 2013)
11 Rep. Mike Honda and Ami C. Carpenter, "What America Can Learn From El
Salvador in Ending Gang Violence," The Huffington Post,
http://www.huffingtonpost.com/rep-mike-honda/what-america-can-learn-
fr_b_2402397.html?utm_hp_ref=fb&src=sp&comm_ref=false (accessed January 21,
2013)
12 IPS Website, "The Power of Dialogue: Peace from Unexpected Places and
Unexpected People," IPS, http://www.ips-
dc.org/events/the_power_of_dialogue_peace_from_unexpected_places_and_unexpecte
d_people, (accessed January 21, 2013)
13 Leading with Love, "Hosts and Sponsors," Leading with Love,
http://domesticworkers.org/leadingwithlove/hosts-and-sponsors, (accessed January 21,
2013)
14 PoliticalWarfare.org, "Congresswoman Barbara Lee: Still stuck in the Cold War,"
PoliticalWarfare.org,
http://jmw.typepad.com/political_warfare/2009/04/congresswoman-barbara-lee-still-
stuck-in-the-cold-war.html (accessed June 15, 2012)
15 Fidel Castro, "The seven Congress members who are visiting us," Digital Granma,
http://www.granma.cu/ingles/2009/april/mar7/Reflections-6april.html (accessed June
15, 2012)
16 LegiStorm, "Center for Democracy in the Americas – Sponsor of Congressional
Travel," LegiStorm,
http://www.legistorm.com/trip/list/by/sponsor/id/10693/name/Center_for_Democracy_
in_the_Americas/page/2.html (accessed January 21, 2013)
17 LegiStorm, "Center for Democracy in the Americas – Sponsor of Congressional
Travel," LegiStorm,
http://www.legistorm.com/trip/list/by/sponsor/id/10693/name/Center_for_Democracy_
in_the_Americas/page/2.html (accessed January 21, 2013)
18 CAPAC Press Release, "CAPAC Chair Judy Chu Leads Historic First Caucus
Congressional Delegation to China," CAPAC, http://capac-chu.house.gov/press-
release/capac-chair-judy-chu-leads-historic-first-caucus-congressional-delegation-
china, (September 12, 2011)
19 Council for A Livable World, "Meet the Candidates," Council for A Livable World,
http://livableworld.org/support/meet_candidates/ (accessed June 15, 2012)

Barbara Lee (D-CA)

Barbara Jean Lee is a Democratic member of the United States House of Representatives, representing the 13th District of California.[1]

She currently serves as Congressional Progressive Caucus Whip and on the Executive Board of the Congressional Asian Pacific American Caucus. She is a member of, and past Chair of, the Congressional Black Caucus.

Background

Born in 1946 in El Paso, Texas, Barbara Lee spent her teenage years in San Fernando, California. She was educated at Mills College and earned a Master's Degree in Social Work from the University of California at Berkeley in 1975.

Lee's radicalism dates at least to the early 1970s, when she was a confidential aide to Black Panther Party "Minister of Defense," Huey Newton.[2]

Barbara Lee was inspired to a political career while a campaign worker for Shirley Chisholm's 1972 presidential campaign. Chisholm was the first black woman to enter Congress. Chisholm had a long history of Communist Party USA (CPUSA) front affiliation, but entered Congress through the Democratic Party in New York's 11th District.[3]

Lee was elected to Congress in 1998 in California's 9th District after the retirement of her former boss Rep. Ron Dellums. The District is now redrawn as the 13th District.

Influence

Lee is the most senior Democratic woman on the House International Relations Committee. She has sponsored legislation disavowing the pre-

245

emptive war doctrine and led bipartisan efforts to end the genocide in Darfur.[4]

Barbara Lee serves on the House Committee on Appropriations, which includes the Subcommittee on Labor, Health and Human Services, Education and Related Agencies and the Subcommittee on State, Foreign Operations and Related Programs. She also serves on the House Committee on The Budget and the House Democratic Steering and Policy Committee.

Lee is the Senior Democratic Whip, she is the Chair on the Social Work Caucus, the Vice-Chair on the LGBT Equality Caucus, the Co-Chair on the Out-of-Poverty Caucus, the Co-Chair on the Congressional HIV/AIDS Caucus, the Co-Chair on the Congressional Sudan Caucus, the Co-Chair on the Health Care Task Force and the Co-Chair on the Peace and Security Task Force.[5]

While most California Democrats initially supported Hillary Clinton, in December 2008, California Congresswoman Barbara Lee became the first California Democrat to endorse Barack Obama.

Lee wrote on December 10, 2008 in the Huffington Post:[6]

> I wanted to share some exciting news with you, as today I announced my endorsement of Senator Barack Obama for President of the United States.
>
> Like so many Americans, I first heard Senator Obama when he delivered his electrifying speech at the 2004 Democratic National Convention in Boston. Deep down, I knew I'd witnessed history in the making.
>
> Barack Obama represents a bridge to the future. He embodies the hope and new direction that our country so desperately needs. As I've watched Senator Obama campaign for the presidency, I am convinced that he is a real agent of change; a man who can lead our nation in a new and positive direction.
>
> This century cries for social, environmental, diplomatic, global, and neighborhood solutions to the misery that confronts far too many people in our own country and around the globe. I share Senator Obama's vision and active commitment to building a society based on activism, progressive values and a keen sense that we must act now and outside of the usual bounds of partisanship and expediency.

Communist Connections

Barbara Lee has extensive ties to two Communist groups—Communist Party USA (CPUSA) and its spinoff, Committees of Correspondence.

Communist Influencers

Both Lee and her boss, Rep. Ron Dellums, were encouraged to enter politics by long-time Berkeley Councilwoman and CPUSA supporter, Maudelle Shirek. Another key influence on Lee was Bay Area doctor and publisher, Carlton Goodlett, a long-time Communist Party member.

Still another was Bay Area radical, Yvonne Scarlett-Golden.

In 2006, Barbara Lee released the following statement in response to the news that Daytona Beach Mayor and long-time San Francisco resident, Yvonne Scarlett-Golden, had died of cancer at the age of 80:[7]

> Yvonne Scarlett-Golden was a friend to me and an inspiration to many. As the first African-American Mayor of Daytona Beach, she knew about breaking down barriers, and the fact that she came to politics after a full career as a teacher and school administrator is a testament to her determination to serve.
>
> I first met Yvonne when she was the principal of Alamo Park High School in San Francisco in the 1970's. I remember very well attending peace conferences with Yvonne, the late Alameda County Supervisor John George, former Berkeley City Council member Maudelle Shirek, and the late Carlton Goodlett, publisher of the Sun Reporter Newspaper, all of whose lives were totally committed to peace and justice. Yvonne was never afraid of controversy, and she was outspoken for what she believed in. We will miss her.

Both Maudelle Shirek and Yvonne Scarlett-Golden went on to join Committees of Correspondence after the Communist Party split in 1991.[8][9]

1980's U.S. Peace Council Executive Board

Barbara Lee was an Executive Board member of the U.S. Peace Council from 1983 to 1985. An affiliate of the Soviet front World Peace Council, the U.S. body was run by the CPUSA. Lee served alongside several known Communist Party members including Sara Staggs, Rob Prince, Michael Myerson, James Jackson, Atiba Mbiwan, Pauline Rosen and Denise Young; as well as several known party sympathizers including

Alice Palmer, who would go on to become a political mentor to Barack Obama in Chicago.[10] [11]

CoC Member

At the Committees of Correspondence founding conference in Berkeley, California on July 17-19, 1992, Barbara Lee was a candidate for the Committees of Correspondence National Coordinating Committee, while serving as a Democratic California State Assembly person.[12]

tian Leadership Conference, later becoming its assistant director. A long-time member of the D.C. Statehood Party, he was elected as a delegate to the D.C. Statehood Convention in 1981. He serves presently as an Advisory Neighborhood Commissioner. A member of the Communist Party, USA, for 20 years, he served as chair of its D.C., Maryland and Virginia districts, as its Legislative Director, and on the National Committee and National Board. He left the party following its support for the coup in the former Soviet Union.

GEOFFREY JACQUES is a poet, journalist, essayist, curator, editor, activist and critic. Born in Detroit, he moved to New York in 1983. He has been active in the peace, trade union and social justice movements for over 20 years, and

HON. BARBARA LEE represents the 13th Assembly District (which includes Oakland, Alameda and Emeryville) in the California State Assembly. She serves on five standing legislative committees and a wide range of commissions. Lee founded a community health center while working on her graduate degree in Social Work in the mid-'70s. She served as a senior advisor and administrative assistant to Rep. Ronald V. Dellums from 1975-87. She is a member of the Rainbow Coalition, Black Women Organized for Political Action, and many other organizations.
Continued on next page

Committees of Correspondence Newsletter – Page 11

CoC National Coordinating Committee Member

In 1993, Barbara Lee was an official member of the Committee of Correspondence's leadership body, the National Coordinating Committee.

When this was publicly exposed, the organization stopped publishing the names of its officers. It is not known when, if ever, Barbara Lee left the Committees of Correspondence.[13]

People's Weekly World Banquet 1997

Elected officials attending the Communist Party's 1997 Bay Area People's Weekly World Banquet at His Lordship's Berkeley Marina, included State Senator Barbara Lee, Assemblywoman Liz Figueroa, Alemeda County

Board of Supervisors President Keith Carson and Berkeley Vice Mayor and City Council member, Maudelle Shirek.[14]

Endorsed Communist Party 1999 PWW Fundraiser

In September 1999, Rep. Barbara Lee co-sponsored a Communist Party fundraising event in Berkeley.[15]

Co-sponsors:

Antonio Abarca, Alameda County LCLAA
Dion Aroner, California State Assembly
Carlos Avitia, Santa Clara County LCLAA
Arnold Becchetti, Alameda County FORUM
Marilyn Bechtel, Friends of the PWW
Richard Benson, President, UFCW Local 870
Delmer Berg, State Bd., Congress of Calif.Seniors
Sue Bierman, San Francisco Board of Supervisors
Willie L. Brown, Jr., Mayor, San Francisco
Everett E. Burdan, Dispatcher, ILWU Local 17
Californians for Justice
Keith Carson, Alameda County Supervisor
Henry Clark, West County Toxics Coalition
Brenda Cochrane, Director, San Francisco State University Labor Studies
Forrest Crumpley, Secretary, Santa Clara County FORUM
Tom Csekey, Vice President, SEIU Local 1877
Pat Dando, San Jose City Council
Amy B. Dean, Exec. Officer, South Bay Labor Council
Ignacio de la Fuente, Pres., Oakland City Council
Libero Della Piana, Co-Chair, N. Calif. Dist., YCL
James DuPont, President, HERE Local 2850
Riva Enteen, Program Dir., Natl. Lawyers Guild
Francis Fink, Pres. Emeritus, South Bay FORUM
Lucille Flato, Co-Chair, Retiree Committee, United Public Employees Local 790
Maria Montes Fink, Chair, SEIU Local 715 Retiree Members Committee
Judith Goff, Exec. Sec'y-Treas., Alameda County CLC
Karega Hart, President, ATU Local 1574
Herb Kaye, N. Calif. correspondent, PWW
Luther Jackson, Executive Officer, The Newspaper Guild Local 98
Walter Johnson, Secretary Treasurer, San Francisco Labor Council

Barbara Lee, Member of Congress

John Lewis, Secretary-Treasurer, ILWU Local 10

People's Weekly World/Nuestro Mundo

Gala Banquet

**Sunday, Sept. 26, 12:30 p.m.
His Lordships Restaurant, Berkeley Marina**

Honoring five who make the difference for labor, peace, democracy, equality and a truly human quality of life:

Maudelle Shirek, Vice Mayor of Berkeley
Cindy Chavez, San Jose City Councilmember
Ruth Holbrook, President, Sacramento Central Labor Council
Lawrence Thibeaux, President, ILWU Local 10
PUEBLO (People United for a Better Oakland) & Executive Director Daniel HoSang

and featuring: **U. Utah Phillips**
story teller, folk singer, song maker

Reservations $35   Information: (510) 436-0477

People's Weekly World (September 11, 1999)

PWW 2001 Banquet

Eliseo Medina, Democratic Socialists of America leader and SEIU International Executive Vice President, received a standing ovation, as keynote speaker at the People's Weekly World Banquet in Berkeley on Nov. 18, 2001.

In addition to Medina, the banquet honored the East Bay Alliance for a Sustainable Economy, the Middle East Children's Alliance and Sacramento Activists for Democratic Trade. The event raised $11,000 for the 2001 fund drive.

Honorees received certificates of Congressional recognition by the office of Rep. Barbara Lee; the event took place in her District. Lee's greeting was presented by her aide, Saundra Andrews.

"At this time of crisis, when world peace hangs in the balance and the rights of immigrants are under attack," Lee's statement said, "it is more important than ever that our community come together to honor the work and legacy of those who struggle to advance the cause of peace and justice for working people everywhere."[16]

PWW 2002 Banquet

In a spirited tribute, the Northern California People's Weekly World Banquet on Oct. 13, 2002, honored "the heroes and heroines of the struggle against corporate greed," and called for a big turnout against Republican "Bush-clones" in the Nov. 5th election. The banquet raised $8,000 for the PWW fund drive.

In her opening, Berkeley Vice Mayor, Maudelle Shirek, spoke of the growing movements in solidarity with West Coast Port Workers and against war. "So there is hope," she said, "…and a new movement that we must help nurture and grow."

That movement includes the bloc in Congress that voted against the Bush war resolution and those who supported Rep. Barbara Lee's peace resolution.

Banquet honorees each received certificates from Rep. Lee.[17]

H.R. 3000

On September 3, 2003, Congresswoman Barbara Lee introduced H.R. 3000, the United States Universal Health Service Act, which would provide health coverage for all Americans. H.R. 3000 would establish a United States Health Service, which "would eliminate profit issues from health care because it would be owned and controlled by the public and administered primarily at the local level."

"The United States is the only industrialized nation in the world that does not provide universal health care," said Lee. "We must become a health care provider, not a denier of this fundamental right."[18]

The Communist Party USA's People's World commented on Lee's proposal:

We will not win the United States Health Service without a massive, prolonged struggle by working people against the corporate defenders of the current for-profit health care industry.

PWW 2004 Banquet

The "mood was both joyous and determined" as Northern California supporters of the People's Weekly World/Nuestro Mundo gathered Oct. 8, 2004, in Oakland to celebrate their favorite newspaper and to rededicate themselves to the banquet's theme—"Beat back Bush!"

The "full-house, rainbow crowd honored leaders and organizations from the labor, anti-war, Cuba and Haiti solidarity movements and enjoyed a rich cultural program." Honorees received certificates of appreciation from area Congresswoman Barbara Lee and from Friends of the People's Weekly World.[19]

PWW 2006 Event

Barbara Lee was involved in a function organized for the People's Weekly World in Oakland, California on December 3, 2006, as was Communist Party supporter, peace activist, Jacqueline Cabasso.

"December 3rd was a day the People's Weekly World can be proud of. Still celebrating the results of the November 7th elections, readers held banquets and dinners in various places across the country, attracting elected officials, leaders of people's movements and rank-and-file fighters for justice and democracy..."

Other honored guests included anti-nuclear-weapons leader Jackie Cabasso, the Blue Diamond Workers Organizing Committee and two Sacramento-based immigrant rights coalitions. All received certificates from U.S. Rep. Barbara Lee.[20]

Socialist Connections

Support from Democratic Socialists of America

San Francisco Bay Area Democratic Socialists of America (DSA) supported Barbara Lee's sole dissenting vote in Congress after the 9/11 attacks:[21]

The DSA national convention passed a resolution condemning the September 11 attacks, supporting in principle the selective use of multilateral armed force, and calling for a halt to the bombing. Its text, along with previous statements by DSA on the war, will presumably be available at the national web site soon. The Sacramento local and the anti-racism commission issued a prior statement, also available as an MS Word document. The East Bay local will be working for the re-election of Barbara Lee, the sole member of Congress to oppose a resolution granting sweeping, vaguely specified war powers to our illegitimate President.

DSA Supported Vaccines Compensation Bill

Democratic Socialists of America backed Dennis Kucinich nationally with his 2002 HR2459 Vaccines Compensation bill. Lynn Woolsey and Barbara Lee both co-sponsored Kucinich's bill.

According to the minutes of a January 5, 2002, SF DSA Steering Committee meeting:[22]

> According to a (fundraising) call from DSA, supporting HR2459 is a national DSA project. The idea is to contact representatives about co-sponsoring the bill, which comes from Dennis Kucinich and is supported by the progressive caucus. Everyone said they would contact their rep. (Woolsey and Lee are co-sponsors).

"Making Trouble"

"Making Trouble—Building a Radical Youth Movement" was held on April 17-19, 1998, in Berkeley, California:

> "Making Trouble" is a conference for young radicals from all over California to meet, form coalitions, and get informed. We will focus on the Prison Industrial Complex and the contemporary Labor Movement, but there will also be workshops on Environmental Justice, the Unz initiative, Art and Revolution, Immigration, Third World Organizing, Economic Globalization, Affirmative Action, Reproductive Rights, and much more.

The Keynote speaker was DSA leader Barbara Ehrenreich.

Invited speakers included DSAers Dolores Huerta, Cornel West and Rep. Ron Dellums, as well as radical leader Tom Hayden, Committees of Correspondence activist Angela Davis and Rep. Barbara Lee.[23]

MAKING TROUBLE
Building a Radical Youth Movement
April 17-19, Berkeley, California
Keynote Speaker: Barbara Ehrenreich

"Making Trouble" is a conference for young radicals from all over California to meet, form coalitions, and get informed. We will focus on the Prison Industrial Complex and the contemporary Labor Movement, but there will also be workshops on Environmental Justice, the Unz initiative, Art and Revolution, Immigration, Third World Organizing, Economic Globalization, Affirmative Action, Reproductive Rights, and much more.

Invited speakers include
> Dolores Huerta
> Donna Haraway
> Tom Hayden
> Angela Davis
> Cornel West
> Barbara Lee
> Jello Biafra
> Ron Dellums

For more information, contact Katie Howenstine at (510) 665.9404 or howenstine@usa.net, or check out the Making Trouble website at www.dsausa.org/trouble.

Democratic Left Issue (1998) p. 6

DSA Campaigner

One time DSA member Nancy Skinner was a Field Manager for Barbara Lee's 2002 Congressional campaign.[24]

Nancy Skinner went on to found ICLEI—Local Governments for Sustainability, an organization dedicated to helping local governments around the world become environmental leaders. As Executive Director of ICLEI's U.S. office, Nancy Skinner launched the Cities for Climate Protection program—the U.S. movement of mayors and cities working to reduce greenhouse gas emissions that now involves over 500 U.S. cities and counties. This is often known as Agenda 21.[25]

Skinner is now a Democratic California State Representative.

21st Century Democrats

On July 28, 2010, Congresswoman Barbara Lee, Congressman Elijah Cummings and Obama's communist former "Green Jobs Czar," Van

Jones, spoke about the future of American politics at the kick-off event for 21st Century Democrats' 2010 Youth Leadership Speaker Series. The event was sponsored by Representative John Lewis and Senator Tom Harkin.[26]

21st Century Democrats was led by one-time DSAer, Jim Scheibel.[27]

"Progressive" Connections

Take Back America Conferences

Barbara Lee was on the list of 153 speakers at the 2006 Take Back America conference, which was organized by the Institute for Policy Studies (IPS) and DSA–initiated Campaign for America's Future.[28]

She was back in 2007.

America's Future Now!

Barbara Lee was one of the 148 speakers who addressed the Take Back America's succeeding America's Future Now Conference on June 7-9, 2010, in Washington, D.C.[29]

Africa Action Connection

In 2009, Barbara Lee served on the Board of Directors of the far left Institute for Policy Studies partner organization, Africa Action.[30]

Leading with Love

Leading with Love was an event to celebrate 5 years of the Marxist-led IPS partnered National Domestic Workers Alliance. It was held in Washington, D.C. on November 14, 2012.

Rep. Barbara Lee served on the Host Committee.[31]

Progressive Democrats of America

Barbara Lee serves on the Advisory Board of the IPS/DSA-led Progressive Democrats of America.[32]

Progressive Democrats of America 2012 Endorsement

In 2012, Barbara Lee was one of 14 leftist Congressional and Senate candidates endorsed by Progressive Democrats of America.[33]

Foreign Policy/National Security

World Peace Council

Barbara Lee told The Progressive magazine that her life was influenced by the late Carlton Goodlett, a dedicated Stalinist and served in the leadership of the international Soviet front, the World Peace Council. He used a newspaper he owned to spread Soviet disinformation and to promote KGB forgeries. In 1981, Lee wrote to the World Peace Council asking that the Soviet front pay for air tickets for California Rep. Ron Dellums and two staffers to attend one of their conferences.34

Supported by Council for a Livable World

Barbara Lee has enjoyed the financial support of Council for a Livable World, founded by reported Soviet agent, Leo Szilard, which seeks to "reduce the danger of nuclear weapons and increase national security," primarily through supporting progressive, Congressional candidates who support their policies.35

No to Use of Force After 9/11

Barbara Lee was the only member of Congress to vote against the resolution broadly authorizing President Bush's use of force after 9/11.[36]

Department of Peace

Speaking to a crowd of 200 peace activists on March 11, 2002, in Oakland, California, Reps. Barbara Lee and Communist Party affiliate Dennis Kucinich (D-OH) took the occasion to condemn the Bush administration's plans to target seven nations with nuclear weapons.

"To think that the nuclear option is on the table as a viable strategy is terrifying," said Lee. "We must keep peace out there as an option."

Kucinich declared, "We have a crisis in the country—a crisis in the lack of belief in the power of peace. The Bush plan," he said, "challenges America morally. It raises the question of what America stands for." Both statements were "warmly applauded by the audience gathered to hear about a proposed Cabinet-level Peace Office initiated by Lee and Kucinich".

They were joined in their stand by Communist Party affiliated activist Jackie Cabasso, spokesperson for the People's Non-Violent Response

Coalition, organizer of the event, who said, "The U.S. position needs to be condemned today, immediately! We need a Department of Peace, but we need some interim measures in the meantime." The PNVRC was formed in the wake of the events of Sept. 11 to promote non-violence as the answer to terrorism.

The bill (HR2459) that would set up the Department of Peace was introduced in Congress on July 11, 2001 by Kucinich; at that point there were 61 co-sponsors, including Lee.

The bill would order the federal government to set up a $3 billion a year agency with a Secretary of Peace who would be a member of the President's Cabinet and seven assistant secretaries. The mission of the Department would include: hold peace as an organizing principle; endeavor to promote justice and democratic principles to expand human rights; develop policies that promote national and international conflict prevention; non-violent intervention; mediation; peaceful resolution of conflict and structured mediation of conflict.

A national "Peace Day" would be declared as an occasion to urge all citizens to create peace.[37]

Anti-Iraq War

An early and outspoken opponent of the Iraq War, Lee repeatedly proposed legislation seeking early U.S. troop withdrawal. In 2007, she successfully blocked funds from being used to establish permanent military bases in Iraq.

Her 2008 amendment requiring that any U.S. agreement to defend Iraq be expressly authorized by Congress, or be included in a Senate approved treaty, was stripped from a defense bill under the threat of a veto by President Bush.[38]

Aiding Grenada Communists

Barbara Lee provided counterintelligence support to the Marxist-Leninist regime in Grenada in the 1980s.

In 1982, together with her colleague Carlottia Scott, Lee accompanied her boss, Rep. Ron Dellums, to communist-ruled Grenada. They wrote a report to the House Armed Services Committee in support of an airport being built on the island, which the U.S. government believed could be used by Soviet bombers aimed at America. Dellums, Lee and Scott provided their draft report to the island's communist leader Maurice

Bishop, to vet before they submitted the final copy to the U.S. House of Representatives.

Lee was Dellums' Administrative Assistant. When she left the job to run for the California legislature in 1987, Scott took her job. When Dellums left Congress in April 1998, Lee won the seat and Carlottia Scott became her Administrative Assistant.

In a handwritten letter to Maurice Bishop addressed to: "My Comrade Leader," Scott wrote: "Grenada is my home and where my deepest love will always remain. I am sincerely committed and dedicated to Grenada. I feel that now, I will be able to convey in a more comprehensive manner, the thoughts and directions of the PRG [People's Revolutionary Government of Grenada] which, based on a solid foundation, will, in eccence [sic] help to keep the REVO [revolution] up in North America."[39]

Lee later opposed the U.S.- led ouster of Grenadian General Hudson Austin, who had murdered Maurice Bishop, his former ally, in a coup just days before.

Documents now stored in the national Archives show the extent of Lee's support for the Grenada revolution.

When Lee received an envelope containing anti-regime material that had been mailed from Bishop's office, she immediately warned Bishop's Ambassador to the Organization of American States, Dessima Williams—who immediately informed Maurice Bishop. The memorandum read:[40]

> Comrade:
>
> On May 14, 1980, Barbara Lee called to say she had received a piece of anti-PRG [People's Revolutionary Government] propaganda stamped from the Prime Minister's Office, post-marked in Grenada. We collected it May 15, and it is herewith attached.
>
> Some obvious questions are:—
>
> What concerns us is: How is it possible for such vicious anti-government propaganda to be mailed and stamped from the Prime Minister's Office to a friendly Congressional Office?
>
> Who?
>
> How?
>
> Barbara says that all those U.S. persons who went to Grenada for The First Anniversary [of the revolution] have been receiving G.I.S. News

Releases regularly. Should this be so? To her knowledge, no one else except she has received this particular piece of anti-PRG material.

Please advise us at an early time if this was a known or unknown error; if a conspiracy and/or sabotage, and how to handle it.

Barack Obama's future Illinois political mentor, Alice Palmer, was one of those invited to the first anniversary celebrations of Grenada's communist revolution.[41]

Influence on Behalf of the Regime

In a typewritten letter to Bishop on U.S. House of Representatives letterhead, dated April 28, 1982, Scott describes how she and Lee involved Dellums in promoting the Grenadan regime.

Addressed to Bishop as "My Dearest, Just a brief note to let you know that I still love you madly," Scott wrote:

> I really need to talk to you face to face to share some thoughts that Ron [Dellums] has. I don't know if you realized it or not but Ron has become truly committed to Grenada and has some very positive political thinking to share with you. He feels that he can best be of assistance in a counseling manner and hopes to be able to discuss these thoughts in the near future. He just has to get all to [sic] his thoughts in order as to how your interests can best be served. Ron, as a political thinker, is the best around and Fidel will verify that in no uncertain terms. When matched against the best of them, Ron always comes out ahead (even with Fidel). He is so far ahead of his time that it scares me at times but I have learned to deal with it over the years.

> When we left Grenada and arrived in Barbados, we met with what I would call a very ugly American, Ludlow Flowers, the Deputy Ambassador to B'dos from the U.S. In the most awesome exchange of dialogue, Ron battled this ass to the bitter end on U.S. policy toward Grenada. You would have been proud.

Scott described what she, Dellums and Lee were doing to run influence operations in Congress on behalf of the Cuban-backed government: "We are now in the process of pulling together the report for the Armed Services Committee, preparing testimony for the Inter-American Affairs Committee Hearings on Grenada, and in the process of trying to come up with a strategy to bring the U.S. and Grenada to the negotiating table."

She told Bishop about the report they were authoring about the Cuban-built airstrip at Point Salines:

> We hope that this report will serve as a basis for a clear understanding and direct counter to the [Reagan] Administration's policy based on their militarist lines of thinking. If the issue can be turned around soon, then we hope that all this insane rhetoric will be stopped by the U.S.

That would take some strategizing with Bishop. Scott continued:

> However, the specifics need to be mapped out very carefully. This is only part of what Ron needs to discuss with you in as much as this has to be a team effort. (smile) Ron also has some very clear ideas on the best procedure that should be followed on your end if you agree to proceed in such a manner. Oh well, I won't bore you with all this until we are able to sit down and really discuss it. It is really very hard to put into a coherent statement at this time. As you are well aware I act on emotion a lot of the time and I am very excited about the role that Ron is willing to play after trying to get him to Grenada for so long. I know now that all our efforts have not been in vain.

Dellums' Chief of Staff then told Bishop that she, the Congressman and Barbara Lee met together in Havana after visiting Grenada:

> Ron had a long talk with Barb and me when we got to Havana and cried when he realized that we had been shouldering Grenada alone all this time. Like I said, he's really hooked on you and Grenada and doesn't want anything to happen to building the Revo and making it strong. He really admires you as a person and even more so as a leader with courage and foresight, principle and integrity. Believe me, he doesn't make that kind of statement often about anyone. The only other person that I know of that he expresses such admiration for is Fidel. (I've known and worked with Ron for many years and the last time I heard him say something like that was in 1977 after a meeting with Fidel).

Scott then told Bishop about a courier who would bring Dellums' materials for the hearings to Grenada and wrote of the report on the Point Salines airstrip:

> Well sweet, I must run. Am doing this as quickly as possible. Just found out that Kojo (Chris) is leaving in a few minutes for the airport. I just wanted you to know that we need to talk and soon. Am sending copies of Ron['s] hearings with him. You will be receiving a formal letter of

appreciation for the wonderful trip from Ron soon, (As soon as I get around to writing it. (SMILE) but I have to finish this report first.) For the... I really need Selwyn's speech to use in this report. Peggy said he had the tape and it had not been transcribed yet. Please see if he has found it yet. It could be very important. Even if we don't use it for the report we could use it for the testimony for the hearings on Grenada in May.

Love you madly and hope to be able to prove it one of these days. Call me soon...

Scott signed her initials, then hand-wrote a postscript: "P.S. This is confidential rap as you well know. Let me know when you or one of the comrades will be taking a trip somewhere in this hemisphere so we can talk. Notice I said this hemisphere. So we can plan to meet and talk. Call me."[42]

First Cuba Trip

In 1977, Barbara Lee and Ron Dellums were part of a delegation to Cuba, which met with Fidel Castro to "discuss health problems."[43]

Lee on Cuban "Self-Determination"

The March 21, 1998 edition of the People's Weekly World, page 16, covered an address by Lee to veterans of the Spanish Civil War's communist-led Abraham Lincoln Brigade, "Lincoln vets honor Robeson." "Greetings to the crowd of more than 1,000 were presented by State Senator Barbara Lee, who is a candidate for Congress to succeed the retiring Ron Dellums. Lee condemned the current blockade against Cuba as 'wrong' and called for its removal, to be replaced by a 'normalizing' of relations with Cuba."

"The Cuban people," said Lee, "should be allowed to determine their own course of action in accordance with self-determination."[44]

1998 Cuba Delegation

In December 1998, newly elected Rep. Barbara Lee hosted an 11 member, five day mission to Cuba. Delegates included far left Oakland City Council members Ignacio De La Fuente, Henry Chang and Jane Brunner, who all paid their own way. On her return, Lee intended to submit a written report to President Bill Clinton and Congress on the delegation's findings. In October that year, Lee had been one of 17

Members of Congress who sent a letter to Clinton calling for a bipartisan commission to review U.S.-Cuba policy.[45]

1999 Cuba Trip

On February 18 1999, 6 members of the U.S. Congressional Black Caucus visited Cuba to evaluate the U.S.-imposed embargo. Among the visitors were Maxine Waters and Barbara Lee of California, Sheila Jackson Lee of Texas and Julia Carson of Indiana.[46]

Staffer's 2004 Trip to Cuba

In May 2004, Julie Nickson from the office of Congresswoman Barbara Lee, spent four days in Havana, Cuba, for the purpose of "fact finding." The trip cost $1,393.16 and was paid for by the leftist Christopher Reynolds Foundation.[47]

Influencing Obama on Cuba

In early April 2009, Rep. Barbara Lee led a congressional delegation to Havana for a 4½ hour meeting with Raul Castro, telling reporters, "All of us are convinced that President Castro would like normal relations and would see normalization, ending the embargo, as beneficial to both countries."

Reuters reported that Lee's delegation "avoided specifics" with Castro, "but were struck by his humor, impressed by his involvement in Third World causes and firm in their belief that he wants to end U.S.-Cuba enmity."

The meeting between Castro, Lee and five other members of the Congressional Black Caucus took place in secret without the customary presence of a U.S. State Department official. No reporters attended and according to the New York Times, Cuban television, which covered the visit, offered no details of what was said.

Lee says she wanted to influence President Barack Obama prior to the upcoming Summit of the Americas in Trinidad and Tobago.

Prior to the trip, Lee told her hometown Oakland Tribune newspaper that the U.S. had to open up to Cuba, but did not demand that the Cuban government open up; she blasted U.S. policy as "based on antiquated Cold War-era thinking."[48]

Barbara Lee with Raul Castro

1 KeyWiki, "Barbara Lee," KeyWiki, http://keywiki.org/index.php/Barbara_Lee (accessed January 18, 2012)
2 Michael Waller, "Congresswoman Barbara Lee: Still stuck in the Cold War," PoliticalWarfare.org, http://jmw.typepad.com/political_warfare/2009/04/congresswoman-barbara-lee-still-stuck-in-the-cold-war.html (April 7, 2009)
3 Jo Freeman, "Shirley Chisholm's 1972 Presidential Campaign," JoFreeman.com, http://www.uic.edu/orgs/cwluherstory/jofreeman/polhistory/chisholm.htm (February 2005)
4 KeyWiki, "Barbara Lee," KeyWiki, http://keywiki.org/index.php/Barbara_Lee (accessed January 16, 2012)
5 Barbara Lee, "Committees and Caucuses," House.gov, http://lee.house.gov/about-me/committees-and-caucuses (accessed April 13, 2013)
6 Rep. Barbara Lee, "Today I Endorsed Barack Obama," The Huffington Post, http://www.huffingtonpost.com/rep-barbara-lee/today-i-endorsed-barack-o_b_76177.html (December 10, 2007)
7 Barbara Lee, "Barbara Lee's Statement on the Passing of Yvonne Scarlett-Golden," House.gov, http://lee.house.gov/press-release/barbara-lee%E2%80%99s-statement-passing-yvonne-scarlett-golden (December 6, 2006)
8 KeyWiki, "Maudelle Shirek," KeyWiki, http://keywiki.org/index.php/Maudelle_Shirek (accessed April 13, 2013)
9 KeyWiki, "Yvonne Scarlett-Golden," KeyWiki, http://keywiki.org/index.php/Yvonne_Scarlett-Golden (accessed April 13, 2013)
10 Yale University, USPC Conference Brochure (November 8-10, 1985)
11 KeyWiki, "Alice Palmer," KeyWiki, http://keywiki.org/index.php/Alice_Palmer (accessed April 13, 2013)

12 CoC Official Ballot Paper

13 Committees of Correspondence, "Proceedings of the Committees of Correspondence Conference: Perspectives for Democracy and Socialism in the '90s" (September 1992)

14 People's Weekly World (December 6, 1997) p. 2

15 People's Weekly World (September 11, 1999)

16 Evelina Alarcon, "N. Calif. PWW banquet raises $11,000," People's World, http://www.peoplesworld.org/n-calif-pww-banquet-raises-11-000/, (December 7, 2001)

17 Marilyn Bechtel, "N. Calif. PWW call: Unity against Bush clones," People's World, http://www.peoplesworld.org/n-calif-pww-call-unity-against-bush-clones/ (October 26, 2002)

18 David Lawrence, "Rep. Lee introduces universal health care bill," People's World, http://www.peoplesworld.org/rep-lee-introduces-universal-health-care-bill/, (October 9, 2003)

19 People's World, "N. Calif. PWW banquet says: Beat back Bush!," People's World, http://www.peoplesworld.org/n-calif-pww-banquet-says-beat-back-bush/ (October 14, 2004)

20 KeyWiki, "Barbara Lee," KeyWiki, http://keywiki.org/index.php/Barbara_Lee (accessed January 18, 2012)

21 Rawbw website, "San Francisco Bay Area Democratic Socialists of America," DSA, http://www.rawbw.com/~ross/dsa/ (June 23, 2012)

22 Rawbw website, "Minutes of Jan. 5, 2002 SF DSA Steering Committee," DSA, http://www.rawbw.com/~ross/dsa/minutes20020105.html (January 5, 2002)

23 Democratic Left (1998) p. 6

24 Nancy Skinner, "About Nancy," Nancy Skinner for Assembly, http://nancyskinnerforassembly.com/about-nancy/ (accessed April 13, 2013)

25 Nancy Skinner, "Re-Elect Assembly member Nancy Skinner," Nancy Skinner for Assembly, http://nancyskinnerforassembly.com/ (accessed April 13, 2013)

26 21st Century Democrats, "2010 Youth Leadership Speaker Series," 21st Century Democrats, http://21stcenturydems.org/index.php/events/sign-up/july-28-2010-speaker-series-kick-off-event (accessed on February 9, 2011)

27 KeyWiki, "Jim Scheibel," KeyWiki, http://keywiki.org/index.php/Jim_Scheibel (accessed April 13, 2013)

28 Campaign For America's Future, "Archives – 2006 Agenda & Speakers," Campaign For America's Future, http://www.ourfuture.org/node/13179 (accessed on May 14, 2010)

29 Campaign For America's Future, "America's Future Now! 2010 Speaker Biographies," Campaign For America's Future, http://www.ourfuture.org/now/speakers (accessed July 12, 2010)

30 Africa Action, "Staff," Africa Action, http://africaaction.org/about/staff.php#board (2009)

31 Leading with Love, "Hosts and Sponsors," Leading with Love, http://domesticworkers.org/leadingwithlove/hosts-and-sponsors, (accessed January 21, 2012)

32 Progressive Democrats of America, "Advisory Board," Progressive Democrats of America, http://pdamerica.org/tools/pda/Adboard.pdf (accessed January 12, 2012)

33 KeyWiki, "Barbara Lee," KeyWiki, http://keywiki.org/index.php/Barbara_Lee (accessed January 18, 2012)

34 Herbert Romerstein, "Who is Barbara Lee?" The Washington Times (September 18, 2001)

35 Council for a Livable World, "Meet the Candidates," Council for a Livable World, http://livableworld.org/support/meet_candidates/ (accessed April 13, 2013)
36 KeyWiki, "Barbara Lee," KeyWiki, http://keywiki.org/index.php/Barbara_Lee (accessed January 18, 2012)
37 People's World, "Reps. Lee, Kucinich call for Peace Dept.," People's World, http://www.peoplesworld.org/reps-lee-kucinich-call-for-peace-dept/, (March 15, 2002)
38 Barbara Lee, "Congresswoman Barbara Lee: A Voice for the People," House.gov, http://lee.house.gov/about-me/full-biography (accessed July 30, 2011)
39 Herbert Romerstein, "Who is Barbara Lee?" The Washington Times (September 18, 2001)
40 Michael Waller, "Congresswoman Barbara Lee: Still stuck in the Cold War," PoliticalWarfare.org, http://jmw.typepad.com/political_warfare/2009/04/congresswoman-barbara-lee-still-stuck-in-the-cold-war.html (April 7, 2009)
41 KeyWiki, "Alice Palmer," KeyWiki, http://www.keywiki.org/index.php/Alice_Palmer (accessed May 24, 2013)
42 Michael Waller, "Congresswoman Barbara Lee: Still stuck in the Cold War," PoliticalWarfare.org, http://jmw.typepad.com/political_warfare/2009/04/congresswoman-barbara-lee-still-stuck-in-the-cold-war.html (April 7, 2009)
43 Fidel Castro, "The seven Congress members who are visiting us," Granma/Havana, http://www.granma.cu/ingles/2009/april/mar7/Reflections-6april.html (April 7, 2009)
44 KeyWiki, "Barbara Lee," KeyWiki, http://keywiki.org/index.php/Barbara_Lee (accessed January 18, 2012)
45 Herb Kay, "Dialogue Delegation to Cuba," People's Weekly World (December 5, 1998)) p. 8
46 Cuba Travel USA, "The Economic Embargo – A Timeline," Cuba Travel USA, http://www.cubatravelusa.com/history_of_cuban_embargo.htm (accessed December 13, 2010)
47 Congressional Staffers Share the Road, "Trips Sponsored by Christopher Reynolds Foundation," American RadioWorks, http://americanradioworks.publicradio.org/features/staffers/travdat/sponsor.php?sponsor_id=T000109 (accessed April 14, 2013)
48 Michael Waller, "Congresswoman Barbara Lee: Still stuck in the Cold War," PoliticalWarfare.org, http://jmw.typepad.com/political_warfare/2009/04/congresswoman-barbara-lee-still-stuck-in-the-cold-war.html (April 7, 2009)

George Miller (D-CA)

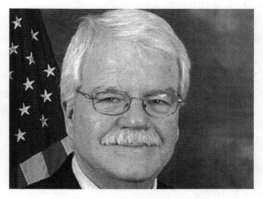

George Miller is a Democratic member of the United States House of Representatives, repre-senting the 7th District of California. He is a long-time member of the Congressional Progressive Caucus.[1]

Background

George Miller was born in Richmond, California on May 17, 1945 and lives in Martinez. He graduated from Diablo Valley Community College, San Francisco State University and earned his law degree from the University of California, Davis Law School. He served on the staff of State Senate Majority Leader George Moscone in Sacramento.[2]

Influence

Congressman Miller is the Senior Democrat of the House Education and Workforce Committee and Chairman of the Democratic Policy Committee. In that role, he helps Democrats "develop and articulate a wide range of policies to benefit all Americans."[3]

In the 111th Congress, George Miller helped craft President Obama's American Recovery and Reinvestment Act.

Miller was one of the three committee chairmen who wrote and passed the Affordable Health Care for America Act, better known as "Obamacare". Miller also worked with President Obama to partially socialize federal student loan programs to "ensure they work in the best interest of students, not big banks."

Under Miller's leadership in the 110th and 111th Congresses, the Education and Labor Committee shepherded 14 bills that were signed into law and dozens of others that passed the House. In fact, according the historian of the House, in the 110th and 111th Congresses, the Education and Labor Committee was the most "productive" committee in the history of the House of Representatives.

Following President Obama's inauguration in January 2009, the first bill he signed into law was written by George Miller and passed out of the Education and Labor Committee. The union inspired Lily Ledbetter Fair Pay Act overturned a Supreme Court ruling that restricted a woman's right to challenge her employer on the basis on pay discrimination.

In response to President Obama's call to action, George Miller passed out of his committee in March of 2009, the GIVE Act, now called the Senator Edward M. Kennedy Service Act, to expand "national service" opportunities. The President signed this bill into law on April 21, 2009.[4]

Miller is the Senior Democrat on the House Committee on Education and the Workforce Committee. He is a member of the Congressional Labor and Working Families Caucus, the International Workers Right Caucus, the Congressional Steel Caucus, the Congressional Native American Caucus and the Congressional LGBT Equality Caucus.[5]

Socialist Connection

In July 1996, the Democratic Socialists of America (DSA) Political Action Committee endorsed George Miller in that year's Congressional elections.[6]

"Progressive" Connections

George Miller has close ties to the Institute for Policy Studies (IPS).

IPS 20th Anniversary Committee

The IPS celebrated its 20th anniversary with an April 5, 1983 reception at the National Building Museum attended by approximately 1,000 IPS staffers and former staff.

The Congressional IPS Anniversary committee members included George Miller and a who's who of the Congressional far left.[7]

IPS Staffer

Congressman Miller, for many years, employed an IPS Associate Fellow, Cynthia Arnson, as his legislative aide, who did most of the legwork and research on Latin American policy.[8]

The Washington School

The Washington School, founded by the IPS in 1978, was an important means of influencing Congress and the Democratic Party. Courses on defence, foreign affairs and domestic policies are taught there by IPS officers and staffers, and other American or foreign radical "experts." A large number of members of Congress and staffers have attended these schools. Several legislators have also taught there, including George Miller.[9]

Take Back America Conference

George Miller was on the list of 153 speakers at the 2006 Take Back America conference, which was organized by the IPS and Democratic Socialists of America initiated Campaign for America's Future.[10]

The Institute for Food and Development Policy/Food First

George Miller is on the list of Congressional Representatives who have participated in hearings/briefings since 1998 with the very radical Institute for Food and Development Policy/Food First, founded by Frances Moore Lappe (DSA/IPS) and Joseph Collins (IPS), authors of the book: "Food First."[11]

Foreign Policy/National Security

Council for a Livable World

The anti-U.S. military Council for a Livable World, brainchild of alleged Soviet agent, Leo Szilard, has supported George Miller in his successful House of Representatives run.[12]

Staffer's Trip to Cuba

In February 2000, David Madland, from the office of Congressman George Miller, spent six days in Havana, Cuba, as part of a delegation of Congressional staffers. The trip cost $1,778.47 and was paid for by the far leftist, Christopher Reynolds Foundation.[13]

---

1 George Miller, "Biography," House.gov, http://georgemiller.house.gov/about-me/full-biography (accessed August 1, 2011)

2 George Miller, "Biography," House.gov, http://georgemiller.house.gov/about-me/full-biography (accessed August 1, 2011)

3 George Miller, "Biography," House.gov, http://georgemiller.house.gov/about-me/full-biography (accessed August 1, 2011)

4 George Miller, "Biography," House.gov, http://georgemiller.house.gov/about-me/full-biography (accessed August 1, 2011)

5 George Miller, "Committees and Caucuses," House.gov, http://georgemiller.house.gov/about-me/committees-and-caucuses (accessed March 29, 2013)

6 Democratic Left (July/August 1996) p. 21

7 Information Digest (April 15, 1983) pp. 77-79

8 Communists in the Democratic Party, p. 71

9 Communists in the Democratic Party, p. 73

10 Campaign for America's Future, "Archives – 2006 Agenda & Speakers," Campaign for America's Future, http://www.ourfuture.org/node/13179 (accessed May 14, 2010)

11 Food First, "Staff," Food First, http://www.foodfirst.org/es/about/staff (accessed March 29, 2013)

12 Council for a Livable World, "Meet the Candidates," Council for a Livable World, http://livableworld.org/support/meet_candidates/ (accessed March 29, 2013)

13 Christopher Reynolds Foundation, "Congressional Staffers Share the Road," American RadioWorks, http://americanradioworks.publicradio.org/features/staffers/travdat/sponsor.php?sponso r_id=T000109 (accessed March 29, 2013)

Nancy Pelosi (D-CA)

Nancy Patricia D'Alesandro Pelosi is a Democratic member of the United States House of Representatives, representing the 12th District of California. She was a leading member of the Congressional Progressive Caucus, until she withdrew when she became Speaker of the House in 2009.[1]

Background

Nancy Pelosi was born in Baltimore, Maryland, the youngest daughter children of Thomas D'Alesandro, Jr., who was a Democratic Party U.S. Congressman from Maryland and a Mayor of Baltimore.[2]

Pelosi graduated from the Institute of Notre Dame, in Baltimore. She then went on to graduate from Trinity College in Washington, D.C. in 1962. As a student at Trinity, she majored in political science and was active in the Political Affairs Club and the International Relations Club.[3]

Nancy Pelosi's husband is millionaire Paul Pelosi. They were married in 1963 and have five children.

Pelosi has represented the San Francisco area in Congress since 1987 and has lived there since 1969.

The Pelosi family has a net worth of over $25 million, mainly in investments of husband Paul Pelosi. Besides a San Francisco Bay area large portfolio of jointly owned real estate, he also has millions of dollars worth of shares in publicly traded companies such as Microsoft, Amazon.com and AT&T. The couple also owns a vineyard in St. Helena, California. Pelosi's husband also owns stock, including $1 million in Apple Inc. and is the owner of the Sacramento Mountain Lions of the United Football League. Nancy Pelosi is among the richest members of Congress.[4]

Influence

Pelosi, is House Minority Leader and in the 111th Congress, was Speaker of the House. As Speaker, Pelosi was second in the line of presidential succession, following Vice President Joe Biden, which made her the highest-ranking female politician in American history.

As a member of the House Permanent Select Committee on Intelligence for 10 years, including two years as the Ranking Democrat, Pelosi worked to "ensure that policymakers and military commanders were provided with intelligence."

Pelosi has also served on the Committee on Standards of Official Conduct (Ethics) and the Banking and Financial Services Committee. She has chaired the Congressional Working Group on China and has served on the Executive Committee of the Democratic Study Group.[5]

According to "progressive" San Francisco author Randy Shaw, writing in March of 2010:[6]

> When the history of the health care reform effort of 2009-10 is written, Speaker Nancy Pelosi deserves chief credit for making it happen. In fact, had Pelosi been given complete control of the health campaign from the start, a public option would have been included in the final bill (as was originally passed by the House).
>
> President Obama did a tremendous selling job in recent weeks, and helped win the votes of wavering Democrats. But Obama spent several months talking about health care without a clear legislative strategy, placing passage in great peril. It took San Francisco Democrat Nancy Pelosi—channeling the spirit of the late, great arm twister Phillip Burton (whose seat she now holds), to bring the health care bill across the finish line...
>
> It is clear that top credit for the health care victory goes to Speaker Nancy Pelosi, who may have finally won over some in her district who have long argued that she was insufficiently progressive. It was Pelosi who stared down Rahm Emanuel when he argued for a scaled down health bill, and who even got in the President's face over his lack of legislative strategy...
>
> I've talked to progressives both locally and across the nation working on a broad range of issues. They overwhelmingly believe that Nancy Pelosi has become the chief political agent for progressive change nationally.

This perspective is backed by political facts. Since 2009, the House has passed the most wide-ranging series of progressive measures since the 1930's, and this is not because Steny Hoyer is Democratic House Majority Leader.

Many of us mistakenly thought Barack Obama would be another Lyndon Johnson, in enacting a progressive domestic agenda. But it is now clear that Nancy Pelosi has the necessary Johnson-type skills, as her upbringing as part of Baltimore's powerful D'Alesandro family, and her long friendship with Phil and John Burton, imparted her with the skills in legislative infighting that the President is only beginning to grasp.

Communist Connections

The Burton Connection

After moving to San Francisco, Pelosi worked her way up in Democratic politics. She became a friend of one of the leaders of the California Democratic Party, 5th District Congressman Phillip Burton.

Phillip Burton died in 1983 and was succeeded by his wife, Sala Burton. In late 1986, Sala became ill with cancer and decided not to run for reelection in 1988. She picked Pelosi as her designated successor, guaranteeing her the support of the Burtons' contacts.[7]

Pelosi won the special election to succeed her, narrowly defeating San Francisco Supervisor and DSA member, Harry Britt on April 7, 1987; then easily defeating Republican candidate Harriet Ross on June 2.[8]

Pelosi was also close to Phillip's brother and sometime fellow Congressman, John Burton. Cesar Chavez historian Randy Shaw tells how in the midst of a legislative battle with the real estate industry in 1999, he told then-State Senator and now California Democratic Party head John Burton, how impressed he was by his tenacity in fighting for their cause. Burton replied, "You think I'm tenacious? I'm a pussycat compared to Nancy." Shaw says he "knew how proud Burton was of his protégé, Nancy Pelosi."[9]

Both Burton brothers were closely allied to the communist movement. Phillip Burton was closely involved with the Soviet controlled World Peace Council and the far left Institute for Policy Studies (IPS).[10]

John Burton, was also involved with the World Peace Council and was sponsoring Bay Area Communist Party USA events well into the 1990s.[11]

Relationship to Hallinan Family

Nancy Pelosi has enjoyed a long and close relationship with San Francisco's famous Hallinan family—especially their late matriarch, Vivian Hallinan. The Hallinans were once under scrutiny by the California Senate Fact-Finding Subcommittee on Un-American Activities for their pro-Soviet propaganda efforts and extensive CPUSA affiliations.

Pelosi has described Vivian Hallinan, who openly held "socialist" views, as a "pioneer" in "a wide range of progressive causes."

These causes included support for Marxist revolutionaries Central America during the 1980s, when Soviet and Cuban-backed forces were fighting for control of the region.[12]

When Vivian Hallinan died in March of 1999, Nancy Pelosi placed a tribute to her in the Congressional Record:[13]

> I am very saddened to know that the leader of one of San Francisco's great Irish families, Vivian Hallinan, passed away last night.
>
> Vivian and her family have deep roots in San Francisco and she has contributed immensely to the fiber of our community during her 88-year lifetime. Throughout her life, Vivian was devoted intellectually and passionately to many causes, well before they became popularly embraced. Her opposition to the war in Vietnam was an example of the courage she displayed in taking an early and fearless stand for her conscience and convictions.
>
> Vivian was a pioneer, a mentor and a leader...

In an article from the San Francisco Examiner, also placed in the Congressional Record, Pelosi described Vivian Hallinan as "a role model for many of us..."[14]

Conn Hallinan, one of Vivian Hallinan's six sons, has said: "My mother and Nancy were pretty close..."

The San Francisco Examiner article described Vivian Hallinan as 'a very committed radical socialist,' and detailed how in the 1980s she had "opposed U.S. policy in Central America" and befriended Daniel Ortega, Nicaragua's Sandinista leader. She also met with Fidel Castro.

From the Canadian Free Press:

The names of the Hallinans, including some of their sons, are included in the annual volumes of the California State Senate Fact-Finding Subcommittee on Un-American Activities. The subcommittee was a well-regarded investigative body which examined not only communist activities in California but right-wing groups such as the John Birch Society and the Minutemen.

In the case of the Hallinans, there was a lot to examine. Vincent Hallinan, a lawyer who died in 1992, was a founding member of the San Francisco chapter of the National Lawyers Guild, officially designated a front of the Communist Party USA, and defended secret Communist Party USA member and labor leader Harry Bridges.

Vincent Hallinan also ran for President on the ticket of the Progressive Party, "a creature of the Communist apparatus and completely dominated by the Communist Party USA from start to finish," the subcommittee said:[15]

A 1961 subcommittee report says that Vincent Hallinan traveled to the Soviet Union with his wife to vouch for the legitimacy of the communist show trial of Francis Gary Powers, the American U-2 pilot shot down over the Soviet Union. Powers' mission had been to document the Soviet missile build-up. It adds, "[Vincent] Hallinan's glowing accounts of the Soviet Union and favorable comments concerning the fairness accorded Powers at his trial were sold in great quantity by the Communist Book Stores both in San Francisco and in Los Angeles."

A 1953 edition of the report states that Vincent Hallinan was a participant in a meeting of the Committee to Secure Justice in the Rosenberg Case, a "Communist front organization." The Rosenbergs were Communists executed for committing atomic espionage against the United States on behalf of the Soviet Union.

A wealthy woman, Vivian Hallinan had contributed financially to one of Pelosi's campaigns. Her only other political contributions on the federal level, as recorded by the Federal Election Commission, went to Senator Barbara Boxer and Reps. Barbara Lee and Ron Dellums.

Vivian Hallinan was also an open supporter of the California District Communist Party—Northern Region in her later years.[16]

Of her six sons, Patrick Hallinan was legal counsel to the W.E.B. DuBois Clubs of America—the youth wing of the CPUSA, while his brother Terence Hallinan was Club National Secretary. Matthew Hallinan was a Communist Party affiliate, turned Democratic Socialists of America member and Conn Hallinan was a decades-long CPUSA member.[17] [18] [19] [20]

Chronicle / Brant Ward

Nancy Pelosi Embracing Terence Hallinan

Tribute to Carlton Goodlett

On February 11, 1997, Congresswoman Nancy Pelosi addressed Congress, paying a tribute to Lenin Peace Prize winner, World Peace Council activist and life-long CPUSA member, Carlton Goodlett.[21]

Sponsored Martinez "Jobs Bill"

In October 1997, Nancy Pelosi became the 54th sponsor of the CPUSA instigated Martinez Jobs Bill (HR-950).[22]

Praising Communist Harry Bridges

In 2001, Nancy Pelosi took to the pages of the Congressional Record to effuse her sentiments on the hundredth anniversary of CPUSA leader Harry Bridges' birth.

Pelosi stated: "Harry Bridges [was] arguably the most significant labor leader of the twentieth century," who was "beloved by the workers of this Nation, and recognized as one of the most important labor leaders in the world." She added: "The (communist controlled) International

Longshoremen's and Warehousemen's Union [was] the most progressive union of the time."

Pelosi delivered this speech nine years after Bridges' membership in the Communist Party USA Central Committee had been publicly revealed.[23]

Socialist Connections

Fred Ross Jr./Marshall Ganz—The Cesar Chavez Connection

Fred Ross, Jr. and other United Farm Workers (UFW) alumni, including Marshall Ganz, helped elect Nancy Pelosi to Congress in 1987. Ross used "house meetings," a strategy that Fred Ross, Sr. taught to Cesar Chavez, a long-time ally of Democratic Socialists of America (DSA), who then used it to build the UFW.

Pelosi attended 120 house meetings in only 60 days and after taking office, joined another Fred Ross, Jr. protege, New York Rep. Louise Slaughter, in leading the fight against military aid to El Salvador's anti-communist government and to Nicaragua's anti-communist contra rebels. Ross, Jr. later became Pelosi's District Chief of Staff.[24]

Fred Ross, Jr. and Marshall Ganz were considered in the 1980s to be among the country's premier political organizers. Ross' father mentored Cesar Chavez

(March 17, circa 1990) Los Angeles Democratic Socialists of America Poster, Advertising Ganz Meeting

and was in many ways the real "power behind the throne." Ross, Jr. and Ganz worked within Pelosi's Congressional team collecting tons of votes by mail and by herding enough volunteers together to cover every precinct. Both men are still working in "progressive"/Democratic politics. Until recently, Ross was working for SEIU and in the summer of 2007, Ganz was a counselor for L.A.'s Camp Obama. He taught key state organizers to share personal narratives and create compelling politics around human experience and emotion, rather than around issues. Ganz can claim a major part of the credit for Obama's success in 2008.[25]

Ganz has been a long-time DSA affiliate.

Fred Ross, Sr.

On the occasion of his 80th birthday, House Minority Leader Nancy Pelosi said, "Fred Ross, Sr. left a legacy of good works that have given many the courage of their convictions, the powers of their ideals, and the strength to do heroic deeds on behalf of the common person."[26]

Democratic Socialists of America Connection

On November 11, 1995, more than 300 Bay Area residents turned out for a public hearing on jobs and economic insecurity in San Francisco. Co-sponsored by San Francisco Democratic Socialists of America and the Full Employment Coalition, the event featured Congresswoman Nancy Pelosi and Congressman Ron Dellums (a DSA member), as Keynote speakers.

Testifiers included Bertram Gross, co-author of HR 1050, "A Living Wage, Jobs for All Act," as well as representatives from the San Francisco Labor Council, Chinese for Affirmative Action, the San Francisco Private Industry Council, the Coalition for Economic Equity and the American Friends Service Committee.[27]

> **CALIFORNIA**
>
> More than 300 Bay Area residents turned out for a public hearing on jobs and economic insecurity in San Francisco on November 11. Co-sponsored by San Francisco DSA and the Full Employment Coalition, the event featured Congresswoman Nancy Pelosi and Congressman Ron Dellums as keynote speakers. Testifiers included Bertram Gross, co-author of HR 1050, "A Living Wage, Jobs for All Act" as well as representatives from the San Francisco Labor Council, Chinese for Affirmative Action, the San Francisco Private Industry Council, the Coalition for Economic Equity, and the American Friends Service Committee.

DSA Endorsement

In July 1996, the Democratic Socialists of America Political Action Committee endorsed Nancy Pelosi in that year's Congressional elections.[28]

Honoring Cesar Chavez

There was a major march through the streets of San Francisco on March 24, 2002, to mark the 75th birthday of United Farm Workers founder Cesar Chavez. Parade Grand Marshalls included two UFW founders: Dolores Huerta (DSA member) and Cesar's brother, Richard Chavez, as well as Rep. Nancy Pelosi.[29]

Besides Pelosi, speakers included Communist Party USA (CPUSA) affiliated, San Francisco Mayor Willie Brown, California Labor Federation Executive Secretary/Treasurer emeritus, John F. Henning (a DSA member), Communist Party affiliates San Francisco Labor Council Secretary/Treasurer Walter Johnson, San Francisco Board of Supervisors President Tom Ammiano, and Evelina Alarcon, Cesar Chavez's Holiday Campaign Leader and CPUSA member.[30] [31] [32] [33] [34]

"Progressive" Connections

Take Back America Conferences

Nancy Pelosi was on the list of 114 speakers at the 2004 Take Back America conference, which was organized by the Institute for Policy Studies and Democratic Socialists of America-dominated Campaign for America's Future.[35]

She was back in 2006.

America's Future Now! 2010

Nancy Pelosi was one of the 148 speakers who addressed the 2010 America's Future Now! conference. The conference was hosted by the Campaign for America's Future and held from June 7-9, 2010 at the Omni Shoreham Hotel, Washington, D.C.[36]

---

1 KeyWiki, "Nancy Pelosi," KeyWiki, http://keywiki.org/index.php/Nancy_Pelosi (accessed April 18, 2013)

2 Jim Puzzanghera, Pelosi's aim for center may steer pundits wrong," Access my Library, http://www.accessmylibrary.com/article-1G1-119973286/pelosi-aim-center-may.html (November 14, 2002)

3 Sam Whiting, "Christine Pelosi's boot camp trains future politicians to avoid the campaign minefield," SFGate, http://www.sfgate.com/magazine/article/Christine-Pelosi-s-boot-camp-trains-future-3295783.php (February 3, 2008)

4 Jennifer Yachnin, Paul Siner and Kristin Coyner, "The 50 Richest Members of Congress (2009)," Roll Call, http://www.rollcall.com/features/Guide-to-Congress_2009/guide/-38181-1.html?page=6 (September 4, 2009)

5 Nancy Pelosi, "Biography," House.gov, http://pelosi.house.gov/about/biography.shtml (accessed April 18, 2013)

6 Randy Shaw, "Nancy Pelosi Deserves Chief Credit for Health Care Victory," BeyondChron, http://www.beyondchron.org/news/index.php?itemid=7930 (March 22, 2010)

7 The Nation, "Is this the new face of the Democratic Party?" The Nation (accessed February 3, 2010)
8 Associated Press, "Democrat Elected in San Francisco," The New York Times (June 3, 1987)
9 Randy Shaw, "Nancy Pelosi Deserves Chief Credit for Health Care Victory," BeyondChron, http://www.beyondchron.org/news/index.php?itemid=7930 (March 22, 2010)
10 KeyWiki, "Phillip Burton," KeyWiki, http://www.keywiki.org/index.php/Phillip_Burton (accessed April 18, 2013)
11 KeyWiki, "John Burton," KeyWiki, http://www.keywiki.org/index.php/John_Burton (accessed April 18, 2013)
12 Cliff Kincaid, "Nancy Pelosi's controversial Marxist connection," Canada Free Press, http://canadafreepress.com/index.php/article/12069 (June 17, 2009)
13 Congresswoman Nancy Pelosi, "On the Passing of Vivian Hallinan," House.gov, http://www.house.gov/pelosi/prvivian.htm (March 17, 1999)
14 Congresswoman Nancy Pelosi, "On the Passing of Three Extraordinary Women," House.gov, http://www.house.gov/pelosi/fltrio.htm (Marcy 25, 1999)
15 Cliff Kincaid, "Nancy Pelosi's controversial Marxist connection," Canada Free Press, http://canadafreepress.com/index.php/article/12069 (June 17, 2009)
16 KeyWiki, "California District Communist Party USA – Northern Region – Page 2," KeyWiki, http://www.keywiki.org/index.php/California_District_Communist_Party_USA_-_Northern_Region_-_Page_2 (accessed April 18, 2013)
17 KeyWiki, "Patrick Hallinan," KeyWiki, http://www.keywiki.org/index.php/Patrick_Hallinan (accessed April 18, 2013)
18 KeyWiki, "Terence Hallinan," KeyWiki, http://www.keywiki.org/index.php/Terence_Hallinan (accessed April 18, 2013)
19 KeyWiki, "Matthew Hallinan," KeyWiki, http://www.keywiki.org/index.php/Matthew_Hallinan (accessed April 18, 2013)
20 KeyWiki, "Conn Hallinan," KeyWiki, http://www.keywiki.org/index.php/Conn_Hallinan (accessed April 18, 2013)
21 JRank Encyclopedia, "Goodlett, Carlton B.(1914-1997) – Chronology, Serves as Publisher, Political Leader, and Mentor, Affiliates with Socialist Activities," JRank Encyclopedia, http://encyclopedia.jrank.org/articles/pages/4263/Goodlett-Carlton-B-1914-1997.html (accessed April 18, 2013)
22 Evelina Alarcon, "National day of action to pass the Martinez Jobs Bill," People's Weekly World (October 4, 1997) p. 1
23 Joshua Muravchik, "Pelosi's Favorite Stalinist Return of the San Francisco Democrats," Weekly Standard (June 25, 2007) Vol. 012, Iss. 39
24 Randy Shaw, "Nancy Pelosi Deserves Chief Credit for Health Care Victory," BeyondChron, http://www.beyondchron.org/news/index.php?itemid=7930 (March 22, 2010)
25 Rochelle Schweizer, "She's The Boss," (2010) pp. 72-73
26 Randy Shaw, "National Campaign Urges Obama to Award Presidential Medal of Freedom to Legendary Organizer Fred Ross," BeyondChron, http://www.beyondchron.org/news/index.php?itemid=10980, (February 13, 2013)
27 Democratic Left (January/February 1996) p. 16
28 Democratic Left (July/August 1996) p. 21
29 People's Weekly World, "Thousands march to commemorate Chavez," People's Weekly World (March 30, 2002)

30 KeyWiki, "Willie Brown," KeyWiki,
http://www.keywiki.org/index.php/Willie_Brown (accessed April 18, 2013)
31 KeyWiki, "Jack Henning," KeyWiki,
http://www.keywiki.org/index.php/Jack_Henning (accessed April 18, 2013)
32 KeyWiki, "Walter Johnson (San Francisco Labor Council)," KeyWiki,
http://www.keywiki.org/index.php/Walter_Johnson_%28San_Francisco_Labor_Counc
il%29 (accessed April 18, 2013)
33 KeyWiki, "Tom Ammiano," KeyWiki,
http://www.keywiki.org/index.php/Tom_Ammiano (accessed April 18, 2013)
34 KeyWiki, "Evelina Alarcon," KeyWiki,
http://www.keywiki.org/index.php/Evelina_Alarcon (accessed April 18, 2013)
35 Campaign For America's Future, "Archives – 2004 Speakers," Campaign For
America's Future, http://www.ourfuture.org/node/13146 (accessed June 11, 2010)
36 Campaign For America's Future, "America's Future Now! 2010 Speaker
Biographies," Campaign For America's Future,
http://www.ourfuture.org/now/speakers (accessed July 12, 2010)

Raul Ruiz (D-CA)

Raul Ruiz is a freshman Democratic member of the United States House of Representatives, representing the 36th District of California. He is a new member of the Congressional Hispanic Caucus.[1]

Background

Just months after he was born in Zacatecas, Mexico, Ruiz's biological mother died. This led to his adoption while still a baby by his father's sister and her husband, and an upbringing in Coachella, California.

In Coachella, "it was the Filipino farm worker strike of 1965 that spurred subsequent strikes across the state for better wages and rights," United Farm Workers (UFW) leader and Democratic Socialists of America member Dolores Huerta recalled.[2]

Huerta and Cesar Chavez were inspired by the Coachella strikers. "It was the Filipino farm workers' courage that helped spur them to action," she said.

Many veteran UFW members from that era still live in the desert. Their influence reflected in groups such as Lideres Campesinas, Pueblo Unido and Promotores Comunitarios del Desierto—a group that Ruiz was involved with.

In the summer of 1990, Ruiz walked from business to business in the Coachella Valley asking them to invest in their community by contributing to his education. He made a promise to "come back home and serve the community as a physician."[3]

After a stint at UCLA, Ruiz studied at Harvard from 1995 to 2003, did residency work in Pittsburgh and then a final academic year in Boston, in 2005-2006. Ruiz then returned to the Coachella Valley in 2007 to work at Eisenhower Medical Center.

While in Boston, Ruiz performed as a "Danzante"—a folkloric dance in traditional Aztecan costume with troupes from across New England.[4]

Influence

Dr. Ruiz currently serves on the House Committee on Natural Resources and the House Committee on Veterans' Affairs.[5]

Communist Connections

While in Boston, Ruiz was involved for several years with the radical North American Indian Center of Boston, a Jamaica Plain-based nonprofit that "provided support services to American Indians."

The North American Indian Center led to Ruiz's connection to the United American Indians of New England (UAINE), a group very closely allied to the pro-Cuba/North Korea Workers World Party.

When leading UAINE activist Bob Gustafson died in 2012, Workers World published an obituary, in the November 21st edition:[6]

> Workers World Party mourns the loss of Bob Gustafson, a Warrior of the Mohawk Nation who was at the historic occupation of Wounded Knee in 1973 and was a longtime United American Indians of New England activist. Gustafson, who passed away on Sept. 21, was a steadfast fighter for Native-American self-determination, sovereignty and freedom, and a comrade in the struggle for socialism. We will pick up his banner and continue the struggle for liberation for all Native nations.

Day of Mourning Arrest

Ruiz participated for over six years in the UAINE's annual Thanksgiving Day protest at Plymouth, MA—including a 1997 arrest with 24 other protesters.

The UAINE-led protest typically started at Cole's Hill, a National Historic Landmark above Plymouth Rock, and the burial site for Pilgrims who died in the first winter after they landed there.

Tensions between authorities and protesters had existed since the first Day of Mourning in 1970. In 1997, tensions boiled over, gaining national attention.

Events turned violent after at least 200 demonstrators left Cole's Hill, marched through Leyden Street, in downtown Plymouth, and approached a central town square.

Police arrested several protesters after scuffles broke out, with both sides blaming the other for initiating the violence.

Raul Ruiz was taken into custody during a second wave of arrests after the Day of Mourning protesters crowded into Plymouth's Town Square. "At some point, police began hitting people with clubs," Ruiz said in his account of the incident. "Another man and I shielded Sam (Sapiel) to prevent him from being hit. The police hit us with clubs, arrested us, and then pepper-sprayed us even though we weren't resisting."

According to the police report, Sapiel was arrested for inciting the crowd after yelling "this is what they wanted," and pointing to an officer to call him "the Mafia." Police had difficulty pulling him away from Ruiz and other protesters and the group fell to the ground, the report stated.

Ruiz (left), with Fellow Arrestees

In 1998, Ruiz pled not guilty to two misdemeanor offenses of disorderly conduct and tumultuous behavior. He faced up to three years in prison, but the charges were later dropped as part of a settlement that also dismissed claims of police brutality.[7]

While awaiting trial in 1998, Ruiz told the Harvard Crimson newspaper that Thanksgiving is "the glorification of an incident in history which has a direct link to the… poverty and oppression which (Latinos and American Indians) experience today."[8]

Of the 25 people arrested that day, three: Steven C. Gillis, 36, of Boston; Kazi A. Toure, 47, of New Hampshire; and Stevan C. Kirschbaum, 44, of Roslindale; were leading supporters of the Workers World Party.[9] [10] [11]

Rally Against Racism

The January 19, 1998, Rally Against Racism in Plymouth was organized by UAINE in response to an "unprovoked police assault on peaceful Native demonstrators and their supporters on November 27th."

UAINE elder Sam Sapiel, opened the program with a greeting and prayer. He was followed by Raul Ruiz's Danza Azteca's ceremonial dances.

Imani Henry of the National People's Campaign, a poet and actor from the lesbian/gay/bi/trans community, co-chaired the rally. One of the two black women arrested at the National Day of Mourning, Henry spoke of the long history of solidarity between the African American and Native struggles, from the Seminole War to the government repression of the Black Panthers and the American Indian Movement.

Henry said of the media: "It is almost laughable to mention Dr. King's legacy of non-violence without mentioning the racist violence with which he was constantly met, including his finally being gunned down. Racism as systemic and systematic oppression is itself an act of violence." Imani Henry is a member of the Workers World Party.

Moonanum James, Co-Leader of UAINE, showed how "the pilgrim mythology continues to be used to justify murder, theft, racism, repression and genocide against Native people today." The crowd cheered when he called for freedom for Leonard Peltier, Mumia Abu-Jamal and all "political prisoners."

Larry Holmes of Workfairness in New York and the Workers World Party, thanked the organizers for "rescuing the struggle essence of Martin Luther King Day from empty platitudes and corporate co-optation".

Holmes said that instead of "grandstanding and pandering to the right" with his "dialogue on race," President Bill Clinton should investigate the police attack on the National Day of Mourning.

Other speakers included Brian Shea of the Boston Disabled People's Liberation Front, also a member of the Workers World Party.

Solidarity messages were read from several chapters of the militant American Indian Movement and from convicted cop killer and Workers World Party cause célèbre, Mumia Abu-Jamal.

Raul Ruiz closed the rally.[12] [13] [14] [15]

30ᵗʰ National Day of Mourning, November 25, 1999

1999's National Day of Mourning was an "activist effort by Native Americans and other indigenous peoples to tell the truth about the genocide—still ongoing in some parts of the world—which is erased by history books and holidays which celebrate the lies that we are all fed as children and adults."

Speaker Teresa Gutierrez demanded freedom for political prisoner, Mumia Abu-Jamal.

Gutierrez noted that she had just returned from supporting the anti-U.S. Navy "struggle" in Vieques, Puerto Rico and the crowd cheered again when she demanded, "U.S. out of Puerto Rico now!"[16]

Gutierrez was later a Workers World Party U.S. presidential candidate.[17]

During the Thanksgiving protest, Raul Ruiz read a letter of support for American Indian activist Leonard Peltier, who had been convicted of killing two FBI agents in North Dakota. Ruiz also read another letter from Sub-Comandante Marcos of the Mexican Marxist/anarchist revolutionary group, Zapatista Army of National Liberation.[18]

Foreign Policy/National Security

In Zapatista Territory

Raul Ruiz spent eight months in Chiapas in 2001, as part of a medical research project while attending Harvard medical school during a period of armed conflict between the Zapatista rebels and Mexican government.[19]

Raul Ruiz, a member of the Partners in Health Chiapas Project, described his experience in seeing the risks women endure when delivering babies:

Julio was wet from the pouring rain and frightened. He ran through the streets of Polho, a community in Chiapas sympathetic to the Zapatista rebels, to find Carlos, the health promoter. He explained to Carlos, in Tzotzil, that his young wife, Ana, had delivered their first child an hour ago and was still heavily bleeding at home. I ran with the student nurse to the clinic's poorly stocked pharmacy to the post-partum hemorrhage kit.

Raul Ruiz was also interested in local herbal medicines which were being investigated by doctors, obviously not sympathetic to anti-Zapatista Mexican Government forces:

> As a Harvard medical student, I spent eight months investigating the use of herbs by health promoters in Chiapas during low intensity warfare. I interviewed several directors from non-government health organizations, doctors, curanderos, and countless health promoters from the highlands and jungle. I worked at two clinics and helped the organization, Equipo de Atención y Promoción de Salud y Educación Comunitario (EAPSEC)—a sister organization of Harvard Medical School based Partners in Health—train health promoters in preventive medicine and primary care. I wanted to better understand the factors that influenced health promoters' use of herbal medicine.

> Since the cease fire agreements in January 1994 between the Mexican Army and the Zapatista Army for National Liberation, the Mexican government militarized Chiapas with a third of its forces and promoted the formation of paramilitary groups to terrorize Zapatista sympathizers. Julio and Ana are two of 5,000 refugees in Polho displaced from their communities.

> Physicians for Human Rights documented multiple violations of the neutrality of health care. Health promoters concurred that the Mexican government cause divisions amongst community members by providing aid only to non-Zapatista sympathizers, use state police and soldiers to assist the Mexican Red Cross deliver medicine, and interrogate clinic patients suspected of being Zapatista sympathizers. Moreover, military and immigration checkpoints are located in strategic entry sites creating fear and limits on community members' ability to travel and organize. They also harass international human rights observers and providers of humanitarian aid, according to Physicians for Human Rights, and local non-governmental organizations.

> To avoid the risk of interrogation and harassment, health promoters see herbal medicine as a means to be independent from government

services. One promoter said, "we need to be prepared with medicinal plants [and] train more people in other collective work in order not to depend on the government." Another questioned, "if there is war and we don't know how to use medicinal plants, how will we treat the indigenous?"

Later in 2008, Ruiz further recounted the experience: "I went in romanticizing the poor and their struggle and issues with social justice. But I came out of there realizing the tremendous nature of poverty and how real policies can actually affect human lives."[20]

Council for a Livable World, 2012 Election Victory

Raul Ruiz was one of the 26 House of Representatives victories chalked up to the anti-U.S. military Council for a Livable World Political Action Committee in the 2012 election cycle.[21]

---

1 KeyWiki, "Congressional Hispanic Caucus," KeyWiki, http://keywiki.org/index.php/Congressional_Hispanic_Caucus (accessed May 15, 2013)

2 KeyWiki, "Dolores Huerta," KeyWiki, http://keywiki.org/index.php/Dolores_Huerta (accessed May 15, 2013)

3 Ruiz for Congress website, http://www.drraulruiz.com/about (accessed April 21, 2013)

4 Marcel Honore, "A look into Raul Ruiz," MyDesert.com, http://www.mydesert.com/article/20121208/NEWS03/312090001/A-look-into-Raul-Ruiz,?nclick_check=1 (December 9, 2012)

5 Raul Ruiz, "Full Biography," House.gov, http://ruiz.house.gov/about/full-biography (accessed May 15, 2013)

6 Editor, "Bob Gustafson," Workers World, http://www.workers.org/2012/11/21/bob-gustafson/ (November 21, 2012)

7 Workers World, "Charges against Plymouth 25 dropped," Workers World, http://www.workers.org/ww/1998/plymouth1029.php, (accessed May 15, 2013)

8 Michael Patrick Leahy, "Dem Congressional Candidate Once Arrested at Plymouth Rock Protesting Thanksgiving," Breitbart, http://www.breitbart.com/Big-Government/2012/10/16/Democratic-Congressional-Candidate-Who-Claimed-Native-American-Heritage-Once-Arrested-at-Plymouth-Rock (October 17, 2012)

9 KeyWiki, "Steven Gillis," KeyWiki, http://keywiki.org/index.php/Steven_Gillis (accessed May 15, 2013)

10 KeyWiki, "Kazi Toure," KeyWiki, http://keywiki.org/index.php/Kazi_Toure (accessed May 15, 2013)

11 KeyWiki, "Steve Kirschbaum," KeyWiki, http://keywiki.org/index.php/Steve_Kirschbaum (accessed May 15, 2013)

12 Frank Neisser, "Fight for Native rights Targets of police attack return to Plymouth Rock," Workers World, http://www.workers.org/ww/1998/plymouth0129.php (1998)

13 KeyWiki, "Imani Henry," KeyWiki, http://keywiki.org/index.php/Imani_Henry (accessed May 15, 2013)

14 KeyWiki, "Larry Holmes," KeyWiki, http://keywiki.org/index.php/Larry_Holmes (accessed May 15, 2013)

15 KeyWiki, "Brian Shea," KeyWiki, http://keywiki.org/index.php/Brian_Shea (accessed May 15, 2013)

16 Workers World, "Native nations say 'No thanks,'" Workers World, http://www.workers.org/ww/1999/dofm1209.php (1999)

17 KeyWiki, "Teresa Gutierrez," KeyWiki, http://keywiki.org/index.php/Teresa_Gutierrez (accessed May 15, 2013)

18 MyDesert.com, "Raul Ruiz lauds Leonard Peltier in tape released by Mary Bono Mack," MyDesert.com (October 19, 2012)

19 Keith Matheny, "Raul Ruiz lauds Leonard Peltier in tape released by Mary Bono Mack," Our Campaigns, http://www.ourcampaigns.com/NewsDetail.html?NewsID=83351&WhenStart=2012-10-19+20%3A00%3A30, (October 19, 2012)

20 Raul Ruiz, "Medicinal Herbs in Times of Low Intensity War, the Case of Chiapas, Mexico," Partners in Health, http://ftp.pih.org/inforesources/essays/medicinal-herbs-chiapas.html, (accessed April 10, 2013)

21 Council for a Livable World, "Meet the Candidates," Council for a Livable World, http://livableworld.org/support/meet_candidates/, (accessed April 10, 2013)

Mark Takano
(D-CA)

Mark Takano is a freshman Democratic member of the United States House of Representatives, representing the 41st District of California. He is a new member of the Congressional Progressive Caucus and serves as Whip for the Congressional Asian Pacific American Caucus.[1] [2]

Background

Mark Takano attended La Sierra High School in the Alvord Unified School District and then attended Harvard where he received his Bachelor's Degree in Government in 1983.

Upon graduation, Takano worked as a substitute teacher for various public school systems in the Boston area.

Mark Takano returned home to California and obtained his secondary teaching credential in Language Arts and Social Studies at the University of California at Riverside. He began teaching in the Rialto Unified School District in 1988. Since 2009, he has served as Adviser to the Rialto High School Gay Straight Student Alliance.

In 1990, Takano was elected to the Riverside Community College District's Board of Trustees and became Board President in 1991.

Mark Takano's public service in Riverside County includes the Board of the Chancellor's Asian Pacific Islander Community Advisory Center at the University of California, Riverside. He has served as Chairman of the Riverside Mayor's Task Force on the Digital Divide, Chairman of the Asian Pacific Islander Caucus of the California Democratic Party, a charter member of the Association of Latino Community College Trustees, a member of the Association of California Asian American Trustees and a member of Asian Pacific Americans in Higher Education.[3]

From a Republican family, Takano switched from the GOP to the Democrats before his first run for Congress in 1992.

Claiming his Harvard education enlightened him: "They [Republicans] were so ideologically conservative, both economically and culturally," said Takano. "They lost their pragmatism."

Takano has cited Central America, trickle-down economics, the pro-life position and treatment of minority groups as issues that influenced his political conversion.

"From the minorities' point of view, the Republicans were incredibly divisive in their rhetoric," Takano said. "Most minorities felt they lost any sort of representation in the government."[4]

Influence

Rep. Takano serves on the Veterans' Affairs and the Science, Space and Technology Committees.[5]

"Progressive" Connections

Though new to Congress, Mark Takano has already forged a close relationship with Progressive Democrats of America (PDA) and their National Director, one-time Orange County Democratic Socialists of America (DSA) leader, Tim Carpenter.[6]

Grayson/Takano Letter

In early 2013, Mark Takano and Florida Rep. Alan Grayson, with PDA's help, drafted a "line in the sand" letter to President Barack Obama, urging no cuts to Medicare, Medicaid and Social Security benefits.

> Dear President Obama:
>
> We join millions of Americans in applauding your Inaugural Address declaration that "we reject the belief that America must choose between caring for the generation that built this country and investing in the generation that will build its future."

Democrats have built the most popular government programs in American history—including Medicare, Medicaid, and Social Security—by working with Republicans whenever possible and by defeating Republican opposition whenever necessary. The torch has been passed to today's elected officials, and we must carry it forward boldly.

That's why we write to let you know that we will vote against any and every cut to Medicare, Medicaid, or Social Security benefits—including raising the retirement age or cutting the cost of living adjustments that our constituents earned and need...

Finally, Americans agree that there is more that must be done to require the rich and giant corporations to pay their fair share. Indeed, it is their patriotic duty to do so.

As you negotiate with Republicans, you deserve to know that millions of Americans and the below signed Members of Congress stand ready to fight for the principles listed above.

The letter was signed by 40 members of Congress, 31 of those members are current or former members of the Congressional Progressive Caucus.[7]

Progressive Democrats of America had input into the letter. According to the PDA website, "Our team on the hill met with Rep. Mark Takano who thanked us for our work on the Grayson/Takano letter."[8]

Prosperity Not Austerity Reception

On April 17, 2013, Progressive Democrats of America hosted a Prosperity Not Austerity reception at a regular Institute for Policy Studies (IPS) venue, Busboys and Poets, in Washington D.C., The event featured Rep. Takano, PDA National Board member Rep. John Conyers, Rep. Keith Ellison, PDA National Board member and DSAer Michael Lighty from National Nurses United, and former IPS Trustee Rev. Lennox Yearwood.

Takano used the opportunity to tell the assembled "progressives" how his letter could be used to pressure moderate Democrats into voting against entitlement cuts.[9] [10]

"My Friend Tim Carpenter"

Mark Takano made clear his strong ties to Tim Carpenter and Progressive Democrats of America in a "dear supporter" letter posted on the PDA website.[11]

Dear Supporter,

As a newly-elected Congressman, I know it takes a lot of work from grassroots volunteers to win election in the first place. It takes even more work to build support and deliver votes on Capitol Hill for humane, progressive policies.

So I wanted to thank all of you in the PDA community who helped me win my election last fall. I also wanted to thank PDA for working to build support for the "Line In The Sand" letter that Rep. Alan Grayson and I drafted to stand up against any cuts to Medicare, Medicaid, or Social Security benefits.

A few weeks ago, I had a good meeting with my friend Tim Carpenter. **We discussed the need to educate people in our fight to save Social Security.** Later, I joined Tim and many PDA supporters at Andy Shallal's great restaurant, Busboys & Poets. I really enjoyed that night. You can **watch the video from that event** and hear me discuss the Grayson / Takano "Line in the Sand" letter.

Tim Carpenter and Rep. Mark Takano

DONATE

From the Progressive Democrats of America Website

As a newly-elected Congressman, I know it takes a lot of work from grassroots volunteers to win election in the first place. It takes even more work to build support and deliver votes on Capitol Hill for humane, progressive policies.

So I wanted to thank all of you in the PDA community who helped me win my election last fall. I also wanted to thank PDA for working to build support for the "Line In The Sand" letter that Rep. Alan Grayson and I drafted to stand up against any cuts to Medicare, Medicaid, or Social Security benefits.

A few weeks ago, I had a good meeting with my friend Tim Carpenter. We discussed the need to educate people in our fight to save Social Security. Later, I joined Tim and many PDA supporters at Andy Shallal's great restaurant, Busboys & Poets. I really enjoyed that night.

I've been impressed with PDA's growing Educate Congress campaign.

Thank you for visiting more than 100 district Congressional offices in both March and April. Thank you for making so many phone calls to support those visits. I can tell you, your hard work is paying off!

I know PDA volunteers will be visiting their local Congressional district offices again this May 15th. This very important work comes at a critical time, and I encourage you to help "Educate Congress" in person and on the phones.

The current battle against Social Security cuts is important for the legacy of the Democratic Party. We're fighting to protect the most important program of FDR's New Deal. I look forward to fighting alongside all of you in PDA for the heart and soul of our party:

Thank you for all you and PDA are doing for progressive politics in America.

Foreign Policy/National Security

Council for a Livable World Support

Council for a Livable World counted Mark Takano among their 26 claimed 2012 House victories.[12]

According to the Council for a Livable World website:

Mark Takano is a forceful progressive champion with a twenty year record as a local elected leader in California's newly created 41st Congressional District...

Takano's Japanese American heritage gives him a unique perspective on peace and nuclear disarmament. Takano's grandfather was born in Hiroshima. Both of his parents and all four of his grandparents were interned by the U.S. Government during World War II. In 2002, Takano visited the Hiroshima Peace Memorial Museum with his Aunt Kikue. This emotional and powerful experience helped reinforce Mark's commitment to peace and nuclear disarmament.

Mark Takano's personal understanding of the horrors of nuclear weapons lends a special credibility to his calls for disarmament. You can amplify this voice by helping to send him to the U.S. Congress.

---

1 Congressional Progressive Caucus, "Caucus Members," Congressional Progressive Caucus, http://cpc.grijalva.house.gov/index.cfm?sectionid=71&sectiontree=2,71, (accessed May 18, 2013)
2 Congressional Asian Pacific American Caucus, "Membership for the 113th Congress," Congressional Asian Pacific American Caucus, http://capac-chu.house.gov/membership (accessed May 18, 2013)
3 Mark Takano, "Meet Mark," Mark Takano Teacher for Congress, http://www.marktakano.com/about/new (accessed May 18, 2013)
4 Geoffrey J. Hoffman, "Harvard Grad Turns Democrat to Win Votes," The Harvard Crimson, http://www.thecrimson.com/article/1992/10/21/harvard-grad-turns-democrat-to-win/?print=1, (October 21, 1992)

5 Mark Takano, "Committees and Caucuses," House.gov,
http://takano.house.gov/legislation/committees-and-caucuses (accessed May 18, 2013)
6 KeyWiki, "Tim Carpenter," KeyWiki, http://keywiki.org/index.php/Tim_Carpenter
(accessed May 18, 2013)
7 Democracy for America, "Be a Citizen Supporter: The Grayson-Takano Letter
Against Benefit Cuts," Democracy for America,
http://act.boldprogressives.org/survey/survey_ss_grayson/ (accessed May 18, 2013)
8 PDA, "PDA Weekly Field Report – 4/19-4/26," Yahoo! Groups,
http://groups.yahoo.com/group/progressivesforobama/message/6413PDA (April 20,
2013)
9 PDA, "Help PDA Continue Our Momentum!," PDA,
http://salsa3.salsalabs.com/o/1987/t/0/blastContent.jsp?email_blast_KEY=1244812,
(accessed May 18, 2013)
10 PDA, "Rep. Mark Takano (CA-41) discusses the Grayson/Takano letter," YouTube,
http://www.youtube.com/watch?v=2nCwKbDkuww (April 25, 2013)
11 PDA, "Tell Them No Cuts to Medicare, Medicaid or Social Security Benefits!,"
PDA,
http://salsa3.salsalabs.com/o/1987/t/0/blastContent.jsp?email_blast_KEY=1245536,
(accessed May 18, 2013)
12 Council for a Livable World, "Meet the Candidates," Council for a Livable World,
http://livableworld.org/support/meet_candidates/, (April 10, 2013)

Maxine Waters (D-CA)

Maxine Waters is a Democratic member of the United States House of Representatives, representing the 35th District of California. She was a founding member of the Congressional Progressive Caucus and a former Chairwoman of the Congressional Black Caucus.[1]

Background

Born on August 15, 1938, in St. Louis, Missouri, Waters was one of thirteen children. In 1961, she moved to Los Angeles where she found work in a garment factory and as a telephone operator. In 1966, Waters was hired as an assistant teacher with the newly formed Head Start program in Watts. Waters attended college while working at Head Start and in 1970 she earned a Sociology Degree from California State University in Los Angeles.

In 1976, Waters successfully ran for election to the California State Assembly. During her tenure in the State Assembly, Waters authored numerous pieces of legislation, including a law requiring state agencies to award a percentage of public contracts to minorities and women; tenants' rights laws; a law restricting police efforts to use strip searches; and the divestment of state pension funds from businesses involved in South Africa.

After serving for fourteen years in the California State Assembly, in 1990 Waters successfully ran for a seat in the 29th Congressional District of California, which formerly belonged to retiring far left Representative Augustus Hawkins. In 1992, Waters ran in the much larger 35th District, winning 83 percent of the vote.[2]

Influence

Following massive civil unrest in Los Angeles in 1992, Waters appeared widely in national media to discuss the despair in urban America. She has called for redirecting resources from the "war on drugs" to prevention and treatment, and for repealing mandatory minimum sentencing laws for minor drug offenses.

Waters made headlines with allegations of CIA involvement in the Contra cocaine drug trafficking in South Central Los Angeles in the mid-1980s—a story widely suspected of having originated with the Soviet KGB.

Waters chaired the Out of Iraq Caucus after having entered Congress in 1991. She was a leader in the movement to end South African Apartheid.[3]

In December 2012, Waters was chosen as the ranking Democratic member of the House Financial Service Committee for the 113th Congress.[4]

Congresswoman Waters also serves as a member of the Steering and Policy Committee, making her an integral part of the House Democratic Leadership led by Democratic Leader Nancy Pelosi, Democratic Whip Steny Hoyer and Assistant Democratic Leader James Clyburn.[5]

Communist Connections

Maxine Waters has enjoyed a long relationship with the Communist Party USA (CPUSA) and its numerous front groups, and to a lesser degree, with the pro-North Korea Workers World Party.

CES Event

On June 3, 1975, Coalition for Economic Survival honored pro-communist Representative Parren Mitchell (D-MD), at a banquet at the Airport Hyatt Inn in Los Angeles. Mitchell was being honored because of his Transfer Amendment—which would redirect several billion from military to social spending.

CES Chair Rev. Al Dortch presided. Sharing the podium with Mitchell were William Robertson, Executive Secretary of the Los Angeles Federation of Labor and Humberto Comacho of the United Electrical Workers.

Ruth Yanatta, newly elected Santa Monica Councilor and CES founder, was also an honored guest. Yanatta is the daughter of one time leading Communist Party member David Goldway.

Honorary co-chairs of the event included Democratic Socialists of America member, actor Ed Asner, communist connected U.S. Representatives Yvonne Braithwaite Burke, John Conyers and Ed Roybal, and actor and decades-long CPUSA member, John Randolph.[6]

Supported Communist Party Front

Waters has supported several CPUSA fronts and causes including the National Alliance Against Racists and Political Repression, which was led by leading Party members Angela Davis and Charlene Mitchell.

In 1982, the California State Assemblywoman Waters lent her name to this NAARPR pamphlet.[7]

RALLY

Saturday, November 6, 1982

at 1st A.M.E. Church
2270 S. Harvard, L.A.
(near Western and Adams)
at 7:00P.M.

U CLA
oct 8

PROFESSOR
Angela Davis
ASSEMBLYWOMAN
Maxine Waters
Charlene Mitchell

SPEAK ON
"THE CAMPAIGN TO FREE MAYOR CARTHAN"

PROFESSOR ANGELA Y. DAVIS
SAN FRANCISCO STATE UNIVERSITY
AUTHOR OF: "WOMEN, RACE AND CLASS,"
CO-CHAIRPERSON OF "NAARPR."

EDDIE CARTHAN, YOUNG, BLACK, LIBERAL MAYOR OF TCHULA, MISS., FACES THE DEATH PENALTY ON A FRAME-UP MURDER CHARGE. AT THE AGE OF 12, CARTHAN WENT TO JAIL FOR MARCHING WITH MARTIN LUTHER KING. AS MAYOR HE WAS CONVICTED OF "INTERFERING" WITH A BOGUS CHIEF OF POLICE WHOM HE HAD NOT APPOINTED; THEN OF FRAUD BECAUSE TWO MEN CONVICTED OF MAKING PHONEY SALES TO TCHULA CLAIMED CARTHAN GAVE THEM PERMISSION TO FORGE HIS NAME; AND NOW HE GOES TO TRIAL ON A MURDER CHARGE

TO WHICH TWO MEN HAVE ALREADY PLEADED GUILTY. AS A POTENTIAL FOUR TIME LOSER, MAY CARTHAN FACES A MANDATORY DEATH PENALTY

SOMETHING IS ROTTEN IN THE STATE OF MISSISSIPPI!
COME AND HEAR THE REAL STORY

CHARLENE MITCHELL
EXECUTIVE SECRETARY, NAARPR

STATE ASSEMBLYWOMAN MAXINE WATERS
48TH ASSEMBLY DISTRICT

SUGGESTED
DONATION $10.00, MORE IF YOU CAN AFFORD IT! BUT COME AND GIVE WHAT YOU CAN.
SPONSORED BY: LOS ANGELES BRANCH,
NATIONAL ALLIANCE AGAINST RACIST AND POLITICAL REPRESSION
FOR FURTHER INFORMATION CALL: 213-731-0789 OR 779-8061
OR WRITE: N.A.A.R.P.R., 3870 S. CRENSHAW BLVD., BOX 104776, L.A., CA. 90008

Greeting Chris Hani

More than 250 labor, peace, civil rights and political leaders greeted South African Communist Party leader Chris Hani at his April 27, 1991 appearance in Los Angeles. The crowd contributed more than $12,000 towards the CPUSA paper People's Weekly World fund drive and the work of the South African Communist Party.

Los Angeles City Council member Robert Farrell, presented Hani with a resolution signed by Mayor Tom Bradley and City Council President

John Ferraro, welcoming him as "one of the most highly respected and powerful voices of the anti-Apartheid movement."

The welcoming committee included Representatives Maxine Waters, Mervyn Dymally and Matthew Martinez, State Senator Diane Watson, Los Angeles School Board President Jackie Goldberg and more than 30 labor, civic and entertainment leaders including Cesar Chavez of the United Farm Workers.

Waters sent a letter of greeting to Hani, saying, "As the struggle within South Africa continues to develop from one stage to the next, please be assured that all of us will continue to be at your side. Your struggle is our struggle."

Evelina Alarcon, Chair of the Southern California District of the CPUSA, introduced Hani. She drew rousing cheers as she pledged, on behalf of the audience and the welcoming committee, continued efforts to maintain sanctions against South Africa.[8]

Supported Communist Party Call

In May 1992, the CPUSA newspaper People's Weekly World published a May Day supplement which included a call to "support our continuing struggle for justice and dignity."

Endorsers of the call included Congresswoman Maxine Waters of California.[9]

MAPA Endorsement

Over 130 delegates attending the Mexican American Retro Region Primary Endorsing Convention in Los Angeles on April 25, 1992, voted to endorse those Congressional, State Senate, Assembly and County Supervisor candidates who took the strongest pro-labor and pro-immigrant stands.

Maxine Waters won the CPUSA dominated Mexican American Political Association's support to be the Democratic candidate for the 35th Congressional District.[10]

CBTU Missouri

In October 1992, Maxine Waters was the Keynote speaker at a Communist Party front Coalition of Black Trade Unionists meeting in St. Louis, Missouri—the 8th annual Ernest and Deverne Calloway Award at the Embassy Suites Hotel.[11]

"Organized labor has suffered mightily in the last few years....Use the lessons of the Civil Rights movement to organize new plants and industries."

Greeting to the Communist Party

In June 1996, the People's Weekly World held a tribute event in Los Angeles for unionists Jerry Acosta and Gilbert Cedillo:[12]

> The Southern California Friends of the People's Weekly World tribute to two of Los Angeles' finest labor leaders, Jerry Acosta and Gilbert Cedillo, became a dynamic rally of elected officials, activists, labor and community leaders in solidarity with labor struggles and in the fight to defeat the ultra-right in November...
>
> "The People's Weekly World and all of us in this room feel very strongly about who we honor today," said Evelina Alarcon, chair of the Southern California District and national secretary of the Communist Party USA, one of the emcees of the tribute. "Jerry Acosta and Gilbert Cedillo represent the new fightback vision of the Sweeney, Trumka, Chavez-Thompson leadership in the AFL-CIO. They represent the rank and file that is pushing from the bottom for that new vision!"

Presentations to the honorees were also made by Clara James, Chair of the Community Affairs Commission of the Second Baptist Church, on behalf of Congresswoman Maxine Waters, and by Antonio Aguilar on behalf of State Senator Hilda Solis, who later went on to become a Congresswoman and Obama Secretary of Labor.

Latino Congreso 2007

Some 2,000 Latino leaders and activists from throughout the United States met in Los Angeles at the Latino Congreso on October 5-9, 2007, to map an action plan and "social justice" program for the 2008 elections. Their goal was to bring out 10 million Latino voters who would play a decisive role in the presidential and Congressional elections.[13]

Helping prepare positions on the Iraq War were Representative Maxine Waters, who chaired the congressional Out of Iraq Caucus; former California State Senator Tom Hayden; United for Peace and Justice organizer and CPUSA leader, Judith LeBlanc; and Lydia Lopez of the Communist Party front, Latinos for Peace. Waters was pictured in the

People's World with Hayden, LeBlanc, Lopez, and another CPUSA member Rosalio Munoz.

"America: not another nickel, not another dime, not another soldier, not this time," Waters declared to a standing ovation. She drew another ovation when she called for African American and Latino unity.

The Congreso unanimously called for complete withdrawal from Iraq starting immediately, no invasion of Iran and support for October 27th regional demonstrations against the war and Iraq Moratorium activities the third Friday of each month.[14]

PEOPLE'S WEEKLY WORLD

eso sets 2008 ag

PWW

Peace workshop participants included, from left, former California state Sen. Tom Hayden, Judith Le Blanc of United for Peace and Justice, Arlene Inouye of the Coalition Against Militarization of our Schools, Rep. Maxine Waters (D-Calif.) of the congressional Out of Iraq Caucus, Canon Lydia Lopez of the Episcopal Diocese of Los Angeles and Rosalio Muñoz of Latinos for Peace.

Left to right: Tom Hayden, Judith LeBlanc, Arlene Inouye, Rep. Maxine Waters, Lydia Lopez, and Rosalio Munos

A.N.S.W.E.R.

Maxine Waters has worked closely with the Workers World Party front group Act Now to Stop War and End Racism (A.N.S.W.E.R.) in the anti-Iraq War movement.

Supporting Aristide with the WWP

On April 7, 2004, in the Whitman Theatre at Brooklyn College, a multinational crowd of 2,000, mainly people from Haiti and the English-speaking Caribbean, packed the hall to hear a program entitled, "An Evening with Friends of Haiti: The Truth Behind the Haiti Coup," in support of Haiti's deposed Marxist President, Jean-Bertrand Aristide.

A broad range of speakers and cultural performers ignited the stage for three-and-a-half hours to express heartfelt anti-imperialist solidarity with the besieged Caribbean country. Haiti has once again suffered a horrific atrocity with the U.S.-orchestrated kidnapping of its democratically elected president, Jean-Bertrand Aristide, on Feb. 29.

The rally was Co-Chaired by Kim Ives and Karine Jean-Pierre from the Haiti Support Network (HSN), with Pat Chin and Sara Flounders from the Workers World Party:

Rep. Maxine Waters electrified the audience as she spoke with great passion about her ongoing contacts with Aristide by cell phone as he was being kidnapped by U.S. forces and sent to the Central African Republic. She was part of a delegation that later traveled to CAR to accompany Aristide to Jamaica, where he and his wife Mildred are now guests of the government.

Waters focused much of her remarks on the complicit roles that Secretary of State Colin Powell and National Security Advisor Condoleezza Rice played. She stated, "Aristide was elected by the people. Rice was not elected by anybody." She ended her rousing remarks with, "I salute Haiti! I salute Aristide! I salute Lavalas! I support real democracy!"[15]

Michigan Coalition for Human Rights

In Detroit on April 19, 2009, Maxine Waters was guest speaker at an event run by the Michigan Coalition for Human Rights, which was then chaired by Workers World Party member Abayomi Azikiwe.[16]

Maxine Waters, Abayomi Azikiwe

Socialist Connections

DSA "Economic Insecurity" Meeting

In 1995, D.C./MD/Northern VA Democratic Socialists of America (DSA) co-sponsored the first of DSA's national series of town meetings on economic security. This hearing was held in a church on September 27th and was scheduled to feature three members of Congress: DSA member Neil Abercrombie (D-HI), DSA supporter Bernie Sanders (I-VT) and Maxine Waters.[17]

DSA Endorsement

In July 1996, the Democratic Socialists of America Political Action Committee endorsed Maxine Waters, California, 35th District, in that year's Congressional elections.[18]

Employed Patrick Lacefield

Patrick Lacefield, a prominent member of DSA, served as Press Secretary and Speechwriter for Congresswoman Waters in the mid-1990s.[19]

Relationship with Stanley Sheinbaum

Maxine Waters has close ties to very wealthy Los Angeles-based DSA member and benefactor, Stanley Sheinbaum.

Representative Maxine Waters said Sheinbaum has "served several important roles in her life: stalwart friend, mentor and an important connection who first introduced her to such politicians as former Presidents Jimmy Carter and Bill Clinton."[20]

> Sheinbaum, a strong proponent of divestment from apartheid-era South Africa during his 12 years as a UC regent, advised her on the subject while she served as a state assemblywoman. Through Sheinbaum, Waters said she learned much about the workings of the investment community and how public pension funds could remain profitable without holdings in South Africa. Armed with that knowledge, she successfully sponsored legislation that called for the divestment of state pension funds.

> "I've used him as a sounding board for years," the congresswoman said. "He has been influencing progressive politics in this country, really the world, for a long time."

"Progressive" Connections

Take Back America Conferences

Maxine Waters was on the list of 153 speakers at the 2006 Take Back America conference, which was organized by the Institute for Policy Studies and Democratic Socialists of America-dominated Campaign for America's Future.[21]

She was also on the list of speakers for 2007.

Progressive Democrats of America

Maxine Waters serves on the Advisory Board of Progressive Democrats of America, which is controlled by the Institute for Policy Studies and Democratic Socialists of America.[22]

Foreign Policy/National Security

Cuba Visit

On February 18, 1999, six members of the U.S. Congressional Black Caucus visited Cuba to evaluate the U.S.-imposed embargo. Among the visitors: Maxine Waters (leader) and Barbara Lee of California, Sheila Jackson Lee of Texas and Julia Carson of Indiana.[23] [24]

Council for a Livable World

The anti-US military Council for a Livable World has supported Maxine Waters in California.[25]

---

1 KeyWiki, "Maxine Waters," KeyWiki, http://keywiki.org/index.php/Maxine_Waters (accessed February 16, 2012)
2 The History Makers, "Hon. Maxine Waters," The History Makers, http://www.thehistorymakers.com/biography/hon-maxine-waters-39 (accessed July 29, 2011)
3 The History Makers, "Hon. Maxine Waters," The History Makers, http://www.thehistorymakers.com/biography/hon-maxine-waters-39 (accessed July 29, 2011)
4 Reuters, "Maxine Waters elected ranking member of House financial panel," Reuters, http://www.reuters.com/article/2012/12/04/us-congress-financialservices-waters-idUSBRE8B31AK20121204 (December 4, 2012)
5 Maxine Waters, "In Congress," House.gov, http://waters.house.gov/biography/incongress.htm (accessed April 1, 2013)
6 People's World Southwest (May 26, 1975) p. 2
7 KeyWiki, "Maxine Waters," KeyWiki, http://keywiki.org/index.php/Maxine_Waters (accessed February 17, 2012)
8 People's Weekly World (May 4, 1991) p. 2
9 People's Weekly World, "May Day Supplement," People's Weekly World (May 2, 1992)
10 Rosalio Munoz, "MAPA endorses pro-labor candidates," People's Weekly World (May 2, 1993) p. 2
11 People's Daily World (October 24, 1992) p. 5
12 People's Weekly World (June 20, 1996)
13 People's Weekly World (October 13, 2007) p. 3
14 Rosalio Munoz and Joelle Fishman, "Latino Congreso sets 2008 agenda," People's World, http://www.peoplesworld.org/latino-congreso-sets-2008-agenda/, (October 12, 2007)
15 Monica Moorehead, "2,000 Rally in Brooklyn To Denounce U.S. Coup in Haiti," IA Center, http://www.iacenter.org/Haitifiles/haiti-rally04rept.htm (April 14, 2004)
16 KeyWiki, "Maxine Waters," KeyWiki, http://keywiki.org/index.php/Maxine_Waters (accessed February 17, 2012)

17 Democratic Left (September/October 1995) p. 40

18 Democratic Left (July/August 1996) p. 21

19 Montgomery County Biography, http://www6.montgomerycountymd.gov/mcgtmpl.asp?url=/content/pio/Overtimes/200 7/janfeb/features.asp (accessed July 24, 2010)

20 Marc Ballon, "Father of the Leftist Guard," JewishJournal.com, http://www.jewishjournal.com/los_angeles/article/father_of_the_leftist_guard_200409 10/ (September 9, 2004)

21 Campaign For America's Future, "Archives – 2006 Agenda & Speakers," Campaign For America's Future, http://www.ourfuture.org/node/13179 (accessed on May 14, 2010)

22 KeyWiki, "Maxine Waters," KeyWiki, http://keywiki.org/index.php/Maxine_Waters (accessed February 17, 2012)

23 Cuba Travel USA, "The Economic Embaro – A Timeline," Cuba Travel USA, http://www.cubatravelusa.com/history_of_cuban_embargo.htm (accessed April 2, 2013)

24 Fidel Castro, "Reflections of Fidel, The seven Congress members who are visiting us," Havana, http://www.granma.cu/ingles/2009/april/mar7/Reflections-6april.html (April 7, 2009)

25 Council for a Livable World, "Meet Our Candidates," Council for a Livable World, http://livableworld.org/support/meet_candidates/ (accessed February 17, 2012)

Rosa DeLauro (D-CT)

Rosa L. DeLauro is a Democratic member of the United States House of Representatives, representing the 3rd District of Connecticut.

She is a long-time member of the Congressional Progressive Caucus and is a member of the Populist Caucus.[1]

Background

Rosa DeLauro grew up in a political family in New Haven, Connecticut and went on to earn degrees from Marymount College and Columbia University.

Prior to serving in Congress, DeLauro served for six years as Chief of Staff to Connecticut Senator Chris Dodd. She was also Executive Director for Countdown '87, a national campaign which successfully campaigned to stop U.S. military aid to the anti-communist Nicaraguan Contras. From 1989 to 1990, she served as Executive Director for EMILY'S List.[2]

Influence

DeLauro has been the Co-Chair of the House Democratic Steering Committee since 2003, where she makes committee assignments. The representative from Connecticut's 3rd Congressional District is the second-highest ranking woman in the U.S. House, after her friend, Nancy Pelosi.

DeLauro is married to prominent Democratic pollster, Stanley Greenberg, who was President Bill Clinton's Chief Pollster from 1991 to 1994 and worked for both Vice President Al Gore and Senator John Kerry (D-MA) during their presidential campaigns. Obama's former

Chief of Staff Rahm Emanuel once lived in DeLauro and Greenberg's basement.

DeLauro sits on the influential House Appropriations and Budget Committees. She serves as Chairwoman of the Agriculture-FDA Appropriations Subcommittee and as a member of the Labor-Health and Human Services-Education and Commerce-Justice-Science Appropriations Subcommittees.[3]

She is the Co-Chair for Steering on the House Democratic Steering and Policy Committee as well.

Communist Connections

Rosa DeLauro has extremely close ties to the Communist Party USA (CPUSA), which is highly influential in the New Haven area.

Sponsored Communist Party "Jobs Bill"

H.R. 950, the Job Creation and Infrastructure Restoration Act of 1997, was introduced in the 105th Congress on March 5, 1997, by Congressman Matthew Martinez of California. It had 33 original co-sponsors, including Rosa DeLauro. The primary purpose of this emergency federal jobs legislation was to "provide much needed jobs at union wages to crisis ridden cities by putting the unemployed to work rebuilding our nation's infrastructure (schools, housing, hospitals, libraries, public transportation, highways, parks, environmental improvements, etc.). $250 billion is authorized for emergency public works jobs over a five year period."

Congressman Martinez had previously introduced this bill in the last Congress (as H.R. 1591) at the request of over 50 prominent labor leaders who formed the Los Angeles Labor Coalition for Public Works Jobs, which is why it is often referred to as the "Martinez Public Works Jobs Bill."

National Coordinator for the bill campaign was Southern California Communist Party District Chair Evelina Alarcon.[4]

Helped Missouri Communist Party Supporter

In 2005, Missouri CPUSA supporter, Melanie Shouse, was diagnosed with terminal breast cancer.

After starting her third round of chemotherapy, Ms. Shouse's insurance company, WellPoint, informed her that it would not continue to cover her latest treatment. Representative DeLauro intervened with WellPoint on Ms. Shouse's behalf, continuing her efforts to get treatments approved for Ms. Shouse through her death in February of 2010.[5]

On February 4, 2010, President Obama, speaking at a Democratic National Committee fundraising event, mentioned Melanie Shouse. This is what he said:[6]

> I got a letter—I got a note today from one of my staff—they forwarded it to me—from a woman in St. Louis who had been part of our campaign, very active, who had passed away from breast cancer. She didn't have insurance. She couldn't afford it, so she had put off having the kind of exams that she needed. And she had fought a tough battle for four years. All through the campaign she was fighting it, but finally she succumbed to it. And she insisted she's going to be buried in an Obama t-shirt.

> But think about this: She was fighting that whole time not just to get me elected, not even to get herself health insurance, but because she understood that there were others coming behind her who were going to find themselves in the same situation and she didn't want somebody else going through that same thing. How can I say to her, "You know what? We're giving up?" How can I say to her family, "This is too hard?" How can Democrats on the Hill say, "This is politically too risky?" How can Republicans on the Hill say, "We're better off just blocking anything from happening?"

Honoring Communist Party Supporter Celestino Cordova

Admirers gathered at the Fair Haven Elderly Apartments community room, New Haven, in June of 2010 to witness U.S. Representative Rosa DeLauro pin on 81 year-old Cordova the Combat Infantry Badge, Sharp Shooter Badge and several others, he was owed, but never awarded, for service in the Korean War.

DeLauro, Celestino Cordova

Cordova earned these honors during service, including hand-to-hand combat, with a reconnaissance unit within the Borinqueneers of the all-Puerto Rican 65th U.S. Army Regiment during the Korean War.[7]

Cordova is a known CPUSA supporter.[8]

Guest of Honor at Communist Run Function

Rosa DeLauro is a regular visitor to the New Haven People's Center, the headquarters of the Connecticut Communist Party.

"The genius of the Social Security system is that it ties generations together," emphasized Congresswoman Rosa DeLauro at the August 2010 kickoff event for Social Security's 75th birthday, held at the New Haven People's Center by the Connecticut Alliance for Retired Americans. "I pay in for my mother during my working life, and in the future my children will pay in for me," she said, adding that it will never become insolvent.

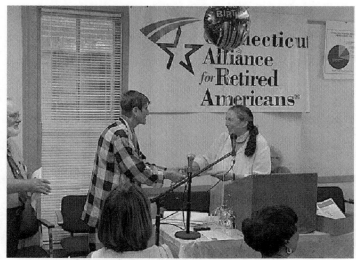

DeLauro Greets Joelle Fishman at the Event

Addressing a packed room, DeLauro decried attempts to privatize or limit Social Security, citing the fact that millions of seniors, disabled and children would fall into poverty without this program.

Communist Party supporter, Celestino Cordova, a Fair Haven resident who works with seniors, presented DeLauro with postcards filled out earlier in the program by the 70 participants, calling on Congress to reject any proposals to raise the retirement age or cut benefits.

"There is a big debate going on in our country about what role government should play," said Communist Joelle Fishman, a board member of both ARA and the People's Center. "Those who want to do away with Social Security want to do away with any role of government for the well-being of people except to protect the corporations and the super rich," she said, urging a large turnout in the November elections.[9]

Embracing a Communist Leader

DeLauro has a very close relationship with Connecticut Communist Party leader Joelle Fishman. According to the August 12, 2010, New Haven Register:

> Joelle Fishman of New Haven, chair of the Communist Party USA's political action commission, second from left, greets Congresswoman Rosa DeLauro, left, before DeLauro speaks at the People's Center in New Haven as local groups gather there together to celebrate the 75th Anniversary of Social Security.

Joelle Fishman's leadership role in the CPUSA's Political Action Commission gives her responsibility for organizing party support for "progressive" Democratic Party candidates at the state, Congressional, Senate and presidential levels. That makes her relationship with DeLauro, one of the most influential policy people in The Democratic Caucus, particularly significant.[10]

Rosa DeLauro Embraces Joelle Fishman

Jobs Roundtable

On August 8, 2011, "Third District voters gave U.S. Rep. Rosa L. DeLauro a simple message to bring back to Washington: "It's all about jobs."

Connecticut AFL-CIO, faith-based groups, community leaders and organizations in the We Are One coalition, coordinated a roundtable discussion with Representative DeLauro of New Haven, at the Second Star of Jacob Church on Chapel Street.[11]

Inez Bell, a recent high school graduate and a supporter of the Young Communist League USA, was one of DeLauro's several radical co-panelists.[12]

Alfred L. Marder 90th Birthday Celebration

The March 2012 Host Committee meeting in honor of Connecticut Communist Party member Alfred Marder's 90th Birthday Celebration, was held at the New Haven People's Center and included communists Joelle Fishman, Henry Lowendorf and Jarvis Tyner; several communist affiliate Connecticut state Senators and Representatives, including Toni Harp, Pat Dillon, Toni Walker and Gary Holder-Winfield; as well as Representative DeLauro.

Rosa DeLauro also inserted a tribute to Alfred Marder in the Congressional Record of March 20, 2012:[13]

> Mr. Speaker, it is a pleasure for me to rise today to join the many friends, family, and community leaders who have gathered to celebrate the outstanding contributions of Alfred L. Marder as he celebrates his 90th birthday. Al is one of our community's most active advocates—dedicating much of his life to fighting for social justice and the improvement of the quality of life for all.
>
> Al Marder is an institution in our community. He is perhaps best known for his work to promote peace, social justice, worker's rights and equality. His commitment to these issues is unwavering—regardless of controversy, he always stands firm in his fight to protect human rights...
>
> Following the war, Al completed his college education at the University of Connecticut and soon found a passion that he would pursue for the rest of his life. During the McCarthy era, Al was one of those singled out for proudly sharing his thoughts and ideas. Standing firm in his support of civil liberties and the right of every American to freely

express themselves, Al discovered his passion for civil and workers rights—two issues to which he has dedicated a lifetime of advocacy...

I am honored to have this opportunity to join all of those gathered today in wishing Alfred L. Marder a very happy 90th birthday. At 90-years young, Al continues his work on behalf of those whose voices are too often silenced...

NEW HAVEN PEOPLES CENTER

A LABOR & COMMUNITY CENTER FOR EDUCATIONAL, SOCIAL AND CULTURAL ACTIVITIES SINCE 1937

TUESDAY, MARCH 6, 2012

Alfred L. Marder 90th Birthday Celebration

HOST COMMITTEE

Hon. Rosa DeLauro, Sen. Toni Harp, Sen. Martin Looney, Rep. Juan Candelaria, Rep. Patricia Dillon, Rep. Toni Edmonds Walker, Rep. Gary Holder-Winfield, Rep. Roland Lemar, Ald. Jorge Perez,President, New Haven Board of Aldermen, Ambassador Sylvester Rowe, Mohammed Barrie, Vinie Burrows, Mary Compton, Joelle Fishman, Craig Gauthier, Emanuel Gomez, Hilda Kilpatrick, Henry Lowendorf, Kenneth Marder, Rev. Scott Marks, William Morico, John Olsen, Quentin Snediker, Jarvis Tyner, Andrea van den Heever, Susan Yolen

Dear Friends and Family of Al Marder,

We are excited to invite you to celebrate the 90th birthday of Al Marder and to recognize his many contributions, international and local, toward world peace, justice and equality.

Please join us in this joyous occasion on Sunday, March 18, at 3:00 pm at the New Haven Peoples Center, 37 Howe Street, New Haven, Connecticut 06511.

New Haven Peoples Center Freedom Trail quilt square block by Susan Klein

Welcome to the New Haven Peoples Center

Site on the CT African American Freedom Trail

37 Howe Street, New Haven 06511

203-624-8664

e-mail: peoplescenter@pobox.com

Meeting place of labor, community, peace and social justice groups

New Haven People's Center Blog

Socialist Connection

Agenda for Shared Prosperity

On May 24, 2007, Agenda for Shared Prosperity, a project of the Democratic Socialists of America-dominated Economic Policy Institute, sponsored an event entitled: "Getting Real About Families." Representative Rosa DeLauro addressed the gathering, sharing the stage with DSA members Larry Mishel of the EPI and Washington Post journalist, Harold Meyerson.[14]

"Progressive" Connections

Take Back America Conference

Rosa DeLauro was on the list of 237 speakers at the 2007 Take Back America conference, which was organized by the Institute for Policy Studies and the Democratic Socialists of America-dominated Campaign for America's Future.[15]

America's Future Now Conference

Rosa DeLauro was on the list of speakers at the 2009 America's Future Now conference, which was the new name for the Take Back America conference.[16]

Foreign Policy/National Security

Council for a Livable World

The anti-U.S. military Council for a Livable World has supported Rosa DeLauro in her successful House of Representatives run as candidate for Connecticut.[17]

Peace Legislation

Legislation: H.Res. (House Resolution) 68, which calls for the U.S. to abide by the Nuclear Proliferation Treaty, is co-sponsored by CT Congress member Rosa DeLauro.[18]

Trip to Cuba

From May 27 to June of 2007, Rosa DeLauro traveled to Havana, Cuba with the purpose: "to examine the transition that is occurring in Cuba and the impact of that transition on U.S. policy, as well as to examine agriculture and trade with the island." The cost of the trip, $1,906.50 was paid by the Institute for Policy Studies affiliated Center for Democracy in the Americas.[19]

Her trip was approved by the late leftist Representative Stephanie Tubbs Jones of Ohio—who at one point employed Young Communist League member Sheltreese McCoy as an intern.[20]

1 KeyWiki, "Rosa DeLauro," KeyWiki, http://www.keywiki.org/index.php/Rosa_DeLauro (accessed March 29, 2013)
2 The Arena, "Arena Profile: Rosa DeLauro," Politico, http://www.politico.com/arena/bio/rosa_delauro.html (accessed March 29, 2013)
3 The Arena, "Arena Profile: Rosa DeLauro," Politico, http://www.politico.com/arena/bio/rosa_delauro.html (accessed March 29, 2013)
4 The Job Creation and Infrastructure Restoration Act of 1997 (H.R. 950), New York State Communist Party, March 16, 1997 Email List (accessed June 14, 2010)
5 Tony Pecinovsky, "Melanie Shouse, health care activist, dies at 41," People's World, http://www.peoplesworld.org/melanie-shouse-health-care-activist-dies-at-4/ (February 4, 2010)
6 Jaelithe, "Why President Obama Should Not Forget Melanie Shouse," MOMocrats, http://momocrats.typepad.com/momocrats/2010/02/why-president-obama-should-not-forget-melanie-shouse.html (February 5, 2010)
7 New Haven Independent (June 8, 2010)
8 KeyWiki, "Celestino Cordova," KeyWiki, http://www.keywiki.org/index.php/Celestino_Cordova (accessed March 29, 2013)
9 People's World, "At Social Security birthday party, Rosa DeLauro cuts the cake," People's World (August 16, 2010)
10 KeyWiki, "Rosa DeLauro," KeyWiki, http://keywiki.org/index.php/Rosa_DeLauro (accessed March 29, 2013)
11 Angela Carter, "Voters in New Haven tell DeLauro: We want jobs (videos)," New Haven Register, http://www.nhregister.com/articles/2011/08/08/news/doc4e409c56c49a6257952287.txt?viewmode=2, (August 8, 2011)
12 KeyWiki, "Inez Bell," KeyWiki, http://www.keywiki.org/index.php/Inez_Bell (accessed March 29, 2013)
13 KeyWiki, "Rosa DeLauro," KeyWiki, http://keywiki.org/index.php/Rosa_DeLauro (accessed March 29, 2013)
14 Agenda for Shared Prosperity, "Getting Real About Families," The Economic Policy Institute, http://www.sharedprosperity.org/av/20070524.html (accessed on November 16, 2010)
15 Campaign for America's Future, "Archives – 2003 Speakers," Campaign for America's Future, http://www.ourfuture.org/node/13211 (accessed June 17, 2010)
16 Confabb, "America's Future Now 2009 Speakers," Confabb, http://now2009.confabb.com/conferences/82401-americas-future-now/speakers (accessed July 13, 2010)
17 Council for a Livable World, "Meet the Candidates," Council for a Livable World, http://livableworld.org/support/meet_candidates/ (accessed March 22, 2012)
18 NoNukes-NoWar.org, "Why Are We Still Living Under The Threat Of Nuclear War?" NoNukes-NoWar.org, http://www.nonukes-nowar.org/files/NukeAbolitionAdHartfordCourantAsPrinted.pdf (accessed March 29, 2013)
19 Legistorm, "Rep. Rosa DeLauro," Legistorm, http://www.legistorm.com/trip/list/by/approver/id/203/name/Rep_Rosa_DeLauro.html (accessed August 30, 2010)
20 KeyWiki, "Stephanie Tubbs Jones," KeyWiki, http://www.keywiki.org/index.php/Stephanie_Tubbs_Jones (accessed March 29, 2013)

Eleanor Holmes Norton (D-DC)

Eleanor Holmes Norton is a non-voting Democratic Delegate of the United States House of Representatives, representing the District of Columbia. She is a long-time member of both the Congressional Progressive Caucus and the Congressional Black Caucus.[1]

Background

Holmes Norton, who taught law full time before being elected, is a tenured Professor of Law at Georgetown University. After receiving her Bachelor's Degree from Antioch College in Ohio, she simultaneously earned her law degree and a Master's Degree in American Studies from Yale University.

Before being elected, Congresswoman Norton served as a trustee on a number of public service boards, including the Rockefeller Foundation and the Board of Governors of the D.C. Bar Association, as well as serving on the boards of civil rights and other national organizations.[2]

While in college and graduate school, Holmes was active in the civil rights movement and an organizer for the Student Nonviolent Coordinating Committee (SNCC). By the time she graduated from Antioch, she had already been arrested for organizing and participating in sit-ins in Washington, D.C., Maryland and Ohio. While in law school, she traveled to Mississippi for the Mississippi Freedom Summer and worked with civil rights stalwarts like Medgar Evers. Her time with the SNCC inspired her life-long "commitment to social activism and her budding sense of feminism".[3]

In the early 1970s, Eleanor Holmes Norton was a signer of the Black Women's Manifesto, a classic document of the black feminist movement.[4]

Influence

Congresswoman Holmes Norton is the Ranking Member of the House Subcommittee on Economic Development, Public Buildings and Emergency Management. She serves on the Committee on Oversight and Government Reform, which includes the Subcommittee on Federal Workforce, Post Office and the District of Columbia and the Subcommittee on Information Policy, Census and National Archives.

She also serves on the Committee on Transportation and Infrastructure, which includes the Subcommittee on Aviation, the Subcommittee on Economic Development, Public Buildings and Emergency Management and the Subcommittee on Water Resources and Environment.

Before her Congressional service, President Jimmy Carter appointed Norton to serve as the first woman to chair the U.S. Equal Employment Commission. She came to Congress as a national figure who had been a civil rights and feminist leader, tenured Professor of Law and board member of three Fortune 500 companies.

Congresswoman Norton has been named one of the 100 most important American women in one survey and one of the most powerful women in Washington in another.[5]

Communist Connections

National Conference of Black Lawyers

Holmes Norton was a founding member in the late '60s of the National Conference of Black Lawyers.

The National Conference of Black Lawyers and its allied organization, the communist initiated National Lawyers Guild, are the U.S. affiliates of the International Association of Democratic Lawyers.[6]

The IADL was a "front" for the former Soviet Union and is still dominated by communist and socialist lawyers and legal organizations.

Employed Gwen McKinney

Gwen McKinney was Press Secretary for Representative Eleanor Holmes Norton during her successful election campaign to the U.S. Congress between June and September of 1990. McKinney assisted in crisis management, advertising and general public relations.[7]

Alice Palmer, Editor of the pro-communist Black Press Review (and Chicago mentor and employer of a young Barack Obama), was elected International Organization of Journalists (IOJ) Vice President for North America at the organization's 10th Congress, October 20-23, 1986, in Prague, Czechoslovakia. She also traveled to the Soviet Union and Bulgaria during the same trip.[8]

Accompanying Alice Palmer were at least two known Communist Party USA members, Simon Gerson and Jose Soler, and Gwen McKinney and Leila McDowell of the National Alliance of Third World Journalists.[9]

The IOJ was a Soviet front operation, based in Prague until its expulsion by the Czech government in 1995.[10]

Socialist Connections

Eleanor Holmes Norton has enjoyed a lifetime's involvement with the socialist movement, particularly with Democratic Socialists of America (DSA).

Early Socialism

According to Boston DSA member Bette Denich, future DSA Founder Michael Harrington:

> ...recruited her friend and future roommate Eleanor Holmes to the Young Socialist League during one of his speaking tours at Antioch College in the late 1950's

> Eleanor Holmes (Norton) went on to be a longtime activist in the civil rights movement before becoming the District of Columbia's elected Congressional delegate.

The Young Socialist League, or Young People's Socialist League, was the youth wing of the Socialist Party USA.[11]

Cablegram to Portuguese Socialists and the M.F.A.

In 1974, after a pro-communist military coup in Portugal:

> More than eighty Americans, all identified with opposition to the Vietnamese war and with various radical and liberal causes, sent on August 9 a cablegram to the Portuguese Armed Forces Movement, to Portuguese president Francisco da Costa Gomes and to Portuguese

socialist leader Mario Soares expressing the hope that "democratic freedoms"... will continue to grow in Portugal.

Michael Harrington, the National Chairman of the Democratic Socialist Organizing Committee, organized the effort. Eleanor Holmes Norton signed the cablegram.[12]

American Solidarity Movement

The American Solidarity Movement was announced in early 1984 by Democratic Socialists of America, as a vehicle to support American labor unions it considered under attack or on strike and in need of support.

Members of the initiating Committee for an American Solidarity Movement were all DSA members or known supporters: Michael Harrington (convener), Stanley Aronowitz, Balfour Brickner, Harry Britt, Harvey Cox., Rep. Ron Dellums, Bogdan Denitch, Barbara Ehrenreich, Cynthia Epstein, Jules Feiffer, Msgr. George Higgins, Irving Howe, Frances Fox Piven, Jose Rivera, Ray Rogers, Gloria Steinem, Peter Steinfels, Ellen Willis and Reps. Barney Frank and Eleanor Holmes Norton.[13]

"New Directions" Conference

In May 1986, Democratic Socialists of America "supported" a New Directions conference in the Washington, D.C. Convention Center. The conference organizer was Jo-Ann Mort of DSA:

> The conference, supported by DSA, will bring together activists, analysts and elected officials to develop new directions for the Democratic Party and the broad democratic left.

Initial sponsors of the event included Reps. Charles Hayes and Barney Frank; labor leaders William Winpisinger and Jack Sheinkman (ACTWU), Joyce Miller (ACTWU and Coalition of Labor Union Women) and Jack Joyce (Bricklayers); feminist leaders Gloria Steinem and Judy Goldsmith policy analysts Robert Kuttner and Jeff Faux and Eleanor Holmes Norton.[14]

Paying Tribute to Michael Harrington

On September 15, 1989, a tribute service was held to commemorate the recently deceased leader of Democratic Socialists of America, Michael Harrington.

Invited guest speakers were Senator Edward Kennedy, former German socialist Prime Minister Willy Brandt, DSA members Irving Howe, Deborah Meier, Bogdan Denitch, Jack Clark and Eleanor Holmes Norton.[15]

Please join the Democratic Socialists of America and Stephanie, Alex, and Teddy Harrington in paying tribute to

MICHAEL HARRINGTON

(Leading American socialist, author, internationalist, activist, radical, husband, father, friend, and comrade.)

at
A Memorial Service

Friday, September 15

7:00 - 9:00 p.m.

Riverside Church
(Riverside Drive and Claremont, between 120th and 122nd Street, New York)
(Take the 1 train to 116th Street)

with invited guests
**Irving Howe ● Senator Edward Kennedy
Willy Brandt ● Deborah Meier
Bogdan Denitch ● Jack Clark
Eleanor Holmes Norton**

Democratic Socialists of America, 15 Dutch Street, Suite 500, NY, NY 10038   (212) 962-0390

16   Washington Socialist

Endorsed by Democratic Socialists of America

The D.C./MD/Northern VA DSA local "plunged into the electoral fray" on June 12, 1990 with a meeting to choose candidates for DSA's endorsement in that year's D.C. elections. Receiving the local's endorsement in September's Democratic Primary were Eleanor Holmes Norton for Congressional Delegate; Jim Nathanson for City Council, Ward 3; and Harry Thomas for City Council from Ward 5.[16]

In July 1996, the Democratic Socialists of America Political Action Committee endorsed Eleanor Holmes Norton, D.C., At Large in that year's Congressional elections.[17]

In 2000, local DSAers endorsed Holmes Norton and her Democratic Party running mate, Florence Pendleton.

The D.C./MD/Northern VA Local held a meeting for endorsements in D.C. races. The endorsed slate included many candidates from the Green Party which pushed progressive ideas (but lost).

The local also endorsed two Democrats, who won easily:

They endorsed Eleanor Holmes Norton as a delegate to Congress (where she serves on committees and speaks but cannot vote) and Florence Pendleton as shadow senator (in essence a lobbyist).

Gay Rights Victory

In 2002, hundreds of District of Columbia activists joined Mayor Anthony Williams, Congresswoman Eleanor Holmes Norton and members of the D.C. Council to celebrate the removal of Congressional restrictions on the District's domestic partnership program after a decade-long struggle.

Even though the Council passed a 1992 act permitting any unmarried partners—gay or straight—to register with the city (DSA National Vice Chair and D.C. Council member Hilda Mason was one of the original backers), conservative members of Congress blocked implementation of the program by placing a rider on the District's budget.

The District, like Puerto Rico and other territories, is subject to budgetary and legislative oversight by Congress. Congress must approve the annual D.C. appropriations bill and it uses this power to impose restrictions on the District.

Gay rights organizations, such as ACT-UP D.C., the Gay and Lesbian Activists Alliance and the Movement for D.C. Democracy joined together to fight the ban with D.C./MD/Northern VA Democratic Socialists of America and its members playing a significant role in the victory. DSA member, Judy Nedrow, chaired a local commission that developed strategy for the domestic partnership struggle and Nedrow's partner, Christine Riddiough, former DSA Political Director, also played an important role on the commission. Riddiough was also the former Chair of the Gertrude Stein Democratic Club, a local gay-lesbian Democratic organization instrumental in convincing the District government to take up the issue.[18]

"Progressive" Connections

Eleanor Holmes Norton has been involved with the Institute for Policy Studies (IPS) since its earliest days.[19]

20ᵗʰ Anniversary Committee

Eleanor Holmes Norton was a member of the Institute for Policy Studies 20th Anniversary Committee, which organized an April 5, 1983 reception at the National Building Museum in Washington D.C. and that was attended by approximately 1,000 IPS staffers and former staff.[20]

30ᵗʰ Anniversary Speaker

On October 2, 1993, the Institute for Policy Studies celebrated its 30th anniversary by holding a conference: "Progressive Thought in the Post WWII Era," featuring discussions about a wide range of public policy issues. The panelists discussed a progressive approach to public policy issues since World War II. A key part of the conference was a panel consisting of Barry Wills, Northwestern University History Professor; Eleanor Holmes Norton, member of the House of Representatives and Marian Kramer, President of the National Welfare Rights Union. It was moderated by IPS founder Richard Barnet.[21]

1 KeyWiki, "Eleanor Holmes Norton," KeyWiki, http://keywiki.org/index.php/Eleanor_Holmes_Norton (accessed March 30, 2013)
2 Eleanor Holmes Norton, "Biography," House.gov, http://www.norton.house.gov/index.php?option=com_content&task=view&id=189&Itemid=94 (accessed August 16, 2011)
3 Eleanor Holmes Norton, "Biography," House.gov, http://www.norton.house.gov/index.php?option=com_content&task=view&id=189&Itemid=94 (accessed August 16, 2011)
4 Answers, "Eleanor Holmes Norton," Answers, http://www.answers.com/search?q=eleanor-holmes-norton%2C (accessed March 30, 2013)

5 Eleanor Holmes Norton, "Biography," House.gov,
http://www.norton.house.gov/index.php?option=com_content&task=view&id=189&It
emid=94 (accessed August 16, 2011)
6 National Lawyers Guild, "News & Opinion," National Lawyers Guild,
http://www.nlg.org/news/statements/SouraniStatement.htm (accessed March 30, 2013)
7 Equal Justice Society, "Speaker: Gwen McKinney, McKinney & Associates," Equal
Justice Society, http://www.equaljusticesociety.org/colorblind/mckinney.html
(accessed March 30, 2013)
8 People's Daily World (December 24, 1986) p. 11
9 IOJ 10th Conference Participants List (1986)
10 Yearbook on International Communist Affairs (1991) p. 437
11 Democratic Socialists of America Boston, "The Yankee Radical – January 2001,"
Democratic Socialists of America, http://www.dsaboston.org/yradical/yr2001-01.pdf
(accessed March 30, 2013)
12 Democratic Left (September 1975) p. 2
13 Democratic Left (January/February 1984) p. 6
14 KeyWiki, "Eleanor Holmes Norton," KeyWiki,
http://keywiki.org/index.php/Eleanor_Holmes_Norton (accessed March 30, 2013)
15 Washington Socialist (September 1989) p. 16
16 Washington Socialist (July 1990) p. 1
17 Democratic Left (July/August 1996) p. 21
18 Democratic Left, http://www.dsausa.org/dl/Spring2002.pdf (Spring 2002) p. 2
19 Institute for Policy Studies – Anniversary Celebration, "U.S. Foreign Policy Since
World War II," Institute for Policy Studies, http://www.c-
spanvideo.org/program/WarII, (October 2, 1993)
20 Information Digest (April 15, 1983) pp. 77-79
21 Institute for Policy Studies – Anniversary Celebration, "U.S. Foreign Policy Since
World War II," Institute for Policy Studies, http://www.c-
spanvideo.org/program/WarII, (October 2, 1993)

Corrine Brown (D-FL)

Corrine Brown is a Democratic member of the United States House of Representatives, representing the 3rd District of Florida. She was elected to Congress in 1992 and has been a member of the Congressional Black Caucus and the Congressional Progressive Caucus for most of that time.[1]

Background

A native of Jacksonville, Florida, Congresswoman Brown served in the Florida House of Representatives for ten years before coming to Washington. Congresswoman Brown attended the Florida Agricultural and Mechanical University where she earned a Bachelor of Science Degree. She also received a Master's Degree and an Education Specialist Degree from the University of Florida. She has been a faculty member at Florida Community College of Jacksonville, the University of Florida and Edward Waters College.[2]

Influence

In the 112th Congress, Brown served as the Ranking Member of the Transportation & Infrastructure Subcommittee on Railroads, Pipelines and Hazardous Materials. She also served as a senior member of the

Subcommittee on Coast Guard and Maritime Transportation, as well as the Subcommittee on Water & Environment. Brown also continues to serve on the Committee on Veterans Affairs and the Veteran Affairs Subcommittee on Health.[3]

Communist Connections

Corrine Brown is close to the Florida Communist Party USA (CPUSA).

In 2002, with the motto, "Protect the real Florida—for working people!" Jacksonville CPUSA Chairman, Russell Pelle, ran for the Soil and Water Conservation Board in Duval County Florida, "hammering Republican Gov. Jeb Bush for coddling corporate polluters and real estate developers."

Pelle called for protection of Florida's fragile environment. "Everywhere I go, I tell voters I am running against Jeb Bush," Pelle told the CPUSA's People's Weekly World. "The Soil and Water Board is pretty low on the electoral totem pole but Bush's policies have been a disaster for the Florida environment. If I am elected, I will fight urban sprawl, fight to protect the people from toxic wastes."

Pelle was endorsed by the North Florida Central Labor Council (NFCLC), Rep. Corrine Brown (D-FL) and by Tony Hill, a community organizer for the SEIU, who won the Democratic nomination for State Senate from Jacksonville in Florida's Sept. 10 primary. Tony Hill, who now works for Jacksonville Mayor Alvin Brown, is a long-time Communist Party supporter and a friend of President Barack Obama.

The Communist Party's People's World of November 2, 2002, claimed that People's World readers and Rep. Corrine Brown were actively helping Pelle's campaign:

> Russell Pelle is running for Soil and Water Conservation Board (District 1) with the help of labor, elected officials, including Corrine Brown and readers of the World.

Rep. Corrine Brown also sent an email reply to the People's World in which she stated, "We can beat Jeb Bush and send a message to his brother that the American people don't support his Robin Hood (in reverse) policies of stealing from the poor to give tax breaks to the rich."[4]

Haitian Earthquake Relief

In January 2010, Communist Russell Pelle held a press conference in Jacksonville, with Rep. Corrine Brown and several pastors to raise support for Haitian earthquake victims.

"I am confident that our nation will provide emergency relief and support to the Haitian people during this critical time," Brown said.[5]

What kind of support Pelle and Brown had in mind, became evident later.

Russell Pelle soon conceived the Haitian Memorial Pyramid Project, a giant pyramid, to be built in Haiti out of earthquake rubble as a giant "make-work scheme for quake survivors." In March 2010, the idea was presented to and supported by then Florida State Senator and CPUSA sympathizer, Tony Hill, at a Haitian-American beach party. An Executive Board was established and the project was incorporated on November 10, 2010. The first formal endorsement came from Senator Hill on November 24, 2010.

Subsequently, the project was endorsed by Jacksonville, Florida Mayor Alvin Brown, U.S. Congresswoman Corrine Brown and U.S. Senator Bill Nelson.[6]

United for Peace and Justice

On October 27th, 2007, the Institute for Policy Studies initiated United for Peace and Justice held an Anti-War National Mobilization near Orlando, Florida at Lake Eola.

Speakers included Congresswoman Corrine Brown and Central Florida CPUSA member and Veterans for Peace activist, Jesse Kern.

Socialist Connection

In July 1996, the Democratic Socialists of America Political Action Committee endorsed Corrine Brown of Florida in that year's Congressional elections.[7]

Foreign Policy/National Security

In May 2004, Roshan Hodge from the office of Congresswoman Corrine Brown spent four days in Havana, Cuba for the purpose of "fact finding." The trip cost $1,350.16 and was paid for by the leftist Christopher Reynolds Foundation.[8]

---

1 KeyWiki, "Corrine Brown," KeyWiki, http://keywiki.org/index.php/Corrine_Brown (accessed March 21, 2013)
2 Corrine Brown, "Biography," Congressional Website, http://corrinebrown.house.gov/index.php?option=com_content&view=article&id=6&It emid=18 (accessed August 4, 2011)
3 Corrine Brown, "Biography," Congressional Website, http://corrinebrown.house.gov/index.php?option=com_content&view=article&id=6&It emid=18 (accessed August 4, 2011)
4 Noel Rabinowitz, "Florida labor, women get out vote to oust Jeb Bush," People's World, http://www.peoplesworld.org/florida-labor-women-get-out-vote-to-oust-jeb-bush/, (November 1, 2002)
5 Larry Hanna, "Jacksonville churches band together to help Haiti," Jacksonville.com, http://jacksonville.com/news/metro/2010-01-17/story/jacksonville_churches_band_together_to_help_haiti (January 17, 2010)
6 The Haitian Earthquake Memorial Pyramid, Botanical Garden & Marine Sanctuary, "Timeline," The Haitian Earthquake Memorial Pyramid, Botanical Garden & Marine Sanctuary, http://www.haitianpyramid.org/timeline.html (accessed March 21, 2013)
7 Democratic Left (July/August 1996) p. 21
8 American Radio Works, "Trips Sponsored by Christopher Reynolds Foundation," Congressional Staffers Share the Road, http://americanradioworks.publicradio.org/features/staffers/travdat/sponsor.php?sponso r_id=T000109 (accessed March 21, 2013)

Alan Grayson
(D-FL)

Alan Grayson is a Democratic member of the United States House of Representatives, representing the 9th District of Florida.[1]

After losing his reelection bid in 2010, Grayson won election back to Congress on November 6, 2012. He is a member and past Vice Chair of the Congressional Progressive Caucus.[2]

Background

Alan Grayson grew up in the tenements of the Bronx, New York. He worked his way through Harvard University, graduating with high honors. Immediately following his undergraduate career, he enrolled in Harvard Law School where he again graduated with honors.

As an attorney, he focused on Contract Law. In 1986, he helped to found the Alliance for Aging Research, serving as an officer of the organization for more than twenty years.

Congressman Grayson was also the first President of IDT Corporation, a publicly traded billion-dollar telecommunications company.

In the 2000s, he worked as a plaintiffs' attorney, specializing in whistleblower fraud cases aimed at Iraq War contractors.[3]

Influence

Grayson serves on the House Committee on Foreign Affairs and the House Committee on Science, Space and Technology. For Foreign Affairs, he serves on two Subcommittees: the Western Hemisphere and the Middle East and North Africa Subcommittees. For Science, Space and Technology, he serves on the Energy and Environment Subcommittees.

Alan Grayson is a member of the House Science and National Labs Caucus and the Congressional Labor and Working Families Caucus.[4]

"Progressive" Connections

21st Century Democrats

Grayson was one of 12 key progressives endorsed by the Democratic Socialists of America (DSA)-led 21st Century Democrats in the 2012 election cycle.

He was one of 17 supported in 2010.[5]

America's Future Now!

Alan Grayson was one of the 148 speakers who addressed the 2010 America's Future Now conference, run by the Institute for Policy Studies (IPS)/DSA initiated Campaign for America's Future.[6]

Progressive Democrats of America Endorsement

In 2012, Alan Grayson was one of 14 leftist Congressional and Senate candidates endorsed by Progressive Democrats of America (PDA), an organization dominated by members or affiliates of DSA and the IPS.[7]

Progressive Central: The Peoples' Inauguration

Progressive Central: The Peoples' Inauguration was held January 19, 2013, at the UDC David A. Clarke School of Law, Washington, D.C.

The event was sponsored by IPS affiliates Progressive Democrats of America, The Nation, National Nurses United and Busboys and Poets. The event was advertised and promoted by the Institute for Policy Studies.[8]

The 2:15 pm - 3:25 pm session, "Organizing for Main Street not Wall Street," was moderated by John Nichols.

It featured Rep. Alan Grayson; Michael Lighty, PDA National Board/National Nurses United and Becky Bond, President CREDO Super PAC.

Participants included PDA National Director Tim Carpenter (DSA); John Nichols of The Nation; DSA and Committees of Correspondence for Democracy and Socialism affiliate; National Nurses United official Michael Lighty (a former DSA National Director) and PDA board member Steve Cobble (IPS). Also included were Phyllis Bennis (IPS); Medea Benjamin (IPS and Committees of Correspondence for Democracy and Socialism affiliate); and Bill Fletcher, Jr., IPS, DSA and Freedom Road Socialist Organization.[9] [10] [11] [12] [13] [14] [15]

PDA National Director Tim Carpenter, John Nichols of The Nation, Rep. Alan Grayson, National Nurses United Michael Lighty and PDA board member, Steve Cobble

Hosting PDA

According to a New Year 2013 press release from Progressive Democrats of America:[16]

> In just a few days, on January 3rd, our team will be on Capitol Hill as special guests of our newly elected and re-elected progressive candidates including our board members our friends Representatives Alan Grayson, Dr. Ami Bera, and Mark Pocan

Foreign Policy/National Security

Supported by Council for a Livable World

The far left, anti-U.S. military Council for a Livable World, supported Alan Grayson in his successful 2008 House of Representatives run as a candidate for Florida.[17] He had also been previously supported by the Council.[18]

---

1 Mark I. Pinsky, "Alan Grayson, Jewish Democrat, Rides Hispanic Support Back to Washington," The Huffington Post, http://www.huffingtonpost.com/mark-i-pinsky/alan-grayson-jewish-democrat-rides-hispanic-support-to-orlando-win_b_2121491.html (November 13, 2012)
2 Alan Grayson, "About Alan," House.gov, http://grayson.house.gov/about/full-biography (accessed April 15, 2013)
3 21st Century Democrats, "Alan Grayson," 21st Century Democrats, http://www.21stcenturydems.org/candidates/rep-alan-grayson/#.UPhv5vLvPGg, (accessed April 15, 2013)
4 Alan Grayson, "Committees and Caucuses," House.gov, http://grayson.house.gov/legislation/committees-and-caucuses (accessed April 15, 2013)
5 21st Century Democrats, "Alan Grayson," 21st Century Democrats, http://www.21stcenturydems.org/candidates/rep-alan-grayson/#.UPhv5vLvPGg, (accessed April 15, 2013)
6 Campaign For America's Future, "America's Future Now! 2010 Speaker Biographies," Campaign For America's Future, http://www.ourfuture.org/now/speakers (accessed July 12, 2010)
7 KeyWiki, "Alan Grayson," KeyWiki, http://keywiki.org/index.php/Alan_Grayson (accessed April 15, 2013)
8 PDA website, http://hq-salsa3.salsalabs.com/o/1987/p/salsa/event/common/public/index.sjs?event_KEY=69575, (accessed January 15, 2013)
9 KeyWiki, "Tim Carpenter," KeyWiki, http://www.keywiki.org/index.php/Tim_Carpenter (accessed April 15, 2013)
10 KeyWiki, "John Nichols," KeyWiki, http://www.keywiki.org/index.php/John_Nichols (accessed April 15, 2013)
11 KeyWiki, "Michael Lighty," KeyWiki, http://www.keywiki.org/index.php/Michael_Lighty (accessed April 15, 2013)
12 KeyWiki, "Steve Cobble," KeyWiki, http://www.keywiki.org/index.php/Steve_Cobble (accessed April 15, 2013)
13 KeyWiki, "Phyllis Bennis," KeyWiki, http://www.keywiki.org/index.php/Phyllis_Bennis (accessed April 15, 2013)
14 KeyWiki, "Medea Benjamin," KeyWiki, http://www.keywiki.org/index.php/Medea_Benjamin (accessed April 15, 2013)
15 KeyWiki, "Bill Fletcher, Jr.," KeyWiki, http://www.keywiki.org/index.php/Bill_Fletcher (accessed April 15, 2013)

16 PDA, "Happy New Year from PDA!," PDA,
http://dir.groups.yahoo.com/group/progressivesforobama/message/6357 (January 1,
2013)
17 Council for a Livable World, "Meet the Candidates," Council for a Livable World,
http://livableworld.org/support/meet_candidates/ (accessed April 15, 2013)
18 Council for a Livable World, "Legacy in Congress: Who We've Helped Elect,"
Council for a Livable World,
http://livableworld.org/what/legacy_in_congress_who_weve_helped_elect/ (accessed
April 15, 2013)

John Lewis (D-GA)

John Lewis is a Democratic member of the United States House of Representatives, representing the 5th District of Georgia.[1]

He is an active member of the Congressional Progressive Caucus[2] and the Congressional Black Caucus.

Background

John Lewis was born the son of sharecroppers on February 21, 1940, outside of Troy, Alabama. He grew up on his family's farm and attended segregated public schools in Pike County, Alabama.

Lewis holds a Bachelor's Degree in Religion and Philosophy from Fisk University. He is a graduate of the American Baptist Theological Seminary as well.[3]

In 1981, Lewis was elected to the Atlanta City Council. He was elected to Congress in 1986 and has served as a United States Representative for Georgia's 5th Congressional District since then.

Influence

John Lewis is the Senior Chief Deputy Whip for the Democratic Party in leadership in the House, a member of the House Ways & Means Committee, a member of its Subcommittee on Income Security and Family Support and Chairman of its Subcommittee on Oversight.[4]

As a student at Fisk University, Lewis organized sit-in demonstrations at segregated lunch counters in Nashville, Tennessee. In 1961, he volunteered to participate in the Freedom Rides, which challenged segregation at interstate bus terminals across the South.[5]

During the height of the movement, from 1963 to 1966, Lewis was named Chairman of the Student Nonviolent Coordinating Committee, which he helped form. The Student Nonviolent Coordinating Committee was largely responsible for organizing student activism in the movement, including sit-ins and other activities.

In Selma, Alabama, Lewis led a march across the Edmund Pettus Bridge straight into a blockade set up by state troopers. The first nightstick came down on Lewis' skull. The troopers used whips, horses and a hose wrapped in barbed wire. Along with Lewis, ninety demonstrators were injured. At the White House, President Lyndon Johnson watched it all on television and deepened his resolve to push the Voting Rights Act.

John Lewis is an icon of the "civil rights movement" and carries huge moral authority across the political spectrum because of it.

Communist Connections

National Committee to Abolish the House Un-American Activities Committee

John Lewis was a Vice Chairman in 1962 of the Communist Party USA (CPUSA) front, National Committee to Abolish the House Un-American Activities Committee.

In 1964, Lewis was also the Chairman of the Student Nonviolent Coordinating Committee and was listed as a sponsor of the National Committee to Abolish the House Un-American Activities Committee.[6]

Freedomways

The CPUSA created Freedomways magazine as a propaganda vehicle with which to reach into the black intellectual and academic community. It was established in the mid-1960s by members of the Communist Party and well-documented sympathizers/supporters. It billed itself as "A Quarterly Review of the Freedom Movement."

Newly declassified documents from Operation SOLO, an FBI program to infiltrate the CPUSA, reveal that Freedomways, which was influential in the black community for decades, was subsidized by the Soviet and Chinese Communist Parties.

Freedomways has been called "one of the most influential African-American literary and political journals of the 1960s and 1970s."

During the 25 years it served as a propaganda organ for the Communist Party and Soviet front organizations such as the World Peace Council, Freedomways published articles by such figures as:

- Derrick Bell, later one of Barack Obama's academic mentors and a Harvard professor.
- Rev. Martin Luther King, Jr.
- Rev. Jesse Jackson, a former aide to King and Democratic candidate for president.

Lewis wrote a 1965 Freedomways article, "Paul Robeson: Inspirer of Youth," about the famous actor and singer who had been a member of the Communist Party and an admirer of Soviet dictator Joseph Stalin.

"He [Robeson] talked and listened to the representatives of the Communist Party," wrote Lewis, then National Chairman of the Student Non-Violent Coordinating Committee. "In many ways," he wrote, "we of SNCC are Paul Robeson's spiritual children."[7]

GI Civil Liberties Defense Committee

In 1969, while Lewis sat on the Southern Regional Council in Atlanta, he was listed as a sponsor of the Trotskyist Socialist Worker's Party-led GI Civil Liberties Defense Committee.[8]

Martinez Jobs Bill

In 1994, John Lewis co-sponsored the CPUSA backed Martinez Jobs Bill (HR-4708).[9]

Communist Party Paper Contribution

John Lewis contributed an article to the Communist Party USA paper People's Weekly World, August 23, 2003, page 8, "An Open letter to my Colleagues in Congress: Remembering the Legacy of Martin Luther King."

8   People's Weekly World   Saturday, August 23, 2003

An Open Letter to My Rei

By John Lewis

My Dear Colleagues:

Forty years ago, Aug. 28, 1963, was a history-making day. The Civil Rights Movement held its largest and perhaps most powerful demonstration. It was called the March on Washington for Jobs and Freedom.

Some of you were not even born, not even a dream during this dramatic period in our nation's history. Others of you were too young

File photo
John Lewis in 1963.

Student Nonviolent Coordinating Committee Anniversary

The Student Nonviolent Coordinating Committee held its 50th Anniversary conference at Shaw University in 2010.

At its founding in 1960, the now legendary civil rights organization adopted its first formal program. Lifelong Communist Party USA activist, Debbie Bell, was a founding member; serving alongside John Lewis; Julian Bond (later a Democratic Socialists of America member); communist affiliated entertainer Harry Belafonte; communist affiliated Sweet Honey in the Rock founder; Bernice Johnson Reagon and radical comedian Dick Gregory.

All of these founders spoke at the anniversary event. There were speeches as well by Attorney General Eric Holder and radical actor Danny Glover.[10]

Socialist Connections

March on Washington

At the age of 23, John Lewis was an architect of and a Keynote speaker at the historic March on Washington in August of 1963. The March was organized primarily by the Socialist Party USA, which tried to hide its role in the event.[11]

According to Boston Democratic Socialists of America's The Yankee Radical, September/October 2010, page 3:

> If anything, one aspect of the 1963 rally, deliberately downplayed at the time for fear of red-baiting, was the influence of members of the Socialist Party..., in both organizing the event and its politics. This began with A. Philip Randolph, who issued the call for the March and MC'd it, his longtime lieutenant Bayard Rustin, and his key assistants who ran the March organizing office in NY—Tom Kahn, Rachelle Horowitz, Norm Hill and others, SPers all... Martin Luther King himself was briefly in the Socialist Party in the early 1950s while attending Boston University.

March on Washington's Bayard Rustin (Socialist Party, left), James Farmer (Socialist Party, second from right) and John Lewis (right)

Socialist Award

In 1965, Lewis was the first recipient of the Eugene Debs Award, presented by the socialist Eugene V. Debs Foundation. The award is to honor an approved social or labor activist.[12]

Tribute to Norman Thomas

In 1967, while Lewis was the Chairman of the Student Nonviolent Coordinating Committee, he paid tribute to Norman Thomas, leader of the Socialist Party USA, on his 80th birthday.[13]

DSA Endorsement

In July 1996, the Democratic Socialists of America (DSA) Political Action Committee endorsed John Lewis, Georgia 5th District, in that year's Congressional elections.[14]

DSA National Conference Guest

In November 2007, Lewis was a special guest at the National Conference of DSA, which was held at the International Brotherhood of Electrical Workers union hall in Atlanta, Georgia. Lewis introduced Senator Bernie Sanders to the conference.[15]

> 7:00PM Convention Dinner
>   First Atlanta Douglass-Debs Dinner
>   Special Guest: Sen. Bernie Sanders (I- Vt.), Hon. John Lewis (D-GA)
>   Honorees: Charlie Flemming, North Georgia Labor Council; Alice Lovelace, Organizer, US Social Forum

Debs-Douglas Dinner Program, Atlanta DSA (2007)

Wellstone Action

In 2009, John Lewis was listed as a member of the Advisory Board[16] of Wellstone Action, a Minnesota organization based on the political legacy of that state's late DSA affiliated Senator Paul Wellstone. Several DSAers members serve on Wellstone Action boards, including Frances Fox Piven, Deborah Olson and Julian Bond.[17]

Standing with DSA

On August 24, 2012, Metro Atlanta DSA's coalition partner Women's Action for New Directions, celebrated the 10th anniversary of its Stand for Peace event that was held in front of Colony Square every Friday at noon, calling for an "end to the wars in Iraq and Afghanistan, reductions in military spending and instead funding for human and environmental needs."

DSA members Barbara Segal and Marcia Borowski, serve on the Steering Committee of the Georgia Coalition for Peace and Justice, which supports Stand for Peace and both were present at the anniversary. DSA member Minnie Ruffin stood with Rep. John Lewis, as he addressed the crowd.[18]

"Progressive" Connections

Institute for Southern Studies

The Institute for Policy Studies (IPS) spinoff, Institute for Southern Studies, was incorporated in the state of North Carolina in 1989. John Lewis was among the founding members listed on the incorporation papers.[19]

21st Century Democrats

In 2010, Congresswoman Barbara Lee, Congressman Elijah Cummings and former Obama communist "Green Jobs Czar," Van Jones, spoke about the future of American politics at the kickoff event for the 21st Century Democrats' 2010 Youth Leadership Speaker Series. The event was sponsored by Representative John Lewis and IPS affiliated Senator Tom Harkin.[20]

Foreign Policy/National Security

Congressional Pink Caucus

In 1989, the Pro-Soviet Nicaraguan Sandinista Government announced that they would no longer comply with the 19 month-old cease-fire agreement with the Contras. This had been considered a prime step forward for the "peace process" that was progressing slowly as part of the Arias Peace Plan.

A resolution was introduced in Congress deploring the Sandinista's actions. The Senate voted unanimously in favor of the resolution, but the House vote was 379 to 29. The 29 Congressmen voting against the resolution were Democrats. The Council for Inter-American Security dubbed these 29 Democrats the "Congressional Pink Caucus." John Lewis of Georgia was one of the 29.[21]

Cuban Connection

In 2004, Michael Collins, from the office of Congressman John Lewis, spent four days in Havana, Cuba for the purpose of "fact finding." The trip cost $1,280.16 and was paid for by the leftist Christopher Reynolds Foundation.[22]

---

1 KeyWiki, "John Lewis," KeyWiki, http://keywiki.org/index.php/John_Lewis (accessed March 29, 2012)

2 Congressional Progressive Congress, "Our Members," Congressional Progressive Caucus, http://cpc.grijalva.house.gov/index.cfm?ContentID=166&ParentID=0&SectionID=4&SectionTree=4&lnk=b&ItemID=164 (accessed March 30, 2012)

3 KeyWiki, "John Lewis," KeyWiki, http://keywiki.org/index.php/John_Lewis (accessed March 29, 2012)

4 KeyWiki, "John Lewis," KeyWiki, http://keywiki.org/index.php/John_Lewis (accessed January 23, 2013)

5 The Arena, "John Lewis," Politico, http://www.politico.com/arena/bio/john_lewis.html (accessed March 29, 2012)

6 KeyWiki, "John Lewis," National Committee to Abolish the House Un-American Activities Committee letterhead circa 1962 – footnote," http://keywiki.org/index.php/John_Lewis#cite_note-2 (accessed March 29, 2012)

7 Cliff Kincaid, "Soviets Funded Black "Freedom" Journal," Accuracy in Media (May 4, 2012)

8 Undated, GI Civil Liberties Defense Committee letterhead (circa 1969)

9 Evelina Alarcon, "PWW Support for jobs bill grows," People's Weekly World (October 1994) p. 3

10 Debbie Bell, "SNCC 50th anniversary meet mixes nostalgia and determination," People's World, http://peoplesworld.org/sncc-50th-anniversary-meet-mixes-nostalgia-and-determination/ (accessed March 30, 2012)

11 David Remnick, "The President's Hero," The New Yorker, http://www.newyorker.com/talk/comment/2009/02/02/090202taco_talk_remnick (accessed January 23, 2013)

12 Eugene V. Debs Foundation, "Eugene Victor Debs," Eugene V. Debs Foundation, http://debsfoundation.org/foundation.html (accessed March 29, 2012)

13 Arkansas Democrat (February 1964) p. 44

14 Democratic Left (July/August 1996) page 21

15 Democratic Socialists of America, "DSA National Convention November 9-11, 2007 – Agenda," Democratic Socialists of America, http://www.dsausa.org/convention2007/Convention%20Agenda.pdf (accessed March 30, 2012)

16 Wellstone Action!, "Board of Directors," Wellstone Action!, http://www.wellstone.org/about-us/board-directors (accessed March 30, 2012)

17 Wellstone Action!, "Our Mission & Goals," Wellstone Action!,
http://www.wellstone.org/about-us/our-mission-goals (accessed March 30, 2012)
18 Democratic Socialists of America, Metro Atlanta Democratic Socialists of America
newsletter (September 2012)
19 KeyWiki, "John Lewis," KeyWiki, http://keywiki.org/index.php/John_Lewis
(accessed March 29, 2012)
20 21st Century Democrats, "2010 Speakers," 21st Century Democrats,
http://21stcenturydems.org/index.php/events/sign-up/july-28-2010-speaker-series-kick-
off-event (accessed March 30, 2012)
21 KeyWiki, "John Lewis," KeyWiki, http://keywiki.org/index.php/John_Lewis
(accessed March 29, 2012)
22 American RadioWorks, "Christopher Reynolds Foundation," American Public
Media,
http://americanradioworks.publicradio.org/features/staffers/travdat/sponsor.php?sponso
r_id=T000109 (accessed March 30, 2012)

Dick Durbin (D-IL)

Dick Durbin is a Democrat and the Senior United States Senator from Illinois. He has been in office since 1997.[1]

Background

Richard Joseph "Dick" Durbin was born in East St. Louis, Illinois, on November 21, 1944. He graduated from the Georgetown University School of Foreign Service and Georgetown University Law Center. Working as State Legal Counsel throughout the 1970s, he made an unsuccessful run for Lieutenant Governor of Illinois in 1978. He was elected to the U.S. House of Representatives in 1982, representing the Springfield-based 20th Congressional District.

Elected to the U.S. Senate on November 5, 1996 and re-elected in 2002 and 2008, Durbin fills the seat left vacant by the retirement of his long-time friend and mentor, far left U.S. Senator Paul Simon.[2]

Influence

Durbin serves as the Assistant Majority Leader, the second highest ranking position in the Senate. Also known as the Majority Whip, Senator Durbin has been elected to this leadership post by his Democratic colleagues every two years since 2006.

Durbin sits on the Senate Judiciary, Appropriations, Foreign Relations and Rules Committees. He is the Chairman of the Judiciary Committee's Subcommittee on the Constitution, Civil Rights and Human Rights and the Appropriations Committee's Financial Services and General Government Subcommittee.[3]

On February 22, 2012, Obama for America announced the selection of the campaign's National Co-Chairs, a diverse group of leaders from around the country committed to re-electing President Obama. The Co-

Chairs serve as ambassadors for the President; advise the campaign on key issues and help engage and mobilize voters in all 50 states. Senator Dick Durbin—U.S. Senator from Illinois, was on the list.[4]

Communist Connections

CoC Support in 1996 Run

When Durbin first ran for the U.S. Senate in 1996, he was supported by the Chicago chapter of the Communist Party splinter group, Committees of Correspondence (CoC).

According to an undated memo from Chicago CoC Co-Chairs Sandy Patrinos and Mildred Williamson, on behalf of the Chicago Chapter Steering Committee:[5]

> Finally, the Steering Committee feels that the U.S. Senate race for the seat vacated by retiring Senator Paul Simon is important enough—and the difference between the candidates significant enough—to merit attention. Democrat Dick Durbin is the best hope to beat Al Salvi, a wealthy "pro-life" ultra right Republican... Polls show Durbin with a significant, but by no means secure lead... Please consider what you can do in the time remaining, to mobilize support for these quite different, but all important campaigns!

Working with Communist Bea Lumpkin

Durbin has worked with senior Chicago CPUSA member, Bea Lumpkin.[6]

Cooperating on Drug Program

On May 3, 2004, Sen. Dick Durbin cautioned seniors against rushing to buy one of the dozens of new discount drug cards available to Medicare recipients.

"Frankly, as soon as you sign up and pay your fee, you're stuck for a year," the Springfield Democrat said, during a news conference at a Chicago pharmacy with two other members of the Illinois Congressional delegation. "What may look like an appealing discount for a drug right now might, in fact, disappear in the next week."

Also joining Durbin was Communist Bea Lumpkin of the communist infiltrated Illinois Alliance for Retired Americans (ARA). All agreed that

Illinoisans may be better off using a new state program that offers drug discounts to people 65 and older and the disabled.[7]

Nursing Home Rally

In 2008, CPUSA member Bea Lumpkin was elected State Secretary of Illinois Alliance for Retired Americans. The ARA was leading the fight for higher standards for nursing homes and home care.

In 2009, she appeared at a press conference with Senator Dick Durbin to protest cuts in federal aid to nursing homes.[8]

Dick Durbin and Bea Lumpkin at Alliance for Retired Americans Rally Against Privatizing Social Security (2009)

Socialist Connections

IPA Endorsement

Chicago Democratic Socialists of America (DSA) and some Communist Party USA (CPUSA) members were heavily involved in Illinois Public Action at IPA's 20th annual convention, held on the weekend of December 8th and 9th, 1995.

The conference had to choose between endorsing two candidates for the U.S. Senate. They heard from Dick Durbin, the Congressman from the 20th District endorsed by Paul Simon and a representative from Patrick Quinn's campaign. The Quinn/Durbin endorsement choice was the major issue of the board. Durbin ultimately got the endorsement.[9]

Speaking Alongside Obama at DSA-Dominated Labor Event

On March 3rd, 2007, Barack Obama was a featured speaker at a meeting of labor unionists at the Hyatt Regency, Chicago Loop Grand Ballroom:

> Speaking in a vernacular and cadence that showed the Harvard Law School and Columbia University trained Barack Obama can connect with working class people, the third year U.S. Senator wowed and energized a mostly labor union crowd of about 1600 supporters this morning...
>
> The event attracted some of Labor's big hitters to join Obama on the dais and speak, including John Sweeney, President of the AFL-CIO and Gerald McEntee, President of AFSCME. Congresswoman Jan Schakowsky [D-Evanston, 9th CD], an early and big-time supporter of Obama's in the 2004 Senate Primary and Senator Dick Durbin [D-IL] also spoke...
>
> Eight other individuals spoke at the rally, including local labor leaders and health care workers, as well as a local favorite for liberals, Dr. Quentin Young.
>
> Cong. Jan Schakowsky [D-Evanston, 9th CD]: ...Employers can intimidate, fire, threaten to move people from the day shift to the graveyard... it is a new day in our nation's capital, it's a new day for Resurrection workers and their friends, it's a new day for immigrant workers, it's a new day for all our working Americans who dream of the justice that ONLY the Union Movement can deliver. And, to the doubters I say, you ain't seen nothing yet. Just wait until we have a Labor Department under President Barack Obama.

Of those speaking with Obama and Durbin, John Sweeney and Quentin Young are confirmed Democratic Socialists of America members. Gerald McEntee is at least a strong supporter and Jan Schakowsky has been a member and is still at least a supporter.[10]

Sponsoring Barack Obama

Chicago activist Adrian Bleifuss Prados, of DSA's youth wing, the Young Democratic Socialists, wrote on their blog, The Activist, on January 29, 2008:[11]

Barack has some real left-wing street cred in Chicago. He is probably the only person running for president who could identify, say, Antonio Gramsci, and that should count for something shouldn't it?

He has often [been] attacked for being less outspoken than the Senior Senator from Illinois, Dick Durbin, but Obama actually takes his cues from Durbin who, along with DSA-friendly Jan Schakowsky, has been his main political sponsor.

Save Our Security Illinois Coalition

In 2005, left opposition to Social Security privatization was organized in Illinois around the Save Our Security Illinois Coalition, which included Chicago Democratic Socialists of America.

The Coalition's first action in Illinois was a 90-person picket line outside the downtown Chicago offices of the Charles Schwab brokerage, a major advocate of privatization. A town hall meeting, with an overflow crowd of 400, on February 28th at Loyola University's Water Tower campus, featured Senators Dick Durbin and Barack Obama and DSA aligned Representative Jan Schakowsky.[12]

Employed Guy Molyneux

Dick Durbin has contracted Guy Molyneux, who is a partner with Hart Research Associates. Molyneux has carried out survey and focus group research projects for a wide variety of nonprofit organizations, government agencies, labor unions, media organizations and political candidates; Durbin being the most notable.[13]

In 1987, Guy Molyneux was Organizational Director of the DSA.[14]

"Progressive" Connections

America's Future Now!

Dick Durbin was one of the 148 speakers who addressed the 2010 America's Future Now! conference. The conference was hosted by the Institute for Policy Studies (IPS) and DSA-dominated Campaign for America's Future. It was held on June 7-9, at the Omni Shoreham Washington D.C.[15][16]

Quoting IPS Report

Senator Dick Durbin spoke about an Institute for Policy Studies Executive Excess Report during a floor speech about how corporate accountability can help the U.S. overcome the current economic crisis.[17]

The 2011 Executive Excess report continues to make waves among members of the media and decision-makers in Congress. This time, Senator Durbin, a progressive Democrat from Illinois, took to the Senate floor to highlight some of the findings of the report. He particularly zeroed in on General Electric, which has highlighted in the report as one of the top ten most creative tax-dodgers.

High IPS Rating

In 2012, in the "Congressional Report Card for the 99 Percent," the Institute for Policy Studies examined 40 different legislative actions in the House and Senate—votes and legislation introduced—to ascertain the real allegiances of sitting members of Congress. These include votes to extend the Bush tax cuts for the wealthy, levy a Wall Street speculation tax, invest in infrastructure and protect workers and student financial aid.

The Report Card also graded politicians for their commitment to reducing inequality and boosting the 99 percent. The report's "Honor Roll" gave an A-plus grade to 5 members of the U.S. Senate, including Senators Sherrod Brown (D-OH), Dick Durbin (D-IL), Al Franken (D-MN), Bernie Sanders (I-VT) and Sheldon Whitehouse (D-RI).[18]

---

1 KeyWiki, "Dick Durbin," KeyWiki, http://keywiki.org/index.php/Dick_Durbin (accessed April 20, 2013)
2 Dick Durbin, "Senator Durbin's Biography," Senate.gov, http://www.durbin.senate.gov/public/index.cfm/about (accessed April 20, 2013)
3 Dick Durbin, "Senator Durbin's Biography," Senate.gov, http://www.durbin.senate.gov/public/index.cfm/about (accessed April 20, 2013)
4 Judy Chu, "Obama For America Announces Rep. Judy Chu As National Campaign Co-Chair," Judy Chu for Congress, http://www.judychu.org/PDF/120222obamacochairrelease.pdf, (February 22, 2012)
5 KeyWiki, "Dick Durbin," KeyWiki, http://keywiki.org/index.php/Dick_Durbin (accessed April 20, 2013)
6 KeyWiki, "Dick Durbin," KeyWiki, http://keywiki.org/index.php/Dick_Durbin (accessed April 20, 2013)
7 Mike Ramsey, "Durbin Cautions Seniors About Medicare Cards," Jan Schakowsky website, https://forms.house.gov/schakowsky/article_5_3_04_Copley_Durbin.shtml, (May 3, 2004)

8 Bea Lumpkin, "Joy in the Struggle," p. 233

9 New Ground 44, "Rallying the Troops in Peoria: Illinois Public Action Convention," Chicago DSA, http://www.chicagodsa.org/ngarchive/ng44.html, (February 1996)

10 Jeff Berkowitz, "The Barack Obama Watch: Today's Labor Rally in Chicago," Public Affairs, http://jeffberkowitz.blogspot.com/2007/03/barack-obama-watch-todays-labor-rally.html (March 3, 2007)

11 Young Democratic Socialists, The Activist (January 29, 2008)

12 Democratic Left, http://www.dsausa.org/dl/Spring_2005.pdf (Spring 2005) pp. 14-15

13 Hart Research, "Guy Molyneux Bio," Hart Research, http://www.hartresearch.com/about/bios/molyneux.html, (accessed April 8, 2013)

14 DSA Letterhead (April 28, 1987)

15 Campaign For America's Future, "America's Future Now! 2010 Speaker Biographies," Campaign For America's Future, http://www.ourfuture.org/now/speakers (accessed July 12, 2010)

16 Campaign For America's Future, "Register On-Site For America's Future Now!" Campaign For America's Future, http://www.ourfuture.org/now/registeronsite (accessed July 12, 2010)

17 Matias Ramos, "Sen. Durbin Floor Speech on IPS CEO Pay Report," PS website, http://www.ips-dc.org/blog/sen_durbin_floor_speech_on_ips_ceo_pay_report_video, (September 9, 2011)

18 Chuck Collins, "Lawmakers Get Graded on Equality Record," Yes! blog, http://www.yesmagazine.org/new-economy/a-voting-guide-for-the-99 (October 9, 2012)

Danny Davis (D-IL)

Danny Davis is a Democratic member of the United States House of Representatives, representing the 7th District of Illinois. He is a member of the Congressional Progressive Caucus and the Congressional Black Caucus.[1]

Background

Danny K. Davis was born a sharecropper's son on September 6, 1941, in Parkdale, Arkansas. He attended Savage High School in Parkdale, where he graduated in 1957. A History major with an Education minor, Davis earned a Bachelor of Arts Degree from Arkansas AM&N College at Pine Bluff, Arkansas in 1961.

Moving to Chicago, Davis clerked for the United States Post Office before going to work as a teacher at Ferdinand Magellan School in 1962. Davis received a Master's Degree in School Guidance from Chicago State University in 1968, while continuing his education in 1969 and 1970 with courses in administration, supervision, psychology and political science. In 1977, he was awarded a Ph.D. in Public Administration by Union Institute.[2]

After graduation, Davis was a public school teacher, health planner and founder of the Westside Center for Community Action. He was later Chair of the National Association of Community Health Centers and later Co-Chair of the Progressive Chicago Area Network. During the 1960s, Davis became involved in the Civil Rights Movement.[3]

In 1969, he became Executive Director of the Greater Lawndale Conservation Commission and then left to become Director of Training for the Martin Luther King, Jr. Health Center.

By 1971, Davis was a manpower consultant for the Westside Health Planning Organization and in 1972 became Executive Director of WHPO. From 1976 through 1981, he served as Special Assistant to the

President of Mile Square Community Health Center. Davis also taught college courses at Malcolm X College, National College of Education, Illinois Benedictine College, Roosevelt University and the University of Illinois, School of Public Health.

In 1979, Davis won the Aldermanic seat for Chicago's 29th Ward as an Independent. He then became a 29th Ward Committeeman in 1984. Active during Chicago's Harold Washington years, Davis served until 1990, when he resigned from the Chicago City Council to take a seat on the Cook County Board of Commissioners. After an unsuccessful bid for mayor in 1991, he ran for and won the U.S. 7th Congressional District seat in 1996.[4]

Influence

In the 113th Congress, Representative Davis serves on the Committee on Ways and Means. His subcommittee assignments are: Oversight and Human Resources.

Congressman Davis is a member of several Congressional Caucuses including the Urban Caucus, the Community Health Center's Caucus and the Congressional Sugar Caucus.[5]

Communist Connections

Danny Davis was also on good terms with the Communist Party USA (CPUSA).

In Chicago, the Communist Party has for many years held an annual fundraising banquet for its paper, the People's Weekly World (formerly the People's Daily World).

1989 Chicago PWW Banquet

Chicago Alderman Danny Davis was Keynote speaker at the June 25th, 1989, People's Daily World Banquet.

1990 Chicago PWW Banquet

According to the People's Daily World of July 28, 1990, Chicago Alderman Danny Davis attended the 1990 banquet on July 15th.

Davis applauded those at the banquet, who, he said, are always in the midst of struggle. PDW readers, he said, are "steadfast in the fight for justice."

The affair netted $2,500 for the PDW fund.[6]

24   People's Daily World   Thursday, May 25, 1989

Illinois to hold P

Special to the PDW

CHICAGO — Illinois will wrap up its '89 PDW Fund Drive with a gala banquet on June 25 by honoring two civic leaders, Frank Rosen, UE District 11 president, and Dr. Margaret Burroughs, founder of the DuSable Museum of African-American History.

Alderman Danny Davis will be the keynote speaker at the banquet, to begin at 4:30 p.m. at the Chiam Restaurant, 2323 S. Wentworth.

Banquet committee member

1998 Chicago PWW Banquet

According to the People's Weekly World on October 3, 1998, Congressman Danny K. Davis interrupted his campaign work for United States Senate candidate Carol Moseley Braun, to present an award at the 1998 Chicago People's Weekly World Banquet. Davis praised the work of Communist Party USA member Harry Gaynor's "active role in tearing [down the] city's segregated walls and working for peace."

This event raised $10,000 towards keeping the Communist Party paper afloat.[7]

2000 Chicago PWW Banquet

The 2000 banquet that was held on October 28th at the House of Fortune restaurant featured Congressman Danny Davis as guest speaker.

Local honorees were: Alice Bush, a Communist Party supporter, Director District 1199, SEIU Local and leader of a strike against Methodist Hospital in Gary, Indiana and Communist Party member Bea Lumpkin.

A special award went to Evelina Alarcon, Coordinator of the Cesar E. Chavez Holiday Campaign and Southern California, Communist Party leader.

Communist Lance Cohn was a banquet organizer.[8]

2011 Chicago PWW Banquet

Labor and community activists, elected officials, readers and supporters of the PeoplesWorld.org and MundoPopular.org gathered in Chicago on Nov. 20th, 2011, for the annual banquet bash at the Parthenon Restaurant. They "feasted on sumptuous Greek food and honored heroes of the growing labor and people's movement."

"Something's terribly wrong when 1% of the population controls 40% of the nation's wealth," said Congressman Danny Davis, who appeared on behalf of his long-time friend, Communist Party supporter, Brenetta Howell Barrett.

Barrett was one of those receiving the Rudy Lozano-Chris Hani Social Justice Award.

Davis said it was the steadfastness of fighters like Barrett, who had been in every fight he could recount, that the movement for justice and equality would be successful.

Barrett, who among other things, is a leader of the Chicago Committee to Defend the Bill of Rights, a former Commissioner in Mayor Harold Washington's administration and a trailblazing fighter for political independence, said it was critical to reelect President Obama in 2012 and blasted the "racist attacks" on him.

"Everyone needs to be involved in that fight if we are to have any meaningful change," said Barrett.[9]

Less Military Spending

In 1997, Danny Davis of Illinois, at the request of the Communist Party-controlled National Labor-Community Coalition for Public Works Jobs, wrote a letter to his colleagues in Congress, asking them to address the real issues and solutions related to the economy, starting with the communist drafted Martinez Jobs Bill. "The debate over the size of the military budget has not been fully aired, has not been conducted with the same vigor and intensity as the scrutiny over other discretionary spending... military experts have earmarked savings of over $200 million over the next ten years, while continuing to maintain our military supremacy."[10]

Attending the Chicago Communist Party's Unity Center

On February 26, 2012, U.S. Representative Danny Davis attended a Celebrating African American History Month 2012 cultural performance at the Chicago Communist Party's Unity Center S. Halsted St. Chicago.[11]

Committees of Correspondence Connection

Davis also had close ties to the Communist Party USA splinter group, Committees of Correspondence (CoC).

Committees of Correspondence Founding Conference

According to Chicago Democratic Socialists of America's New Ground of September 1994:

> Over 500 delegates and observers (including 140 from Chicago) attended the founding convention of the Committees of Correspondence held here in Chicago in July.

New Ground reported that speakers included Charles Nqukula, General Secretary of the South African Communist Party; Dulce Maria Pereira, a senatorial candidate of the Worker's Party of Brazil; Angela Davis of Committees of Correspondence and Andre Brie of the Party of Democratic Socialism of Germany (a revamp of the old East German Communist Party).

Guests during the Convention included Cook County Commissioner Danny Davis, Chicago Aldermen Helen Shiller and Rick Munoz, a representative of the Green Left Weekly of Australia and a "representative of the Cuban Interest Section."[12]

CoC Contacts List

In 1994, Danny Davis was listed on a "Membership, Subscription and Mailing List" for the Chicago Committees of Correspondence.[13]

Chicago Committee to Defend the Bill of Rights

Congressman Davis has a close relationship to the Chicago Committee to Defend the Bill of Rights—founded in 1960 as a CPUSA front, but now also heavily influenced by members and supporters of DSA and particularly the Committees of Correspondence for Democracy and Socialism.[14]

CCDBR Bicentennial Celebration

On November 10, 1991, Danny K. Davis was listed as the Master of Ceremonies for the Chicago Committee to Defend the Bill of Rights Bicentennial Celebration.[15]

Richard Criley Memorial

In 2000, Danny K. Davis served as Honorary Chairperson on the welcoming committee for the Chicago Memorial Service for Richard Criley, a long-time activist with the Communist Party and a leader of the Chicago Committee to Defend the Bill of Rights.[16]

Honoring Frank Wilkinson

The Chicago Committee to Defend the Bill of Rights organized a "Celebration of the Dynamic Life of Frank Wilkinson (1914-2006)" on Sunday, October 29, 2006. Wilkinson had been a leader of the CPUSA, the New American Movement and DSA.

Honoring Committee members included Danny Davis.[17]

Socialist Connections

Danny Davis is the only current member of Congress who is an open member of Democratic Socialists of America (DSA).

Supporting Timuel Black

In the late 1970s, Communist Party USA (CPUSA) member Harold Rogers served on a "Citizen's Committee" supporting socialist Timuel Black's unsuccessful campaign for State Representative in the 22nd District.

The "Citizen's Committee" included "former" communist Charles Hayes, radical journalist Don Rose, socialist Chicago Alderman Leon

Despres, future DSA members Saul Mendelson (a former Trotskyite), Danny Davis and Milt Cohen (another former communist).

Timuel Black would also go on to join DSA and to befriend and mentor a young Barack Obama.[18]

Committee in Support of Southern Africa

The Committee in Support of Southern Africa was an anti-Apartheid group active in Chicago in the early 1980s.

Members of the committee included: DSA/Communist Party affiliated politicians Rep. Charles Hayes, Rep. Harold Washington and future U.S. Senator Carol Moseley Braun; the Communist-controlled Coalition of Black Trade Unionists, pro-communist labor unionist, Frank Rosen; communist Harold Rogers and DSAers Alderman Danny Davis, Milt Cohen and Timuel Black.[19]

Socialist School

In the fall of 1983, Alderman Danny Davis lectured at the Chicago Democratic Socialists of America's Socialist School.[20]

1989 Debs Dinner

In 1989, Danny Davis gave the opening address to Chicago Democratic Socialists of America's annual Debs Dinner.[21]

Democratic Left (January/February 1992) p. 13

DSA Conference

Cook County Commissioner Danny Davis welcomed Democratic Socialists of America's 1991 National Convention to Chicago.[22]

DSA Endorsements

In 1990, Chicago DSA endorsed Danny Davis for the Chicago mayoralty.[23]

In July 1996, the Democratic Socialists of America Political Action Committee endorsed Danny Davis, running in Illinois' 7th District in that year's Congressional elections.[24]

Chicago Democratic Socialists of America endorsements in the March 19th 1995 Primary Election, went to Danny Davis, Patricia Martin, Willie Delgado and Barack Obama.[25]

DSA Member

When Danny Davis ran for Congress in 1998, DSA did not officially endorse any candidates, but he was "recommended" as worthy of a vote by Chicago DSA, citing his membership in the Congressional Progressive Caucus and his support for Progressive Challenge:[26]

Danny Davis, U.S. House of Representatives, 7th District

Danny Davis is a member of the Progressive Caucus, an old friend of DSA and a member of the New Party.

Davis was named as a DSA member during his 2006 Congressional race according to DSA's Democratic Left Summer 2006.[27]

DSA has also endorsed DSAer and Congress member Danny Davis in his bid for re-election in Chicago.

"African Americans and the 1996 Elections"

In conjunction with the Chicago Chapter of the Committees of Correspondence, the University of Chicago DSA hosted a panel discussion on "African Americans and the 1996 Elections." Panelists included Danny Davis, Cook County Commissioner and Democratic Party nominee for Illinois' 7th Congressional District; Barbara Ransby, Chair of the Center for African American Research at DePaul University and Salim Muwakkil, columnist for In These Times and the Chicago Sun-Times. Long-time political activist Timuel Black moderated.[28]

The New Party

Danny Davis joined the Chicago New Party (along with Barack Obama) during his successful Congressional 1996 campaign on the Democratic Party ticket.

The New Party News, Spring 1996, page 1, celebrated the Davis' Congressional victory and went on to say:[29]

"New Party members won three other primaries this Spring in Chicago: Barack Obama (State Senate), Michael Chandler (Democratic Party

Committee) and Patricia Martin (Cook County Judiciary)... These victories prove that small 'd' democracy can work" said Obama.

The New Party was founded and led by ACORN, SEIU, Institute for Policy Studies and Democratic Socialists of America.[30]

New Party News (Spring 1996) p. 2, Danny Davis (center), Barack Obama (right)

1 KeyWiki, "Danny K. Davis," KeyWiki, http://keywiki.org/index.php/Danny_Davis (accessed April 11, 2013)
2 Political Makers, "Hon. Danny K. Davis," The History Makers, http://www.thehistorymakers.com/biography/hon-danny-k-davis-38 (accessed August 24, 2011)
3 People's Weekly World (January 19, 1991) p. 12
4 Political Makers, "Hon. Danny K. Davis," The History Makers, http://www.thehistorymakers.com/biography/hon-danny-k-davis-38 (accessed August 24, 2011)
5 Danny K. Davis, "Committees," House.gov, http://davis.house.gov/index.php?option=com_content&task=view&id=20&Itemid=40 (accessed April 11, 2013)
6 KeyWiki, "Danny K. Davis," KeyWiki, http://keywiki.org/index.php/Danny_Davis (accessed April 11, 2013)
7 People's Weekly World, "Chicago Banquet Nets $10,000 for 'World'," p. 3
8 People's Weekly World (October 7, 2000)
9 John Bachtell, "Chicago PeoplesWorld.org readers celebrate growing fightback," People's World http://peoplesworld.org/chicago-peoplesworld-org-readers-celebrate-growing-fightback/, (December 1, 2011)
10 People's Weekly World (June 28, 1997) p. 2
11 People's World, "Chicago: "Tea party" Congress can't stop the fight for equality!" People's World, http://peoplesworld.org/events/647CHICAGO: (accessed February 13, 2011)
12 Jim Williams, "Committees of Correspondence Meet in Chicago," Chicago DSA/New Ground 36, http://www.chicagodsa.org/ngarchive/ng36.html#anchor810069 (September 1994)
13 Chicago CoC, "Membership, Subscription and Mailing List" (October 14, 1994)

14 KeyWiki, "Danny K. Davis," KeyWiki, http://keywiki.org/index.php/Danny_Davis (accessed April 11, 2013)

15 Chicago Committee to Defend the Bill of Rights Bicentennial Celebration Program (November 10, 1991)

16 Memoriam Service Program (2000)

17 CCDBR, "Wilkinson Committee," CCDBR, http://www.ccdbr.org/events/wilkinson/Wilkinson_Committee.html (accessed April 11, 2013)

18 KeyWiki, "Timuel Black," KeyWiki, http://www.keywiki.org/index.php/Timuel_Black (accessed April 11, 2013)

19 CSSA Supporters Letter (September 4, 1981)

20 Chicago Socialist (February/March 1983) p. 7

21 Chicago DSA, "1989 Norman Thomas – Eugene V. Debs Dinner," DSA, http://www.chicagodsa.org/d1989/index.html (May 6, 1989)

22 Democratic Left (January/February 1992) p. 13

23 New Ground (Winter 1990-1991) Volume 4, Number 6

24 Democratic Left (July/August 1996) p. 21

25 New Ground 45 (March/April 1996)

26 Chicago DSA, "New Ground 60," DSA, http://www.chicagodsa.org/ngarchive/ng60.html#anchor566085 (September/October 1998)

27 Democratic Left (Summer 2006) p. 3

28 Democratic Left (May/June 1996)

29 New Party News (Spring 1996) p. 1

30 KeyWiki, "New Party," KeyWiki, http://keywiki.org/index.php/New_Party#DSA_supporters (accessed April 11, 2013)

Luis Gutierrez (D-IL)

Luis V. Gutierrez is a Democratic member of the United States House of Representatives, representing the 4th District of Illinois. He is an active member of the Congressional Progressive Caucus and the Congressional Hispanic Caucus.

Background

Luis Gutierrez was born in Chicago, Illinois on December 10, 1953 and later moved to Puerto Rico, his parent's birthplace, before returning to Chicago to attend college. He received his Bachelor of Arts Degree from Northeastern Illinois University in 1975 and then worked as a teacher, cab driver, community activist and a social worker for ten years. He taught in the public schools of Puerto Rico and Chicago from 1975 to 1977. He was a social worker for the Illinois State Department of Children and Family Services from 1979 to 1983.[1]

Gutierrez was first elected to office through the efforts of the same "progressive coalition of blacks, Latinos and whites" that brought pro-communist Harold Washington into power in 1983 as Mayor of Chicago.[2]

Gutierrez worked in the Harold Washington administration from 1984 to 1985 as the Administrative Assistant for the Mayor's Subcommittee on Infrastructure.[3]

He won election in 1986 as Alderman from the city's 26th Ward.

Although Gutierrez rode the Harold Washington wave into the Chicago City Council, it was his alliance with the Richard Daly, Jr. machine that gave him backing to enter the United States House of Representatives in 1992.[4]

Influence

As a key lieutenant in Mayor Harold Washington's "progressive multi-ethnic coalition" in the Chicago City Council, Gutierrez led the fight for "affordable housing, tougher ethics rules and a law to ban discrimination based on sexual orientation."[5]

In 1996, several Illinois Latino political leaders, including Congressman Luis Gutierrez and three far leftists: State Senators Miguel del Valle, Jesus Garcia and Alderman Rick Munoz, held a press conference in Chicago to condemn what they determined was "bad faith" on the part of the Immigration and Naturalization Service over immigration raids and citizenship applications.[6]

Because of the Congressman's work on immigration issues, he was appointed Chair of the Congressional Hispanic Caucus Immigration Task Force and has previously served as Chair of the Democratic Caucus Immigration Task Force. He is the Democratic Party's leading strategist and spokesperson on immigration issues. During the 110th and 111th Congresses, he served as a member of the Judiciary Committee's Immigration, Citizenship, Refugees, Border Security and International Law Subcommittee.[7]

Gutierrez was the Chair of the House Subcommittee on Financial Institutions and Consumer Credit as well.

In 2010, Gutierrez was appointed to the prestigious House Permanent Select Committee on Intelligence by Minority Leader Nancy Pelosi.[8]

In 2008, the Obama Campaign announced the formation of its National Latino Advisory Council, Luis Gutierrez was a member of the Council, as was Democratic Socialists of America (DSA) leader and Service Employees International Union Vice President Eliseo Medina, now one of the country's key "immigration reform" activists.[9] Gutierrez works closely with Medina on immigration issues.

Communist Connections

Puerto Rican Socialist Party

Harold Washington's electoral coalition included many members of the Marxist-Leninist/pro-Cuba Puerto Rican Socialist Party. Luis Gutierrez belonged to the Puerto Rican Socialist Party and was able to secure city funds for a Party run "cultural center."[10]

Endorsed Communist Affiliate

In 2011, well known Communist Party USA (CPUSA) supporter, Rudy Lozano, Jr., announced his second bid for State Representative for the 21st District, standing as a Democrat. Luis Gutierrez was one of his endorsers.[11]

Socialist Connections

"Progressive Forces"

When Luis Gutierrez was elected to Congress in 1992, Chicago Democratic Socialists of America regarded it as a "progressive" move:[12]

Progressive forces in Illinois made history November 3 by electing Carol Moseley Braun as the first African-American woman to the U.S. Senate.

Chicago City Council member Luis Gutierrez was elected the first Latino to the U.S. House of Representatives from the Midwest.

DSA "Recommendation"

When Gutierrez ran for Congress in 1998, DSA did not officially endorse any candidates, but he was "recommended" as worthy of a vote by Chicago Democratic Socialists of America who cited his membership in the Congressional Progressive Caucus and his support for the Institutes for Policy Studies' Progressive Challenge.[13]

Globalization from Below

'Globalization From Below' was a conference held in 1998 in Chicago and was organized by Democratic Socialists of America.

Invited speakers included Rep. Luis Gutierrez; Profirio Munoz-Ledo, PRD-Mexico; Audrey MacLaughlin, New Democratic Party-Canada; Rev. Jesse Jackson; Dolores Huerta (United Farm Workers and DSA); Clare Short, Secretary of State for Overseas Development, United Kingdom; Representative Danny Davis (DSA); Jose LaLuz (AFCSME and DSA); Karen Nussbaum (AFL-CIO, veteran of the radical Venceremos brigade to Cuba); Stanley Gacek (AFL-CIO and DSA); and Stephen Yokich, United Auto Workers and DSA supporter.[14]

REGISTRATION: $10. To register, or to get more information, call the DSA Youth Section Coordinator, Kevin Pranis, at 212 727 8610. *For information* on co-sponsorship or to join planning teams, call Daraka Larimore at 773 955 6371.

INVITED SPEAKERS INCLUDE: Profirio Munoz-Ledo, PRD-Mexico; **Audrey MacLaughlin,** NDP-Canada; **Rev. Jesse Jackson; Dolores Huerta,** United Farm Workers; **Clare Short,** Secretary of State for Overseas Development, UK; **Rep. Luis Gutierrez; Rep. Danny Davis;** Jose **LaLuz,** AFSCME, **Karen Nussbaum,** AFL-CIO; **Stan Gacek,** AFL-CIO; **Stephen Yokich,** United Auto Workers; **Enrique Herandez, Han Young/** Hyudnai plant organizer, Tijuana.

page 10 •Democratic Left • Issue #1 1998

Housing Foreclosures

Chicago DSA has lobbied Luis Gutierrez over the housing foreclosure issue. According to Boston DSA's The Yankee Radical:[15]

> One of the community banks affected by the financial crisis was the Park National Bank in Chicago, which was seized by the FDIC in 2009 and turned over to U.S. Bankcorp. The Park National Bank had a well-deserved reputation as one of the most community-minded banks in the country, and its seizure caused the people of Chicago's Westside to rise up, forming the Coalition to Save Community Banking. (DSA's Chicago chapter is a member). They have been pressuring their own Congressman, Luis Gutierrez, to arrange a meeting with the FDIC and hearings in Congress—and they need our help!

Illinois Public Action

In 1995, Luis Gutierrez was a member of the Board of Directors of Illinois Public Action, an organization heavily influenced by both the CPUSA and DSA.[16]

In 1996, members of the 120-strong Board of Illinois Public Action included Rep. Gutierrez, DSA member Quentin Young, CPUSA affiliated State Senator Alice Palmer, DSA member, and State Representative Jan Schakowsky and Cook County Clerk David Orr, also a DSA affiliate.[17]

Immigration Rally

8,000 working people joined the March and Rally for a New Amnesty in Chicago in 2000. "Si se puede," was the chant of the day at the rally for the millions of immigrant workers in the United States. Janitors, home health care workers, garment workers and meat packers were among those at the event.

The demonstration was sponsored by the Grassroots Collaborative, the Illinois Coalition for Immigrant and Refugee Rights, SEIU Local 880, ACORN, American Friends Service Committee, the Chicago Coalition for the Homeless, the Interfaith Leadership Project and others.[18]

Statements of support came from AFL-CIO, President John Sweeney (DSA member) and Representative Danny Davis (DSA member).

Representative Jan Schakowsky (one time DSA member) told the crowd, "I support complete amnesty, total restoral of benefits... and an end to employer sanctions." Danny Davis' message echoed these themes.

Representative Luis Gutierrez told the assembly that he would introduce legislation to accomplish amnesty... into the House of Representatives and asked for the pressure to be kept up.[19]

Coalition to Save Community Banking

The Coalition to Save Community Banking is a group of several dozen metro Chicago organizations and individuals, including Chicago DSA leader Peg Strobel, who came together after the Federal Deposit Insurance Corporation seized the assets of a local community bank, Park National Bank with two branches in Oak Park, Illinois in 2009.

Gutierrez held a Congressional hearing on the issue of First Bank of Oak Park, Inc./Park National Bank and community banks. He sent more than 60 people to Washington.[20]

"Progressive" Connections

Progressive Challenge

Chicago DSA member, Rob Roman, wrote of a 1998 Institute for Policy Studies (IPS) organized Progressive Challenge meeting attended by Illinois Congressmen Jesse Jackson, Jr., Luis Gutierrez and Danny Davis:[21]

On the evening of Monday, April 21, the Progressive Challenge came to Chicago. Starting off with a town hall style meeting that brought together about 150 people in the UNITE hall at 333 S. Ashland in Chicago, the meeting was structured to present testimony from representatives of various local organizations to local Congressional members of the Progressive Caucus.

Congressmen Jesse Jackson, Jr., Luis Gutierrez and Danny Davis attended the meeting...

The Progressive Challenge is an effort to link the Congressional Progressive Caucus with the larger left grass roots network of single issue, constituent, labor and ideological organizations. The Institute for Policy Studies is very much the keystone organization of this project, which has brought together some 40 organizations including DSA, Americans for Democratic Action, United Electrical Workers, NETWORK, National Jobs for All Coalition to name a few.

2004 Take Back America Conference

Luis Gutierrez was on the list of 114 speakers (which included leftist financier George Soros) at the 2004 Take Back America conference, which was organized by the IPS and DSA co-founded Campaign for America's Future.[22]

Foreign Policy/National Security

Puerto Rican Rebel Prisoners

In 1999, eleven imprisoned Puerto Rican independence fighters were released on parole from long prison terms in the United States. The clemency offers came after a long campaign that saw 75,000 people sign a petition in Puerto Rico and the United States for their release. The campaign, led by the Pro-Human Rights Committee of Puerto Rico, involved such activists as Coretta Scott King, Reverend Jesse Jackson, Bishop Desmond Tutu, Rigoberta Menchu and Dr. Aaron Tolen, President of the World Council of Churches.

Political leaders who supported the prisoners included Representatives Luis Gutierrez, Nydia Velazquez (D-NY), Jose Serrano (D-NY) and two prominent Democratic Socialists of America members Ron Dellums (D-CA) and former New York City Mayor David Dinkins.[23]

Progressive Political Agenda

More than 250 Puerto Rican activists and leaders met in the Bronx "to discuss the state of our communities" and to begin the development of a "progressive political agenda" for Puerto Ricans in 2004. The Boricua Roundtable met at Hostos Community College in 2004.

A major theme of the meeting was mobilizing the Puerto Rican vote against the ultra-right in the White House and in Congress.

The three Puerto Rican members of Congress—Representatives Luis Gutiérrez, Nydia Velázquez (D-NY) and José Serrano (D-NY)— participated in a panel on key issues facing Puerto Ricans.

The Boricua Roundtable ended with the singing of the anti-imperialist version of the Puerto Rican national anthem—La Borinqueña.[24]

---

1 KeyWiki, "Luis Gutierrez," KeyWiki, http://keywiki.org/index.php/Luis_Gutierrez (accessed April 5, 2012)

2 KeyWiki, "Luis Gutierrez," KeyWiki, http://keywiki.org/index.php/Luis_Gutierrez (accessed April 5, 2012)

3 KeyWiki, "Luis Gutierrez," KeyWiki, http://keywiki.org/index.php/Luis_Gutierrez (accessed April 5, 2012)

4 KeyWiki, "Luis Gutierrez," KeyWiki, http://keywiki.org/index.php/Luis_Gutierrez (accessed April 5, 2012)

5 KeyWiki, "Luis Gutierrez," KeyWiki, http://keywiki.org/index.php/Luis_Gutierrez (accessed April 5, 2012)

6 People's Weekly World (August 1996) p. 8

7 KeyWiki, "Luis Gutierrez," KeyWiki, http://keywiki.org/index.php/Luis_Gutierrez (accessed April 6, 2012)

8 KeyWiki, "Luis Gutierrez," KeyWiki, http://keywiki.org/index.php/Luis_Gutierrez (accessed April 6, 2012)

9 KeyWiki, "Luis Gutierrez," KeyWiki, http://keywiki.org/index.php/Luis_Gutierrez (accessed April 6, 2012)

10 KeyWiki, "Luis Gutierrez," KeyWiki, http://keywiki.org/index.php/Luis_Gutierrez (accessed January 21, 2013)

11 Lozano for State Representative, http://www.rudylozanoforstaterep.com/bio/, (accessed April 6, 2012)

12 New Ground (December 1992 – January 1993)

13 Chicago Democratic Socialists of America, "New Ground 60," Chicago Democratic Socialists of America, http://www.chicagodsa.org/ngarchive/ng60.html#anchor566085 (accessed April 6, 2012)

14 Democratic Left (Issue #1 1998) p. 10

15 Democratic Socialists of America, "The Yankee Radical," Democratic Socialists of America, http://www.dsaboston.org/yradical/yr2010-02.pdf (accessed April 6, 2012)

16 Illinois Public Action 20th Anniversary Leaflet

17 Chicago Democratic Socialists of America, "New Ground 44," Chicago Democratic Socialists of America, http://www.chicagodsa.org/ngarchive/ng44.html (accessed April 6, 2012)

18 KeyWiki, "Luis Gutierrez," KeyWiki, http://keywiki.org/index.php/Luis_Gutierrez (accessed April 6, 2012)

19 People's Weekly World (October 2000)

20 KeyWiki, "Luis Gutierrez," KeyWiki, http://keywiki.org/index.php/Luis_Gutierrez (accessed April 6, 2012)

21 Chicago Democratic Socialists of America, "New Ground 58," Chicago Democratic Socialists of America, http://www.chicagodsa.org/ngarchive/ng58.html (accessed April 6, 2012)

22 Campaign For America's Future, "Archives – 2004 Speakers," Campaign For America's Future, http://www.ourfuture.org/node/13146 (accessed January 21, 2013)

23 Jose Cruz, "Puerto Ricans accept clemency offer," People's Weekly World (September 1999) p. 4

24 People's World, "Puerto Ricans chart progressive agenda," People's World, http://www.peoplesworld.org/puerto-ricans-chart-progressive-agenda/, (accessed April 6, 2012)

Bobby Rush (D-IL)

Bobby L. Rush is a Democratic member of the United States House of Representatives, representing the 1st District of Illinois. He is a member of the Congressional Black Caucus and a former member of the Congressional Progressive Caucus.[1]

Background

Rush is an ordained minister with a Master's Degree in Theology. In addition to his Congressional responsibilities, he is the Pastor of the Beloved Community Christian Church of Chicago.[2]

Bobby Rush was born in Albany, Georgia on November 23, 1946. His family moved to Chicago when he was young, where they settled on the West Side. Rush attended Marshall High School.

After dropping out of high school, Rush joined the U.S. Army in 1963, then joined the radical Student Non-Violent Coordinating Committee in 1966. He went AWOL in 1968, co-founded the state's Black Panther Party while stationed in Chicago and received an Honorable Discharge in 1968.

The Maoist leaning Black Panthers, made Rush their "Defense Minister" in 1968.

Rush's late son, Huey, was named after Panther leader, Huey Newton.

"We were reacting to police brutality, to the historical relationship between African-Americans and recalcitrant racist whites," Rush later told People Magazine. "We needed to arm ourselves."

Rush was present when fellow Black Panther Fred Hampton was killed in a police raid and later made an official statement that the police, referred only to as "pigs" by Rush, had murdered Hampton.

Rush's own apartment was raided in December 1969, where police discovered an unregistered pistol, rifle, shotgun and pistol ammunition, training manuals on explosives and booby traps, a small amount of marijuana and an assortment of Communist literature, including works by Che Guevara and Mao Tse Tung.[3]

Bobby Rush served six months in prison for illegal possession of firearms.

Rush graduated with honors from Chicago's Roosevelt University in 1973. A year later, he left the Panthers, who were already in decline.

"We started glorifying thuggery and drugs," he told People Magazine. He went on to say that, "I don't repudiate any of my involvement in the Panther Party—it was part of my maturing."[4]

Rush ran for a seat on Chicago's City Council in 1974. The first of several black militants who later sought political office, he was defeated.

In 1983, however, Chicago's political career was bolstered by the election of far leftist Harold Washington to the Mayoralty.

That same year, Rush was elected Alderman from the Second Ward on Chicago's South Side. He was one of the pro-Harold Washington members on the Council during the "Council Wars" that began in 1983, following Washington's election as Mayor of Chicago in a racially-polarized contest.

Rush was elected to the U.S. House of Representatives in 1992.

Influence

Bobby Rush currently serves on the Committee on Energy and Commerce, which includes the Subcommittee on Energy and Power, where he is a Ranking Member; the Subcommittee on Communications and Technology and the Subcommittee on Commerce, Manufacturing and Trade.

He serves on many caucuses and task forces. Presently, he Co-Chairs the Community College Caucus, the Congressional African Partnership for Economic Growth Caucus, the Congressional Caucus on Access to Capital and Credit, the Congressional Caucus on Educating, Engaging and Employing America's Youth and the Congressional Collegiate Sports Caucus.[5]

Communist Connections

GI Civil Liberties Defense Committee

Circa 1969, Bobby Rush, Minister of Defense, Illinois Black Panther Party, was listed as a sponsor of the Socialist Workers Party-led GI Civil Liberties Defense Committee.[6]

Canter Connection

Long-time Communist Party USA member, David Canter, served as an adviser to Bobby Rush.

At Canter's memorial service, Congressman Bobby Rush addressed the mourners, saying that the highest praise he could give David Canter was that there wasn't a racist bone in his body.[7]

Canter, who at one time, was paid by the Soviet Embassy in Washington, D.C. to distribute Russian and Soviet literature throughout the United States, was also a friend and mentor to Barack Obama's future confidante and Campaign Strategist, David Axelrod.[8]

Chicago Committee to Defend the Bill of Rights

On November 16, 1989, Bobby Rush and his wife Carolyn, served on the Tribute Committee for the Communist Party-controlled Chicago Committee to Defend the Bill of Rights Tribute to Leon Golub and Lucy Montgomery, held at the Congress Hotel in Chicago.[9]

In 2000, Bobby Rush served as Co-Chairperson on the welcoming committee for the Chicago Memorial Service for Richard Criley, a long-time leader of the CPUSA and an activist for the Chicago Committee to Defend the Bill of Rights.[10]

Addie Wyatt Connection

Rev. Addie Wyatt's home in Chicago was used to carry out meetings with public figures such as Rev. Jesse Jackson, Barack Obama and U.S. Rep. Bobby Rush.[11]

Wyatt was a life-long affiliate of the CPUSA.[12]

People's World Dinner Speaker

Bobby Rush was the guest speaker at the Chicago Communist Party's annual People's Weekly World fundraising banquet on September 20, 1997, which raised $6,000 to support the radical newspaper. Rep. Rush urged support for the Martinez Jobs Bill (HR-950), then before Congress. His sentiments were echoed by Congressman Danny Davis.

Rush was introduced by Katie Jordan of the Coalition of Labor Union Women.[13]

2   People's Weekly World   Saturday, September 20, 1997

Chicago banquet ra

By Mike Giocondo

CHICAGO – *People's Weekly World* supporters at its annual banquet here were moved by U.S. Rep. Bobby Rush's talk and pledged to take action to get the public works jobs bill now before Congress (HR-950) adopted. The banquet raised $6,000 for the *People's Weekly World's* 1997 fund drive.

Speaking to nearly 200 *World* supporters Sept. 7, Rush said it was up to the people to mobilize and get behind the bill if it is going to pass.

He urged them to build for the national rally day Oct. 18 in support of HR-950 (see related

stories, p. 3, 10-11). "We have to raise the consciousness of the country, and mobilize people around this," Rush said, "and we can do it."

He told the audience that, while 53 members of Congress have signed on to the bill, more pressure has to be applied. "This bill won't pass on just the good will of Congress," he said.

Rep. Rush was the main speaker at the banquet. His remarks were seconded by Congressman Danny Davis. Both are Democrats from Chicago.

The banquet honored veteran trade unionist Norm Roth, former present of UAW Local 6

Chicago Martinez Jobs Bill Support Rally

On October 18, 1997, Communist Party affiliate Tom Balanoff, President of SEIU Local 73 and Chicago Jobs with Justice, and Rep. Bobby Rush addressed a Chicago "show us the living wage jobs" rally as part of a national day of action, calling on Congress to pass the Martinez Jobs Bill. There were concurrent rallies in nearly 20 cities, organized by the Communist Party USA-dominated National Labor Community Coalition For Public Works Jobs.[14]

2002 Chicago PWW Banquet

Ishmael Flory, long-time member of the CPUSA, headed the list of honorees at the 2002 annual Chicago People's Weekly World/Nuestro Mundo Banquet. Barbara Moore, Vice President of the Coalition to Protect Public Housing and a representative of the Carousel Linen workers, rounded out the list of those who had been nominated to receive the Chris Hani/Rudy Lozano Award.

The Chris Hani/Rudy Lozano Award is named in honor of Chris Hani, a one-time commander of the armed wing of African National Congress and General Secretary of the South African Communist Party, and Rudy Lozano, a Mexican-American activist and key player in the campaign that elected Harold Washington as Chicago Mayor in 1983. Both were gunned down by assassins.

Banquet sponsors included local Communist Party leader John Bachtell; Communist Party supporters Rev. Willie Barrow and Katie Jordan, of the Coalition of Labor Union Women; Rep. Bobby Rush and Tom Balanoff, President, SEIU Local 1.[15]

Socialist Connections

Mayoralty Tilt

In 1998, Bobby Rush was busy preparing for a tilt at the Chicago Mayoralty.

At his campaign launch, Rush was introduced by Democratic Socialists of America (DSA) member Representative Danny Davis and Mexican-American activist and Committees of Correspondence affiliate, Emma Lozano.[16]

According to Charity Crouse of Chicago DSA:[17]

> With months to go until a formal announcement, Congressman Bobby Rush (D-1) has been preparing the groundwork for a full-scale grassroots campaign to take him to the fifth floor of City Hall by organizing the disenfranchised majority of Chicago's residents. The South Sider promises to provide a voice for poor and working people in city policies concerning housing, wages and economic opportunities.
>
> Since the end of August, Rush has been meeting with community residents and campaign volunteers in what has come to be called the

Rush for Change Organizing Committee. Setting a minimum goal of 50,000 registered voters and $250,000 in campaign funds by November before he officially announces his candidacy for mayor, Rush has been working to form a coalition of African Americans, Latinos and progressives into what he calls the democratic vanguard of the possible to help him unseat Richard M. Daley in the Spring.

DSA endorsed Rush's Mayoralty bid after some debate:[18]

After some consideration, the December 12th, 1998, General Membership meeting of Chicago DSA voted to endorse Bobby Rush for Mayor of Chicago and a mix of nine incumbent and insurgent aldermanic candidates.

Bobby Rush lost the race, receiving less than 30% of the vote.

DSA "Recommendation"

When Bobby Rush ran for Congress in 1998, DSA did not officially endorse any candidates, but he was "recommended" as worthy of a vote by Chicago DSA:[19]

Bobby Rush, U.S. House of Representatives, 1st District. Bobby Rush is not a member of the Progressive Caucus, though he should be.

Foreign Policy/National Security

Supporting Communist Youth

In 1997, the old Soviet front World Federation of Democratic Youth (WFDY), based in Budapest, denounced the U.S. Treasury Department's denial of a license for hundreds of young people from all over the U.S. to attend the 14th World Festival of Youth and Students in Havana, Cuba.

WFDY, an initiator of the festival, scheduled for July 28th to August 5th, assailed the anti-democratic character of the decision and pledged an international campaign to demand that the U.S. government lift the travel ban.

According to the CPUSA paper People's Weekly World:[20]

Nationally, the broad list of sponsors and endorsers has already begun to mount a campaign.

Members of the U.S. Congress, Ron Dellums (D-CA), Jesse Jackson, Jr. and Bobby Rush, both Illinois Democrats, have offered support.

Cuba Trip

In early April 2009, Rep. Barbara Lee led a Congressional delegation to Havana for a 4½ hour meeting with Raul Castro.

Delegation member, Bobby Rush, said he found Raul Castro "to be just the opposite of how he's being portrayed in the media." AP quotes Rush as saying, "I think what really surprised me, but also endeared [me] to him was his keen sense of humor, his sense of history and his basic human qualities." At times, Rush said, the lawmakers and Castro chatted "like old family members."[21]

Shortly afterwards, Rep. Rush introduced the U.S.-Cuba Trade Normalization Act, which would repeal the Helms-Burton and Torricelli Acts and end the embargo against Cuba. The bill had 55 co-sponsors, but was unsuccessful.[22]

1 KeyWiki, "Bobby Rush," KeyWiki, http://keywiki.org/index.php/Bobby_Rush (accessed April 1, 2012)
2 Bobby L. Rush, "Biography," House.gov, http://rush.house.gov/about-me/biography (accessed April 14, 2014)
3 Bill Matney on CBS Evening News, "Bobby Rush Kept Handgun and Communist Literature in Apartment," YouTube, http://www.youtube.com/watch?v=WTUFIRd32FM (December 4, 1969)
4 Kevin Klose, "A Black Panther on Little Cat Feet; Bobby Rush Drops the Clenched Fist," The Washington Post (August 11, 1984)
5 Bobby L. Rush, "Committees and Caucuses" House.gov, http://rush.house.gov/about-me/committees-and-caucuses (accessed April 14, 2014)
6 GI Civil Liberties Defense Committee, Letterhead (circa 1969)
7 Walter Roth, "David and Miriam Canter: Doing Right from the Left," Chicago Jewish History (Spring 2010)
8 KeyWiki, "David Canter," KeyWiki, http://www.keywiki.org/index.php/David_Canter (accessed May 23, 2013)
9 Chicago Committee to Defend the Bill of Rights, "Tribute to Golub and Montgomery: Program," Chicago Committee to Defend the Bill of Rights (November 16, 1989)
10 Memoriam Service Program (2000)
11 Glenn Marshall, "Rev. Addie Wyatt Memorialized," NBC Chicago, http://www.nbcchicago.com/news/local/Rev-Addie-Wyatt-Memorialized-146428745.html, (April 7, 2012)
12 KeyWiki, "Addie Wyatt," KeyWiki, http://www.keywiki.org/index.php/Addie_Wyatt (accessed April 14, 2013)
13 People's Weekly World (September 20, 1997) p. 2
14 People's Weekly World (October 11, 1997) p. 6
15 Evelina Alarcon & John Pappademos, "Chicago PWW banquet set for Oct. 20," People's World, http://peoplesworld.org/chicago-pww-banquet-set-for-oct-20/ (October 3, 2002)

16 Chicago DSA, "New Ground 60," DSA, http://www.chicagodsa.org/ngarchive/ng60.html#anchor566085 (September-October 1998)
17 Chicago DSA, "New Ground 62," DSA, http://www.chicagodsa.org/ngarchive/ng62.html (January-February 1999)
18 Chicago DSA, "New Ground 63," DSA, http://www.chicagodsa.org/ngarchive/ng63.html (March-April 1999)
19 Chicago DSA, "New Ground 60," DSA, http://www.chicagodsa.org/ngarchive/ng60.html#anchor566085 (September-October 1998)
20 People's Weekly World (June 14, 1997) p. 4
21 Michael Waller, "Congresswoman Barbara Lee: Still stuck in the Cold War," Political Warfare, http://jmw.typepad.com/political_warfare/2009/04/congresswoman-barbara-lee-still-stuck-in-the-cold-war.html (April 7, 2009)
22 People's World, "Pressure mounts to end Cuban travel ban," People's World, http://www.peoplesworld.org/pressure-mounts-to-end-cuban-travel-ban/ (July 18, 2009)

Jan Schakowsky (D-IL)

Jan Schakowsky is a Democratic member of the United States House of Representatives, representing the 9th District of Illinois.

She is a member of the Congressional Progressive Caucus and the Populist Caucus. She is also a former Associate Member of the Congressional Asian Pacific American Caucus.[1]

Background

Jan Schakowsky resides in Evanston, Illinois with her husband, "progressive" political consultant, Robert Creamer. She graduated from the University of Illinois in 1965 with a Bachelor of Science Degree in Elementary Education.

Prior to her election to Congress, Schakowsky represented the 18th District in the Illinois General Assembly for eight years. She served as a Democratic Floor Leader and as Secretary of the Conference of Women Legislators.

Before her election to the State House, Schakowsky was the Program Director of Illinois Public Action (1976-1985), the state's largest leftist "public interest" organization. She was Director of the Illinois State Council of Senior Citizens from 1985-1990.[2]

Influence

Schakowsky serves in the House Democratic Leadership as Chief Deputy Whip and as a member of the Steering and Policy Committee. She is a member of the Energy and Commerce Committee, where she is working to accomplish her top priority in Congress—providing "universal healthcare coverage for all Americans." On that Committee, she serves as Vice-Chair of the Subcommittee on Commerce, Trade and Consumer Protection and as a member of the Subcommittee on Health and the Subcommittee on Oversight and Investigations.

In 2010, Speaker Nancy Pelosi appointed Schakowsky to serve on the House Select Committee on Intelligence. Schakowsky opposed the Iraq War resolution and was a founding member of the Out-of-Iraq Caucus.

During the 110th Congress, Schakowsky served as Democratic Vice-Chair of the bipartisan Women's Caucus.[3]

Jan Schakowsky has long been one of Barack Obama's greatest allies in Chicago and national politics.

On February 22, 2012, Obama for America announced the selection of the campaign's National Co-Chairs, a diverse group of leaders from around the country committed to reelecting President Obama. The co-chairs serve as ambassadors for the President; advise the campaign on key issues and help engage and mobilize voters in all 50 states.

Representative Jan Schakowsky, representing the 9th District of Illinois, was on the list.

Communist Connections

Richard Criley Memorial

In 2000, Jan Schakowsky served on the welcoming committee for the Chicago Memorial Service for Richard Criley, a long-time activist with the Communist Party USA (CPUSA), and a leader of the Committees of Correspondence front Chicago Committee to Defend the Bill of Rights.[4]

Working with Communists to Lower Gas Bills

In the winter of 2001, "the gas bills for heating Chicago homes rose. Members of Bea Lumpkin's South Side Communist Party Club were angry too when they saw their huge gas bills".

So, on February 7, 2001, the Communist Club took the first step to start the fight back. They talked to their coalition partners and together acted fast. Within days, they held a rally of 130 people to demand lower gas prices.

On February 13, 2001, USWA and Save Our Jobs Committee co-sponsored a rally in the steel union hall in South Chicago. They formed a new group, "Angry Utility Consumers." They included presidents of three USWA locals, Communists Bea Lumpkin and Frank Lumpkin of Save Our Jobs Committee, communist supporter Katie Jordan of Chicago Coalition of Labor Union Women and Rev. Bill Hogan, Saint Bride Catholic Church, a Catholic priest and a card carrying member of the Communist Party.[5]

Bea Lumpkin and her group met with Rep. Jan Schakowsky after changing its name to the more positive Utility Consumers United for Justice on May 14, 2001. They were granted an interview even though the group was comprised of South Siders, far from Schakowsky's district on the North Side.

Schakowsky listened and warmly supported the demands:[6]

> "Our people are angry but discouraged," we added. Schakowsky tried to pick up our spirits. "Don't be discouraged," she said. "This is war, class war, war on working families. We did not declare it, but we will fight it and win! We must fight this (Bush) budget that does not include money to solve the energy crisis and we must take back Congress in 2002!"

Communist Funeral

On April 24, 2011, Congress members Jan Schakowsky and Danny Davis addressed the funeral service of Chicago CPUSA identity Frank Lumpkin. Among those who also paid tribute to Lumpkin's lifelong work was Governor of Illinois, Pat Quinn.

Communist Party leaders in attendance included Scott Marshall, Roberta Wood, Pepe Lozano, Rudy Lozano, Jr. and Jarvis Tyner.[7]

Schakowsky on Tax Rates for Millionaires and Billionaires

On June 7, 2011, Rep. Schakowsky, joined by senior citizens and labor representatives, called for higher tax rates for the wealthy on the 10th anniversary of the Bush tax cuts.

Schakowsky slammed the failed promises of the Bush administration that claimed the tax cuts would reduce the national debt in 10 years. Instead, Schakowsky pushed for the scheduled expiration of the Bush tax cuts in 2012 as well as additional revenue measures to address the deficit without endangering Medicare and many programs important to the middle class.

Other speakers included Joe Persky, of the Democratic Socialists of America-dominated Chicago Political Economy Group; Bea Lumpkin, senior citizen activist and CPUSAer and Communist Party supporter William McNary, Co-Director of Citizen Action/Illinois and President of USAction.

In March 2011, Schakowsky introduced the Fairness in Taxation Act to create new tax brackets for millionaires and billionaires.[8]

Emergency Jobs Bill

A crowd of local union members, advocating for the unemployed and elected officials were on hand outside the Gould Elementary School in Chicago on August 10, 2011, for the unveiling of a new jobs bill.

Rep. Jan Schakowsky, who then sat on President Obama's 18-member Fiscal Commission, announced she would introduce the Emergency Jobs to Restore the American Dream Act, which will put "over 2 million people to work for two years."

"It begins with this simple idea: If we want to create jobs, then create jobs," the Congresswoman declared. "I'm not talking about incentivizing companies in the hope they'll hire someone, or cutting taxes for the so-called job creators who have done nothing of the sort. My plan creates actual new jobs."

"For months," Schakowsky declared, "They have been talking about the deficit, but the worst deficit this country faces isn't the budget deficit. It's the jobs deficit. We need to get our people and our economy moving again."

Schakowsky called Janet Edburg, a jobless factory worker and Communist Party USA supporter, who has exhausted her 99 weeks of unemployment benefits, to the speaker's platform. Not able to hold back her tears, but speaking in a loud, firm voice, Edburg told the hushed crowd: "You cannot imagine how it feels to lose your job, to be homeless and have to be taken in by a friend." Pounding on the podium, she declared, "It is about time that something be done."

Schakowsky stepped back up and, putting her arm around Edburg, said, "This is America and we can do better than this."[9]

Marching with a Communist

At an Occupy Chicago protest on October 10, 2011, Jan Schakowsky marched alongside comrade Bea Lumpkin; Jordan Farrar of the Young Communist League also participated.[10]

Honoring Bea Lumpkin

Illinois Alliance for Retired Americans honored labor leader and CPUSA activist, Bea Lumpkin, at their 2012 luncheon. Among those who paid tribute to Lumpkin's 80 years of labor activism were Rep. Jan Schakowsky and Chicago Teachers Union President, Karen Lewis.[11]

Socialist Connections

Jan Schakowsky has a long history as a member and supporter of Democratic Socialists of America (DSA).

Grape Boycott

Schakowsky was recruited to help with the famous 1970's Chicago Grape Boycott by a young United Farm Workers union leader named Eliseo Medina.

A lifelong socialist, Medina is today Executive Vice President of the SEIU and an Honorary Chair of DSA. Medina and Schakowsky crossed paths at Chicago DSA's 2004 Debs-Thomas-Harrington Dinner. Eliseo Medina was honored for his union work at the dinner, while Jan Schakowsky was the Keynote speaker.

From Chicago DSA's New Ground:[12]

> Carl Shier introduced the second honoree, SEIU Executive Vice President Eliseo Medina. Shier first met Medina when Medina was a young man sent to Chicago by Cesar Chavez to organize the UFW's grape boycott in Chicago on $5 dollars a week. Medina worked miracles (including roping young suburban women like Jan Schakowsky into the effort).

Chicago Socialist

In 1983, Jan Schakowsky penned an article for DSA's Chicago Socialist in the February/March issue, pages 4 and 5: "Hopes and fears dominate IPAC conference."[13]

Confirmed DSA Member

Jan Schakowsky was named as an "Evanston DSA member" in the DSA News, January 1986, page 2.

Schakowsky was confirmed as a DSA member in DSA News, June 9, 1986, page 2, in which an article entitled: "DSAers on the move," reported on some of Schakowsky's early electoral forays.[14]

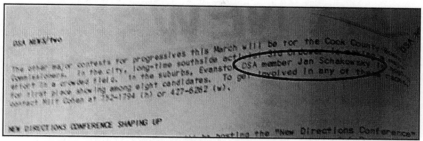

DSA News (January 1986) p. 2

DSA Endorsement

When Jan Schakowsky ran for Congress in 1998, she was endorsed by Chicago DSA, as was fellow DSA member Danny Davis:[15]

> Jan Schakowsky, U.S. House of Representatives, 9th District
>
> Jan Schakowsky is running for Sid Yates old position. Like Danny Davis, she's an old friend of DSA and a real fighter.

DSA Honor

Jan Schakowsky was herself honored at the May 2000 Dinner for her work in Congress and the community.[16]

Schakowsky received her 2000 Debs Dinner Award from Chicago DSA leader Carl Shier:

> In your early days as a consumer advocate, you began the fight for freshness dates on products sold in supermarkets. As Program Director of Illinois Public Action, you fought for energy reform and stronger protection from toxic chemicals. As Executive Director of the Illinois State Council of Senior Citizens, you helped organize across the state for universal and comprehensive health care, for lowering the cost of prescription drugs, for financial protection for spouses of residents in nursing homes.
>
> As an Illinois State Representative, you served your constituency well for four terms. You were an outstanding Chair of the Labor and Commerce Committee. You served on the Human Services,

Appropriation, Health Care, and Electric Deregulation Committees. You were a Democratic Party Floor Leader and served as Secretary of the Conference of Women Legislators.

Your dedication to the people was rewarded by a great grassroots campaign, with hundreds of street volunteers, when you chose to run for the United States House of Representatives. Your first term in Congress has been outstanding. You have been an outstanding voice for seniors, labor union members, women and children. You have continued your advocacy of universal health care through your membership on the Health Care and Medicare Task Forces. Through your work, you were appointed to a leadership whip position.

Your work and your life honors the memory of Eugene V. Debs, Norman Thomas and Michael Harrington and continues their legacy of struggle for social justice.

For your dedication to the fight for a just society, the Debs-Thomas-Harrington Dinner Committee hereby presents to you its annual award on this 5th day of May, 2000.

Jan Schakowsky also attended the 35th Annual Eugene V. Debs–Norman Thomas–Michael Harrington Dinner on May 7th, 1993.[17]

Supporting DSA

Schakowsky for Congress placed a paid ad in the Chicago Democratic Socialists of America, May 10, 2002, 44th Annual Eugene V. Debs–Norman Thomas–Michael Harrington Dinner program.[18]

Immigrant "Rights" Rally

Some 8,000 working people joined the March and Rally for a New Amnesty in Chicago on September 23, 2000. Hundreds of signs read: "It's Time For Amnesty!" "Living Wage For All Workers," "Union Organizing Is A Human Right!" and "Amnesty Means Workers' Rights."

The demonstration was sponsored

Congratulations Chicago DSA On your Annual Debs-Thomas-Harrington Dinner.

Congresswoman Jan Schakowsky
Paid for and authorized by Schakowsky for Congress.

by the Grassroots Collaborative, the Illinois Coalition for Immigrant and Refugee Rights, Service Employees International Union Local 880, ACORN, American Friends Service Committee, Chicago Coalition for the Homeless, the Interfaith Leadership Project and others.[19]

Statements of support came from DSA members AFL-CIO President John Sweeney and Rep. Danny Davis.

Rep. Jan Schakowsky told the crowd, "I support complete amnesty, total restoral of benefits… and an end to employer sanctions".[20]

"Osama" Remark

At the 2004, 46th Annual Eugene V. Debs–Norman Thomas–Michael Harrington Dinner in Chicago, Jan Schakowsky told the story of a meeting in Washington with U.S. President George Bush.

The Congressional Black Caucus had demanded a meeting with President Bush to discuss the situation in Haiti.

Schakowsky had also been invited because of her strong interest in the issue.

According to Chicago DSA's New Ground:[21]

> Bush finally, at the insistence of caucus members, made it to this meeting and spent enough time to display his ignorance of the issue. He noticed Jan, a lone white face, and seemed to "jump back" when he saw her button. Osama? No, Mr. President. Barack Obama, and you'll be hearing from him when he becomes the Senator from Illinois.

2011 Debs Dinner

The 53rd Debs Thomas Harrington Dinner was held in 2011, at the Crowne Plaza Chicago Metro on the 13th of May, 2011.

Chicago DSA Co-Chair Ron Baiman presented the Dinner award to AFSCME's John Cameron. In accepting the award, Cameron noted that while both public and private employees may be represented in the workplace by a union, public employees, as voters, have some say in the meaning of their work and this is the essence of socialism.

U.S. Representative Jan Schakowsky seized the time and the podium to second the Dinner's endorsement of Cameron's work. Despite now being in the minority in Congress, Schakowsky noted in passing, she was extremely optimistic as the conservatives in Congress have "seriously over-reached themselves."[22]

"Progressive" Connections

IPS Grades "Progressive"

In 1998, fourteen new members of Congress were elected on "progressive" platforms.

The fourteen were gauged "progressive" by the Institute for Policy Studies (IPS) after comparing their campaign literature and past activities with the IPS' Progressive Challenge "Fairness Agenda for America."

On issues "ranging from shifting budgetary priorities from military spending and corporate giveaways, to health care and education, to promoting worker and environmental rights, fair trade and equality, these fourteen candidates stood for the liberal values that recent polls show Americans embrace." The fourteen new progressive members included:[23]

> Jan Schakowsky, a Democrat from Illinois' 9th District, "has long been an advocate for consumers, senior citizens and women's rights. She has spoken out about human rights and demilitarization as well as supported campaign finance reform."

Letelier-Moffitt Awards

On September 23, 2003, the IPS held its 27th annual Letelier-Moffitt Memorial Human Rights Awards.

The International Award recipient was Nancy Sanchez Mendez. Her award was presented by Rep. Jan Schakowsky.

A Special Recognition Award was presented in-absentia to Brazil's Marxist President Luis Ignacio Lula de Silva by AFL-CIO President and DSA Member, John Sweeney.[24]

Take Back America Conferences

Jan Schakowsky was on the list of 129 speakers at the 2003 Take Back America conference, which was organized by the Institute for Policy Studies and the Democratic Socialists of America-dominated Campaign for America's Future[25]

Schakowsky was on the list of 114 speakers (which included leftist financier George Soros) at the 2004 Take Back America conference.[26]

She was back in 2005, 2006, 2007 and 2008, as well as at the succeeding America's Future Now conference in 2009 and was one of the

158 speakers who addressed the related Take Back the American Dream conference in 2011.[27] [28]

1 KeyWiki, "Jan Schakowsky," KeyWiki, http://keywiki.org/index.php/Janice_Schakowsky (accessed April 9, 2013)
2 Jan Schakowsky, "Biography," House.gov, http://schakowsky.house.gov/index.php?option=com_content&view=article&id=2577 &Itemid=109 (accessed August 6, 2011)
3 Jan Schakowsky, "Biography," House.gov, http://schakowsky.house.gov/index.php?option=com_content&view=article&id=2577 &Itemid=109 (accessed August 6, 2011)
4 Criley Memoriam Service Program (2000)
5 Bea Lumpkin, "Joy in the Struggle," p.220
6 Bea Lumpkin, "Joy in the Struggle," p.222
7 People's World, "Frank Lumpkin always brings a crowd," People's World, http://peoplesworld.org/frank-lumpkin-always-brings-a-crowd/, (May 14, 2010)
8 Jan Schakowsky, "On 10th Anniversary of the Bush Tax Cuts, Rep. Schakowsky Calls for New Tax Rates for Millionaires and Billionaires," House.gov, http://schakowsky.house.gov/index.php?option=com_content&view=article&id=2942: on-10th-anniversary-of-the-bush-tax-cuts-rep-schakowsky-calls-for-new-tax-rates-for-millionaires-and-billionaires&catid=22:2011-press-releases (June 7, 2011)
9 John Wojcik, "Congresswoman introduces emergency jobs bill," People's World, http://peoplesworld.org/congreswoman-introduces-emergency-jobs-bill/, (August 11, 2011)
10 Eagfoundation, "CPUSA Marches With Jan Schakowsky At #OccupyChicago," EAG News, http://www.youtube.com/watch?v=HHG6dfjXpUY (October 10, 2011)
11 John Bachtell, "Illinois Alliance for Retired Americans Flickr page," People's World, http://www.flickr.com/photos/peoplesworld/sets/72157631792853219/comments/, (accessed 2011)
12 Chicago DSA, "New Ground 94," DSA, http://www.chicagodsa.org/ngarchive/ng94.html (May-June 2004)
13 Jan Schakowsky, "Hopes and fears dominate IPAC conference," Chicago Socialist (1983)
14 DSA News (January 1986) p. 2
15 Chicago DSA, "New Ground 60," DSA, http://www.chicagodsa.org/ngarchive/ng60.html#anchor566085 (September-October 1998)
16 Chicago DSA, "Eugene V. Debs–Norman Thomas–Michael Harrington Dinner," DSA, http://www.chicagodsa.org/d2000.html (May 5, 2000)
17 Chicago DSA, "New Ground 30," DSA, http://www.chicagodsa.org/ngarchive/ng30.html (July-August 1993)
18 DSA, "44th Annual Eugene V. Debs–Norman Thomas–Michael Harrington Dinner program," DSA (May 10, 2002)
19 Lisa Potash, "Chicago rally for immigrant rights draws 8,000," The Militant, http://www.themilitant.com/2000/6438/643862.shtml, (October 9, 2000) Vol. 64/No. 38
20 People's Weekly World (October 7, 2000)
21 Chicago DSA, "New Ground 94," DSA (May-June 2004)

22 Chicago DSA, "2011 Debs Dinner," DSA (May 13, 2011)
23 Democratic Left (Winter 1998) p. 2
24 KeyWiki, "Jan Schakowsky," KeyWiki,
http://keywiki.org/index.php/Janice_Schakowsky (accessed April 9, 2013)
25 Campaign For America's Future, "Archives – 2003 Speakers," Campaign For
America's Future, http://www.ourfuture.org/node/13211 (accessed June 17, 2010)
26 Campaign For America's Future, "Archives – 2004 Speakers," Campaign For
America's Future, http://www.ourfuture.org/node/13146 (accessed June 11, 2010)
27 Confabb website, "America's Future Now 2009 Speakers," Confabb website,
http://now2009.confabb.com/conferences/82401-americas-future-now/speakers
(accessed July 13, 2010)
28 Campaign For America's Future, "Speakers At Take Back The American Dream,"
Campaign For America's Future, http://www.ourfuture.org/conference/speakers
(accessed September 22, 2011)

Tom Harkin
(D-IA)

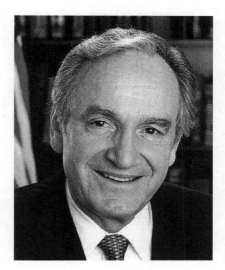

Tom Harkin is a Democratic member of the United States Senate, representing Iowa. He is due to retire in 2014.[1]

Background

Tom Harkin was born in Cumming, Iowa (pop. 150) on November 19, 1939, the son of an Iowa coal miner father and a Slovenian immigrant mother.

After graduating from Dowling High School in Des Moines, he attended Iowa State University on a Navy ROTC scholarship, earning a degree in government and economics.

Following graduation, Harkin served in the Navy as a jet pilot on active duty from 1962 to 1967. Later, he continued to fly in the Naval Reserves. He is an active member of American Legion Post 562 in Cumming and the Commander of the Congressional Squadron of the Civil Air Patrol.

In 1972, Harkin and his wife Ruth Raduenz graduated in the same class at Catholic University of America Law School in Washington, D.C. They returned to Iowa and settled in Ames. He worked with Polk County Legal Aid, assisting low-income Iowans who could not afford legal help.

In 1974, Tom Harkin was elected to Congress from Iowa's 5th Congressional District.

In 1984, after serving 10 years in the U.S. House of Representatives, Harkin challenged an incumbent Senator and won. Iowans returned him to the Senate in 1990, 1996, 2002 and 2008.[2]

Influence

Tom Harkin serves on the Health, Education, Labor and Pensions Committee, where he is Chairman. This also includes the Public Health Subcommittee and the Employment, Safety and Training Subcommittee. He also serves on the Agriculture, Nutrition and Forestry Committee, the Small Business and Entrepreneurship Committee and the Appropriations Committee.

The Appropriations Committee also includes the Subcommittee on Labor, Health and Human Services, and Education where he is the Chairman, the Subcommittee on Agriculture, Rural Development, FDA, the Subcommittee on Energy and Water Development, the Subcommittee on Defense, the Subcommittee on State, Foreign Operations and the Subcommittee on Transportation, Treasury, the Judiciary, HUD and Related Agencies.[3]

"Progressive" Connections

21st Century Democrats

21st Century Democrats is a Political Action Committee which was founded in 1986 by Senator Harkin and two DSA affiliated politicians, then Texas Agriculture Secretary Jim Hightower and Illinois Congressman Lane Evans.[4]

Harkin was himself endorsed by 21st Century Democrats in 2002.

On July 28, 2010, Congresswoman Barbara Lee, Congressman Elijah Cummings and President Obama's communist former "Green Jobs Czar," Van Jones, spoke about the future of American politics at the kick-off event for 21st Century Democrats' 2010 Youth Leadership Speaker Series.

The event was sponsored by Representative John Lewis and Senator Tom Harkin.[5]

FightingBobFest Speaker

Tom Harkin was a guest speaker at Wisconsin's annual progressive FightingBobFest in 2006 and 2009. The festival is a gathering place for communists, socialists, anarchists and "progressives."[6]

An Almost "Progressive" Cabinet "Nominee"

In September 2008, Chicago based Democratic Socialists of America/Institute for Policy Studies affiliated journal In These Times asked its editors and writers to suggest their top progressive choices for a potential Obama Cabinet:

> We asked that contributors weigh ideological and political considerations, with an eye toward recommending people who have both progressive credentials and at least an arguable chance at being appointed in an Obama White House.

> This group of people would represent at once the most progressive, aggressive and practical Cabinet in contemporary history. Of course, it is by no means a definitive list. It is merely one proposal aimed at starting a longer discussion about the very concept of a progressive Cabinet—and why it will be important to a new administration, especially if that administration is serious about change.

David Moberg suggested Jim Hightower for Agriculture Secretary—he also spoke highly of Tom Harkin:[7]

> Two current U.S. senators would make excellent secretaries of agriculture. One is Sen. Tom Harkin (D-Iowa). Harkin has been a committee chair and leader on agriculture issues, opposing deregulation and favoring supply management, conservation, antitrust actions and many progressive policies—only some of which he has managed to put into law.

Institute for Policy Studies Connections

Tom Harkin has a 30 year history with the Institute for Policy Studies.

Center for International Policy

In 1980, Congressman Harkin served on the Advisory Board of the Center for International Policy, a project of the Institute for Policy Studies.[8]

IPS 20th Anniversary Committee

The Institute for Policy Studies celebrated its 20th Anniversary with an April 5th, 1983 reception at the National Building Museum attended by approximately 1,000 IPS staffers and former staff.

The Congressional IPS Committee members included Les Aspin (D-WI); George Brown, Jr. (D-CA); Philip Burton (D-CA); George Crockett (D-MI); Ron Dellums (D-CA); former Texas Congressman Robert Eckhardt; Don Edwards (D-CA); Chairman of the Subcommittee on Civil and Constitutional Rights, Robert Kastenmeier (D-WI); Chairman of the Subcommittee on Courts, Civil Liberties and the Administration of Justice, George Miller (D-CA); Richard Ottinger (D-NY); Leon Panetta (D-CA); Henry Reuss (D-WI); Chairman of the Joint Economic Committee, Patricia Schroeder (D-CO); John Seiberling (D-OH); Ted Weiss (D-NY) and Tom Harkin (D-IA).[9]

IPS "In My Office a Lot"

At an Institute for Policy Studies reception in 1984, Harkin said, "I want to thank the Institute for Policy Studies and the people who worked so hard... and have been in my office a lot."[10]

The Washington School

The Washington School, founded by the Institute for Policy Studies in 1978, was an important means of influencing Congress and the Democratic Party. Courses on defense, foreign affairs and domestic policies are taught there by IPS officers, staffers and other American or foreign radical "experts." A large number of members of Congress and staffers have attended these schools. Several legislators have also taught there, including Tom Harkin.[11]

Interlink

By 1984, under the leadership of Brennon Jones, Interlink, the U.S. affiliate of the communist-influenced, Rome based Inter Press Service, had contracts servicing such prestigious media outlets as the New York Times, the Baltimore Sun, the Wall Street Journal's Los Angeles bureau, the Atlanta Journal and Constitution, the San Francisco Examiner, the Christian Science Monitor, the Long Island Newsday, CBS News, National Public Radio, Cable Network News and Metromedia's Channel 5 in New York City.

Under a Board of Directors that included Peter Weiss of IPS, Richard Falk of Princeton (later a presenter at the New York Marxist School), Sen. Tom Harkin and Dwain Epps of the World Council of Churches,

Interlink developed into a major outlet for Inter Press "propaganda" in the United States.[12]

Dinges Book Party

On March 23, 2004, at Mott House, 122 Maryland Ave. in Washington, D.C., a Book Party for IPS affiliate John Dinges' new book: "The Condor Years: How Pinochet and his Allies Brought Terrorism to Three Continents" (The New Press 2004), was hosted by Senator Tom Harkin and Rep. Maurice Hinchey (D-NY) in conjunction with the Fund for Constitutional Government, the IPS and the National Security Archive.[13]

Take Back America Conferences

Tom Harkin was on the list of 153 speakers at the 2006 Take Back America conference, which was organized by the IPS and the DSA-dominated Campaign for America's Future.[14]

Financial Transactions Tax

In November 2011, two U.S. lawmakers introduced measures to impose a transaction tax on financial firms that resembles a proposal released by the European Union.

Senator Tom Harkin, an Iowa Democrat, and Representative Peter DeFazio, an Oregon Democrat, introduced the bills in their respective chambers.

A "Briefing on Financial Transaction Taxes" was held.

The briefing was sponsored by Senator Tom Harkin, Representative Peter DeFazio and the Congressional Populist Caucus:

> Friday, October 21st 10:30am—12:00pm
>
> U.S. Capitol Building S-115
>
> Presented by:
>
> Americans for Financial Reform, AFL-CIO, Institute for Policy Studies, the Center for Media and Democracy and the Center for Economic and Policy Research.[15] [16]
>
> A small tax on financial transactions would raise tens of billions of dollars a year and curb dangerous high speed trading. Support for a transaction tax is growing in the U.S. and around the world.

Foreign Policy/National Security

SANE

From 1978 to at least 1982, Tom Harkin served on the Board of Directors of SANE—"A Citizens' Organization for a Sane World." One of the longest running and most influential "peace" groups in America (now called Peace Action); SANE was run by radicals from both the Institute for Policy Studies (IPS), Communist Party USA (CPUSA) and the Socialist Party USA—part of which later became Democratic Socialists of America (DSA).[17]

Supported by Council for a Livable World

The Anti-U.S. military Council for a Livable World supported Tom Harkin in his successful Senate run as a candidate in Iowa.[18]

Nicaragua Conference

The Communist Party USA-controlled U.S. Peace Council organized a National Conference on Nicaragua in 1979, along with several other radical groups, to discuss a strategy to ensure that the Marxist-Leninist Sandinistas took control.

Three Congressmen and two Senators lent support to this Conference: Ron Dellums, Walter Fauntroy and Tom Harkin in the House; and Mark Hatfield and Edward Kennedy in the Senate.[19]

The Chile Letter

On August 1, 1979, thirty-five U.S. Congressmen signed a letter to President Jimmy Carter demanding that private bank loans to Chile be barred unless the Chilean government chose to extradite three military officials, including the former Director of the Chilean Intelligence Service. The three had been indicted for complicity in the assassination of Marxist Unidad Popular; government member and KGB agent, Orlando Letelier; and the killing of Institute for Policy Studies staffer Ronni Moffitt in Washington, D.C. in 1976.

In May of 1978, the Chief Justice of the Chilean Supreme Court rejected the U.S.'s request for extradition.

Chief sponsor of the letter was Rep. Tom Harkin.

The Harkin letter characterized the Chilean government as "an enemy of the American people" and urged the President to "take strong action against this terrorist government." The letter was released at 9 AM on August 1, 1979, at the same time a press statement from the Washington, D.C., Chile Legislative Center of the National Coordinating Center in Solidarity with Chile, staffed by veterans of the pro-Cuba Venceremos Brigade and the Communist Party USA, supported the Congressional letter and urged pressure so that the State Department would not accept a military trial of the three Chileans in Chile as a substitute for extradition and trial in the U.S.[20]

Promoting IPS Propaganda

In the 1980s, the IPS often acted as the ideological center and hub of activism of the autonomous groups in the pro-Sandinista, Latin American network. For instance... in early 1985, IPS brought together various players in the Latin network to compile "the Reagan record of deceit and illegality on Central America." "In Contempt of Congress" was a "mishmash of contradictory data and not particularly persuasive." But it was mainly intended to confuse and sow distrust of the Reagan administration. It got wide circulation in Congress. Senator Harkin offered his praise for it and Sen. John Kerry called it "essential reading for every American who remembers Vietnam or Watergate."[21]

Nicaragua Visit

John Kerry, Tom Harkin and Daniel Ortega

When the $14 million aid package for the anti-communist Nicaraguan "Contras" came up in the spring of 1985, Congress initially voted it down. Just forty-eight hours before the vote, Senators. Harkin and Kerry traveled to Nicaragua. Their much publicized meetings with Sandinista junta leaders helped sway Congress and were arranged by Peter Kornbluh, a fellow at IPS.

Within a week, the Sandinista President, Daniel Ortega, flew to Moscow and secured $200 million in Soviet aid. Shocked and embarrassed, Congress backtracked and granted $27 million in humanitarian aid to the Contras.[22]

Supporting "Veteran's Fast for Life"

On September 1st, 1986, four veterans began a water-only "fast for life" on the Capitol steps in Washington, D.C. They wanted to draw attention to and protest President Reagan's "illegal and extraordinarily vicious wars against the poor of Nicaragua, El Salvador and Guatemala:"

> The veterans believed that the President's explicit policy of directing the contra terrorists in Nicaragua to commit wanton murder and destruction, enabled by appropriations passed by a majority of members of the U.S. Senate and House of Representatives, amounted to grotesque, unconscionable violent behavior in violation of both U.S. Constitutional and international law, and the egregious breach of the human rights of virtually all Nicaraguan citizens. The veterans believed that the President was clearly vulnerable to Constitutional impeachment and that all members of the Senate and House of Representatives should have been subjected to criminal prosecution under international law as well, whether they were re-elected or not.

On October 7th, several U.S. Congressmen and Senators spoke at a press conference in support of the fasters' cause. They included Senator Charles Mathias (R-MD), Claiborne Pell (D-RI), Don Edwards (D-CA), Senator Ted Kennedy (D-MA), Leon Panetta (D-CA), Senator John Kerry (D-MA), David Bonior (D-MI), Lane Evans (D-IL), Senator Patrick Leahy (D-VT) and Senator Tom Harkin (D-IA).[23]

Staffer's Trip to Cuba

Sen. Harkin sent Brian Ahlberg to Cuba for a number of days in August of 2009. The trip was courtesy of a $1,681.70 grant from the IPS-connected

Center for Democracy in the Americas. Ahlberg "attended tours and meetings to learn about the impact of U.S. policy toward Cuba."[24]

"Tiger Cages"

Tom Harkin went to Washington in 1969 to join the staff of Iowa Congressman Neal Smith.

In 1970, President Nixon sent a delegation of ten Congressmen to Vietnam to investigate pacification. A part of their mandate included a visit to a prison in South Vietnam as a way to be allowed to visit a prison where U.S. POWs were held in the North. This visit led to Harkin's involvement with anti-War activist Don Luce, and his participation in a huge propaganda coup for the North Vietnamese communists.[25]

The Don Luce Connection

After a previous stint teaching agriculture, serving with International Voluntary Services (IVS), an overseas volunteer program similar to the Peace Corps, Cornell graduate Don Luce returned to Vietnam in 1969, as an investigative journalist for Cornell University and for the United Methodist Church's Vietnam Education Project. He also became affiliated with the World Council of Churches, an international religious body which had been infiltrated by the Soviet Union through front groups such as the Prague-based Christian Peace Conference. Networking with other religious antiwar groups, Luce along with former IVS colleagues Gene Stolzfus and Tom Fox, joined a campaign to publicize allegations of torture against the South Vietnamese government, involving what were called "Tiger Cages," allegedly located at Con Son Island Prison.

Luce's public involvement in the "Tiger Cages" story was preceded by the more subtle involvement of Stolzfus and Fox. After quitting IVS, Fox began working as a foreign correspondent for National Catholic Reporter, TIME, The New York Times and Dispatch News Service International. Dispatch News was the same news service that helped Seymour Hersh break the My Lai Massacre story in 1969. It was funded by Philip Stern, nephew of Soviet spy Alfred Stern and a financier and board member of the Institute for Policy Studies. Dispatch News also employed known Soviet propaganda agent Wilfred Burchett.

Fox and Stoltzfus served as the Saigon staff of the U.S. Study Team on Religious & Political Freedom in Vietnam. This was a human rights investigating body consisting primarily of a group of religious antiwar leaders that included Fox's friend Robert Drinan, a far left Catholic priest from Massachusetts, soon to run for Congress in a 1970 campaign chaired by future Obama Secretary of State John Kerry. Also part of the team was communist affiliated Congressman John Conyers, Jr.

The Study Team's research was conducted in May-June 1969 and the results were presented to the Senate Foreign Relations Committee in February 1970 by anti war Senator J. William Fulbright. The Team's report stated that "prison authorities denied the existence of "Tiger Cages," that "Team members were unable to elicit any more from the prison officials than that the "Tiger Cages" were no longer in existence," and that "Team members observed no brutality." However, an unidentified prisoner "speaking surreptitiously to the Team members said, in answer to a question, 'Yes, the "Tiger Cages" are here, behind Camp No. 2 and Camp No. 3. You looked in the wrong place.'"

To give this story traction, Don Luce started his own campaign. One of Luce's former agricultural students had been imprisoned at Con Son. Students protesting the imprisonment had written a report on conditions at the prison, which Luce translated and sent to newspapers all around the U.S. While Luce was preparing the report for distribution, he persuaded Congressmen William Anderson and the extreme left Augustus Hawkins, as well as Congressional Aide Tom Harkin to stray from an official Congressional delegation to Saigon for a private fact-finding trip to Con Son in July 1970.

Harkin forced his Vietnamese hosts to let him into the prison and shot some photos of prison cells with bars in the ceiling under catwalks, which shouting prisoners reportedly alleged were used for abusing inmates by dumping things from the ceiling. Luce's team then went back to Saigon and collected abuse allegations from five former inmates who had been imprisoned as suspected Communists. The allegations collected by Luce's team were disputed by officials who claimed the catwalks were used merely for observing inmates. USAID's Senior Advisor to the South Vietnamese Director of Corrections, Don Bordenkircher, would later heavily criticize the Luce team's allegations, arguing, "The Tiger Cage story put out in 1970 stands as one of the most successful operations ever undertaken by Hanoi's Department of Psychological Warfare." The majority of other Congressmen investigating the matter did not find the Luce team's allegations credible enough to include in their official report.

Disregarding his colleagues' objections, Harkin called a press conference to denounce the official report as "a whitewash or a snow job." He allowed Luce to provide some of his photographs for a pictorial essay in the July 17, 1970 issue of LIFE. Luce also supplied photographs to the underground paper Liberation News Service (supported by the Institute for Policy Studies) and wrote pieces on the subject for several Vietnamese newspapers. The South Vietnamese government then withdrew Luce's press card.

No longer welcome in South Vietnam, Luce began telling his "Tiger Cages" story around the United States as he toured the country from 1971 to 1974 with what he called the Indochina Mobile Education Project. This involved Luce traveling by bus around the country and presenting visual aids designed to arouse opposition to the war and pressure Congress to cut off aid to South Vietnam.[26] [27]

Harkin Returns to Vietnam

In July 2010, Tom Harkin returned to now communist controlled Vietnam, as part of a delegation led by Senator Al Franken, who had been working closely with the Vietnam Agent Orange Relief and Responsibility Campaign to win financial compensation for Vietnam for damage caused by U.S. defoliant usage during the war.[28] [29]

Coincidentally, one of Vietnam Agent Orange Relief and Responsibility Campaign's Advisory Board members was Tom Harkin's old Vietnam colleague, Don Luce.[30]

---

1 KeyWiki, "Tom Harkin," KeyWiki, http://keywiki.org/index.php/Tom_Harkin (accessed April 15, 2013)
2 Tom Harkin, "Biography," Senate.gov, http://www.harkin.senate.gov/abouttom.cfm (accessed April 15, 2013)
3 Tom Harkin, "Committee Assignments," Senate.gov, http://www.harkin.senate.gov/committees.cfm (accessed April 15, 2013)
4 21st Century Democrats, Facebook, https://www.facebook.com/21stCenturyDemocrats (accessed April 15, 2013)
5 21st Century Democrats, "2010 Youth Leadership Speaker Series," 21st Century Democrats, http://21stcenturydems.org/index.php/events/sign-up/july-28-2010-speaker-series-kick-off-event (accessed February 9, 2011)
6 FBF website, "Speakers Page," FBF website, http://www.fightingbobfest.org/speakers.cfm, (accessed December 28, 2012)
7 In These Times, "22 to Know," In These Times, http://inthesetimes.com/article/3933/ (September 26, 2008)
8 Center for International Policy Letterhead (April 11, 1980)
9 Information Digest (April 14, 1983) pp. 77-79

10 Communists in the Democratic Party, p. 72
11 Communists in the Democratic Party, p. 73
12 S. Steven Powell, "Covert Cadre: Inside the Institute for Policy Studies," p. 142
13 John Dinges, "Speaking Engagements, Events and Media Appearances," John Dinges, http://www.johndinges.com/condor/Speaking.htm (2004)
14 Campaign For America's Future, "Archives – 2006 Agenda & Speakers," Campaign For America's Future, http://www.ourfuture.org/node/13179 (accessed May 14, 2010)
15 John Dinges, "A Briefing On Financial Transaction Taxes," John Dinges, http://www.johndinges.com/condor/Speaking.htm (accessed April 16, 2013)
16 Americans for Financial Reform, "Americans 50+ Demand Protections from Financial Abuse," Americans for Financial Reform, http://ourfinancialsecurity.org/2010/02/americans-50-demand-protections-from-financial-abuse/ (February 22, 2010)
17 KeyWiki, "SANE," KeyWiki, http://www.keywiki.org/index.php/SANE (accessed April 15, 2013)
18 Council for a Livable World, "Meet the Candidates," Council for a Livable World, http://livableworld.org/support/meet_candidates/ (accessed April 16, 2013)
19 Communists in the Democratic Party, p. 67
20 Information Digest (August 10, 1979) p. 244
21 S. Steven Powell, "Covert Cadre: Inside the Institute for Policy Studies," Ch. 14, pp. 226-227
22 S. Steven Powell, "Covert Cadre: Inside the Institute for Policy Studies," Ch. 14, pp. 226-227
23 Ivan's Place, "Veterans Fast for Life for Peace in Central America," Ivan's Place (accessed June 2, 2010)
24 Legistorm, "Center for Democracy in the Americas – Sponsor of Congressional Travel," Legistorm, http://www.legistorm.com/trip/list/by/sponsor/id/10693/name/Center_for_Democracy_in_the_Americas/page/2.html (accessed August 30, 2010)
25 Don Luce, "The Tiger Cages of Viet Nam," Historians Against the War, http://www.historiansagainstwar.org/resources/torture/luce.html (accessed May 29, 2013)
26 Fedora Goodfellow's Bedfellows, "Who's in Bed with the Washington Post," Fedora Goodfellow's Bedfellows (July 2006)
27 Tom Harkin, "Biography," Senate.gov, http://www.harkin.senate.gov/abouttom.cfm (accessed August 1, 2011)
28 Joe Kimball, "Al Franken to visit Vietnam with Senate group, then head to Laos," MinnPost, http://www.minnpost.com/political-agenda/2010/07/al-franken-visit-vietnam-senate-group-then-head-laos, (July 1, 2010)
29 KeyWiki, "Al Franken," KeyWiki, http://keywiki.org/index.php/Al_Franken (accessed May 29, 2013)
30 Vietnam Agent Orange Relief & Responsibility Campaign website, "About," Vietnam Agent Orange Relief & Responsibility Campaign website, http://www.vn-agentorange.org/about.html (accessed December 13, 2010)

Mike Michaud
(D-ME)

Michael H. Michaud is a Democratic member of the United States House of Representatives, representing the 2nd District of Maine. He is a member of the Populist Caucus.[1]

Background

Mike Michaud was raised in Medway, Maine, and worked at the Great Northern Paper Company. He is a member of United Steel Workers Local #4-00037.

Michaud attended the John F. Kennedy School of Government Program for Senior Executives in State and Local Government at Harvard University. He has also been awarded an honorary Doctorate of Public Service from Unity College, Husson College and Maine Maritime Academy.

Citing a desire to help clean up the badly polluted Penobscot River near his home, Mike Michaud first ran for and was elected to the Maine House of Representatives in 1980 where he went on to serve seven consecutive terms. In 1994, he defeated a Republican incumbent in his first bid for the Maine Senate.

Michaud was sworn in as a U.S. Congressman in January of 2003.[2]

Influence

In the U.S. House of Representatives, Mike Michaud serves on the Committee on Veterans' Affairs, where he is the Ranking Member, and the Committee on Transportation and Infrastructure. The Committee on Transportation and Infrastructure includes the Subcommittee on

Highways and Transit, the Subcommittee on Economic Development, Public Buildings and Emergency Management, the Subcommittee on Railroads, Pipelines and Hazardous Materials and the Subcommittee on Water Resources and Environment.[3]

Michaud is one of Congress' strongest advocates for protectionist trade policies.

On June 24th, 2009, Rep. Mike Michaud introduced the TRADE (Trade Reform Accountability Development and Employment) Act in the House of Representatives with 106 co-sponsors.

The TRADE Act called for Congress to re-examine all current free trade agreements, evaluate their overall impact on both U.S. and trade-partner citizens and "chart a new path towards trade agreements that benefit workers and the environment".[4]

On June 5, 2008, the Ohio Conference on Fair Trade, led by President Simone Morgen of Columbus Jobs with Justice and Democratic Socialists of Central Ohio, commended Sen. Sherrod Brown and five members of Ohio's Congressional delegation for co-sponsoring the Trade Reform, Accountability, Development and Employment (TRADE) Act, introduced by Sen. Brown and Rep. Mike Michaud the day before in Washington D.C.

Ohio Conference on Fair Trade President Simone Morgen said, "We have the opportunity for a new beginning that can spread the benefits of fair trade to the widest possible number of people. This is change we can really believe in!"[5]

"Progressive" Connections

Mike Michaud has close ties to the Institute for Policy Studies (IPS).

IPS Award Presenter

Community leaders from El Salvador received the IPS' 2009 Letelier-Moffitt Human Rights Award on behalf of the National Roundtable on Mining. This "broad coalition of environmental, faith-based and community activists, has successfully worked to block permits for potentially environmentally devastating mining in El Salvador."

> The coalition will speak about the investor-state suits recently filed under the Central American Free Trade Agreement (CAFTA) by U.S.

and Canadian mining companies against El Salvador. They will also discuss their work to oppose mining, and the attacks and threats that they and other members of the National Roundtable have suffered in El Salvador.

Mike Michaud speaks to Vidalina Morales de Gamez of la Mesa Nacional Frente a la Mineria en El Salvador

Speakers at the event were:

- Representatives of El Salvador's National Roundtable on Mining: William Castillo, Center for Research on Investment and Trade (CEICOM) and Francisco Pineda, Environment Coordinating Committee of Cabañas.
- Sarah Anderson, Global Economy Project Director at the Institute for Policy Studies. Anderson reported on her recent experience serving on an official advisory committee to the Obama Administration on Bilateral Investment Treaties (BITs). The administration is currently reviewing the U.S. Model BIT, which includes rules that are similar to those in the investment chapter of CAFTA and other trade agreements.
- Rep. Michael Michaud, Democratic Congressman from and the lead sponsor of the Trade Reform, Accountability, Development and Employment (TRADE) Act. One provision of the TRADE Act would ensure that trade agreements no longer permit foreign investors to sue governments in international tribunals over domestic regulatory policies that protect public health and the environment.

Contact for the event was Manuel Perez-Rocha from the IPS.

The event was organized by the IPS, Oxfam America and the radical Washington Office on Latin America. It was sponsored by Rep. Michael Michaud.[6]

Sponsored IPS Presentation

Institute for Policy Studies Global Economy Director Sarah Anderson presented a slideshow on the negative impacts of the Korea-U.S. Free Trade Agreement at a Congressional briefing sponsored by Rep. Mike Michaud on July 19, 2010.[7]

Foreign Policy/National Security

Supported by Council for a Livable World

The Council for a Livable World, is a non-profit advocacy organization that seeks to "reduce the danger of nuclear weapons and increase national security," primarily through supporting "progressive" Congressional candidates who support their anti-military policies. The Council supported Mike Michaud in his successful House of Representatives run as candidate for Maine.[8]

Meeting Mexican Labor Leaders

Mexican labor leaders representing independent unions held a Congressional briefing on September 13th, 2011, in Washington, D.C. to highlight Mexico's "ongoing repression and assault on the rights and wages of Mexican workers."

"Workers in Mexico are facing repression from the Mexican government and corporations," say the labor leaders. "And more and more working people in Mexico are being driven into poverty through the erosion of their wages and human rights," they added.

U.S. Rep Mike Michaud sponsored the briefing on behalf of the Congressional Labor Caucus and the International Worker Rights Caucus.

"More than 15 years ago, we were told that NAFTA would create a thriving middle class in Mexico," said Rep. Michaud. "Economists and government officials said the agreement would lead to growing trade surpluses and that hundreds of thousands of jobs would be gained. As our friends from Mexico can attest, NAFTA did not bring these benefits.

Instead, workers' rights are being violated on a regular basis, and both the U.S. and Mexico are worse off."

The labor leaders said they plan to meet with U.S. members of Congress to discuss worker rights and safety standards for Mexican workers. They intend to highlight the repeated efforts by Mexico's government under "conservative and right-wing President Felipe Calderon." The Calderon Administration is trying to strip union members with Los Mineros of its right to exist as the union continues a four-year strike by 1,100 copper miners over safety issues against the company, Grupo Mexico.

Del Toro noted, "We are taking this opportunity to paint a picture of the status of worker rights in Mexico and to outline the persecution faced by unions and leaders there. The diminishing of workers' rights and very low wages produce an unequal standard between wage levels in Mexico and the U.S. This is affecting the U.S., which is looking to create jobs for workers here," he said.

Leo Gerard, President of the United Steelworkers and a Democratic Socialists of America supporter, joined the Mexican labor officials.[9]

1 KeyWiki, "Mike Michaud," KeyWiki, http://keywiki.org/index.php/Mike_Michaud (accessed April 29, 2013)

2 Mike Michaud, "Biography," House.gov, http://michaud.house.gov/about-mike/full-biography (accessed April 29, 2013)

3 Mike Michaud, "Biography," House.gov, http://michaud.house.gov/about-mike/full-biography (accessed April 29, 2013)

4 Globalgoodspartners, "Free Trade vs. Fair Trade: Where are we headed?" Handmade Stories, http://globalgoodspartners.wordpress.com/2009/07/09/free-trade-vs-fair-trade-where-are-we-headed/ (July 9, 2009)

5 Karen Hansen, "Congressional Leaders Launch Bold New Trade Reform Act," Ohio Conference on Fair Trade, http://www.citizenstrade.org/ctc/wp-content/uploads/2011/01/20080605_LeadersLaunchTradeAct_OhioCFT2.pdf (June 5, 2008)

6 IPS DC, "Briefing: Investment Rules in Trade Agreements – Who Benefits? The Case of Mining in El Salvador," IPS, http://www.ips-dc.org/events/investment_rules_in_trade_agreements (accessed April 29, 2013)

7 Sarah Anderson, "Investment Rules in Trade Agreements: Korea-U.S. and Beyond," IPS DC, http://www.ips-dc.org/articles/investment_rules_in_trade_agreements_korea-us_and_beyond, (July 21, 2010)

8 Council for a Livable World, "Meet the Candidates," Council for a Livable World, http://livableworld.org/support/meet_candidates/ (accessed April 29, 2013)

9 Pepe Lozano, "Mexican labor officials meet with Congress about worker abuses," People's World, http://peoplesworld.org/mexican-labor-officials-meet-with-congress-about-worker-abuses/, (September 14, 2011)

Barbara Mikulski (D-MD)

Barbara Mikulski is the Senior Democratic member of the United States Senate, representing Maryland.[1]

Background

Growing up in the Highlandtown neighborhood of East Baltimore, Mikulski trained as a social worker, earning her Bachelor's Degree at Mount St. Agnes College in Baltimore and then continuing her studies at the University of Maryland. She graduated in 1965 with a Master's Degree in Social Work.

Mikulski first worked for the Associated Catholic Charities and then the Baltimore Department of Social Services. By 1966, she was an Assistant Chief of Community Organizing for the City Social Services Department.

Mikulski expressed many of her concerns in an essay entitled, "Who Speaks for Ethnic America?" for the New York Times in September of 1970. Ethnic immigrants who came to the United States at the turn of the century, she wrote, "Constructed the skyscrapers, operated the railroads, worked on the docks, factories, steel mills and in the mines. Though our labor was in demand, we were not accepted. Our names, language, food and cultural customers were the subject of ridicule. We were discriminated against by banks, institutions of higher learning and other organizations controlled by the Yankee Patricians. There were no protective mechanisms for safety, wages and tenure." Mikulski maintained that it was smarter for these groups to organize than to fight, "to form an alliance based on mutual issues, interdependence and respect."

Mikulski got her start in politics in 1968 with the organization of a coalition of black, Polish, Greek, Lithuanian and Ukrainian Americans to block construction of a 16-lane highway that would have destroyed areas of East Baltimore. Called SCAR (Southeast Council Against the Road), the neighborhood group fought against an entrenched Democratic political organization at City Hall that supported the highway project. Despite the strength of the opposition, SCAR, led by Mikulski, was successful in blocking the highway proposal.[2]

Mikulski's first election was a successful run for Baltimore City Council in 1971, where she served for 5 years. In 1976, she ran for Congress and won, representing Maryland's 3rd District for 10 years. In 1986, she ran for the Senate and won, becoming the first Democratic woman Senator elected in her own right. She was re-elected with large majorities in 1992, 1998, 2004 and 2010.[3]

Influence

A leader in the Senate, Mikulski is the Dean of the Women—serving as a mentor to other women Senators when they first take office.

Mikulski is the first woman to serve as Chairwoman of the Senate Appropriations Committee. The Committee's role is defined by the U.S. Constitution, which requires "appropriations made by law" prior to the expenditure of any money from the Federal Treasury. The Committee writes the legislation that allocates federal funds to the numerous government agencies, departments and organizations on an annual basis.

She is also the Chairwoman of the Subcommittee on Commerce, Justice and Science. The CJS Subcommittee oversees funding for several key federal departments, agencies and programs, including NASA, the FBI, the National Science Foundation, the National Oceanic and Atmospheric Administration, the Bureau of Census, the Department of Commerce and the Federal Trade Commission.

Mikulski also serves on the following Appropriations Subcommittees which are tasked with drafting legislation to allocate funds to government agencies within their jurisdictions. These Subcommittees are responsible for reviewing the President's budget requests, hearing testimony from government officials and drafting the spending plans for the coming fiscal year: the Subcommittee on Defense, the Subcommittee on State, Foreign Operations and Related Programs, the Subcommittee on Transportation, Housing and Urban Development and Related Agencies and the Subcommittee on Labor, Health and Human Services, Education and Related Agencies.

Mikulski is a senior member of the Senate Select Committee on Intelligence, which oversees all intelligence activities of the United States government. The panel monitors the Central Intelligence Agency (CIA) and other U.S. intelligence operations "in order to safeguard American interests abroad."[4]

Socialist Connections

Barbara Mikulski has a long history with Democratic Socialist Organizing Committee (DSOC)/Democratic Socialists of America (DSA).

Democratic Agenda

More than 1,200 people attended the DSOC-initiated Democratic Agenda conference held on November 16-18, 1979, at the International Inn and Metropolitan AM Church in Washington, D.C. The conference focused on "corporate power" as the key barrier to "economic and political democracy," concepts many Democratic Agenda participants defined as "socialism."

The Democratic Agenda meetings attempted to develop anti-corporate alternatives through influencing the direction of the Democratic Party during the period leading up to the July 1980, Democratic National Convention in New York.

The opening speaker was U.S. Rep. Barbara Mikulski (D-MD), who set the stage for the DA conference with the proclamation, "I come to you with a message of hype—hope—well, it is hype." The Baltimore Congresswoman proceeded with a speech that was a collection of slogans such as "change comes from the bottom!" and "people power!" which were "received with warm applause."[5]

"Knows About DSOC"

Nancy Lieber, International Committee Chair of the Democratic Socialist Organizing Committee, wrote a June 30, 1981 letter to Danielle Page, a staffer for Canadian Member of Parliament, Ian Waddell:[6]

Dear Danielle Page,

I'm sending along a list of Congress people and senators who know about us, democratic socialism, and—perhaps Canada.

Only the first one is an open socialist, but the others are sympathetic in varying degrees.

- Congressman Ron Dellums
- Congressman Byron Dorgan
- Congressman Steven Solarz (D-NY)
- Congressman Ted Weiss (D-NY)
- Congressman Barney Frank (D-NY)
- Congressman Gerry Studds (D-MA)
- Congressman Robert Kastenmeier (D-WI)
- Congressman John Conyers (D-MI)
- Congressman Harold Washington
- Congressman David Obey (D-WI)
- Congressman Les Aspin
- Congresswoman Barbara Mikulski
- Senator Ted Kennedy (D-MA)
- Hope this is of help and you recruit them to the cause!
- In Solidarity,
- Nancy Lieber
- Chair, Intl. Committee

Democratic Agenda Conference

DSOC

DEMOCRATIC SOCIALIST
ORGANIZING COMMITTE
853 Broadway, Suite 801
New York, N.Y. 10003
Tel. (212) 260-3270
Cable: SOCIALISTS

National Chair
Michael Harrington

Political Director
Ben Tafoya

Organizational Director
Selma Lenihan

National Vice-Chairs
Harry Britt
Marjorie Phyfe
Michael Germinal Rivas
Trudy Robideau
Rosemary Ruether
William Winpisinger

Advisory Committee Co-Chairs
Ralph Helstein
Victor Reuther

Executive Committee
Bogdan Denitch
Brian Doherty

February 17, 1982

To: East Coast DSOC locals
From: Ben Tafoya
Re: May 1 Democratic Agenda Conference in Newark, New Jersey.
DA News #2.

As we mentioned at the National Board meeting in January, we are hard at work on the East Coast Democratic Agenda conference. We are at the point of inviting speakers -- indeed invitations to our major plenary speakers have already gone out. They include: Mike Harrington, Congresswoman Barbara Mikulski, SEIU President John Sweeney, CLUW President Joyce Miller, ADA President Robert Drinan, N.Y. City Councilmember Ruth Messinger and others. We are also collecting endorsements from a variety of local and national unions including the IAM, the UAW, ACTWU, DC 37 AFSCME (N.Y. City municipal workers), the California Federation of Teachers, etc...

405

Congresswoman Barbara Mikulski was invited as a speaker to the DSOC organized Democratic Agenda conference, scheduled for 1982 in Newark, New Jersey.

Other invited speakers included New York City Councilor Ruth Messinger, SEIU President John Sweeney, Coalition of Labor Union Women President Joyce Miller and Americans for Democratic Action President Robert Drinan.[7]

Homage to Harrington

In 1988, 600 activists gathered in the Roseland Hotel in New York to pay homage to Democratic Socialists of America leader Michael Harrington, then age 60 and undergoing treatment for cancer.

Co-Chairs of the event were DSA members William Winpisinger, Gloria Steinem, Jack Sheinkman and Stanley Sheinbaum.

Congresswoman Barbara Mikulski was listed among the prominent attendees.[8]

Working with Pappas

Dean Pappas is a Baltimore activist whose strong antiwar views were formed during the Vietnam War era, when he stood, often shoulder to shoulder, with the late Philip Berrigan, the "Dissenter Emeritus," in "opposing the evils of the American Empire."

Pappas said: "I have actually known [Sen.] Barbara Mikulski for over 40 years. We worked together. I was really proud of what she did in standing up to U.S. imperialism in Central America."[9]

Pappas was, for many years, a leading Baltimore Democratic Socialists of America activist.[10]

Foreign Policy/National Security

Supported by Council for a Livable World

The anti-U.S. military Council for a Livable World supported Barbara Mikulski in her successful Senate run as candidate for Maryland.[11]

Tour to Nicaragua

In January 1981, three Congressional Democrats (all connected to DSA), Gerry Studds of Massachusetts, Bob Edgar of Pennsylvania and

Barbara Mikulski of Maryland, toured Nicaragua and met with Sandinista leaders.

A follow-up report by Studds claimed that the Marxist-Leninist Sandinista's main "accomplishment has been to create within Nicaragua a universal commitment to social equity, and a concern for the country's multitude of poor, ill clothed, ill fed and sick people. There is a fully shared sense that the revolution is necessary and just."[12]

After her February 1981 visit to Nicaragua and other countries in Central America, Mikulski "provided further evidence of atrocities committed by right-wing forces."

Mikulski reported that, "In each and every conversation [with Salvadoran civilian refugees], it was verified that the military aid from the United States was aiding and abetting the killing and torture of innocent people."[13]

Mikulski, took the communist propaganda line so far that she even claimed that children were used as target practice, "and macheted up to be eaten by dogs" and "rape is used as a systematic form of social control." She also said terrorists "disemwombed" pregnant women.[14]

Opposed Aid to El Salvador

On February 6, 1990, Senators Edward Kennedy and John Kerry introduced a Bill to cut off all aid to El Salvador for its fight against communist guerillas, just a few days after El Salvador's President Cristiani had come to Washington to discuss the need for such support.

This bill was backed by four other far left Democratic Senators: Barbara Mikulski of Maryland, Paul Simon of Illinois, Alan Cranston of California and Brock Adams of Washington State.

The Senators and Congressmen who voted against providing aid to the government of El Salvador were effectively handicapping the democratically-elected government in that area and paralleling the Communist Party line of the time.

The Communist Party USA newspaper, the People's Daily World of January 30, 1990, stated:[15]

> Last weekend's meeting of the Communist Party, USA resolved to Mobilize to build the March 24 demonstration in Washington, D.C. demanding an end to military aid to El Salvador and intervention in Central America.

1 KeyWiki, "Barbara Mikulski," KeyWiki, http://keywiki.org/index.php/Barbara_Mikulski (accessed May 1, 2013)
2 Gale Encyclopedia of Biography, "Barbara Mikulski," Gale Encyclopedia of Biography, http://www.answers.com/topic/barbara-mikulski, (accessed May 1, 2013)
3 Barbara A. Mikulski, "About Barbara Mikulski," Senate.gov, http://www.mikulski.senate.gov/about/biography.cfm (accessed August 8, 2011)
4 Barbara A. Mikulski, "Committee Assignments," Senate.gov, http://www.mikulski.senate.gov/about/committeeassignments.cfm (accessed May 1, 2013)
5 Information Digest (December 14, 1979) p. 372
6 KeyWiki, "Barbara Mikulski," KeyWiki, http://keywiki.org/index.php/Barbara_Mikulski (accessed May 1, 2013)
7 KeyWiki, "Barbara Mikulski," KeyWiki, http://keywiki.org/index.php/Barbara_Mikulski (accessed May 1, 2013)
8 Reading Socialist (September/October 1988) Vol. 6, Number 3, pp. 3-4
9 MediaMonitors, "Bearing Witness to Sen. Mikulski's Complicity in the War," MediaMonitors, http://newswire.mediamonitors.net/layout/set/print/content/view/full/45391, (August 3, 2007)
10 KeyWiki, "Dean Pappas," KeyWiki, http://www.keywiki.org/index.php/Dean_Pappas (accessed May 2, 2013)
11 Council for a Livable World, "Meet the Candidates," Council for a Livable World, http://livableworld.org/support/meet_candidates/ (accessed May 2, 2013)
12 Roger C. Peace, "A Call to Conscience: The Anti/Contra War Campaign," p. 18
13 PBS, "PBS debates, Should the US congress have provided military aid for the Salvadorean Government in the 1980s?" PBS, http://www.pbs.org/wnet/justice/elsalvador_debate.html, (accessed May 2, 2013)
14 Eagle, "Democrats sue over El Salvador," Eagle, http://news.google.com/newspapers?nid=1955&dat=19810501&id=Kg0iAAAAIBAJ&sjid=0aAFAAAAIBAJ&pg=3424,103186Reading (May 1, 1981)
15 Communists in the Democratic Party, p. 9

Donna Edwards (D-MD)

Donna F. Edwards is a Democratic member of the United States House of Representatives, representing the 4th District of Maryland. She is a member of the Congressional Progressive Caucus, the Populist Caucus and the Congressional Black Caucus.[1]

Background

Donna Edwards was born June 1958, into a military family that traveled throughout the country during her childhood. She returned to North Carolina, her birth state, to attend Wake Forest University. She subsequently earned a law degree from Franklin Pierce Law Center in New Hampshire and settled in Maryland in 1989.[2]

Donna Edwards has served as either a Chairperson, Trustee, Board Member or Executive Director of the National Network to End Domestic Violence, which she co-founded; Citizens for Responsibility and Ethics in Washington; Common Cause; the League of Conservation Voters; the Center for a New Democracy and the Funders' Committee for Civic Participation. She was a lobbyist for the nonprofit, Public Citizen organization.[3]

She co-founded and served as the first Executive Director of the National Network to End Domestic Violence and received national recognition for her work leading the effort to pass the Violence Against Women Act of 1994.[4]

Edwards began her career at the United Nations Development Program and was a Systems Engineer for Lockheed Corporation with NASA's Space Shuttle program.[5]

Just prior to serving in Congress, she was the Executive Director of the Arca Foundation in Washington, D.C.[6]

Influence

Edwards serves on the Transportation and Infrastructure Committee where she sits on the Subcommittee on Highways and Transit, the Subcommittee on Water Resources and Environment and the Subcommittee on Economic Development, Public Buildings and Emergency Management. She also serves on the Science and Technology Committee where she sits on the Subcommittee on Investigations and Oversight (she is a Ranking Member) and the Subcommittee on Space and Aeronautics. Edwards serves on the House Committee on Standards of Official Conduct and is a member of the Tom Lantos Human Rights Commission.[7]

"Progressive" Connections

21st Century Democrats Support

Donna Edwards was one of 71 key "progressives" endorsed by 21st Century Democrats in the 2008 election cycle, second round.[8]

Progressive Agenda?

Writing on the website of the Maoist leaning Freedom Road Socialist Organization (FRSO), Bill Fletcher Jr. of FRSO, Democratic Socialists of America (DSA) and the Institute for Policy Studies (IPS) explained:[9]

> The radical Left can engage in electoral work to raise issues. This can take place at the level of local or statewide initiatives or referenda, or it can take place in the context of battling over the platform of a particular candidate. Initiatives and referenda are very straight to the point. With candidates such as that of Democratic nominee for Congress Donna Edwards (from Maryland), their candidacy can become a means to push a very progressive agenda—in her case, around the war.

Institute for Policy Studies Ties

Donna Edwards is a long-time affiliate of the Institute for Policy Studies.

Letelier-Moffit Award Presenter

On October 15, 2008, the IPS hosted the 32nd annual Letelier-Moffitt Human Rights Awards at the National Press Club in Washington D.C.

Rep. Donna Edwards presented Francisco Soberon and the Peruvian-based Asociacion Pro Derechos Humanos with the International Award for being the driving force behind the current trial of former Peruvian President Alberto Fujimori. DSAer and IPS trustee, Barbara Ehrenreich, presented The Indian Workers Congress with the Domestic Award for their "courageous stand against modern-day slavery:"

> This year's program marks the 32nd anniversary of the September 21, 1976 car bombing that killed Chilean diplomat Orlando Letelier and American Ronni Moffitt. IPS has continued to host the annual human rights awards in the names of Letelier and Moffitt to honor these fallen colleagues while celebrating new heroes of the human rights movement from the U.S. and elsewhere in Latin America.

According to a YouTube version of the speech, the IPS' John Cavanagh introduced Edwards with the words, "she will help us end the war in Iraq... she will help us build an economy that serves people and the planet..."

Edwards stated that she had attended several previous award ceremonies as an audience member and she was "among friends."[10]

Take Back America Conferences

Donna Edwards was on the list of 153 speakers at the 2006 Take Back America conference, which was organized by the IPS and DSA initiated Campaign for America's Future.

She was back in 2007.[11]

On March 17, 2008, at the Take Back America conference in Washington D.C., Institute for Policy Studies board member, Robert Borosage, Donna Edwards and self-proclaimed communist, Van Jones, spoke in the Opening Plenary entitled: "The Progressive Plan for Victory."

America's Future Now!

Donna Edwards was on the list of speakers at the 2009 America's Future Now! conference, also organized by the Campaign for America's Future.[12]

She also spoke at the America's Future Now! 2010 conference.[13]

"Progressive Maryland" Event, Silver Spring

On September 20, 2011, Progressive Maryland convened a "Take Back the Budget Debate" at the Silver Spring Civic Center, Ellsworth and Veterans Place, Silver Spring, Maryland: "Turn Your Anger to Action on the Economy and Federal Budget—Come, spread the word, and bring everyone you can!"

Panel speakers included: U.S. Rep. Donna Edwards, MD State Senators Roger Manno and Jamie Raskin (son of Institute for Policy Studies founder Marcus Raskin), Center for American Progress Senior Economist Heather Boushey and IPS Fellow Karen Dolan. The event was moderated by Progressive Maryland Board President, Elbridge James.[14]

Town Hall Tonight
Take Back the Budget Debate
Tues. Sept 20, 7:30 p.m.

**FUND OUR COMMUNITIES
BRING THE WAR $$ HOME**

-- As President Seeks Jobs, Fairer Taxes

**Turn Your Anger to Action on the Economy and Federal Budget
- *Come, spread the word, and bring everyone you can!***

Panel speakers include *(left to right)*: US Rep. Donna Edwards, MD State Senators Roger Manno and Jamie Raskin, Center for American Progress Senior Economist Heather Boushey, and Institute for Policy Studies Fellow Karen Dolan. Moderated by Progressive Maryland Board President and NAACP's Elbridge James (below).
(FLASH: Rep. John Conyers also hopes to join us)

Silver Spring Civic Center, Ellsworth and Veterans Place, Silver Spring

"Progressive Maryland" Event, Prince George

On November 7, 2011, Progressive Maryland convened a "Shift the Budget Debate" at Prince George's Town Hall in Largo, Maryland.

Panel speakers included: U.S. Rep. Donna Edwards; Maryland State Senator and DSA supporter Paul Pinsky; Delegate Aisha Braveboy; IPS fellow Karen Dolan; activist and former State Senator David Harrington (moderator).[15]

Progressive Democrats of America

Donna Edwards serves on the Advisory Board of Institute for Policy Studies/Democratic Socialists of America-led Progressive Democrats of America.[16]

Progressive Democrats of America 2012 Endorsement

In 2012, Donna Edwards (MD-4) was one of 14 leftist Congressional and Senate candidates endorsed by Progressive Democrats of America.[17]

Leading with Love

Leading with Love was an event to celebrate 5 years of the Marxist-led IPS partner organization National Domestic Workers Alliance. It was held in Washington D.C. on November 14, 2012.

Members of the Host Committee included Donna Edwards.[18]

May 12, 2010—Donna Edwards with PDA National Director and Former Orange County, CA Democratic Socialist of America Activist, Tim Carpenter

Foreign Policy/National Security

Supported by Council for a Livable World

The Council for a Livable World, supported Donna Edwards in her successful House of Representatives run as candidate for Maryland.[19]

Iraq: The Legacy of the 7-Year U.S. Occupation

On August 29th, 2010, at Busboys and Poets, 5th and K Sts. NW, Washington, D.C., an event: "Iraq: The Legacy of the 7-Year U.S. Occupation," was held:

> Is the U.S. military really leaving Iraq or just rebranding? What is the toll of seven years of occupation on Iraqis, U.S. soldiers and our economies? What is the status of Iraqi refugees around the world? Is it still possible to hold accountable those who dragged us into the war or committed crimes such as torture? What role did Congress and the media play in facilitating the invasion/occupation? We'll also look at the role of the peace movement—its strengths and weaknesses—and draw key lessons to make our work for peace, including in Afghanistan, more effective.

Speakers/performers included:

- Congresswoman Donna Edwards
- Phyllis Bennis, IPS
- Raed Jarrar, Peace Action
- Bill Fletcher, Jr., IPS, DSA, Progressive Democrats of America
- Josh Stieber, Iraq Veterans Against the War
- Medea Benjamin, CODEPINK, Global Exchange, Progressive Democrats of America
- Andy Shallal, Iraqi artist, owner Busboys and Poets, IPS
- David Swanson, Progressive Democrats of America
- Gene Bruskin, U.S. Labor Against the War

The event was sponsored by CODEPINK, Peace Action, IPS, Fellowship of Reconciliation, Global Exchange, Just Foreign Policy, Veterans for Peace, Iraq Veterans Against the War, Military Families Speak Out, Progressive Democrats of America, U.S. Labor Against the War, ANSWER, World Can't Wait, Voices for Creative Nonviolence, War is a Crime, the Rivera Project and the Washington Peace Center.[20]

Anti-Israel

Donna Edwards was a member of the Republican chaired House Ethics Committee as of August of 2011. It is well known that she is anti-Israel in her leanings. She voted to bar members of Congress from attending Glenn Beck's Restoring Courage rally in Jerusalem, Israel during the week of August 24th, 2011. Also during this time, she received substantial campaign cash from the Democratic Socialists of America infiltrated, anti-Israel organization, J Street.[21]

1 KeyWiki, "Donna Edwards," KeyWiki, http://keywiki.org/index.php/Donna_Edwards (accessed April 16, 2013)
2 Donna F. Edwards, "Biography," House.gov, http://donnaedwards.house.gov/biography/ (accessed January 15, 2013)
3 PDA, "Board of Directors," PDA, http://pdamerica.org/about/board.php (accessed April 16, 2013)
4 Donna F. Edwards, "Biography," House.gov, http://donnaedwards.house.gov/biography/ (accessed January 15, 2013)
5 PDA, "Board of Directors," PDA, http://pdamerica.org/about/board.php (accessed April 16, 2013)
6 Donna F. Edwards, "Biography," House.gov, http://donnaedwards.house.gov/biography/ (accessed August 11, 2011)
7 Donna F. Edwards, "Legislation & Committee Assignments," House.gov, http://donnaedwards.house.gov/legislation-committee-assignments/ (accessed April 16, 2013)
8 21st Century Democrats, "Biography," 21st Century Democrats, http://21stcenturydems.org/candidates/2008-candidates/, (2008)
9 Freedom Road, http://freedomroad.org/content/view/576/231/lang,en/ (accessed 2011)
10 Institute for Policy Studies, "2008 Letelier-Moffitt Human Rights Awards, YouTube, http://www.youtube.com/watch?v=4mg0SkJAsrA (August 5, 2011)
11 Campaign For America's Future, "Archives – 2006 Agenda & Speakers," Campaign For America's Future, http://www.ourfuture.org/node/13179 (accessed May 14, 2010)
12 Confabb website, "America's Future Now 2009 Speakers," Confabb website, http://now2009.confabb.com/conferences/82401-americas-future-now/speakers (accessed July 13, 2010)
13 Campaign For America's Future, "America's Future Now! 2010 Speaker Biographies," Campaign For America's Future, http://www.ourfuture.org/now/speakers (accessed July 12, 2010)
14 KeyWiki, "Progressive Maryland," KeyWiki, http://keywiki.org/index.php/Progressive_Maryland (September 20, 2011)
15 KeyWiki, "Progressive Maryland," KeyWiki, http://keywiki.org/index.php/Progressive_Maryland (September 20, 2011)
16 PDA website, "Advisory Board," PDA website, http://pdamerica.org/tools/pda/Adboard.pdf (accessed April 17, 2013)
17 KeyWiki, "Donna Edwards," KeyWiki, http://keywiki.org/index.php/Donna_Edwards (accessed April 16, 2013)

18 Leading with Love, "Hosts and Sponsors," Leading with Love,
http://domesticworkers.org/leadingwithlove/hosts-and-sponsors, (accessed January 21,
2012)
19 Council for a Livable World, "Meet the Candidates," Council for a Livable World,
http://livableworld.org/support/meet_candidates/ (accessed April 17, 2013)
20 David Swanson, "The Last Combat Politician," Pacific Free Press,
http://www.pacificfreepress.com/news/1/6899-the-last-combat-politician.html (August
29, 2010)
21 JoshuaPundit, "House Ethics Committee Prohibits Members From Attending Glenn
Beck's Pro-Israel Rally," JoshuaPundit,
http://joshuapundit.blogspot.com/2011/08/house-ethics-committe-prohibits-
members.html (August 19, 2011)

Elizabeth Warren (D-MA)

Elizabeth Warren was elected to the U.S. Senate for Massachusetts on November 6, 2012.[1]

Background

A native Oklahoman, Warren was a Leo Gottlieb Professor of Law at Harvard Law School.

She has written eight books and more than a hundred articles dealing with credit and economic stress. Her latest two books, "The Two-Income Trap" and "All Your Worth," were both on national bestseller lists. She has been the principal investigator on empirical studies funded by the National Science Foundation and more than a dozen private foundations. Warren was the Chief Adviser to the National Bankruptcy Review Commission and she was appointed as the first academic member of the Federal Judicial Education Committee.[2]

Warren is married to Bruce Mann, a legal historian and law professor also at Harvard Law School. She has a daughter, Amelia Warren Tyagi, with whom she has co-authored two books and several articles.[3]

Influence

The National Law Journal named Warren one of the Most Influential Lawyers of the Decade.

In the aftermath of the 2008 financial crisis, Elizabeth Warren served as Chair of the Congressional Oversight Panel for the Troubled Asset Relief Program. Her "independent and tireless efforts to protect taxpayers, to hold Wall Street accountable and to ensure tough oversight of both the Bush and Obama Administrations, won praise from both sides of the aisle."[4]

Warren serves on the Committee on Banking, Housing and Urban Affairs, which includes the Subcommittee on Economic Policy. She also sits on the Committee on Health, Education, Labor and Pension, which includes the Subcommittee on Children and Families, the Subcommittee on Employment and Workplace Safety and the Subcommittee on Primary Health and Aging. Warren also serves on the Committee on Aging.

In 2009, Elizabeth Warren appeared in Michael Moore's anti-free market film: *Capitalism: A Love Story.*[5]

Socialist Connections

Elizabeth Warren has close ties to Democratic Socialists of America (DSA).

DSA Fundraisers

Maryland State Senator Jamie Raskin announced a fundraising event for Elizabeth Warren in Maryland on April 21, 2012, to be held at the home of his friend Damon Silvers and Elissa McBride:[6]

> District 20 is the progressive Democratic heartland of Maryland so it makes sense that the sensational progressive Democratic nominee for U.S. Senate from Massachusetts, Elizabeth Warren, is coming to visit us here tomorrow! Please join me and true-blue Democrats from all over our community and state in giving Elizabeth Warren a rousing Maryland welcome tomorrow, Saturday, April 21, between 2:00 and 3:30 pm at the home of my friend Damon Silvers, a key force in the labor and consumer movement, in Takoma Park. We have the opportunity to give a big financial boost to Elizabeth's campaign, which is essential to holding the U.S. Senate and taking back Congress in November. Join us!
>
> As you know, Elizabeth Warren is America's passionate champion of the struggling middle class and has proven herself time and again willing to fight against corporate fraud and the capture of government by predatory special interests. The populist thinker who came up with the idea for the Consumer Financial Protection Bureau, she has done more to advance the cause of consumers and workers over the last decade than anyone else in America. Imagine what she can do in the U.S. Senate seat held by Teddy Kennedy when she beats Scott Brown!

Jamie Raskin is a DSA supporter, a member of the communist affiliated National Lawyers Guild and the son of Institute for Policy Studies Founder Marcus Raskin.

Damon Silvers is Director of Policy and Special Counsel for the AFL-CIO and former leader of Harvard Democratic Socialists of America.[7]

Elissa McBride is AFSCME Director of Education and Leadership Training, a graduate of the Saul Alinsky based Midwest Academy and former DSA National Youth Organizer.[8]

The Heather Booth Connection

Heather Booth is one of America's most influential socialists. She is married to DSA member and AFSCME official, Paul Booth and has been participating in Democratic Socialist Organizing Committee/DSA events and campaigns for more than 40 years. She is also the long-time head of Chicago's Midwest Academy, a DSA-dominated school for "community organizers."

Heather Booth was an ardent champion of Elizabeth Warren, promoting her at every opportunity for the role of Consumer Financial Protection Bureau head.

Booth did this through her position as head of Americans for Financial Reform (AFR), which is basically a tool of DSA unionists in the leadership of AFSCME, SEIU and the AFL-CIO.

AFR's Steering Committee includes Alan Charney, former National Director of DSA; Richard Ferlauto, AFSME and DSA; and Robert Kuttner of Demos, himself a long-time DSA supporter.[9] [10]

Consumer Financial Protection Bureau Possibility

In 2010, Americans for Financial Reform circulated an online petition asking President Barack Obama to appoint Elizabeth Warren to head the new Consumer Financial Protection Bureau and a rap song urging the same—Got a New Sheriff, by the Main Street Brigade, also appeared.

"Elizabeth Warren is one of the great experts in the country on the economics of middle class families and supporting them and protecting them," said Heather Booth. "There's no one who has a background with the depth on the issues and the willingness to stand up to those biggest banks."[11]

Working with Booth in 2009

According to Dave Johnson, a fellow with the DSA/Institute for Policy Studies (IPS) founded Campaign for America's Future; the Booth/Warren relationship was strong as early as 2009, on proposals for a Consumer Finance Protection Act (CFPA):[12]

> I was on a blogger call today with Elizabeth Warren to discuss this bill. This call was hosted by Heather Booth, Americans for Financial Reform, a coalition of 200 organizations fighting for this other reforms of our banking and financial system. Warren is Chair of the Congressional Oversight Panel—COP—but was not on the call in that capacity. She was on the call to explain why we need the CFPA. Warren originally proposed the idea of a CFPA.

Warren/Booth Webinar

On April 6th, 2010, Americans for Financial Reform and its "progressive" ally Americans for Fairness in Lending hosted a special webinar discussion with Elizabeth Warren and AFR Director Heather Booth for the general public. It focused on "where things stand in the movement for financial reform and how everyday citizens can get involved in the fight to rein in the big banks and get the economy back on track."[13]

- Find out about reform efforts in Congress—including the Senate bill currently being debated and the House bill which passed in December.
- Learn why we need a Consumer Financial Protection Agency to protect us from abusive financial products.
- Ask Professor Warren and Heather Booth your question about financial reform.
- Hear about ways to join the fight around the country and online.

Young Professionals Event

On March 21, 2012, a Young Professionals Event fundraiser was held at the International Brotherhood of Electrical Workers in Boston, for Elizabeth Warren.

Hosts included Heather Booth, her DSAer husband Paul Booth, IPS Trustee Robert Borosage and former Iowa DSA member and prominent Democratic Party strategist, Mike Lux.[14] [15] [16]

Midwest Academy Awards

When DSA-controlled Midwest Academy held its annual award ceremony on December 12, 2012, at the Eatonville Restaurant in Washington, D.C., Elizabeth Warren was guest speaker.

Elizabeth Warren, Midwest Academy Awards Dinner

Bob Creamer, Heather Booth, Roberta Lynch and Elizabeth Warren

At the event, Elizabeth Warren mingled with Heather Booth, Democratic Party strategist and long-time DSA associate Bob Creamer, his wife, one time Evanston DSA member Rep. Jan Schakowsky and well known Chicago DSAer Roberta Lynch.

Long-time DSA member Julian Bond was given a "Lifetime Achievement Award," while two other one-time DSAers Mike Lux and Damon Silvers were given Progressive Leadership Awards.[17] [18] [19]

AFL-CIO "Teach-In" with DSAers

Massachusetts Senate hopeful, Elizabeth Warren, was scheduled to appear at an AFL-CIO sponsored "National Teach-In," on October 12, 2011, with two leading members of Democratic Socialists of America.

The AFL-CIO urged activists to join "Elizabeth Warren, Frances Fox Piven, Barbara Ehrenreich and student activists for a national teach-in on the jobs crisis and student activists' fight for worker's rights, equal access to education, fair taxation and economic and social justice."

According to the AFL-CIO press release:[20]

> America wants to work, and a new movement of students and young people is growing to demand that our leaders get to work creating good jobs. As part of that movement, we are organizing a National Teach-In at the University of California Washington Center on Oct. 12 that will be webcast live across the country. Frances Fox Piven, other featured speakers and student activists will discuss the roots of the jobs crisis and how unions, students and community groups are fighting back to defend the core values of our country... The National Teach-In is part of a nationwide campaign that week to impress upon our political leaders and corporate power-brokers: Now is the time for big, bold action to put America back to work, retain good jobs and rebuild the U.S. economy.

> The teach-in will examine the disaster caused by corporate control of our economic and political system... as corporate profits soar. The big banks are stripping away the wealth of consumers, homeowners, students and young workers. Schools, day care centers, senior citizen facilities, health clinics, parks and firehouses are starved for funds so corporations and the wealthy can get billions of dollars in tax break...

> Unions, student organizations and community groups are fighting back against these abuses of corporate power and the efforts of the right wing to reduce wages, maintain tax breaks for the wealthy and eliminate social safety net programs...

We are on the cusp of a new social movement to resist and roll back the corporate domination of political and economic systems by the banks, big corporations and Wall Street profiteers. Please join the National Teach-In: Students Rising for Jobs and Economic Justice to be part of this movement.

Barbara Ehrenreich was a Co-Founder of Progressives for Obama in 2008. Frances Fox Piven endorsed the organization.[21]

"Progressive" Connections

Elizabeth Warren has close to ties to the New York based non-profit Demos, a formal partner organization of the Institute for Policy Studies (IPS). Warren's daughter, Amelia Warren Tyagi, chairs the Demos Board of Trustees, on which both Barack Obama and Obama's communist former "Green Jobs Czar," Van Jones have served.[22]

Demos 10th Anniversary Honor

On Tuesday, May 11th, 2010, Demos honored TARP Oversight Committee Chair Elizabeth Warren, PBS Host Tavis Smiley and AFL-CIO Secretary-Treasurer Elizabeth Shuler at its 10th Anniversary celebration in New York City.[23]

Stephen Heinz, President of the Rockefeller Brothers Fund, was also an honoree.[24]

Demos Support

Miles Rapoport, President of the "nonpartisan research and advocacy organization Demos," issued the following statement on July 20, 2010, on the upcoming nomination of the inaugural Director of the Consumer Financial Protection Bureau (CFPB):[25]

> "Our country is at a critical turning point. By enacting the Dodd-Frank Wall Street Reform and Consumer Protection Act, Congress has declared the end of the era of deregulation and delinquent government oversight that enabled the financial sector to reap oversized profit at the expense of American households and investors, ultimately caving our weakened economy in on itself. The centerpiece of this landmark legislation is the creation of the Consumer Financial Protection Bureau, a first-of-its-kind federal agency whose sole mission is to shield the

credit and savings of everyday Americans from unfair and deceptive lending practices. However, the fledgling Bureau will only be as strong as its director is effective. We can think of no more qualified public leader than Elizabeth Warren...

In making the case for the establishment of the CFPB—a notion originated by Professor Warren herself—she has become known as a passionate advocate for regular Americans.

"The President should nominate, and the Senate should confirm, Elizabeth Warren as Director of the Consumer Financial Protection Bureau. The appointment of, and a vote for, Professor Warren will be a vote for America's middle class."

Miles Rapoport was a youthful activist with the radical Students for a Democratic Society. He has since been a very close and long-term affiliate of DSA.[26]

"Demos Has Long Been a Vocal Supporter of Elizabeth Warren"

Demos President Miles Rapoport issued a press release in July of 2011, praising her "leadership" in designing the CFPB:[27]

Demos has long been a vocal supporter of Elizabeth Warren and commends her for working tirelessly to set up the CFPB all while defending it from unrelenting and unfounded attacks...

21st Century Democrats Support

Warren was one of 12 key progressives endorsed by DSA and IPS affiliated Political Action Committee 21st Century Democrats in the 2012 election cycle.[28]

Progressive Democrats of America Endorsement

In 2012, Elizabeth Warren, was one of 14 leftist Congressional and Senate candidates endorsed by Progressive Democrats of America (PDA):[29]

Elizabeth Warren...was one of the nine victorious congressional candidates backed by PDA, which favors an 'inside-outside' strategy for change.

Warren with PDA head Tim Carpenter—
once a leader of Orange County DSA (2011)

NNU and PDA

Wrote Michael Lighty, Director of Public Policy, National Nurses United, DSA leader and PDA America Advisory Board member:[30] [31]

The RNs of NNU have found a natural alliance with PDA, who are never slow in the fight against austerity to win prosperity for all. RNs and PDA activists joined in campaigns across the country for insurgent progressives like Elizabeth Warren, now Senator-elect from Massachusetts…

Foreign Policy/National Security

Council for a Livable World Endorsement

Council for a Livable World announced its endorsement of Elizabeth Warren for Senate from Massachusetts on October 20, 2011.

Council President Gary Collins called Warren: "Intelligent, articulate and unwavering in her commitment to strong principles."

Ira Lechner, the Council's Chairman, added, "We are excited to get involved early in a campaign that has impressed voters in Massachusetts and supporters around the country."[32]

council for
A LIVABLE WORLD

JOIN US! REC

Email address

WHO WE ARE   WHAT WE STAND FOR   SUPPORT   MEDIA CEN

Home » Elections » 2012 » candidates » senate   Email   Print

Elizabeth Warren

Party: Democrat
State: Massachusetts
What you need to know: Warren
supports the Kissinger-Schulz-Nunn-
Perry vision of moving toward a world
free of nuclear weapons.

Democrat - Challenger
Endorsed for U.S. Senate by Council for a Livable World

The Massachusetts Senate contest between Democrat Elizabeth Warren and Republican Senator Scott Brown remains where it has been for several months: a toss-up.

A Western New England College poll conducted at the end of May for the Springfield Republican put Elizabeth's

According to the Council for a Livable World's website:[33]

> Elizabeth Warren supports the Kissinger-Shultz-Nunn-Perry vision of moving toward a world free of nuclear weapons. She strongly backs President Obama's goal of securing and retrieving vulnerable nuclear-weapons usable materials worldwide within four years. She opposed the Iraq War and would accelerate the withdrawal of American troops out of Afghanistan. If elected to the Senate, Warren would vote to approve the Comprehensive Nuclear Test Ban Treaty.

The organization raised more than $200,000 to support Elizabeth Warren's successful campaign against Republican Senator Scott Brown.[34]

Council for a Livable World, 50th Anniversary

On June 6, 2012, Council for a Livable World, along with its sister organizations Center for Arms Control and Non-Proliferation and Council for a Livable World's PeacePAC celebrated the 50th Anniversary of their founding by Leo Szilard in 1962.

An evening celebration was held at the Newseum in Washington, D.C. DSA affiliated Congressman Barney Frank acted as the Master of Ceremonies and, in the process, received a lifetime achievement award from DSA supported former Rep. Tom Downey, a member of the Council's Board of Directors. The Robert F. Drinan Peace and Human Award was presented to former Representative and PeacePAC Chairman, David Bonior, a bona fide DSA member.

Videos were shown in which Vice President Joe Biden and Massachusetts Senate candidate Elizabeth Warren celebrated the organization's 50 years, although they were not able to attend.[35] [36]

---

1 KeyWiki, "Elizabeth Warren," KeyWiki, http://keywiki.org/index.php/Elizabeth_Warren (accessed April 19, 2013)

2 Demos, "Elizabeth Warren, TARP Oversight Chair, Among Honorees at Demos 10th Anniversary Celebration," Demos, http://www.demos.org/press.cfm?currentarticleID=830E848E-3FF4-6C82-5502304D7FF28D98 (May 10, 2010)

3 Elizabeth Warren, "About Elizabeth," Senate.gov, http://www.warren.senate.gov/?p=about_senator (accessed April 19, 2013)

4 Elizabeth Warren, "About Elizabeth," Senate.gov, http://www.warren.senate.gov/?p=about_senator (accessed April 19, 2013)

5 Democratic Left, http://www.dsausa.org/dl/Fall_2009.pdf (Fall 2009)

6 Senator Jamie Raskin, "Montgomery County Progressive Alliance › Tomorrow! Elizabeth Warren in Mont County!," Google Groups, https://groups.google.com/forum/?fromgroups#!topic/mcprogressivealliance/X2Inae8JLVQ (April 20, 2012)

7 KeyWiki, "Damon Silvers," KeyWiki, http://www.keywiki.org/index.php/Damon_Silvers (accessed June 5, 2013)

8 KeyWiki, "Elissa McBride," KeyWiki, http://www.keywiki.org/index.php/Elissa_McBride (accessed June 5, 2013)

9 KeyWiki, "Heather Booth," KeyWiki, http://www.keywiki.org/index.php/Heather_Booth (accessed April 20, 2013)

10 KeyWiki, "Americans for Financial Reform," KeyWiki, http://www.keywiki.org/index.php/Americans_for_Financial_Reform (accessed April 20, 2013)

11 The Yankee Radical, http://dsaboston.org/yradical/yr2010-08.pdf, (September/October 2010) p. 2

12 Dave Johnson, "Stopping Banks From Fleecing, Looting, Scamming, Robbing, Swindling, Tricking, Cheating, Conning, and Generally Ripping Us Off," Seeing the Forest blog, http://seeingtheforest.com/tag/elizabeth-warren/, (October 13, 2009)

13 Daryl Rodriguez, "PS, Reminder April 6 Webinar with Elizabeth Warren on the CFPA," Back and Forth, http://darylrodrigues.com/2010/04/04/reminder-april-6-webinar-with-elizabeth-warren-on-the-cfpa/Bicker, (April 4, 2010)

14 OpenSecrets.org, "Fundraising Events—Senator Elizabeth Warren," OpenSecrets.org, http://www.opensecrets.org/politicians/partytime.php?cid=N00033492. (accessed May 17, 2013)

15 KeyWiki, "Paul Booth," KeyWiki, http://www.keywiki.org/index.php/Paul_Booth (accessed May 17, 2013)

16 KeyWiki, "Mike Lux," KeyWiki, http://www.keywiki.org/index.php/Mike_Lux (accessed May 17, 2013)

17 Midwest Academy, "Academy Awards 2012!," Facebook, https://www.facebook.com/media/set/?set=a.10151302762413491.495653.5549354849 0&type=1 (accessed May 17, 2013)

18 KeyWiki, "Roberta Lynch," KeyWiki, http://www.keywiki.org/index.php/Roberta_Lynch (accessed May 17, 2013)

19 KeyWiki, "Julian Bond," KeyWiki, http://www.keywiki.org/index.php/Julian_Bond (accessed May 17, 2013)

20 United Students Against Sweatshops, "National Teach-In: Students Rising for Jobs and Economic Justice," Facebook, https://www.facebook.com/events/266229340078002/ (October 12, 2011)

21 KeyWiki, "Progressives for Obama," KeyWiki, http://www.keywiki.org/index.php/Progressives_for_Obama (accessed April 20, 2013)

22 KeyWiki, "Demos," KeyWiki, http://www.keywiki.org/index.php/Demos (accessed April 20, 2013)

23 Demos, "Elizabeth Warren, TARP Oversight Chair, Among Honorees at Demos 10th Anniversary Celebration," Demos, http://www.demos.org/press.cfm?currentarticleID=830E848E-3FF4-6C82-5502304D7FF28D98 (May 10, 2010)

24 Demos, "Elizabeth Warren, TARP Oversight Chair, Among Honorees at Demos 10th Anniversary Celebration," Demos, http://www.demos.org/press.cfm?currentarticleID=830E848E-3FF4-6C82-5502304D7FF28D98 (May 10, 2010)

25 Demos, "Press Release," CisionWire, http://www.cisionwire.com/demos--a-network-for-ideas-and-action-ltd/r/demos-supports-elizabeth-warren-to-head-new-consumer-protection-bureau,g504196, (July 20, 2010)

26 KeyWiki, "Mile Rapoport," KeyWiki, http://www.keywiki.org/index.php/Miles_Rapoport (accessed April 20, 2013)

27 Miles Rapoport, "Demos President Miles Rapoport Issues Statement In Support of CFPB Director Nominee Richard Cordray; Praises Elizabeth Warren's Leadership," Demos, http://www.demos.org/press-release/demos-president-miles-rapoport-issues-statement-support-cfpb-director-nominee-richard- (July 18, 2011)

28 21st Century Democrats, "Elizabeth Warren," 21st Century Democrats, http://www.21stcenturydems.org/candidates/2012-candidates/elizabeth-warren/#.UPh5d_LvPGg, (accessed April 19, 2013)

29 Cole Stangler, "A People's Inauguration," ITT, http://inthesetimes.com/article/14423/progressive_democrats_hold_a_peoples_inaugur ation, (January 15, 2013)

30 PDA, "Let's Tax Wall Street, Create Jobs, and Save the Social Safety Net," PDA, http://salsa3.salsalabs.com/o/1987/t/0/blastContent.jsp?email_blast_KEY=1233025, (accessed May 17, 2013)

31 KeyWiki, "Michael Lighty," KeyWiki, http://www.keywiki.org/index.php/Michael_Lighty (accessed May 17, 2013)

32 John Isaacs, "Foreign Policy/National Security: Council for a Livable World Endorses Elizabeth Warren for Senate," Council for a Livable World, http://blog.livableworld.org/story/2011/10/20/123320/40, (October 20, 2011)

33 Council for a Livable World, "Democrat – Challenger, Endorsed for U.S. Senate," Council for a Livable World, http://livableworld.org/elections/2012/candidates/senate/ewarren/, (accessed May 17, 2013)

34 Robert Rizzuto, "Council for Livable World directors endorse U.S. Rep. Edward Markey in anticipated Senate run," Massachusetts Live, http://www.masslive.com/politics/index.ssf/2013/01/congressman_ed_markey_lands_a n.html, (January 18, 2013)

35 Center for Arms Control and Non-Proliferation website, "Foreign Policy/National Security: Council for a Livable World 50th Anniversary Celebration," Center for Arms Control and Non-Proliferation website, http://www.masslive.com/politics/index.ssf/2013/01/congressman_ed_markey_lands_a n.html, (accessed May 17, 2013)

36 KeyWiki, "David Bonior," KeyWiki, http://www.keywiki.org/index.php/David_Bonior (accessed May 17, 2013)

Ed Markey (D-MA)

Ed Markey is a Democratic member of the United States Senate, representing Massachusetts. He was elected to the position in June 2013, when the previous Senator John Kerry became U.S. Secretary of State.

While serving in the House of representatives Ed Markey was a long-time member of the Congressional Progressive Caucus.[1] [2]

Background

Ed Markey was born in Malden, Massachusetts, on July 11, 1946. He attended Boston College (B.A., 1968) and Boston College Law School (J.D., 1972). He served in the U.S. Army Reserve and was elected to the Massachusetts State House where he served two terms representing Malden and Melrose, until his election to Congress in 1976.[3]

Influence

From 2007 to 2010, Rep. Markey served as Chairman of the Select Committee on Energy Independence and Global Warming. The Select Committee has held 80 hearings and briefings and contributed to the "advancement of smarter energy and climate policies, including the first increase in fuel economy standards in three decades, which Rep. Markey authored."

During the 111th Congress, Rep. Markey also chaired the Energy and Environment Subcommittee of the House Energy & Commerce Committee. Perhaps the most powerful Subcommittee in the House of

Representatives, it had "unprecedented jurisdiction over national energy and environmental policy." As Chairman, Markey co-authored the Waxman-Markey "American Clean Energy and Security Act," which was approved by the House of Representatives in June 2009.

Gene Karpinski, the President of the League of Conservation Voters of the United States, has said "there is no greater environmental champion in Congress than Ed Markey as we fight to head off the looming catastrophe of climate change." Kevin Knobloch, President of the far left Union of Concerned Scientists, has said that Rep. Markey "is part of an exciting, game-changing leadership in the Congress on climate and energy."

Markey served for 20 years as Chair or Ranking Member of the Subcommittee on Telecommunications and the Internet, where he was the principal author of many of the laws now governing the U.S.'s telephone, broadcasting, cable television and broadband communications systems.

From 2003 to 2009, Rep. Markey also served as a senior member of The House Homeland Security Committee.[4]

"Progressive" Connections

Physicians for Social Responsibility Press Conference

The far left Physicians for Social Responsibility (PSR), Rep. Ed Markey and the Institute for Policy Studies' (IPS) Robert Alvarez, held a joint press conference on April 26, 2011, at the National Press Club in Washington, D.C. on the ongoing impact of the Chernobyl nuclear disaster to public health 25 years after the accident, the continuing nuclear catastrophe in Fukushima, Japan and the lessons for both U.S. public health and safety.

PSR also unveiled a new online interactive Evacuation Zone Map:[5]

> PSR doctors will outline how accidents such as Chernobyl and Fukushima pose a threat to the public's health and the real challenges of implementing evacuation plans in the event of an accident, especially near major metropolitan areas. Speakers will cover the latest findings regarding radiation exposure, the medical response to nuclear reactor accidents, and the implications of Fukushima and Chernobyl for U.S. energy policy.

Progressive Democrats of America

Progressive Democrats of America (PDA) formally voted to endorse Ed Markey in his 2013 U.S. Senate run.[6]

Ed Markey with PDA National Director and former Orange County Democratic Socialists of America leader, Tim Carpenter

PDA organized phone banking teams for Markey:[7]

> Our core phone team has been working hard making calls for the past few weeks, and response has been great. But since Ed showed the sensitivity to suspend campaigning during the days after the tragedy in Boston, we now find ourselves a bit behind on our goal of total voter touches.

> The election is next Tuesday, April 30, so we have no time to waste...

> It's time for us to show solidarity with Ed Markey... The vast majority like what Ed stands for. We just have to make sure they know they have to get out and vote April 30th!

> We regularly put thousands and thousands of calls into targeted endorsed candidates' races. Whether it was Norman Solomon in CA or Alan Grayson in FL, PDA members from all across the country have poured the calls in from out of state to make a real difference.

Thank you, thank you, thank you for anything you can do to bring this win home for all of us.

Solidarity!

Mike "Phone Guy" Fox, National Phone Bank Coordinator

Progressive Round Table

On April 18, 2013, Progressive Democrats of America held a Progressive Round Table in Washington D.C. with staffers Joseph Wender from Rep. Ed Markey's office, Jenny Perrino from Rep. John Conyers' office and Jamie Long from Rep. Keith Ellison's office, who "reported on key legislation and joined them discussing austerity pressure, budget priorities and more."

Also attending were Ethan Rosenkranz from the Project on Defense Alternatives (a project of the Democratic Socialists of America-controlled Commonwealth Institute), Miriam Pemberton from the IPS, Joan Stallard from IPS affiliate CODEPINK and Michael Lighty of PDA, DSA and National Nurses United.[8]

Foreign Policy/National Security

Despite serving on the Homeland Security Committee, Ed Markey has probably done more to undermine U.S. national security than any other serving Congressman.

Grossman Relationship

While serving in the U.S. Army Reserves in the early 1970s, Ed Markey met Steve Grossman, an aspiring politician from a wealthy Massachusetts envelope manufacturing family. "We were always talking about politics," Markey remembers. When Markey announced that he was running for a Congressional seat in 1976, Grossman called to offer his family's support.

Steve Grossman's uncle, Jerome Grossman, was a very influential political power broker and as a long-time Chair of Council for a Livable World, one of the country's leading nuclear disarmament activists.[9]

As Markey had been inspired to work for nuclear disarmament at an early age by the far left Dr. Benjamin Spock, Markey was a good fit for the Grossman operation.[10]

In 1962, Jerome Grossman had been Campaign Manager for the Senate run (against Ted Kennedy) of Independent peace candidate Harvard Prof. H. Stuart Hughes, Chair of the Committee for a SANE Nuclear Policy. This campaign was supported by the Socialist Party USA, to which both Grossman and Hughes were very close. Jerome Grossman claimed that the Hughes campaign set up a political structure that later elected "progressive" Congressmen and Senators such as Markey, Gerry Studds, Barney Frank and John Kerry, which made Massachusetts an almost impregnable Democratic stronghold.[11]

Ed Markey worked very closely with SANE in the 1970s and 80s, despite it being heavily infiltrated by the Communist Party, the Socialist Party and later, Democratic Socialists of America.[12]

The "Freeze" Movement

During the 1979 SALT II debate, Oregon's far left Republican Senator Mark Hatfield, a long-time IPS affiliate, introduced an amendment that called for a "strategic weapons freeze," which helped provide the impetus for the popular Nuclear Weapons Freeze Campaign.

On March 10, 1982, Hatfield and Kennedy joined House proponents of the freeze, including Rep. Markey, to introduce a "sense of Congress" resolution based directly on a widely disseminated document, "Call to Halt the Nuclear Arms Race," developed by Randall Forsberg, a Massachusetts Institute of Technology defense policy expert who would later join the Board of Directors of the far left Arms Control Association. With the backing of Hatfield and Kennedy, the effort gained "broad-based popular and expert support, national attention and increasing political momentum."

Like Barack Obama, Forsberg was later active in the New Party, a creation of the Institute for Policy Studies and Democratic Socialists of America.[13]

She was also honored by Boston Democratic Socialists of America at their May 1984, Debs-Thomas-Bernstein Award Dinner.[14]

In July 1985, Soviet leader Mikhail Gorbachev announced that the Soviet Union would cease nuclear tests and would not test "until and unless" the United States began testing. The Reagan Administration refused to take the bait. In October 1986, a bipartisan group of 63 House and Senate members, led by Hatfield, far left Senator Alan Cranston (D-CA) and IPS affiliate, Rep. Les Aspin (D-WI), sent a letter to President

Reagan urging him to reciprocate and call off the next scheduled test in Nevada, code-named Glencoe.

Cranston and Hatfield also introduced legislation seeking to bar expenditure to carry out U.S. nuclear tests, if the Soviet Union was not testing. Their initiative failed, but it would get another chance.[15]

Until March 1983, the anti-nuclear movement was focusing mainly on the INF missiles for Europe and the MX missiles for the United States. When President Reagan announced the Strategic Defense Initiative program, "Star Wars," the far left Union of Concerned Scientists and the Federation of American Scientists launched a campaign against the project, calling the "immensely costly project scientifically unworkable and strategically unsound."

The Freeze Campaign wanted to block Star Wars and ban all nuclear weapons. By 1984, the freeze organization was calling itself "Freeze Voter '84."

Freeze Voter '84 was partially successful. It raised almost $1.5 million for the 1984 elections. Out of eight Senate candidates whom it supported, four won. Out of the 37 House candidates it supported, 24 won. But unfortunately for the Freeze Campaigners, and fortunately for the Free World, Ronald Reagan was re-elected.

In 1986, the Freeze Campaign merged with SANE.

Although the freeze movement was the most prominent American political campaign of the eighties, it was supported by older existing groups such as the Socialist Party-led War Resisters League, SANE and the Council for a Livable World.[16]

Public "Wants Test Ban"

On April 17, 1986, SANE said a poll it commissioned with Opinion Research Corp. showed that " 60percent of U.S. citizens believe the United States should halt nuclear weapons testing as long as the Soviet Union stops its tests".

"The poll shows beyond a doubt that the vast majority of Americans want President Reagan to stop nuclear testing, especially before any second summit meeting," said David Cortright, Executive Director of the group.

The poll results were announced as several members of Congress pushed for House consideration of an amendment to cut off money for nuclear weapons testing.

"What we're trying to do is break the administration's testing habit— cold turkey," Rep. Ed Markey said at a news conference with officials from SANE.

Markey said he and Reps. Patricia Schroeder, (D-CO) and Tom Downey, (D-NY), had planned to offer their amendment cutting off nuclear test funds, but were "denied by a parliamentary maneuver."

According to SANE, governors or legislatures in five states—Washington, New York, Hawaii, Ohio and Rhode Island—had adopted test ban resolutions.[17]

Tribute to Randall Forsberg

Ed Markey placed a tribute in the Congressional Record on October 23, 2007, to mark the death of "Nuclear Freeze" activist Randall Forsberg:[18]

> Madam Speaker, it is with great sadness that I rise to mark the passing of my friend Randall Forsberg, but it is with pride, admiration, and thankfulness that I remember her enormous contributions to the cause of nuclear disarmament.
>
> Randy Forsberg was the mother of the Nuclear Freeze movement. When she was a doctoral candidate at the Massachusetts Institute of Technology in 1980, she put forward a simple and inspired proposal: to end the "testing, production, and deployment" of all nuclear weapons everywhere. With her "Call to Halt the Nuclear Arms Race," and her tireless advocacy for a nuclear weapons freeze, Randy galvanized a national grassroots campaign to end the threat of nuclear weapons.
>
> I was proud to introduce the very first nuclear freeze resolution in the Congress, and to work for its successful passage on the House floor in the spring of 1983. That vote shocked many within the dusty confines of the foreign policy establishment, who simply could not comprehend that ordinary citizens understood the unique and intolerable threat of nuclear weapons and that the American public would demand a fundamentally different course be set.

Effects of the "Freeze" Movement

"What the freeze movement did in the United States, like the Greens in Europe, was to bring nuclear strategy out of the elite foreign policy salons and move it to the grassroots," said Representative Ed Markey, a leader of the Freeze Campaign. "Public education led to public activism and public activism has seriously constrained decision-makers' options over the last six or seven years."

"It was the movement, combined with the rise of Mikhail Gorbachev in the Soviet Union that created an irreversible momentum toward reduction of nuclear weapons on both sides."[19]

Markey Attempts to Revive the "Freeze"

After 9/11, Rep. Markey and a group of "veteran anti-nuclear activists" sought to revive the movement for a nuclear freeze—to "reinvigorate a worldwide campaign against the use and proliferation of nuclear weapons."

In a news conference on June 11, 2002, Markey urged President Bush to renounce proposals that the U.S. adjust its strategic doctrine to allow the first use of nuclear weapons and said the United States should agree to a permanent end to the testing of nuclear warheads.

Markey introduced a joint resolution that called for an end to the development, testing and production of nuclear weapons and the ratification of the Comprehensive Test Ban Treaty.

SANE Reincarnated

Rep. Markey introduced House Bill 7394, entitled "The Smarter Approaches to Nuclear Expenditures (SANE) Act of 2012," in the House of Representatives in February 2012. He was joined by 34 co-sponsors. Numerous organizations around the country signed on in support of the legislation as it was being prepared.

Markey's bill called for a dramatic reduction in the number of delivery vehicles for nuclear weapons, for the termination of the B61 and W78 Life Extension Programs and the termination of the Uranium Processing Facility at Oak Ridge, as well as the CMRR-NF in Los Alamos and the MOX plant at Savannah River.[20]

Former SANE Director David Cortright wrote in his self-named blog on March 7, 2012:[21]

> I was delighted in early February to see that Representative Ed Markey has introduced a new bill in Congress, the SANE (Smarter Approach to Nuclear Expenditures) Act. Markey's bill calls for significant reductions in nuclear weapons, for a savings of about $100 billion over the next 10 years. Markey remains, as he has been for more than 30 years, the most significant leader and articulate voice in Congress for nuclear arms reduction. I'm glad to see he is still at it.
>
> As the former executive director of SANE, I was thrilled to see renewed reference to the venerable SANE brand. When I was with

SANE in the 1980s we worked closely with Markey. I continued to cooperate with him on disarmament initiatives after that—including the Urgent Call, a nuclear abolition appeal launched in 2002 with Jonathan Schell and Randy Forsberg.

When I contacted Markey's office recently to congratulate him for introducing the SANE Act and making reference to our organization, his staff said the SANE acronym was intentional, to recall the halcyon days of the 1980s when the Nuclear Weapons Freeze Campaign was sweeping across the country like a populist prairie fire and SANE was growing rapidly into a formidable mass membership organization.

Peace Action Endorsement

SANE—now known as Peace Action and still thoroughly infiltrated by the Communist Party and DSA, endorsed Ed Markey in his 2013 Senate race:[22]

Ed Markey is a key leader in Congress on nuclear disarmament, nuclear power and climate change. He opposes the Afghanistan war and favors reducing military spending to fund social needs.

Markey has worked for nuclear disarmament for decades. Markey's Smarter Approach to Nuclear Expenditures (SANE) Act, named for Peace Action's predecessor organization, would cut $100 billion in nuclear weapons spending from the Federal budget. He is a constant critic of the Nuclear Regulatory Commission's lax oversight of nuclear power plant safety and was joint sponsor of the Waxman-Markey climate change bill.

Markey has voted repeatedly against funding for the Afghanistan war and against the defense authorization and appropriation bills. He is a member of the Congressional Progressive Caucus, voted for its Budget for All progressive budget amendment in 2011, and supported the Budget for All non-binding question which the voters of 91 Massachusetts cities and towns passed by an average 3 to 1 margin in.

Peace Action "Ally"

A 2013 Peace Action email blast signed by Paul Kawika Martin, described Ed Markey as a Peace Action ally:[23]

On April 30th, there will be a special election to fill the Senate vacancy left by the now Secretary of State, John Kerry. Please help Peace Action ally, Rep. Ed Markey, become the next Senator of Massachusetts.

Rep. Ed Markey is a key leader in Congress on abolishing nuclear weapons. He is the U.S. co-president of Parliamentarians for Nuclear Non-proliferation and Disarmament, and his "SANE Act," named for Peace Action's predecessor organization, calls for cuts in spending on nuclear bomb production facilities, nuclear-armed bombers and submarines, the end of U.S. bombers' nuclear mission, and reduction in number of deployed weapons.

You can send Markey to the Senate now. With your support, Markey can become a Senator with more power to enact your, and Peace Action's, values.

Council for a Livable World Endorses Markey

Ed Markey landed another endorsement in January of 2013, as his old friend Jerome Grossman's Council for a Livable World, gave him a "nod of support" for his bid to become a U.S. Senator.

"As a Bay Stater, I'm proud to have voted to endorse Rep. Markey's candidacy for the Senate," said Priscilla McMillan, an "expert on U.S.-Russia relations" and one of the group's board members. "Markey's courage and far-sightedness in nearly four decades of public service leading the effort for greater control of nuclear weapons and better protection of the environment make him the perfect successor to Senator Kerry."

The organization said that it raised more than $200,000 to support Democratic U.S. Sen. Elizabeth Warren's successful campaign against ex-Republican Senator Scott Brown, and that it "will throw its financial weight behind Markey."[24]

---

1 KeyWiki, "Edward Markey," KeyWiki, http://keywiki.org/index.php/Ed_Markey (accessed May 17, 2013)

2 Congressional Progressive Caucus, "Caucus Members," Congressional Progressive Caucus, http://cpc.grijalva.house.gov/caucus-members/ (accessed May 17, 2013)

3 Ed Markey, "About Ed," House.gov, http://markey.house.gov/about-ed (accessed August 11, 2011)

4 Ed Markey, "About Ed," House.gov, http://markey.house.gov/about-ed (accessed August 11, 2011)

5 Democratic Underground, "Press Conference Tuesday by Ed Markey, Robert Alvarez, and Physicians for Social Responsibility," Democratic Underground, http://www.democraticunderground.com/discuss/duboard.php?az=view_all&address=1 15x290710, (April 26, 2011)

6 KeyWiki, "Progressive Democrats of America," KeyWiki, http://www.keywiki.org/index.php/Progressive_Democrats_of_America (accessed May 17, 2013)

7 Mike Fox, "Get on the Phones to Secure Victory for Ed Markey!," PDA, http://salsa3.salsalabs.com/o/1987/t/0/blastContent.jsp?email_blast_KEY=1245334, (accessed May 17, 2013)

8 PDA, "Help PDA Continue Our Momentum!," PDA, http://salsa3.salsalabs.com/o/1987/t/0/blastContent.jsp?email_blast_KEY=1244812, (accessed May 17, 2013)

9 Seth Gitell, "Is Grossman our next governor?," The Boston Phoenix, http://www.bostonphoenix.com/archive/features/00/03/16/TALKING_POLITICS.html , (March 16-23, 2000)

10 The Quarterly Newsletter of Peace Action and the Peace Action Education Fund (Winter 2007) vol. 46, no. 3

11 Jerome Grossman, "Ted Kennedy: His First Election," The Relentless Liberal Blog, http://www.articlealley.com/article_811556_13.html (February 16, 2009)

12 KeyWiki, "SANE," KeyWiki, http://www.keywiki.org/index.php/SANE (accessed May 17, 2013)

13 KeyWiki, "New Party," KeyWiki, http://www.keywiki.org/index.php/New_Party (accessed May 17, 2013)

14 The Yankee Radical (May 1984) p. 1

15 Daryl G. Kimball, "ACA in Memoriam: Mark O. Hatfield (1922-2011)," ArmsControl.org, http://www.armscontrol.org/2011_09/In_Memoriam_Mark_Hatfield, (accessed May 17, 2013)

16 Russian Peace and Democracy, "The Surge of the Eighties," Russian Peace and Democracy, http://russianpeaceanddemocracy.com/the-surge-of-the-eighties (1996)

17 Jill Lawrence, "Anti-Nuclear Group Maintains Public Wants Test Ban," AP, www.apnewsarchive.com/1986/Anti-Nuclear-Group-Maintains-Public-Wants-Test-Ban/id-970cef7c8daddae8c79ce066e96ba9d6, (April 17, 1986)

18 KeyWiki, "Edward Markey," KeyWiki, http://keywiki.org/index.php/Ed_Markey (accessed May 17, 2013)

19 Robert Pear, "Washington Talk; Diplomacy," The New York Times, http://www.nytimes.com/1989/06/05/us/washington-talk-diplomacy.html, (June 5, 1989)

20 Ed Markey, "Markey Calls for Cuts to U.S. Nuclear Weapons Budget," House.gov, http://markey.house.gov/press-release/markey-calls-cuts-us-nuclear-weapons-budget, (February 8, 2012)

21 David Cortright, "SANE is Back," David Cortright, http://davidcortright.net/2012/03/07/sane-is-back/ (March 7, 2012)

22 Massachusetts Peace Action, "Ed Markey for Senate!," Massachusetts Peace Action, http://masspeaceaction.org/2542 (March 11, 2013)

23 Peace Action, Email Blast, http://org.salsalabs.com/o/161/t/0/blastContent.jsp?email_blast_KEY=1273074 (accessed May 17, 2013)

24 Robert Rizzuto, "Council for Livable World directors endorse U.S. Rep. Edward Markey in anticipated Senate run," The Republican, http://www.masslive.com/politics/index.ssf/2013/01/congressman_ed_markey_lands_a n.html, (January 18, 2013)

Mike Capuano
(D-MA)

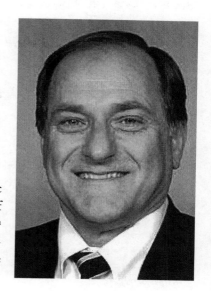

Michael Capuano is a Democratic member of the United States House of Representatives, representing the 7th Congressional District of Massachusetts. He is an active member of the Congressional Progressive Caucus.

Background

Michael "Mike" Everett Capuano was born in Somerville, Massachusetts in 1952.

Capuano graduated from Somerville High School, received a Bachelor of Arts Degree from Dartmouth College in 1973 and a law degree from Boston College Law School in 1977. He passed the Massachusetts Bar in 1977.[1]

Prior to serving in Congress, Capuano was the Mayor of Somerville, Massachusetts from 1990 through 1998.

Michael Capuano is serving his eighth term as a Representative in Congress for Massachusetts' 7th District, which includes Cambridge, Chelsea, Somerville and approximately 75% of Boston.

He has also campaigned to become a United States Senator for Massachusetts.[2]

Influence

On the local level, Capuano serves as Massachusetts' member of the Committee on Transportation and Infrastructure. Through his efforts, Massachusetts received more than $5 billion over six years.

He is a member of the House Committee on Transportation and Infrastructure and the House Committee on Financial Services. In 2006,

Capuano was appointed to head the Transition Team by then Democratic Leader Nancy Pelosi as Democrats prepared for a majority role in the 110th Congress. In 2007, Speaker Pelosi appointed him to Chair the Special Task Force on Ethics Enforcement.[3]

In 2011, Capuano fired up a group of union members in Boston with a speech urging them to work down in the trenches to fend off limits to workers' rights like those proposed in Wisconsin:

> I'm proud to be here with people who understand that it's more than just sending an email to get you going. Every once and awhile you need to get out on the streets and get a little bloody when necessary.[4]

Socialist Connections

DSA Greetings

In 2002, Boston Democratic Socialists of America (DSA) held their 24th annual Debs-Thomas Bernstein awards. Capuano sent greetings to the 25th annual dinner in 2002—as did fellow Congressman James McGovern and Senator John Kerry.[5]

Socialized Health Care

In 2004, DSA supporting Congressman Barney Frank was one of the sponsors of House Concurrent Resolution 99 (H. Con Res. 99), directing Congress to enact legislation by October of 2004 that provided access to comprehensive health care for all Americans. Mike Capuano sponsored the legislation, as did several DSA connected Representatives, including John Conyers, Jan Schakowsky, John Tierney, David Bonior, Dennis Kucinich, Maurice Hinchey, Jerry Nadler and John Lewis.[6]

In December 2005, Mike Capuano became a co-sponsor to John Conyers' "single payer" socialized health care bill HR 676.[7]

"Progressive" Connection

Progressive Democrats of America Support

In 2009, Mike Capuano was endorsed by Progressive Democrats of America, during his unsuccessful run for the U.S. Senate.

"Members of the Progressive Democrats of America feel that Mike's strong progressive record as a Member of Congress and his forthright, commonsense positions on a range of critical issues from support for single payer to his vote against the resolution authorizing the use of force in Iraq set him apart from the other candidates," said National Executive Director Tim Carpenter... "There is tremendous enthusiasm for Mike's candidacy."

"I appreciate the endorsement of the Progressive Democrats of America," stated Congressman Capuano. "It is an honor to receive recognition for my steadfast commitment to progressive principles and for my efforts to advance the important issues of our time, from ending the wars and bringing our men and women in uniform home, to fighting for real health care reform."[8]

Capuano (left), DSA and PDA leader Michael Lighty, (April) 2013

Foreign Policy/National Security

Cuban Trip

In 2001, Michelle Mancini from the office of Congressman Michael Capuano spent seven days in Havana, Cuba, for the purpose of "meeting with officials and discussing embargo and human rights." The trip cost $1,923.32 and was paid for by the leftist Christopher Reynolds Foundation.[9]

1 KeyWiki, "Mike Capuano," KeyWiki, http://keywiki.org/index.php/Mike_Capuano (accessed April 24, 2012)
2 KeyWiki, "Mike Capuano," KeyWiki, http://keywiki.org/index.php/Mike_Capuano (accessed April 24, 2012)
3 KeyWiki, "Mike Capuano," KeyWiki, http://keywiki.org/index.php/Mike_Capuano (accessed April 24, 2012)
4 Michael O'Brian, "Democrat urges unions to 'get a little bloody when necessary,'" The Hill, http://thehill.com/blogs/blog-briefing-room/news/145627-dem-lawmaker-on-labor-protests-get-a-little-bloody-when-necessary (accessed April 24, 2012)
5 The Yankee Radical, http://www.dsaboston.org/yradical/yr2002-09.pdf (September/October 2002) (accessed April 24, 2012)
6 Democratic Left, http://www.dsausa.org/dl/Summer_2002.pdf (Summer 2002) (accessed April 24, 2012)
7 People's World, http://www.peoplesworld.org/this-week-in-labor-12623/ (December 3, 2005) (accessed January 20, 2013)
8 SomervilleNews, "The Progressive Democrats of America Endorse Michael Capuano for Senate," SomervilleNews, http://somervillenews.1upprelaunch.com/main.asp?SectionID=15&SubSectionID=15&ArticleID=2448&TM=63826.12 (November 9, 2009)
9 American Radio Works, "Christopher Reynolds Foundation," American Public Media, http://americanradioworks.publicradio.org/features/staffers/travdat/sponsor.php?sponsor_id=T000109 (accessed April 24, 2012)

Jim McGovern (D-MA)

Jim McGovern is a Democratic member of the United States House of Representatives, representing the 2nd District of Massachusetts.

He is an active member of the Congressional Progressive Caucus.

Background

James (Jim) McGovern was born on November 20, 1959 in Worcester, Massachusetts. He earned a Master's of Public Administration Degree at American University in Washington, D.C.[1]

Jim McGovern has been a Representative since 1997.

McGovern was previously a staff member for leftist Senator George McGovern of South Dakota (no relation) and for equally radical Representative Joe Moakley of Massachusetts.[2]

Influence

Rep. McGovern is the Vice Chairman of the powerful House Rules Committee, which sets the terms for debate and amendments on most legislation and he is a member of the House Budget Committee.

McGovern is also Co-Chair of both the Tom Lantos Human Rights Commission and the House Hunger Caucus.[3]

Socialist Connections

Greeting Socialists

In 2001, Boston Democratic Socialists of America (DSA) honored Dessima Williams, a member of the Communist Party USA splinter group, Committees of Correspondence, at their 24th annual Debs-Thomas-Bernstein awards:[4]

> Dessima Williams recounted how as a young graduate student in the U.S. in 1979 she suddenly found herself appointed UN Ambassador from Grenada's new revolutionary government...

> Thanks to all who helped make this event a success, including Kathy Casavant of the AFL-CIO, Harris Gruman of Boston DSA, and civic activist Eleanor LeCain for their eloquent introductions of the awardees... and Congressman Jim McGovern, who again sent his greetings.

McGovern also sent greetings to the 25th annual dinner in 2002—as did fellow Congressman Michael Capuano and Senator John Kerry:[5]

> Thanks to everyone who helped make this evening a success, including Barbara Ackerman of MASS-CARE, Jim St. George of TEAM, and longtime DSAers Fran and Jake Schlitt for their eloquent introductions... and Congressmen Mike Capuano and Jim McGovern, Senator John Kerry, and last year's awardee Dessima Williams, who sent greetings.

Part of Democratic Socialists of America's "5 Year Plan"

According to Boston DSA's magazine, The Yankee Radical, January 2001:[6]

> Three years of hard work for the Working Family Agenda coalition (which includes DSA) came to a head in this year's election. In February we found a progressive candidate, Jim Leary, to take on Bill McManus, the worst of Worcester's conservative State Reps. McManus, who had the worst voting record of any Democrat in the State House, served in the leadership team of House Speaker Finneran, and was a supporter of Republican Governor Cellucci, knew we could beat him in a primary, so he switched from Democrat to Independent to garner the Republican and centrist votes of a presidential election while holding on to his Democratic hacks.

446

So Neighbor to Neighbor, the AFL-CIO, the Teachers Association, and the Commonwealth Coalition fielded an army (all DSA led). For the primary we had a voter universe of 6000 likely voters, who we contacted three times each (at their door, by phone, and by mail). Our July poll showed the opponent ahead of us by 14 points, mostly due to name recognition. On primary day, September 19th, we beat him 62 to 38%!

For the general election we had a voter universe of 16,000 presidential voters. Again we contacted them all three times before the election, and all our ID'd voters six times between Saturday and election day (over 150 people worked for Leary on election day). At 8:30 p.m., precinct captains began calling in results, and we won 71 to 29%—possibly the largest margin of victory against a leadership incumbent in the state's history!

The progressive resurgence in Worcester began with the victory of Congressman Jim McGovern in 1996, and seems to be building to a progressive bid for Mayor in 2001. Not a bad five-year plan..!

These three forces were present in almost equal measure in Northeast Worcester: Great Brook Valley and Lincoln Village housing projects (2500 voters), the unions (2500 members), and the progressive middleclass Irish-American community (that produced candidates like Jim McGovern and Jim Leary). Together a coalition like this is unstoppable, and it shows that the Working Family Agenda strategy can become the majoritarian movement we need to win progressive power.

The article was written by Harris Gruman—Chair of Boston DSA and Campaigns Director for Neighbor to Neighbor.[7]

Working with Socialists to End the Iraq War

In the Fall of 2008, Shelagh Foreman, Angela Kelly and DSA member John Maher, of Massachusetts Peace Action, went to ask Congressman Jim McGovern the question, "What the hell does it take to get us out of Iraq?"

McGovern used the opportunity to advise Peace Action, how they could build public pressure, in order to help give the Democrats a public mandate to pull U.S. troops out of Iraq.

According to Maher, writing in the November 2008 edition of Boston DSA's The Yankee Radical:

"We have some problems," Jim said. "For one thing when we argue for withdrawal the other side accuses us of abandoning the Iraqis to a bloodbath and the Middle East to chaos. We don't have an answer for this. We don't have a plan for withdrawal. We seem irresponsible. Worse, we are irresponsible." "So what can be done about that?" we asked. "You guys can organize a conference of Middle East experts to make a responsible plan for withdrawal, one that focuses on the non-military issues that need to be addressed. Have it at Harvard so people will take it seriously. Publish a report. We'll help you put on a big press event and I'll distribute it to Congress. We'll make how to withdraw an issue that Congress and the public have to deal with."

Within a week the activists had recruited DSA member Charles Knight of the Project on Defense Alternatives at the DSA-controlled Commonwealth Institute and Chris Toensing, Editor of Middle East Report, to make up a task force with the skills and contacts to get the job done.[8]

The trio then recruited 14 Middle East experts and charged them with answering this question:

> The President has announced that a complete military withdrawal from Iraq will take place over the next 12 to 18 months. What concrete steps can the U.S. government take, immediately and during withdrawal, to encourage peace and stability in Iraq?

Harvard University's Weatherhead Center for International Affairs hosted the round table in March of 2008. Chris Toensing drafted the report. "Quickly, Carefully, and Generously: The Necessary Steps for a Responsible Withdrawal from Iraq," was released at a call-in press conference in June. That same day, Representatives Jim McGovern, Bill Delahunt and John Tierney distributed the report to all members of the House and Senate accompanied by a "Dear Colleague" letter.

Medicare for All

According to Boston DSA leader Rand Wilson, in September of 2005, Congressmen John Tierney and Maurice Hinchey heard testimony in Boston in support of a "Medicare for All" solution to the health care crisis. Lobbyists at the meeting included members of DSA and there ally Sandy Eaton of Committees of Correspondence for Democracy and Socialism:

> The growing severity of this crisis brought together over 40 grassroots organizations for an impressive—and unusual—showing of political unity for health care reform based on extending Medicare to everyone.

According to Wilson, Representatives Barney Frank, Jim McGovern, John Olver and John Tierney were sponsoring legislation in the House, John Conyers' HR 676 that would implement this approach.[9]

"Progressive" Connections

Progressive Democrats of America

Jim McGovern serves on the Advisory Board of Progressive Democrats of America PDA), an organization heavily influenced by DSA and the far left Institute for Policy Studies (IPS).[10]

One time Orange County DSA leader, and Progressive Democrats of America Director Tim Carpenter, claimed that PDA had chalked up several achievements in its short life, successfully promoting initiatives by PDA board members John Conyers and James McGovern."[11]

PDA's Tim Carpenter interviews Jim McGovern during a PDA Progressive Central event at the DNC, Denver (Sept. 2008)

Progressive Democrats of America, 2012 Endorsement

In 2012, Jim McGovern was one of 14 leftist Congressional and Senate candidates endorsed by Progressive Democrats of America.[12]

The Peoples' Inauguration

Progressive Central—The Peoples' Inauguration, a conference to mark President Obama's inauguration, was held January 19, 2013, at the UDC David A. Clarke School of Law in the 5th Floor Moot Court Room at 4340 Connecticut Avenue NW, Washington, D.C.

The event was sponsored by Progressive Democrats of America, The Nation, National Nurses United and Democrats.com. The event was advertised and promoted by the IPS.

The 11:15 am-12:30 pm session, "What will the Progressive Agenda be in 2013?," was moderated by Wisconsin socialist activist and journalist

John Nichols and featured Rep. Jim McGovern, Rep. John Conyers, Andrea Miller of the PDA National Team and Randy Parraz, Citizens for a Better Arizona.[13]

Foreign Policy/National Security

Council for a Livable World

The far left, anti-U.S. military Council for a Livable World supported Jim McGovern in his successful House of Representatives run as a candidate for the state of Massachusetts.[14]

The Council has also supported McGovern in his 2010 Congressional election campaign.[15]

When endorsing McGovern in 2010, the Council praised McGovern's work as a Congressional aide, in getting U.S. aid cut to anti-communist forces in El Salvador and his opposition to the wars in Iraq and Afghanistan:[16]

> As a congressional aide, McGovern earned recognition for his tireless efforts to end U.S. support for oppressive right-wing regimes in Central America. In 1989, McGovern was the lead investigator on the investigation into the murders of 6 Jesuit priests, their housekeeper and her daughter in 1989. The investigation ultimately led to a cut off in U.S. aid when the Salvadoran military was implicated in the murders.

> McGovern was a vocal opponent of the invasion of Iraq and a leader in attempts to bring U.S. troops home. In February 2007, he sponsored legislation to withdraw troops from Iraq on a 6-month timeline. It was the toughest anti-war legislation to reach the House floor, where it was defeated by a surprisingly narrow 74-vote margin.

> McGovern has been a leading critic of the escalation of American troops in Afghanistan. He is a sponsor of bipartisan legislation calling for a flexible timetable for withdrawal of U.S. troops.

Drinan Award

The Father Robert F. Drinan National Peace and Human Rights Award was established in 2006. It is named after far left former Massachusetts Congressman and Jesuit priest, Fr. Robert Drinan. The award is annually presented by the Center for Arms Control and Non-Proliferation and

Council for a Livable World to individuals who "exemplify the late Father Drinan's commitment to peace and human justice."

2010 awardees were Rep. Jim McGovern and United Auto Workers President Bob King, a Democratic Socialists of America supporter.[17] [18]

Cuba Trip

In December of 2006, a Congressional delegation of ten Congressmen and women from the United States House of Representatives visited Havana, Cuba. Leading the delegation were Jeff Flake and Bill Delahunt. The other participants were Hilda Solis, Jo Ann Emerson, Jerry Moran, Michael Conaway, Jane Harman, Lincoln Davis, Gregory Meeks and Jim McGovern.

The delegation met with Cuban Foreign Minister, Felipe Perez Roque and other communist officials. The delegation asked to meet with Raul Castro during their weekend visit to Cuba, but there was no word on whether such a meeting took place.[19]

Campaigning to Remove Cuba from "Terrorism Sponsors" List

At the National Press Club in Washington, D.C., a consortium of organizations announced a new push to get Cuba taken off the State Department's "State Sponsors of Terrorism" list in early March 2013.

The event, in the form of a panel discussion, was sponsored by the Institute for Policy Studies founded Center for International Policy and the IPS "partner" Washington Office on Latin America (WOLA).

The MC was Wayne Smith, Senior Fellow at the Center for International Policy, who was the head of the U.S. Interests Section (instead of embassy) in Havana from 1979 to 1982, having been appointed by Jimmy Carter. Other participants were Rep. McGovern, former Ambassador Anthony Quainton who is now "Diplomat in Residence" at American University, Robert Muse of Muse and Associates and Adam Isacson of WOLA.

Congressman McGovern, who "has followed U.S. Cuba policy closely," had just returned from a visit to Cuba with a bipartisan delegation headed by Senator Patrick Leahy of Vermont.

There McGovern had participated in a two hour meeting with Cuban President Raul Castro. He and the other speakers pushed for an overall change in U.S.-Cuba policy, of which removal of Cuba from the State Sponsors of Terrorism would be a "useful first step."[20]

451

1 Jim McGovern, "Jim McGovern Biography," Jim McGovern Campaign Website, http://jimmcgovern.com/about/ (accessed April 20, 2012)
2 Jim McGovern, "Jim McGovern Biography," Jim McGovern Campaign Website, http://jimmcgovern.com/about/ (accessed April 20, 2012)
3 Jim McGovern, "Jim McGovern Biography," Jim McGovern Campaign Website, http://jimmcgovern.com/about/ (accessed April 20, 2012)
4 The Yankee Radical, http://www.dsaboston.org/yradical/yr2001-08.pdf (August 2001) (accessed April 20, 2012)
5 The Yankee Radical, http://www.dsaboston.org/yradical/yr2002-09.pdf (September/October 2002) (accessed April 20, 2012)
6 The Yankee Radical, http://www.dsaboston.org/yradical/yr2001-01.pdf (January 2001) (accessed April 20, 2012)
7 KeyWiki, "Harris Gruman," KeyWiki, http://www.keywiki.org/index.php/Harris_Gruman (accessed June 1, 2013)
8 The Yankee Radical, http://www.dsaboston.org/yradical/yr2008-11.pdf (November 2008) (accessed April 20, 2012)
9 The Yankee Radical, http://www.dsaboston.org/yradical/yr2005-11.pdf (November 2005) (accessed April 20, 2012)
10 KeyWiki, "Jim McGovern," KeyWiki, http://keywiki.org/index.php/Jim_McGovern (accessed April 20, 2012)
11 KeyWiki, "Jim McGovern," KeyWiki, http://keywiki.org/index.php/Jim_McGovern (accessed April 20, 2012)
12 KeyWiki, "Jim McGovern," KeyWiki, http://keywiki.org/index.php/Jim_McGovern (accessed January 23, 2013)
13 PDA Website (accessed January 23, 2013)
14 Council for a Livable World, "Meet the Candidates," Council for a Livable World, http://livableworld.org/support/meet_candidates/ (accessed April 20, 2012)
15 Council for a Livable World, "Meet the Candidates," Council for a Livable World, http://livableworld.org/support/meet_candidates/ (accessed April 20, 2012)
16 Council for a Livable World, "Meet the Candidates," Council for a Livable World, http://livableworld.org/support/meet_candidates/ (accessed April 20, 2012)
17 The Center for Arms Control and Non-Proliferation, "Council Center 50th Anniversary," The Center for Arms Control and Non-Proliferation, http://armscontrolcenter.org/issues/recent/council_center_50th_anniversary/, (accessed June 1, 2013)
18 KeyWiki, "Bob King," KeyWiki, http://www.keywiki.org/index.php/Bob_King (accessed June1, 2013)
19 Anita Snow, "Fidel Castro and US Congressional trip to Cuba update," Havana Journal, http://havanajournal.com/politics/entry/fidel-castro-and-us-congressional-trip-to-cuba-update/ (accessed April 20, 2012)
20 Emile Schepers, "Groups fight to remove Cuba from "terrorism sponsors" list," People's World (March 11, 2013)

John Tierney (D-MA)

John Tierney is a Democratic member of the United States House of Representatives, representing the 6th District of Massachusetts. He is a member of the Congressional Progressive Caucus.[1]

Background

Born in Salem, Massachusetts, Congressman Tierney attended Salem Public Schools and graduated from Salem State College. He earned a law degree from Suffolk University and until he took office in January 1997, was a partner in the law firm Tierney, Kalis and Lucas for over 20 years.[2]

Influence

Rep. Tierney serves on the Committee on Education and the Workforce, serving on the Subcommittee on Higher Education, Lifelong Learning and Competitiveness and the Subcommittee on Health, Employment, Labor and Pensions in the 113th Congress. His "hard work and commitment" to ensuring the Legislative Branch conducts vigorous oversight, has earned Congressman Tierney the Chairmanship of the National Security and Foreign Affairs Subcommittee on the Committee on Oversight and Government Reform from 2007 through 2010 and a Speaker-appointed seat on the House Permanent Select Committee on Intelligence.

Chairman Tierney "undertook a variety of investigations to ensure that our national security policy prioritizes a robust military and an intelligence capability focused on 21st century threats, meaningful diplomatic

TREVOR LOUDON: THE ENEMIES WITHIN

initiatives, serious attention to nuclear non-proliferation efforts and a defense budget that efficiently uses taxpayer dollars."[3]

Socialist Connections

DSA Support in 1996

In 1996, Democratic Socialists of America (DSA) sent six staff members into the field for the final weeks of that year's election campaign.

These staff and DSA volunteers "contributed to the reelection of Senator Paul Wellstone, Congressman Maurice Hinchey (D-NY) and aided in the narrow victory of pro-labor John Tierney (D-MA) over "moderate" Republican Pete Torkildsen in Massachusetts."

> termed Abercrombie "a hippie leftist."
> DSA sent six staff members into the field for the final weeks of the campaign. These staff and DSA volunteers contributed to the re-election of Senator Paul Wellstone, Congressperson Maurice Hinchey (D-upstate NY) and aided in the narrow victory of pro-labor John Tierney (D-MA) over "moderate" Republican Pete Torkildsen in Massachusetts. DSA also contributed to the near-upset victories of first-time Democratic challengers Joe Hoeffel
>
> **Democratic Left • Nov**

According to Colorado-based DSA leader Barb Ferrill:[4]

> In Massachusetts' 6th district DSA was an integral part of a campaign that made the critical difference in unseating Republican incumbent Peter Torkildsen and electing John Tierney, a progressive Democrat. We did it through a non-partisan get-out-the-vote campaign that targeted people acutely affected by economic insecurity.

> One week before the election I joined the staff of Lynn Voter Power, an effort coordinated by Neighbor to Neighbor, Project '96 of the AFL-CIO, Boston Voter Power and other community organizations. Instead of the usual "win-this-election-now" campaign which is run with no real concern for the community, this project was started a year ago with the

mission of building a long-term grassroots coalition to increase voter participation—and clout—in the most disaffected neighborhoods of Lynn. The campaign integrated the traditional elements of an intensive GOTV: voter registration, literature drops, door-knocking, phone banking, and providing rides to the polls, with a concerted effort to bring together community leaders, organizations, and unions.

When I arrived they put me to work coordinating nearly 100 volunteers who had signed up to work on election day. Because funding for stipends was provided by one of the unions, a very diverse range of people were able to volunteer, people who otherwise might not have participated...

Tierney's margin of victory was smaller than the number of "infrequent voters" we brought to the polls, and who voted for him. Overall turnout in our precincts was significantly higher than the national average, and most of these people would probably not have voted without our work.

DSA member, Harris Gruman, also ran Tierney's field operations in his successful 1996 race.[5]

DSA Endorsement

This announcement appeared in the September/October 1996 issue of Democratic Socialists of America's newsletter, Democratic Left:[6]

In the last issue of Democratic Left, we reported that Carlos Romero-Barcelo (Puerto Rico at-large), a member of the Progressive Caucus, was endorsed by DSA PAC. We realize that this endorsement was a mistake and have withdrawn it.

In addition, DSA PAC voted to endorse candidate John Tierney, who is running in the 6th district of MA against Republican incumbent Peter Torkildsen; and to endorse candidate Shirley Baca, running in the 2nd district of NM against Republican incumbent Joe Skeen.

Boston Health Care Meeting with Socialists

According to Boston DSA member Rand Wilson, on September 1, 2005, Congressman John Tierney and Maurice Hinchey (D-NY) heard testimony in Boston in support of a "Medicare for All" solution to the health care crisis:

The growing severity of this crisis brought together over 40 grassroots organizations for an impressive—and unusual—showing of political unity for health care reform based on extending Medicare to everyone.

Reps. Barney Frank, Jim McGovern, John Olver and John Tierney were sponsoring legislation in the House—HR 676—that would implement this approach.

The hearing, initiated by Massachusetts Jobs with Justice and cosponsored by numerous health care, labor and community groups, including Boston Democratic Socialists of America, was attended by over a hundred people.

"Over fifteen years of privatization, deregulation, job reengineering, managed care, hospital closures and cuts in essential services has resulted in an industrial model of health care that I call mangled care," said long-time reform advocate Sandy Eaton, a member of Committees of Correspondence for Democracy and Socialism, who worked as an RN at Quincy Medical Center.

"When we started organizing the hearing, only one member of the Massachusetts Congressional delegation had signed on. Now we have four out of the ten," said Paul Cannon, President of Teamsters Local 122 and Co-Chair of Jobs with Justice's Health Care Action Committee.

"Skyrocketing costs, deteriorating quality of care, loss of insurance coverage and access to essential services is affecting everyone's health care," said Rep. Tierney. "Common sense solutions like extending Medicare to cover everyone can save money while improving quality and access to health care for all."[7]

Foreign Policy/National Security

Supported by Council for a Livable World

The anti-U.S. military Council for a Livable World supported John Tierney in his successful House of Representatives run as candidate for Massachusetts.[8]

2012 Council for a Livable World House victories included John Tierney.[9]

---

1 KeyWiki, "John Tierney," KeyWiki, http://keywiki.org/index.php/John_Tierney (accessed April 10, 2013)

2 John F. Tierney, "Biography," House.gov, http://tierney.house.gov/index.php?option=com_content&view=article&id=107:englis h-detailed-version&catid=39:biography&Itemid=398 (accessed August 11, 2011)

3 John F. Tierney, "About John – detailed version," House.gov, http://tierney.house.gov/index.php?option=com_content&view=article&id=107:englis h-detailed-version&catid=39:biography&Itemid=398 (accessed April 10, 2013)

4 Democratic Left (November/December 1996)

5 Our Communities Bio, http://ourcommunities.org/author.php?n=harris-gruman, (accessed March 30, 2013)

6 Democratic Left (September/October 1996) p. 6

7 The Yankee Radical, http://www.dsaboston.org/yradical/yr2005-11.pdf (November 2005)

8 Council for a Livable World, "Meet the Candidates," Council for a Livable World, http://livableworld.org/support/meet_candidates/ (accessed April 10, 2013)

9 Council for a Livable World, "Meet the Candidates," Council for a Livable World, http://livableworld.org/support/meet_candidates/ (accessed April 10, 2013)

Debbie Stabenow (D-MI)

Debbie Stabenow is the Junior Democratic member of the United States Senate, representing Michigan.[1]

Background

Growing up in Clare, Michigan, Debbie Stabenow was the daughter of an Oldsmobile dealer and the Director of Nursing at the local hospital. She graduated at the top of her class from Clare High School and went on to receive her Bachelor's and Master's Degrees from Michigan State University. She worked with youth in the public schools before running for public office.

Senator Stabenow was inspired to first run for office after leading a successful effort to stop the closure of a local nursing home. She was elected to the Ingham County Board of Commissioners when she was 24 years old and in just two years was elected Chair of the Board. She was elected to the Michigan House of Representatives where she served for twelve years (1979-90) and to the State Senate where she served for four years (1991-94).

Elected to the U.S. Congress in 1996, representing Michigan's 8th Congressional District, she made history in 2000 when she became the first woman from the State of Michigan to be elected to the United States Senate.[2]

Influence

As Chair of the Senate Agriculture Committee and a member of the Senate Energy, Finance and Budget Committees, Stabenow has a "powerful and unique role to play in shaping our nation's manufacturing, health care and agriculture policies, which are so critical to our future."[3]

Debbie Stabenow currently serves on the Committee on Agriculture, Nutrition and Forestry and the Committee on the Budget. She also sits on the Committee on Energy and Natural Resources, which includes the Subcommittee on National Parks, the Subcommittee on Energy and the Subcommittee on Water and Power. Stabenow also serves on the Committee on Finance, which includes the Subcommittee on Energy, Natural Resources and Infrastructure where she is the Chair, the Subcommittee on International Trade and Global Competitiveness and the Subcommittee on Health Care.[4]

Socialist Connections

Like many Michigan politicians, Debbie Stabenow has a long-term relationship with Democratic Socialists of America (DSA).

The Millie Jeffrey Connection

Stabenow was particularly close to the late Michigan DSA leader, Millie Jeffrey.

An extremely influential Marxist, in the 1950s and '60s, Jeffrey was a Democratic Party National Committeewoman from Michigan. In 1960, she helped campaign for John F. Kennedy as a Michigan member of the Democratic National Committee.

After mobilizing the Michigan Democratic Party behind JFK in 1960, she then reportedly pushed JFK to initiate the Peace Corps, a haven for leftists ever since. Jeffrey also played a role in the establishment of the radical Students for a Democratic Society in the early 1960s. In the 80s, she was instrumental in getting Geraldine Ferraro her historic Democratic vice presidential candidacy under Walter Mondale:[5]

> Millie then became "the unelected leader," in the words of her co-conspirator Joanne Howes, of a committee of seven Democratic women promoting the idea of a female vice presidential candidate on the 1984 ticket. "By the fall of 1983," recalls Howes, "we came to the conclusion that the right person was Gerry Ferraro"—then an obscure member of Congress from Queens. That required augmenting Ferraro's visibility and bona fides, and as a result of "Millie's strategic thinking," says Howes, the group successfully pressured the party and Walter Mondale to make Ferraro chair of the convention platform committee. The rest is herstory.

In 1994, Mildred Jeffrey was a leader on the Stabenow for Governor Committee.[6]

In 2000, Millie Jeffrey was part of Team Stabenow—actively supporting her friend's successful bid for the U.S. Senate.[7]

On Millie Jeffrey's death in 2004, Debbie Stabenow wrote:[8]

> ...today I have lost a very dear friend, as have the people of Michigan and hundreds of thousands of people across the country. Millie Jeffery is an icon in the State of Michigan and in our country for civil rights, women's rights, and workers' rights. Her life has epitomized the principles by which we all strive to live our lives—justice, equality, and compassion...
>
> Millie is the "political godmother" for many of us, and we are extremely grateful for her love and support.

Then Governor Jennifer Granholm and Stabenow spoke of their debt of gratitude to her work:[9]

> When Millie died last week, both Michigan Gov. Jennifer Granholm and Senator Debbie Stabenow told the media that they would not be in their current positions without the decades of work that Millie had put in on behalf of equal opportunities for women.

Honoring Millie Jeffrey

On May 15, 2004, the Michigan Democratic Party held their annual Jefferson Jackson Day Dinner. At the dinner, an iron sculpture representing equality, created by Wayne State University students, was presented to the family of Millie Jeffrey.

Michigan Democrats' Chair Melvin Hollowell stated that the Lifetime Achievement Award was given in tribute to "Millie's wonderful and enduring legacy of fighting for the equal rights of all people, particularly women." U.S. Senator Debbie Stabenow, U.S. Representative Carolyn Kilpatrick and Governor Jennifer Granholm presented the award.[10]

Co-Sponsored Resolution Honoring DSA Leader

On May 20, 2004, Debbie Stabenow and Carl Levin co-sponsored Senate Resolution 367: A resolution honoring the life of Mildred McWilliams "Millie" Jeffrey (1910-2004) and her contributions to her community and to the United States. The resolution passed with unanimous consent.[11]

"Passing the Torch"

In celebration of Women's History Month in March of 2006, the Michigan Veteran Feminists of America presented the documentary: "Passing the Torch," on March 25th on PBS (WTVS, Channel 56).

The documentary, narrated by Lily Tomlin, explored Michigan women's motivations to participate in "one of the most profound social movements of the 20th Century."

Luminaries such as Communist Party supporter Erma Henderson; the first African American woman elected to the Detroit City Council, UAW executive Millie Jeffrey; Senator Debbie Stabenow and Governor Jennifer Granholm, "reminisce about the protest marches, consciousness raising sessions and the excitement they felt when opening doors that had been closed to women."[12]

The Justice Caucus

On August 28, 2010, The Justice Caucus, a Democratic Socialists of America initiated pressure group in the Michigan Democratic Party, held a meeting at the 2010 Michigan Democratic Party Convention which took place on August 28-29, 2010.

Speakers on the panel included Governor Jennifer Granholm and Senator Debbie Stabenow.

At the meeting, the Caucus presented Governor Jennifer Granholm with the "Spirit of Millie Award," honoring her contribution to Michigan's judiciary via judicial appointments.[13] [14] [15]

Helped by Socialist Elizabeth Bunn

DSA member, Elizabeth Bunn, was the creator of the United Auto Workers Woman-to-Woman campaign that helped elect Senator Debbie Stabenow in 2000 and Governor Jennifer Granholm in 2002.[16]

Foreign Policy/National Security

Supported by Council for a Livable World

The Council for a Livable World supported Debbie Stabenow in her successful Senate run as a candidate for Michigan.[17] She has also been previously supported by the Council in her House of Representatives run for Michigan.[18]

According to the Council website:[19]

> In 2000, Stebenow challenged incumbent Republican Senator Spencer Abraham. The contest was close, with the challenger trailing until the end. However, she beat Abraham by 49%-489%, a margin of about 66,000 votes out of four million cast.

> During her re-election bid in 2006, she scored a solid victory with 57% of the vote. Council for a Livable World enthusiastically supported her in both of those races.

> Senator Stabenow has taken a thoughtful and common sense approach to national security issues. She voted to stop the development of new nuclear weapons in order to prevent a new and dangerous arms race. She has also opposed wasteful spending on a national missile defense system that has yet to work. Additionally, she voted for the New START Treaty to reduce U.S. and Russian nuclear arsenals.

Soviet Trip

Debbie Stabenow visited Moscow, Leningrad and Tbilisi, Georgia in the Soviet Union in 1989, as a delegate with Women for a Meaningful Summit, a group designed to give credibility to Soviet "disarmament" proposals. She traveled with DSA leader Millie Jeffrey and far left future Detroit City Councilmember, JoAnn Watson.[20]

> "Millie was open to everything and everybody. She made friends with everyone—young and old, men and women, big and small, those who

spoke English and those who didn't," said her friend, Michigan Sen. Debbie Stabenow, who was with her on a delegation of women to the Soviet Union

"Every place we went women would walk in off the street and ask if Millie was there. And they may have been speaking another language, but they would walk in and they would be looking for Millie Jeffrey."[21]

Beijing UN Women's Conference

In 1995, Debbie Stabenow accompanied Millie Jeffrey to China to the UN's Fourth World Conference on Women in Beijing—a major gathering point for communist and socialist women.[22]

> Millie's capacity for connecting with people was unmatched. As one who traveled with her to the Fourth World Conference on Women in Beijing, it was amazing to see people from all over the world, hearing we were from Michigan, asking if we knew Millie Jeffrey and if we could tell them where she was; or that their grandmother, their aunt, suggested they meet Millie Jeffrey...

Opposed Iraq War

Six of the eight U.S. Senators from the four upper Midwest states voted against the resolution to authorize force against Iraq, all of them "progressive" Democrats: Mark Dayton and Paul Wellstone (MN), Russ Feingold (WI), Dick Durbin (IL) and Carl Levin and Debbie Stabenow (MI).[23]

Aspen Institute

From May 23-28, 2004, Stabenow traveled to Barcelona, Spain to participate in a conference on political Islam. The trip, which cost $7,511, was paid for by the leftist Aspen Institute.

From August 10-16, she traveled to Moscow to participate in a conference on U.S.-Russia relations.[24]

Staffer's Trip to Cuba

Sen. Stabenow sent Amanda A. Renteria to Cuba for three days in July 2007. The trip was courtesy of a $1,681.70 grant from the Institute for Policy Studies-connected Center for Democracy in the Americas. Renteria "attended [a] fact-finding mission to learn more about Cuba's leadership transition and ongoing program of reforms in Cuban government."[25]

Cuba Trip

A delegation of American lawmakers led by Senator Patrick Leahy (D-VT), arrived in Cuba on Monday, Feb. 18, 2013, in order to gauge the island's economic changes and to lobby on behalf of Alan Gross, an American whose detention had "chilled relations between the two countries." The trip was the first to the Communist-run country by high-level U.S. politicians since President Barack Obama's re-election in November.

The delegation also included Republican Senator Jeff Flake, Democrat Senators Sherrod Brown, Debbie Stabenow and Sheldon Whitehouse, and Democratic Congressmen James McGovern (MA) and Chris Van Hollen from Maryland, Gross's home state.[26]

---

1 KeyWiki, "Debbie Stabenow," KeyWiki, http://keywiki.org/index.php/Debbie_Stabenow (accessed April 20, 2013)
2 Debbie Stabenow, "About Debbie," Senate.gov, http://www.stabenow.senate.gov/?p=about_senator (accessed April 20, 2013)
3 Debbie Stabenow, "About Debbie," Senate.gov, http://www.stabenow.senate.gov/?p=about_senator (accessed April 20, 2013)
4 Debbie Stabenow, "Committee Assignments," Senate.gov, http://www.stabenow.senate.gov/?p=committee_assignments (accessed April 20, 2013)
5 KeyWiki, "Mildred Jeffrey," KeyWiki, www.keywiki.org/index.php/Millie_Jeffrey (accessed April 20, 2013)
6 Opinion, "In Michigan School-Tax Shift, the Poor Lose; Give Her the Credit," The New York Times, http://www.nytimes.com/1994/04/01/opinion/l-in-michigan-school-tax-shift-the-poor-lose-give-her-the-credit-643602.html (April 1, 1994)
7 Google News, http://news.google.com/newspapers?nid=1350&dat=20000917&id=-oQUAAAAIBAJ&sjid=vgMEAAAAIBAJ&pg=4552,347985 (accessed, April 20, 2013)
8 Vote Smart, "Speech Details," Vote Smart, http://www.votesmart.org/speech_detail.php?sc_id=105109&keyword=&phrase=&contain (accessed April 20, 2013)
9 DSA, "Spring 2004," DSA, http://www.dsausa.org/dl/Spring_2004.pdf (Spring 2004)
10 David Romas, "Michigan Democratic Party taps Wayne State University for tribute sculpture to Mildred Jeffrey," Wayne State University, http://media.wayne.edu/2004/05/05/michigan-democratic-party-taps-wayne-state-university-for-tribute-sculpture-to-mildred-jeffrey (May 5, 2004)
11 Govtrack.us, "S. Res. 367: A resolution honoring the life of Mildred McWilliams "Millie" Jeffrey (1910-2004) and her..." Govtrack.us (accessed January 28, 2011)

12 University of Michigan's Institute for Research on Women and Gender, "News," University of Michigan (Fall 2012)

13 KeyWiki, "The Justice Caucus," KeyWiki, www.keywiki.org/index.php/The_Justice_Caucus (accessed April 20, 2013)

14 West Michigan Rising, "Justice Caucus at the Convention," West Michigan Rising, http://www.westmichiganrising.com/diary/1620/justice-caucus-at-the-convention (accessed February 17, 2011)

15 Justice 4 Michigan, "Justice Caucus to Honor Governor Granholm's Contribution to Michigan Judiciary," Justice 4 Michigan, http://www.justice4michigan.org/node/76 (August 20, 2011)

16 Mark Brewer, "DNC Michigan Superdelegates," The Huffington Post, http://www.huffingtonpost.com/off-the-bus-reporter/dnc-michigan-superdelegat_b_89004.html (February 28, 2008)

17 Council for a Livable World, "Meet the Candidates," Council for a Livable World, http://livableworld.org/support/meet_candidates/ (accessed April 20, 2013)

18 Council for a Livable World, "Legacy in Congress: Who We've Helped Elect," Council for a Livable World, http://livableworld.org/what/legacy_in_congress_who_weve_helped_elect/ (accessed April 20, 2013)

19 Council for a Livable World, "Debbie Stabenow," Council for a Livable World, http://livableworld.org/elections/2012/candidates/senate/dstabenow/, (accessed May 15, 2013)

20 KeyWiki, "JoAnn Watson," KeyWiki, www.keywiki.org/index.php/JoAnn_Watson (accessed April 20, 2013)

21 CBS News Opinion, "Thoroughly Marvelous Millie CBS' Lynch Reflects On The Life Of Activist Mildred McWilliams Jeffrey," CBS News Opinion (March 29, 2004)

22 Vote Smart, "Speech Details," Vote Smart, http://www.votesmart.org/speech_detail.php?sc_id=105109&keyword=&phrase=&contain (accessed April 20, 2013)

23 Watchdog Milwaukee, http://watchdogmilwaukee.com/ (January 4, 2005)

24 LegiStorm, "Sen. Debbie Stabenow (D-Michigan) – Privately Financed Travel," LegiStorm, http://www.legistorm.com/trip/list/by/approver/core_person_id_page/51236/id/91/name/Sen_Debbie_Stabenow/page/2.html (accessed January 17, 2010)

25 LegiStorm, "Sen. Debbie Stabenow (D-Michigan) – Privately Financed Travel," LegiStorm, http://www.legistorm.com/trip/list/by/approver/core_person_id_page/51236/id/91/name/Sen_Debbie_Stabenow/page/2.html (accessed January 17, 2010)

26 The Guardian, "Senator Patrick Leahy leads US group to Cuba to seek release of Alan Gross," The Guardian, http://www.guardian.co.uk/world/2013/feb/18/patrick-leahy-cuba-alan-gross (February 18, 2013)

John Conyers (D-MI)

John Conyers, Jr. is a Democratic member of the United States House of Representatives, representing the 13th District of Michigan. He is the second most senior member of the House and Dean of the Congressional Black Caucus. He was also a founding member of the Congressional Progressive Caucus and an original member of President Nixon's Enemies List.[1]

Background

John Conyers, Jr. was born in 1929 in Detroit, Michigan, the son of Lucille Simpson and United Auto Workers activist John Conyers, Sr. After graduating from Detroit public schools, Conyers earned his Bachelor of Arts Degree in 1957 and his Juris Doctorate Degree in 1958 from Wayne State University. Before beginning a career as a private attorney, Conyers served one year in Korea as an officer in the U.S. Army Corps of Engineers and was awarded combat and merit citations.

In 1958, Conyers began his work in politics as an aide to Congressman John Dingell, whom he served until 1961. Conyers made history when he was elected to the House of Representatives in 1964 on a platform of "jobs, justice and peace."

Conyers has served as Trustee of the Martin Luther King, Jr. Center for Non-Violent Social Change, past Director of United Auto Workers Local 900, a member of the Advisory Council of the Michigan Civil Liberties Union, General Counsel for the Trade Union Leadership Council, Vice-Chair for the Advisory Council of Michigan Civil Liberties

Union and a member of the Executive Board of Directors of the Detroit Branch of the NAACP.

Conyers was re-elected in November 2012 to his twenty-fourth term in the House.[2]

Influence

Among his accomplishments in Congress: the Violence Against Women Act of 1994, the Motor Voter Bill of 1993, the Martin Luther King Holiday Act of 1983, the Alcohol Warning Label Act of 1988 and the Jazz Preservation Act of 1987.

John Conyers is the second most senior member in the House of Representatives. He served as Chairman of the House Committee on Government Operations (now renamed Committee on Oversight and Government Reform) from 1989 until 1994. In 2006, Congressman Conyers was elected by his Congressional colleagues to lead, as Chairman, the pivotal House Committee on the Judiciary in the 110th and 111th Congress. In addition to its oversight of the Department of Justice (including the FBI) and the Federal Courts, the Judiciary Committee has jurisdiction over copyright, civil rights, consumer protection and constitutional issues. Congressman Conyers was also a member of the Judiciary Committee during its 1974 hearings on the Watergate impeachment scandal.

Conyers serves currently on the Committee on the Judiciary as the Ranking Member. He also serves on the Subcommittee on the Constitution and the Subcommittee on Intellectual Property, Competition and Internet.[3]

Conyers has been a major advocate of federal aid to black communities, as "reparations" for slavery.

Conyers first introduced HR 40, the "Forty Acres and a Mule Bill," as he called it, in 1989. The bill would not implement reparations, but would develop a federal government commission, appointed by the President and Congressional leaders, to study the issue. Included in the study would be the work of academics and politicians, but also discussions of ordinary people in town hall meetings.

Conyers said that since slavery was a national issue, the repair, both economic and psychological, of the effects must also be considered a "national obligation; slavery is a national fact and ought to be treated as such, not as a personal issue."[4]

Communist Connections

Conyers has almost 60 years of history with the Communist Party USA (CPUSA).

Sugar/Crockett Connection

Detroit law partners Maurice Sugar and George Crockett (later a Democratic Congressman), both lifelong affiliates of the CPUSA, encouraged the young John Conyers to first stand for Congress in 1964.[5]

Chicago Committee to Defend the Bill of Rights

In 1965, John Conyers was a guest speaker with CPUSA member Frank Wilkinson at a March 27th supper-workshop-conference of the Communist Party-controlled Chicago Committee to Defend the Bill of Rights at McGiffert House in Chicago.[6]

On March 1, 2003, John Conyers was the Keynote speaker at an event entitled: "Assembly to Reclaim Our Rights," which was held at Bethel AME Church in Chicago. The event was organized by the Chicago Committee to Defend the Bill of Rights and the Bill of Rights Foundation.

Trade Unionists for Peace

In 1966, Conyers spoke at the founding convention of Trade Unionists for Peace which was established by leftist labor leaders as a lobby against United States forces remaining in Vietnam. (TUP was run by Charles Walters, a shop steward for the United Automobile Workers. Former Communist Bereniece Baldwin testified under oath, in 1954, before the House Committee on Un-American Activities, that Walters was a member of the Communist Party). In 1966, Walters was Editor of Labor Today, a communist-controlled publication. Conyers has written for Labor Today.[7]

Black Voting "Bloc"

In 1968, Conyers told The Worker, a CPUSA publication, that he was organizing a committee of blacks to evaluate candidates for the 1968 election. It was part of his overall program to organize American Negroes into one voting bloc. For his evaluating committee, he had chosen, among others, the revolutionaries Stokely Carmichael, Ralph Abernathy and Floyd B. McKissick.[8]

National Alliance Against Racist and Political Repression

The 10th Anniversary Conference of the Communist Party USA front, National Alliance Against Racist and Political Repression, was held in Chicago on May 13-15, 1983, at the McCormick Inn—featured speakers included John Conyers.[9]

Labor Research Association Award

In November 1982, Reps. George Crockett and John Conyers of the Congressional Black Caucus were honored at the CPUSA controlled Labor Research Association's Banquet Luncheon. Rep. Major Owens of Brooklyn was also present.[10]

Communist Party "Ally"

In a report: "What Can We Learn From the Movement for Health Care Reform?" prepared as part of the discussion leading up to the Communist Party USA's 29th National Convention on May 21-23, 2010, CPUSA member David Bell wrote on the partial failure of the Party's health care agenda:[11]

> Did we forget the fact that many of the same unions, hundreds of locals, and the rank and file supported single payer? We also turned away from our allies in Congress, the Progressive Caucus, and John Conyers.

Detroit Angela Davis Gathering

A standing room only crowd of nearly 2,000 people welcomed former CPUSA leader Angela Davis on October 24, 2012, to Detroit to celebrate the 40th anniversary of her acquittal on charges of murder, kidnapping and conspiracy. The event, held at Fellowship Chapel on the city's northwest side, was a "powerful demonstration of the respect and affection Detroiters have for Professor Davis and her history of struggle for economic, racial and gender justice."

The program included Congressman John Conyers, far left Detroit City Councilperson JoAnn Watson, Retired Wayne County Circuit Court Judge and long time Communist Party supporter Claudia Morcom and Metro AFL-CIO Civil Rights Committee Chair Michele Artt, a well known CPUSA member.

A common thread running through the remarks of all speakers was the importance of the November 6 election. Alluding to the fact that Prof. Davis had come to Detroit thirteen days before the election, Congressman Conyers said it was a "night where we not only remember history but plan how we're going to make history... Dr. Davis, you're right on time!"[12]

Socialist Connections

John Conyers has a more than 50 year relationship with Democratic Socialists of America (DSA) and the preceding Democratic Socialist Organizing Committee (DSOC).

DSOC "Initiator"

According to the December 29, 1979 issue of Information Digest, the "initiators" of the Democratic Socialist Organizing Committee, formed in 1973 as a result of a split within the Socialist Party USA, largely over the issue of cooperation with communists (the Socialist party was against it), included John Conyers.[13]

"Democracy '76"

DSOC organized a Democracy '76 seminar in Chicago in June of 1976, one of the organizations earliest attempts to influence and infiltrate the Democratic Party.

The conference lineup included Michigan Congressman John Conyers.[14]

Democratic Agenda/Socialist Caucus

The Democratic National Convention of 1980 witnessed the formation of a Socialist Caucus of delegates. It was organized by the DSOC and by the Democratic Agenda, which was DSOC's cadre and had supporters within the Democratic Party. The event was based in DSOC's New York office (1730 M Street, NW, Washington, D.C.). Some 31 delegates and alternates from twelve states and Democrats Abroad attended the Socialist Caucus.

As a preliminary to the convention's Socialist Caucus meeting, the Democratic Agenda sponsored a convention rally at New York's Town

Hall. The speakers included John Conyers, radical labor leader Cesar Chavez and several DSOCers, including future San Francisco Supervisor, Harry Britt, New York City Councilor Ruth Messinger and feminist Gloria Steinem.

"DSOC works within the Democratic Party," said leader Michael Harrington, "because of the party's relationships with organized workers, blacks, feminists, environmentalists and other "progressive groups.""[15]

DSA Founding Convention

John Conyers was a special guest on day one of the Democratic Socialist Organizing Committee/New American Movement Unity Convention in Detroit on March 21-22, 1982, that resulted in the formation of Democratic Socialists of America.[16]

2003 DSA Convention

In 2003, John Conyers was a Keynote speaker at the DSA conference in Detroit with DSAers Cornel West, Holly Sklar and Harold Meyerson.[17]

Conyers opened by saying that, "with a crypto-fascist administration, there's no singular purpose more important than unelecting the unelected president."

Conyers with DSA members Cornel West, Harold Meyerson and Holly Sklar, Detroit (2003)

DSA "Ally"

In 2005, DSA's Democratic Left—Spring edition, called Congressman John Conyers "a key DSA ally in Congress."[18]

Speaking at a DSA Meeting

On October 2, 2010, Congressman John Conyers spoke at a Democratic Socialists of America meeting following the One Nation Rally which had taken place earlier that day. Among those present at the meeting were DSAers Frank Llewellyn (chair) and David Green, Chair of DSA's Detroit local.

During his talk, Conyers stated that he was supporting Congressman Dennis Kucinich's measure to make a United States Department of Peace in the Federal Government. He referred to Barack Obama as his beloved 44th President, however he stated that:[19]

> "I see that us making him more cooperative with our plans is going to strengthen him and not weaken him... The whole point is that, trashing progressives and the left, and at the same time watching your ratings go down—gee... what's so difficult about figuring that out? Whose job do you think it is to get him straightened out and get him on the right track? Ours! Ours!" (applause)

DSA "Friend"

According to Chicago DSA's New Ground No. 135, March/April 2011:[20]

> The need for Federal action should be obvious. To that end, DSA supports H.R. 870, The Humphrey-Hawkins 21st Century Full Employment and Training Act, introduced into the House of Representatives by John Conyers, U.S. Representative from Detroit, and friend of DSA. This bill introduces several strategies to generate jobs, including the establishment of a National Full Employment Trust Fund to create employment opportunities for the unemployed, financed (budget-neutral) by a tax on securities transactions.

Rev. David Bullock, Rep. John Conyers, Jr., Marjorie Mitchell

2012 DSA Fundraiser

Democratic Socialists of America Political Action Committee held a fundraising reception for Representative John Conyers, Jr. in Detroit on May 27th, 2012. The guest of honor was Jim Hightower, noted "progressive" radio commentator and Editor of the Hightower Lowdown.

Co-Hosts were David Bullock, President of the Detroit branch of Operation PUSH; DSAer Tim Carpenter, Executive Director of Progressive Democrats of America; DSAer David Hecker, President of the American Federation of Teachers-Michigan and Marjorie Mitchell, Executive Director of the DSA dominated Michigan Universal Health Care Access Network.[21]

> As you may know, Congressman Conyers faces a serious primary challenge in a new district. In the past, he has never needed to raise much money for his campaigns. This time is different. We anticipate significant negative advertising will be directed against him. He will require sufficient resources with which to respond.

> John Conyers is an icon to the progressive community. He is the only elected official ever to be endorsed by Reverend Martin Luther King, Jr. As the ranking member of the House Judiciary Committee, he opposed the Patriot Act and has been a staunch defender of civil liberties. He is the sponsor of the Medicare for All Act (HR 676), a single-payer health insurance bill which would provide comprehensive health care benefits to all Americans while simultaneously containing health care costs. He is the sponsor of the Humphrey-Hawkins 21st Century Full Employment and Training Act (HR 870), a bill which would use a tax on financial transactions to create a national jobs program aimed at producing three to four million new jobs per year in infrastructure improvement, social services, and green energy. In short, Congressman Conyers shares our politics.

Health Care

Conyers has worked for years with DSA to promote "single payer"-socialized health care.

According to Michael Lighty, a former National Director of DSA and Director of Public Policy for the California Nurses Association/National Nurses Organizing Committee, writing in DSA's Democratic Left, Winter 2007/2008:[22]

There's a growing movement for single-payer universal healthcare. The movement is led by activists in Healthcare-Now!, doctors in the Physicians for a National Health Program, nurses in the California Nurses Association/National Nurses Organizing Committee, leaders in labor unions such as United Steelworkers of America and Communication Workers of America, activists in the Progressive Democrats of America, and Congressman John Conyers...

"Progressive" Connections

Conyers also has deep ties to the Institute for Policy Studies (IPS) and its spinoffs.

"Alternative Budgets"

In 1975, a group of 47 members of Congress, led by John Conyers, asked radical Washington D.C. "think tank," the IPS, to prepare an "alternative budget" to that proposed by President Ford. This request was repeated in 1976 and 1978 by 56 legislators.

The 1978 document called for "a socialist housing program... radical social change in the educational system... a 50% cut in the defense budget" and "disengagement" from America's overseas commitments.[23]

The Washington School

The Washington School, founded by the IPS in 1978, was an important means of influencing Congress and the Democratic Party. Courses on defense, foreign affairs and domestic policies are taught there by IPS officers, staffers and other American or foreign radical "experts." A large number of members of Congress and staffers have attended these schools. Several legislators have also taught there, including John Conyers.[24]

Take Back America Conferences

John Conyers was on the list of 153 speakers at the 2006 Take Back America conference, which was organized by the IPS and DSA-initiated Campaign for America's Future.[25]

Progressive Democrats of America

John Conyers serves on the Advisory Board of Institute for Policy Studies-dominated Progressive Democrats of America.[26]

PDA Claimed Successes

Tim Carpenter claimed that Progressive Democrats of America had chalked up several achievements in its short life, successfully promoting initiatives by PDA board members John Conyers and James McGovern:[27]

Foreign Policy/National Security

John Conyers' foreign policy positions have consistently favored America's enemies.

Against the Vietnam War

Conyers adopted the position that the Vietnam War was a racist conflict and he was one of only four members of the House of Representatives to vote against military support for U.S. troops in Vietnam.[28]

World Peace Council Connection

From September 29 to October 12, 1975, the Soviet front World Peace Council (WPC) sent a delegation on a ten-day tour of the United States of America, where it was "warmly and enthusiastically received."

The WPC delegates were guests of a number of members of Congress at a luncheon in the House of Representatives' dining room and at a reception. Among those present were several members of the Congressional Black Caucus, including Congress members John Conyers, Ronald Dellums, Ralph Metcalfe and others.[29]

In 1978, Congressmen John Burton, Ted Weiss, Ron Dellums, John Conyers, Don Edwards, Charles Rangel and others attended a World Peace Council organized meeting on Capitol Hill.

The WPC delegation was led by its President, Romesh Chandra, a member of the Communist Party of India. Conyers welcomed this group, saying, "You have joined us to give courage and inspiration in our fight for disarmament and against the neutron bomb."[30]

In 1981, another World Peace Council delegation led by Romesh Chandra of the Communist Party of India, toured the U.S. to publicize the "nuclear freeze" then being promoted by Leonid Brezhnev.

This group met with several Congressmen at the Capitol, including John Conyers, George Crockett, Ron Dellums and Don Edwards.[31]

These Democratic Congressmen made House offices available for meetings with the WPC delegates.

During one of the meetings in these Congressmen's offices, an official of the CPUSA was present and made a speech recommending that the "peace movement" unite in supporting the cause of several terrorist groups including the PLO and the Communist guerillas in EI Salvador.[32]

1 Participants in the meeting of the Bureau of the World Peace Council held in Copenhagen in January 1982.

2 Congressman John Conyers, Jr., member of the U.S. House of Representatives from Detroit (Michigan) addressing the members of the Bureau of the WPC and other participants at the "Discussion on Disarmament and Security in Europe" in Copenhagen (Denmark).

WPC's New Perspectives, Vol. 11 (May, 1982)

1982 WPC Bureau Meeting

In January 1982, Conyers addressed a World Peace Council Bureau meeting: "Discussions on Disarmament and the Security in Europe," in Copenhagen, Denmark.[33]

U.S. Peace Council

On the weekend of November 12-13, 1979, the Communist Party USA front, U.S. Peace Council, was established in a meeting at International House on the campus of the University of Pennsylvania in Philadelphia. U.S. Rep. John Conyers twice addressed the conference.[34]

"Agent Orange" Campaign Connection

From November 1-14, 2007, leading Vietnamese communist official, Dr. Nguyen Thi Ngoc Phuong, a leading clinician/researcher on the effects of Agent Orange on women and children in Vietnam, from Tu Du Hospital, Ho Chi Minh City, visited Washington, D.C. on a Vietnam Agent Orange Public Health Tour.

Dr. Phuong, Vice President of the Vietnam Association for Victims of Agent Orange toured Washington, D.C. where a policy of the American Public Health Association on Agent Orange (Vietnamese version) was passed on November 6, 2007. Dr. Phuong was accompanied by Merle Ratner of the Committees of Correspondence for Democracy and Socialism and Susan Schall (both leaders of the Committees of Correspondence-dominated Vietnam Agent Orange Relief & Responsibility Campaign).

The delegation met several members of Congress including John Conyers and Sheila Jackson Lee.[35]

During the visit to John Conyers' office, Dr. Phuong was also accompanied by Jeanne Mirer, a leader of the old Soviet front, International Association of Democratic Lawyers.

Members of the U.S. Congress showed their support for Vietnamese "victims of Agent Orange/Dioxin" during a visit to the U.S. by a delegation from the Vietnam Association of Victims of Agent Orange/Dioxin.

John Conyers stated that the U.S. administration must attach more importance to settling the aftermaths of Dioxin in Vietnam.[36]

1 DAAHP, "Biography – John Conyers, Jr.," DAAHP, http://www.daahp.wayne.edu/biographiesDisplay.php?id=75 (accessed February 8, 2011)
2 John Conyers, Jr., "Biography," House.gov, http://conyers.house.gov/index.cfm/biography (accessed April 13, 2013)
3 John Conyers, Jr., "Committee Assignments," House.gov, http://conyers.house.gov/index.cfm/committee-assignments (accessed April 13, 2013)
4 People's World, "Conyers speaks about reparations," People's World, http://peoplesworld.org/conyers-speaks-about-reparations/, (February 8, 2002)
5 Dudley W. Buffa, "Union power and American democracy: the UAW and the Democratic Party, 1935-72," p. 148
6 CCDBR, Letterhead (February 1965)
7 Francis X. Gannon, "Biographical Dictionary of the Left," v. 1, pp. 292-293
8 Francis X. Gannon, "Biographical Dictionary of the Left," v. 1, pp. 292-293
9 NAARPR, Newsletter (March 24, 1983) p. 1
10 Barry Cohen, "Honor Black Legislators," Daily World (November 25, 1982)
11 David Bell, "Convention Discussion: What Can We Learn From the Movement for Health Care Reform?" Communist Party USA, http://www.cpusa.org/convention-

discussion-what-can-we-learn-from-the-movement-for-health-care-reform/ (February 2, 2010)

12 Mark Walton, "Angela Davis speaks to 2,000 at Michigan rally," People's World, http://peoplesworld.org/angela-davis-speaks-to-2-000-at-michigan-rally/, (October 25, 2012)

13 Margrit Pitman, "DSOC meet urge butter not guns," People's Daily World (June 11, 1981)

14 KeyWiki, "John Conyers," KeyWiki, http://keywiki.org/index.php/John_Conyers (accessed May 12, 2012)

15 KeyWiki, "John Conyers," KeyWiki, http://keywiki.org/index.php/John_Conyers (accessed May 12, 2012)

16 Conference Program Brochure

17 Democratic Left (Fall 2003)

18 Democratic Left, Spring Edition (2005)

19 YouTube, "John Conyers speaking at Democratic Socialists of America meeting," http://www.youtube.com/watch?feature=player_embedded&v=JLv0xeu9VyA (October 13, 2010)

20 Chicago DSA, "New Ground 135," DSA, http://www.chicagodsa.org/ngarchive/ng135.html (March/April 2011)

21 DSA, "DSA Newsletter, DSA, http://detroitdsa.com/May2012Newsletter.pdf, (May 2012)

22 Democratic Left, http://www.dsausa.org/dl/Winter_2008.pdf (Winter 2007/2008)

23 Communists in the Democratic Party, p. 71

24 Communists in the Democratic Party, p. 73

25 Campaign For America's Future, "Archives – 2006 Agenda & Speakers," Campaign For America's Future, http://www.ourfuture.org/node/13179 (accessed May 14, 2010)

26 PDA America, "Advisory Board," PDA America, http://pdamerica.org/tools/pda/Adboard.pdf (accessed April 13, 2013)

27 PDA website, http://pdamerica.org/about/strategy.php (accessed 2009)

28 Political Makers, "Hon. John Conyers," The History Makers, http://www.thehistorymakers.com/biography/hon-john-conyers-40 (accessed April 13, 2013)

29 World Peace Council Tour USA (1975) pp. 6-7

30 Communists in the Democratic Party, p. 50

31 Communists in the Democratic Party, p. 50

32 Communists in the Democratic Party, p. 66

33 WPC, "New Perspectives, Vol. 11" (May 1982)

34 Terry Cannon, "New national body to push peace fight," Daily World (November 13, 1979) p. 1

35 Vietnam Agent Orange Relief & Responsibility Campaign website, "November 1-14, 2007 Vietnam Agent Orange. Public Health Tour Featuring: Dr. Nguyen Thi Ngoc Phuong," Vietnam Agent Orange Relief & Responsibility Campaign website, http://www.vn-agentorange.org/Nov2007_public_health_tour.html (accessed December 12, 2010)

36 BaoMoi.com, "Vietnamese AO victims receive great support in the US," BaoMoi.com, http://en.baomoi.com/Info/Vietnamese-AO-victims-receive-great-support-in-the-US/3/91846.epi (accessed April 13, 2013)

Gary Peters
(D-MI)

Gary Peters is the U.S. Representative for Michigan's 14th Congressional District, serving Congress since 2009. He previously represented Michigan's 9th Congressional District from 2009 to 2013. Following the redrawing of the Congressional District boundaries after the 2010 United States Census, Peters announced that he would run for reelection, running in the newly redrawn 14th District and won. Peters is now considering running in 2014 for the seat being vacated by the retiring Senator Carl Levin in the United States Senate.[1]

Background

U.S. Representative Gary Peters was born in Pontiac and has lived his entire life in the Greater Detroit area. His father worked as a public school teacher for more than 30 years and his mother worked at a local nursing home where she helped organize her workplace as an SEIU union steward.

Peters graduated from Rochester High School and went on to Alma College where he earned a Bachelor of Arts Degree in Political Science.

He later went on to earn a Master's in Business Administration Degree in Finance from the University of Detroit Mercy, a law degree from Wayne State University Law School and a Michigan State University Master's Degree in Philosophy.

Prior to his election to Congress, Peters represented the 14th District in the Michigan Senate and was a political science professor at Central Michigan University.[2]

Influence

In Congress, U.S. Rep. Peters "partnered with the Obama Administration to ensure the survival of the auto industry in Michigan." In other words, he assisted with and facilitated the auto industry bailout.

As a member of the Financial Services Committee, Peters has worked vigorously to go after big business and Wall Street. As one of just 10 House Democrats selected to serve on the Wall Street Reform Conference Committee, Peters played a central role in shaping financial reform law. Congressman Peters serves on the House Financial Services committee where he works to advance policies that are progressive in nature as well as Keynesian in theory.[3]

Socialist Connections

Detroit DSA Connection

In 2008, the Peters campaign turned down offers from Democratic Socialists of America (DSA) for help. According to the newsletter of the Greater Detroit DSA, January 2009:[4]

> Having been rebuffed in our offers of assistance to progressive Congressional candidates Gary Peters (9th district) and Mark Schauer (7th district)—both of whom were afraid of being red-baited—Detroit DSA focused instead on local and state races.

Greater Detroit DSA Chair, David Green, said that the candidates themselves were happy to have Detroit DSA's involvement, but that "handlers" from the Democratic National Committee refused the support, for fear that the candidates would be "red-baited or branded socialist."[5]

Peters has maintained low key ties to DSA since that time.

The Agenda for the May 2, 2009 Greater Detroit Democratic Socialists of America General Membership Meeting included the following item:[6]

- Report on Meeting with Gary Peters' Staff

The Agenda for the July 11, 2009 Greater Detroit Democratic Socialists of America General Membership Meeting included the following item:[7]

- Report on Meeting with Representative Gary Peters

Spirit of Millie Jeffrey

The Spirit of Millie Jeffrey Award Dinner is the Democratic Socialists of America-initiated Michigan Democratic Party's The Justice Caucus' annual award and fundraising dinner in honor of the life of "progressive" activist, Millie Jeffrey.

Jeffrey was both a high ranking Democrat and a long time DSA leader. Congressman Peters was the Keynote Speaker at the June 7, 2009 dinner.[8]

21ˢᵗ Century Democrats

Peters has also been endorsed and supported by the progressive 21st Century Democrats Political Action Committee, long led by DSA member Jim Scheibel.[9]

Occupy Detroit

Peters allied himself with the Occupy Wall Street movement, making an appearance at Occupy Detroit on November 6, 2011. Speaking to reporters, he stated: "It's speculation on Wall Street that we're still paying the price for here, particularly in Detroit that almost brought the auto industry to a collapse because of what we saw on Wall Street. So we put in restrictions, or put in regulations necessary to rein that in, and right now in Washington I'm facing a Republican majority that wants to undo that."[10]

Occupy Detroit was heavily infiltrated by DSA and members of the pro-North Korean Workers World Party.

Foreign Policy/National Security

Council for a Livable World

Gary Peters received donations from Council for a Livable World, founded in 1962 by long-time socialist activist and reported Soviet agent, Leo Szilard.[11]

---

1 KeyWiki, "Gary C. Peters," KeyWiki, http://keywiki.org/index.php/Gary_C._Peters (accessed March 22, 2013)
2 Gary Peters, "Biography," U.S. Representative's website, http://peters.house.gov/biography/ (accessed March 22, 2013)

3 Gary Peters, "Biography," U.S. Representative's website,
http://peters.house.gov/biography/ (accessed March 22, 2013)
4 Democratic Socialist of America Greater Detroit Local, "Detroit DSA Succeeds in
2008 Electoral Effort," Democratic Socialists of America,
http://detroitdsa.com/january2009newsletter.pdf (January 2009)
5 Seth A. Maxon, "Mobilized in Motor City," In These Times,
http://inthesetimes.com/article/5317/mobilized_in_motor_city (December 25, 2009)
6 Democratic Socialists of America Greater Detroit Local, "Innovation Broker
Developing Detroit as Green Manufacturing Center," Democratic Socialists of
America, http://detroitdsa.com/newsletter2.0.pdf (May 2009)
7 Democratic Socialists of America Greater Detroit Local, "DSA Healthcare
Resolution," Democratic Socialists of America,
http://detroitdsa.com/july2009newsletter.pdf (July 2009)
8 Flickr, "Jim Kruer & Congressman Gary Peters, flickr,
http://www.flickr.com/photos/40034830@N07/3681465993/ (accessed January 31,
2011)
9 21st Century Democrats, "2008 Bio," 21st Century Democrats website,
http://www.21stcenturydems.org/candidates/2008-candidates/, (accessed March 22,
2013)
10 CBS Detroit, "Occupy Detroit Gets Union Support," CBS Detroit,
http://detroit.cbslocal.com/2011/11/06/233330/, (November 6, 2011)
11 Council for a Livable World, "Legacy in Congress, Who We've Helped Elect,"
Council for a Livable World,
http://livableworld.org/what/legacy_in_congress_who_weve_helped_elect/ (accessed
March 22, 2013)

Al Franken (D-MN)

Alan Stuart "Al" Franken is a Democratic-Farmer-Labor Party member of the United States Senate, serving as the Junior Senator for Minnesota. The Democratic-Farmer-Labor Party is unique to Minnesota and is affiliated with the Democratic Party.[1]

Background

Al Franken was born on May 21, 1951 and grew up in St. Louis Park, Minnesota. He graduated from Harvard in 1973 and married Franni Franken.

Franken achieved note as a writer and performer for the television show Saturday Night Live from its inception in 1975, before moving to writing and acting in films and television shows. He then became a political commentator, author of five books and a host of a nationally syndicated radio show on the Air America Radio Network.

He has taken part in seven USO tours, visiting U.S. troops overseas in Germany, Bosnia, Kosovo and Uzbekistan—as well as visiting Iraq, Afghanistan and Kuwait four times.

Franken was a Founder and leading voice on the Air America radio network.[2]

He was elected to the U.S. Senate in 2008.

Influence

Franken serves on the Committee on Health, Education, Labor and Pensions, which includes the Subcommittee on Employment and Workplace Safety and the Subcommittee on Children and Families. Franken also sits on the Committee on the Judiciary, which includes the Subcommittee on Privacy, Technology and the Law, the Subcommittee on Antitrust, Competition Policy and Consumer Rights, the Subcommittee on Human Rights and the Law and the Subcommittee on Administrative Oversight and the Courts. He also serves on the Committee on Indian Affairs and the Committee on Energy and Natural Resources.[3]

Communist Connections

Al Franken won his U.S. Senate seat in 2008, against Republican Norm Coleman after an extremely close election night result, followed by a long and controversial recount process, supervised by Minnesota Secretary of State and secret Communist Party USA (CPUSA) "friend," Mark Ritchie.[4]

Communist Party Commentary

In the Communist Party's People's World, November 22, 2008, Barb Kucera wrote of the controversial Minnesota U.S. Senate election, quoting both Minnesota Secretary of State Mark Ritchie and his known associate CPUSA member, Mark Froemke:[5]

> Whether Minnesota labor's massive effort to mobilize members in the 2008 elections was a success will ultimately turn on the results of a recount in the U.S. Senate race, Labor 2008 coordinators say.

> While most AFL-CIO and Change to Win unions backed Democratic-Farmer-Labor (DFL) challenger Franken, a few labor organizations—notably the Carpenters and Pipe Trades—endorsed Coleman. After all the results were turned in, Coleman led Franken by only 215 votes out of just under 3 million cast. An official recount began Nov. 18 and could take a month, Secretary of State Mark Ritchie said.

> Franken's race against GOP incumbent Norman Coleman is important nationally. To get pro-worker bills through the Senate, workers and their allies need 60 votes, out of 100 senators, to cut off GOP filibusters. That includes a presumed GOP talkathon against the

Employee Free Choice Act, which is designed to help level the playing field between workers and bosses in union organizing and bargaining first contracts...

Independence Party candidates made the difference in the Bachmann and Paulsen races and definitely affected the Senate race, said Mark Froemke, president of the West Area Labor Council that spans the western half of the state. 'The Independence Party got a better number than I would have expected in this area,' he said. Negativity of campaign commercials in the final days of the Senate race also had an effect.

Endorsed by Communist Mark Froemke

Interestingly, Minnesota/Dakota's Communist Party leader, Mark Froemke, had already endorsed Al Franken.

On July 14, 2008, the Al Franken for U.S. Senate campaign announced that four new labor organizations have "joined its ever-growing coalition that's fighting to send a senator to Washington who will stand with Minnesota's middle class."

The new endorsements were:

- Bakery, Confectionary, Tobacco Workers and Grain Millers Union
- Minnesota State Council of UNITE HERE!
- Minnesota Postal Workers Union
- International Union of Bricklayers and Allied Craftworkers, Local Union 1

"Minnesotans need a Senator who understands the needs of Minnesota families, and who won't abandon them in a time of need," declared Mark Froemke, Education Director of the Bakery, Confectionary, Tobacco Workers and Grain Millers Union, Local 167G.

"Norm Coleman had a chance to support the families of the Red River Valley on CAFTA and, instead, he supported President Bush," Froemke noted. "Al Franken will stand with farmers and workers and Minnesotans, and that's why we stand with him in this election."[6]

Mark Ritchie's Communist Party Connection

Minnesota Secretary of State Mark Ritchie was also a covert "friend" of the Communist Party.[7]

In December of 1999, a Communist Party meeting was held at the May Day Bookstore in Minneapolis, Minnesota, for the purpose of reestablishing the CPUSA Farm Commission.

Party members present were Erwin Marquit, Helvi Savola, Jack Brown, Peter Molenaar, Morgan Soderburg, Bill Gudex, Mark Froemke, Scott Marshall, Gary Severson, Mike Madden, Becky Pera, Charlie Smith and Tim Wheeler.

Mark Ritchie also attended and addressed the meeting. In a written report on the meeting by Tim Wheeler, Ritchie is referred to as a "non-party friend" of the Communist Party. The report was marked "not for publication."[8]

Report on the CPUSA farm meeting, Minneapolis, Dec. 5, 1999 (Not for publication)

The Communist Party USA convened a day-long meeting at the May Day Bookstore in Minneapolis Dec. 5. to discuss the crisis of family and independent farmers.

Those present: Erwin Marquit, Helvi Savola, Jack Brown, Peter Molenaar, Morgan Soderberg, Bill Gudex, Mark Froemke, Scott Marshall, Gary Severson, Mike Madden, Becky Pera, Charlie Smith, Tim Wheeler.

The meeting took place in an atmosphere of great enthusiasm because four of those present had just returned from Seattle where farmers were strongly represented in the fightback against the WTO and globalized monopoly capitalism. All four gave reports on the "Battle in Seattle."

Mark Ritchie, a non-party friend, executive director of the Minneapolis-based Institute on Trade and Agricultural Policy, had chaired the farm-agricultural rally of over 5,000 people in Seattle. He opened our meeting with a report on Seattle and gave us an in-depth analysis of the current farm crisis. He spent the entire morning session with us.

His main points: The powerful new coalition in Seattle based on farmers-labor-environmental-religious and other human rights organizations "stopped the WTO. It is a tremendous victory." Ritchie, who is also a member of the U.S. delegation to the WTO, said the key to the collapse of the WTO Ministerial meeting was a "revolt by Third World delegates who looked out their hotel windows and saw what was happening in the streets and said to themselves, 'We are not alone. Millions of Americans agree with us! We don't have to just go along with the dictates of the big capitalist powers.'" They rejected the U.S. diktat and the whole meeting ended in failure.

"It is one thing to stop something, another to come forward with a democratic alternative." That is the challenge now, he said.

On October 11, 2003, Mark Ritchie's article, "A new beginning for WTO after Cancun," was published in the CPUSA's newspaper, People's Weekly World. Ritchie was listed on the People's Weekly World website as an author. The article had originally been published at the Institute for Agriculture and Trade Policy website.[9] [10]

Ritchie also received approval from the CPUSA for his 2006 campaign.

In a July 8, 2006, People's World article: "This Battle Can be Won!" the author underlined the importance of the elections for Secretary of State, "whose job is mandated as protecting voting rights and election practices." They stated of Ritchie:[11]

In Minnesota the DFL candidate for Secretary of State Mark Ritchie, of the League of Rural Voters could play a valuable national role.

Working with Communist Mark Froemke

U.S. Sen. Al Franken, (D-MN) and Mark Froemke, an AFL-CIO representative and Communist Party USA member, left the Grand Forks International Airport on January 11, 2012, after Franken flew into Grand Forks to spend two days talking to locked-out American Crystal Sugar Co. workers in the Red River Valley.[12]

Al Franken (left), Mark Froemke

Socialist Connections

Socialist Wellstone Tribute

As the 2004 Democratic National Convention was about to commence in Boston, Jobs with Justice hosted a living tribute to the late Senator Paul Wellstone on July 25th. Hundreds filled the historic Old West Church to confront the question, "What must the Democratic Party do to live up to the progressive vision of Paul Wellstone?"

Wellstone, who died in office in a 2002 plane crash, was a long-time supporter of Democratic Socialists of America (DSA) and this was reflected in the speaking lineup.

"Paul had the courage to stand the pain that comes with standing for something and not fall for anything," said United Steelworkers of America Union International President Leo Gerard, a long-time DSA affiliate. "That's what the Democratic Party needs right now. He gave people a reason to fight, to hope."

Rep. Major Owens (D-NY), a DSA member, pointed out that too many liberals, including Owens himself, voted for "welfare reform" in 1996. He praised Wellstone as the lone voice defending welfarism at the time.

Another DSA member, Boston City Councilor Chuck Turner, fired up the audience with a call for "direct action" to ensure accountability from a John Kerry administration. "We need Kerry there and we need to be there to purge the cancer (of the Bush administration) from the soul of the body politic."

Moderator Horace Small was also a DSA member, while speaker Jim Hightower, an author and radio personality, is a long-time DSA supporter.

Other panelists included Columbia University professor and DSA leader, Frances Fox Piven; Anna Burger, Vice President of the DSA-dominated SEIU; and "media personality," Al Franken.[13]

Wellstone Action

In 2009, Al Franken was listed as a member of the Advisory Board of Wellstone Action, a Minnesota based organization based on the political legacy of that state's late 'progressive' Senator Paul Wellstone.

Franken shared duty on the Advisory Board with Democratic Socialists of America supporters or members Julian Bond, Heather Booth, Peter Edelman, Frances Fox Piven, Leo Gerard, Jim Hightower, Gerald McEntee, Deborah Olson and economist Robert Reich. SEIU boss Andy Stern and Communist Party affiliate and Minnesota Secretary of State, Mark Ritchie, were also on the roster.[14] [15]

DSA Support

The minutes of a Metro Atlanta Democratic Socialists of America membership meeting, held at the Friends Meeting House in Decatur, Georgia on March 1, 2008, included reference to a report by Milt Tambor on DSA support for Congressional and Senate candidates in the 2008 election:[16]

> 4) Milt reported that DSA is calling on locals to support progressive candidates for Congress and the Senate, mainly through fundraisers and volunteering. Al Franken (MN) and one other have been suggested; more details will follow…

Foreign Policy/National Security

Supported by Council for a Livable World

The Council for a Livable World supported Al Franken in his successful Senate run as candidate for Minnesota.[17]

Council for a Livable World, 50th Anniversary

On June 6, 2012, Council for a Livable World, along with its sister organizations Center for Arms Control and Non-Proliferation and Council for a Livable World's PeacePAC celebrated the 50th Anniversary of their founding by Leo Szilard in 1962.

Council for a Livable W Celebration

Senator Al Franken addresses the crowd at the Council's 50th anniversary celebration.

There were speeches and toasts by Senator Al Franken, Representative Shelley Berkley (D-NV), former Representative and PeacePAC Chairman Tom Andrews (D-ME), former Cabinet Secretary Norman Mineta and Communications Workers of America President, Larry Cohen.

"Agent Orange" Campaign Connection

In July of 2010, Dr. Nguyen Thi Ngoc Phuong, a leading clinician/researcher on the effects of Agent Orange on women and children in Vietnam (from Tu Du Hospital, Ho Chi Minh City), visited Washington, D.C. with "Agent Orange victim" and student, Ms. Tran Thi Hoan.

On July 15, 2010, at the Third Hearing on Agent Orange in Vietnam: Recent Developments in Remediation, Rayburn House Office Building, VAVA (Vietnam Association of Victims of Agent Orange/Dioxin), Tran Thi Hoan testified before the U.S. House of Representatives Committee on Foreign Affairs, Subcommittee on Asia, the Pacific and the Global Environment.

This was the first time a victim of Agent Orange had spoken to Congress. The "victim, the well-received Ms. Tran Thi Hoan, who has no legs, received a lot of attention."

Front Left, Dr. Nguyen Thi Ngoc Phuong, Al Franken, Tran Thi Hoan (seated), Susan Schall and Merle Ratner (July 15, 2010)

Dr. Phuong and Tran Thi Hoan were accompanied by Merle Ratner of the Committees of Correspondence for Democracy and Socialism and Susan Schall (both leaders of the Committees of Correspondence-dominated Vietnam Agent Orange Relief & Responsibility Campaign).

This Marxist led campaign was set up to extract money from the U.S. taxpayers for the Committees of Correspondence's communist friends in Vietnam.

The party met with Minnesota Senator Al Franken.[18]

---

1 KeyWiki, "Al Franken," KeyWiki, http://keywiki.org/index.php/Al_Franken (accessed April 19, 2013)

2 Al Franken, "Al's Biography," Senate.gov, http://www.franken.senate.gov/?p=about_al (accessed April 19, 2013)

3 Al Franken, "Committees and Subcommittee Assignments," Senate.gov, http://www.franken.senate.gov/?p=committees (accessed April 19, 2013)

4 KeyWiki, "Mark Ritchie," KeyWiki, http://keywiki.org/index.php/Mark_Ritchie (accessed April 19, 2013)

5 Barb Kucera, "Minnesota euphoria over Obama win tempered by Senate recount," People's World, http://transitional.pww.org/minnesota-euphoria-over-obama-win-tempered-by-senate-recount/ (November 22, 2008)

6 Kari Larson, "Franken Announces New Labor Endorsements," UnionWorld, http://www.unionworld.us/2008/07/franken-announces-new-labor-endorsements-by-kari-larson/ (July 2008)

7 KeyWiki, "Mark Ritchie," KeyWiki, http://keywiki.org/index.php/Mark_Ritchie (accessed April 19, 2013)

8 Tim Wheeler, "CPUSA Farm Commission report," CPUSA (December 16, 1999)

9 Mark Ritchie, "A new beginning for WTO after Cancun," People's World, http://www.peoplesworld.org/a-new-beginning-for-wto-after-cancun/ (October 10, 2003)

10 Mark Ritchie, "A new beginning for WTO after Cancun," WayBackMachine/People's Weekly World, http://web.archive.org/web/20050503204123/www.pww.org/article/author/view/653 (March 5, 2005)

11 Communist Party USA, "This Battle Can Be Won!" Communist Party USA, http://www.cpusa.org/this-battle-can-be-won- (June 24, 2006)

12 AGWEEK, "Sen. Al Franken, D-Minn., and Mark Froemke," AGWEEK, http://www.agweek.com/event/image/id/55223/headline/Sen.%20Al%20Franken,%20D-Minn.,%20and%20Mark%20Froemke/publisher_ID/40/AG (January 11, 2012)

13 People's World, "Wellstone legacy: Stand up and fight," People's World, http://www.peoplesworld.org/wellstone-legacy-stand-up-and-fight/, (July 31, 2004)

14 Wellstone, "Board and Advisors," Wellstone, http://www.wellstone.org/about/board-and-advisors (accessed April 19, 2013)

15 KeyWiki, "Wellstone Action," KeyWiki, http://www.keywiki.org/index.php/Wellstone_Action (accessed April 19, 2013)

16 Atlanta Democratic Socialists of America, "Metro Atlanta Democratic Socialists of America membership meeting minutes," DSA, http://www.dsa-atlanta.org/minutes/Minutes_2008_03_01.pdf, (March 1, 2008)

17 Council for a Livable World, "Meet the Candidates," Council for a Livable World, http://livableworld.org/support/meet_candidates/ (accessed April 19, 2013)

18 Vietnam Agent Orange Relief & Responsibility Campaign website, "Third Hearing on Agent Orange in Vietnam: Recent Developments in Remediation," Vietnam Agent Orange Relief & Responsibility Campaign website (accessed December 12, 1010)

Keith Ellison (D-MN)

Keith Maurice Ellison is a Minnesota Democratic-Farmer-Labor Party member of the United States House of Representatives, representing the 5th District of Minnesota. He is also a Co-Chair on the Congressional Progressive Caucus, a member of the Congressional Black Caucus and of the Populist Caucus.[1]

Background

Keith Ellison was born and raised in Detroit, Michigan. He moved to Minnesota in 1987 to attend the University of Minnesota, Law School, where he earned his law degree in 1990.

Keith Ellison has represented the 5th Congressional District of Minnesota in the U.S. House of Representatives since taking office on January 4, 2007. The 5th District includes the City of Minneapolis and the surrounding suburbs. He previously served two terms representing Legislative District 58B in the Minnesota State House of Representatives, from 2003 to 2007.[2]

Ellison is a Muslim convert and was affiliated with the radical Nation of Islam from at least the late 1980s, until he ran for Minnesota State Representative in 1998.[3]

Influence

Keith Ellison was elected as Co-Chair of the Congressional Progressive Caucus for the 112th Congress. Working together with other members of the Caucus, "Keith helped shape historic health care and Wall Street reform, raise the federal minimum wage, start the process to end the War in Iraq, strengthen veterans' benefits, combat hate crimes and create guarantees of pay equality for women."[4]

Ellison serves on the House Financial Services Committee and the House Democratic Steering Committee which determines the party's platform and committee assignments for Democratic members.

The House Financial Services Committee has jurisdiction over the banking system, stock exchanges and the housing and insurance industries. The committee also handles policy matters including monetary policy, international finance and combating terrorist financing.

The Committee also oversees the Federal Reserve, the U.S. Treasury Department, the Federal Deposit Insurance Corporation, the Securities and Exchange Commission, the National Credit Union Administration, the Office of the Comptroller of the Currency (OCC), the U.S. Department of Housing and Urban Development, the Federal Housing Finance Agency and the Export-Import Bank.[5]

Communist Connections

Kathleen Soliah

In February 2000, Ellison gave a speech at a fundraising event sponsored by the Minnesota chapter of the pro-communist National Lawyers Guild, on whose Steering Committee he had served. The event was a fundraiser for a former member of the Maoist-terrorist Symbionese Liberation Army, Kathleen Soliah, after her arrest in St. Paul (under the name "Sara Jane Olson") for the attempted murder of Los Angeles police officers in 1975.

Though she is white, Ellison referred to Soliah/Olson as a "black gang member" and thus a victim of government persecution. He described her as one of those who had been "fighting for freedom in the '60s and '70s" and called for her release. (She subsequently pleaded guilty to charges in Los Angeles and to an additional murder charge in Sacramento; she is serving time in California.) He also spoke favorably of cop killers Mumia Abu-Jamal and Assata Shakur, a former Black Liberation Army member who has been hiding in Cuba since 1984—last year she was placed on the FBI's domestic terrorist's list with a one million dollar reward for her capture.[6]

Communist Party Approval

In August 2006, the Communist Party USA (CPUSA) welcomed Ellison's probable election to Congress, comparing him to the late far left senator Paul Wellstone:[7]

> If Keith Ellison is elected in November to represent Minnesota's 5th Congressional District, he will bring to the U.S. House of Representatives a fresh progressive voice in [the] tradition of Paul Wellstone. He will also be the first African American congressman from Minnesota and the first Muslim in the U.S. Congress.
>
> Ellison is a well-known civil rights attorney and an established progressive leader in the Minnesota House of Representatives. He received the Democratic Farmer-Labor (DFL) Party's endorsement at the district convention in May, enjoys strong support from organized labor, and has been endorsed by the state AFL-CIO.
>
> Peace and justice activists have been volunteering in increasing numbers in the Ellison campaign to refocus attention on Ellison's program. Ellison calls for immediate withdrawal of U.S. troops from Iraq, a universal, single-payer health care system, protection and extension of civil rights to all, including gays and lesbians, and responsible stewardship of the environment.
>
> In the Minnesota House, Ellison supported legislation to raise the minimum wage. He has spoken at peace rallies in the Twin Cities area. He pledged to fight all attempts to erode the Voting Rights Act. He founded the Environmental Justice Advocates of Minnesota.

Coalition of Black Trade Unionists Conference

From May 22 to May 25, 2008, the CPUSA founded Coalition of Black Trade Unionists held their 37th International Convention in St. Louis, Missouri.[8]

Rep. Ellison urged delegates to put the housing crisis "in its proper context. We've had 30 years of frozen wages. However, in 1984, CEOs made 42 times more than the average worker. But in 2005, CEOs made 411 times more than the average worker. As a result we consume less and borrow more. Our wages stagnate, while the rich get richer."

Ellison called for a "grassroots movement married to legislation."[9]

Michigan Coalition for Human Rights

Detroit Workers World Party leader Abayomi Azikiwe greeted Congressman Keith Ellison of Minnesota during the Michigan Coalition for Human Rights annual dinner on April 6, 2008. Azikiwe serves as Chairman of the MCHR board.[10]

Abayomi Azikiwe, Keith Ellison   (April 6, 2008)

Meeting with Activists from the September 24, 2010, FBI Raids

On November 5, 2010, Rep. Ellison held a meeting with five of the activists, mainly members of the Marxist-Leninist Freedom Road Socialist Organization, FightBack! faction, who were raided by the FBI in September. "While unclear about what legislative action he could take on their behalf, Ellison conveyed dismay with the raids." The activists encouraged Ellison to circulate a "Dear Colleague" letter to other members of the Progressive Caucus asking for support of an investigation of the FBI's actions. "Ellison reminded them that he could not interfere with an ongoing investigation."[11]

FRSO member Sarah Martin, one of the activists who attended the meeting stated:

> It was a reasonably good meeting. He certainly understands the seriousness of this and although political times are pretty horrible right now... he's gonna pursue doing a "dear colleague" letter with the progressive caucus... He kept saying of course, he can't stop this Grand Jury but he's gonna do everything he can. He met with us! This is

Congressman Keith Ellison, and he met with us in person and gave us you know, a good time—which is—didn't happen at the Senator's office.

FRSOer Tracy Molm, another of the activists who attended the meeting, stated:[12]

> [We asked Ellison to write] a "dear colleague" letter to Obama directly... He said that he's going to look into a "dear colleague" letter, and try to get other progressive people in Congress to sign onto it also.

Socialist Connections

Wellstone Action

In 2009, Keith Ellison was listed as a member of the Advisory Board of Wellstone Action, a Minnesota based organization founded on the political legacy of that state's late Democratic Socialists of America (DSA) affiliated Senator Paul Wellstone.

Ellison served on the board alongside DSA members Frances Fox Piven, Julian Bond and Deborah Olson, as well as DSA affiliates Heather Booth, Peter Edelman, Leo Gerard, Jim Hightower, Gerald McEntee and former U.S. Secretary of Labor, Robert Reich.[13]

21st Century Democrats Support

21st Century Democrats is a Political Action Committee that has stood for Progressive causes for over 20 years.

The long-time Board Chair of 21st Century Democrats was Democratic Socialists of America member Jim Scheibel, a former Mayor of Saint Paul, Minnesota.

Keith Ellison was one of 17 key progressives endorsed by 21st Century Democrats in the 2010 election cycle.

Ellison was also supported by them in 2006.[14]

Midwest Academy Awards

In 2011, Keith Ellison was honored with a "Progressive Leadership Award" by the Democratic Socialists of America-controlled Midwest Academy—a school based on the teachings of radical "community organizer" Saul Alinsky.

Then Massachusetts Rep. Barney Frank, a long time DSA supporter, was given a "Lifetime Achievement Award," at the same event.[15]

Economic Policy Institute

In 2013, Keith Ellison was listed as a member of the Board of Directors of the Washington D.C., Economic Policy Institute.[16]

The EPI is led by long-time Democratic Socialists of America member Larry Mishel and the Board has always been dominated by DSA affiliated labor unionists and academics.

On the current board, Ellison serves alongside DSAers Mishel and Teresa Ghilarducci, and DSA affiliates Barry Bluestone, Jeff Faux, Leo Gerard, Bob King, Robert Kuttner, Gerald McEntee and Robert Reich.[17]

"God Willing... Border Will Become an Irrelevancy"

In June 2010, Ellison spoke at a Network of Spiritual Progressives conference, during which he stated the following on border security:

> No security policy position can be premised on military might. ...The way it works is we are a country guided by ideals of equity, generosity and engagement in our relations with other nations and those philosophical ideals create safe borders... and, God willing, one day the border will become an irrelevancy.

Also speaking at the conference was avowed Marxist and onetime DSAer, Michael Lerner, Editor of the pro-Palestinian Tikkun Magazine. According to an account of the conference by Baltimore Sun columnist Marta Mossburg, who attended the two-day event, Lerner compared Tea Party activists to Hitler at least five times.

Another speaker at the event was DSA "friend" Heather Booth, founder of the DSA-dominated Midwest Academy, which teaches the community organizing tactics of radical, Saul Alinsky.[18] [19] [20]

Young Socialist Staffer

Irene Schwoeffermann, an affiliate of the DSA youth wing Young Democratic Socialists, has worked for Rep. Ellison.[21]

"Progressive" Connections

Take Back America Conferences

Keith Ellison was on the list of 237 speakers at the 2007 Take Back America conference, which was organized by the Institute for Policy

Studies (IPS) and the DSA of America-dominated Campaign for America's Future.[22]

Keith Ellison was also on the list of speakers at the follow-up 2009 America's Future Now conference, which was also organized by the Campaign for America's Future.

He was back in 2010 at the aligned Take Back the American Dream conference in 2011.[23] [24]

Demos Event

On May 31, 2012, the Institute for Policy Studies' stated that their "partner" organization Demos, The American Prospect and "our supporters, celebrated our work over the past year. We also honored three incredible leaders who have advanced our vision of shared economic prosperity, inclusive democracy, and effective government. Thanks to all for helping us be at our best in this critical moment."

2012 Transforming America Awardees were Sheila Bair, Leo Gerard and Ai-jen Poo.

Honorary Chairs included Congressman Keith Ellison.[25]

Progressive Democrats of America

Keith Ellison has close ties to the IPS/DSA-led Progressive Democrats of America (PDA).[26]

The Peoples' Inauguration

Progressive Central: The Peoples' Inauguration was held on January 19, 2013, at the UDC David A. Clarke School of Law, Washington, D.C.

The event was sponsored by PDA, The Nation, National Nurses United, Democrats.com and Busboys and Poets, a restaurant owned by IPS Trustee Andy Shallal. The event was advertised and promoted by the IPS.

Keith Ellison addressed the lunchtime session by video.[27]

According to PDA—"In the 113th Congress, some PDA-backed Democrats planned to introduce pieces of legislation that enjoy widespread support among the American left—but would, in all likelihood, be met with stiff opposition."

Rep. Keith Ellison pledged to introduce a bill backed prominently by the DSA-led National Nurses United Union, to implement a tax on all financial transactions, the so-called Robin Hood tax.[28]

Progressive Democrats of America 2012 Endorsement

In 2012, Keith Ellison (MN) was one of 14 leftist Congressional and Senate candidates endorsed by Progressive Democrats of America.[29]

---

1 KeyWiki, "Keith Ellison," KeyWiki, http://keywiki.org/index.php/Keith_Ellison (accessed July 3, 2012)

2 Keith Ellison, "Keith's Biography," House.gov, http://ellison.house.gov/index.php?option=com_content&view=article&id=21&Itemid=146 (accessed August 15, 2011)

3 Scott W. Johnson, "Louis Farrakhan's First Congressman," The Weekly Standard, http://www.weeklystandard.com/Content/Public/Articles/000/000/012/764obcsx.asp?page=3, (October 9, 2006)

4 Keith Ellison, "Keith's Biography," House.gov, http://ellison.house.gov/index.php?option=com_content&view=article&id=21&Itemid=146 (accessed August 15, 2011)

5 Keith Ellison, "Committee Assignments," House.gov, http://ellison.house.gov/index.php?option=com_content&view=article&id=67&Itemid=147 (accessed April 25, 2013)

6 Scott W. Johnson, "Louis Farrakhan's First Congressman," The Weekly Standard, http://www.weeklystandard.com/Content/Public/Articles/000/000/012/764obcsx.asp?page=3, (October 9, 2006)

7 People's World, "Progressive for Congress comes under fire," People's World, http://www.peoplesworld.org/progressive-for-congress-comes-under-fire/ (accessed April 27,2013)

8 Broadcast Urban, "37th International Convention – Town Hall Meeting," Broadcast Urban, http://www.broadcasturban.net/webcast/cbtu2008/fri_townhall.htm (accessed December 19, 2011)

9 Tony Pecinovsky, "Black trade unionists gear up for election," People's World, http://www.peoplesworld.org/black-trade-unionists-gear-up-for-election/ (June 1, 2008)

10 KeyWiki, "Keith Ellison," KeyWiki, http://keywiki.org/index.php/Keith_Ellison (accessed July 3, 2012)

11 Bill Sorem, "Congressmen Ellison Meets FBI Raid Victims," The UpTake, http://www.theuptake.org/2010/11/07/congressmen-ellison-supporting-fbi-raid-victims/ (November 7, 2010)

12 US Peace Council, "Report on Congressional Delegation From the Committee to Stop FBI Repression," US Peace Council, http://uspeacecouncil.org/?p=334 (November 20, 2010)
13 KeyWiki, "Wellstone Action!" KeyWiki, http://www.keywiki.org/index.php/Wellstone_Action (accessed April 25, 2013)
14 21st Century Democrats, "Rep. Keith Ellison," 21st Century Democrats, http://www.21stcenturydems.org/candidates/rep-keith-ellison/#.UXndF8rTAyE (accessed April 25, 2013)
15 Midwest Academy, "Midwest Academy Awards 2012," Midwest Academy, www.midwestacademy.com/midwest-academy-awards-2012, (accessed June 5, 2013)
16 Economic Policy Institute, "Board of Directors," Economic Policy Institute, http://www.epi.org/about/board/ (accessed April 26, 2013)
17 KeyWiki, "Economic Policy Institute," KeyWiki, http://www.keywiki.org/index.php/Economic_Policy_Institute (accessed April 26, 2013)
18 Naked Emperor News, "Progressive Vision of Borderless US: Rep Says 'God Willing... Border Will Become an Irrelevancy," YouTube, http://www.youtube.com/watch?v=aC6UDLSQ42k (June 2010)
19 KeyWiki, "Michael Lerner," KeyWiki, http://www.keywiki.org/index.php/Michael_Lerner (accessed April 26, 2013)
20 KeyWiki, "Heather Booth," KeyWiki, http://www.keywiki.org/index.php/Heather_Booth (accessed April 26, 2013)
21 KeyWiki, "Irene Schwoeffermann," KeyWiki, http://www.keywiki.org/index.php/Irene_Schwoeffermann (accessed April 26, 2013)
22 Campaign For America's Future, "Archives – 2003 Speakers," Campaign For America's Future, http://www.ourfuture.org/node/13211 (accessed June 17, 2010)
23 Confabb website, "America's Future Now 2009 Speakers," Confabb website, http://now2009.confabb.com/conferences/82401-americas-future-now/speakers (accessed July 13, 2010)
24 Campaign For America's Future, "Speakers At Take Back The American Dream," Campaign For America's Future, http://www.ourfuture.org/conference/speakers (accessed September 22, 2011)
25 Demos, "2012 Transforming America, Honorary Chairs," Demos, http://www.demos.org/gala-2012, (accessed April 27, 2013)
26 KeyWiki, "Keith Ellison," KeyWiki, http://keywiki.org/index.php/Keith_Ellison (accessed July 3, 2012)
27 PDA website, http://hq-salsa3.salsalabs.com/o/1987/p/salsa/event/common/public/index.sjs?event_KEY=6957 5, (accessed January 15, 2013)
28 Cole Stangler, "Progressive Democrats: Inside and Outside," ITT, http://www.inthesetimes.com/article/14463/progressive_democrats_inside_and_outside, (January 22, 2013)
29 KeyWiki, "Keith Ellison," KeyWiki, http://keywiki.org/index.php/Keith_Ellison (accessed July 3, 2012)

Bennie Thompson (D-MS)

Bennie G. Thompson is a Democratic member of the United States House of Representatives, representing the 2nd District of Mississippi. He is a long-time member of the Congressional Black Caucus and the Congressional Progressive Caucus.[1]

Background

As a young man growing up in rural Bolton, Mississippi, Thompson "was well aware of the realities that plagued the South. The experiences that his family endured made him determined to be an advocate for those of who were oftentimes underserved."

While earning his Bachelor of Science and Master's Degrees from Tougaloo College and Jackson State University, respectively, Thompson began to develop his grassroots political activism. He joined the Student Nonviolent Coordinating Committee and helped to organize voter registration drives for African Americans in the Mississippi Delta.

After graduating from college, Thompson worked as a schoolteacher and began to pursue a career in politics.

From 1968 to 1972, Thompson served as Alderman and then went on to serve as Mayor from 1973 to 1980 in Bolton, Mississippi. He was also founding President of the Mississippi Association of Black Mayors.

In 1975, Thompson filed a lawsuit to increase funding at Mississippi's historically black universities. With Thompson as lead plaintiff, the case was subsequently settled for an unprecedented $503 million. From 1980 to 1993, Thompson served as County Supervisor for Hinds County and was the founding member and President of the state's Association of Black Supervisors. He was elected to Congress in 1993.[2]

Influence

In 2000, Thompson authored legislation creating the National Center for Minority Health and Health Care Disparities, which subsequently became law. He also received a Presidential appointment to serve on the National Council on Health Planning and Development.

In 2006, during the 109th Congress, he served as the first Democratic Chairman of the Homeland Security Committee. As Chairman, Congressman Thompson introduced and engineered House passage of the most comprehensive homeland security package since September 11, 2001—H.R. 1, the "9/11 Commission Recommendations Act of 2007."

As a ranking member of the Committee on Homeland Security, Thompson may serve as an ex officio member of all subcommittees.

He also belongs to the Congressional Rural Caucus, the Congressional Sunbelt Caucus, the Renewable Energy and Energy Efficiency Caucus, the Congressional Travel and Tourism Caucus and the Tennessee Valley Authority Caucus.

He is also involved in the Congressional Children's Working Group and the National Guard and Reserve Components Congressional Members Organization.[3]

Communist Connections

Supported Communist Party Front

In 1982, Bennie Thompson served on the National Coordinating Committee of a Communist Party USA (CPUSA) front, the National Alliance Against Racists and Political Repression, which was led by leading Party members Angela Davis and Charlene Mitchell.[4]

Martinez Jobs Bill

In 1994, the CPUSA backed Martinez Jobs Bill (H.R.-4708), was co-sponsored by California Democratic Party Reps. Howard Berman, Xavier Becerra and Lucille Roybal-Allard, as well as Robert Scott (D-VA), Tom

Foglietta (D-PA), John Lewis (D-GA), Ed Pastor (D-AZ) and Bennie Thompson (D-MS).[5]

Talking to the "World"

The Communist Party front Coalition of Black Trade Unionists held their 34th annual convention in Tucson, AZ on May 26, 2005.

At a "town hall meeting" on African American, Native American, Asian American and Latino relations, including leaders from these communities, panels pointed out the importance of united action to defeat the ultra-right attacks on labor and the poor.

After addressing the meeting, Representative Bennie Thompson told the Communist Party USA paper People's World, "The issue for people of color in the labor movement is that they have to stay together. As organizations change sometimes people of color are overlooked. And if they don't stick together they lose out. And one of the things I want to share with them is if you don't stick together then you come in on the short end of the stick."[6]

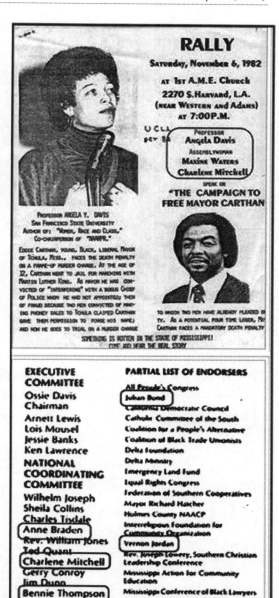

503

Introduced by Communist Party Supporter

From May 22nd through the 25th, 2008, the Coalition of Black Trade Unionists held their 37th International Convention in St. Louis, Missouri.

Representative Bennie Thompson was one of the speakers from the May 22nd opening session. He was introduced by Tony Hill of Florida, a state politician, labor unionist and well known Communist Party supporter.[7]

Tony Hill made a personal endorsement in the Communist Party's People's Weekly World of June 2, 2007, on page 2 of the publication.

Socialist Connections

Democratic Agenda

More than 1,200 people attended the Democratic Socialist Organizing Committee (DSOC) initiated Democratic Agenda Conference held November 16-18, 1979, at the International Inn and Metropolitan AM Church in Washington, D.C.

Bennie Thompson was a panelist in a workshop entitled: "Relating Local Issues to the Democratic Party," alongside Ruth Messinger, a Democratic Socialist Organizing Committee/Democratic Socialists of America member and a future New York City Councilor.[8]

DSA Endorsement

In July 1996, the Democratic Socialists of America Political Action Committee endorsed Bennie Thompson, Mississippi 2nd District, in that year's Congressional elections.[9]

Young Socialist Staffer

Irene Schwoeffermann, an affiliate of DSA's youth wing, the Young Democratic Socialists, has served as a staffer for Congressman Thompson.[10]

Foreign Policy/National Security

Staffer's Trip to Cuba, 2000

In February 2000, Marsha McCraven from the office of Congressman Bennie Thompson spent five days in Havana, Cuba, for the purpose of "information gathering." The trip cost $1,778.47 and was paid for by the leftist Christopher Reynolds Foundation.[11]

Promoting America Medical Training in Cuba

In June 2000, a group from the Congressional Black Caucus visited Cuban President Fidel Castro, led by then Caucus President James Clyburn.

Delegation member, Representative Bennie Thompson, described huge areas in his district where there were no doctors and Castro responded with an offer of full scholarships for U.S. citizens to study at the Latin American School of Medical Sciences in Havana.[12]

Congressman Thompson's visit to Cuba in June 2000, "paved the way to exploring the possibility of trading agricultural and medical products with the communist state. In addition, he has sought to explore medical education and training opportunities that may exist for Second District students in Cuba."[13]

Why Cuba?

Hon. Bennie Thompson, U.S. House of Representatives, Mississippi:[14]

> Of 23 counties that I represent, 22 of them are medically underserved.... One of the reasons the Congressional Black Caucus wanted to go to Cuba is that as we traveled around the world, in some of the most remote places we would always run up on Cuban doctors. So we went to Cuba.

Back to Cuba, 2005

In May 2005, Congressman Thompson and two of his staff members, Timla Washington and Steve Gavin, spent four days in Havana, Cuba, for the purpose of "Cuba business, fact finding." The trip cost $1,298.26 and was again paid for by the Christopher Reynolds Foundation.[15]

---

1 KeyWiki, "Bennie Thompson," KeyWiki, http://keywiki.org/index.php/Bennie_Thompson (accessed May 9, 2012)
2 Bennie Thompson, "About Bennie," House.gov, http://benniethompson.house.gov/index.php?option=com_content&view=article&id=4 6&Itemid=91 (accessed August 15, 2011)

3 Bennie Thompson, "About Bennie," House.gov, http://benniethompson.house.gov/index.php?option=com_content&view=article&id=4 6&Itemid=91 (accessed August 15, 2011)

4 NAARPR, "National Alliance Against Racist and Political Repression Pamphlet" (1982)

5 Evelina Alarcon, "Support for jobs bill grows," People's Weekly World (October 1, 1994) p. 3

6 Martin Frazier, "Black trade unionists urge labor unity," People's World, http://www.peoplesworld.org/black-trade-unionists-urge-labor-unity/ (June 4, 2005)

7 CBTU, "Broadcast Urban: 37th International Convention – May 24 Opening Session," CBTU, http://www.broadcasturban.net/webcast/cbtu2008/sat_opening.htm (accessed December 19, 2011)

8 Information Digest (December 14, 1979) pp. 370-371

9 Democratic Left (July/August 1996) p. 21

10 KeyWiki, "Bennie Thompson," KeyWiki, http://keywiki.org/index.php/Bennie_Thompson (accessed May 9, 2012)

11 Christopher Reynolds Foundation, "Congressional Staffers Share the Road," American RadioWorks, http://americanradioworks.publicradio.org/features/staffers/travdat/sponsor.php?sponso r_id=T000109 (accessed April 3, 2013)

12 Mika, "U.S. Rep. (MS) Bennie Thompson promotes Cuba med program," Democratic Underground, http://www.democraticunderground.com/discuss/duboard.php?az=view_all&address=4 05x6433 (July 26, 2008)

13 Re-elect Bennie G Thomson for Congress (accessed January 10, 2010)

14 Salud!, "Clips & Quotes," Salud!, http://www.saludthefilm.net/ns/clips-quotes.html (accessed May 9, 2012)

15 Christopher Reynolds Foundation, "Congressional Staffers Share the Road," American RadioWorks, http://americanradioworks.publicradio.org/features/staffers/travdat/sponsor.php?sponso r_id=T000109 (accessed April 3, 2013)

William Lacy Clay, Jr. (D-MO)

William (Lacy) Clay, Jr. is a Democratic member of the United States House of Representatives, representing the 1st District of Missouri. He is a member of the Congressional Black Caucus (which was Co-Founded by his father) and the Congressional Progressive Caucus.[1]

Background

William Lacy Clay, Jr., usually known as Lacy Clay (born July 27, 1956), attended the University of Maryland-College Park, from which he earned a degree in Political Science and certification to be a Paralegal.

Prior to his election, Clay served for 17 years in both chambers of the Missouri Legislature.

He resides in St. Louis and attends St. Nicholas Catholic Church.

As a result of the 2010 Census redistricting, Clay was placed into a district with fellow Democratic incumbent Russ Carnahan. In the 2012 Democratic Primary, Clay defeated Carnahan.[2][3]

Influence

Clay is a senior member of the powerful House Financial Services Committee.

He is the Ranking Member on the newly-created House Financial Services Subcommittee on Domestic and International Monetary Policy and Technology. This key Subcommittee will have major oversight responsibilities over the Federal Reserve, the Export-Import Bank of the United States, the World Bank and the International Monetary Fund.

Clay also serves on the Oversight and Government Reform Committee, which has major oversight and investigative responsibilities for the operations of the federal government.[4]

Communist Connections

Lew Moye

Clay has close ties to the Coalition of Black Trade Unionists (CBTU), which in Missouri is completely controlled by the local Communist Party USA (CPUSA), through its leader, long-time Communist Party supporter, Lew Moye. Though nominally a Democrat and a strong Obama supporter, Moye has been involved with the Communist Party for almost 40 years.

The CPUSA's People's Weekly World 1997, May Day Supplement, listed Moye as one of the St. Louis Friends of the People's Weekly World.[5]

CPUSA Member Tony Pecinovsky (left), Lew Moye (center left) and CPUSA Member Zenobia Thompson (right) at the 19th Annual Hershel Walker Peace and Justice Awards Breakfast (July 2011)

In his successful 2000 Congressional campaign, Clay employed Lew Moye as a campaign adviser.[6]

Coalition of Black Trade Unionists Conference

From May 22 to May 25, 2008, the CBTU held their 37th International Convention in St. Louis, Missouri.

Rep. William Lacy Clay, Jr. was one of the speakers at the May 22nd opening session and was introduced by Lew Moye.[7]

Calloway Awards Banquet

The St. Louis Chapter of the CBTU's Ernest and De Verne Calloway Awards Banquet was held on October 13, 2012 at the Renaissance Grand Hotel in downtown St. Louis. Speakers included Congressman William Lacy Clay, Jr., Secretary of State Candidate Jason Kander, Governor Nixon, Representative Damion Trasada and CPUSA-aligned State Representative Karla May.

CBTU Chapter President Lew Moye stated: "We can win Missouri for President Obama with a massive turnout from the African American Communities."[8]

Lew Moye and Jason Kander

Congressman Clay at 2012 Calloway Awards

"Socialist Issues"

In reference to the above meeting, Missouri CPUSA member E.E.W. Clay commented on a People's World article: "Mega-storm now underway a taste of what may be," by John Bachtell, October 29, 2012:[9]

> Democrats, especially since the base of their Party is so working class, so multi-generational, multi-ethnic, and multi-racial, demands change- and basic change.

> The thrust of the more progressive elements, the NAACP and labor influences, through John Conyers's, the John Lewis's and the tradition of the Digg's, the Stokes's and the Barbara Lee's, and now, Emanuel Cleaver and Lacy Clay, is guiding the country to a more inclusive and a substantive democracy, based on bread, butter and peace, and therefore, socialist issues.

That is why Democratic Congressperson Lacy Clay recently urged with Lew Moye, local President of The Coalition of Black Trade Unionists, at the annual Ernest and Laverne Calloway Awards Banquet (these two close friends of our CPUSA's icon, James E. Jackson Jr.) to get out the vote on 6 November to support people's progress, the African American base of the Democratic Party, the ballot, continuing Social Security, Medicaid, trade unionism, and expanding health care for all Americans.

Supported Communist-Led Student Action

In April of 2005, Washington University in St. Louis, Missouri, committed "at least $1 million over the next two years toward higher salaries and better benefits for low-paid contract employees as a result of a 19-day sit-in by students demanding a living wage for service workers." Washington University's Student Worker Alliance reached a "groundbreaking agreement" with campus officials on April 22nd:

> The new agreement is a significant step towards a living wage for campus service workers, who were making an average of $7.50 an hour. The university agreed to continue working towards a living wage and to form a joint student-university committee, with SWA representation, to improve university policy of freedom of association for all workers directly or indirectly employed by the university. Also, the university will join the Workers' Rights Consortium, which ensures that factories producing university clothing and other goods respect workers' rights.

At the April 22nd victory rally, Rep. William Lacy Clay told SWA members, "You students risked a lot. But it was a worthwhile victory."[10]

Student Worker Alliance was led and supported by Katie Castellano and several other known supporters of the Young Communist League USA.[11]

Relationship with Jamala Rogers

Writing in the St Louis American on March 14, 2013, Jamala Rogers, a Missouri member of the Marxist-Leninist, Freedom Road Socialist Organization, claimed to have a "long relationship" with both Missouri State Senator Jamilah Nasheed and Congressman William Lacy Clay, Jr.[12]

William Lacy Clay, Jr. spoke alongside Jamala Rogers at the August 2007 Veterans for Peace convention in St. Louis. Veterans for Peace has always been heavily infiltrated by the Communist Party and other Marxist groups.[13]

Foreign Policy/National Security

Staffer's 2004 Trip to Cuba

In May 2004, Robert Odom, from the office of Congressman William Lacy Clay, spent four days in Havana, Cuba for the purpose of "fact finding," as a part of a Congressional staff delegation. The trip cost $1,340.16 and was paid for by the leftist Christopher Reynolds Foundation.[14]

1 KeyWiki, "William Lacy Clay, Jr.," KeyWiki, http://keywiki.org/index.php/William_Lacy_Clay%2C_Jr. (accessed April 27, 2013)
2 Wm. Lacy Clay, "About Lacy," House.gov, http://clay.house.gov/about-lacy/ (accessed April 27, 2013)
3 Kevin McDermott, "William Lacy Clay wins easily over Russ Carnahan," Political Fix, http://www.stltoday.com/news/local/govt-and-politics/william-lacy-clay-wins-easily-over-russ-carnahan/article_ca33460d-8ce4-5f0b-8a3e-7f31e70b9403.html (April 8, 2012)
4 Wm. Lacy Clay, "Committees," House.gov, http://clay.house.gov/committees/ (accessed April 27, 2013)
5 KeyWiki, "Lew Moye," KeyWiki, http://www.keywiki.org/index.php/Lew_Moye (accessed April 27, 2013)
6 William L. Clay, "Bill Clay: a political voice at the grass roots," p. 299
7 Broadcast Urban, "37th International Convention – May 24 Opening Session," Broadcast Urban, http://www.broadcasturban.net/webcast/cbtu2008/sat_opening.htm (accessed December 19, 2011)
8 Metro Sentinel Journal, "2012 CBTU Ernest and De Verne Calloway Awards," Metro Sentinel Journal, http://www.metrosentineljournal.com/wp-content/uploads/2012/10/Sentinel-10-25-12-final-review-pgs-1-8.pdf (October 25, 2012)
9 John Bachtell, "Mega-storm now underway a taste of what may be," People's World, http://peoplesworld.org/mega-storm-now-underway-a-taste-of-what-may-be/ (October 29, 2012)
10 Tony Pecinovsky, "Victory for Wash U students in living wage," People's World, http://www.peoplesworld.org/victory-for-wash-u-students-in-living-wage/ (April 29, 2005)
11 KeyWiki, "Student Worker Alliance," KeyWiki, http://www.keywiki.org/index.php/Student_Worker_Alliance (accessed April 27, 2013)
12 Jamala Rogers, "A defeat and a victory," The St. Louis American, http://m.stlamerican.com/news/columnists/article_a8965c1e-8c4e-11e2-92ca-0019bb2963f4.html?mode=jqm, (March 2013)
13 KeyWiki, "Veterans for Peace," KeyWiki, http://www.keywiki.org/index.php/Veterans_for_Peace (accessed April 27, 2013)
14 Congressional Staffers Share the Road, "Christopher Reynolds Foundation," American RadioWorks, http://americanradioworks.publicradio.org/features/staffers/travdat/sponsor.php?sponsor_id=T000109 (accessed April 27, 2013)

Carolyn Maloney (D-NY)

Carolyn Maloney is a Democratic member of the United States House of Representatives, representing the 12th District of New York. She is a long-time member of the Congressional Progressive Caucus.[1]

Background

After graduating from Greensboro College, Maloney worked for several years as a teacher and an administrator for the New York City Board of Education. In 1977, she went to work for the New York State legislature and held senior staff positions in both the State Assembly and the State Senate. In 1982, Maloney ran for public office, winning a seat on the New York City Council.

In 1986, she founded the Council's Committee on City Contracts and used this position to write a series of new laws setting up a computerized system to monitor the $7 billion which the city awards each year in contracts.

She was also the principal author of the landmark New York City Campaign Finance Act.[2]

Influence

Carolyn Maloney is a senior member of both the House Financial Services Committee and the House Oversight and Government Reform Committee. She is Vice-Chair of the House Democrats' Steering and Policy Committee and immediate past Chair of the Joint Economic Committee.[3]

Communist Connections

Asian Americans for Equality

Carolyn Maloney has ties to Asian Americans for Equality (AAFE); a Chinatown based rebranding of the pro-Communist China, Communist Workers Party.

Marching with Margaret Chin, Chinese Flags

In 2011, Reps. Nydia Velazquez and Carolyn Maloney marched with Margaret Chin at the Lunar New Year Parade in Chinatown, complete with American and Chinese flags. Chin is a New York City Councilor, long-time President of AAFE and a former leader of the Communist Workers Party.[4]

Velazquez, Chin, Maloney, Communist Flags

Supporting AAFE

On November 25, 2009, at a press conference in Chinatown, AAFE announced it had become a charter member of NeighborWorks America.[5]

While unable to attend the event, Congresswoman Carolyn Maloney also applauded AAFE's membership in the NeighborWorks network. "I am delighted that AAFE will be one of the first Asian-American charter members of the NeighborWorks," said Congresswoman Maloney. "For decades, AAFE has been a force for positive change in lower Manhattan, helping thousands access affordable housing and granting millions in low-cost loans to small businesses and entrepreneurs. AAFE exemplifies the spirit of civic involvement that makes New York the greatest city in the world."[6]

"Stop the Violence" Rally

On January 31, 2013, Carolyn Maloney addressed a "Stop the Violence" rally supported by AAFE and several other radical and community groups.[7]

Socialist Connections

Greeting the Peace Marchers

The Great Peace Marchers for Global Nuclear Disarmament arrived in New York, October 23, 1986, after trekking 3,500 miles from Los Angeles with their message of global nuclear disarmament.

They were greeted at the George Washington Bridge by Mark Green, Democratic Socialists of America (DSA) and Institute for Policy Studies-affiliated Democratic candidate for the U.S. Senate; DSA member David Dinkins (Manhattan Borough President); DSAer David Livingston (President of District 65 UAW); DSA Assembly member Jerry Nadler; City Council members Ruth Messinger (DSA) and Miriam Friedlander (Communist Party USA); and Rep. Carolyn Maloney.

The following Friday, the Communist Party USA's People's Daily World sponsored a reception for 25 of the marchers at Unity Auditorium on West 23rd St.[8]

Hiroshima Day

On August 6, 1993, a rally to commemorate Hiroshima Day was held at the United Nations, Dag Hammarskjold Park in New York. The rally was designed "to kickoff a national campaign to collect a million signatures supporting a Comprehensive Test Ban Treaty, commend President Clinton for extending the nuclear testing moratorium, urge renewal of the Non-Proliferation Treaty and urge swift and complete nuclear disarmament."

The event was sponsored by the Metro New York Peace Action Council and several other "peace" groups.[9]

Speakers included: Leslie Cagan, Cuba Information Project and Committees of Correspondence; David McReynolds, War Resisters League, Socialist Party USA and Democratic Socialists of America; three more DSA comrades: Ruth Messinger; Manhattan Borough President; Congressman Jerry Nadler; and Congressman Major Owens; as well as Rep. Carolyn Maloney.

"Progressive" Connection

Leading with Love

Leading with Love was an event to celebrate 5 years of the Marxist led, Institute for Policy Studies partner organization, the National Domestic Workers Alliance. It was held in Washington, D.C. on November 14, 2012.

Members of the Host Committee included Rep. Carolyn Maloney and Barack Obama's communist former "Green Jobs Czar," Van Jones.[10]

---

1 KeyWiki, "Carolyn Maloney," KeyWiki, http://keywiki.org/index.php/Carolyn_Maloney (accessed April 5, 2013)
2 Carolyn B. Maloney, "Biography," House.gov, http://maloney.house.gov/about-me/extended-biography (accessed August 21, 2011)
3 Carolyn B. Maloney, "Committees," House.gov, http://maloney.house.gov/about-me/committees-and-caucuses (accessed August 21, 2011)
4 Ed Litvak, "Asian Politicians Celebrate Gains, Plan for the Future," The Lo-Down, http://www.thelodownny.com/leslog/2011/03/asian-politicians-celebrate-gains-plan-for-the-future.html#more-30620, (March 25, 2011)
5 Ed Litvak, "Asian Americans for Equality Joins NeighborWorks," The Lo-Down, http://www.thelodownny.com/leslog/2009/11/asian-americans-for-equality-joins-neighborworks.html, (November 25, 2009)
6 NeighborWorks America, "Two Newly Chartered NeighborWorks Organizations Celebrate their Affiliation in the Northeast District," NeighborWorks, http://www.nw.org/network/newsroom/articles/netNews120309.asp, (accessed January 12, 2012)
7 KeyWiki, "Carolyn Maloney," KeyWiki, http://keywiki.org/index.php/Carolyn_Maloney (accessed April 5, 2013)
8 Richard Hoyen, "Full schedule in NYC for peace marchers," People's Daily World (October 1986) p. 3
9 People's Weekly World (June 1993)
10 Leading with Love, "Hosts and Sponsors," Leading with Love, http://domesticworkers.org/leadingwithlove/hosts-and-sponsors, (accessed January 12, 2012)

Greg Meeks
(D-NY)

Gregory W. Meeks is a Democratic Congressman representing the 5th District of New York. He is a member of the Congressional Black Caucus.[1]

Background

Gregory Weldon Meeks was born on September 25, 1953, in East Harlem, New York City and raised in a housing project.

Congressman Meeks earned his Bachelor's Degree at Adelphi University and he received his law degree from Howard University.

He worked as an Assistant District Attorney and Special Narcotics Prosecutor for the City of New York before joining the Investigations Commission on Official Misconduct and Organized Crime. He then was Supervising Judge for the New York State Workers Compensation System.

Meeks was elected to the New York State Assembly in 1992.[2]

Influence

Congressman Meeks is a senior member of the House Financial Services Committee and is the former Chairman of the Subcommittee on International Monetary Policy and Trade.

He currently serves as Ranking Member of the Subcommittee on Financial Institutions and Consumer Credit, which oversees all components of the nation's housing and financial services sectors including banking, insurance, real estate, public and assisted housing and securities.

The Committee reviews the laws relating to the U.S. Department of Housing and Urban Development, the Federal Reserve Bank, the Federal Deposit Insurance Corporation, Fannie Mae and Freddie Mac and international development and finance agencies such as the World Bank and the International Monetary Fund.

Congressman Meeks serves as a senior member of the House Foreign Affairs Committee where he is the former Ranking Member of the Subcommittee on Europe and Eurasia. He sits on the Subcommittee on the Western Hemisphere and the Subcommittee on Europe and Eurasia.

The Committee is responsible for oversight and legislation relating to: foreign assistance; the Peace Corps; national security developments affecting foreign policy; strategic planning and agreements; war powers; treaties; executive agreements; the deployment and use of United States Armed Forces; peacekeeping; peace enforcement and enforcement of United Nations or other international sanctions; arms control and disarmament issues; the United States Agency for International Development; activities and policies of the State, Commerce and Defense Departments and other agencies related to the Arms Export Control Act and the Foreign Assistance Act.

Congressman Meeks is a Co-Chair of the Brazil Caucus and Colombia Caucus. He also Co-Chairs the New Dem Task Force on Trade, the Services Caucus to promote the advancement of trade in services and the Organization of American States Caucus to "facilitate a stronger, more cooperative hemisphere."[3]

Foreign Policy/National Security

Staffer's 2000 Trip to Cuba

In February 2000, Faith Blackburne, from the office of Congressman Meeks, spent six days in Havana, Cuba, for the purpose of "improving US/Cuba relations." The trip cost $1,778.47 and was paid for by the leftist Christopher Reynolds Foundation.[4]

First Cuba Visit

Meeks was part of the June 2000 delegation from the Congressional Black Caucus that visited Cuban President Fidel Castro.[5]

Second Cuba Trip

From December 15th through the 18th of 2006, a Congressional Delegation of ten Congressmen and women from the U.S. House of Representatives visited Havana, Cuba.

Leading the delegation were Jeff Flake and Bill Delahunt. The other participants were Hilda Solis, Jo Ann Emerson, Jerry Moran, Michael Conaway, Jane Harman, Lincoln Davis, Gregory Meeks and Jim McGovern. The delegation met with Cuban Foreign Minister, Felipe Perez Roque and other communist officials. The delegation asked to meet with Raul Castro, but there was no word on whether such a meeting took place.[6]

Congressional Delegation meets with Cuban Foreign Minister, Felipe Perez Roque; Greg Meeks, partially obscured

Staffer's 2007 Trip to Venezuela

Rep. Meeks sent Sophie Atlee King to Marxist-led Venezuela for four days in July of 2007. The trip was courtesy of a $1,606.25 grant from the Institute for Policy Studies-connected Center for Democracy in the Americas... "To examine U.S. policy toward Venezuela and to better understand how government policies are affecting foreign investment in the energy sector."[7]

Chavez's Funeral

In March of 2013, Rep. Meeks announced he would officially represent the United States at former Venezuelan President Hugo Chávez's funeral, a "country he's dealt with in the past as a senior member on the House Foreign Affairs Committee."

"I thought that the trip was very good," Meeks later said. "I was welcomed there by both members of the opposition as well as people close to President Chávez. As you know, I got to know President Chávez quite well. I think that though controversial—there were many things that

I disagreed with—that he did have his heart on the poor. When you look at the thousands upon thousands of people that were in the streets mourning his death, Venezuela is clearly a country that is in mourning."

"It was an opportunity to hope that we have a better relationship with Venezuela in the future," he explained. "There were world leaders from many of our allies—Colombia, all of the Caribbean, and everyone who was there—so it was an opportunity to talk to them also about where we go from here and how we can improve relationships. Before Chávez was president poor people had no hope. Chavez gave them hope and that someone was on their side."

"I believe in democracy and the people of Venezuela elect its leaders just like we elect ours," he said. "So that's for the people of Venezuela to decide and move together. Chávez was democratically elected three times. So I would never disparage a people's choice for their president just like I don't want anyone to disparage the American people's choice for president."[8]

---

1 KeyWiki, "Gregory Meeks," KeyWiki, http://keywiki.org/index.php/Gregory_Meeks (accessed April 28, 2013)

2 Gregory W. Meeks, "Full Biography," House.gov, http://meeks.house.gov/about-me/full-biography (accessed April 29, 2013)

3 Gregory W. Meeks, "Full Biography," House.gov, http://meeks.house.gov/about-me/full-biography (accessed April 29, 2013)

4 Congressional Staffers Share the Road, "Christopher Reynolds Foundation," American RadioWorks, http://americanradioworks.publicradio.org/features/staffers/travdat/sponsor.php?sponso r_id=T000109 (accessed April 29, 2013)

5 Fitzhugh Mullan, M.D., "Cuba Trains Physicians for Wealthy United States," University of Dayton, http://academic.udayton.edu/health/02organ/providers01.htm (December 23, 2004)

6 Anita Snow, "Fidel Castro and US Congressional trip to Cuba update," Havana Journal, http://havanajournal.com/politics/entry/fidel-castro-and-us-congressional-trip-to-cuba-update/ (December 17, 2006)

7 LegiStorm, "Center for Democracy in the Americas – Sponsor of Congressional Travel," LegiStorm, http://www.legistorm.com/trip/list/by/sponsor/id/10693/name/Center_for_Democracy_ in_the_Americas/page/2.html (accessed August 30, 2010)

8 Colin Campbell, "NY Congressman Gregory Meeks Reports Back After Attending Hugo Chavez's Funeral," Politicker, http://politicker.com/2013/03/congressman-gregory-meeks-reports-back-after-attending-hugo-chavezs-funeral/oliticker (March 2013)

Grace Meng (D-NY)

Grace Meng is a freshman Democratic member of the United States House of Representatives, representing the 6th District of New York. She is a member of the Congressional Asian Pacific American Caucus.[1]

Background

Born in Corona, Queens, Grace Meng graduated from Stuyvesant High School and the University of Michigan. She then earned a law degree from Yeshiva University's Benjamin Cardozo School of Law. Prior to entering public service, she worked as a public interest lawyer.

Prior to serving in Congress, Grace Meng was a member of the New York State Assembly. While she was in the Assembly, she was a "dedicated bridge builder and a fighter for equality."[2]

Influence

While in the State Assembly, Meng served on Governor-elect Andrew Cuomo's transition team for the areas of human services and housing.

Meng served alongside several key leftists including Chung-Wha Hong, Executive Director of the New York Immigrant Coalition; City Council Speaker Christine Quinn; Stuart Appelbaum, President of the Retail, Wholesale and Department Store Union; Christopher Kui, Executive Director of Asian Americans for Equality and Ross Levi, Legislative Director of New York State Pride Agenda.[3]

Grace Meng is a member of the House Foreign Affairs Committee and its Subcommittee on the Middle East and North Africa. The Foreign Affairs Committee oversees United States foreign policy towards all nations around the world and has jurisdiction over foreign aid, the State Department and key international organizations such as the United Nations.

Meng also serves on the House Small Business Committee where she sits on two subcommittees: Contracting and Workforce—of which she is the Ranking Member—and Agriculture, Energy and Trade. The Small Business Committee has oversight over financial aid, regulatory matters and the Small Business Administration.[4]

Communist Connections

Grace Meng has a very close relationship with Asian Americans for Equality (AAFE), a powerful New York Chinatown organization formed, by the pro-China Communist Workers Party (CWP).

NeighborWorks America Event

On November 25, 2009, at a press conference in Chinatown, AAFE announced it has become a charter member of NeighborWorks America. A non-profit created by Congress, NeighborWorks provides financial support and training for community-driven revitalization projects. As a start, AAFE was presented with a check for nearly a quarter of a million dollars. Several elected officials were on hand to celebrate the occasion. Among them: Assembly Speaker Sheldon Silver, Rep. Nydia Velazquez, State Senator Daniel Squadron, Assembly member Grace Meng and City Council member Rosie Mendez. Margaret Chin, District 1's new City Council member, former AAFE President and CWP member, was there as well.[5]

Supporting John Choe

A new AAFE project called the One Flushing Community Economic Development Center opened its doors on December 15, 2012, marking the occasion with an open house.

The project's Executive Director, John Choe, said his role "is to bring people together and connect people to existing resources."

That August, Choe had left his job as Chief of Staff for then-City Council member John Liu, and began working in conjunction with AAFE on the One Flushing project.

Choe left Liu's service not long after controversy erupted over his pro-North Korean views and activism.

Grace Meng (left); John Choe (microphone)

In 1999, he helped found a community-development organization called Nodutdol, which is Korean for "stepping stone." The organization's mission, according to its website, is "to contribute to a global people's struggle against war and militarism as part of a Korean struggle for national unification and democracy, and as part of a U.S.-based peoples' struggle for racial, social and economic justice in New York City."

As part of that mission, the group organizes trips to North Korea. It's what the group calls its "Democratic People's Republic of Korea Exposure & Education Program."

"Because of the biased and negative portrayal of North Korea by the U.S. government and mainstream media, most of us (even Koreans who are already committed to social justice), are poorly informed about the DPRK," reads the program description available on the site. "This program helps to demystify the DPRK and build person to person understanding to organize in this collective, socialist society."

Choe also told a 2006 Workers World Party "Global Struggle for Socialism" conference that North Korea was "at the front line of the liberation struggles against imperialism."[6]

At the open house, Choe said he would count on AAFE to help him identify private foundations and government agencies that could provide One Flushing with much-needed resources.

Several elected officials and community leaders attended the open house, including Christopher Kui, Executive Director of AAFE, who said, "We want to push Flushing forward. Small business is a key to help the area become a major economic center."

Assemblywoman Grace Meng called One Flushing a "very important project. I'm proud to join all of you."[7]

John Choe later gathered signatures on a Meng petition in April of 2012 for her Congressional primary race.[8]

AAFE Community Development Conference

In celebration of Asian Pacific American Heritage Month, AAFE convened its 5th Community Development Conference on May 17, 2012, in New York to examine the "socio-economic contributions of New York's growing Asian Pacific American community."

The summit brought together over 300 leaders from housing and community organizations, corporations, foundations, government agencies and academic institutions, as well as local, state and national elected officers.

Keynote speakers included: New York City Council member and "former" Maoist, Margaret Chin; State Assembly person Grace Meng; U.S. Dept. of Labor Official Patricia Shiu; HUD official Francey Lim Youngberg and Hyeok Kim, representing the White House Initiative on Asian Americans and Pacific Islanders.[9]

The moderator of Meng's plenary, "Mobilizing Our Community from the Margins to the Center," was Bill Chong, NYC Department for the Aging, a former member of the Communist Workers Party and an AAFE Board President.[10] [11]

Asian Americans for Equality Award

AAFE's 39th Annual Lunar New Year Banquet was held on March 21, 2013 at the Jing Fong Restaurant in Manhattan's Chinatown. At every banquet, AAFE presents the "Dream of Equality Award" to several honorees.

2013 honorees included Congress members Grace Meng and Joseph Crowley, as well as State Assembly member Ron Kim:[12]

Last year, Grace Meng became the first Asian American member of Congress from New York, representing the 6th Congressional District, including west, central and northeast Queens. Rep. Meng has dedicated herself to fighting for New York's hard-working families, protecting Medicare and Social Security, focusing on economic growth and job creation, advocating for equal access to quality education and championing critical infrastructure projects. Before winning election to the U.S. Congress, Meng served in the New York State Assembly. She passed laws extending unemployment coverage during the worst economic crisis since the Great Depression, fought human trafficking, cracked down on those who abuse women and children and protected seniors from rising property taxes.

Grace Meng (center); Margaret Chin next to her; Chris Kui (far right)

Lunar New Year, School Holiday

Grace Meng has worked many years with AAFE affiliates, to promote legislation making the Chinese Lunar New Year a school holiday in New York.

On January 31, 2013, a press conference was held outside P.S. 20 in Flushing. State Senators Daniel Squadron (D-Chinatown) and Toby Ann Stavisky (D-Flushing), Assembly member Ron Kim (D-Flushing) and Congresswoman Grace Meng (D-Queens), urged the city to make the Asian Lunar New Year a school holiday so that New York City's growing number of Asian American students can celebrate with their families without missing class.

"When I served in the State Legislature, I led the effort to make the Lunar New Year a public school holiday, and worked with Speaker Sheldon Silver to pass the bill in the Assembly," said Grace Meng. "I am glad that my successor Ron Kim will now be taking up the cause. Making the Lunar New Year a school holiday would recognize the important customs and culture of Asian Americans, and it would highlight the vital role that the Asian American community plays in our city. I am happy to continue my support for this important measure."

"Designating the Asian Lunar New Year as an official school holiday is long overdue," said former AAFE President, Council member Margaret Chin.

"Lunar New Year is a time of coming together and renewal for the nearly 1 million Asian New Yorkers of different ethnicities who celebrate the holiday," said Christopher Kui, Executive Director of AAFE. "Children whose families celebrate Lunar New Year should not have to miss a day of school, and passing this legislation brings an opportunity to raise cultural awareness about Asian heritage and traditions within the school system."[13]

Foreign Policy/National Security

UN Chinese Friendship Association

On December 28, 2011, Charles Lee, Secretary-General of the United Nations Chinese Friendship Association, visited Grace Meng:[14]

Ms. Grace Meng highly "evaluated UN Chinese Friendship Association and decided to cooperate with Charles Lee, Secretary-General of UN Chinese Friendship Association, and called on all of the Chinese in U.S. to consolidate".

---

1 KeyWiki, "Grace Meng," KeyWiki, http://keywiki.org/index.php/Grace_Meng (accessed April 10, 2013)
2 Grace Meng, "Full Biography," House.gov, http://meng.house.gov/about/full-biography (accessed March 23, 2012)
3 Kenny Schaeffer, "Cuomo Names Housing Transition Team," Metropolitan Council on Housing, http://metcouncilonhousing.org/news_and_issues/tenant_newspaper/2010/december/cuomo_names_housing_transition_team, (December 2010)
4 Grace Meng, "Full Biography," House.gov, http://meng.house.gov/about/full-biography (accessed March 23, 2012)
5 Ed Litvak, "Asian Americans for Equality Joins NeighborWorks," The Lo-Down, http://www.thelodownny.com/leslog/2009/11/asian-americans-for-equality-joins-neighborworks.html, (November 25, 2009)
6 KeyWiki, "John Choe," KeyWiki, http://www.keywiki.org/index.php/John_Choe (accessed April 10, 2013)
7 Queens Chronicle, "New group helps small businesses," Queens Chronicle, http://www.qchron.com/editions/north/new-group-helps-small-businesses/article_6bc789d5-fa44-5f1e-907f-684a0d3a4134.html, (December 15, 2011)
8 Michael Gartland, "Kim pal aids pol," New York Post, http://www.nypost.com/p/news/local/queens/kim_pal_aids_pol_xhojHacsJIkJC1jguGbW8N, (April 29, 2012)
9 AAFE blog, "Recap: 5th Annual Community Development Conference," AAFE blog, http://www.aafe.org/2012/07/recap-5th-annual-community-development-conference.html, (accessed April 29, 2012)
10 5th Annual Asian American Community Development Conference page (accessed March 25, 2013)
11 KeyWiki, "Bill Chong," KeyWiki, http://www.keywiki.org/index.php/Bill_Chong (accessed April 10, 2013)
12 AAFE blog, "Crowley, Meng, Kim, Wright, Garza To Be Honored at AAFE Banquet," AAFE blog, http://www.aafe.org/2013/02/crowley-meng-kim-wright-garza-to-be-honored-at-aafe-banquet.html, (accessed April 10, 2013)
13 Amy Spitalnick, "Squadron, Stavisky, Kim, Meng Urge Lunar New Year School Holiday," Daniel Squadron website, http://www.nysenate.gov/press-release/squadron-stavisky-kim-meng-urge-lunar-new-year-school-holiday, (January 31st, 2013)
14 UNCFA, "Charles Lee visited Ms. Grace Meng, American New York State's only congresswoman," UNCFA, http://www.uncfa.org/english/html/2012/pps_0201/48.html, (January 2, 2012)

Jerrold Nadler (D-NY)

Jerrold Nadler is a Democratic member of the United States House of Representatives, representing the 8th District of New York. He is a long-time member of the Congressional Progressive Caucus.[1]

Background

Jerry Nadler was born in Brooklyn in June 1947. Nadler attended Crown Heights Yeshiva and Later Stuyvesant High School, from which he graduated in 1965. He also graduated from Columbia University and Fordham Law School.

At Columbia University, Nadler "began his political career as a founder of a group of students known as the 'West End Kids,' (referring to the West Side of Manhattan) which focused on reforming New York City Democratic Party politics through support of liberal and anti-Vietnam War candidates.

The Kids developed their political base by engaging in community organizing to improve local housing and education conditions. Nadler's West End Kids at Columbia University wrote, "Also led the 'Clean for Gene' McCarthy campaign that brought thousands of students to New Hampshire for the 1968 Democratic Presidential campaign of Senator Eugene McCarthy against [Democratic President] Lyndon Johnson and the Vietnam War."

In 1970, Nadler graduated from Columbia University and worked a stint as a legislative staffer. Then in 1976, he won election to a seat in the lower house of the New York state legislature, where he served until 1992.

That year, far left Democratic Congressman Ted Weiss died one day before the primary election for a newly-redrawn 8th District. Nadler replaced Weiss on the November ballot, winning easily.[2]

Influence

In 2007, with the Democrats in control of Congress, Representative Nadler was given the honor of serving as the Chair of the House Judiciary Subcommittee on the Constitution, Civil Rights and Civil Liberties. He is also the highest ranking Northeastern member of the House Transportation and Infrastructure Committee, an Assistant Democrat Whip and the New York State Congressional Delegation's representative on the Democratic Steering and Policy Committee, "affording him the opportunity to work on a daily basis to craft and shape the policy and major laws that govern our country."

In 2010, Nadler still held the position of Chair of the House Judiciary Subcommittee on the Constitution, Civil Rights and Civil Liberties.[3]

Currently, Nadler still serves on the Judiciary Committee, which includes the Subcommittee on the Constitution where he is a Ranking Member and the Subcommittee on Intellectual Property, Competition and the Internet. He also serves on the Transportation and Infrastructure Committee, which includes the Subcommittee on Highways and Travel and the Subcommittee on Railroads, Pipelines and Hazardous Materials.[4]

Socialist Connections

DSOC Member

According to Democratic Socialist Organizing Committee (DSOC) Founder and Chairman Michael Harrington, the influence of the group was disproportionate to its size because of the positions held by some DSCO members within the Democratic Party.

In 1980, prominent DSOC members working through the Democratic Party included Rep. Ronald Dellums (D-CA); Hilda Mason, D.C. City Council; Harlan Baker, Maine State Legislature; Perry Bullard, Michigan State Legislature; Ruth Messinger, New York City Council; Harry Britt, San Francisco Board of Supervisors and Jerry Nadler, New York State Legislature.[5]

Identified DSA Member

Jerry Nadler was identified as a member of Democratic Socialists of America (DSA) in DSA's Democratic Left, January 1983 issue, page 14:[6]

In New York, DSA State assembly members now include Eileen Dugan, Denny Farrell, and Jerry Nadler. Ed Wallace remains on the New York City Council, as an at large member, while Ruth Messinger was re-elected to the council...

Socialist Scholars Conferences

In the 1990s, Jerry Nadler was a regular speaker at New York's annual DSA organized Socialist Scholars Conference (SSC).

In 1995, Jerrold Nadler was prominent at the SSC, April 7-9 in New York City. Nadler was involved in Panel 1: "Crisis in the City," with DSAer Frances Fox Piven.[7]

Jerrold Nadler attended the 14th Annual SSC: "Two Cheers for Utopia: Reimagining Socialism," April 12-14, 1996 in New York City.

Nadler shared a panel with DSAers Frances Fox Piven and Stanley Aronowitz entitled: "The Left and the Job Agenda in the U.S."[8]

Nadler was listed as a speaker at the 1997 Socialist SSC held March 28-30 at the Borough of Manhattan Community College in New York.[9]

1995 DSA National Conference

Jerry Nadler addressed the 1995 Democratic Socialists of America National Conference.[10]

DSA Endorsement

In July 1996, the Democratic Socialists of America Political Action Committee endorsed Jerrold Nadler in that year's Congressional elections.[11]

DSA "People's Hearing on Economic Insecurity"

New York DSA held a "People's Hearing on Economic Insecurity," on October 28, 1995. The hearing, chaired by Congress member Major Owens (a DSA member) and Jerry Nadler, was the second of twelve planned by DSA locals during the next year. With Republicans controlling both Houses of Congress, "progressive" legislation such as DSA member Ron Dellums' Living Wage/Jobs for A|1 Act and DSA affiliate Bernie Sanders' Corporate Responsibility Act "can't get a hearing these days." Congressman Ron Dellums thus asked DSA to organize town meetings around the country that could begin to "refocus the public debate and unite poor, working and middle-class people around a program for economic justice and growth."

"It's shocking to me that no one is questioning whether the conservative way is the best way to promote growth," agreed Congress member Nadler. "Many economists show that putting more money in the hands of the poor and middle class is more effective, and that one dollar spent by the government has greater impact on the economy than one dollar spent by the private sector."

"We have to put an end to the sterile debate," Nadler added, "between conservatives who argue for growth through removing regulatory fetters and putting more money in the hands of the rich by reducing taxes, and liberals who argue for redistribution. We need growth with fairness and equity, an industrial policy and investment in infrastructure and human capital."[12]

Social Security Briefing

According to DSA's Democratic Left of April 1, 1999:[13]

Recently, Congressional Representative Jerrold Nadler briefed DSA activists from around the country on the state of the Social Security situation. According to Nadler, the Social Security "crisis" isn't financial, it's political.

Nadler pointed out, however, that it's hard to stop something with nothing: "People on our side of the aisles have to have a positive plan." To this end, Nadler has proposed a bill, H.R. 1043, that addresses some of the perceived problems with Social Security.

Nadler Updates DSA on Sc

BY STEVE OLIVER

Recently, Congressional Representative Jerrold Nadler briefed DSA activists from around the country on the state of the Social Security situation. According to Nadler, the Social Security "crisis" isn't financial, it's political. Analyses of the Social Security Trust Fund that point to the looming insolvency of the fund in 2032 (or 2034) are based on an unrealistically low growth rate in the economy of 1.5%. A more realistic assumption of 2.4% means the Trust Fund is flush for the statutory requirement of 75 years.

The publicity generated around these analyses, pumped by right wing politicians and think tanks, has caused the public to think that Social Security is in trouble (see DL, Winter 1999). Congressman Nadler, a New York City Democrat and a member of the House Progressive Caucus, attacked conservative assumptions, and called the "assault on social insurance a danger to the health and well-being of the ous "carve out" proposals that would have some percentage of the S.S. tax reduced for individuals who set up their own private investment accounts. Others prefer one of over thirty variations floating around their caucus. Nadler believes that this right wing division of opinion, coupled with delay until after the 2000 national elections "would be the best thing to happen." Congressman

Democratic Left, April 1, 1999

Union Park Square Event

According to Democratic Left, Summer 2004, page 11:[14]

> In March, New York City DSA arranged several panels and a reception at the Socialist Scholars Conference.

> For May Day (also known as Law Day in the United States), the local held an event in Union Square Park with Congressman Jerry Nadler and other speakers about the erosion of the rule of law under the Bush administration and about the promises of the Brown vs. Board of Education decision still unfulfilled on its 50th anniversary.

National Jobs For All Coalition

In 2010, Jerry Nadler was listed as serving on the Advisory Board of the DSA-dominated National Jobs For All Coalition.[15]

Saving ACORN

When DSA-connected Congressman John Conyers called for an investigation of the DSA-connected ACORN, the effort was brought to a halt by the DSA-connected Jerry Nadler.

Rep. Jerry Nadler, Chairman of the Subcommittee on the Constitution, made the case that the bill to deny federal funding to ACORN, may not, if signed into law, stand up to court challenges.

The ACORN bill, Nadler claimed was essentially a "Bill of Attainder," a measure targeted to benefit or penalize an individual or group which is prohibited in the Constitution, Article 1, Sections 9 and 10.

In a floor speech, Nadler said:[16]

> A little while ago, the House passed an amendment to the bill that we were considering that says no contract or federal funds may ever go to ACORN, a named organization, or to any individual or organization affiliated with ACORN. Unfortunately, this was done in the spirit of the moment and nobody had the opportunity to point out that this is a flat violation of the Constitution, constituting a Bill of Attainder. The Constitution says that Congress shall never pass a Bill of Attainder. Bills of Attainder, no matter what their form, apply either to a named individual or to easily ascertainable members of a group, to inflict punishment. That's exactly what this amendment does.

> It may be that ACORN is guilty of various infractions, and, if so, it ought to be vetted, or maybe sanctioned, by the appropriate

administrative agency or by the judiciary. Congress must not be in the business of punishing individual organizations or people without trial.

Working Families Party

Under New York's "fusion" system, Jerry Nadler has run on the tickets of both the Democratic Party and New York's ACORN and DSA infiltrated Working Families Party.[17]

1 KeyWiki, "Jerry Nadler," KeyWiki, http://keywiki.org/index.php/Jerrold_Nadler (accessed April 4, 2013)
2 Jerrold Nadler, "Full Biography," House.gov, http://nadler.house.gov/about-me/full-biography (accessed April 4, 2013)
3 Jerrold Nadler, "Full Biography," House.gov, http://nadler.house.gov/about-me/full-biography (accessed April 4, 2013)
4 Jerrold Nadler, "My Committees," House.gov, http://nadler.house.gov/legislative-work/my-committees (accessed April 4, 2013)
5 Information Digest (September 19, 1980) p. 331
6 Democratic Left (January 1983) p. 14
7 Radio Free Maine, "1995 Socialist Scholars Conference – flyer," Radio Free Maine, http://www.radiofreemaine.com/RFMDSA.html (accessed February 8, 2011)
8 Radio Free Maine, "14th Annual Socialist Scholars Conference: Two Cheers for Utopia: Reimaging Socialism," Radio Free Maine, http://www.radiofreemaine.com/RFMDSA96.html (accessed February 8, 2011)
9 Karl Carlile, "Socialists Scholars Conference," The Mail Archive, http://www.mail-archive.com/pen-l@galaxy.csuchico.edu/msg18263.html (accessed February 8, 2011)
10 Democratic Socialists of America, "1995 National Conference Report"
11 Democratic Left (July/August 1996) p. 21
12 Democratic Left (November/December 1995) p. 7
13 Democratic Left (April 1, 1999)
14 Democratic Left, http://www.dsausa.org/dl/Summer_2004.pdf (Summer 2004)
15 National Jobs For All Coalition, "Who We Are," National Jobs For All Coalition, http://www.njfac.org/whoweare.html (accessed November 156, 2010)
16 Glenn Thrush, "Nadler: ACORN ban unconstitutional," Politico, http://www.politico.com/blogs/glennthrush/0909/Nadler_ACORN_ban_unconstitutional.html (September 17, 2009)
17 Mathew Vadum, "Nadler's ACORN Ethics," The American Spectator, http://spectator.org/archives/2009/10/26/nadlers-acron-ethics (October 26, 2009)

Charles Rangel (D-NY)

Charles B. Rangel is a Democratic member of the United States House of Representatives, representing the 15th District of New York. Rangel was one of the founding members of the Congressional Black Caucus and served at one time as its Chairman. He is also a long-time member of the Congressional Progressive Caucus and an associate member of the Congressional Asian Pacific American Caucus.[1]

Background

Charlie Rangel was born in New York on June 11, 1930. Raised by his mother and maternal grandfather, an elevator operator, Rangel grew up in the streets of New York. After dropping out of high school, Rangel served in the U.S. Army during the Korean War, where he was seriously wounded in battle and received the Bronze Star and Purple Heart.

After his return from Korea, Rangel enrolled at New York University, earning a B.A. in 1957 and receiving his law degree from St. John's University Law School in 1960.[2]

In 1961, Attorney General Robert Kennedy appointed Rangel Assistant U.S. Attorney for the Southern District of New York. In 1967, Rangel won election to the New York State Assembly and in 1971, he ran against the famous Reverend Adam Clayton Powell, Jr. in an historic election. Rangel's victory inaugurated the first of his more than 40 years of consecutive terms as Harlem's Representative to Congress.

Influence

In 1987, Rangel, one of the leading opponents to South African Apartheid, pushed the Internal Revenue Service to eliminate tax credits for taxes paid to the Apartheid government of South Africa. In 1995, he helped to create a federal "empowerment zone" in Manhattan and authored the low-income tax credit to stimulate the development of affordable housing in urban areas.

Early in 2003, Rangel proposed the reinstatement of the military draft as a way to deter the use of force and promote a peaceful resolution to the War in Iraq.[3] In 2007, Rangel became the Chairman of the House Ways and Means Committee.

Communist Connections

Harlem 5

One time New York City Mayor David Dinkins rose through the Democratic Party organization in Harlem and became part of an influential group of African-American politicians that included Percy Sutton, Basil Paterson, Denny Farrell and Charles Rangel. The group ran Harlem politics for decades. Of the five, Dinkins and Farrell (a senior New York state legislator) have been members of Democratic Socialists of America (DSA), while Sutton, Patterson and Rangel leaned more towards the Communist Party USA (CPUSA).[4][5]

National Conference of Black Lawyers

Charlie Rangel was a founding member of the National Conference of Black Lawyers.[6]

According to the National Conference of Black Lawyers website:[7]

> In 1968, young people of African descent in America were growing impatient with the slow pace of social change. Despite modest advances brought on by two decades of non-violent resistance, from one end of the country to the other, the cry for Black Power was raised in the midst of a sea of clinched fists. At the same time, this new militant spirit had moved many to don black berets and carry rifles. On street corners in practically every Black community, passers-by heard demands for Nation Time and Power to the People!

The National Conference of Black Lawyers and its allied organization, the National Lawyers Guild, are the U.S. affiliates of the former Soviet front International Association of Democratic Lawyers.[8].

First Annual Fannie Lou Hammer Awards Dinner

According to an article, "Plan awards dinner to honor activists," in the CPUSA's Daily World, Feb. 19, 1983, page 4:

> Women for Racial and Economic Equality will honor civil rights activists Julia Wilder and Maggie Bozeman at its First Annual Fannie Lou Hammer Awards dinner on Saturday, February 26.
>
> Joining WREE will be city and state officials; leaders from civil rights organizations and liberation movement, and representatives from church and women's groups.

Women for Racial and Economic Equality was a CPUSA front. Representative Charles Rangel was among the participants.[9]

Communist Party Award Ceremony

On November 4, 1999, New York State Assemblyman Richard Gottfried (a Communist Party supporter) presented State Assembly citations to honorees, including Elizabeth Hall, a member of the National Committee of the CPUSA and her comrade Bobbie Rabinowitz, a Founder of the New York City Labor Chorus, at the People's Weekly World 75th Anniversary celebrations at the Henry Winston Unity Auditorium in New York.

U.S. Representative Charles Rangel sent a letter regretting that he was unable to attend, but congratulated the honorees and the World.[10]

2000 People's Weekly World Award Luncheon

On October 22, 2000, the People's Weekly World held its 4th annual celebration luncheon in New York at the Henry Winston Auditorium.

Speakers included City Council members Bill Perkins and Christine Quinn, Assembly member Richard Gottfried, State Senator Tom Duane, Larry Moskowitz of the CPUSA and Working Families Party, and Elena Mora for the Communist Party.

U.S. Representative Charles Rangel sent greetings.[11]

Henry Winston's Centenary Celebration Greeting

A standing room only crowd gathered in Winston Unity Center, New York, on the occasion of Henry Winston's centenary celebration. Winston, who was born in 1912, was the National Chairman of the Communist Party for two decades until his death in 1986.

The multimedia celebration of this great African American leader included speeches, music, a slideshow and greetings from former coworkers and friends—including one from New York Congressman Charles Rangel.[12]

Socialist Connection

DSA Endorsement

In July 1996, the Democratic Socialists of America Political Action Committee endorsed Charles Rangel (NY-15) in that year's Congressional elections.[13]

Foreign Policy/National Security

World Peace Council

Rangel was associated with the Soviet front World Peace Council (WPC).

The first official WPC conference in the U.S. was the Dialogue on Disarmament and Détente held January 25-27, 1978, in Washington, D.C.

Congressman Charles Rangel (left) and Congressman Don Edwards addressing participants in the WPC events.

It was sponsored by a small committee including World Peace Council Presidium member CPUSA functionary and Amalgamated Meatcutters Union Vice-President, Abe Feinglass.

A luncheon was held to honor WPC President Romesh Chandra that was attended by California Congressmen Philip Burton, Don Edwards, Ron Dellums and New York Representative Charles Rangel.

WPC delegation members included President Romesh Chandra, KGB Colonel Radomir Bogdanov and Oleg Kharkhardin of the Communist Party of the Soviet Union International Department.[14]

Voted Against Support for "Contras"

The Congressional Record of February 3, 1988, shows that Charlie Rangel was one of several leading Democratic Party Congressmen who voted against aid to the Nicaraguan Freedom Fighters—the "Contras"—then fighting against the Marxist-Leninist Sandinista government of Nicaragua.[15]

"Congressional Pink Caucus"

In October of 1989, Nicaragua's Marxist-Leninist Sandinista Government announced that they would no longer comply with the 19 month-old cease-fire agreement with the Contras. This had been considered a prime step forward for the "peace process" that was progressing slowly as part of the Arias Peace Plan.

A resolution was introduced in Congress deploring the Sandinistas' action. The Senate voted unanimously in favor, but in the House the vote was 379-29. All of the 29 Congressmen voting against the resolution were Democrats.

The Council for Inter-American Security dubbed these 29 people the "Congressional Pink Caucus."[16] Charlie Rangel was, of course, one of them.

Cuba Recognition Drive

Charlie Rangel has long been one of communist Cuba's best friends in the U.S. Congress.

In 1972, a coalition of Congressmen, radical activists and some communists spearheaded a drive to relax relations with Fidel Castro's Cuba.

Under the auspices of Senator Ted Kennedy (D-MA) and Senator Harold Hughes (D-IA), a two day conference of liberal scholars assembled in April, in the New Senate Office Building to thrash out a fresh U.S. policy in Cuba.

Charlie Rangel was among the Congressional sponsors of the event.

Secretary of the New York State Communist Party, Michael Myerson, was among the observers.[17]

Cuba Bill

In mid-1993, a meeting of the radical National Network on Cuba in Chicago endorsed a call for strong lobbying support for HR 1943, the Free Trade with Cuba Act, introduced into Congress by Charlie Rangel.[18]

Peace for Cuba Appeal

In 1994, Charlie Rangel was an initiator of the International Peace for Cuba Appeal, an affiliate of the Workers World Party dominated International Action Center.

Other prominent initiators included Cuban Intelligence agent Philip Agee, DSA academic/activist Noam Chomsky and Congressman John Conyers.[19]

Welcoming Castro

Charles Rangel attended an October 1995 meeting in Harlem to welcome Cuban leader Fidel Castro to New York.

According to CPUSA paper People's Weekly World:[20]

> Almost 1,600 Harlemites and solidarity activists packed the Abyssinian Baptist Church to give a hero's welcome to Fidel Castro, the president of Cuba.

> The mainly African American audience, which included New York Democratic representatives Charles Rangel and Nydia Velazquez, enthusiastically greeted the Communist leader with a 10-minute standing ovation. Chants of "Cuba si, Bloqueo no!" resounded from the rafters and sent a strong message of protest to New York Mayor Rudolph Giuliani and President Clinton for excluding the Cuban leader from their sponsored events.

> The audience erupted in shouts of "Fidel, Fidel" when Elombe Brath, head of the Patrice Lumumba Coalition and chair for the meeting, asked the audience, "Who would you rather come to Harlem, Fidel or Giuliani?"

Charlie Rangel, Fidel Castro

Controversial Trip to Cuba

Representative Charles Rangel, a frequent critic of the U.S. embargo against Cuba, met with Fidel Castro on a trip to the island in 2002, but only acknowledged that the Cuban government picked up part of the tab when pressed on the issue.

Rangel changed his travel disclosure form for the April 2002 trip and reimbursed the Cuban government and a New York grocery store owner $1,922 for his son's expenses after the Center for Public Integrity, a "nonpartisan group that focuses on open records", raised questions about the trip. House ethics rules permit private sponsors of lawmakers' trips to cover the cost of the member of Congress and one relative—in Rangel's case, his wife Alma, who also went on the trip.

The government watchdog group, which released an extensive review of Congressional travel, noted that Congressional travel disclosure forms "are supposed to make the sponsor and purpose of privately funded trips transparent to the public."

But according to the group, Rangel initially listed a group that was conducting a bird study in Cuba at the time, the Minneapolis-based Sian Ka'an Conservation Foundation, as the sponsor of the trip. On a later amended form, Rangel added the Cuban government and grocery store owner, John Catsimatidis, as sponsors.

In 2009, John Catsimatidis of the Red Apple Group; turned up on the board of the leftist Drum Major Institute.[21]

Rangel's Chief of Staff, George Dalley, told the center that Rangel and his staff did not know the Cuban government had paid for part of the trip until they were contacted by the group.

"The most important thing is that Rangel corrected the mistake he made," Dalley said.

Rangel, who met with Castro as far back as 1988 as part of a Congressional trip, reported the 2002 trip was for "education and fact finding."[22]

Supporting Medical Training in Cuba

In 2004, there were 88 U.S. students at the Latin American School of Medicine in Havana—a school sponsored by the Cuban government and dedicated to training mainly Marxist doctors to treat the poor of the Western hemisphere and Africa.

The Bush administration's restrictions on travel to Cuba had been added to the program from the beginning. Since the Cuban government paid the students' room, board, tuition and a stipend, the ban was not initially applied to them. But the "Bush administration's further attempts to curtail Cuban travel threatened the students and sent their families looking for political help." Representatives Barbara Lee and Charles Rangel led a campaign of protest and 27 members of Congress signed a letter to Secretary of State Colin Powell asking that the ELAM students be exempted from the ban. In August, the administration relented and granted the students permission to remain in Cuba.[23]

---

1 KeyWiki, "Charles B. Rangel," KeyWiki,
http://keywiki.org/index.php/Charles_B_Rangel (accessed March 25, 2013)
2 KeyWiki, "Charles B. Rangel," KeyWiki,
http://keywiki.org/index.php/Charles_B_Rangel (accessed June 18, 2012)

3 Charles B. Rangel, "Biography," The History Makers, http://www.thehistorymakers.com/biography/hon-charles-b-rangel-39 (accessed March 25, 2013)

4 KeyWiki, "David Dinkins," KeyWiki, http://www.keywiki.org/index.php/David_Dinkins (accessed March 25, 2013)

5 KeyWiki, "Denny Farrell," KeyWiki, http://www.keywiki.org/index.php/Denny_Farrell (accessed March 25, 2013)

6 National Conference of Black Lawyers, "Founding Members of The National Conference of Black Lawyers," National Conference of Black Lawyers, http://www.ncbl.org/PDF/NCBLFoundingMbrs.pdf (accessed March 25, 2013)

7 National Conference of Black Lawyers, "Our History," National Conference of Black Lawyers, http://www.ncbl.org/history.htm (accessed March 25, 2013)

8 National Lawyers Guild, "News & Opinion," National Lawyers Guild, http://www.nlg.org/news/statements/SouraniStatement.htm (accessed March 25, 2013)

9 Daily World (February 19, 1983) p. 4

10 People's Weekly World December 11, 1999) p. 12

11 People's Weekly World ... in NYC (November 4, 2000) p. 2

12 Sam Webb, "Angele Davis headlines tribute for CPUSA's Henry Winston," People's World, http://peoplesworld.org/angela-davis-headlines-tribute-for-cpusa-s-henry-winston/, (February 23, 2012)

13 Democratic Left (July/August 1996) p. 21

14 Communists in the Democratic Party, p. 65

15 KeyWiki, "Charles B. Rangel," KeyWiki, http://keywiki.org/index.php/Charles_B_Rangel (accessed March 26, 2013)

16 KeyWiki, "Charles B. Rangel," KeyWiki, http://keywiki.org/index.php/Charles_B_Rangel (accessed June 19, 2012)

17 Human Events (April 29, 1972) p. 3

18 People's Weekly World (July 10, 1993) p. 10

19 International Peace for Cuba Appeal – letterhead (November 14, 1994)

20 People's Weekly World (October 28, 1995)

21 Drum Major Institute, "Board," Drum Major Institute, http://www.drummajorinstitute.org/board.php#NAC (2009)

22 Lesley Clark, "Castro pitched in for lawmaker's visit," Cubanet, http://www.cubanet.org/CNews/y06/jun06/08e6.htm (June 8, 2006)

23 Fitzhugh Mullan, M.D., "Cuba Trains Physicians for Wealthy United States," New England Journal of Medicine Volume 351:2680-2682, http://academic.udayton.edu/health/02organ/providers01.htm (December 23, 2004)

Jose Serrano (D-NY)

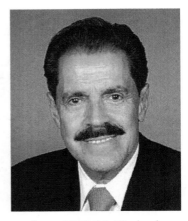

Jose Enrique Serrano is a Democratic member of the United States House of Representatives, representing the 15th District of New York. He is an active member of the Congressional Hispanic Caucus and has served as Chair of the Caucus from 1993-94. He is also a longstanding member of the Congressional Progressive Caucus.[1]

Background

Born in Mayagüez, Puerto Rico, on October 24, 1943, Serrano moved to the Bronx with his family when he was a young boy. He grew up in the Mill Brook housing project in the South Bronx and attended local public schools. From 1964-66, Serrano served in the 172nd Support Battalion of the U.S. Army Medical Corps. After an honorable discharge from the Army, he returned to the Bronx and worked in a bank and as a school administrator, before his election to the New York State Assembly in 1974.

In Albany, Assemblyman Serrano chaired the Committee on Education for eight years, during which he authored legislation that doubled state funding for bilingual education programs. He also served as Chairman of the Committee on Consumer Affairs and Protection.[2]

In 1976, Serrano successfully ran for the New York Assembly in the 75th District. In 1990, Serrano won a special election for the seat vacated by resigning U.S. Congressman Robert García with 92% of the vote. He has never won re-election with less than 92% of the vote in what is considered one of the safest and most "progressive" seats in Congress.

Influence

In 1993, Serrano joined the powerful Appropriations Committee, which is responsible for shaping expenditures of discretionary federal funds. That same year he was also elected by his colleagues to serve as Chairman of the Congressional Hispanic Caucus during the 103rd Congress. As Chairman, Serranostrong contributed to the passage of several bills of "interest to Hispanics and other minorities. During this same period, the CHC helped to defeat a number of pieces of legislation that were widely criticized as attempts at "immigrant-bashing" and veiled bigotry."

As a Member of the House Appropriations Committee, Serrano has managed to secure millions of dollars in federal funding for his Bronx Congressional District.

The Committee on Appropriations also includes the Subcommittee on Commerce, Justice and Related Agencies; the Subcommittee on Financial Services and General Government (where Serrano is a Ranking Member) and the Subcommittee on Interior, Environment and Related Agencies.[3]

Communist Connections

Asian Americans for Equality Award

On Feb. 23, 1993, the Asian Americans for Equality announced their 19th Annual Chinese New Year Celebration dinner to be held at the Silver Palace in New York City on Feb. 27th.

California Congressman Robert Matsui and New York Congressman Jose Serrano were honored by this well known front for the pro-China Communist Workers Party.[4]

Article in the People's World

Rep. Serrano had an article published in the Communist Party USA's People's Weekly World on June 11, 1994, entitle, "Immigrant bashing—a dirty political sport."[5]

Supporting Lucius Walker

On September 17, 2010, Harlem's Convent Avenue Baptist Church filled with people celebrating the example, ongoing legacy and life of the Rev. Dr. Lucius Walker, a long-time affiliate of the Communist Party USA and long-time pro-Cuba activist. Walker, 80, had died suddenly at his home in New Jersey.

The headline in Granma, the daily newspaper of the Cuban Communist Party, announcing his death stated, "We do not want to think of a world without Lucius Walker."

"Joining the wide representation of Cuba solidarity, socialist and progressive activists" were Cuba's United Nations Ambassador Pedro Núñez Mosquera; Nicaraguan Ambassador María Eugenia Rubiales de Chamorro; two Workers World Party affiliates: New York City Council person and Freedom Party candidate for Governor, Charles Barron and former U.S. Attorney General Ramsey Clark; as well as Akbar Mohammed of the Nation of Islam.

Messages and resolutions came from author and former Maoist leader, Jane Franklin, and elected officials, including Congressional Reps. Charles Rangel, Maxine Waters and Jose Serrano.[6]

Socialist Connections

Majority Coalition for a New New York

In 1991, on the initiative of Democratic Socialists of America (DSA) supporter, Local 1199 President Dennis Rivera, DSAer Rep. Major Owens, Deputy Mayor Bill Lynch and Rep. Jose Serrano, a citywide labor/community coalition called the Majority Coalition for a New New York was formed to unite disparate forces for a solution to the city's financial crisis "reflecting the interests of working people."

The coalition aimed to focus on an "issue driven" approach to supporting candidates in Council elections.[7]

Endorsed Nydia Velazquez

In her 1992 New York Democratic primary, Nydia Velazquez ran against two other Puerto Ricans: Elizabeth Colon and Ruben Franco, President of the Puerto Rican Legal Defense and Education Fund.

Velazquez won the primary, receiving endorsements from New York Mayor and DSA member David Dinkins, DSA affiliated Rev. Jesse Jackson, DSA affiliated Local 1199 leader Dennis Rivera and Congressmen Jose Serrano.[8]

DSA Endorsement

In July 1996, the Democratic Socialists of America Political Action Committee endorsed Jose Serrano in that year's Congressional elections.[9]

Supported Puerto Rican Rebel Prisoners

In 1999, eleven imprisoned Puerto Rican Marxist-inspired "independence fighters" were released on parole from long prison terms in the U.S.

Political leaders who supported the prisoners included DSA affiliated Reps. Luis Gutierrez (D-IL) and Nydia Velazquez (D-NY), as well as DSA members Ron Dellums (D-CA) and former New York City Mayor David Dinkins. This also included Rep Jose Serrano.[10]

Foreign Policy/National Security

Representative Serrano is a big fan of Latin American Marxist regimes.

"Sensible" Approach to Cuba

According to Congressman Serrano's website:[11]

> Since his earliest days in Congress, Congressman Serrano has been actively involved in ending the embargo against Cuba. He has sponsored legislation and worked tirelessly to educate other Members of Congress about how the embargo harms American businesses and American farmers. While Serrano was once part of a tiny group in Congress to support a changed approach to Cuba, growing numbers of Members join Congressman Serrano in signing on to his Bridges to the Cuban People Act each year.

Staffers Trip to Cuba

Rep. Jose Serrano sent George A. Sullivan to Cuba for a number of days in July of 2003. The trip was courtesy of a $1,825.00 grant from the Institute for Policy Studies connected Center for Democracy in the Americas, "To examine U.S. policy toward Cuba, the impact of the American trade embargo and the economy of Cuba."[12]

Promoting Medical Training in Cuba

Serrano has aided the Cuban Communist Party's program of recruiting young, mainly leftist Americans for medical training and indoctrination in Cuba.

Teresa Glover, from New York, was recruited in the mid-2000s for training at the Latin American School of Medicine (ELAM) in Havana—a school sponsored by the communist Cuban government.

Glover's mother heard about ELAM from her Congressman, Rep. José Serrano.[13]

Chavez Heating Oil Deal

On Dec. 6, 2005, Rep. Jose Serrano, along with CITGO CEO Felix Rodriguez, leaders of neighborhood organizations and Venezuela's Ambassador to the United States, Bernardo Alvarez, delivered the first installment of 8 million gallons of CITGO heating oil earmarked for New York City, to be sold to those in need at a substantially reduced rate.[14]

The deal was a huge propaganda victory for Venezuela's late Marxist dictator, Hugo Chavez, a man long idolized by Rep. Serrano.

Chavez Eulogy

On March 5, 2013, Serrano issued a release mourning the death of President Hugo Chavez of Venezuela:

> "I met President Chavez in 2005 when he came to my district at my invitation," said Congressman Serrano. "His focus on the issues faced by the poor and disenfranchised in his country made him a truly revolutionary leader in the history of Latin America. He understood that after 400 years on the outside of the established power structure looking in, it was time that the poor had a chance at seeing their problems and issues addressed. His core belief was in the dignity and common humanity of all people in Venezuela and in the world.

Serrano also issued a tweet to mark the occasion.[15]

Jose E. Serrano ✓
@RepJoseSerrano

[1▾] [🐦 Follow]

Hugo Chavez was a leader that understood the needs of the poor. He was committed to empowering the powerless. R.I.P. Mr. President.

◄ Reply ↻ Retweet ★ Favorite ••• More

1 KeyWiki, "Jose Serrano," KeyWiki, http://keywiki.org/index.php/Jose_Serrano (accessed June 29, 2012)

2 Jose E. Serrano, "Biography," House.gov, http://serrano.house.gov/about-me/full-biography (accessed April 21, 2013)

3 Jose E. Serrano, "Biography," House.gov, http://serrano.house.gov/about-me/full-biography (accessed April 21, 2013)

4 The Free Library, "New York Life Sponsors Asian Americans for Equality 19th Annual Chinese New Year Celebrations," The Free Library, http://www.thefreelibrary.com/NEW+YORK+LIFE+SPONSORS+ASIAN+AMERICANS+FOR+EQUALITY+19TH+ANNUAL...-a013120335 (February 23, 1993)

5 People's Weekly World (June 11, 1994)

6 Cheryl LaBash, "Lucius Walker built solidarity with Cuba," Workers World, http://www.workers.org/2010/us/lucius_walker_0930/ (September 26, 2010)

7 People's Weekly World (August 10, 1991) p. 19

8 People's Weekly World (August 29, 1992) p. 15

9 Democratic Left (July/August 1996) p. 21

10 People's World, "Puerto Ricans chart progressive agenda," People's World, http://www.peoplesworld.org/puerto-ricans-chart-progressive-agenda/, (May 28, 2004)

11 Jose E. Serrano, "Biography," House.gov, http://serrano.house.gov/about-me/full-biography (accessed April 21, 2013)

12 LegiStorm, "Center for Democracy in the Americas – Sponsor of Congressional Travel," LegiStorm, http://www.legistorm.com/trip/list/by/sponsor/id/10693/name/Center_for_Democracy_in_the_Americas/page/2.html (accessed August 30, 2010)

13 Fitzhugh Mullan, M.D., "Cuba Trains Physicians for Wealthy United States," University of Dayton, http://academic.udayton.edu/health/02organ/providers01.htm (December 23, 2004)

14 People's World, "Poor people in the U.S. also benefitted from Venezuelan oil," People's World, http://www.peoplesworld.org/poor-people-in-the-u-s-also-benefitted-from-venezuelan-oil/, (March 11, 2013)

15 Jose Serrano, "Chavez Changed the Conversation In Latin America," House.gov, http://serrano.house.gov/press-release/serrano-%E2%80%9Cchavez-changed-conversation-latin-america%E2%80%9D, (March 5, 2013)

Louise Slaughter (D-NY)

Louise McIntosh Slaughter is a Democratic member of the United States House of Representatives, representing the 25th District of New York. She is a member of the Congressional Progressive Caucus and the Populist Caucus.[1]

Background

Rep. Slaughter, who was first elected to Congress in 1986, holds a Bachelor of Science Degree (1951) in Microbiology and a Master of Science Degree (1953) in Public Health from the University of Kentucky. Prior to entering Congress, she served in the New York State Assembly (1982-86) and the Monroe County (NY) Legislature (1976-79). She also served as Regional Coordinator to then Secretary of State Mario Cuomo from 1976 to 1978 and then to Lt. Gov. Mario Cuomo from 1979 to 1982.

A native of Harlan County, Kentucky, Congresswoman Slaughter has lived most of her life in the Rochester area.

Influence

As one of the "leading advocates in Congress for women's rights," Rep. Slaughter is consistently engaged in legislation and advocacy on both a local and national level. She previously served as Co-Chair of the Congressional Caucus for Women's Issues in the 108th Congress and continues to serve as Co-Chair of the Bipartisan Congressional Pro-Choice Caucus.

Along with Vice President Joe Biden and others, Slaughter co-authored the historic Violence Against Women Act in 1994 and wrote legislation to make permanent the Department of Justice's Violence Against Women Office.[2]

Congresswoman Slaughter, a member of the House Democratic Leadership, is one of the most powerful figures in the House of Representatives. In 2007, she became the first woman to serve as Chairwoman of the influential House Committee on Rules, a position that allowed her to influence nearly every single piece of legislation that comes to the House floor for a vote. She held that position from 2007 until 2011. Congresswoman Slaughter also serves on the prestigious Democratic Steering & Policy Committee and is Chair of two Congressional caucuses: the Congressional Arts Caucus and the Bipartisan Congressional Pro-Choice Caucus, of which she was a founding member.

Currently, Slaughter serves on the Rules Committee, where she is a Ranking Member; the Congressional Bipartisan Upstate New York Caucus, where she is the Chair; the Congressional Arts Caucus, where she is the Co-Chair, the Congressional Bipartisan Pro-Choice Caucus, where she is the Co-Chair and the Congressional Caucus for Women's Issues.[3] She also belongs to a long list of member organizations.[4]

Socialist Connections

DSA Support

In 1987, Democratic Socialists of America (DSA) helped in Slaughter's election campaign:[5]

> Rochester DSAers helped elect progressive Louise Slaughter...

Fred Ross, Jr. Connection

New York Rep. Louise Slaughter was also the first Congress member whose election was assisted by DSA allied Neighbor to Neighbor, the national grassroots organization opposed to U.S. military aid to Central America, headed by United Farm Workers (UFW) veteran, Fred Ross, Jr. Ross learned from the UFW how to target swing districts and representatives, and his group helped build the grassroots field campaign that brought Slaughter her narrow victory.

Less than a year after Slaughter's election, Ross and other UFW alums helped elect Nancy Pelosi to Congress. Pelosi joined Slaughter in leading the fight against military aid to El Salvador's "right-wing government" and to Nicaragua's anti-communist contra rebels.[6]

Democratic Alternatives

In 1987, Louise Slaughter was listed as a proposed speaker at the DSA-organized Democratic Alternatives conference. This conference, organized by DSA leaders Michael Harrington and Jo-Ann Mort, was part of a series of gatherings designed to give the Democratic Party "a positive, progressive program."

Besides Slaughter, other listed speakers included DSAers Robert Lekachman, Barbara Ehrenreich, William Julius Wilson, Steve Max, Ruth Messinger, Nancy Kleniewski and future New York City Mayor David Dinkins.[7]

"Progressive" Connection

Leading with Love

Leading with Love was an event to celebrate 5 years of the Marxist-led, Institute for Policy Studies "partner" organization, National Domestic Workers Alliance. It was held in

DEMOCRATIC ALTERNATIVES
Dedicated to the proposition that the Democratic Party can be a winner if it presents a positive progressive program, the folks who brought you New Directions last spring (Michael Harrington and Ann Lewis, Conveners, Jo-Ann Mort, Coordinator) are now launching a series of regional conferences. Below is the program at its present stage of planning.

Democratic Alternatives Conference
Albany Hilton
February 27, 28, 1987

Friday Night Plenary
8:00 PM "Growth Though Equity"
Bob Lekachman, Barbara Ehrenreich

Saturday
9:00 AM Plenary: "Social Needs and the Changing Economy"
William Julius Wilson, Ruth Messinger, Steve Max, Moderator: Michael Harrington
10:30-12 noon Workshops
Education, Phil Ramore, Buffalo NEA
Family Policy, Noreen Connell, NY NOW; David Blankenhorn
National Health Policy
Economic Development and Social Needs, Nancy Kleniewski, SUNY Geneseo
Affirmative Action, Courts and Social Policy
12:00-1:00 Lunch Break
1:00-2:30 PM Workshops
Political Terrain for 88, Jan Pierce, Linda Davidoff, Ethel Klein
Campaign Reform and Voter Registration, Gerry Goldfeder
Foreign Policy
National Budget Priorities, Stan Hill
Interreligious Response to Bishops Letter, Evan Bayer, AJ Congress
2:30-4:00 PM Plenary: "Where Do We Go From Here?"
Ann Lewis, David Dinkins (?), Louise Slaughter (?)

At least one car will be going from Ithaca. Call Theresa Alt 273-3009 or Jeanne Fudala 277-0387 for arrangements.

WORKING PRESS
The January Working Press is out. To get your copy, stop by 109 W. State St. Or, better yet, subscribe—send $5.00 to the Tompkins-Cortland Labor Coalition, 109 W. State St., Ithaca NY 14850.

The Ithaca Socialist relies on your subscriptions of $6 to cover costs. Checks payable to Ithaca DSA.

Ithaca Socialist (January 1987)

Washington, D.C. on November 14, 2012.

Members of the Host Committee included Louise Slaughter.[8]

Foreign Policy/National Security

Supported by Council for a Livable World

The Council for a Livable World, a non-profit advocacy organization that seeks to "reduce the danger of nuclear weapons and increase national security," primarily through supporting "progressive" Congressional candidates who forward their policies, supported Louise Slaughter in her successful House of Representatives run as candidate for New York.[9]

---

1 KeyWiki, "Louis Slaughter," KeyWiki, http://keywiki.org/index.php/Louise_Slaughter (accessed April 14, 2013)

2 Louise M. Slaughter, "Biography," House.gov, http://www.louise.house.gov/index.php?option=com_content&view=article&id=39&Itemid=61 (accessed April 14, 2013)

3 Louis M. Slaughter, "Committee Assignments," House.gov, http://www.louise.house.gov/index.php?option=com_content&view=article&id=42&Itemid=63 (accessed April 14, 2013)

4 Louis M. Slaughter, "Additional Member Organizations," House.gov, http://www.louise.house.gov/index.php?option=com_content&view=article&id=43&Itemid=118 (accessed April 14, 2013)

5 Democratic Left (January/February 1987) p. 18

6 Randy Shaw, "Nancy Pelosi Deserves Chief Credit for Health Care Victory," BeyondChron, http://beyondchron.org/news/index.php?itemid=7930 (March 22, 2010)

7 Ithaca Socialist (January 1987)

8 Leading with Love, "Hosts and Sponsors," Leading with Love, http://domesticworkers.org/leadingwithlove/hosts-and-sponsors, (accessed April 14, 2013)

9 Council for a Livable World, "Meet the Candidates," Council for a Livable World, http://livableworld.org/support/meet_candidates/ (accessed April 14, 2013)

Nydia Velazquez (D-NY)

Nydia Margarita Velazquez is a Democratic member of the United States
House of Representatives, representing
the 12th District of New York. She is a member of the Congressional Progressive Caucus and a former Chair of the Congressional Hispanic Caucus.[1]

Background

Velazquez was born in Yabucoa, Puerto Rico in 1953. At the age of 16,
she entered the University of Puerto Rico in Rio Piedras. She graduated
Magna Cum Laude in 1974 with a degree in Political Science. After
earning a Master's Degree on scholarship from NYU, Velazquez taught
Puerto Rican studies at CUNY's Hunter College in 1981.

In 1983, Velazquez was appointed Special Assistant to Congressman
Edolphus Towns (D-Brooklyn). One year later, she became the first
Latina to serve on the New York City Council. In 1992, Velazquez was
elected to the House of Representatives to represent New York's 12th
District.[2]

Influence

By 1986, Velázquez served as the Director of the Department of Puerto
Rican Community Affairs in the United States.[3]

In 2008, Nydia Velazquez served on candidate Obama's National
Latino Advisory Council.

Congresswoman Velazquez is a Ranking Member of the House Small
Business Committee. She is a senior member of the Financial Services
Committee, which includes the Subcommittee on Financial Institutions

and Consumer Credit and the Subcommittee on Housing and Insurance. She also serves on the following: the Democratic Caucus, the Women's Issues Caucus, the Out of Iraq Caucus, the Congressional Caucus on the Census, the Congressional Children's Caucus, the Congressional Jobs and Fair Trade Caucus, the Empowerment Zone and Enterprise Community (EZ/EC) Caucus, the Human Rights Caucus, the Older Americans' Caucus and the Urban Caucus.[4]

Communist Connections

Ackerman Connection

As campaign manager for Nydia Velazquez in 1992, Karen Ackerman ran a successful campaign against incumbent Steven Solarz for the newly created Congressional seat in the 12th District of New York. Moving to Washington, D.C. after the race, Ackerman served as Chief of Staff for Congresswoman Velazquez until 1996.[5]

Ackerman had once been active with the Communist Party USA (CPUSA) youth wing, the Young Workers Liberation League and in 1970, was a member of the second Venceremos Brigade to Cuba, where she cut sugar cane for Castro.[6]

Praised Puerto Rican Communist

In her speech to the Rainbow Coalition Leadership Summit, February 19, 1993, Nydia Velazquez paid tribute to the late Jesus Colon, a garment worker, CPUSA member and author of: "A Puerto Rican in New York."

Said Velasquez, "the plight of the America today, particularly the nation's people of color, reminds me of the stories of Jesus Colon, a writer, who with piercing accuracy, poignantly chronicled the struggles of early Puerto Rican migrants in this country. Sixty years after the experiences of Colon, I would arrive in New York, and like him, would be shocked at the unbearable conditions of the people. I too would be subject to harsh and threatening words, merely for the olive tone of my skin, or the sound of my name. I too would feel the sting of discrimination."[7]

Article Re-Printed in the People's World

A speech Velazquez gave to Rev. Jesse Jackson's communist heavy Rainbow Coalition in February 1993, was re-printed with full credit in the CPUSA's People's Weekly World of March 6, 1993.[8]

Asian Americans for Equality

Nydia Velazquez has long-term ties to Asian Americans for Equality (AAFE), a powerful and very wealthy (thanks to U.S. taxpayers) Chinatown, New York based organization, founded by former members of the pro-Communist China and North Korean Communist Workers Party (CWP).[9]

Freddie Mac Funding for AAFE

U.S. Senator Charles Schumer (D-NY) and Rep. Nydia Velazquez joined AAFE, June 2, 2003, to announce Freddie Mac's $1.5 million grant to the newly created Lower Manhattan Affordable Housing Trust Fund. The fund supports the development and preservation of affordable housing in the Lower Manhattan neighborhoods most affected by the September 11th World Trade Center disaster.

"Rebuilding and revitalizing Lower Manhattan is one of my top priorities," said Congresswoman Nydia Velazquez. "Increased home ownership has been shown to promote community development through increased neighborhood involvement and investment in local businesses. Freddie Mac's generous contribution is an important step towards this goal and will help place more local residents on the road to home ownership."[10]

NeighborWorks America Event

On November 25, 2009, at a press conference in Chinatown, AAFE announced it has become a charter member of NeighborWorks America, a non-profit created by Congress. On hand to celebrate the occasion, were several elected officials including Rep. Nydia Velazquez, AAFE Executive Director Chris Kui and Margaret Chin, District 1's new city council member, former AAFE President and one time CWP member.[11]

Rep. Velazquez offered her congratulations to AAFE. "By joining forces with NeighborWorks, AAFE will have additional funding and support for their efforts to create equal opportunities for all New Yorkers. I am committed to working with AAFE to address the shortage of affordable housing, increase financial literacy and improve lending practices. With unemployment rising above 10 percent and families struggling to make ends meet, this help is needed in New York City now more than ever."[12]

Asian Americans for Equality, 38th Anniversary

Dignitaries including U.S. Rep. Nydia Velazquez, New York City; Comptroller John Liu; and City Council member Margaret Chin came to Chinatown, March 2012, to help Asian Americans for Equality celebrate its 38th anniversary.

A fundraiser for more than one-thousand supporters was held at the Jing Fong restaurant on Elizabeth Street.

AAFE honored San Francisco Mayor Ed Lee, a former pro-China student radical who was elected November 2011, as that city's first Asian-American mayor.[13]

Velazquez has been a past recipient of the annual AAFE award, in her own right.[14]

Socialist Connections

Dinkins Support

New York Mayor and Democratic Socialists of America (DSA) member David Dinkins was an early supporter of Nydia Velazquez's political career.[15]

DSA Endorsements

In 1992, New York DSA endorsed Nydia Velazquez during her successful run for Congress.[16]

In July 1996, the DSA Political Action Committee endorsed Nydia Velazquez, New York 12th District, in that year's Congressional elections.[17]

New York DSA Awards Dinner

On June 24, 1993, New York City DSA held its annual Debs-Thomas-Harrington Awards Dinner. Local 1199 President Dennis Rivera and DSA member Deborah Meier of the Central Park East Secondary School received awards. Featured speakers included New York State Comptroller H. Carl McCall, Manhattan Borough President; DSA member Ruth Messinger and DSA Honorary Chair Cornel West. U.S. Rep. Nydia Velazquez, who was unable to attend because of Congressional commitments, sent greetings.[18]

Working Families Party Co-Chair

In 1998, Co-Chairs of the Democratic Socialists of America initiated Working Families Party included DSA member and former New York Mayor David Dinkins and Brooklyn Rep. Nydia Velazquez.[19]

Supported Puerto Rican Rebel Prisoners

In 1999, eleven imprisoned Puerto Rican Marxist independence fighters were released on parole from long prison terms in the U.S.

Political leaders who supported the prisoners included Nydia Velazquez (D-NY) and two DSA members, Ron Dellums (D-CA) and former New York City Mayor David Dinkins.[20]

Foreign Policy/National Security

United for Peace and Justice

Nydia Velazquez was listed as an endorser of the January 27, 2007, "Act Now to End the War" event, organized by Institute for Policy Studies partner organization, United for Peace & Justice. Also endorsing the event was Democratic Socialists of America, Socialist Party USA, Committees of Correspondence for Democracy & Socialism, National Lawyers Guild, National Organization for Women and the Communist Party USA. At the event, peace activists "converge[d] from all around the country in Washington, D.C. to send a strong, clear message to Congress and the Bush Administration: 'The people of this country want the war and occupation in Iraq to end and we want the troops brought home now!'"[21] [22]

WIDF Affiliated United States "Regional Workshops"

Circa 2007, Nydia Velazquez—"Congressista," was a member of the United States "Regional Workshop" of the former Soviet front Women's International Democratic Federation.[23]

1 KeyWiki, "Nydia Velazquez," KeyWiki, http://keywiki.org/index.php/Nydia_Velazquez (accessed June 15, 2012)
2 Nydia M. Velazquez, "Biography," House.gov, http://velazquez.house.gov/about/bio.shtml (accessed August 16, 2011)
3 Nydia M. Velazquez, "Biography," House.gov, http://velazquez.house.gov/about/bio.shtml (accessed August 16, 2011)
4 Nydia M. Velazquez, "Committees and Caucus Memberships," House.gov, http://velazquez.house.gov/about/committees-caucuses.shtml (accessed August 16, 2011)
5 The Arena, "Karen Ackerman," Politico, http://www.politico.com/arena/bio/karen_ackerman.html (accessed June 16, 2012)
6 KeyWiki, "Karen Ackerman," KeyWiki, http://www.keywiki.org/index.php/Karen_Ackerman (accessed June 16, 2012)
7 People's Weekly World (February 20, 1993) p. 4
8 People's Weekly World (March 6, 1993)
9 KeyWiki, "Nydia Velazquez," KeyWiki, http://keywiki.org/index.php/Nydia_Velazquez (accessed June 15, 2012)
10 PR Newswire, "Senator Schumer, Rep. Velazquez Join Asian Americans for Equality to Celebrate Freddie Mac's $1.5 Million Grant to Promote Affordable Housing in Lower Manhattan," PR Newswire, http://www.prnewswire.com/news-releases/senator-schumer-rep-velazquez-join-asian-americans-for-equality-to-celebrate-freddie-macs-15-million-grant-to-promote-affordable-housing-in-lower-manhattan-71179012.html, (June 2, 2003)
11 The Lo-Down, "Asian Americans for Equality Joins NeighborWorks Ed Litvak in Community Organizations on November 25, 2009," The Lo-Down, http://www.thelodownny.com/leslog/2009/11/asian-americans-for-equality-joins-neighborworks.html, (November 25, 2009)
12 NeighborWorks America, "Two Newly Chartered NeighborWorks Organizations Celebrate their Affiliation in the Northeast District," NeighborWorks America,

http://www.nw.org/network/newsroom/articles/netNews120309.asp, (December 3, 2009)

13 Ed Litvak, "AAFE Celebrates 38 Years, Honors San Francisco Mayor," The Lo-Down, http://www.thelodownny.com/leslog/2012/03/aafe-celebrates-38-years-honors-san-francisco-mayor.html#more-57148, (March 26, 2012)

14 Douglas Lim, "AAFE 2013 Banquet Journal," AAFE (March 26, 2013)

15 People's Weekly World (1993) p. 18

16 Democratic Left (September/October 1992) p. 20

17 Democratic Left (July/August 1996) p. 21

18 Democratic Left (July/August 1993) p. 10

19 People's Weekly World (September 19, 1998) p. 5

20 Jose Cruz, "11 Puerto Ricans accept clemency offer," People's Weekly World (September 11, 1999) p. 4

21 UFPJ Website, "January 27th Endorsers – Individuals," UFPJ Website, http://www.unitedforpeace.org/article.php?id=3458 (accessed on January 26, 2011)

22 UFPJ Website, "January 27th Endorsers – Organizations," UFPJ Website, http://www.unitedforpeace.org/article.php?id=3454 (accessed on January 26, 2011)

23 Women's International Democratic Federation, regional workshops, USA, http://www.fdim-widf.com.br/indexingles.htm (accessed February 22, 2011)

Mel Watt (D-NC)

Mel Watt is a Democratic member of the United States House of Representatives, representing the 12th District of North Carolina. He is a long-time member of the Congressional Black Caucus and the Congressional Progressive Caucus.

Background

Mel Watt was born in Mecklenburg County, North Carolina on August 26, 1945. He is a graduate of York Road High School in Charlotte. He was a Phi Beta Kappa graduate of the University of North Carolina at Chapel Hill in 1967 with a Bachelor of Science Degree in Business Administration. In 1970, he received a Juris Doctorate Degree from Yale University Law School and was a published member of the Yale Law Journal.

He practiced law from 1970 to 1992, specializing in minority business and economic development law in a general practice law firm best known for its civil rights reputation.

Watt is a life member of the NAACP. He served as President of the Mecklenburg County Bar and has been a member of many professional, community and civic boards and organizations.[1]

In 1992, he was elected to the United States House of Representatives from North Carolina's 12th Congressional District.[2]

Influence

Watt is a member of the House Judiciary Committee, where he is the Ranking Member of the Subcommittee on Intellectual Property, Competition and the Internet and serves on the Subcommittee on Courts, Commercial and Administrative Law. He is also on the House Financial Services Committee, where he serves on the Subcommittee on Financial Institutions and Consumer Credit and the Subcommittee on Insurance, Housing and Community Opportunity. He was elected Chairman of the Congressional Black Caucus in 2005-2006.[3]

Socialist Connections

Democratic Socialists of America Endorsement

Mel Watt was the Campaign Manager of leftist Harvey Gantt's campaigns for City Council, for Mayor of Charlotte and for the United States Senate in 1996—the same year Watt stood for Congress. In July 1996, the Democratic Socialists of America (DSA) Political Action Committee endorsed Mel Watt, North Carolina's 12th District and Harvey Gantt for Senate in that year's election cycle.[4]

"Progressive Caucus" Meeting

In 1996, Democratic Socialists of America sponsored a Progressive Caucus meeting at the Democratic National Convention. Among the participants was Congressman Mel Watt from North Carolina. In his remarks, he "crystallized completely the problem facing progressives inside (and also outside) the Democratic Party"… "The problem," he said, "is that we have lowered our expectation of what is possible."[5]

"Progressive" Connections

Take Back America Conference

Mel Watt was on the list of 153 speakers at the 2006 Take Back America conference, which was organized by the Institute for Policy Studies and DSA founded Campaign for America's Future.[6]

The Institute for Food and Development Policy/Food First

Mel Watt is on the list of Congressional Representatives who have participated in hearings/briefings since 1998, with the very radical Institute for Food and Development Policy/Food First, founded by Frances Moore Lappe (DSA member, Institute for Policy Studies affiliate) and Joseph Collins (Institute for Policy Studies), authors of the book: "Food First."[7]

Foreign Policy/National Security

Council for a Livable World

The Council for a Livable World, supported Mel Watt in at least one Congressional race.[8]

2005 Cuban Trip

In March 2005, Mel Watt spent three days in Havana, Cuba with a Congressional Black Caucus delegation.

The trip cost $1,329.23 and was paid for by the leftist Christopher Reynolds Found.[9]

Back to Cuba

In early April 2009, Representative Barbara Lee led a congressional delegation to Havana for a 4½ hour meeting with Raul Castro, telling reporters, "All of us are convinced that President Castro would like normal relations and would see normalization, ending the embargo, as beneficial to both countries."

Mel Watt was accompanied by his wife, Eulada Watt.[10]

Mel Watt in Havana

1 KeyWiki, "Melvin L. Watt," KeyWiki, http://keywiki.org/index.php/Mel_Watt (accessed July 6, 2012)
2 Mel Watt, "Congressman Melvin L. Watt—Biography," House.gov, http://www.watt.house.gov/index.php?option=com_content&view=article&id=2576&Itemid=73 (accessed August 16, 2011)
3 Mel Watt, "Committee Assignments," House.gov, http://www.watt.house.gov/index.php?option=com_content&view=article&id=2577&Itemid=74 (accessed August 16, 2011)

4 Democratic Left (July/August 1996) p. 21
5 Democratic Left (September/October 1996) p. 31
6 Campaign For America's Future, "Archives – 2006 Agenda & Speakers," Campaign For America's Future, http://www.ourfuture.org/node/13179 (accessed May 14, 2010)
7 Food First, "Staff," Food First, http://www.foodfirst.org/es/about/staff (accessed April 1, 2013)
8 Council for a Livable World, "Meet the Candidates," Council for a Livable World, http://livableworld.org/support/meet_candidates/ (accessed July 6, 2012)
9 American RadioWorks, "Christopher Reynolds Foundation," American Public Media, http://americanradioworks.publicradio.org/features/staffers/travdat/sponsor.php?sponsor_id=T000109 (accessed July 6, 2012)
10 PoliticalWarfare.org, "Congresswoman Barbara Lee: Still stuck in the Cold War," PoliticalWarfare.org, http://jmw.typepad.com/political_warfare/2009/04/congresswoman-barbara-lee-still-stuck-in-the-cold-war.html (April 7, 2009)

Sherrod Brown
(D-OH)

Sherrod Brown is a Democratic member of the United States Senate, representing Ohio. Previously, he was a member of the House of Representatives from 1993 to 2006, during which time he was an active member of the Congressional Progressive Caucus.[1]

Background

Sherrod Brown is a native of Mansfield, Ohio, where he spent summers working on his family's farm. He is married to Pulitzer Prize-winning columnist, Connie Schultz.

Prior to serving in the United States Senate, Brown served as a United States Representative for the 13th District, as Ohio's Secretary of State, as a member of the Ohio General Assembly and has taught in Ohio's public schools and at Ohio State University.

In the early 1990s, Brown taught democracy and government in Poland as that nation was making the transition from communism.

A member of the Evangelical Lutheran Church of America, Sherrod Brown is committed to "social and economic justice."[2] [3]

Influence

Brown serves on the Senate Committee on Finance. He also serves on the Senate Banking Committee, where he played an instrumental role in passing the "historic Wall Street reform law" and is Chairman of its Financial Institutions and Consumer Protection Subcommittee.

Brown serves on the Senate Agriculture, Nutrition and Forestry Committee and as Chairman of the Subcommittee on Jobs, Rural Economic Growth and Energy Innovation.

He also serves on the Senate Veterans Affairs Committee.

A strong opponent of international "free trade agreements," Brown led the bipartisan opposition to NAFTA in 1993—as a freshman in the U.S. House of Representatives—and to CAFTA in 2005.

As a Senator, Brown is working with the Obama Administration on the creation of a national manufacturing policy that would "invest in manufacturing innovation, strengthen our component supply chain, connect workers with emerging industries and align our trade policies to promote our national interests."[4]

Communist Connections

Rick Nagin connection

In 1990, the office of Ohio Secretary of State Sherrod Brown gave a Certificate of Recognition to Rick Nagin, Chairman of the local Communist Party USA (CPUSA). Nagin collected the award in Columbus for registering more than 2,000 voters during his losing campaign for Cleveland City Council.[5]

In 2006, Rick Nagin served on the staff of the AFL-CIO Labor 2006 campaign for Sherrod Brown and gubernatorial candidate, Ted Strickland.[6]

Rick Nagin, speaking to a meeting on June 25th of the CPUSA's National Committee in New York, said, "the labor movement and other progressive forces are using a ballot referendum to raise Ohio's minimum wage to reach out to voters in rural and southern Ohio, a bastion of the Republican Party. The referendum could prove decisive in Rep. Sherrod Brown's drive to oust Republican Sen. Michael DeWine."[7]

Column Reprinted in Communist Paper

Sherrod Brown wrote a commentary on Medicare privatization for the St. Louis Post-Dispatch on Dec. 11, 2003. It was reprinted by permission of the author in the Communist Party USA's People's World publication of December 19, 2003.[8]

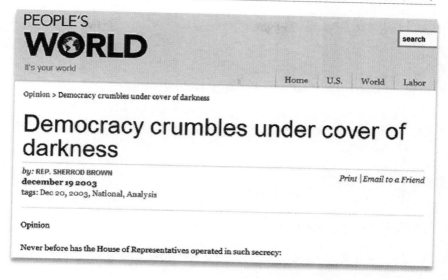

Opinion > Democracy crumbles under cover of darkness

Democracy crumbles under cover of darkness

by: REP. SHERROD BROWN
december 19 2003
tags: Dec 20, 2003, National, Analysis

Print | Email to a Friend

Opinion

Never before has the House of Representatives operated in such secrecy:

Socialist Connections

DSA Support in Senate Race

Ohio Democratic Socialists of America members campaigned for Brown in his successful 2006 Senate race:[9]

> Former Representative, now Senator Sherrod Brown is the most visible symbol of this change... A longtime critic of "free trade" agreements, frequently characterized as far left and out of the mainstream, Brown handily defeated the relatively moderate but free-trade proponent Mike DeWine.
>
> Trade was also an issue in the narrow loss of Mary Jo Kilroy to Deborah Pryce. Local DSAers worked in both the Brown and Kilroy campaigns.

Mary Jo Kilroy, though standing as a Democrat, had been a member of Democratic Socialists of America (DSA).[10]

Jobs with Justice

On April 21, 2009, Sherrod Brown spoke alongside DSA affiliates Heidi Hartmann and Ai-Jen Poo, and DSA member Barbara Ehrenreich at the D.C. Lobby Day for members of the Workers Rights Board of DSA infiltrated Jobs with Justice.[11]

21ˢᵗ Century Democrats Support

Sherrod Brown was one of 12 key progressives supported by Democratic Socialists of America, SA initiated and led, 21ˢᵗ Century Democrats Political Action Committee in the 2012 election cycle:[12]

> A longtime ally, 21ˢᵗ Century Democrats provided Brown active support in his Senate election in 2006. One of our first endorsees, we first helped this true progressive win his House seat in 1992.

"Progressive" Connections

Take Back America Conferences

Sherrod Brown was on the list of 153 speakers at the 2006 Take Back America conference, which was organized by the Institute for Policy Studies (IPS) and the Democratic Socialists of America-dominated Campaign for America's Future.[13]

He was back in 2007.

Sherrod Brown was on the list of speakers at the 2009 America's Future Now conference, the new name for Take Back America.[14]

Progressive Democrats of America Support

Sherrod Brown has close ties to IPS/DSA-controlled Progressive Democrats of America PDA).

National Director Tim Carpenter (a long-time DSA member) claimed that PDA had chalked up several achievements in its short life.[15]

During the 2006 election cycle, PDA staff and activists backed progressives in dozens of Congressional races. PDA wins included Rep. John Hall (D-NY) and Sen. Sherrod Brown (D-OH).[16]

Brown with PDA, Ohio (April 2009)

High IPS Rating

In 2012, in the "Congressional Report Card for the 99 Percent," the Institute for Policy Studies examined 40 different legislative actions in the

House and Senate—votes and legislation introduced—to ascertain the real allegiances of sitting members of Congress. These include votes to extend the Bush tax cuts for the wealthy, levy a Wall Street speculation tax, invest in infrastructure and protect workers and student financial aid.

The Report Card also graded politicians for their commitment to reducing inequality and boosting the 99 percent. The report's "Honor Roll" gave an A-plus grade to 5 members of the U.S. Senate, including Senator Sherrod Brown.[17]

IPS Donors

Lynn Raskin, a Washington D.C. realtor and her husband, Marcus Raskin, a Co-Founder of the Institute for Policy Studies, contributed to progressive candidates in several tight Congressional races during the 2012 election cycle. They donated to Rep. Tammy Baldwin (D-WI), Rep. John Conyers (D-MI), Elizabeth Warren, running for U.S. Senate in Massachusetts, and Sherrod Brown.[18]

Foreign Policy/National Security

Supported by Council for a Livable World

The anti-U.S. military, pro-disarmament Council for a Livable World, supported Sherrod Brown in his successful Senate run as a candidate for Ohio.[19] He has also been previously supported by the Council.[20]

In 2012, Council for a Livable World helped fund 17 successful Senate victories, including that of Sherrod Brown.[21]

Cuba Trip

A delegation of American lawmakers, led by Senator Patrick Leahy, arrived in Cuba on February 18, 2013, in order to gauge the country's economic changes and to lobby on behalf of Alan Gross, an American whose detention has "chilled relations between the two countries".

The delegation included Senators Sherrod Brown.[22]

---

1 KeyWiki, "Sherrod Brown," KeyWiki, http://keywiki.org/index.php/Sherrod_Brown (accessed April 20, 2013)
2 Sherrod Brown, "Biography," Senate.gov, http://www.brown.senate.gov/biography (accessed April 20, 2013)

3 21st Century Democrats, "Sherrod Brown," 21st Century Democrats, http://www.21stcenturydems.org/candidates/2012-candidates/senator-sherrod-brown/#.UPhxaPLvPGg, (accessed April 20, 2013)
4 Sherrod Brown, "Biography," Senate.gov, http://www.brown.senate.gov/biography (accessed April 10, 2012)
5 Yemi Toure, "Newsmakers," Los Angeles Times, http://articles.latimes.com/1990-03-02/news/vw-1593_1_dog-days (March 2, 1990)
6 Rick Nagin, "Resume Compare," Nagin for Council, http://www.naginforcouncil.com/resume_compare.html (2006)
7 People's World, "GOP can be beat in November, CPUSA says," People's World, http://peoplesworld.org/gop-can-be-beat-in-november-cpusa-says/, (July 7, 2006)
8 KeyWiki, "Sherrod Brown," KeyWiki, http://keywiki.org/index.php/Sherrod_Brown (accessed April 20, 2013)
9 DSA, http://www.dsausa.org/dl/Winter_2007.pdf (Winter 2007)
10 KeyWiki, "Mary Jo Kilroy," KeyWiki, http://www.keywiki.org/index.php/Mary_Jo_Kilroy (accessed April 20, 2013)
11 Martin Rafanan, "Jobs with Justice April 22, 2009 Lobbying EFCA," flickr, http://www.flickr.com/photos/martinrafanan/sets/72157617204962072/with/3466911049/ (April 21, 2009)
12 21st Century Democrats, "Sherrod Brown," 21st Century Democrats, http://www.21stcenturydems.org/candidates/2012-candidates/senator-sherrod-brown/#.UPhxaPLvPGg, (accessed April 20, 2013)
13 Campaign For America's Future, "Archives – 2006 Agenda & Speakers," Campaign For America's Future, http://www.ourfuture.org/node/13179 (accessed May 14, 2010)
14 Confabb website, "America's Future Now 2009 Speakers," Confabb website, http://now2009.confabb.com/conferences/82401-americas-future-now/speakers (accessed July 13, 2010)
15 PDA website, http://pdamerica.org/about/strategy.php (accessed 2009)
16 PDA National, "PDA History," PDA website, http://www.pdamerica.org/about-pda/history, (December 10, 2011)
17 Chuck Collins, "Lawmakers Get Graded on Equality Record," Yes! Blog, http://www.yesmagazine.org/new-economy/a-voting-guide-for-the-99 (October 9, 2012)
18 Deanna Pan, "How Google Mixed Up Sherrod and Scott Brown" Mother Jones, http://www.motherjones.com/mojo/2012/08/google-adwords-scott-brown-sherrod-brown, (August 31, 2012)
19 Council for a Livable World, "Meet the Candidates," Council for a Livable World, http://livableworld.org/support/meet_candidates/ (accessed April 10, 2013)
20 Council for a Livable World, "Legacy in Congress: Who We've Helped Elect," Council for a Livable World, http://livableworld.org/what/legacy_in_congress_who_weve_helped_elect/ (accessed April 10, 2013)
21 Council for a Livable World, "Meet the Candidates," Council for a Livable World, http://livableworld.org/support/meet_candidates/ (accessed April 10, 2013)
22 The Guardian, "Senator Patrick Leahy leads US group to Cuba to seek release of Alan Gross," The Guardian, http://www.guardian.co.uk/world/2013/feb/18/patrick-leahy-cuba-alan-gross (February 18, 2013)

Marcy Kaptur (D-OH)

Marcy Kaptur is a Democratic member of the United States House of Representatives, representing the 9th District of Ohio. She is a member of the Congressional Progressive Caucus and the Populist Caucus.[1]

Background

Congresswoman Kaptur came from a family who operated a small grocery, where her mother worked after serving on the original organizing committee of an auto trade union at the Champion Spark Plug Company.

Kaptur is a native of Toledo, Ohio. She is a member of the Little Flower Roman Catholic Church and a graduate of St. Ursula Academy. She earned a Bachelor of Arts Degree in History from the University of Wisconsin in 1968 and a Master's Degree in Urban Planning from the University of Michigan.

Kaptur worked as a city and regional planner for fifteen years in Toledo and throughout the country. Appointed as an Urban Advisor to the Carter White House, she helped maneuver seventeen housing and neighborhood revitalization bills through the Congress during those years.

While pursuing a Doctorate in Urban Planning and Development Finance at the Massachusetts Institute of Technology, the local Democratic Party recruited her to run for the U.S. House seat in Ohio in 1982.

Kaptur had been a well-known party activist and volunteer since the age of thirteen. Although she was outspent by a 3-to-1 margin, she "parlayed her deep roots in the blue-collar neighborhoods of Toledo and the rural areas of the district to pull the national upset of 1982."[2]

Influence

Congresswoman Kaptur is the senior Democratic woman on the House Appropriations Committee. She has secured appointments to three important subcommittees: Defense, Agriculture (the leading industry in her state) and Transportation/Housing and Urban Development (HUD).

Congresswoman Kaptur was also appointed by Party leadership to serve on the powerful House Budget Committee for the 112th Congress.

Kaptur is the first Democratic woman to serve on the Defense Subcommittee. During her legislative career, she has also served on the Banking and Veterans Affairs Committees.

Kaptur belongs to the Congressional Ukrainian Caucus where she is the Co-Chair, the Congressional Caucus on Poland and the Congressional Caucus on Central and Eastern Europe.[3]

"Progressive" Connections

Marcy Kaptur has campaigned extensively with the Institute for Policy Studies (IPS) and other elements of the "progressive" movement against U.S. "free trade" agreements.

Anti-NAFTA Activism

In November 1993, Democratic Socialists of America (DSA)-infiltrated Jobs with Justice and Cleveland Women Against NAFTA organized an anti-NAFTA rally in the Sheet Metal Workers Local 13 Hall in Cleveland. Congresswoman Marcy Kaptur gave a "ringing indictment" of NAFTA and called for intense last minute lobbying to ensure its defeat. "Keep the pressure on," she said, "we can win this one."[4]

Anti-NAFTA Bill

In 1995, Congressional Progressive Caucus members Marcy Kaptur, Peter DeFazio, Nydia Velazquez and Bernie Sanders, co-sponsored a bill to force the U.S. to withdraw from NAFTA within 90 days. The bill was unsuccessful.[5]

Capitalism: A Love Story

In 2009, Marcy Kaptur appeared in radical filmmaker Michael Moore's anti-free market "documentary"—*Capitalism: A Love Story*.[6]

"NAFTA at Seven"

The Democratic Socialists of America dominated Economic Policy Institute (EPI), convened a conference on May 23, 2001, at the Cannon House Office Building, U.S. Congress, Washington, D.C. to read "NAFTA at Seven."

Panelists included:[7]

- Rep. Marcy Kaptur (D-OH)
- Jeff Faux, President, EPI, IPS and DSA Affiliate
- Robert Scott, Director of International Programs EPI
- Bruce Campbell, Executive Director, Canadian Centre for Policy Alternatives
- Lisa Fuentes, Board Member, Washington Office on Latin America and the IPS

"A Critical Look at NAFTA Past, Present and Future"

On March 5, 2008, co-sponsoring organizations: Global Exchange, Institute for Agriculture and Trade Policy, Washington Office on Latin America, Heinrich Boll Foundation, Alliance for Responsible Trade, National Alliance of Latin American and Caribbean Communities, Labor Council for Latin American Advancement... all affiliated with the Institute for Policy Studies and IPS itself, convened "A Critical Look at NAFTA Past, Present and Future" conference at The Carnegie Endowment for International Peace, Washington, D.C.

Keynote Presentation: "From NAFTA and now toward a U.S. trade agenda that works for people, at home and abroad:"[8]

- Introduction: Tom Loudon, Alliance for Responsible Trade
- The Honorable Marcy Kaptur, U.S. House of Representatives
- The Honorable Victor Quintana, Deputy of the State of Chihuahua, Mexico
- The Honorable Peter Julian, Member of Parliament, Canada

"Progressive" Cabinet "Nominee"

In September 2008, Chicago based Institute for Policy Studies/Democratic Socialists of America affiliated journal, In These Times, asked its editors and writers to suggest their top progressive choices for a potential Obama cabinet.

David Sirota suggested Marcy Kaptur for U.S. Trade Representative:[9]

No voice for trade reform has been more dogged than Rep. Marcy Kaptur's (D-Ohio).

A 13-term House member, Kaptur serves on the Appropriations Committee—one of Congress' most powerful panels. As Toledo's representative, she has seen firsthand the devastation that comes with unfair trade pacts, and has led the fight against every major lobbyist-written deal that has come through Congress—from NAFTA to China PNTR to CAFTA.

That personal connection to the trade issue would serve Kaptur well in international negotiations where compromise too often means selling out the American worker. Similarly, Kaptur's longtime experience in the House would be critical in powering fair-trade deals through what remains a corporate-dominated Congress.

Presidents of both parties have treated the trade representative position as an ambassadorship to a banana republic, appointing go-along-to-get-along hacks—such as former Clinton campaign chairman Mickey Kantor—who use the department as a taxpayer-funded training program for their post-government career in the corporate whorehouse.

Kaptur would be far different.

The Institute for Food and Development Policy/Food First

Marcy Kaptur is on the list of Congressional Representatives who have participated in hearings/briefings since 1998 with the very radical Institute for Food and Development Policy/Food First, founded by Frances Moore Lappe (DSA, IPS) and Joseph Collins (IPS), author of the book: "Food First."[10]

Foreign Policy/National Security

Cuba Trip

Rep. Charles Rangel, a frequent critic of the U.S. embargo against Cuba, met with Fidel Castro on a trip to the island in 2002, but only acknowledged that the Cuban government picked up part of the cost when a watchdog group began investigating.

Rep. Marcy Kaptur, who was also on the trip, said at the time that she and Rangel met with Castro and discussed the case of an American who fought in the Cuban Revolution, but was later executed.

Kaptur said at the time that top Cuban officials assured her they would consider returning Yanqui Comandante William Morgan's remains.

The body was never returned.[11]

Anti-U.S.-South Korea FTA Briefing

On June 7, 2006, Korea Policy Institute (an IPS affiliate) co-organized a press briefing in Congress, sponsored by Ohio Congressman Dennis Kucinich.

Speakers included Congresswoman Marcy Kaptur, Assembly member Kang Ki Kap of Korea's far left Democratic Labor Party, Kim Tae Il, the General Secretary of the Korean Confederation of Trade Unions, Lee Heung Se of the leftist Korean Advanced Farmers Federation and Lee Kang Sil of the Korean Hospital and Medical Workers Union. All spoke of their deep misgivings over the proposed Korea-U.S. FTA.

Many Korea Policy Institute leaders are affiliated with Nodutdol, a pro-North Korean group which organizes trips to Kim Jong-Un's "workers' paradise." It's what the group calls its "Democratic People's Republic of Korea Exposure & Education Program."[12]

South Korean Assembly member Kang Ki Kap and Congress Member Marcy Kaptur speaking at the Congressional Press Conference on the Proposed U.S.-Korea Free Trade Agreement

Far Left "Council of Canadians" Connection

In late June 2011, Stuart Trew, Trade campaigner for the far left Council of Canadians, spent two days in Washington, D.C. for meetings with U.S. allies and other organizations on the Beyond the Border perimeter deal.

Trew met with the IPS, Center for Economic Policy Research, Hudson Institute, AFL-CIO and a staffer in Congresswoman Marcy Kaptur's office.[13]

---

1 KeyWiki, "Marcy Kaptur," KeyWiki, http://keywiki.org/index.php/Marcy_Kaptur (accessed April 8, 2013)

2 Marcy Kaptur, "Biography," House.gov, http://www.kaptur.house.gov/index.php?option=com_content&view=article&id=98&Itemid=300248 (accessed August 1, 2011)

3 Marcy Kaptur, "Biography," House.gov, http://www.kaptur.house.gov/index.php?option=com_content&view=article&id=98&Itemid=300248 (accessed August 1, 2011)

4 People's Weekly World (November 13, 1993) p. 7

5 People's Weekly World (January 21, 1995) p. 4

6 Democratic Left, http://www.dsausa.org/dl/Fall_2009.pdf (Fall 2009)

7 Economic Policy Institute, "NAFTA at seven," Economic Policy Institute, http://www.epi.org/event/nafta-at-seven/ (May 23, 2001)

8 IPS website, "A Critical Look at NAFTA Past, Present and Future, IPS website, http://www.ips-dc.org/events/a_critical_look_at_nafta_past_present_and_future, (accessed April 9, 2013)

9 In These Times Editors and Contributors, "22 to Know," In These Times, http://inthesetimes.com/article/3933/ (September 26, 2008)

10 Food First, "Staff Page," Food First, http://www.foodfirst.org/es/about/staff (accessed April 9, 2013)

11 Lesley Clark, "Castro pitched in for lawmaker's visit," Cuba News/Miami Herald, http://www.cubanet.org/CNews/y06/jun06/08e6.htm (June 8, 2006)

12 Press Conference on the Proposed U.S.-Korea Free Trade Agreement: Mobilize and Organize to Resist the U.S.-South Korea FTA and Neoliberal Globalization (MORFNG)* Los Angeles, CA, http://www.kpolicy.org/documents/press/statement061606suhseunghyefta.html, (June 16, 2006)

13 Stuart Trew, "Report back on the fact-finding trip to Washington, D.C." Council of Canadians blog, http://canadians.org/blog/?p=9642#more-9642 (June 29th, 2011)

Ron Wyden (D-OR)

Ron Wyden is a Democrat and is the Senior United States Senator, for Oregon.

Background

Born in 1949 in Wichita, Kansas, Senator Wyden attended the University of California at Santa Barbara on a basketball scholarship. He later earned a B.A. Degree with Distinction from Stanford University and received a J.D. Degree from the University of Oregon, School of Law in 1974. He also served as the Director of the Oregon Legal Services for the Elderly from 1977 to 1979 and as a member of the Oregon State Board of Examiners of Nursing Home Administrators during that same time period.

Ron Wyden was first elected to Congress in 1980 to represent Oregon's 3rd District. In 1996, he was elected to the U.S. Senate in a special election, becoming the first U.S. Senator to be elected in a vote-by-mail election. He was sworn in on February 5, 1996, to the seat once held by his mentor, far left U.S. Senator Wayne Morse. He was re-elected in 2004 and in 2010.[1]

Influence

Wyden serves on the Committees on Finance, Budget, Aging, Intelligence and Energy and Natural Resources. He is Chairman of the Senate Energy and Natural Resources Committee and chairs the Senate Finance Subcommittee on International Trade, Customs and Global Competitiveness.[2]

Socialist Connections

Gray Panthers

Following law school, Ron Wyden taught gerontology and co-founded the Oregon chapter of the Gray Panthers, a socialist leaning advocacy group for the elderly.

According to Chicago Democratic Socialists of America's New Ground, May/June 2010, "The organization was born in 1970, when Maggie Kuhn, leading a group of friends fighting ageist employment practices, joined forces with students demonstrating against the Vietnam War. The press compared "their militancy to that of the Black Panthers, and so the first Gray Panthers network was born: age and youth working together for social and economic justice and peace."[3] [4]

Maggie Kuhn was a leading member of Greater Philadelphia Democratic Socialists of America and the Panthers worked closely with the socialists for years.[5]

GRAY PANTHERS Salute The Democratic Socialists
The Gray Panther Project Fund
1424 16th Street, NW, Suite 602
Washington, D.C. 20036
(202) 387-3111

Democratic Left, September 1991, page 28

Foreign Policy/National Security

"Congressional Pink Caucus"

In October 1989, the Marxist-Leninist Nicaraguan Sandinista Government announced that they would no longer comply with the 19 month-old cease-fire agreement with the anti-communist Contras.

A resolution was introduced in Congress deploring the Sandinistas' action. The Senate voted unanimously in favor, but in the House the vote was 379-29. All the 29 Congressmen voting against the resolution were Democrats.

The Council for Inter-American Security dubbed these 29 people the "Congressional Pink Caucus." Representative Ron Wyden was one of them.

Supported by Council for a Livable World

The anti-U.S. Defense Council for a Livable World supported Ron Wyden in his successful Senate run as a candidate for Oregon.[6]

Council for a Livable World, 50ᵗʰ Anniversary

On June 6, 2012, Council for a Livable World, along with its sister organizations Center for Arms Control and Non-Proliferation and Council for a Livable World's PeacePAC celebrated the 50th Anniversary of their founding by Leo Szilard in 1962.

Additionally, prior to the celebration, Senator Ron Wyden (D-OR) inserted a statement in the Congressional Record congratulating the Council on "our" 50th Anniversary stating:[7]

> In a time when our country continues to face a host of global threats, it is important that we recognize the vital work that the Council for a Livable World carries out each and every day to mitigate these threats, and to make our world a more peaceful, a more livable place.

> The Council for a Livable World is honored and humbled by everyone who joined in the 50th Anniversary Celebration. Thank you to all those who attended the events and to the many supporters who generously contributed to our work. The event exceeded all of our expectations and we are excited and determined as we look forward to another 50 years working on arms control and non-proliferation.

The Sustainable Defense Task Force

The Sustainable Defense Task Force was formed in response to a request from Representative Barney Frank (D-MA), working in cooperation with Representative Walter B. Jones (R-NC), Representative Ron Paul (R-TX) and Senator Ron Wyden, to explore possible defense budget contributions to deficit reduction efforts that would "not compromise the essential security of the United States."

The Project on Defense Alternatives coordinated the work of the Task Force. Carl Conetta drafted the main body of the Task Force report in ongoing consultation with Task Force members who developed or digested proposals from the diverse sources cited in the report. A subcommittee of the Task Force reviewed the final draft before publication.[8]

On June 11 2010, the Task Force report identified $960 billion in Pentagon budget savings that can be generated over the next ten years from realistic reductions in military spending.

"Leaders from the left, right and center agree on two major policy changes: the U.S. deficit must be reduced and the Pentagon budget can reverse its exponential growth while keeping Americans safe," claimed Paul Kawika Martin, Policy and Political Director of Peace Action (the nation's largest grassroots peace organization) and a member of the task force.

"At a time of growing concern over federal deficits, all elements of the budget must be subjected to careful scrutiny. The Pentagon should be no exception," said Carl Conetta of the Project on Defense Alternatives, an author of the report.

Major options for reductions in Pentagon spending cited in the report include the following:

- Over $113 billion in savings by reducing the U.S. nuclear arsenal to 1,050 total warheads deployed on 450 land-based missiles and seven Ohio-class submarines.
- Over $200 billion in savings by reducing U.S. routine military presence in Europe and Asia to 100,000 while reducing total uniformed military personnel to 1.3 million.
- Over $138 billion in savings by replacing costly and unworkable weapons systems with more practical, affordable alternatives. Suggested cuts would include the F-35 combat aircraft, the MV-22 Osprey and the Expeditionary Fighting Vehicle.
- Over $60 billion in savings by reforming military health care.
- Over $100 billion in savings by cutting unnecessary command, support and infrastructure funding.

The report also included a set of possible reductions based on a strategy of restraint that would emphasize the ability to bring force from the sea to defeat and deter enemies rather than putting large numbers of troops ashore in extended operations. The savings from this approach would total $1.1 trillion.

Calls for massive defense cuts were predictable given who was charged with writing the report. Wyden, Frank, Paul and Jones had given "respectable" cover to several far left groups, well known for their anti-defense/U.S. military agenda.[9]

The report's authors included Project on Defense Alternatives coordinators:[10]

- Carl Conetta—A former fellow at the Institute for Defense and Disarmament Studies, which in turn has been affiliated with the Institute for Policy Studies (IPS) and the Soviet front World Peace Council.
- Charles Knight—A onetime member of Democratic Socialists of America (DSA).

And contributors:

- William D Hartung—Represents the leftist New America Foundation on the Advisory Committee of the IPS' Foreign Policy in Focus.
- Christopher Hellman—From the IPS partner organization National Priorities Project.
- Heather Hurlburt—National Security Network and a Senior Adviser to the U.S. in the World Project of IPS partner organization Demos.
- Lawrence J. Korb—From the leftist, IPS and DSA infiltrated Center for American Progress.
- Paul Kawika Martin—Peace Action, (formerly SANE) the U.S.'s largest "peace" network, Peace Action is heavily infiltrated by DSA and other Marxist groups, including its national Field Director Judith LeBlanc, a leader of the Communist Party USA's "Peace and Solidarity Commission."
- Laicie Olson—Center for Arms Control and Non-Proliferation, Senior Policy Analyst for Center for Arms Control and Non-Proliferation, Council for a Livable World.
- Miriam Pemberton—IPS.
- Prasannan Parthasarathi—Boston College and husband of DSA member Juliet Schor.
- Laura Peterson—Of the leftist Taxpayers for Common Sense.
- Winslow Wheeler—From the IPS spinoff Center for Defense Information.

Democratic Socialists of America and Institute for Policy Studies had their fingerprints all over Wyden and friends' anti-defense report. This is not surprising, because the Cambridge Massachusetts based Commonwealth Foundation, which runs the Commonwealth Institute, of which the Project on Defense Alternatives is part and parcel of, is a front for DSA.

Of the Commonwealth Foundation's seven board members in 2011, five of them: Richard Healey, Charles Knight, S. M. Miller, Guy Molyneux and Cynthia Ward, are known members or supporters of Democratic Socialists of America. Richard Healey is the son of well known Los Angeles Communist Party leader turned DSAer, Dorothy Ray Healey.

At one point, the Project on Defense Alternatives' Advisory Board included Philip Morrison, Professor, Emeritus, Massachusetts Institute of Technology, a former Manhattan Project scientist, Communist Party front activist and suspected Soviet spy.[11] [12] [13] [14] [15] [16]

Report Coordinator Charles Knight revealed his views on U.S. National Security in Boston DSA's The Yankee Radical, October issue, 2001, entitled: "Defense Budget Blues."

> It is important to note that George Bush has now fully joined the ranks of wartime Keynesians. He has a majority coalition with Democrats to spend the country out of the recession it is now entering. In the short term the left in this country cannot hope to advance a better option. We must instead focus on deepening our analysis and story of this time in history so that when our country tires of vengeful war and its repercussions we have done the groundwork to lead the country in a different direction.

> Part of that story should be that 90+% of military investments have nothing to do with countering terrorism or with defending our homeland and that if we desire not to be a target of terrorist hate in the future we need to change our country's stance in the world.

> Furthermore, I think this is a good time for the left to reexamine a piece of its dogma: that it is the economic interests of defense contractors that keep defense budgets high. The economic self-interest of contractors is an important fact of the political economy, but the central impetus for high military budgets comes from the utility of military power to U.S. elites in their efforts to enhance their position of dominance across the globe. We are seeing that power in action now.

> Nevertheless, I believe that the majority of Americans do not share that interest in dominance with conservative elites. We must learn to provide a viable security option for this majority of Americans.[17]

So a Marxist group that effectively believes that America should not be able to lead the world militarily was covertly allowed to try and influence U.S. defense spending and priorities. Republicans Ron Paul and Walter Jones almost certainly had no idea that they were commissioning

IPS and DSA to write Defense Budget recommendations. However it is difficult to believe that Ron Wyden and Barney Frank, both of who have worked with Democratic Socialists of America run organizations in the past, did not realize who they were dealing with.[18]

1 Ron Wyden, "Meet Ron Wyden," Senate.gov. http://www.wyden.senate.gov/meet-ron/biography (accessed April 21, 2011)

2 Ron Wyden, "Meet Ron Wyden," Senate.gov. http://www.wyden.senate.gov/meet-ron/biography (accessed April 21, 2011)

3 Chicago DSA, "New Ground 130," DSA (May/June 2010)

4 DSA, "Democratic Left," DSA (September/October 1991) p. 28

5 KeyWiki, "Maggie Kuhn," KeyWiki, http://www.keywiki.org/index.php/Maggie_Kuhn (accessed June 8, 2013)

6 Council for a Livable World, "Meet the Candidates," Council for a Livable World, http://livableworld.org/support/meet_candidates/ (accessed June 8, 2013)

7 Center for Arms Control and Non-Proliferation website, "Foreign Policy/National Security: Council for a Livable World 50th Anniversary Celebration," Center for Arms Control and Non-Proliferation website (accessed June 8, 2013)

8 COMW, "Sustainable Defense Task Force Report," COMW (June 2010)

9 Peace Action blog, "New Report Urges Pentagon Cuts for Deficit Reduction," Peace Action (June 11, 2010)

10 KeyWiki, "The Sustainable Defense Task Force," KeyWiki, http://www.keywiki.org/index.php/The_Sustainable_Defense_Task_Force (accessed June 8, 2013)

11 KeyWiki, "Philip Morrison," KeyWiki, http://www.keywiki.org/index.php/Philip_Morrison (accessed June 8, 2013)

12 KeyWiki, "Project on Defense Alternatives," KeyWiki, http://www.keywiki.org/index.php/Project_on_Defense_Alternatives (accessed June 8, 2013)

13 KeyWiki, "Cynthia Ward," KeyWiki, http://www.keywiki.org/index.php/Cynthia_Ward (accessed June 8, 2013)

14 KeyWiki, "Richard Healey," KeyWiki, http://www.keywiki.org/index.php/Richard_Healey (accessed June 8, 2013)

15 KeyWiki, "Commonwealth Institute," KeyWiki, http://www.keywiki.org/index.php/Commonwealth_Institute (accessed June 8, 2013)

16 KeyWiki, "Guy Molyneux," KeyWiki, http://keywiki.org/index.php/Guy_Molyneux (accessed June 8, 2013)

17 DSA Boston, "Yankee Radical," DSA (October 2001)

18 KeyWiki, "Barney Frank," KeyWiki, http://www.keywiki.org/index.php/Barney_Frank (accessed June 8, 2013)

Jeff Merkley (D-OR)

Jeff Merkley is a Democrat and is the Junior U.S. Senator from Oregon.

Background

Born in Myrtle Creek Oregon, in 1956, Jeff Merkley earned a Bachelor of Arts Degree in International Relations from Stanford University in 1979 and a Master of Public Policy Degree from the Woodrow Wilson School at Princeton University in 1982.

Merkley was selected as a Presidential Management Fellow, working at the Office of the Secretary of Defense on the security of American military technology. After his fellowship, he worked in the Congressional Budget Office, analyzing nuclear weapons policies and programs.[1]

In 1991, Merkley returned to Oregon to lead Portland's leftist Habitat for Humanity, where he "led the neighborhood in shutting down Portland's worst crack market, developed the Habitat Home Building Center and launched a pilot project to establish Portland Youthbuilders, a program dedicated to helping gang-affected youth get back on their feet."

Merkley later served as President of the Oregon World Affairs Council, expanding the K-12 education program and launching an International Speakers Series that has brought many "distinguished leaders" to Oregon, including former Soviet premier Mikhail Gorbachev.

Merkley won his first campaign for State Representative in 1998. He was elected Democratic Leader in 2003 and Speaker of the Oregon House in 2007:

> As Oregon's House Speaker, Merkley emphasized replacing bitter partisan warfare with a culture of bipartisan problem solving. The result was what many termed the most successful session in decades. The legislature increased education funding, expanded access to affordable prescription drugs, passed landmark environmental and energy legislation, established domestic partnerships, cracked down on

predatory payday and title lending, and created Oregon's first ever Rainy Day fund.

Jeff Merkley was elected to the U.S. Senate in 2008.[2]

Influence

In the U.S. Senate Merkley has "released a nationally recognized plan to eliminate overseas oil by 2030 by boosting deployment of electric vehicles, increase travel options and improve infrastructure, develop alternative transportation fuels and reduce the use of oil to heat buildings."

To "take on the high-risk Wall Street trading that got us into the financial crisis," Merkley worked with Senator Carl Levin of Michigan to include in the Wall Street Reform and Consumer Protection Act new limits on risky trading by banks.

Merkley also successfully included a provision in the 2010 health care reform law that ensures new mothers have the time and space to pump milk at work.

Merkley serves on the Appropriations Committee; the Banking, Housing and Urban Affairs Committee; the Environment and Public Works Committee and the Budget Committee.[3]

Progressive Connections

"Progressive" Darling

Jeff Merkley is a darling of the U.S. "progressive" movement.

Writing in the Institute for Policy Studies (IPS) affiliated "The Nation," John Nichols named Jeff Merkley to the "The Progressive Honor Roll of 2012," as Most Valuable Senator:

> Among the new generation of Democratic senators elected in the past several years, none has been so steadfastly determined to forge progressive solutions as Oregon's Jeff Merkley. A frequent ally of stalwarts like Sanders and Tom Harkin, Merkley has also been willing to strike out on his own to pick big fights for big reforms.

As one of America's leading open socialists, affiliated with both Democratic Socialists of America (DSA) and Committees of

Correspondence for Democracy and Socialism, John Nichols is in a good position to judge "progressive" credentials.[4] [5]

The Merkley/Hatfield Relationship

Jeff Merkley's public service began as a 19-year-old intern with Oregon's former Republican Senator, Mark Hatfield. He was elected as a Democrat to Hatfield's old Senate seat, 33 years later in 2008.

Senator Merkley paid tribute to Senator Mark Hatfield, who passed away in August of 2011, in a eulogy to the U.S. Senate. Jeff Merkley described Mark Hatfield as a "mentor." In 2007, Merkley asked Hatfield to swear him in as Speaker of the Oregon House. When Merkley came to the U.S. Senate chamber, he asked for Senator Hatfield's old desk.

This relationship is significant for a number of reasons. While nominally a Republican, Hatfield, especially on Defense and Foreign Policy was one of the most far left members in the history of the U.S. Senate.

A "pacifist," Hatfield was a vocal opponent of the Vietnam War. While he was Governor of Oregon, the National Governors' Association passed a resolution reaffirming its support for the war in Vietnam. Hatfield cast the only dissenting vote.

In 1970, Hatfield partnered with ultra-left Democratic Senator George McGovern of South Dakota to propose legislation that would have set a deadline for the end of U.S. military operations in Vietnam. Strongly opposed by President Richard Nixon, the so-called McGovern-Hatfield amendment was defeated, 55 to 39.[6]

As Chairman of the Senate Appropriations Committee for the first six years of Ronald Reagan's presidency, Hatfield succeeded in diverting $100 billion from Reagan's military buildup to social programs. He joined Democrats in mocking Reagan's plans for the space-based missile-defense system known as Star Wars.

In 1982, he joined with Democrat Edward Kennedy of Massachusetts to propose an immediate nuclear weapons freeze in the U.S.—an idea promoted by the socialist/communist controlled SANE "peace" organization.[7]

On July 28, 1970, the F.B.I. issued a top secret memo entitled CONTACTS BETWEEN REPRESENTATIVES OF THE SOVIET UNION AND MEMBERS OR STAFF PERSONNEL OF THE UNITED STATES CONGRESS INTERNAL SECURITY—RUSSIA.

OFFICE OF THE DIRECTOR

UNITED STATES DEPARTMENT OF JUSTICE

FEDERAL BUREAU OF INVESTIGATION

WASHINGTON, D.C. 20535

July 28, 1970

CONTACTS BETWEEN REPRESENTATIVES OF THE
SOVIET UNION AND MEMBERS OR STAFF PERSONNEL
OF THE UNITED STATES CONGRESS
INTERNAL SECURITY - RUSSIA

A review of information we have developed through
our coverage of Soviet officials and establishments in
Washington, D. C., has disclosed a continuing interest by
representatives of the Union of Soviet Socialist Republics
(USSR) to maintain contacts with and cultivate members or
staff personnel of the U. S. Congress. There appears below
a compilation of such contacts which have come to our
attention from January 1, 1967, to date:

	Senators	Representatives	Staff Employees
1967	77	55	265
1968	34	23	224
1969	53	10	239
1970 to date	16	6	104

Based on a review of the information disclosed
through our coverage, it appears that Soviet officials are
making more contacts with the following Congressmen or members
of their staff than with other U. S. Legislators:

Senator Edward W. Brooke of Massachusetts
Senator Allen J. Ellender of Louisiana
Senator J. W. Fulbright of Arkansas
Senator Mark O. Hatfield of Oregon
Senator Edward M. Kennedy of Massachusetts
Senator Michael J. Mansfield of Montana
Senator Eugene J. McCarthy of Minnesota
Senator George S. McGovern of South Dakota
Senator Walter F. Mondale of Minnesota
Senator Edmund S. Muskie of Maine
Representative James G. Fulton of Pennsylvania
Representative Robert L. Leggett of California
Representative Donald W. Riegle, Jr., of Michigan

Group 1
Excluded from automatic
downgrading and
declassification

DECLASSIFIED
E.O. 12900, Sec. 3.6

By ____ Date 9/13/97

The memo stated:

A review of information we have developed through our coverage of
Soviet officials and establishments in Washington, D.C., has disclosed a
continuing interest by representatives of the Union of Soviet Socialist
Republics (USSR) to maintain contacts with and cultivate members or
staff personnel of the U.S. Congress. There appears below a
compilation of such contacts which have come to our attention from

January 1, 1967, to date: Based on a review of the information disclosed through our coverage, it appears that Soviet officials are making more contacts with the following Congressmen or members of their staff than with other U.S. Legislators...

Senator Mark O. Hatfield of Oregon was on the list, as were prominent leftist anti-Vietnam War Senators Edward M. Kennedy of Massachusetts, Eugene J. McCarthy of Minnesota, George S. McGovern of South Dakota, Walter F. Mondale of Minnesota and Edmund S. Muskie of Maine.

The memo was de-classified in 1997.

The Communist Party USA-controlled U.S. Peace Council organized a National Conference on Nicaragua in 1979, along with several other radical groups, to discuss a strategy to ensure that the communist Sandinistas took control of the country. Three Congressmen and two Senators lent support to this conference: Ron Dellums, Tom Harkin and Walter Fauntroy in the House and Mark Hatfield and Edward Kennedy in the Senate.[8]

Hatfield was also a very active supporter of the Institute for policy Studies, even teaching at the organization's radical Washington School.[9]

Predictably, Hatfield was one of the few Republicans ever supported by the far left, anti-U.S. defense, Council for a Livable World.[10]

America's Future Now Conference

Jeff Merkley was on the list of speakers at the 2009 America's Future Now conference, which was organized by the IPS and DSA dominated Campaign for America's Future.[11]

21st Century Democrats

The DSA/IPs affiliated 21st Century Democrats Political Action Committee supported Jeff Merkley in his successful 2008 U.S. Senate race.

Endorsing "Progressive" Candidates

On September 23, 2010, Merkley sent an email to supporters in which he requested donations for "six progressive candidates in tough races who aren't afraid to stand up to the big Wall Street banks and the corporate machine." He states that the 2010 election offers a choice "between giving power to extreme radical Republicans or strengthening progressive voices in the Senate." The six candidates for U.S. Senate Merkley endorsed were:[12]

- Patty Murray, Washington
- Paul Hodes, New Hampshire
- Russ Feingold, Wisconsin
- Chris Coons, Delaware
- Jack Conway, Kentucky
- Barbara Boxer. California
- Foreign Policy/National Security

Council for a Livable World

The Council for a Livable World, founded in 1962 by long-time socialist activist and alleged Soviet agent, Leo Szilard, supported Jeff Merkley in his successful 2008 Senate run as candidate for Oregon. He has also been previously supported by the Council.[13] [14]

According to the Council's website, Merkley warranted their support because:

Council for a Livable World has endorsed Jeff Merkley because he is an electoral winner who is also an expert on nuclear weapons and acutely aware of the dangers. In 1982, Merkley was selected as a Presidential Fellow and served in the Office of the Secretary of Defense. There he worked on verification for theater nuclear arms agreements, assisting the U.S. delegation to NATO and coordinating a committee on technology transfer to other countries. His next assignment was at the Congressional Budget Office, where he prepared reports on the Trident II missiles installed on our nuclear-powered submarines and the B-1B bomber program.

For the past decade he has been immersed in Oregon politics but remained involved in national security issues by serving as president and then a board member of the World Affairs Council of Oregon. In the United States Senate, Jeff Merkley will have the knowledge and capability to be a leader on nuclear and national security matters...

He interned for former Republican Senator Mark Hatfield, a patron saint of arms control...

Jeff Merkley opposes building a new generation of nuclear weapons and says that he "strongly supports the idea of the United States leading an international effort to reduce nuclear weapons stockpiles." He has endorsed the Kissinger-Shultz-Nunn-Perry vision of moving toward a world free of nuclear weapons.

He rejects deployment of National Missile Defense, pointing out that missile defenses "cannot stop either low-tech enemies who have other delivery mechanisms such as suitcase bombs or sophisticated enemies who can overcome expensive and complex sensor and intercept technologies with much simpler countermeasures." He opposes proposals to place weapons in space and instead endorses an international ban on space weapons. Merkley urges the Senate to approve the Comprehensive Test Ban Treaty and to greatly expand nuclear non-proliferation programs.

Merkley will be an important progressive leader in the Senate. His background on nuclear weapons, his knowledge of national security issues and his political experience clearly indicate that we need him in the U.S. Senate.

Council for a Livable World, 50th Anniversary

On June 6, 2012, Council for a Livable World, along with its sister organizations Center for Arms Control and Non-Proliferation and Council for a Livable World's PeacePAC celebrated the 50th Anniversary of their founding by Leo Szilard in 1962.

Jeff Merkley, Council for a Livable World

Six sitting Senators joined Council for a Livable World in an afternoon national security forum in the U.S. Capitol to speak on the issues the Council has been working on for 50 years. Sen. Jeff Merkley (D-OR), Sen. Jack Reed (D-RI), Sen. John Kerry (D-MA), Sen. Tom Udall (D-NM), Sen. Carl Levin (D-MI) and Sen. Ben Cardin (D-MD), "all spoke eloquently on these pressing issues."

Vietnam Delegation

U.S. Sen. Al Franken is part of a Senate delegation that traveled to communist Vietnam in July of 2010.

The group "look[ed] into environmental remediation of dioxin and the joint funding of medical services for people with disabilities, and meet with Vietnamese government officials to discuss education initiatives, labor issues and trade relations."

Other Senators on the Vietnam leg of the trip were Tom Harkin of Iowa, Bernie Sanders of Vermont and Jeff Merkley of Oregon.[15]

China Visit

In 2011, Jeff Merkley was part of a bipartisan group of 10 senators that met with China's senior leadership, including Vice President Xi Jinping and Foreign Minister Yang Jiechi.

Merkley had visited China for the first time 14 years before.

The topics were trade, jobs and economic issues, including U.S. complaints that China is manipulating its currency to make U.S. imports more expensive. Other talks focused on clean energy, international security and human rights.

Merkley said he "saw both the promise and the problem that China poses when it comes to economic matters and jobs. Fourteen years ago, he said, you could find dirt roads just beyond the limits of China's major cities. Today, the roads are both smooth and large, a testament to China's huge investments in new infrastructure. The county is spending roughly 10 percent of its gross domestic product to build roads and bridges, rail lines and airports. The U.S., by comparison, spends about 2 percent of its GDP."

That is good, Merkley said. "But the jury is still out on if it can be sustained."

Yet another difference from 14 years ago, Merkley said, is how China is liberalizing its rules on religion. Merkley went to Easter service in one of China's registered churches which have multiplied in recent years. Fourteen years ago, he said, he could not find open churches.[16]

1 Jeff Merkley, "Meet Jeff Merkley," Jeff Merkley for Oregon, http://www.jeffmerkley.com (January 21, 2008)
2 Jeff Merkley, "Biography," Senate.gov, http://www.merkley.senate.gov/about/biography/ (accessed May 2013)
3 Jeff Merkley, "Biography," Senate.gov, http://www.merkley.senate.gov/about/biography/ (accessed May 2013)
4 John Nichols, " The Progressive Honor Roll of 2012," The Nation (December 19, 2012)
5 KeyWiki, "John Nichols," KeyWiki, http://keywiki.org/index.php/John_Nichols (accessed June 8, 2013)
6 Laurence Arnold, "Mark Hatfield, Anti-War Republican Senator, Dies," Bloomberg (August 9, 2011)
7 KeyWiki, "SANE," KeyWiki, http://www.keywiki.org/index.php/SANE (accessed June 8, 2013)
8 Communists in the Democratic Party, p. 67
9 Communists in the Democratic Party, p. 73
10 Council for a Livable World, "Meet the Candidates," Council for a Livable World, http://livableworld.org/support/meet_candidates/ (accessed June 8, 2013)
11 Confabb website, "America's Future Now 2009 Speakers," Confabb website (accessed July 13, 2010)
12 Email from Senator Jeff Merkley to Supporters (September 23, 2010)
13 Council for a Livable World, "Meet the Candidates," Council for a Livable World, http://livableworld.org/support/meet_candidates/ (accessed June 8, 2013)
14 Council for a Livable World, "Who We've Helped Elect," Council for a Livable World, http://livableworld.org/what/legacy_in_congress_who_weve_helped_elect/ (accessed June 8, 2013)
15 Joe Kimball, "Al Franken to visit Vietnam with Senate group, then head to Laos," Minn Post (July 1, 2010)
16 Charles Pope, "Sen. Jeff Merkley confronts China's reality and contradictions during week-long visit," Oregon Live, http://www.oregonlive.com/politics/index.ssf/2011/04/sen_jeff_merkley_confronts_chi .html (April 26, 2011)

Peter DeFazio (D-OR)

Peter A. DeFazio is a Democratic member of the United States House of Representatives, representing the 4th District of Oregon. He was a Founder of the Congressional Progressive Caucus and is also a member of the Populist Caucus.[1]

Background

Peter Anthony DeFazio was born on May 27, 1947.

Congressman Peter DeFazio was first elected to the U.S. Congress in 1986. The 4th District includes Eugene, Springfield, Roseburg and part of Corvallis. As Oregon's most senior member of Congress, he is the Dean of the Oregon House Delegation, representing Southwest Oregon.

DeFazio was born in Needham, Massachusetts, a suburb of Boston. He credits his great-uncle with shaping his politics. As a boy, that great-uncle almost never said "Republican" without including "bastard" at the end of the phrase. He served in the United States Air Force from 1967 to 1971. He received a Bachelor of Arts Degree from Tufts University in 1969 and a Master of Arts Degree from the University of Oregon in 1977.

After graduation, DeFazio worked as a Gerontologist. From 1977 to 1982, DeFazio worked as an aide for U.S. Representative Jim Weaver. He was elected as a Lane County Commissioner in 1983 and served as Chairman from 1985 to 1986.[2]

Influence

DeFazio is a senior member of the House Transportation and Infrastructure Committee where he serves as Ranking Member of the Highways and Transit Subcommittee. He currently also serves on the Aviation Subcommittee and Railroad, Pipelines and Hazardous Materials Subcommittee. DeFazio also serves on the House Natural Resources Committee, where he sits on the National Parks, Forests and Public Lands Subcommittee and the Energy and Mineral Resources Subcommittee.[3]

Oregon Communist Party Connections

Peter DeFazio seems to be very popular with the Eugene, Oregon based John Reed Club of the Communist Party USA.

Endorsing DeFazio

Eugene, Oregon CPUSA leader Steve McAllister endorsed Peter DeFazio in the Graduate Teaching Fellows Federation, Local 3544, AFT Oregon, newsletter, The Agitator on Oct. 1st, 2012.[4]

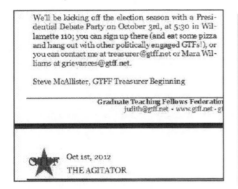

We'll be kicking off the election season with a Presidential Debate Party on October 3rd, at 5:30 in Willamette 110; you can sign up there (and eat some pizza and hang out with other politically engaged GTFs!), or you can contact me at treasurer@gtff.net or Mara Williams at grievances@gtff.net.

Steve McAllister, GTFF Treasurer Beginning

Graduate Teaching Fellows Federation
judith@gtff.net · www.gtff.net · gt

Oct 1st, 2012
THE AGITATOR

Oregon 4th Congressional District, U.S. House of Representatives
Peter DeFazio (D, Incumbent)*
Art Robinson (R)

Peter DeFazio is Oregon's most senior congressman, having served as the 4th District Representative since 1986. He has been a tireless ally of labor, and an unusually independent lawmaker who has a unique leadership style suited to his extremely politically diverse district. He has handily won re-election every time his seat is on the ballot, but the campaign of Republican Art Robinson in 2010, immediately on the heels of the Citizens United Supreme Court decision, eroded his lead with an influx of out-of-state corporate money so large it attracted national comment. Peter needs our support now more than ever.
(con't Pg 5)

Speaking Alongside Communist

On October 3, 2012, a "new coalition of students, teachers and workers at the University of Oregon rallied and marched against rising tuition and plans to privatize governance of the university. The event drew over a hundred participants and observers to the student union amphitheater."

Sponsored by the League of Educators and Students Slashing Tuition, the rally included a wide variety of speakers who addressed the rising cost of higher education in Oregon and around the country."

Congressman Peter DeFazio, representing Oregon's 4th Congressional District, also spoke, "about the dismal state of support for students from the federal government. He pointed out that during the budget crisis last year the one thing Republican lawmakers insisted on was cutting subsidized federal loans to graduate students. That was met with loud jeers from members of the graduate teaching fellows union, GTFF, who helped organize the rally."

"A 1 percent addition to the taxes of people who earn over $350,000 a year would pay for the low-interest rates forever for national direct student loans," DeFazio said.

"These people are already paying a lot less in taxes than they were in the Clinton era," he continued, referring to the super-wealthy who continue to enjoy George W. Bush's tax cuts. "They've already made it, and they made it by virtue, probably, of a good education."

Greg Rose, a retired professor and Chairman of the Communist Party of Oregon, told the crowd that this issue demands activism and resistance from the current generation of students, likening it to the struggle against the Vietnam War a generation ago.

"You must throw yourselves athwart the machine that is devouring this generation, capitalism," Rose said to cheers and waving signs. "It has commodified education, it has commodified teachers, and it has commodified students. It must stop, it must stop here; it must stop now!"[5]

Communist Petition

Eugene, Oregon Communist Party USA affiliate Jillian Littell, addressed an online petition to Congressman Peter DeFazio in February of 2013.[6]

Socialist Connections

Congressional Progressive Caucus

The Congressional Progressive Caucus was founded in 1991 by freshman Congressman Bernie Sanders, a supporter of Democratic Socialists of America (DSA). Sanders' CPC Co-Founders included House members Ron Dellums (DSA member), Lane Evans (DSA supporter), Tom Andrews, Peter DeFazio and Maxine Waters (DSA and Communist Party affiliate).

The CPC, now nearly 80 strong, has worked closely with DSA to promote socialist policies ever since.[7]

DSA Endorsement Given Then Revoked

This announcement appeared in the September/October 1996 issue of Democratic Socialists of America's newsletter, Democratic Left:

> In the last issue of Democratic Left, we reported that Carlos Romero-Barcelo (Puerto Rico at-large), a member of the Progressive Caucus, was endorsed by DSA PAC. We realize that this endorsement was a mistake and have withdrawn it.
>
> Likewise, DSA PAC voted to withdraw endorsements of Peter DeFazio (OR-4th District) and Elizabeth Furse (OR-1st District).

No explanation was given.[8]

"Progressive" Connections

Progressive Caucus SOTU Address

On January 27, 2000, the Congressional Progressive Caucus held its 3rd Annual Congressional Progressive Caucus' State of the Union Address. This event was also sponsored by the Institute for Policy Studies' (IPS) Progressive Challenge coalition, whose Fairness Agenda for America was "endorsed by 200 public interest groups nationally."

Caucus Chair Rep. Peter DeFazio stated: "The Progressive Caucus Alternative State of the Union will provide a much needed reality check to politicians who would rather ignore the priorities of Americans left out of the economic boom—priorities like access to quality health care and education, repairing crumbling schools, addressing the growing gap between the rich and poor, and creating a sustainable global economy that works for everyone, not just the corporate architects."

From their press release:[9]

> The Congressional Progressive Caucus, Chaired by Rep. Peter DeFazio (D-OR), consists of over a quarter of the House Democrats, one Independent and Senator Paul Wellstone. The Caucus will be releasing position papers on Health Care and Income Inequality, with reports on the Alternative Federal Budget, Social Security, Minimum Wage, Education and the Global Economy.

The press release on this event was issued by Karen Dolan of the IPS and Tom Vinson and Kathie Eastman from the Office of Rep. DeFazio.[10]

Financial Transactions Tax

In November of 2011, two U.S. lawmakers introduced measures to impose a transaction tax on financial firms that resembles a proposal released by the European Union.

Senator Tom Harkin, of Iowa, and Representative Peter DeFazio, introduced the bills in their respective chambers.

A "Briefing on Financial Transaction Taxes" was held and it was sponsored by Senator Tom Harkin, Representative Peter DeFazio and the Populist Caucus. It was held on October 21st at the U.S. Capitol Building—S-115. The briefing was presented by:

Americans for Financial Reform, (led by Democratic Socialists of America supporter Heather Booth); AFL-CIO; Institute for Policy Studies; The Center for Media and Democracy and The Center for Economic and Policy Research.[11]

The Institute for Food and Development Policy/Food First

Peter DeFazio is on the list of Congressional Representatives who have participated in hearings/briefings since 1998, with the very radical Institute for Food and Development Policy/Food First, founded by Frances Moore Lappe (DSA member, IPS affiliate) and Joseph Collins (IPS affiliate), authors of the book "Food First."[12]

Foreign Policy/National Security

Supported by Council for a Livable World

The Council for a Livable World, supported Peter DeFazio in his successful House of Representatives run as candidate for Oregon.[13]

The Council also supported DeFazio in his 2010 Congressional election campaign.[14]

"Congressional Pink Caucus"

In October of 1989, the Nicaraguan Sandinista Government announced that they would no longer comply with the 19 month-old cease-fire agreement with the Contras. This had been considered a prime step forward for the "peace process" that was progressing slowly as part of the Arias Peace Plan.

A resolution was introduced in Congress deploring the Sandinistas' action. The Senate voted unanimously in favor, but in the House the vote was 379-29. All of the 29 Congressmen voting against the resolution were Democrats.

The Council for Inter-American Security dubbed these 29 people the "Congressional Pink Caucus." Peter Defazio was one of them.[15]

---

1 KeyWiki, "Peter DeFazio," KeyWiki, http://keywiki.org/index.php/Peter_DeFazio (accessed April 21, 2013)

2 Peter DeFazio, "Biography," House.gov, http://www.defazio.house.gov/index.php?option=com_content&view=article&id=22& Itemid=45 (accessed April 21, 2013)

3 Peter DeFazio, "Committee Assignments," House.gov, http://www.defazio.house.gov/index.php?option=com_content&view=article&id=533 &Itemid=44 (accessed April 21, 2013)

4 Steve McAllister, "Peter DeFazio Endorsement," The Agitator (October 1, 2012)

5 Steve McAllister, "Students, teachers protest university privatization, tuition hikes," People's World, http://www.peoplesworld.org/students-teachers-protest-university-privatization-tuition-hikes/,v (October 5, 2012)

6 KeyWiki, "Peter DeFazio," KeyWiki, http://keywiki.org/index.php/Peter_DeFazio (accessed April 21, 2013)

7 KeyWiki, "Congressional Progressive Caucus," KeyWiki, http://www.keywiki.org/index.php/Congressional_Progressive_Caucus (accessed April 21, 2013)

8 Democratic Left (September/October 1996) p. 6

9 Progressive Newswire, "Progressive Groups And Congressional Caucus To Present Their Third Annual Alternative State Of The Union Address," Common Dreams, http://www.commondreams.org/news2000/0126-103.htm (January 26, 2000)

10 Progressive Newswire, "Progressive Groups And Congressional Caucus To Present Their Third Annual Alternative State Of The Union Address," Common Dreams, http://www.commondreams.org/news2000/0126-103.htm (January 26, 2000)

11 Admin, "Americans 50+ Demand Protections from Financial Abuse," Americans for Financial Reform, http://ourfinancialsecurity.org/2010/02/americans-50-demand-protections-from-financial-abuse/ (February 22, 2010)

12 Food First, "Staff Page," Food First, http://www.foodfirst.org/es/about/staff (accessed April 22, 2013)

13 Council for a Livable World, "Meet the Candidates," Council for a Livable World, http://livableworld.org/support/meet_candidates/ (accessed April 22, 2013)

14 Council for a Livable World, "Meet the Candidates," Council for a Livable World, http://livableworld.org/support/meet_candidates/ (accessed April 22, 2013)

15 KeyWiki, "Peter DeFazio," KeyWiki, http://keywiki.org/index.php/Peter_DeFazio (accessed April 21, 2013)

Chaka Fattah
(D-PA)

Chaka Fattah is a Democratic member of the United States House of Representatives, representing the 2nd District of Pennsylvania. He is a member of the Congressional Progressive Caucus and the Congressional Black Caucus.[1]

Background

Chaka Fattah was born to Russell Davenport and Frances Brown on November 21, 1956, under the name Arthur Davenport. His parents divorced when he was young and his mother soon remarried, this time to a man she met at a national conference on "black power" in 1968. Following this conference, his mother decided to change her name to Falaka Fattah, to acknowledge her African ethnicity and she renamed her son, Chaka Fattah.

When Fattah was 14, his mother and stepfather decided to develop a home for homeless boys and gang members and it eventually became the House of Umoja Boystown and the initiator of Fattah's political career. Fattah's next political act, undertaken while attending Shoemaker Junior High School in Philadelphia in 1968, was campaign volunteer for Mayor Hardy Williams.

In 1976, Fattah received his Associate's Degree from the Community College of Philadelphia. In 1977, he completed his Bachelor's Degree in Economics and Business at the University of Pennsylvania's Wharton School. Next, he attended Harvard University's John F. Kennedy School of Government, where he completed the Senior Executive Program for State Officials. Finally, in 1986, Fattah attended the University of

Pennsylvania Fels Institute of State and Local Government, receiving a Master's Degree in Government Administration.

Immediately following his schooling, Fattah served six years as a State Representative and six more as a State Senator, until being elected to Congress in 1994.[2]

Influence

Fattah is a senior member of the House Appropriations Committee. This committee is responsible for setting spending priorities for over $1 trillion in annual discretionary funds.

Congressman Fattah is the Ranking Member on the Subcommittee on Commerce, Justice, Science and related agencies (CJS). The Subcommittee on CJS oversees close to $51 billion in discretionary spending including the Commerce and Justice Departments, NASA, NOAA and the National Science Foundation.

Fattah is also Chair of the Congressional Urban Caucus, a bipartisan group of 47 members representing America's metropolitan centers. These members work collaboratively with other stakeholders to address the "unique challenges facing America's urban communities."

Congressman Fattah was appointed by former House Speaker Nancy Pelosi to Chair the Congressional Urban Caucus.[3]

Socialist Connections

DSA Endorsement

In July 1996, the Democratic Socialists of America (DSA) Political Action Committee endorsed Chaka Fattah in that year's Congressional elections.[4]

Nicholas Relationship

Fattah is very close to socialist labor leader Henry Nicholas, an International Vice President for the American Federation of State, County and Municipal Employees from Philadelphia, Pennsylvania.

Nicholas has been involved with Democratic Socialists of America or its predecessor, the Democratic Socialist Organizing Committee (DSOC), since at least the early 1980s.[5]

He has also been close to the Communist Party USA.

According to the CPUSA newspaper Daily World on October 21, 1982, p. 4, "Salute Black Caucus at labor luncheon," Henry Nicholas, President, National Union of Hospital and Health Employees, was a sponsor of a Labor Research Association event scheduled for November 21, 1982. The Labor Research Association had been cited several times by Congress and the government as a CPUSA front organization.

Nichols is also very active in the Communist Party/Democratic Socialists of America-controlled Coalition of Black Trade Unionists.

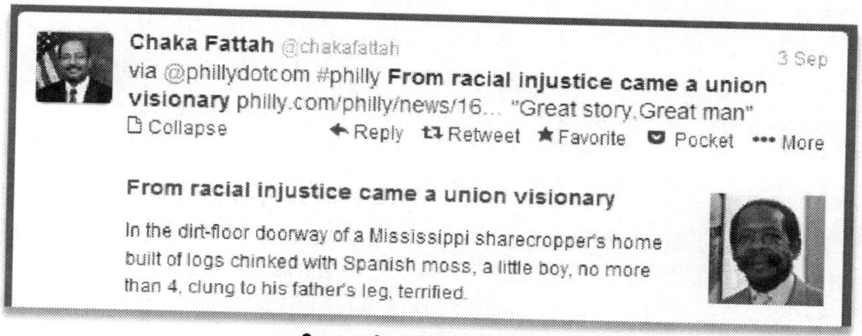
Chaka Fattah @chakafattah
3 Sep
via @phillydotcom #philly From racial injustice came a union visionary philly.com/philly/news/16... "Great story.Great man"
Collapse
Reply
Retweet
Favorite
Pocket
More
From racial injustice came a union visionary
In the dirt-floor doorway of a Mississippi sharecropper's home built of logs chinked with Spanish moss, a little boy, no more than 4, clung to his father's leg, terrified.

September 2012, Fattah Tweet

Nicholas Protégé

Labor boss Henry Nicholas, talked about running for Mayor of Philadelphia as an Independent in the November 1995 election against Democratic Mayor Ed Rendell.

"When I am a candidate, I expect them all to come out," Nicholas said. "They would be hard-pressed not to because I'm not just any candidate. I'm a candidate who paid dues already."

According to the Daily News, March 13, 1995, "If he runs, he puts his latest political protégé, Democratic U.S. Rep. Chaka Fattah, on the hot seat."

Nicholas helped Fattah beat U.S. Rep. Lucien Blackwell, who was Rendell's candidate in the Congressional race in 1994:[6]

> It's hard for Fattah to represent the city in Washington, D.C., without being at peace with the mayor, and Fattah is a practical politician. He didn't want to talk about Nicholas last week.

Pro-Democracy Convention

The Pro-Democracy Convention was held June 29th through July 1st in 2001. It started with a National Town Hall Meeting at Annenberg Center, University of Pennsylvania:

Come to a National Town Hall Meeting! Hear speakers representing a wide range of communities, including academics, labor leaders, lawyers, organizers, and elected officials, speak out about Election 2000, recommendations for electoral reform, and how we all can build the movement to expand democracy in the U.S.

Speakers included CPUSA and DSA affiliate Ron Daniels of the far left Center for Constitutional Rights; Marxist Ted Glick of the Independent Progressive Politics Network; "Red Diaper Baby" Lani Guinier of Harvard University; Reverend Al Sharpton of the National Action Network; William Lucy of Coalition of Black Trade Unionists and DSA; Henry Nicholas of the National Union of Hospital and Health Care Employees and Representative Chaka Fattah.[7]

Town Meeting for Jobs Not Wars

A Town Meeting for Jobs Not Wars was held Saturday, October 30th, 2010 at the Community College of Philadelphia, Bonnell Hall.

Speakers included Rep. Chaka Fattah; Henry Nicholas, AFSCME and Mike Prokosch, Community Organizer and Co-Author of "The Global Activist's Manual: Local Ways to Change the World," and an affiliate of both DSA and Committees of Correspondence for Democracy and Socialism.[8] [9]

Sharpton Rally

The Communist Party-connected Rev. Al Sharpton and his militant National Action Network, along with AFSCME and partners in labor, civil rights and clergy from across the country, held rallies in over 25 cities on December 9th, 2011, to "bring attention to the growing economic disparity in these cities, lack of employment and equality issues surrounding our current economic state:"

The 25-city rallies will call attention to key issues that have not yet been remedied such as the disproportionate layoffs of Blacks, Latinos, and other minority groups, and the growing wealth gap. The rallies will be held in cities that are most impacted by joblessness and attacks on workers' rights.

Philadelphia speakers included Rep. Chaka Fattah and Henry Nicholas of AFSCME.[10] [11]

CLUW Awards

On June 16th, 2011, the Philadelphia Chapter of the Communist Party/Democratic Socialists of America-dominated Coalition of Labor Union Women held their annual Working Women's Awareness Week Awards Reception.

A proclamation from U.S. Representative Chaka Fattah and a Citation from State Representative Babette Josephs (a DSA member) were presented to awardee, Labor Justice Radio.[12]

Other honorees included Debbie Bell, retired PFT leader; civil, workers and human rights activist and long-time Philadelphia CPUSA member.[13] [14]

Chaka Fattah, Center

CLUW Staffer

Coalition of Labor Union Women activist Cindy Bass is a policy formulator and community activist in Philadelphia. She is a former Senior Policy Advisor on Urban and Domestic Policy to Congressman Fattah.[15]

Foreign Policy/National Security

Venezuela Oil Deal

On Jan. 27, 2006, Rep. Chaka Fattah announced that CITGO, a U.S. subsidiary of the publicly-owned Venezuelan national oil company PDVSA, was going to begin shipping 5 million gallons of discounted heating oil to Philadelphia as part of a plan to provide assistance to 25,000 low-income families throughout the city.[16]

The first CITGO delivery was made the next day to Geraldine Shields in the West Oak Lane section of Philadelphia. Neighbors and friends applauded, waving U.S. and Venezuelan flags, as they welcomed the oil delivery to their community.

Fattah, Venezuelan Ambassador to the U.S., Bernardo Alvarez and CITGO CEO Felix Rodriguez participated in welcoming Shields' home delivery.

Ambassador Alvarez said Venezuela welcomes the opportunity to show true friendship to the American people; especially those in need. CITGO's Rodriguez said the gift was possible because PDVSA is publicly-owned: "Our shareholders are the Venezuelan people," he said.

Fattah planned to meet with Gov. Ed Rendell's staff the following week to discuss whether the program can be expanded throughout the state.

The previous September, Venezuela's Marxist President Hugo Chávez had announced that he would help lead a campaign in making oil from PDVSA (Petroleos de Venezuela, SA) available to low-income families within the U.S.

Chavez toured Manhattan and the Bronx communities in New York City after he attended the United Nations World Summit. Afterward, CITGO began to work with nonprofit groups to supply low cost oil to low-income families in New York City, Rhode Island, Vermont and Indian reservations in Maine.

In a radio interview, Fattah was asked why he was "embarrassing the U.S. government," since the Bush administration considers Chávez, a socialist and an enemy. "This is not a political matter. We have the ability to keep families in Philadelphia warm. I'm deeply appreciative of this humanitarian gesture," he said.[17]

---

1 KeyWiki, "Chaka Fattah," KeyWiki, http://keywiki.org/index.php/Chaka_Fattah (accessed April 27, 2013)

2 Chaka Fattah, "Fattah, Chaka," PA Book Libraries, http://pabook.libraries.psu.edu/palitmap/bios/Fattah__Chaka.html (accessed April 27, 2013)

3 Chaka Fattah, "About Congressman Chaka Fattah," House.gov, http://fattah.house.gov/index.cfm?sectionid=18 (accessed April 27, 2013)

4 Democratic Left (July/August 1996) p. 21

5 KeyWiki, "Henry Nicholas," KeyWiki, http://www.keywiki.org/index.php/Henry_Nicholas (accessed April 27, 2013)

6 Cynthia Burton, "Nicholas' Hat In The Ring? He Eyes Ed's Seat Amid Skepticism," Philly.com, http://articles.philly.com/1995-03-13/news/25698068_1_henry-nicholas-chaka-fattah-first-black-mayor (March 13, 1995)

7 impeach_bush, "National Town Hall Meeting," Yahoo! Groups, http://groups.yahoo.com/group/internetdemocrats1/message/4715 (June 4, 2001)

8 Marlene Santoyo, "Political Allies – ActionCalendar: Call DC to ease Cuba travel restrictions," AFSC, http://list.afsc.org/pipermail/political_allies_i/2010q3/000782.html (August 11, 2010)
9 KeyWiki, "Mike Prokosch," KeyWiki, http://www.keywiki.org/index.php/Mike_Prokosch (accessed April 28, 2013)
10 KeyWiki, "Al Sharpton," KeyWiki, www.keywiki.org/index.php/Al_Sharpton (accessed April 28, 2013)
11 National Action Network, "Along With Labor & Civil Rights Leaders To Attack Joblessness & Voter ID Laws That Are Threatening People's Voter Rights Across the Country on December 9th in 25-City Rally For Jobs & Justice," National Action Network, http://nationalactionnetwork.net/press/nan%E2%80%99s-annual-community-health-fair/ (accessed April 28, 2013)
12 KeyWiki, "Babette Josephs," KeyWiki, http://www.keywiki.org/index.php/Babette_Josephs (accessed April 28, 2013)
13 Labor Justice Radio website, "Labor Justice Radio Honored with Award from the Coalition of Labor Union Women," Labor Justice Radio website, http://www.mediamobilizing.org/updates/labor-justice-radio-honored-award-coalition-labor-union-women, (accessed April 28, 2013)
14 KeyWiki, "Debbie Bell," KeyWiki, http://keywiki.org/index.php/Debbie_Bell (accessed April 28, 2013)
15 Cindy Bass, "About Cindy," Cindy Bass for 8th District Council, http://cindybass.com/?page_id=2, (accessed April 28, 2013)
16 People's World, "Poor people in the U.S. also benefitted from Venezuelan oil," People's World, http://www.peoplesworld.org/poor-people-in-the-u-s-also-benefitted-from-venezuelan-oil/, (March 11, 2013)
17 Rosita Johnson, "Venezuelan discounted oil arrives in Philly," People's World, http://www.peoplesworld.org/venezuelan-discounted-oil-arrives-in-philly/, (February 3, 2006)

Jim Clyburn (D-SC)

James "Jim" E. Clyburn is a Democratic member of the United States
House of Representatives, representing the 6th District of South Carolina.
He is a leader and former Chairman of
the Congressional Black Caucus.[1]

Background

Jim Clyburn started life as the eldest son of an activist fundamentalist
minister and an "independent civic minded beautician." He was elected
President of his NAACP youth chapter when he was 12 years old and
helped organize many civil rights marches and demonstrations as a
student leader at South Carolina State College. He met his wife Emily in
jail during one of his incarcerations.[2]

Influence

President Barack Obama has said he is, "One of a handful of people who,
when they speak, the entire Congress listens." As Assistant Democratic
Leader in the 112th Congress, the number three Democrat in the House,
James E. Clyburn was the leadership liaison to the Appropriations
Committee and one of the Democratic Caucus primary liaisons to the
White House. Working with the internal caucuses, he plays a prominent
role in messaging and outreach.

When Clyburn came to Congress in 1993, he was elected Co-President
of his freshman class and quickly rose through leadership ranks. He was
elected Chairman of the Congressional Black Caucus in 1999 and won a
difficult three-way race for House Democratic Caucus Vice Chair in 2002.
Three years later, he was unanimously elected by his colleagues to House
Majority Whip.[3]

He is a member of the Democratic Faith Working Group and the Democratic Steering and Policy Committee.

Foreign Policy/National Security

Cuban Medical Training

The invitation for U.S. Students to earn a free medical education in Cuba dates to June 2000, when a group from the Congressional Black Caucus visited Cuban President Fidel Castro. It was led by the then Caucus President Jim Clyburn and was made up of Bennie Thompson from Mississippi and Gregory Meeks from New York.

Representative Thompson described huge areas in his district where there were no doctors and Castro responded with an offer of full scholarships for U.S. citizens to study at the Latin American School of Medicine (ELAM).

Later that year, Castro spoke at the Riverside Church in New York, reiterating the offer and committing 500 slots to U.S. Students who would pledge to practice in poor U.S. communities. Castro opened the doors of the program to 500 U.S. students who began enrolling two years later.

Communist Party affiliate, Reverend Lucius Walker, also got involved through his embargo breaking Pastors for Peace organization. Some of the students selected for free training are the children of U.S. Communist Party members.[4]

Castro's Version of Events

Writing in Granma, April 7, 2009, Fidel Castro gave his version of the Clyburn visit:[5]

> In May 2000, another Caucus delegation visited us. It was presided over by the then Caucus President James Clyburn, from North Carolina... These congressmen were the first to learn from me of Cuba's disposition to grant a number of scholarships to low-income youths, to be selected by the Congressional Black Caucus, so that they could come to Cuba and study medicine. We made a similar offer to the "Pastors for Peace" NGO, which is presided over by Reverend Lucius Walker, who sent the first students to the Latin American School of Medicine.
>
> When the anti-Cuban pressures and activities of the Bush administration were intensified with respect to travel and the presence

in Cuba of persons under U.S. jurisdiction, Black Caucus legislators addressed Secretary of State Colin Powell and managed to secure a license that legally allowed American youths to continue their medical studies—which they had already begun—in Cuba.

Staffer's Trip to Cuba

Rep. Clyburn sent Congressional staffer, David Francis Grimaldi, Jr., to Cuba for three days in March/April 2010. The trip was courtesy of a $2,127.40 grant from the Institute for Policy Studies (IPS) affiliated Center for Democracy in the Americas. It was a "fact-finding mission to understand the importance and culture of U.S. policy toward Cuba."[6]

Staffer's Trip to Venezuela

Rep. Clyburn sent staffer, Adam Arguelles, to Marxist-led Venezuela for three days in February 2010. The trip was courtesy of a $2,219.70 grant from the IPS affiliated Center for Democracy in the Americas. It was a "fact-finding trip in Venezuela and other Latin American countries with the mission of fostering dialogue and improving U.S. policy and bilateral relations."[7]

---

1 James E. Clyburn, "Biography," House.gov, http://clyburn.house.gov/about-me/full-biography (accessed August 16, 2011)

2 James E. Clyburn, "Biography," House.gov, http://clyburn.house.gov/about-me/full-biography (accessed August 16, 2011)

3 James E. Clyburn, "Biography," House.gov, http://clyburn.house.gov/about-me/full-biography (accessed August 16, 2011)

4 Fitzhugh Mullan, M.D., "Cuba Trains Physicians for Wealthy United States," New England Journal of Medicine Volume 351:2680-2682, http://academic.udayton.edu/health/02organ/providers01.htm (December 23, 2004)

5 Fidel Castro, "Reflections of Fidel, The seven Congress members who are visiting us," Granma, http://www.granma.cu/ingles/2009/april/mar7/Reflections-6april.html (April 7, 2009)

6 Legistorm, "Center for Democracy in the Americas – Sponsor of Congressional Travel," Legistorm, http://www.legistorm.com/trip/list/by/sponsor/id/10693/name/Center_for_Democracy_in_the_Americas/page/2.html (accessed August 30, 2010)

7 Legistorm, "Center for Democracy in the Americas – Sponsor of Congressional Travel," Legistorm, http://www.legistorm.com/trip/list/by/sponsor/id/10693/name/Center_for_Democracy_in_the_Americas/page/2.html (accessed August 30, 2010)

Sheila Jackson Lee (D-TX)

Sheila Jackson Lee is a Democratic member of the United States House of Representatives, representing the 18th District of Texas. She is a member and a former Vice Chair of the Congressional Progressive Caucus, as well as a member of the Congressional Black Caucus.[1]

Background

Sheila Jackson Lee was born on January 12, 1950. She is married to Dr. Elwyn C. Lee, who holds a dual position of Vice Chancellor and Vice President for Student Affairs at the University of Houston System and the University of Houston, respectively.

Congresswoman Jackson Lee earned a Bachelor of Arts Degree in Political Science from Yale University with Honors, followed by a Juris Doctorate from the University of Virginia, Law School.[2]

Congresswoman Sheila Jackson Lee is serving her ninth term representing the 18th Congressional District, centered in Houston, which is the energy capital of the world.[3]

Jackson Lee made three unsuccessful attempts at local judgeships before becoming a municipal judge from 1987 to 1990. In 1989, she won the At Large position for a seat on the Houston City Council, serving until 1994.

Influence

Sheila Jackson Lee sits on two Congressional Committees—the House Committees on the Judiciary and Homeland Security. The Congresswoman has authored several immigration bills, such as HR 750, the "Save America Comprehensive Immigration Act of 2007." Jackson Lee introduced legislation to enhance federal enforcement of hate crimes with HR 254, the "David Ray Hate Crimes Prevention of 2007." She also played a significant role in the recent renewal and reauthorization of the Voting Rights Act. Congresswoman Jackson Lee contributed an amendment to the NASA reauthorization bill this year that will ensure "equal access for minority and economically disadvantaged students to NASA's education programs."

Congresswoman Jackson Lee is a Founder, member and Co-Chair of the Congressional Children's Caucus, the Pakistan Caucus, the Afghan Caucus and the newly formed Algerian Caucus.[4]

Communist Connections

Houston "Progressives"

According to James Thompson of the Communist Party USA paper People's World:[5]

> Houston also has a strong union movement which is very progressive and is active in electoral politics. The city's three Congress people Al Green, Gene Green and Sheila Jackson Lee are at the forefront of the progressive struggle in the House of Representatives.

Stoney Cooks

In the mid-2000s, far left activist Stoney Cooks, served as Sheila Jackson Lee's Chief of Staff and Administrative Assistant.

In 1967, Cooks was one of forty-one Americans who traveled to communist Czechoslovakia to meet with representatives of the North Vietnamese communist government and the Viet Cong.

The American delegation included members of Students for a Democratic Society and other leftist groups. According to one participant, the meeting had been initiated by the North Vietnamese and the Americans "were expected not only to oppose the war in Vietnam but also to favor, on balance, an NLF (National Liberation Front) victory."

Stoney Cooks was among the sponsors of a United States Preparatory Committee for the 10th World Festival of Youth and Students held during 1973 in East Berlin. The committee operated from the offices of the official youth front for the Communist Party USA and its promotional literature was printed by a firm characterized by the Attorney General of the United States as "reliably known to be owned by the Communist Party."[6]

"Progressive" Connections

Appeal for Redress

The Appeal for Redress held a press conference, on October 17, 2007, on Capitol Hill, in the Rayburn Building. The group of 2,050 active duty military members called on the U.S. Congress "to end the occupation of Iraq." It also warned the "Bush-Cheney Gang" about "repeating the same mistake in Iran." Sharing her views in support of the group's goals was Rep. Sheila Jackson Lee. Sponsoring the event was the Institute for Policy Studies.[7]

Take Back America

Jackson Lee was a speaker at the March 2007, Take Back America Conference, which was hosted by the Democratic Socialists of America/Institute for Policy Studies affiliated Campaign for America's Future in Washington, D.C.[8]

Foreign Policy/National Security

Cuban Delegation

In February of 1999, six members of the United States Congressional Black Caucus visited Cuba to evaluate the United States-imposed embargo. Among the visitors was Sheila Jackson Lee of Texas.[9] [10]

Committees of Correspondence/Aid to Vietnamese Communists

In November of 2007, two representatives of the communist government of Vietnam, Dr. Nguyen Thi Ngoc Phuong, a leading clinician/researcher on the effects of Agent Orange on women and children in Vietnam and another from Tu Du Hospital, Ho Chi Minh City, visited Washington, D.C. on a Vietnam Agent Orange Public Health Tour.

Dr. Phuong, Vice President of the Vietnam Association for Victims of Agent Orange, toured Washington, D.C. and attended a conference where a policy of the socialist infiltrated American Public Health Association on Agent Orange (Vietnamese version) was passed in November of 2007.

Dr. Phuong was accompanied by Merle Ratner of the Committees of Correspondence for Democracy and Socialism and Susan Schall, both leaders of the Committees of Correspondence-dominated Vietnam Agent Orange Relief & Responsibility Campaign.

The delegation met several members of Congress including John Conyers, Bob Filner and Sheila Jackson Lee.[11]

November 7, 2007: (second from left) Merle Ratner, Sheila Jackson Lee, Dr. Nguyen Thi Ngoc Phuong, (far right) Susan Schall

Dr. Phuong has held many senior positions in Vietnam's communist government and was touring the USA under communist guidance to extract United States taxpayers' money for the communist government of Vietnam.[12]

---

1 Congressional Black Caucus Foundation, "The Congressional Black Caucus Members of the 112th Congress," Congressional Black Caucus Foundation, http://www.cbcfinc.org/cbc/cbc-members.html (accessed June 13, 2012)

2 Sheila Jackson Lee, "Biography," U.S. Congresswoman Sheila Jackson Lee, http://jacksonlee.house.gov/Biography/,/ (accessed June 13, 2012)

3 Sheila Jackson Lee, "Biography," U.S. Congresswoman Sheila Jackson Lee, http://jacksonlee.house.gov/Biography/,/ (accessed June 13, 2012)

4 Sheila Jackson Lee, "Biography," U.S. Congresswoman Sheila Jackson Lee, http://jacksonlee.house.gov/Biography/,/ (accessed June 13, 2012)

5 James Thompson, "Houston elects first openly gay mayor," People's World, http://www.peoplesworld.org/houston-elects-first-openly-gay-mayor/ (accessed June 13, 2012)

6 James M. Klatell, "Here's The Thing: It's Not Race," CBS News, http://www.cbsnews.com/stories/2006/04/05/politics/main1472724_page2.shtml (accessed June 12, 2012)

7 Rep. Sheila Jackson-Lee: "Let Us Wake Up America!," YouTube, http://www.youtube.com/watch?v=ZtFbSQhv8Uk, (accessed January 20, 2013)

8 Campaign For America's Future, "Archives – 2007 Speakers," Campaign For America's Future, http://www.ourfuture.org/node/19968 (accessed June 13, 2012)

9 Cuba Travel USA, "The Economic Embargo – A Timeline," Cuba Travel USA, http://www.cubatravelusa.com/history_of_cuban_embargo.htm (accessed June 13, 2012)

10 Digital Granma Internacional, "The seven Congress members who are visiting us," Digital Granma Internacional, http://www.granma.cu/ingles/2009/april/mar7/Reflections-6april.html (accessed June 13, 2012)

11 "November 1-14, 2007 Vietnam Agent Orange Public Health Tour Featuring Dr. Nguyen Thi Ngoc Phuong," Vietnam Agent Orange Relief & Responsibility Campaign, http://www.vn-agentorange.org/Nov2007_public_health_tour.html (accessed June 13, 2012)

12 BaoMoi.com, "Vietnamese AO victims receive great support in the US," BaoMoi.com, http://en.baomoi.com/Info/Vietnamese-AO-victims-receive-great-support-in-the-US/3/91846.epi (accessed June 13, 2012)

Eddie Bernice Johnson (D-TX)

Eddie Bernice Johnson represents the Dallas area 30th Congressional District of Texas. She is a member of the Congressional Progressive Caucus and in the 107th Congress served as Chair of the Congressional Black Caucus.[1]

Background

From Waco Texas, Congresswoman Johnson studied nursing at St. Mary's College at the University of Notre Dame. She returned to Texas, where she became Chief Psychiatric Nurse at the VA Hospital in Dallas. She received a Bachelor's Degree in Nursing from Texas Christian University in 1967 and a Master's Degree in Public Administration from Southern Methodist University in 1976.

Johnson was elected to the Texas House of Representatives in 1972 and went on to lead the Labor Committee. She was appointed by President Jimmy Carter to serve as Regional Director of the Department of Health, Education and Welfare in 1977. In 1986, she was elected as a Texas State Senator, serving until she was elected to Congress in 1992.[2]

Influence

In December 2010, Rep. Johnson was elected as the Ranking Member of the House Committee on Science, Space and Technology. From 2000 to 2002, she was the Ranking Member of the Subcommittee on Research and Science Education.

Rep. Johnson has been a member of the House Transportation and Infrastructure Committee since 1993. In 2007, Congresswoman Johnson was appointed by House Transportation and Infrastructure Committee Chairman James L. Oberstar (D-MN) to serve as Chairwoman of the

Subcommittee on Water Resources and Environment during the 110th and 111th Congresses. The Subcommittee on Water Resources and Environment has jurisdiction over water conservation, pollution control, infrastructure and hazardous waste cleanup. The Subcommittee is also responsible for reauthorizing the Clean Water Act.

Johnson has also served in the position of Senior Democratic Deputy Whip. Congresswoman Johnson is credited with originally authoring and co-authoring more than 150 bills that were passed by the House and Senate and signed into law.[3]

Communist Connections

Eddie Bernice Johnson has connections to the Communist Party USA, particularly with a Dallas based activist, a former Socialist Workers Party leader turned Communist Party supporter, named Gene Lantz.[4]

People's World Article

Eddie Bernice Johnson, then Chair of the Congressional Black Caucus, contributed an article to the Communist Party's People's World, of Dec. 7, 2001, entitled, "Drug czar assures repeat of past failures:"[5]

> While the national drug movement and voter reform efforts move toward humane, effective strategies, John Walters, President Bush's choice for drug czar is a giant step backwards.

> Walters' nomination for director of the Office of National Drug Control Policy is pending before the Senate after being approved by the Judiciary Committee. I strongly disagree that if confirmed, Walters is the right man for the job. A protégé of former drug director William J. Bennett, Walters is considered a hardliner in the drug fight. His writings depict him as viewing drug addiction as a

problem to be solved by courts and prisons rather than a public health issue that can be resolved through hospitals and treatment...

Critics have noted that decades of the law enforcement, lock-'em-up approaches supported by Walters have helped land 500,000 Americans behind bars and consumed tens of billions of tax dollars without reducing the demand whatsoever.

Yet, Walters would continue that failed policy, according to his writings on drug policy. In a recent op-ed piece Walters wrote that research showing that the criminal justice system is imprisoning too many people for drug possession, unjustly punishes Black men and the sentencing is too long and harsh are "the three greatest myths of our time."

The choice of Walters is an embodiment of policies that have failed. They are mistakes we can't afford to repeat.

Honored by Gene Lantz

Judy Bryant of the Education Workers Union (Alliance/AFT) and Gene Lantz, a leader of the AFL-CIO affiliated and communist infiltrated Alliance of Retired Americans, honored Congresswoman Johnson for "her work on health care" at the union hall at 334 W. Center, Dallas, TX on August 21, 2008.[6]

Gratitude from the Left

At noon on November 13, 2009, activists from MoveOn, Organizing for America, Jobs with Justice (led by local leader Gene Lantz) and the Progressive Center of Texas, "poured into the offices" of Congresswoman Johnson. They were there to express their gratitude for her vote on the House version of national health care reform.[7]

They were greeted by District Director Rod Givens, who told them that, "it is folks like you who keep the Congresswoman propped up!"

The group brought a giant "thank you" card that each of them had signed. They also brought bouquets of yellow roses. Many of them carried pledges to work several hours in her next campaign.[8]

Speaking Alongside Gene Lantz

Retirees from all over North Texas "cooperated to celebrate Congresswoman Eddie Bernice Johnson's lifelong commitment to health care reform" at the Alliance/AFT hall in Dallas on August 21, 2011. The bills for the event were shared by members of the Retired Members Committee of the Communication Workers of America, Alliance/American Federation of Teachers, United Auto Workers Local 848 and Jobs with Justice.

The event was chaired by AFT leader Judy Bryant. Gene Lantz showed the 11 minute introductory video for the Alliance for Retired Americans and conducted a discussion on the importance of organizing for such legislative goals as the Employee Free Choice Act. Congresswoman Johnson gave a "thorough analysis of the need for health care reform and how to accomplish it through Congress."[9]

TARA Honor

The Texas Alliance of Retired Americans, presided over by Gene Lantz, held a Fiesta Dinner to Honor Congresswoman Eddie Bernice Johnson in Dallas, Texas on May 3, 2013.

Tony Padilla, Secretary of the organization welcomed the guests:[10]

> Greetings and Good evening Brothers and Sisters, President Gene Lantz, Officers of Board of the TARA, Vice President Emeritus of the National AFL-CIO Linda Chavez Thompson, Congresswoman Eddie Bernice Johnson, Congressman Marc Veasey, Officers of the National Board of ARA, Members and Distinguished Guests.

> Today is a very special night as we honor Congresswoman Eddie Bernice Johnson, and it is a historical night for seniors.

> So, on behalf of the 4 million members of the National Alliance for Retired Americans with the AFL-CIO as our parent organization, it is with great pleasure and honor to pay tribute to you Congresswoman Eddie Bernice Johnson, a longtime friend and supporter of issues affecting Seniors and working families...

Gene Lantz (front rear) with Marc Veasey, Linda Chavez Thompson, and Eddie Bernice Johnson

Foreign Policy/National Security

Eddie Bernice Johnson is a long-time friend of Cuba and a supporter of easing restrictions on the communist dictatorship.

2005 Trip to Cuba

In July 2005, Congresswoman Johnson and her Chief of Staff Murat Gokcigdem spent three days in Havana, Cuba, "to explore firsthand the issues facing the people of Cuba. An opportunity to foster a more pragmatic approach towards dealing with the Cuban government and finding constructive solutions to U.S./Cuba policy concerns." Johnson's trip cost $1,555.29 and was paid for by the leftist Christopher Reynolds Foundation.[11]

Pastors for Peace

Pastors for Peace styles itself as "a special ministry of the Interreligious Foundation for Community Organization, and was created in 1988 to pioneer the delivery of humanitarian aid to Latin America and the Caribbean." In reality, it is a support network for Cuba and Latin American revolutionary movements. The organization sends regular "aid" caravans to Cuba in an attempt to overturn the U.S. trade embargo on the island.[12]

Its long-time head, the late Rev. Lucius Walker, was a lifelong supporter of Communist Party USA fronts and causes.[13]

One of Eddie Bernice Johnson's first aides was Texas radical Ernest McMillan, who has been very active in Pastors for Peace.[14]

In August 2005, Pastors for Peace was in Dallas, "networking with local churches and peace and justice networks, and doing media outreach." The group held a vigil in front of Dallas City Hall, along with representatives of the Dallas Peace Center, Pax Christi and the homeless veteran population. Some computers bound for Cuba had recently been seized by U.S. Authorities:[15]

Then we had the honor of receiving a two-hour visit from Rep. Eddie Bernice Johnson (D-TX), former chair of the Congressional Black Caucus. Rep. Johnson has visited Cuba twice, and pledged to increase her advocacy for the release of the computers for Cuba.

When the July 2007 Pastors for Peace Caravan went through Dallas, one of the Caravanistas, "Ernest," wrote on the IFCO/Pastors for Peace 2007 Caravan to Cuba blog:[16]

I can't end this note and go back to my personal chores and diversions without thanking the Dallas Peace Center, the Jobs with Justice brothers and sisters, Congresswoman Eddie Bernice Johnson, the Presbyterian "Peacemakers", the Pan African Connection Bookstore (and any others I may have unintentionally left out) for their contributions—in word and in deed—to the overall efforts.

Rep. Johnson sent a congratulatory message to the Pastors for Peace 20th Cuba Friendship Caravan as it passed through Dallas in August of 2009.[17]

---

1 KeyWiki, "Eddie Bernice Johnson," KeyWiki, http://keywiki.org/index.php/Eddie_Bernice_Johnson (accessed May 18, 2013)

2 Eddie Bernice Johnson, "About Eddie Bernice Johnson," House.gov, http://ebjohnson.house.gov/index.cfm?sectionid=2&sectiontree=2, (accessed May 18, 2013)

3 Eddie Bernice Johnson, "About Eddie Bernice Johnson," House.gov, http://ebjohnson.house.gov/index.cfm?sectionid=2&sectiontree=2, (accessed May 18, 2013)

4 KeyWiki, "Gene Lantz," KeyWiki, www.keywiki.org/index.php/Gene_Lantz (accessed May 18, 2013)

5 Rep. Eddie Bernice Johnson, "Drug czar assures repeat of past failures," People's World, http://www.peoplesworld.org/drug-czar-assures-repeat-of-past-failures/ (December 7, 2001)

6 Grand Prairie Democrats, "Health Care Event," Grand Prairie Democrats, http://dir.groups.yahoo.com/group/gpdems/message/980, (August 21, 2008)

7 Gene Lantz, "Thanks to Congresswoman Johnson for Health Care Reform Vote," YouTube, http://www.youtube.com/watch?v=5udy8Fc0ej8 (November 13, 2009)

8 Jim Lane, "Activists Say "Thanks" for Health Care Reform," Texas CPUSA, http://tx.cpusa.org/ebjthank.htm, (accessed May 18, 2013)

9 UAW 848, "Dallas Retirees Cooperate to Win Health Care Reform," Retirees Corner, http://www.uaw848.org/retirees_corner.htm,UAW (accessed May 18, 2013)

10 International Association of Machinists, "Retiree Tony Padilla and others Honors Congresswoman Eddie Bernice Johnson," International Association of Machinists, http://www.goiam.org/index.php/headquarters/departments/retirees-community-and-membership-services/retirees/11414-retirees-honor-congresswoman-eddie-bernice-johnson, (May 6, 2013)

11 American RadioWorks, "Trips sponsored by Christopher Reynolds Foundation," American Public Media, http://americanradioworks.publicradio.org/features/staffers/travdat/sponsor.php?sponsor_id=T000109 (accessed May 18, 2013)

12 KeyWiki, "Interreligious Foundation for Community Organization," KeyWiki, http://www.keywiki.org/index.php/Pastors_for_Peace#Pastors_for_Peace (accessed May 18, 2013)
13 KeyWiki, "Lucius Walker," KeyWiki, http://www.keywiki.org/index.php/Lucius_Walker (accessed May 18, 2013)
14 Roy Appleton, "Dallas men gave voices to those working for peace and justice," The Dallas Morning News, http://www.wfaa.com/news/local/64545162.html (August 15, 2009)
15 PFP Caravan, "Pastors for Peace Update and Action Alert: We're Headed to Washington! For Immediate Release, Greetings from Dallas, Texas!," PFP Caravan, http://caravan16.blogspot.co.nz/ (August 2005)
16 Ernest, "Beautiful Letter from Dallas," IFCO/Pastors For Peace 2007 Caravan to Cuba, http://18thcubacaravan.blogspot.co.nz/2007/07/beautiful-letter-from-dallas.html, (July 16, 2007)
17 Dallas Peace Times (August 2009) p. 3

Bernie Sanders (I-VT)

Bernard Sanders is an openly Socialist member of the United States Senate, representing Vermont. Though technically Independent, he usually caucuses with the Democrats.

In 1991, Sanders founded the Congressional Progressive Caucus as a freshman Congressman. He is currently the Senate's only official Progressive Caucus member.[1]

Background

Born in Brooklyn, Bernie Sanders was educated in Chicago. After graduation from the University of Chicago in 1964, he moved to Vermont, where he worked as a carpenter, filmmaker, writer and researcher. Early in his career, Sanders was Director of the American People's Historical Society.

In 1971, he became a candidate for the U.S. Senate for the far-left Liberty Union Party—an alternative to the Democratic and Republican parties. Sanders picked up 2 percent of the vote. He ran as a candidate for Liberty Union three more times, achieving 6 percent of the vote before finally quitting. Sanders promoted programs that included nationalizing all U.S. banks, public ownership of all utilities and establishing a worker-controlled government.[2]

Elected Mayor of Burlington by 10 votes in 1981, he served four terms.

In 1990, Sanders was elected to Congress from Vermont, as a socialist, on a third party ticket. At the time, Sanders was a leading member of Jesse Jackson's National Rainbow Coalition. He was supported by the AFL-CIO, environmentalists, anti-Apartheid activists and Democratic Party leaders.[3]

Before his election as Vermont's At Large member in Congress, Sanders lectured at the John F. Kennedy School of Government at Harvard and at Hamilton College in upstate New York.[4]

Influence

Bernie Sanders serves on the Environment and Public Works Committee, the Energy and Natural Resources Committee, the Health, Education, Labor and Pensions Committee, the Budget Committee, the Veteran's Affairs Committee and the Joint Economic Committee.[5]

Communist Connections

U.S. Peace Council

An ad/notice was placed in the Guardian, November 8, 1989, concerning an upcoming U.S. Peace Council national conference. The text of the notice was:

"End The Cold War Fund Human Needs"—U.S. Peace Council's Tenth Anniversary National Conference—Boston, Mass., Nov. 10-12, 1989.

Bernie Sanders addressed the conference, as did pro-Cuba activist Leslie Cagan, scientist and Communist Workers Party affiliate Michio Kaku, DSA members Holly Sklar and Manning Marable, Communist Party affiliate Gerald Horne and Zehdi Terzi of the terrorist Palestine Liberation Organization.

All willing followers of an agenda set by the Communist Party USA and the Soviet controlled World Peace Council.[6]

Communist John Case on Sanders' Political Skills

In response to an organized campaign to draft Sanders for a presidential run in 2012, CPUSA member John Case wrote on the Political Affairs blog:[7]

> The complexity of the U.S. political process at this moment requires shrewd and careful AND BOLD calculations. There are few, if any, politicians on the left more shrewd than Bernie Sanders. I am not convinced about Bernie's denials. I got to know him somewhat in my years as a UE rep in VT, and later as DO for the Communist Party in N. New England. With a few arguable exceptions, he has always—both

ideologically and politically—pursued a working class line. As important, he become a demonstrated master of very concrete tactics directed at isolating the right, without appearing irresponsible or reckless to center forces. He kept focused on the concretes—especially economics, and non-corrupt governance—that blunted repeated attempts by the right to isolate him.

Communist Mike Bayer on Sanders

December 3, 2006, "was a day the People's Weekly World can be proud of. Still celebrating the results of the Nov. 7 elections, readers held banquets and dinners in various places across the country, attracting elected officials, leaders of people's movements and rank-and-file fighters for justice and democracy."

In Connecticut, guests packed the Communist Party-run New Haven People's Center to "Carry the People's Election Victories Forward"...

Mike Bayer, a leading Communist Party member and treasurer of the Sanders supporting Vermont Progressive Party, spoke about: "left Independent Bernie Sanders' election to the U.S. Senate as a fighter for working-class people." Bayer also stressed the continuing need to pressure Congress for universal health care, minimum wage increases, the right to belong to a union and U.S. troops returning home from Iraq.[8]

The event was described this way in an earlier edition of People's Weekly World:[9]

> Special guest Michael Bayer, state treasurer of Vermont's Progressive Party, will address "Building Independent Political Action on behalf of Working Families." The Progressive Party was inspired by Congressman Bernie Sanders, who is a founder of the Congressional Progressive Caucus and is newly elected U.S. Senator from Vermont.
>
> The event will celebrate a year of activism against the war in Iraq and for immigrant rights and workers' rights, reflected in major get out the vote efforts by labor and community groups which changed control of Congress. Projections will be made for next steps to change the direction of the country and achieve an end to the war, good jobs and health care.
>
> The program, to be held at the New Haven People's Center, 37 Howe Street, will include poetry, music, an international holiday gift table and a home-cooked light supper. The annual reception is hosted by the

People's Weekly World in Connecticut on the occasion of the 87th anniversary of the Communist Party USA.

Socialist Connections

Bernie Sanders has been part of the socialist movement since his college days.

Young People's Socialist League

After one year at Brooklyn College, Sanders spent four years at the University of Chicago, where he joined the Young People's Socialist League, the youth wing of the Socialist Party USA, the Congress on Racial Equality and the Student Peace Union. He also worked briefly for the communist-led United Packinghouse Workers Union.[10]

I.F. Stone's Endorsement Letter

In October of 1988, journalist I.F. Stone, a former secret Communist Party USA member and Soviet agent, by then a Democratic Socialists of America (DSA) sympathizer if not member, wrote a letter endorsing Burlington Mayor Bernie Sanders' Congressional run:[11]

Dear Friend,

I've been politically active all my life. I was a member of the Executive Committee of the Socialist Party in New Jersey, before I was old enough to vote.

Now I'd like to ask you to join me in a historic step forward in American politics. My favorite Mayor—Bernie Sanders of Burlington, Vermont—is running for Congress and with our help he can win an unprecedented victory for us all.

Bernie is a unique figure in our political system. He's an unapologetic socialist who has been elected Mayor of Vermont's largest city four times. He has proved that a socialist, running as an Independent against the combined opposition of Republicans and Democrats, can be successful by speaking out for working people, the elderly and the poor.

Under Bernie's leadership, Burlington has become a vibrant, innovative city, nationally recognized for its accomplishments. The U.S. Conference of Mayors recently gave it the "Most Livable City" award, and even the conservative U.S. News and World Report has spotlighted Bernie as one of the country's Top Twenty Mayors (December 21, 1987).

Bernie has been a leader in the struggle for peace and justice. His activism was instrumental in Vermont's strong support of the Nuclear Freeze in its town meetings in 1982. He has traveled to Nicaragua to speak out against the Reagan Administration's war, and to establish a Sister City relation between Burlington and Puerto Cabezas. More recently, he went to the Soviet Union to set up a Sister City program with Yaroslavl.

While socialism has a long and proud history in America, extending back to the utopian experiments of the early 1800s, it's been a long time since we've had a socialist voice in Congress. Not since Victor Berger of Milwaukee in the twenties, has the debate gone beyond the limits set by the conventional two-party system.

I.F. STONE

Dear Friend,

I've been politically active all my life. I was a member of the Executive Committee of the Socialist Party in New Jersey, before I was old enough to vote.

Now I'd like to ask you to join me in a historic step forward in American politics. My favorite Mayor -- Bernie Sanders of Burlington, Vermont -- is running for Congress, and with our help he can win an unprecedented victory for us all.

Bernie is a unique figure in our political system. He's an unapologetic socialist who has been elected Mayor of Vermont's largest city four times. He has proved that a socialist, running as an Independent against the combined opposition of Republicans and Democrats, can be successful by speaking out for working people, the elderly and the poor.

Under Bernie's leadership, Burlington has become a vibrant, innovative city, nationally recognized for its accomplishments. The U.S. Conference of Mayors recently gave it the "Most Liveable City" award, and even the conservative U.S. News and World Report has spotlighted Bernie as one of the country's Top Twenty Mayors (December 21, 1987).

Bernie has been a leader in the struggle for peace and justice. His activism was instrumental in Vermont's strong support of the Nuclear Freeze in its town meetings in 1982. He has traveled to Nicaragua to speak out against the Reagan administration's immoral war, and to establish a Sister City relation between Burlington and Puerto Cabezas. More recently, he went to the Soviet Union to set up a Sister City program with Yaroslavl.

While socialism has a long and proud history in America, extending back to the utopian experiments of the early 1800s, it's been a long time since we've had a socialist voice in Congress. Not since Victor Berger of Milwaukee in the twenties, has the debate gone beyond the limits set by the conventional two-party system.

Having Bernie in Washington will widen out the limits of political discussion. He'll speak up loudly, as he has in Vermont, for real alternatives. He'll show that we need a pragmatic socialism to deal with the grave problems of our economic system.

Having Bernie in Washington will widen out the limits of political discussion. He'll speak up loudly, as he has in Vermont, for real alternatives. He'll show that we need a pragmatic socialism to deal with the grave problems of our economic system.

I.F. STONE

Democratic Socialists of America

Though technically Independent, Bernie Sanders has been a close ally of DSA, since at least the early 1990s.

Ties to Democratic Socialists of America

Sanders is a regular speaker at DSA conferences and the organization is a major fundraiser for his campaigns.

From a Spring 2000, Democratic Left editorial:[12]

> Electoral tactics are only a means for DSA; the building of a powerful anti-corporate and ultimately socialist movement is the end. Where third party or non-partisan candidates represent significant social movements DSA locals have and will continue to build such organizations and support such candidates. DSA honored Independent socialist Congressperson Bernie Sanders of Vermont at our last convention banquet, and we have always raised significant funds nationally for his electoral campaigns.

DSA Endorsements

In 1990, the DSA Political Action Committee endorsed two Congressional candidates, "DSAer Democrat" Neil Abercrombie, seeking to regain the House seat representing Honolulu and Vermont Independent candidate, Bernie Sanders.[13]

In July 1996, the Democratic Socialists of America Political Action Committee endorsed Bernard Sanders, Vermont At Large, in that year's Congressional elections.[14]

DSA Conferences

In November 1991, Sanders spoke at the Democratic Socialists of America national convention at Mundelin College, Chicago.[15]

In November 1999, Bernie Sanders was keynote speaker at DSA's national convention in San Diego. He was introduced by local congressman, Bob Filner.

Sanders addressed the Greater Detroit Democratic Socialists of America conference in June 2006.

Bernie Sanders and Detroit DSA Leader David Green (June 25th, 2006)

In November 2007, Senator Sanders addressed the national Conference of Democratic Socialists of America, held at the IBEW union hall in Atlanta, Georgia.[16]

> I want to thank the DSA for the support that they gave me in the last campaign. And I want to thank DSA, not only for what they are doing today, but also for keeping alive what in my view is the most important vision that we as human beings can hold. It's a vision that has been passed on from generation to generation, literally for thousands of years: the vision of peace, the vision of brotherhood.

> And the vision tells us that peace is better than war that greed should not be the dominant factor in our society today, and that people can come together beyond race and creed and country of origin to create a very different world than the world in which we are living today.

DSA Support in Senate Campaign

DSA's 2005 National Conference in Los Angeles committed the organization to supporting Sanders' 2006 U.S. Senate race and to using it to recruit some new members along the way:[17]

> From now through November 2006, the Sanders for Senate campaign in Vermont will focus national media attention on the most serious socialist electoral effort in the United States since the Debsian period. Bernie Sanders has been an articulate voice for democratic socialist politics among the 435 members of the House of Representatives and has spoken at DSA events on many occasions.

> Sanders would become a much more visible national spokesperson for socialist politics if and when he serves as one of 100 members of the more powerful United States Senate.

> His election is by no means assured and he will need the financial and organizational help of the broad democratic left around the country. In addition, Sanders support work provides a natural vehicle in any locality for DSA to reach out to—and potentially recruit—unaffiliated socialists and independent radicals.

> Thus, this convention commits itself to:

> a. The national staff and NPC developing feasible, legal, ways that DSA locals, networks, individuals, and campus groups can aid the Sanders for Senate campaign.

b. The national leadership providing guidance as to how local groups engaged in aiding the Sanders campaign can utilize such efforts to recruit for and build DSA.

In 2006, Bernie Sanders received $15,387 from the Democratic Socialists of America Political Action Committee for his campaign as the Independent candidate for the Vermont seat in the U.S. Senate primary and general elections.[18]

Boston Democratic Socialists of America leader David Knuttunen and the DSA National Political Committee wrote in The Yankee Radical, August 2006:[19]

> So it is no surprise that DSA's National Convention, in November 2005, voted to make support for Bernie Sanders a priority for the organization.

> DSA's staff and leadership responded to the Convention vote by forming a Political Action Committee (the Democratic Socialists of America, Inc. PAC), which then launched a project to hold house parties across the country to raise money for the Sanders Campaign.

The events are organized by DSA activist volunteers, who pay the associated costs out of their own pockets—all proceeds go directly to the Sanders Campaign. The list of house party locales reminds one of the words of "Joe Hill": "from San Diego on up to Maine..." To date, the DSA PAC campaign has resulted in events in Boston, Atlanta, Detroit, Central Ohio, Portland ME and Boulder CO. Events are being planned for San Diego, San Francisco, Sacramento, Central Indiana, Washington DC, Minneapolis/St. Paul, New York City, and Springfield MA, with a few more under discussion. Over $28,000 has been raised for the Sanders Campaign so far. DSA PAC expects that the campaign will eventually generate well over $50,000—not bad for a tiny little organization, and a campaign run almost entirely with volunteer effort.

Even more important than the fundraising, though, in the eyes of many DSAers, is the opportunity for political education. The house parties give DSA volunteers the opportunity to expose people to DSA and political ideas that Bernie Sanders and DSA both hold.

The Democratic Socialists of America PAC raised over $50,000 nationally to support Sanders' campaign.[20]

Foreign Policy/National Security

Soviet Flag

Sanders hung the Soviet flag in the Mayoral office in Burlington, in honor the city's Soviet sister city, Yaroslavl.[21]

Nicaragua Visit

In 1985, while Mayor of Burlington, Sanders celebrated the sixth anniversary of the Sandinista victory in Managua, with Nicaragua's Marxist-Leninist dictator Daniel Ortega.[22]

Staffer's 2000 Trip to Cuba

In February of 2000, Sandra Caron from the office of Congressman Bernie Sanders, spent six days in Havana, Cuba, for the purpose of "fact-finding, [and to] study effects of [the] U.S. embargo." The trip cost $1,778.47 and was paid for by the far left Christopher Reynolds Foundation.[23]

Supported by Council for a Livable World

The Council for a Livable World, supported Bernie Sanders in his successful Senate run as a candidate for the state of Vermont.[24]

When backing Sanders again in 2012, the Council website explained:

Bernie, as he is universally known, has a perfect record on Council for a Livable World's voting scorecard on key national security issues...

He opposed the authorization for war in Iraq when in the House and supported measures in both the Senate and House to withdraw troops...

He also opposed additional funding for national missile defence and efforts to cut U.N. peacekeeping funds. He enthusiastically endorsed the New START treaty and opposed all Republican attempts to cripple the agreement. ..

Council for a Livable World endorses Bernie Sanders for U.S. Senate with the greatest enthusiasm. His frank, open, no-nonsense style is a breath of fresh air in the U.S. Senate. He is committed to the elimination of weapons of mass destruction, opposes pre-emptive wars and works hard on these issues.[25]

---

1 KeyWiki, "Bernie Sanders," KeyWiki, http://keywiki.org/index.php/Bernie_Sanders (accessed April 12, 2013)
2 Dateline D.C., Pittsburgh Tribune-Review (November 12, 2006)
3 People's Weekly World (November 10, 1990) p. 23
4 The Arena, "Bernie Sanders," Politico, http://www.politico.com/arena/bio/bernie_sanders.html (accessed April 12, 2013)
5 Bernie Sanders, "About Bernie," Senate.gov, http://www.sanders.senate.gov/about/ (accessed April 12, 2013)
6 KeyWiki, "U.S. Peace Council," KeyWiki, http://keywiki.org/index.php/U.S._Peace_Council (accessed April 12, 2013)
7 John Case, "Sanders for President," Political Affairs, http://politicalaffairs.net/sanders-for-president/?utm_source=feedburner&utm_medium=feed&utm_campaign=Feed%3A+P aeditorsblog+%28PA+Editors+Blog%29 (December 29, 2010)
8 People's Weekly World, "PWW events salute peoples leaders," People's Weekly World, http://www.peoplesworld.org/pww-events-salute-people-s-leaders/ (December 15, 2006)
9 People's Weekly World, "Three Connecticut Leaders to be Honored," KeyWiki, http://keywiki.org/cache/2010/8/Three-Connecticut-leaders-to-be-honored-Dec3-2006.htm (November 28, 2006)
10 Bernie Sanders, "Outsider in the House," Huck Gutman, p. 14
11 KeyWiki, "Bernie Sanders," KeyWiki, http://keywiki.org/index.php/Bernie_Sanders (accessed June 4, 2012)

12 DSA, http://www.dsausa.org/dl/sum2kindex.html (accessed April 12, 2013)
13 Democratic Left, http://www.dsausa.org/dl/sum2kindex.html (November/December 1990) p. 4
14 Democratic Left (July/August 1996) p. 21
15 Democratic Left (November/December 1991) p. 11
16 Democratic Left, http://www.dsausa.org/dl/Winter_2008.pdf (Winter 2007-2008) p. 5
17 DSA, http://www.dsausa.org/dl/Winter_2006.pdf (Winter 2006)
18 CampaignMoney.com, "Democratic Socialists of America PAC," CampaignMoney.com, http://www.campaignmoney.com/political/committees/democratic-socialists-of-america-pac.asp?cycle=06 (accessed April 12, 2013)
19 DSA Boston, The Yankee Radical, http://www.dsaboston.org/yradical/yr2006-08.pdf (August 2006)
20 DSA Boston, The Yankee Radical, http://www.dsaboston.org/yradical/yr2007-04.pdf (April 2007)
21 Wall Street Journal (September 1990) p. A16
22 Wall Street Journal (September 24, 1990) p. A16
23 American RadioWorks, "Christopher Reynolds Foundation," American Public Media, http://americanradioworks.publicradio.org/features/staffers/travdat/sponsor.php?sponsor_id=T000109 (accessed June 6, 2012)
24 Council for a Livable World, "Meet the Candidates," Council for a Livable World, http://livableworld.org/support/meet_candidates/ (accessed June 6, 2012)
25 Council for a Livable World, "Bernie Sanders," Council for a Livable World, http://livableworld.org/elections/2012/candidates/senate/bsanders/ (accessed May 20, 2013)

Patty Murray (D-WA)

Patricia Lynn "Patty" Murray is the Senior Democratic member of the United States Senate, representing the State of Washington.[1]

Background

Born in Bothell, Washington, in 1950, Patty Murray received her Bachelor of Arts Degree in Physical Education from Washington State University in 1972. She was a preschool teacher for several years and taught a parenting class at Shoreline Community College from 1984 to 1987.[2]

In the 1980's, Patty Murray led a grassroots coalition of 13,000 parents to save a local preschool program from budget cuts. She went on to serve on the local School Board and in 1988 was elected to the Washington State Senate.

In 1992, Murray ran for the United States Senate as a "voice for Washington families who were not being heard in the Senate." Dramatically outspent, Murray ran a grassroots campaign of family, friends, supporters and "public interest groups" to beat a 10-year veteran of the U.S. House of Representatives. Senator Murray was re-elected in 1998, 2004 and 2010.[3]

Influence

Murray has served as the Senate Majority Conference Secretary since 2007, making her the fourth-highest-ranking Democrat in the Senate. Chairman of the Democratic Senatorial Campaign Committee from 2001 to 2003 and again from 2011 to 2013, Murray currently chairs the Senate Budget Committee and previously served as Co-Chair of the United

States Congress Joint Select Committee on Deficit Reduction. She is also the Chairman of the Senate Committee on Veterans' Affairs.

As of 2012, leaders of the Democratic National Committee included Senator Patty Murray, Democratic Senatorial Campaign Committee Chair.[4][5][6][7]

Communist Connections

Patty Murray has a pattern of association with the Washington State Communist Party USA (CPUSA).

Coalition of Labor Union Women, 1997 Conference

Speakers at the November 1997 Coalition of Labor Union Women (CLUW) conference in Seattle included Richard Trumka and Linda Chavez-Thompson of the AFL-CIO; Nancy Riche, Executive VP of the Canadian Labor Congress; Rep. Jim McDermott of Washington State and Senator Patty Murray.[8]

While a Communist Party/Democratic Socialists of America (DSA) front nationwide, in Washington State CLUW was almost exclusively a CPUSA creation. CPUSA members, such as Irene Hull and Lonnie Nelson, founded and ran the Puget Sound branch of CLUW for many years.[9][10][11]

Washington Senator Patty Murray was one of CLUW's featured convention speakers.

CLUW 2003 Seattle Conference

CPUSA supporter Pat Stell, Vice-President of the Washington State CLUW, welcomed the 800 delegates from local chapters and national unions to that organization's biennial convention in Seattle on October 9, 2003.

CLUW President Gloria Johnson, a DSA supporter, set a tone of determined defiance to the Bush administration "running roughshod over our schools and reproductive rights, invading our privacy, and other nations." Taking on the Patriot Act and its assault on civil liberties, Johnson challenged the assembly, "Do we want to go back to the days of McCarthyism?" "No!" they roared back. "Hell no!"

Health care was a major focus of the delegates, with five chapters introducing resolutions in support of HR 676, Rep. John Conyers' bill that would provide expanded and improved Medicare-type coverage for all Americans.

Senator Patty Murray pointed to the convention's theme, "Vision, Voices, Votes," as the same plan of attack that led to victory recently in stopping the Bush administration's attack on overtime pay. "We need to give people the vision, make their voices heard, and count the votes," she said.

"In the scheme of things, there are them and us," said DSA member and Coalition of Black Trade Unionists President William Lucy, going on to describe "all-out class warfare between those who have the power to make the rich richer and the rest of us who just want a good life."

Communist Party reporter Roberta Wood recorded the event for the People's World and noted that comrade Irene Hull was among the attendees.[12]

Communist Party Support

In 1998, according to then Washington State Communist Party Chair, B. J. Mangaoang; the "Party weighed in to re-elect Democratic Senator Patty Murray and to unseat three ultra-right GOP house members."[13]

Lonnie Nelson's Policy Input

CPUSA member, Lonnie Nelson, "has worked in packing, sorting, vegetable processing and child care, but has never earned more than $8.50 an hour. Now she says she relies on the Puget Sound Labor Agency to keep food on the table, and she wants the unions that support the PSLA food bank to know she is grateful."

Nelson was part of a roundtable discussion held at the Seattle Labor Temple on August 18, 2008, with Sen. Patty Murray and several clients and directors of area food banks.

Sen. Murray toured the Puget Sound Labor Agency food bank and then participated in the discussion on growing needs at area food banks caused by food and fuel inflation and a slumping national economy. She added that events like Monday's tour and forum have made her "increasingly aware that as food prices increase, many more families are going hungry."

"This (forum) has been very helpful," Murray said. "At the federal level, we have got to pass a supplemental bill (on food assistance). That's the message I will take back to Congress."[14]

Social Security Birthday

A 75th Birthday Celebration of Social Security, featuring Senator Patty Murray and U.S. Rep. Jim McDermott, was held on August 16, 2010 at the Phinney Neighborhood Association's Greenwood Senior Center in Seattle.

The event was organized by the Puget Sound Alliance for Retired Americans and Social Security Works—Washington, which included the Coalition of Labor Union Women; the Puget Sound Chapter of the Asian Pacific American Labor Alliance; the Seattle Chapter of the DSA-led Physicians for a National Health Program; and the Western Washington Chapter of the Washington State Jobs with Justice, a Communist Party influenced organization.[15] [16]

At the time, Puget Sound Alliance for Retired Americans Board was led by its founder CPUSA member Will Parry and Communist Party affiliated board members Gene Lux and Rachael Levine.[17] [18] [19]

Grant to Communist Led Board

Roslyn, Washington's Old City Hall building was affected by the 2001 Nisqually earthquake, revealing major structural issues with the old building. A committee appointed by the city began working on finding ways to address needed changes in the structure. Fundraising began. A major grant made possible by Sen. Patty Murray, "sealed the deal" for the first phase of the improvements in September 2010.

Marc Brodine, Chairman of the Roslyn Library Board of Directors and of the Washington State Communist Party, said many in the community were looking forward to the day the project would start.[20] [21]

Communist Party Campaigners

In 2010, Communist Party leaders Tim Wheeler and Joyce Wheeler worked in Patty Murray's campaign in Sequim, Washington State.

Tim Wheeler wrote in the People's World:[22]

The highest profile election victory here Nov. 2 was the reelection of Sen. Patty Murray. She defeated Republican Dino Rossi by more than 100,000 votes.

I was asked to coordinate street-corner "waves" for Murray here in my hometown. We could tell Murray was doing well by the number of motorists, especially women, who honked and gave us the thumbs-up salute, far outnumbering the Republicans who gave us a sour look and the thumbs-down.

My wife Joyce and I spent one afternoon canvassing for Murray up on Bell Hill...

One wealthy resident told me she had already mailed in her ballot, marked for Patty Murray, and was "praying for our country," that voters reject the lies of the rightwing demagogues...

Washington State voters helped put up a firewall against the ultra-right in reelecting Murray, blocking a GOP majority takeover of the Senate. Victory was won when the coalition of unions and other progressive organizations succeeded in getting out the vote.

Tim Wheeler (center)

Foreign Policy/National Security

Supported by Council for a Livable World

The anti-U.S. military Council for a Livable World supported Patty Murray in her successful Senate run as candidate for Washington in 1992 and again in 2010.

According to the 2010 Patty Murray endorsement on the Coalition's website:[23] [24]

Patty Murray has made a difference, particularly on arms control, nuclear disarmament and foreign policy. In 2002, Murray was one of 23 Senators to vote against the President's request for authority to take military action in Iraq... In key Senate votes, she supported amendments to bring U.S. troops out of Iraq, opposed funding for a new generation of nuclear weapons and voted against amendments to increase national missile defense funding.

---

1 KeyWiki, "Patty Murray," KeyWiki, http://keywiki.org/index.php/Patty_Murray (accessed May 18, 2013)
2 Patty Murray, "Biographical Directory," Congress.gov, http://bioguide.congress.gov/scripts/biodisplay.pl?index=m001111, (accessed May 18, 2013)
3 Patty Murray, "Biography," Senate.gov, http://www.murray.senate.gov/public/index.cfm?p=Biography (accessed July 28, 2011)
4 Patty Murray, "Biography," Senate.gov, http://www.murray.senate.gov/public/index.cfm?p=Biography (accessed July 28, 2011)
5 Sahil Kapur, "Patty Murray To Chair The Senate Budget Committee," TPM, http://livewire.talkingpointsmemo.com/entry/patty-murray-to-chair-senate-budget-committee (November 15, 2012)
6 Deidre Walsh, "Reid taps Sen. Murray to co-chair debt committee," CNN Politics, http://www.cnn.com/2011/POLITICS/08/09/debt.committee.appointments/index.html?eref=rss_topstories&utm_source=feedburner&utm_medium=feed&utm_campaign=Feed%3A+rss%2Fcnn_topstories+%28RSS%3A+Top+Stories%29 (August 9, 2011)
7 Democrats.org, "Our Party," Democrats.org, http://www.democrats.org/about/our_party (accessed May 18, 2013)
8 People's Weekly World (November 8, 1997) p. 3
9 KeyWiki, "Coalition of Labor Union Women," KeyWiki, http://www.keywiki.org/index.php/Coalition_of_Labor_Union_Women (accessed May 18, 2013)
10 KeyWiki, "Lonnie Nelson," KeyWiki, www.keywiki.org/index.php/Lonnie_Nelson (accessed May 18, 2013)
11 KeyWiki, "Irene Hull," KeyWiki, http://www.keywiki.org/index.php/Irene_Hull (accessed May 18, 2013)
12 People's World, "Labor women chart fightback," People's World, http://www.peoplesworld.org/labor-women-chart-fightback/, (October 18, 2003)
13 People's Weekly World (November 7, 1998) p. 4
14 WSLC blog, "Murray: More must be done for struggling working families," WSLC blog, http://www.wslc.org/reports/2008/august/19.htmTUESDAY, (August 19, 2008)
15 Social Security Works, "Celebrate Social Security's 75th Today with Murray, McDermott," Social Security Works, http://ssworkswa.org/2010/08/16/celebrate-social-securitys-75th-today-with-murray-mcdermott/, (August 16, 2010)
16 SS Works Washington, "Members of Social Security Works – Washington," SS Works Washington, http://ssworkswa.org/2010/08/01/members-of-social-security-works-washington/ (August 1, 2010)

17 KeyWiki, "Will Parry," KeyWiki, http://www.keywiki.org/index.php/Will_Parry (accessed May 18, 2013)

18 KeyWiki, "Gene Lux," KeyWiki, http://keywiki.org/index.php/Gene_Lux (accessed May 18, 2013)

19 KeyWiki, "Rachael Levine," KeyWiki, http://keywiki.org/index.php/Rachael_Levine (accessed May 18, 2013)

20 Mary Swift, "Work on Roslyn's old City Hall begins next week," Daily Record, http://www.dailyrecordnews.com/news/article_2a1c758e-c5af-11df-9639-001cc4c03286.html, (September 22, 2010)

21 KeyWiki, "Marc Brodine," KeyWiki, http://www.keywiki.org/index.php/Marc_Brodine (accessed May 18, 2013)

22 Tim Wheeler, "The thumbs up win in Washington State," People's World, http://peoplesworld.org/the-thumbs-up-win-in-washington-state/ (November 12, 2010)

23 Council for a Livable World, "Meet the Candidates," Council for a Livable World, http://livableworld.org/support/meet_candidates/ (accessed December 31, 2010)

24 Council for a Livable World, "Senator Patty Murray," Council for a Livable World, http://livableworld.org/elections/2010/candidates/senate/pmurray/ (accessed December 31, 2010)

Maria Cantwell (D-WA)

Maria Cantwell is the Junior Democratic member of the United States Senate, representing the State of Washington.[1]

Background

Maria Cantwell was born on October 13, 1958 in Indianapolis, Indiana. She received her Bachelor of Arts Degree in Public Administration from Miami University.

She also pursued an academic course at the Miami University European Center, Luxembourg.

Cantwell moved to Seattle, Washington in 1983 to campaign for far left California Senator Alan Cranston in his unsuccessful bid for the 1984 Democratic Presidential nomination.[2]

In 1986, Cantwell was elected to the Washington State House of Representatives at the age of 28. As a State Representative, she helped write Washington's Growth Management Act of 1990, which required cities to develop comprehensive growth plans.

Cantwell was Washington State Representative from 1987 through 1993; was elected as a Democrat to the 103rd Congress (January 3, 1993-January 3, 1995); and was an unsuccessful candidate for reelection to the 104th Congress before being elected to the U.S. Senate in 2000.[3]

Influence

Maria Cantwell serves on the Senate Committee on Commerce, Science and Transportation, where she is the Chairwoman on the Subcommittee on Aviation Operations, Safety and Security. She is also a member of the

Subcommittee on Communications, Technology and the Internet, a member of the Subcommittee on Surface Transportation and Merchant Marine Infrastructure, Safety and Security and a member of the Subcommittee on Oceans, Atmosphere, Fisheries and Coast Guard.

She also serves on the Committee on Energy and Natural Resources, where she is a member on the Subcommittee on Energy and Natural Resources, the Subcommittee on Water and Power and the Subcommittee on Public Lands, Forests and Mining.

Cantwell sits on the Committee on Finance, where she is a member of the Subcommittee on Energy, Natural Resources and Infrastructure, the Subcommittee on Taxation and IRS Oversight and Long-term Growth, the Subcommittee on Health Care and the Subcommittee on International Trade, Customs and Global Competitiveness.

She is the Chairwoman of the Senate Committee on Indian Affairs and also sits on the Senate Committee on Small Business and Entrepreneurship.[4]

Communist Connection

The Washington State Communist Party apparently backed Maria Cantwell in her 2006 Senate race.

According to the Seattle Post Intelligencer on November 8, 2006:[5]

> (Communist Party member) Irene Hull, a supporter of U.S. Senate candidate Maria Cantwell, keeps her fingers crossed, one for the U.S. Senate and one for the U.S. House, to fall into Democratic control during an election return party on Tuesday November 7, 2006 at the Sheraton Hotel in downtown Seattle.

> Irene Hull was there, crossing her fingers, watching returns projected on a screen at the Sheraton and telling the story of many of her comrades within the Democratic Party.[6]

Socialist Connection

Washington Public Campaigns' Banquet

Senator Maria Cantwell gave the Keynote Address for Washington Public Campaigns' Fourth Annual Awards Banquet on June 19, 2010, at South

Seattle Community College. Cantwell had been selected by the Institute for Policy Studies (IPS) affiliated The Nation magazine, as "Most Valuable Senator" in 2009 for "her effort challenging fellow members of Congress to get serious about financial services reform. As this year's guest speaker, Cantwell lent her voice to the call for fair elections nationally."

The awards banquet generated financial support for Washington Public Campaigns to support their efforts to achieve voter-owned elections (public funding of election campaigns) in Washington State. Writing about the Awards Banquet, WPC Director Craig Salins, former Washington State head of Democratic Socialists of America (DSA), stated:[7]

> At the 4th Annual Awards Banquet June 19th—with guest speaker Senator Maria Cantwell—Washington Public Campaigns will celebrate our progress in the past year, and recognize individuals and groups who have contributed mightily to our work.

"Progressive" Connections

NEXT AGENDA Conference

NEXT AGENDA was held at the National Press Club in Washington D.C. on February 28, 2001. It was organized by the Institute for Policy Studies/Democratic Socialists of America initiated Campaign for America's Future:

> At Feb. 28 Conference on NEXT AGENDA, progressive activists, [and] Congressional leaders will unite to forge strategy for "working families" agenda—the day after President Bush delivers his plans to [a] joint session of Congress.

> Calling themselves the real "democratic majority," organizers and thinkers, led by the Campaign for America's Future, to release [a] new book outlining an agenda for changes they insist most voters endorsed in 2000 elections.

> On Feb. 28, a national conference on the NEXT AGENDA, will bring together progressive activists, intellectuals and allies in the Congress for the first time since the disputed election and battles over President Bush's cabinet nominees. It will frame the next two year's debate.

Sponsored by the progressive advocacy group, the Campaign for America's Future and its sister research organization, the Institute for America's Future, the Conference on the Next Progressive Agenda has been endorsed by a who's who of prominent leaders from the labor unions, women's organizations, civil rights groups, environmentalists and individual members of the House and Senate. Their goal: to forge a progressive movement to fight for the "working family" agenda they insist was endorsed by a majority of the voters in the 2000 election.

Organizers of the conference would release a new book, THE NEXT AGENDA: Blueprint for a New Progressive Movement, edited by IPS Trustee Robert Borosage and Roger Hickey.

Maria Cantwell was one of seven "Special Guests" at the conference.[8]

Apollo Alliance

Maria Cantwell was a Founder of the far left controlled Apollo Alliance, a Marxist scheme to unite labor unions, the environmental movement and some businesses behind a "green jobs" movement—essentially huge government make work programs designed to funnel taxpayer's money to socialist causes.

From Common Dreams.org, here is an Apollo Alliance press release from January 14, 2004:[9]

> An unusual alliance of labor, environmental, civil rights, business, and political leaders today laid out a vision for a "New Apollo Project" to create 3.3 million new jobs and achieve energy independence in ten years. Named after President Kennedy's moon program, which inspired a major national commitment to the aerospace industry, the Apollo Alliance aims to unify the country behind a ten-year program of strategic investment for clean energy technology and new infrastructure.

> The Alliance also announced that it has received support from 17 of America's largest labor unions, including the United Auto Workers, the Steelworkers and Machinists, as well as a broad cross section of the environmental movement, including the Sierra Club, the NRDC, the Union of Concerned Scientists, and Greenpeace.

> The press conference was held as President Bush is expected to make a final push for his energy agenda, which was defeated under widespread criticism last November. The press conference was attended by co-chairs of the Apollo Alliance, Senator Maria Cantwell (by phone), Leo Gerard, president of the United Steelworkers of America, Carl Pope,

executive director of the Sierra Club, as well as by California State Treasurer Phil Angelides, Congressman Jay Inslee (by phone), John Podesta, president of the Center for American Progress and Bracken Hendricks, executive director of the Apollo Alliance...

Sen. Maria Cantwell (D-Wash.) said, "At the time of Kennedy's moon shot, we were in space race with the Soviet Union. Now we are in an economic race with the Europeans and Japanese. Bush is focused on the past, the New Apollo Project for energy independence is focused on the future. America led the electronic and communications revolutions. Now we must lead the clean energy revolution if we are to maintain our global economic leadership."

In 2006, Senator Maria Cantwell served on the National Advisory Board of the Apollo Alliance, alongside such "progressive" socialist notables as Chairman Julian Bond (Democratic Socialists of America), Leo W. Gerard, United Steel Workers of America (DSA affiliate) and Bill Lucy, Secretary/Treasurer, AFSCME (DSA member). Later Apollo Alliance boards included Robert Borosage of the IPS and Gerry Hudson, International Executive VP, SEIU and a DSA member.[10]

Foreign Policy/National Security

Council for a Livable World Support

The Council for a Livable World, supported Maria Cantwell in her successful Senate run as candidate for Washington. She has also been previously supported by the Council.[11] [12]

Cuban Business Conference

On February 19, 2003, Cuban President Fidel Castro met with participants of the U.S.-Cuba Business Conference at Palacio de Convenciones in Havana. Participants included Raul de la Nuez, Cuban Minister of Trade; Ricardo Alarcon, President of Cuba's National Assembly; U.S. Senator Maria Cantwell; Juanita Vera; President Fidel Castro; Kirby Jones, President of Alamar Associates, a long time advocate of U.S.-Cuba trade; U.S. Democratic Senator for North Dakota, Kent Conrad; Pedro Alvarez, Chairman of Alimport; and John Moore, Lt. Gov. of Kansas.[13]

**From Left: Senator Maria Cantwell, President Castro and Kirby Jones
(Juanita Vera, Translator is Standing)**

1 KeyWiki, "Maria Cantwell," KeyWiki, http://keywiki.org/index.php/Maria_Cantwell (accessed May 16, 2013)
2 KeyWiki, "Alan Cranston," KeyWiki, http://www.keywiki.org/index.php/Alan_Cranston (accessed May 16, 2013)
3 Maria Cantwell, "Home/About Maria," Senate.gov, http://www.cantwell.senate.gov/public/index.cfm/about-maria (accessed May 16, 2013)
4 Maria Cantwell, "Home/About Maria/Committees," Senate.gov, http://www.cantwell.senate.gov/public/index.cfm/committees (accessed May 16, 2013)
5 KeyWiki, "Irene Hull," KeyWiki, http://www.keywiki.org/index.php/Irene_Hull (accessed May 16, 2013)
6 Post Intelligencer, "How to meet an 8:15 deadline on election night," Post Intelligencer, http://blog.seattlepi.com/photo/category/how-to/page/4/Seattle (November 8, 2006)
7 Chad Shue, "Cantwell to be guest speaker at upcoming awards banquet," Examiner.com, http://www.examiner.com/article/cantwell-to-be-guest-speaker-at-upcoming-awards-banquet, (June 3, 2010)
8 News Advisory, "Morning After Bush's Speech, Progressive Activists to Unite Feb. 28 for Conference on 'Working Family' Agenda," Common Dreams, http://www.commondreams.org/news2001/0226-05.htm (February 26, 2001)
9 Common Dreams, "Apollo Alliance Press Release," Common Dreams (January 14, 2004)
10 KeyWiki, "Apollo Alliance," KeyWiki, http://www.keywiki.org/index.php/Apollo_Alliance (accessed May 16, 2013)
11 Council for a Livable World, "Meet the Candidates," Council for a Livable World, http://livableworld.org/support/meet_candidates/ (accessed May 16, 2013)
12 Council for a Livable World, "Legacy in Congress: Who We've Helped Elect," Council for a Livable World, http://livableworld.org/what/legacy_in_congress_who_weve_helped_elect/ (accessed May 16, 2013)
13 Alamar Associates website, http://www.alamarcuba.com/photogallery5.html (accessed December 15, 2010)

Jim McDermott (D-WA)

Jim McDermott is a Democratic member of the United States House of Representatives, representing the 7th District of Washington. He is a member of the Congressional Progressive Caucus.

Background

Jim McDermott was born in Chicago, Illinois on December 28, 1936.

McDermott graduated from Wheaton College, Illinois. He then went to medical school, earning an MD from the University of Illinois, College of Medicine in Chicago in 1963 after completing an internship from 1963 to 1964 at Buffalo General Hospital in Buffalo, New York, a two-year psychiatry residency at the University of Illinois Research and Educational Hospital and fellowship training in Child Psychiatry from 1966 to 1968 at the University of Washington Medical Center in Seattle. He served in the United States Navy Medical Corps as a Psychiatrist in California during the Vietnam War.[1]

McDermott made his first run for public office in 1970 and was elected to the State Legislature from the 43rd Legislative District of Washington State. In 1974, he successfully ran for the State Senate and subsequently was re-elected three times.

In 1987, McDermott left politics to serve as a Foreign Service Medical Officer based in Zaire, providing psychiatric services to Foreign Service, Agency for International Development and Peace Corps personnel in sub-Saharan Africa. When the 7th District Congressional seat became open, he returned from Africa to seek election to the United States House of Representatives. He was elected in 1988 to the 101st Congress.[2]

Influence

As a senior member of the Ways and Means Committee, Representative McDermott is the Ranking Member of its Trade Subcommittee and also serves on its Human Resources Subcommittee and its Oversight Subcommittee.[3]

Communist Connections

McDermott has a long pattern of connections to the Washington State Communist Party.

Communist Linked Aide

Washington State Communist Party USA (CPUSA) supporter, Pat Stell, was an aide to Rep. McDermott from 1989 to 1993. While nominally a Democrat, Stell was involved in the CPUSA/ Democratic Socialists of America (DSA)-led Coalition of Labor Union Women and other communist causes.[4]

On May 25, 1989, Pat Stell accepted an award on behalf of the Puget Sound Chapter, Coalition of Labor Union Women, at a fundraiser for the Communist Party's People's Daily World newspaper:

> Friends and supporters of the People's Daily World gathered here last weekend for the highlight of their 1989 fund

Program

MC	Maryamu Eltayeb-Givens
Greetings	Marjorie Prince, *chair,Task Force on South Africa, Church Council of Greater Seattle*
	Rev. Robert Jeffrey, *New Hope Baptist Church*
A Special Appeal	Marc Auerbach

Introducing...

Chris Hani

Welcoming Committee

Larry Gossett, *chair, Washington State Rainbow Coalition**
Pat Stell, *Coalition of Labor Union Women**
BJ Mangnoang, *chair, Washington State Communist Party*
Dr. and Mrs. Fred Dube, *ANC Senior Members*
Maseko and Mokeshane Nxumalo, *Task Force on South Africa, Church Council of Greater Seattle*
Rev. Robert Jeffrey, *New Hope Baptist Church**

Organizations listed for identification purposes only

drive, the third annual "Northwest Newsmaker Awards" banquet. PDW editor Barry Cohen spoke on "Remaking the world: how people make history."

Pat Stell told the audience of her recent trip to the Soviet Union.[5]

On April 25, 1991, Pat Stell was a member, with Washington State Communist Party Chair B. J. Mangaoang, of a People's Weekly World welcoming committee for a visit to Seattle by South African Communist Party Chairman Chris Hani.

In May of 1995, The Communist Party USA newspaper People's Weekly World published a May Day supplement. Included was a page of greetings to CPUSA veteran Will Parry, sending "warmest greetings" for his 75th birthday. Almost all of the more than 100 endorsers listed were identified members or supporters of the Washington State Communist Party.

The list included Pat Stell.[6]

Coalition of Labor Union Women

Speakers at the November 1997 conference in Seattle of the Communist Party founded Coalition of Labor Union Women, included Richard Trumka of the AFL-CIO, Washington State's Senator Patty Murray and Rep. Jim McDermott.[7]

Will Parry

At his 90th birthday party in April of 2010, CPUSA member Will Parry picked up his guitar and led 400 union brothers and sisters, family, comrades and friends in singing "Carry It On," ending with, "No more tears, for we're still singing."

Jim McDermott's aide, David Loud, read a letter from the Congressman hailing Will Parry as a leader of the fight for comprehensive, universal health care reform. "We are indebted to you for your years of service," McDermott wrote.[8]

Congratulating Communist Irene Hull

Seattle Communist Party member Irene Hull was honored for her 66 years of activism by Congressman Jim McDermott at his 2010 annual "Potato Fest."[9]

A few years earlier, Hull had solicited signatures at her residence, the Council House, for a petition about American policy on Iraq. It was initiated by Rep. McDermott. McDermott's mother lived in the same residence at the time.[10]

Socialist Connections

Jim McDermott has enjoyed a long and close relationship with Washington State Democratic Socialists of America (DSA), particularly its late leader, Craig Salins.

Craig Salins, Jim McDermott

Democratic Socialists of America Endorsement

In July 1996, the Democratic Socialists of America Political Action Committee endorsed James A. McDermott in that year's Congressional elections.[11]

Socialized Health Care

In 1994, Jim McDermott and DSA supporters Rep. John Conyers and Senator Paul Wellstone promoted a "single-payer" health care bill (HR 1200/S 491).[12] Ellen Shaffer, a member of Wellstone's staff, told the CPUSA's People's Weekly World that the authors had been "working closely" with Hillary Clinton. "She knows what they are doing," Shaffer said.[13]

HR 676

In February of 2003, Reps. Jim McDermott, John Conyers, Dennis Kucinich (another DSA and CPUSA affiliate) and more than 20 others introduced legislation entitled: "Medicare for All" (HR 676).[14]

Washington "Single Payer" Conference

350 health care activists attended a conference at Seattle University in June of 1996, organized by the Washington Single Payer Action Network. Democratic Socialists of America member Craig Salins, the organization's President, hoped the conference could become a launching pad for a "greatly broadened crusade to win affordable, quality health care for all Washingtonians."

McDermott addressed the conference. He (the prime sponsor of HR 1200, the Single Payer bill in Congress) predicted a social upsurge in which the people will demand "get the profiteers out of health care. Period!"

DSA member Quentin Young, of Physicians for a National Health Program, criticized the centralization of fewer and fewer health care providers.[15]

Washington Public Campaigns

Congressman Jim McDermott was a Guest Speaker at Craig Salins' Washington Public Campaigns on June 13, 2009:[16]

Congressman Jim McDermott connected the dots between campaign finance and health care reform.

He felt this year featured a convergence of situations which made the passage of health care reform, with publicly funded health care funding, a practical possibility.

Seattle Anti-Corporate Personhood/Occupy Rally

On January 21st, 2012, a Coalition of Occupy Seattle, Peace and Justice activists; campaign finance reform advocates; Move to Amend (overturn Citizens United) and "Get Money Out of Politics" street performers assembled at Westlake Center to protest on the 2nd anniversary of the Supreme Court's Citizens United decision.

Craig Salins introduced Rep. McDermott to the audience.[17]

Physicians for a National Health Program

The March 3, 2012, 7th Physicians for a National Health Program, Western Washington's Annual Public Meeting, featured speakers Quentin Young, MD, National Coordinator for Physicians for a National Health

Program and Rep. Jim McDermott, Congressman for the Washington 7th Congressional District.

DSAer Quentin Young, the father of the U.S. socialized health care movement, leads Physicians for a National Health Program. It is effectively a front for Democratic Socialists of America and the Communist Party.

The Physicians for a National Health Program board of Western Washington awarded its 2012 John Geyman Health Justice Advocate Award to David Loud, a former student radical, turned health reform activist, who has worked as a hospital worker, union organizer and currently is Jim McDermott's staff aide for community outreach.[18]

In 2012, Jim McDermott was Honorary Chair of Physicians for a National Health Program, Western Washington.[19]

"Progressive" Connection

Progressive Cabinet Nominee

In September of 2008, Chicago based DSA/Institute for Policy Studies (IPS) affiliated journal, In These Times, asked its editors and writers to suggest their top progressive choices for a potential Obama Cabinet:[20]

Phyllis Bennis, of the IPS, suggested Jim McDermott for Secretary of State:

> Secretary of state has two major tasks: To define and represent U.S. interests in the world, and to bring the rest of the world's interests to the United States. Rep. Jim McDermott (D-Wash.)—a 10-term member of Congress and a Progressive Caucus stalwart—would do both.

> McDermott has been a consistent voice for single-payer healthcare, for increased funding for the U.S. and global HIV/AIDS crisis, and for maintaining the estate tax. And he has stated unequivocally that Big Oil and the Iraq War are causing skyrocketing oil prices.

> Like any U.S. politician, his record isn't perfect, particularly on trade. But unlike most of his colleagues, McDermott is independent and willing to think and act outside the Washington box.

> McDermott actively opposes U.S. threats of war against Iran, and he has challenged Israel directly, saying it's "both appropriate and urgent for the U.S. to raise questions about [Israel's] intentions" toward Iran.

Secretary McDermott would not only call for redeploying combat troops out of Iraq, he would also press for bringing home all U.S. troops and mercenaries. He would enforce ignored laws prohibiting U.S. bases there. And he would immediately renounce U.S. efforts to control Iraq's oil…

Secretary of State Jim McDermott would reclaim the primacy of diplomacy in U.S. foreign policy.

Foreign Policy/National Security

Iraqi Spy Connection

In 2002, Michigan Rep. David Bonior (later an identified member of Democratic Socialists of America) and two other Democratic Congressmen: Jim McDermott and Mike Thompson traveled to Iraq on a fact-finding mission. It was later revealed that Iraqi intelligence had funded the trip through a Michigan based Muslim group headed by Muthanna Al-Hanooti.

Before he was indicted for allegedly spying for Saddam Hussein, Muthanna Al-Hanooti's charity work and political activism "provided him with access to the highest echelons of government."

Iraqi intelligence agents reportedly had confidence that Al-Hanooti would be able to persuade Congress to lift economic sanctions against Iraq. A federal indictment unsealed in March of 2008 accused him of using his work with the Michigan-based Life for Relief and Development, formerly known as the International Relief Association, Inc., todo Saddam Hussein's bidding.

According to the indictment, Al-Hanooti hatched a plan to undermine the sanctions for the Iraqis, listing members of Congress who would support the move. He then led tours to Iraq, indirectly funded by the Iraqi government, with Congressional leaders including David Bonior, Jim McDermott and Mike Thompson.[21]

Life for Relief and Development issued a statement in advance of the 2002 trip, saying it was designed to help the representatives "gain a better understanding of the humanitarian plight faced by innocent Iraqi civilians still suffering from the destruction caused by the 1991 Gulf War and the continuation of the 12-year embargo."

According to the indictment, a "cutout" for the Iraqis gave Al-Hanooti $34,000 in late 2002 to cover trip expenses. The indictment also claims he was given the right to buy 2 million barrels of oil under Iraq's Oil for Food program.

Baghdad Airport: (R-L) U.S. Rep. Mike Thompson, Muthanna Al-Hanooti, U.S. Rep. Jim McDermott, U.S. Rep. David Bonior

FBI agents interviewed Al-Hanooti in 2007. He denied knowingly meeting with any Iraqi intelligence officials and denied being offered the oil contract. That led to three counts in the indictment of providing false statements to federal agents.[22]

Anti-War Rally—Iraq Trip Report

Jim McDermott called for putting "a million people in the street" to stop a United States attack on Iraq. "We're here because we're engaged in a national debate about life and death," McDermott told the crowd who came to the Jefferson Park Community Center in Seattle on October 6, 2002, to hear his report on his recent visit to Iraq.

Iraq is a subtitle to "a much bigger issue, which is the kind of country we live in, where the government derives its power from the people, from Congress, not the President—such as its power to declare war," McDermott said.

"If we don't derail this coup that's going on, we'll be in a government that's run by the President of the U.S. and the rest of us will be just standing around wondering what's happening," he declared.

"If you are thinking of defending the Republic, you had better get up on your feet," McDermott told the crowd. "The power is in your hands."

"Though the U.S. is now the most powerful country in the world," he commented, "history is full of the histories of powerful countries that fell because they reached beyond what the people would put up with."

During their visit to Iraq, Reps. McDermott, Bonior and Thompson, spoke to 15 members of Iraq's Parliament and told each, "If you don't allow unfettered inspections, you will get a war." Now that Iraq has agreed to inspections, Bush has been trying to "submarine" the process, McDermott told the Seattle meeting.

"The Iraqi people are suffering elevated cancer rates and birth defects today from exposure to depleted uranium in ammunition used by the U.S. during the Gulf War," McDermott charged. "And we're planning to send our soldiers to walk around in that poison dust?" he asked.

"The fact is we have created a disaster and we have driven the people into the arms of Saddam," McDermott said. "When so many supplies have been withheld by our sanctions," he said, "those items that get through are being distributed by Hussein, and Iraqi people who may have opposed him ten years ago are now grateful." "If we go into Iraq, there will be no uprising. They're going to defend him," McDermott said.

Following the meeting, McDermott joined an anti-war rally in progress, which brought out 5,000 to 7,000 people.[23]

2ⁿᵈ International Islamic Unity Conference

Speakers from around the globe gathered at the Omni Shoreham Hotel in Washington, D.C. in August of 1998, to discuss Muslim issues at the 2nd International Islamic Unity Conference. Under the auspices of the Islamic Supreme Council of America and its founder, Shaykh Muhammad Hisham Kabbani, religious and political leaders alike gathered to address concerns facing the Islamic community and to "condemn the oppression of Muslims worldwide."

In the opening session, Congressman Jim McDermott addressed the lack of understanding of Islam in the United States. As he criticized the "unfair, ignorant image [of Muslims] presented in the media," McDermott urged audience members to contact their governmental representatives to express their concerns. He emphasized that the United States is neither a Christian nor a Jewish nor a Muslim nation, but rather a nation where "people of all faiths can live together in religious freedom."[24]

Trip to Cuba

From June 30th to July 3rd, 2007, McDermott travelled with staffer Sean Hughes to Havana, Cuba on a "fact-finding" trip. The cost of the trip was $3,603.60 and was paid by the Institute for Policy Studies linked Center for Democracy in the Americas.[25]

Gaza

In December of 2009, thirty-three United States Representatives wrote to Secretary of State Hillary Clinton, calling on her to request that the Israeli Government end the ban on student travel from Gaza to the West Bank. Jim McDermott was one of the signatories of the letter.[26]

In January of 2010, United States Representatives Keith Ellison (a Muslim), and Jim McDermott led 52 other members of Congress in signing a letter addressed to President Barack Obama, calling for him to use diplomatic pressure to resolve the blockade affecting Gaza.[27]

---

1 Jim McDermott, "Biography," Congressman Jim McDermott, http://mcdermott.house.gov/index.php?option=com_content&view=article&id=2&Ite mid=9 (accessed June 26, 2012)

2 Jim McDermott, "Biography," Congressman Jim McDermott, http://mcdermott.house.gov/index.php?option=com_content&view=article&id=2&Ite mid=9 (accessed June 26, 2012)

3 Jim McDermott, "Biography," Congressman Jim McDermott, http://mcdermott.house.gov/index.php?option=com_content&view=article&id=2&Ite mid=9 (accessed June 26, 2012)

4 KeyWiki, "Pat Stell," KeyWiki, http://www.keywiki.org/index.php/Pat_Stell (accessed May 16, 2013)

5 People's Daily World (May 25, 1989) p. 5

6 People's Weekly World May Day Supplement (May 6, 1995)

7 People's Weekly World (November 1997) p. 3

8 Tim Wheeler, "Hero of labor, Will Parry, celebrates 90th birthday," People's World, http://peoplesworld.org/hero-of-labor-will-parry-celebrates-90th-birthday/ (accessed June 26, 2012)

9 People's Memorial Association, "Irene Hull," People's Memorial Association, http://funerals.coop/irene-b-hull-2/, (accessed May 16, 2013)

10 Contra Cabal, "Irene H. Hull," Contra Cabal, http://contracabal.org/801-56-00.html, (accessed May 16, 2013)

11 Democratic Left (July/August 1996) p. 21

12 Democratic Left (January/February 1994) p. 2

13 People's Weekly World (March 1993) p. 1

14 People's Weekly World (August 2003) p. 14

15 People's Weekly World (June 1996)

16 WPC blog, "Guest speaker Congressman Jim McDermott," WPC blog, http://www.washclean.org/banquet09-pics.htm, (accessed May 16, 2013)

17 Dinazina, "Photos! Seattle Anti-Corporate Personhood/Occupy Rally," The Daily Kos, http://www.dailykos.com/story/2012/01/24/1058149/-Photos-Seattle-Anti-Corporate-Personhood-Occupy-Rally (January 24, 2012)

18 Blog, "Health Care and Social Justice, How We Get There, Where We Came From, Where We Are," PNHPWW Annual Public Meeting (March 3rd, 7th)

19 Physicians for a National Health Program Western Washington, "About Us Page," Physicians for a National Health Program Western Washington, http://pnhpwesternwashington.org/about.htm (accessed May 31, 2013)

20 In These Times, "22 to Know," In These Times http://www.inthesetimes.com/article/3933/ (accessed June 26, 2012)

21 Steven Emerson, "Exclusive Photos Show Al-Hanooti's Political Clout," The Investigative Project On Terrorism, http://www.investigativeproject.org/628/exclusive-photos-show-al-hanootis-political-clout (accessed June 26, 2012)

22 Steven Emerson, "Exclusive Photos Show Al-Hanooti's Political Clout," The Investigative Project On Terrorism, http://www.investigativeproject.org/628/exclusive-photos-show-al-hanootis-political-clout (accessed June 26, 2012)

23 KeyWiki, "Jim McDermott," KeyWiki, http://keywiki.org/index.php/Jim_McDermott (accessed June 26, 2012)

24 Washington Report on Middle East Affairs, "Muslim-American Activism, Washington, DC Hosts 2nd International Islamic Unity Conference," Washington Report on Middle East Affairs (October/November 1998) p. 107

25 LegiStorm, Rep. Jim McDermott," LegiStorm, http://www.legistorm.com/trip/list/by/approver/id/361/name/Rep_Jim_McDermott.htm l (accessed June 26, 2012)

26 John Dingell, "Letter to Hillary Clinton," John Dingell's Website, http://dingell.house.gov/pdf/091222gaza.pdf (accessed June 26, 2012)

27 Andy Birkey, "Ellison, McCollum and Oberstar urge Obama to lift Gaza blockade," The Minnesota Independent, http://minnesotaindependent.com/54474/ellison-oberstar-and-mccollum-urge-lifting-of-gaza-blockade (accessed June 26, 2012)

Tammy Baldwin (D-WI)

Tammy Baldwin is a Junior Democratic member of the United States Senate, representing Wisconsin. When formerly in the House, she was a leader of the Congressional Progressive Caucus.

Background

Tammy Baldwin was born on February 11, 1962, in the area she later represented in Congress. Raised in Madison, Wisconsin, Baldwin graduated first in her class of 510 students at Madison West High School in 1980. She received an Artium Baccalaureatus Degree from Smith College in Northampton, Massachusetts in 1984 with majors in Government and Mathematics. In 1989, while an active member of the Dane County Board of Supervisors, Baldwin earned her Juris Doctorate from the University of Wisconsin Law School and practiced law from 1989-1992.[1]

Tammy Baldwin served four terms as a Dane County Supervisor (1986-1994), representing the downtown Madison area, including the University of Wisconsin-Madison campus. In 1986, Baldwin also served briefly on the Madison Common Council, filling an Aldermanic vacancy. She served three terms as a Wisconsin State Representative for the 78th Assembly District (comprising central and south Madison) from January 1993 to January 1999.

She represented the 2nd District of Wisconsin in the House of Representatives from 1999 to 2013.[2]

Influence

Tammy Baldwin led successful efforts in the House in 2009 to pass expanded hate crimes legislation. As Co-Founder and Co-Chair of the Congressional LGBT Equality Caucus, she led efforts to advance the Employment Non-Discrimination Act and other civil rights initiatives. She is the lead author of legislation to extend benefits to same-sex partners of federal employees. Baldwin also has crafted legislation to "repeal antiquated antitrust exemptions protecting freight railroads from competition."[3]

Communist Connection

Tribute to Communist Clarence Kailin

In 1999, Tammy Baldwin honored Madison Communist Party USA (CPUSA) veteran Clarence Kailin and the communist-led Abraham Lincoln Brigade, in which she effectively credited the communist movement for leading the charge against Fascism.

From the Congressional Record, Volume 145, Number 149, Page E2209m, Extensions of Remarks, Oct. 28, 1999:[4]

> Mr. Speaker, I rise to honor Mr. Clarence Kailin of Madison, and the brave men and women who volunteered to serve in the Abraham Lincoln Brigade during the Spanish Civil War, especially those courageous volunteers from my home state of Wisconsin.
>
> They, along with 45,000 volunteers from over 50 different countries, fought side by side during the early struggle against fascism. Their foresight in recognizing the rising tyranny of fascism was a call to arms that went unheeded by the free world, and resulted in the long and bloody conflict that became World War II.
>
> Mr. Speaker, I want to express my gratitude to these men and women who helped to defend the democratic Spanish Republic from fascist aggression, at a time when the fate of democracy in Europe was being threatened by all sides of the political spectrum.
>
> On October 31st, in James Madison Park, in the state capitol of Wisconsin, a memorial will be dedicated to those sons and daughters of the "Badger State" that joined the Abraham Lincoln Brigade. A volunteer unit comprised of American citizens from all ethnic and religious backgrounds and walks of life were all equal in their resolve to stem the tide of fascism. Our country's reluctance to aid the Spanish Republican government did not deter these brave people who understood what the consequences were if a legitimately elected government were to fall.

Mr. Speaker, for the first time in our country's long history of isolationism, United State's citizens were reacting to threats to liberty and freedom on the international level more passionately than ever before. Mr. Kailin was one of those citizens, had it not been for him and other brave volunteers in the Lincoln Brigade, the tide of fascism would have swept over Europe unchecked. The corps of international volunteers who came together in Spain would be the same volunteers to comprise the victorious armies of the allied forces that triumphed over the fascist dictators Adolf Hitler and Benito Mussolini.

Mr. Speaker, I ask you and my colleagues to honor these dedicated men and women in the same rightful fashion as my state. The strength of character of Clarence Kailin and others from Wisconsin who volunteered in the Abraham Lincoln Brigade are the qualities which we all can take pride in and celebrate in this Congress.

Socialist Connections

"Strong Progressive"

After the 1998 Congressional elections, Bob Roman of Chicago Democratic Socialists of America wrote:[5]

In addition, the increase in numbers of Democrats in the House was due to the election of Progressives. These include: Tammy Baldwin (WI2), the first open lesbian to be elected to Congress and a strong progressive.

DSA Support—2004

In 2004, Democratic Socialists of America targeted local races where control of State Houses were up for grabs and where statewide electoral-vote outcomes hinged on successful local district turnouts:[6]

Incumbent Tammy Baldwin vocally supports equal rights, gay rights, and expanded health insurance benefits, and her public posture as an out lesbian is symbolically important. Left critics widely view her leadership, however, as disappointing and ineffective. Like Feingold, she faces well-funded right wing opposition. DSAers also are backing what they call "old-fashioned democrat" Dave Obey in the northwestern part of the state.

In Democratic Socialists of America's Democratic Left Winter 2004/2005, Theresa Alt wrote:

> We reported on the candidates that DSAers were supporting in the last issue of Democratic Left. How did they do?
>
> In Wisconsin, progressive incumbents Feingold, Baldwin and Obey won. In a race for an open state senate seat, the favored Mark Miller won handily. However, progressive insurgent Bryan Kennedy lost badly.

DSAers Back Candidates
continued from page 4

incumbent Senator Arlen Specter. Philly DSAers also like Democrat Lois Murphy, who is challenging Republican Party incumbent and Bush loyalist Jim Gerlach in the 6th CD, south and west of Philadelphia. Murphy has made national healthcare system one of her major issues. The

incumbent Tammy Baldwin vocally supports equal rights, gay rights, and expanded health insurance benefits, and her public posture as an out lesbian is symbolically important. Left critics widely view her leadership, however, as disappointing and ineffective. Like Feingold, she faces well-funded right wing opposition. DSAers also are backing what they call "old-fashioned democrat" Dave Obey in the northwestern part of the state, and are pulling for Bryan Kennedy to

Democratic Left (Fall 2004) p. 6

Conyers Health Care Bill

Democratic Socialists of America and CPUSA affiliated Representative John Conyers promoted House Concurrent Resolution 99 (H. Con. Res. 99), directing Congress to enact legislation by October of 2004 that provided access to comprehensive health care for all Americans. Tammy Baldwin was a sponsor of the bill.[7]

DSA Support—2012

Speaking to Reuters in May 2012, SEIU Wisconsin Vice President of Politics and Growth and DSA member, Bruce Colburn said of Wisconsin Senate candidate Tammy Baldwin: "We were looking for a champion, and Tammy fit the bill."

Baldwin won endorsement from the local SEIU.

"Progressive" Connections

Tammy Baldwin is heavily involved in the "progressive movement" and has close ties to the Institute for Policy Studies (IPS).

IPS Approval

In 1998, fourteen new members of Congress were elected who ran on "progressive" platforms.

The fourteen were gauged "progressive" by the IPS after comparing their campaign literature and past activities with the Progressive Challenge "Fairness Agenda for America." Tammy Baldwin was one of those listed:

> Tammy Baldwin won in Wisconsin's 2nd district after a tough grassroots campaign. She has led the fight on progressive issues throughout her career in the Wisconsin state legislature, proposing bills on a range of issues from living wage and workers rights, to support for public education and strong environmental protection. She has advocated a progressive tax system, universal health care and women's rights. She is also the first openly gay, non-incumbent elected to Congress.

"This vote represents a vital shift in the U.S. Congress towards progressive Democrats," said Karen Dolan of the IPS. "It is important to point out that Tammy Baldwin and the other new progressives in Congress won by impressive mobilization at the grassroots," concluded Shelley Moskowitz, Political Director of Neighbor to Neighbor (a DSA affiliated organization). "Baldwin, for example, had 1,500 volunteers in the field on primary day."[8]

Progressive Challenge Coalition

In January of 2000, the Congressional Progressive Caucus held its 3rd Annual Congressional Progressive Caucus' State of the Union Address. This event was also sponsored by the Institute for Policy Studies' Progressive Challenge coalition, whose "Fairness Agenda for America was endorsed by 200 public interest groups nationally."

Tammy Baldwin was one of the speakers.[9]

IPS Award Presenter

Every year, the IPS grants two awards—one domestic and one international—to what are described as "heroes of the progressive movement."

In 2011, representatives from Madison Teachers Inc. accepted the national Letelier-Moffitt Human Rights Award on behalf of Wisconsin "progressives" involved in demonstrations that last spring against anti-union legislation proposed by Republican Gov. Scott Walker.

The Madison Teachers Union was cited for its role in helping organize last spring's massive protests at the state Capitol in response to "Walker's efforts to eliminate collective bargaining rights for most public workers, as well as other legislation including strict voter ID requirements that are likely to limit voting by college students, the elderly, the poor and immigrants."

In a release from the IPS, Executive Director John Cavanagh wrote, "MTI, along with a rainbow of other groups, were leaders in the demonstrations against Walker's proposed legislation in February and March."

They were described as "gallantly fighting to preserve workers' rights and dignity in Wisconsin."

John Matthews, Executive Director of MTI for 43 years and Peggy Coyne, a middle school teacher and MTI President, accepted the award in Washington, D.C. on Oct. 12. Rep. Tammy Baldwin presented the award.[10]

Progressive Democrats of America

Tammy Baldwin is also supported by the Democratic Socialists of America/Institute for Policy Studies-led Progressive Democrats of America (PDA).

PDA Across Wisconsin

On November 2nd, 2012, PDA hosted a guided discussion at the Wisconsin Federation of Nurses & Health Professionals offices in Milwaukee, moderated by John Nichols (The Nation, an MSNBC Contributor and DSA supporter). Guest speakers included: PDA's National Director and DSAer Tim Carpenter, NNU's Director of Public Policy and DSAer Michael Lighty, Communist Party leader and Peace Action field organizer Judith LeBlanc and Dr. Robert Kraig from Citizen Action of Wisconsin.

Lighty and Carpenter joined with author/commentator and DSA affiliate, Jim Hightower, at the UAW Local 95 Hall in Janesville on November 3rd. Rob Zerban—who was challenging Paul Ryan in Wisconsin's 1st District—and John Nichols also appeared. That afternoon, Carpenter and Lighty appeared in Madison, WI with Mark Pocan, Congressional candidate in Wisconsin's 2nd District.

All three Wisconsin events also sought to "help Congresswoman Tammy Baldwin win her close race for the U.S. Senate."[11] [12] [13] [14]

Hightower on Baldwin

DSA supporter Jim Hightower said, "PDA, NNU, and I are joining together to make sure Tammy Baldwin carries Wisconsin. She is now under a slanderous last-minute attack from Karl Rove! I once wrote a book called 'If the Gods Had Meant Us to Vote They Would Have Given Us Candidates.' Well, the Gods mean for us to vote—and donate—and make phone calls—this year, because you don't find great progressive candidates like Tammy Baldwin and Mark Pocan and Rob Zerban every day."[15] [16]

Hosting PDA

According to a New Year's 2013 press release from PDA:[17]

Progressive Democrats of America accomplished a lot in 2012—thanks to your help and support.

In just a few days, on January 3rd, our team will be on Capitol Hill as special guests of our newly-elected Senators Tammy Baldwin and Elizabeth Warren.

RadFest 2002

RadFest 2002 was held May 31st through June 2nd at Aurora University's George Williams Lake Geneva Campus.

RadFest was sponsored by the A.E. Havens Center for the Study of Social Structures and Social Change. Its Director, Patrick Barrett, said that "the central goal of the conference is to provide an opportunity for progressive activists, organizers and intellectuals to come together to discuss issues of mutual interest and concern, strengthen networks and devise strategies for progressive social, economic and political change."

The annual event is attended by communists, socialists and progressives from all over Wisconsin and beyond.

The second conference plenary, titled: "The State of Progressive Politics: Where Are We? Where Are We Going?," featured Medea Benjamin, David Newby of the South Central Wisconsin Coalition of Labor, Madison-based The Nation columnist and avowed socialist John

Nichols, Rep. Tammy Baldwin and the Green Party USA's George Martin. "We're all here to see how we can make this a bigger movement when we leave here," said Martin.[18]

FightingBobFest

Wisconsin's FightingBobFest, named in honor of the state's former "Progressive" Republican, Senator Robert LaFollette, attracts socialists and radicals from all over the U.S. to the annual event.

Tammy Baldwin has been a guest speaker at the event every year from 2004 to 2012.[19]

Foreign Policy/National Security

Supported by Council for a Livable World

The far left, anti-U.S. military Council for a Livable World, supported Tammy Baldwin in her successful House of Representatives run as a candidate for the state of Wisconsin.[20]

The Council for a Livable World also counted Tammy Baldwin among its sixteen 2012 Senate victories.[21]

661

The Colombia Connection

Tammy Baldwin has been an active defender of the Colombian Marxist revolutionary movement.

Colombia Support Network

On November 7, 2012, the pro-Colombian revolution Madison Wisconsin Colombia Support Network, issued this statement:[22]

> Colombia Support Network (CSN) celebrates the election last night of two great friends: Tammy Baldwin, elected to the United States Senate, and Mark Pocan, elected to the United States House of Representatives. Tammy, with the assistance of Mark, drafted our sister community resolution for Dane County and Apartadó...

> Tammy and Mark have provided great support to our human rights and sister community work on Colombia. We look forward to their solidarity from their new positions as Senator and Representative in Washington D.C. We congratulate them on their election and on their commitment to good government and support for a sensible U.S. foreign policy toward Colombia.

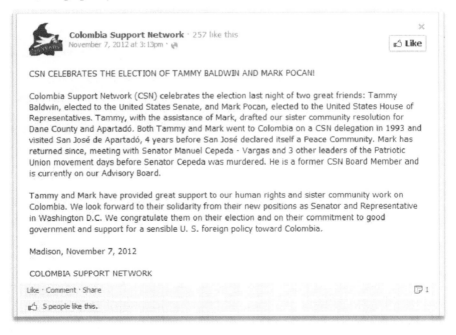

Colombia Support Network · 257 like this
November 7, 2012 at 3:13pm ·

Like

CSN CELEBRATES THE ELECTION OF TAMMY BALDWIN AND MARK POCAN!

Colombia Support Network (CSN) celebrates the election last night of two great friends: Tammy Baldwin, elected to the United States Senate, and Mark Pocan, elected to the United States House of Representatives. Tammy, with the assistance of Mark, drafted our sister community resolution for Dane County and Apartadó. Both Tammy and Mark went to Colombia on a CSN delegation in 1993 and visited San José de Apartadó, 4 years before San José declared itself a Peace Community. Mark has returned since, meeting with Senator Manuel Cepeda - Vargas and 3 other leaders of the Patriotic Union movement days before Senator Cepeda was murdered. He is a former CSN Board Member and is currently on our Advisory Board.

Tammy and Mark have provided great support to our human rights and sister community work on Colombia. We look forward to their solidarity from their new positions as Senator and Representative in Washington D.C. We congratulate them on their election and on their commitment to good government and support for a sensible U. S. foreign policy toward Colombia.

Madison, November 7, 2012

COLOMBIA SUPPORT NETWORK

Like · Comment · Share   1

5 people like this.

Open Letter to the Colombian People, Press and Government, August 1996

In the open letter, "Stop the Bloodshed in Uraba, Due Process for Jose Antonio Lopez, Nelson Campo and others, and an End to Faceless Justice and Political Repression," the following was stated:

> We, the undersigned, are North Americans and others who are deeply disturbed by the human rights situation in Colombia.
>
> Massacres, disappearances and torture happen continually in the anguished region of Uraba. We cannot understand how paramilitary groups operate so freely in this militarized region where the Colombian army is present in massive numbers, and which does not perform its constitutional function of defending the civilian population. And we cannot understand why the regional paramilitary leader is not apprehended and brought to justice for his crimes against humanity.
>
> We call upon all armed parties—paramilitary units, guerrillas, army, police, urban militias and commandos—to immediately cease all attacks upon both the civilian population and upon each other. Justice, peace and a fruitful life is never found through murder, torture, kidnapping and intimidation.

Tammy Baldwin signed the letter from the Colombia Support Network, as did several well-known Marxists, including Democratic Socialists of America supporters Ed Asner, Blasé Bonpane and Noam Chomsky; Communist Party USA supporters Gary Grass, Babette Grunow, Michael Parenti, Fr. Bill Hogan and Clarence Kaillin; Institute for Policy Studies affiliate Medea Benjamin and former Weather Underground terrorist leader and Obama friend, Bernardine Dohrn.[23]

No to Military Aid to Colombia

On the same day in 2000 that President Clinton used a White House press conference to promote the $1.7 billion Colombian military aid package—Rep. Tammy Baldwin, took to the floor of the House to attack the aid package as "a misguided initiative that will not help the peace process in Colombia."

The aid package pushed by Clinton and Congressional Republicans "would spend a fortune to make everything in that Latin American country worse. It seeks to direct U.S. money into Colombia's military, while failing to address fundamental problems such as economic inequality, lack of economic development and a corrupt judiciary."

"Peace is what Colombia needs. Peace will allow democracy to flourish; peace will permit law enforcement officials to combat the flow of illicit drugs; and peace will create the conditions to address the income inequalities, the problems of displaced persons and economic development issues that will truly improve the lives of Colombian people," said Baldwin.[24]

"Dear Colleagues" Letter on Colombia

In September 2009, Rep. Tammy Baldwin was circulating a 'Dear Colleague' letter, which urged members of Congress to sign a letter to President Obama. This letter expressed concern and urged caution regarding a U.S. military base agreement with Colombia.[25]

1 KeyWiki, "Tammy Baldwin," KeyWiki,
http://keywiki.org/index.php/Tammy_Baldwin (accessed June 11, 2012)
2 KeyWiki, "Tammy Baldwin," KeyWiki,
http://keywiki.org/index.php/Tammy_Baldwin (accessed June 11, 2012)
3 KeyWiki, "Tammy Baldwin," KeyWiki,
http://keywiki.org/index.php/Tammy_Baldwin (accessed June 11, 2012)
4 KeyWiki, "Tammy Baldwin," KeyWiki,
http://keywiki.org/index.php/Tammy_Baldwin (accessed June 11, 2012)
5 Chicago Democratic Socialists of America, "New Ground 61," Chicago Democratic
Socialists of America, http://www.chicagodsa.org/ngarchive/ng61.html (accessed June 11, 2012)
6 Theresa Alt and Michael Hirsch, "Beyond Kerry DSAers Back Local Candidates,"
Democratic Left, http://www.dsausa.org/dl/DLFall2004.pdf (Fall 2004) (accessed June 11, 2012)
7 Democratic Left, http://www.dsausa.org/dl/Summer_2002.pdf (Summer 2002) (accessed June 11, 2012)
8 Democratic Left (Winter 1998) p. 2
9 Karen Dolan, "Progressive Groups And Congressional Caucus To Present Their
Third Annual Alternative State Of The Union Address," Common Dreams Progressive
Newswire, http://www.commondreams.org/news2000/0126-103.htm (accessed June 11, 2012)
10 Susan Troller, "Chalkboard: MTI to accept national award for helping organize
protests," The Cap Times,
http://host.madison.com/news/local/education/blog/article_f5cae6fc-e886-11e0-b1a0-001cc4c03286.html (accessed January 21, 2013)
11 PDA Press Release, "Jim Hightower, John Nichols, Michael Lighty and Tim
Carpenter in Janesville," PDA, http://www.prlog.org/12014034-jim-hightower-john-nichols-michael-lighty-and-tim-carpenter-in-janesville.html (November 1, 2012)
12 KeyWiki, "John Nichols," KeyWiki, http://keywiki.org/index.php/John_Nichols
(accessed May 18, 2013)

13 KeyWiki, "Judith LeBlanc," KeyWiki,
http://keywiki.org/index.php/Judith_LeBlanc (accessed May 18, 2013)
14 KeyWiki, "Michael Lighty," KeyWiki,
http://keywiki.org/index.php/Michael_Lighty (accessed May 18, 2013)
15 PDA Press Release, "Jim Hightower, John Nichols, Michael Lighty and Tim
Carpenter in Janesville," PDA, http://www.prlog.org/12014034-jim-hightower-john-
nichols-michael-lighty-and-tim-carpenter-in-janesville.html (November 1, 2012)
16 KeyWiki, "Jim Hightower," KeyWiki, http://keywiki.org/index.php/Jim_Hightower
(accessed May 18, 2013)
17 PDA, "Happy New Year from PDA!," Yahoo! Groups,
http://dir.groups.yahoo.com/group/progressivesforobama/message/6357 (January 1,
2013)
18 Fred Gaboury, "RadFest 2002," People's World,
http://www.peoplesworld.org/radfest-2002/ (accessed January 21, 2013)
19 FBF, "FBF Speakers Page," http://www.fightingbobfest.org/speakers.cfm,
(accessed December 28, 2012)
20 Council for a Livable World, "Meet the Candidates," Council for a Livable World,
http://livableworld.org/support/meet_candidates/ (accessed June 11, 2012)
21 Council for a Livable World, "Meet the Candidates," Council for a Livable World,
http://livableworld.org/support/meet_candidates/ (accessed April 10, 2013)
22 Colombia Support Network, "CSN Celebrates The Election Of Tammy Baldwin
And Mark Pocan," Facebook,
https://www.facebook.com/ColombiaSupportNetwork/posts/485402191491296,
(November 7, 2012)
23 ColombiaSupport.net, "Open Letter to the Colombian People, Press and
Government: Stop the Bloodshed in Uraba, Due Process for Jose Antonio Lopez,
Nelson Campo and others, and an End to Faceless Justice and Political Repression,"
ColombiaSupport.net, http://colombiasupport.net/archive/199608/open.html, (August
1996)
24 Common Dreams, "A Disaster For Colombia," Common Dreams,
http://www.commondreams.org/views/033100-109.htm, (March 31, 2000)
25 Mennonite Central Committee, "Oppose the U.S. military base agreement with
Colombia," Democracy in Action,
http://org2.democracyinaction.org/o/5764/t/5764/content.jsp?content_KEY=1507,
(accessed May 18, 2013)

Mark Pocan (D-WI)

Mark Pocan is a freshman Democratic member of the United States House of Representatives, representing the 2nd District of Wisconsin. In his victory speech, Pocan emphasized the deep "progressive" roots of the 2nd Congressional District. "This is the district of Fighting Bob La Follette. This is the seat of Bob Katenmeier. And this is the seat of Tammy Baldwin. This is the seat where we expect our representatives to work hard for progressive values and the middle class and lower income families of Wisconsin, and I will do that."[1]

In January 2013, Mark Pocan was listed as a new member of the Congressional Progressive Caucus.[2]

Background

Mark Pocan got his start in politics in blue-collar Kenosha, Wisconsin, where at age eight he was delivering campaign literature door-to-door for his father, a long-time city Alderman.

Pocan came to Madison to attend college and shortly after earning a degree in Journalism in 1986, opened up his own small business—a printing company he continues to own and operate today. His active years at UW-Madison in College Democrats, led to his election in 1991 to the Dane County Board of Supervisors where he served Madison's downtown community for three terms. In 1998, he was elected to succeed his long-time friend and ally Tammy Baldwin as the State Representative from the 78th District, when she left for Congress.[3]

In his six terms as a member of the Wisconsin State Assembly, Pocan helped create the Wisconsin Quality Home Care Commission, authored the American Jobs Act and the Compassionate Care for Rape Victims Act, and was "deeply involved in many progressive initiatives focused on collective bargaining rights, public financing of clean elections, domestic partner protections and corrections reform."

For six years, Pocan sat on the state's powerful budget writing Joint Finance Committee, including a term as Co-Chair last session.

During the recent labor union instigated turmoil, Pocan took a "visible, leading role, fighting hard for what he believes in as a legislator and a union member of the International Union of Painters and Allied Trades."

He has also been active in international affairs with his travel and involvement in Dane County's sister community in Apartado, Colombia.[4]

Influence

Pocan identifies as a progressive Democrat and is a member of a number of organizations, including Wisconsin Citizen Action, the American Civil Liberties Union, Fair Wisconsin and the Midwest Progressive Elected Officials Network.[5]

In Congress, he serves on both the Budget Committee and the Committee on Oversight and Government Reform, and has been appointed as Assistant Minority Whip.[6]

"Progressive" Connections

RadFest

In the early 2000s, Mark Pocan spoke several times at RadFest, an annual Madison, Wisconsin gathering of communists, socialists and "progressive" activists.

RadFest was sponsored by the A.E. Havens Center for the Study of Social Structures and Social Change. Its Director, Patrick Barrett, said that "the central goal of the conference is to provide an opportunity for progressive activists, organizers and intellectuals to come together to discuss issues of mutual interest and concern, strengthen networks and devise strategies for progressive social, economic and political change."[7] Pocan addressed RadFest 2002 on LGBT Issues, Civil Rights and Progressive Coalition Building.

In 2003, Pocan participated in the RadFest, "Moving toward Tax Fairness in Wisconsin" forum.[8]

DSA Connection

Mark Pocan also has ties to Democratic Socialists of America (DSA). Madison area DSA sponsored a workshop on equitable taxation at RadFest 2002, which featured Pocan and DSA and Committees of Correspondence affiliate Mike Prokosch. The moderator was another CoC affiliate, Frank Emspak.

"Coalition for Wisconsin Health" Health Care Bill

In the Summer of 2005, leftist Wisconsin State Senator Mark Miller reintroduced Coalition for Wisconsin Health's Wisconsin Universal Health Program legislation. Originally known as LRB-2576, the Bill would get a new number when introduced.

Coalition for Wisconsin Health worked to help Miller recruit new co-sponsors for the bill.

Other co-sponsors of the WUHP in the 2003-2004 legislative session who had returned in 2005 were Representatives Mark Pocan, and fellow "progressive" Spencer Coggs.

Coalition for Wisconsin Health Treasurer at the time was George Robson of Wisconsin United Methodist Federation for Social Action and Madison Democratic Socialists of America, while Vice Chair was Linda Farley, MD, from the DSA front Physicians for a National Health Program.9

Progressive Democrats of America

Tim Carpenter, PDA's Rob Hansen, Mark Pocan, Michael Lighty, Wisconsin 2012

Mark Pocan is very closely tied to the DSA/Institute for Policy Studies (IPS) dominated Progressive Democrats of America (PDA), and it's National Director Tim Carpenter, a former leader of Orange County DSA, and PDA Advisory Board member Michael Lighty, a former DSA National Director.

In 2012, Mark Pocan was one of 14 leftist Congressional and Senate candidates endorsed and supported by Progressive Democrats of America.

"Progressive Central"

PDA helped celebrate their man's victory at the Progressive Central— The Peoples' Inauguration, held on January 19, 2013, at the UDC David A. Clarke School of Law, Washington, D.C.

The event was sponsored by Progressive Democrats of America and IPS affiliates: The Nation, National Nurses United and Busboys and Poets. The event was advertised and promoted by the Institute for Policy Studies. The 1:00 pm - 2:10 pm session: "Organizing the Progressive Movement Inside and Outside the Democratic Party," was moderated by DSA affiliate John Nichols and featured PDA's Rep. Raul Grijalva; Thom Harman, a journalist and long-time radical and freshman Rep. Mark Pocan.[10]

Foreign Policy/National Security

The Colombian Connection

Mark Pocan has close ties to leftist forces in Colombia and has worked hard to stop attempts to oppose efforts to defeat that county's FARC/Communist Party-led Marxist insurgency.

Colombia Support Network

On November 7, 2012, the communist-influenced Madison Wisconsin based Colombia Support Network issued this statement:[11]

> Colombia Support Network (CSN) celebrates the election last night of two great friends: Tammy Baldwin, elected to the United States Senate, and Mark Pocan, elected to the United States House of Representatives. Tammy, with the assistance of Mark, drafted our sister community resolution for Dane County and Apartadó. Both Tammy and Mark

went to Colombia on a CSN delegation in 1993 and visited San José de Apartadó, 4 years before San José declared itself a Peace Community. Mark has returned since, meeting with Senator Manuel Cepeda—Vargas and 3 other leaders of the Patriotic Union movement days before Senator Cepeda was murdered. He is a former CSN Board Member and is currently on our Advisory Board.

According to Communist Party USA member W.T. Whitney, writing in Marxism-Leninism Today. The Patriotic Union was a front for the Colombian Communist Party and FARC terrorists:[12]

> In 1985, Colombia's Communist Party, elements of the Revolutionary Armed Forces of Colombia (FARC), and other leftists formed the Patriotic Union, an electoral coalition competing for local, regional, and national political offices. Under the peace initiative launched by the Belisario Betancur government and the FARC, armed insurgents joined regular political processes.

Lobbying Feingold on Behalf of the CSN

Not long after leftist Russ Feingold was elected to the United States Senate for his first term (circa 1993), several members of the Colombia Support Network Board went to meet him at his office, accompanied by future Congresswoman Tammy Baldwin and future Wisconsin State Representative Mark Pocan, at the time both members of the Dane County Board:[13]

> Senator Feingold listened carefully to our concerns about the dramatic situation in our sister community of Apartado, even though he had no particular reason to be interested in Colombia, South America.

School of Americas Resolution

While in the Wisconsin Legislature, Pocan introduced a resolution to urge Congress to close the School of Americas, an organization dedicated to training Latin American military officers in countering Marxist insurgencies in their native countries. The resolution is a perfect example of the anti-School of the America's propaganda commonly disseminated by the U.S. far left:[14]

> This institution is one of the bigger wastes of taxpayer dollars at the federal level. It is responsible for the training of foreign military officers

associated with high profile massacres, killings, kidnappings and tortures in Central and South America.

I have seen firsthand the effects of the bloodshed caused by those trained by the School of Americas in both El Salvador and Colombia on Sister City visits. The cost in human and financial terms is significant. Many religious and human rights organizations support its closure.

The Committee on Veteran's Affairs held a hearing on this issue in mid-September. Over 30 people spoke and or registered in favor of the resolution. No one opposed it. I have sent a request to the Chair of the Committee asking for a vote on the resolution. I hope the resolution will be voted on and move to the Assembly floor soon.

Colombia Support Network Advisory Board

As of 2008, the Colombia Support Network Advisory Board included Marxist academic Noam Chomsky (Democratic Socialists of America, Committees of Correspondence for Democracy and Socialism), DSA supporter Larry Birns, DSA affiliate Blase Bonpane, Marxist academic and DSA affiliate Robert McChesney, Marxist labor unionist Daniel Kovalik, former secret Communist Party member, DSA affiliate and "people's historian" Howard Zinn and Mark Pocan.[15 16 17 18 19 20 21]

---

1 Judith Davidoff, "Sexual orientation a non-issue in Mark Pocan's historic congressional victory," The Daily Page (accessed on November 7, 2012)
2 Congressional Progressive Caucus website, "Members," Congressional Progressive website, http://cpc.grijalva.house.gov/index.cfm?sectionid=71&sectiontree=2,71, (accessed January 15, 2013)
3 Progressive Democrats of America, "Mark Pocan Biography," Progressive Democrats of America, http://www.pdamerica.org/candidates/mark-pocan, (accessed January 15, 2012)
4 Progressive Democrats of America, "Mark Pocan Biography," Progressive Democrats of America, http://www.pdamerica.org/candidates/mark-pocan, (accessed January 15, 2012)
5 KeyWiki, "Mark Pocan," KeyWiki, http://keywiki.org/index.php/Mark_Pocan (accessed March 21, 2013)
6 Mark Pocan, "Meet Congressman Mark Pocan," House.gov, http://pocan.house.gov/about/full-biography (accessed <au 15. 2013)
7 Fred Gaboury, "RadFest 2002," People's World, http://www.peoplesworld.org/radfest-2002/ (June 14, 2002)
8 Brian Lutenegger, "Invitation to RadFest 2003: Midwest Social Forum," Yahoo! Groups, http://groups.yahoo.com/group/greens/message/6621, (April 1, 2003)
9 Health Coalition for Wisconsin (Summer 2005) vol. 7, p. 2

10 Progressive Democrats of America website, http://hq-salsa3.salsalabs.com/o/1987/p/salsa/event/common/public/index.sjs?event_KEY=6957 5, (accessed January 15, 2013)

11 Colombia Support Network, "CSN Celebrates the Election of Tammy Baldwin and Mark Pocan!," Facebook, https://www.facebook.com/ColombiaSupportNetwork/posts/485402191491296, (November 7, 2012)

12 MLToday, "Colombia's Patriotic Union Tragedy: Lessons Learned," MLToday, http://mltoday.com/subject-areas/national-liberation/colombia-s-patriotic-union-tragedy-lessons-learned-1001.html, (2004-10)

13 CSN, "Senator Feingold: Oh how we miss you!," CSN, http://colombiasupport.net/2011/02/senator-feingold-oh-how-we-miss-you/, (February 23, 2011)

14 Mark Pocan, "Capitol View: By State Representative Mark Pocan," Danenet, http://www.danenet.org/tlna/web-data/news/news11/1199poca.html, (accessed May 16, 2013)

15 Colombia Support Network, "The Colombian Army: Terrorism, Thievery, Bungling and Massacres," Colombia Support Network, http://colombiasupport.net/2009/colombian_army_csn_report_08_09.pdf (August 24, 2009)

16 KeyWiki, "Lawrence Birns," KeyWiki, http://www.keywiki.org/index.php/Lawrence_Birns (accessed May 16, 2013)

17 KeyWiki, "Blasé Bonpane," KeyWiki, http://www.keywiki.org/index.php/Blase_Bonpane (accessed May 16, 2013)

18 KeyWiki, "Noam Chomsky," KeyWiki, http://www.keywiki.org/index.php/Noam_Chomsky (accessed May 16, 2013)

19 KeyWiki, "Robert McChesney," KeyWiki, http://www.keywiki.org/index.php/Robert_McChesney (accessed May 16, 2013)

20 KeyWiki, "Daniel Kovalik," KeyWiki, http://www.keywiki.org/index.php/Daniel_Kovalik (accessed May 16, 2013)

21 KeyWiki, "Howard Zinn," KeyWiki, http://www.keywiki.org/index.php/Howard_Zinn (accessed May 16, 2013)

Epilogue:

America's Greatest Security Weakness

The United States suffers from a major security weakness.

There is no political will or mechanism in place to prevent obvious "security risks" from entering the House of Representatives or the Senate, or for exposing or removing them once they are there.

If any young Marxist firebrand puts on a suit and tie and tries to get a low level, federal government job, he will be investigated by the FBI. His family background, his associates, his education, travel… all will be checked. In some instances, the FBI practically goes through the applicant's underwear drawers.

Yet, if that same young radical, who may have been to Cuba several times, associated with known terrorist supporters or has been a card carrying member of a totalitarian Marxist Party, gets elected to Congress, he is home free.

The young radical may serve on highly sensitive committees, with access to highly sensitive material. He may take occasional unsupervised trips to Cuba or Venezuela. He may even attend meetings with his former comrades. But no one will challenge him, criticize him or demote him. As long as he is part of the club, no one will touch him on either side of the aisle.

Once, the public could rely on the media to expose such people. But since the left took over most of the journalism schools from the 1950s onwards and most journalists self-identify as "liberal" or now even "progressive," that is a very false hope.

The Founding Fathers never foresaw Marxism-Leninism or socialism. They couldn't comprehend that one day, whole blocs of followers of an international revolutionary movement would be serving in the U.S. Congress, subverting the Constitution, steering the country towards statism and undermining national security at every opportunity.

Nobody could have predicted such a scenario in the 18th century. European kings, or Barbary Pirates were the only foreseeable threat in those days. Nothing like an organized, worldwide revolutionary movement was even comprehensible.

After the Bolshevik Revolution, the U.S. government got a little more serious about internal security, clamping down on communist agitators and Soviet spies.

After World War II and the Communist conquest of Eastern Europe and China, the United States really got serious. NATO was established, the military was expanded and new weapons systems were developed. The U.S. spent billions competing with the Soviet Union in the greatest arms race the world had ever seen. At home spies were uncovered in the Roosevelt Administration. Hearings were held into communist subversion all across the country. A near panic gripped the nation as communists were rooted out from every nook and cranny.

I remember talking to an Australian former communist about this period—often called the McCarthy era after the communist hunting Senator from Wisconsin, Joseph McCarthy. I asked Geoff McDonald what the Australian communists thought of McCarthy. "We were shit scared of him," said Geoff. "But he didn't go anywhere near far enough."

And he didn't either. Despite all the great work McCarthy did and the tremendous and largely unsung efforts of Democrats such as Senator Thomas J. Dodd of Connecticut and Rep. Larry McDonald of Georgia, the State Department was never properly cleaned out and the Congress itself was never touched.

By the 1970s and 1980s, both the House and Senate internal security committees had been abolished by leftist Democrats, working hand in glove with the Communist Party.

America was invincible abroad, but the heart of the American Government was being taken over from within by radical leftists working through the Democrat Party. Once, many Democrats were more conservative than a lot of Republicans. Today, Harry Truman or John Kennedy wouldn't even be able to stand for Congress for the Democrats, let alone lead the Party. Both of them would be considered "right wing extremists" by the Democrats of today.

So now with socialism and communism on the upsurge all over the world, America in general and certainly the U.S. House of Representatives and the Senate are virtually unprotected against it.

Today, America spends itself bankrupt to project power abroad, while its own legislature is being rotted away by extremists who couldn't get a security clearance to clean the latrines at any military base in the country.

If Congressional candidates were required to pass an FBI security clearance before standing, a very substantial number of today's representatives would never have gotten to Washington. If current Congress members or Senators had to pass a security clearance before they could serve on any Congressional or Senate Committee, a shockingly high percentage would have to excuse themselves.

That is the heart of the problem. These "Enemies Within" have an agenda. They plan to weaken America militarily and socialize the U.S. economy. They are destroying the Constitutional heritage that made America great and they are putting millions of lives at stake.

Worse—they are endangering the life and liberty of the entire free world.

If America loses its economic and military dominance, the combined forces of Russia, China, Iran, Cuba, Venezuela, Vietnam, North Korea, Nicaragua and radical Islam will carve up the globe amongst themselves. Who will be strong enough to stop them?

So, the whole world is in danger because tiny Marxist groups such as Democratic Socialists of America and Communist Party USA have been able to penetrate and influence the U.S. Congress.

If Americans think of national security at all, they mainly worry about radical Islam, maybe North Korea, or possibly China. Nobody talks about the Russia/China/Iran alliance or the fact that Islamic terrorism has long worked closely with Russia and the communist powers.

And virtually nobody talks about the biggest threat of all... the infiltration and subversion of the U.S. Congress.

Nobody is talking about the most deadly enemy of all, the "Enemies Within."

Maybe it's time to put cowardice and "political correctness" aside for the sake of America.

For terrible though treason is, it is nothing compared to cowardice in the face of a threat to one's own family's life and liberty.

The first step in defeating an enemy is to name him.

America can be saved, but not if no one is brave enough to name that enemy.

If the enemy goes unnamed, he goes unchallenged. If he goes unchallenged, he will win.

Who will be brave enough to name and challenge America's "Enemies Within?"

About the Author

New Zealander Trevor Loudon is an internationally known blogger, writer and researcher, noted among other things for exposing the communist background of Obama's "Green Jobs Czar" Van Jones, which led to his eventual resignation from his White House position. Loudon was also the first to publicize Barack Obama's ties to Hawaiian Communist Party member Frank Marshall Davis.

Trevor Loudon's research has been cited by Glenn Beck, Rush Limbaugh, countless articles, blog posts and in books by well known authors Paul Kengor, Aaron Klein and Jerome Corsi. He has addressed more than 200 audiences in more than 30 states in his four tours of the United States.

He is also the author of the 2011 book *Barack Obama, and the Enemies Within*.

INDEX

D

E

F

P